Money and Banking

Version 3.0

Robert E. Wright

Money and Banking
Version 3.0

Robert E. Wright

Published by:

FlatWorld
175 Portland Street
Boston, MA 02114

Brief Contents

Contents

About the Author

Robert E. Wright

The Face Behind the Text
Robert E. Wright

I attribute my enduring interest in money and banking, political economy, and economic history to the troubled economic conditions of my youth. Born in 1969 in Rochester, New York, to two self-proclaimed factory rats, I recall little of my earliest days except the Great Inflation and oil embargo, which stretched the family budget past the breaking point. The recession in the early 1980s also injured my family's material welfare and was seared into my brain. My only vivid, noneconomic memories are of the *Planet of the Apes* films (all five of them!) and the 1972 Olympics massacre in Munich; my very young mind conflated the two because of the aural similarity of the words *gorilla* and *guerilla*.

After taking degrees in history from Buffalo State College (B.A., 1990) and the University of Buffalo (M.A., 1994; Ph.D., 1997), I began teaching a variety of courses in business, economics, evolutionary psychology, finance, history, and sociology at Temple University, the University of Virginia, sundry liberal arts colleges, New York University's Stern School of Business, and, since 2009, Augustana University, where I am additionally the director of the Thomas Willing Institute for the Study of Financial Markets, Institutions, and Regulations. I've also been an active researcher, editing, authoring, and coauthoring books about the development of the U.S. financial system (*Origins of Commercial Banking, Hamilton Unbound, Wealth of Nations Rediscovered, The First Wall Street, Financial Founding Fathers, One Nation Under Debt, Genealogy of American Finance*), construction economics (*Broken Buildings, Busted Budgets*), life insurance (*Mutually Beneficial*), publishing (*Knowledge for Generations*), bailouts (*Bailouts*), entrepreneurship (*Little Business on the Prairie*), public policy (*Fubarnomics, The C.Q. Guide to U.S. Economic Policy, Corporation Nation, The Poverty of Slavery*), and investments (*The Wall Street Journal Guide to the 50 Economics Indicators That Really Matter*). Due to my unique historical perspective on public policies and the financial system, I was once something of a media maven, showing up on NPR and other talk radio stations, as well as various television programs, and getting quoted in major newspapers like the *Wall Street Journal, New York Times, Chicago Tribune*, and the *Los Angeles Times*. I still publish op-eds and make regular public speaking appearances nationally and, occasionally, internationally. I am the treasurer of Historians Against Slavery, an NGO dedicated to ending all forms of bonded labor, and am also active in the Museum of American Finance and sit on the editorial board of its magazine, *Financial History*.

I wrote this textbook because I strongly believe in the merits of financial literacy for all. Our financial system struggles sometimes in part because so many people, including some of its top political leaders, remain feckless financially. My hope is that people who read this book carefully, dutifully complete the exercises, and attend class regularly will be able to follow the financial news and even critique it when necessary. I also hope they will make informed choices in their own financial lives and raise their voices against untoward public policies, like the politicization of monetary policy.

Acknowledgments

Many people have helped to make this project a reality. At FlatWorld, Shannon Gattens and Jeff Shelstad helped to shepherd the concept and the manuscript through the standard trials and tribulations. Along the way, a score of anonymous academic readers helped to keep our economic analyses and prose on the straight and narrow. Paul Wachtel and Richard Sylla, two colleagues at New York University's Stern School of Business, also aided us along the way with measured doses of praise and criticism. I thank them all. Thanks, too, to the University of Virginia's Department of Economics, especially the duo of economic historians and "money guys" there, Ron Michener and John James, for putting up with me during my various stints in Charlottesville. John's recent passing saddened me to the core. Very special thanks go to the members of Wright's Summer I 2007 Money and Banking class at the University of Virginia, who suffered through a free but error-prone first draft, mostly with good humor and always with helpful comments: Kevin Albrecht, Adil Arora, Eric Bagden, Michelle Coffey, Timothy Dalbey, Karina Delgadillo, Christopher Gorham, Joshua Hefner, Joseph Henderson, Jamie Jackson, Anthony Jones, Robert Jones, Risto Keravuori, Heather Koo, Sonia Kwak, Yiding Li, Patrick Lundquist, Maria McLemore, Brett Murphy, Daniel Park, Bensille Parker, Rose Phan, Patrick Reams, Arjun Sharma, Cole Smith, Sandy Su, Paul Sullivan, Nedim Umur, Will van der Linde, Neal Wood, and June Yang. The students and professors who provided feedback on versions 2.0 and 3.0 of this book also have my hearty gratitude. Especially worthy of thanks are Augustana University students Areesha Najam and Justin Kautz for convincing me to cover Islamic finance in the context of fighting financial fiascos (Section 13.7).

It's customary at this point for authors to assume full responsibility for the facts and judgments in their books. I will not buck that tradition: the buck stops here! Unlike a journal article or academic monograph, textbooks afford ample room for revision in subsequent editions, of which I hope there will be many more. So if you spot a problem, contact the publisher and we'll fix it at the earliest (economically justifiable) opportunity.

Robert E. Wright, July 2017, Sioux Falls, S.D.

Preface

"Dad," my kids used to regularly ask me, "why do you write such boring books?" They would then giggle and run away before I had a chance to tickle them to tears. They were too young to realize that boring, like beauty, is in the eye of the beholder. This book is exciting, or at least not boring, in part because of the writing style I've employed. Multiple humorous examples are provided, and slang terms are peppered throughout. Seemingly complex subjects like money, interest rates, banking, financial regulation, and the money supply are treated in short, snappy sections, not long-winded treatises. Yet I have sacrificed little in the way of analytical rigor.

Moreover, the financial crisis of 2007–2008 has made the study of money and banking almost as exciting as sex, drugs, and rock 'n' roll because it has made clear to all observers just how important the financial system is to our well-being. Version 1 was the first textbook to emerge after that crisis, and the crisis and its aftermath have shaped this second edition in important ways. Most of the book explains what economists currently consider to be "facts," statements that the majority of academic researchers agree to be true. Sometimes, however, the narrative becomes more controversial because what economists consider true is changing, partly due to new ideas and discoveries and partly due to new perspectives ushered forth by the financial crisis. I share those new ideas whenever I think them important to financial literacy. Readers should also know from the outset that I have been called a "pragmatic libertarian." In other words, I believe governments should venture into the economy only when they demonstrate that their actions actually improve people's lives. Some readers may call this a "bias," but they need to understand that I came to this view after two decades of intense study. It's an expert judgment, not an ideological predilection. Where I am agnostic on an issue, I "teach the controversy" and narrate all sides of the debate. Where I believe one side has conquered another, however, I take the side of the conqueror and mention the conquered only in passing. For example, if this were a biology text, to refer to a commonly understood issue of this type, I would explain the theory of evolution by means of natural selection and mention creationism only to provide historical or current events context.

Not all experts share my pragmatic libertarianism, and even your professor may question some of my claims. Such controversies are key learning opportunities because they will help you understand that money and banking, like most other subjects you study in college, is not a static body of knowledge to be swallowed and regurgitated on an examination but an evolving concept that is constantly improved by its interactions with reality. And participating in clashes of ideas with each other and with reality can be much more exciting than blasting a video game alien or passively watching a sporting event (even in HD).

In case you haven't surmised it yet, this book is designed to help you *internalize* the basics of money and banking. There is a little math, some graphs, and some sophisticated vocabulary, but nothing terribly difficult, if you put your brain to it. The text's most important goal is to get you to think for yourselves. To fulfill that goal, each section begins with one or more questions, called Learning Objectives, and ends with Key Takeaways that provide short answers to the questions and smartly summarize the section in a few bullet points. Most sections also contain a sidebar called Stop and Think. Rather than ask you to simply repeat information given in the chapter discussion, the Stop and Think sidebars require that you apply what you (should have) learned in the chapter to a novel situation. You won't get them all correct, but that isn't the point. The point is to stretch your brain.

Where appropriate, the book also drills you on specific skills, like calculating bond prices. Key terms and chapter-level objectives also help you to navigate and master the subject matter. The book is deliberately short and chatty but right to the point. If you hunger for more, read one or more of the books listed in the Suggested Reading section at the end of each chapter. Keep in mind, however, that the goal is to internalize, not to memorize. Allow this book to inform your view of the world and you will be the better for it, and so will your loved ones, a hypothesis developed more thoroughly in the first chapter.

CHAPTER 1
Money, Banking, and Your World

Chapter Objectives

By the end of this chapter, students should be able to:

1. Describe how ignorance of the principles of money and banking has injured the lives of everyday people.
2. Describe how understanding the principles of money and banking has enhanced the lives of everyday people.
3. Explain how bankers can simultaneously *be* entrepreneurs and *lend* to entrepreneurs.

1.1 Dreams Dashed

Learning Objective

1. How can ignorance of the principles of money and banking destroy your dreams?

At 28, Ben is in his prime. Although tall, dark, and handsome enough to be a movie star, Ben's real passion is culinary, not thespian. Nothing pleases him more than applying what he learned earning his degrees in hospitality and nutrition to prepare delicious yet healthy appetizers, entrées, and desserts for restaurant-goers. He chafes, therefore, when the owner of the restaurant for which he works forces him to use cheaper, but less nutritional, ingredients in his recipes. Ben wants to be his own boss and thinks he sees a demand for his style of tasty, healthy cuisine. Trouble is, Ben, like most people, came from humble roots. He doesn't have enough money to start his own restaurant, and he's having difficulty borrowing what he needs because of some youthful indiscretions concerning money. If Ben is right, and he can obtain financing, his restaurant could become a chain that might revolutionize America's eating habits, rendering Eric Schlosser's exposé of the U.S. retail food industry, *Fast Food Nation* (2001),[1] as obsolete as *The Jungle* (1901),[2] Upton Sinclair's infamous description of the disgusting side of the early meatpacking industry. If Ben can get some financial help but is wrong about Americans preferring natural ingredients to hydrogenized this and polysaturated that, he will have wasted his time and his financial backers may lose some money. *If he cannot obtain financing, however, the world will never know whether his idea was a good one or not.* Ben's a good guy, so he probably won't turn to drugs and crime but his life will be less fulfilling, and Americans less healthy, if he never has a chance to pursue his dream.

negative amortization mortgage

A mortgage with periodic payments lower than what would be required to pay the interest on the loan. Instead of declining over time, the principal owed increases as unpaid interest is added to it.

balloon payment

A principal payment due in a large lump sum, usually at the end of the loan period.

interest rate

The price of borrowed money.

Married for a decade, Rose and Joe also had a dream, the American Dream, a huge house with a big, beautiful yard in a great neighborhood. The couple could not really afford such a home, but they found a lender that offered them low monthly payments. *It seemed too good to be true because it was.* Rose and Joe unwittingly agreed to a **negative amortization mortgage** with a **balloon payment**. Their monthly payments were so low because they paid just part of the interest due each year and none of the (growing) principal. When housing prices in their area began to slide downward, the lender foreclosed, although they had never missed a payment.[3] They lost their home and, worse, their credit. The couple now rents a small apartment and harbors a deep mistrust of the financial system.

Rob and Barb had a more modest dream of a nice house in a good location with many conveniences, a low crime rate, and a decent public school system. They found a suitable home, had their offer accepted, and obtained a conventional thirty-year mortgage. But they too discovered that their ignorance of the financial system came with a price when they had difficulty selling their old house. They put it up for sale just as the Federal Reserve,[4] America's central bank (monetary authority), decided to raise the **interest rate** because the economy, including the housing market, was too hot (growing too quickly), portending a higher price level across the economy (inflation). Higher interest meant it was more expensive to borrow money to buy a house (or anything else for that matter). To compensate, buyers decreased the amount they were willing to offer and in some cases stopped looking for new homes entirely. Unable to pay the mortgage on both houses, Rob and Barb eventually sold their old house for much less than they had hoped. The plasma TV, new carpeting, playground set in the yard, sit-down mower, and other goods they planned to buy evaporated. *That may have been good for the economy by keeping inflation in check, but Rob and Barb, like Rose, Joe, and Ben, wished they knew more about the economics of money, banking, and interest rates.*

foreign exchange

Buying and selling of foreign currencies, for example, the British pound, the Japanese yen, and the European Union's euro.

Samantha too wished that she knew more about the financial system, particularly **foreign exchange**. Sam, as her friends called her, had grown up in Indiana, where she developed a vague sense that people in other countries use money that is somehow different from the U.S. dollar. But she never gave the matter much thought, until she spent a year in France as an exchange student. With only $15,000 in her budget, she knew that things would be tight. As the dollar depreciated (lost value) vis-à-vis France's currency, the euro, she found that she had to pay more and more dollars to buy each euro. Poor Sam ran through her budget in six months. Unable to obtain employment in France, *she returned home embittered, her conversational French still vibrating with her Indiana twang.*

Jorge would have been a rich man today if his father had not invested his inheritance in U.S. government bonds in the late 1960s. The Treasury promptly paid the interest contractually due on those bonds, but high rates of inflation and interest in the 1970s and early 1980s reduced their prices and wiped out most of their purchasing power. Instead of inheriting a fortune, Jorge received barely enough to buy a midsized automobile. That his father had worked so long and so hard for so little saddened Jorge. If only his father had understood a few simple facts: when the supply of money increases faster than the demand for it, prices rise and inflation ensues. When inflation increases, so too do nominal interest rates. And when interest rates rise, the prices of bonds (and many other types of assets that pay fixed sums) fall. Jorge's father didn't lack intelligence, and he wasn't even atypical. Many people, even some otherwise well-educated ones, do not understand the basics of money, banking, and finance. And they and their loved ones pay for it, sometimes dearly.

life insurance

A contract that promises to pay a sum of money to beneficiaries upon the death of an insured person.

Madison knows that all too well. Her grandparents didn't understand the importance of portfolio diversification (the tried-and-true rule that you shouldn't put all of your eggs in one basket), so they invested their entire life savings in a single company, Enron.[5] They lost everything (except their Social Security checks)[6] after that bloated behemoth went bankrupt in December 2001. Instead of lavishing her with gifts, Madison's grandparents drained resources away from their granddaughter by constantly seeking handouts from Madison's parents. When the grandparents died—without **life insurance**, yet another misstep—Madison's parents had to pay big bucks for their "final expenses."[7]

Stop and Think Box

History textbooks often portray the American Revolution as a rebellion against unjust taxation, but the colonists of British North America had other, more important grievances. For example, British imperial policies set in London made it difficult for the colonists to control the supply of money or interest rates. When money became scarce, as it often did, interest rates increased dramatically, which in turn caused the value of colonists' homes, farms, and other real estate to decrease quickly and steeply. As a consequence, many lost their property in court proceedings and some even ended up in special debtors' prisons. Why do history books fail to discuss this important monetary cause of the American Revolution?

Most historians, like many people, generally do not fully understand the principles of money and banking.

Key Takeaway

- People who understand the principles of money and banking are more likely to lead happy, successful, fulfilling lives than those who remain ignorant about them.

1.2 Hope Springs

Learning Objective

1. How can knowledge of the principles of money and banking help you to achieve your dreams?

Of course, sometimes things go right, especially when one knows what one is doing. Henry Kaufman,[8] who as a young Jewish boy fled Nazi persecution in the 1930s, is now a billionaire because he understood what made interest rates (and as we'll see, by extension, the prices of all sorts of financial instruments) rise and fall. A little later, another immigrant from Central Europe, George Soros, made a large fortune correctly predicting changes in the **exchange rate**.[9] David did not become uberwealthy trading **financial derivatives** for a Wall Street firm, but he did earn enough money to retire at the age of forty. Instead of missing the early years of his two children's lives in a maze of meetings and dying early from a heart attack, David spends his days raising his kids and living healthily.

Millions of other individuals have improved their lot in life by making astute life decisions informed by knowledge of the economics of money and banking. Over several decades, Henri leveraged his knowledge of the financial system by regularly buying low and selling high. A confirmed bachelor, he died of cancer at a relatively young age but felt blessed that he was able to share his substantial nest egg with online **microlender** Kiva[10] and several other worthy charities. Songho doesn't earn much tutoring Korean, but he is single and frugal so he can save a little each month in conservative (low risk) investments that he will one day use to aid his aging parents or to bring his brother and neice to America. Aesha, a single mom and nurse, can't afford to invest, let alone retire, but she uses her knowledge of the financial system to minimize her borrowing costs, thus freeing up resources that she uses to send Kelton to a private school that provides him with a far better educational experience than his public school did. Your instructor and I cannot guarantee you riches and fame, but we can assure you that, if you read this book carefully, attend class dutifully, and study hard, your life will be the better for it.

exchange rate

The price of one currency in terms of another.

financial derivatives

Financial contracts, like forwards, futures, options, and swaps, the value of which derives from the price of some underlying asset such as a commodity, an interest rate, or a foreign currency.

microlender

A company or nonprofit entity that makes very small loans to impoverished, self-employed individuals.

The study of money and banking can be a daunting one for students. *Seemingly familiar terms here take on new meanings.* **Derivatives** refer not to calculus (though calculus helps to calculate their value) but to financial instruments for trading risks. Interest is not necessarily interesting; stocks are not alive nor are they holding places for criminals; zeroes can be quite valuable; CDs don't contain music; blockchains unleash and unchain rather than impede or weigh down; yield curves are sometimes straight lines; and the principal is a sum of money or an owner, not the administrative head of a high school. In finance, unlike in retail or publishing, returns are a good thing. *Military-style acronyms and jargon also abound*: 4X, A/I, Basel II, B.I.G., CAMELS, CRA, DIDMCA, FIRREA, GDP, IMF, LIBOR, *m*, NASDAQ, NCD, NOW, OTS, *r*, SOX, TIPS, TRAPS, and on and on.[11]

People who learn this strange new language and who learn to think like a banker (or other type of financier) will be rewarded many times over in their personal lives, business careers, and civic lives. *They will make better personal decisions, run their businesses or departments more efficiently, and be better-informed citizens.* Whether they seek to climb the corporate ladder or start their own companies, they will discover that interest, inflation, and foreign exchange rates are as important to success as are cell phones, computers, and soft people skills. And a few will find a career in banking to be lucrative and fulfilling. Some, eager for a challenging and rewarding career, *will try to start their own banks from scratch.* And they will be able to do so, provided they are good enough to pass muster with investors and with government regulators charged with keeping the financial system, one of the most important sectors of the economy, safe and sound.

One last thing. This book is almost entirely about Western financial systems, not Islamic ones. Islamic finance performs the same functions as Western finance but tries to do so in a way that is sharia-compliant, or, in other words, in a way that accords with the teachings of the Quran and its modern interpreters, who frown upon interest. To learn more about Islamic finance, which is currently growing and developing very rapidly, you can refer to one of the books listed in Suggested Readings and/or read Section 13.7 "Islamic Banking and Financial Stability."

Stop and Think Box

Gaining regulatory approval for a new bank has become so treacherous that consulting firms specializing in helping potential incorporators to navigate regulator-infested waters have arisen and some, like Nubank,[12] have thrived. Why are regulations so stringent, especially for new banks? Why do people bother to form new banks if it is so difficult?

Banking is such a complex and important part of the economy that the government cannot allow just anyone to do it. For similar reasons, it cannot allow just anyone to perform surgery or fly a commercial airliner. People run the regulatory gauntlet because establishing a new bank can be extremely profitable and exciting.

Key Takeaway

- Not everyone will, or can, grow as wealthy as Henry Kaufman, George Soros, and other storied financiers, but everyone can improve their lives by understanding the financial system and their roles in it.

1.3 Suggested Browsing

Practical Money Skills for Life

http://www.practicalmoneyskills.com

Developed and approved by educators and funded by Visa, this site provides free educational resources, including personal finance articles and games. Similar organizations include the Community Foundation for Financial Literacy (http://www.thecommunityfoundation-ffl.org) and the Institute for Financial Literacy (http://www.financiallit.org).

Museum of American Finance

http://www.moaf.org/index

In addition to its website and its stunning new physical space at the corner of William and Wall in Manhattan's financial district, the Museum of American Finance publishes a financial history magazine (http://www.moaf.org/publications-collections/financial-history-magazine/index).

Best Books on Islamic Finance

https://blogs.cfainstitute.org/investor/2013/05/03/a-selection-of-books-in-islamic-finance-by-professor-rodney-wilson/

If the suggested readings in Section 1.4 are not enough to quench your thirst for knowledge, try this site for numerous additional quality titles regarding Islamic finance.

1.4 Suggested Reading

Ayub, Muhammed. *Understanding Islamic Finance*. Hoboken, NJ: John Wiley and Sons, 2008.

Hayat, Usman and Adeel Malik. *Islamic Finance: Ethics, Concepts, Practice*. CFA Institute Research Foundation, 2014.

Kaufman, Henry. *On Money and Markets: A Wall Street Memoir*. New York: McGraw Hill, 2001.

Soros, George. *Soros on Soros: Staying Ahead of the Curve*. Hoboken, NJ: John Wiley and Sons, 1995.

Endnotes

1. www.amazon.com/Fast-Food-Nation-Eric-Schlosser/dp/0060838582/sr=8-1/qid=1168386508/ref=pd_bbs_sr_1/104-9795105-9365527?ie=UTF8&s=books
2. sinclair.thefreelibrary.com/Jingle, babel.hathitrust.org/cgi/pt?id=mdp.39015026866577;view=1up
3. Traditionally, one has to miss several payments before a lender can foreclose, but several new types of mortgages developed during the housing boom of the mid-2000s have "call" features that allow lenders to ask for immediate repayment of the principal if the value of the home sinks, leaving the lender undersecured.
4. www.federalreserve.gov
5. www.investopedia.com/terms/e/enron.asp
6. www.ssa.gov
7. www.settlerslife.com/what-are-final-expenses
8. http://topics.nytimes.com/top/reference/timestopics/people/k/henry_kaufman/index.html
9. www.georgesoros.com
10. www.kiva.org
11. www.acronym-guide.com/financial-acronyms.html, www.garlic.com/~lynn/fingloss.htm
12. www.nubank.com

CHAPTER 2

The Financial System

Chapter Objectives

By the end of this chapter, students should be able to:

1. Critique cultural stereotypes of financiers.
2. Describe the financial system and the work that it performs.
3. Define asymmetric information and sketch the problems that it causes.
4. List the major types of financial markets and describe what distinguishes them.
5. List the major types of financial instruments or securities and describe what distinguishes them.
6. List the major types of intermediaries and describe what distinguishes them.
7. Describe and explain the most important trade-offs facing investors.
8. Describe and explain borrowers' major concerns.
9. Explain the functions of financial regulators.

2.1 Evil and Brilliant Financiers?

Learning Objective

1. Are bankers, insurers, and other financiers innately good or evil?

A ubiquitous stereotype portrays financiers as evil, brilliant, or both. While instances of uberintelligent, unfathomly selfish financiers can be adduced, most people working in the financial services sector are normal folks and not unusually greedy or smart. To understand the financial system in all its glorious complexity, readers need to expunge stereotypes of financiers from their minds. One way to do that is to cultivate critiques of media portrayals of all things financial.

Ever notice that movies and books tend to portray financiers as evil and powerful monsters, bent on destroying all that decent folks hold dear for the sake of a fast buck? In his best-selling 1987 novel *Bonfire of the Vanities*,[1] for example, Tom Wolfe depicts Wall Street bond trader Sherman McCoy (played by Tom Hanks in the movie version)[2] as a slimy "Master of the Universe": rich, powerful, and a complete butthead. Who could forget Danny DeVito[3] as the arrogant, donut-scarfing "Larry the Liquidator" juxtaposed against the adorable, old factory owner Andrew Jorgenson (played by Gregory Peck)[4] in *Other People's Money*?[5] And moviegoers have now been treated to two flicks called *Wall Street*,[6] which revile the nation's largest and most important financiers and financial firms under thinly disguised names and circumstances. Since the financial crisis, a slew of movies like *The Big Short*[7] have emerged to titillate audiences.[8]

Bashing finance and financiers is not a passing fad; you may recall the unsavory Shylock character from Shakespeare's play *The Merchant of Venice*.[9] Even the Christmas classic *It's a Wonderful Life*[10] contains at best a dual message. In the film, viewers learn that George Bailey, the lovable president of the local building and loan association (a type of community bank) played by Jimmy Stewart, saved Bedford Falls from the clutches of a character portrayed by Lionel Barrymore, actress Drew Barrymore's grand-uncle, the ancient and evil financier Henry F. Potter. (No relation to Harry, I'm sure.) That's hardly a ringing endorsement of finance.[11]

Truth be told, some financiers have done bad things. Then again, so have members of every occupational, geographical, racial, religious, and ethnic group on the planet. *But most people, most of the time, are pretty decent, so we should not malign entire groups for the misdeeds of a few, especially when the group as a whole benefits others.* Financiers and the financial systems they inhabit benefit many people. The financial system does so much good for the economy, in fact, that some people believe that financiers are brilliant rocket scientists or at least "the smartest guys in the room."[12] This positive stereotype, however, is as flawed as the negative one. While some investment bankers, insurance actuaries, and other fancy financiers could have worked for NASA, they are far from infallible. The financial crisis that began in 2007 reminds us, once again, that complex mathematical formulas are less useful in economics (and other social sciences) than in astrophysics. *Financiers, like politicians, religious leaders, and, yes, college professors, have made colossal mistakes in the past and will undoubtedly do so again in the future.*

So rather than lean on stereotypes, this chapter will help you to form your own view of the financial system. In the process, it will review the entire system. *It's well worth your time and effort to read this chapter carefully because it contains a lot of descriptive information and definitions that will help you later in the text, as well as later in life.*

Key Takeaways

- Financiers are not innately good or evil but rather, like other people, can be either, or can even be both simultaneously.
- While some financiers are brilliant, they are not infallible, and fancy math does not reality make.
- Rather than follow prevalent stereotypes, students should form their own views of the financial system.
- This important chapter will help students to do that, while also bringing them up to speed on key terms and concepts that will be used throughout the book.

2.2 Financial Systems

Learning Objective

1. What is a financial system and why do we need one?

A **financial system** is a densely interconnected network of intermediaries, facilitators, and markets that serves three major purposes: allocating capital, sharing risks, and facilitating all types of trade, including intertemporal exchange. That sounds mundane, even boring, but it isn't once you understand how important it is to human welfare. The material progress and technological breakthroughs of the last two centuries, ranging from steam engines, cotton gins, and telegraphs, to automobiles, airplanes, telephones, computers, DNA splicing, and cell phones, would not have been possible without the financial system.[13] Efficiently linking borrowers to lenders is the system's main function. Borrowers include inventors, entrepreneurs, and other economic agents, like domestic households, governments, established businesses, and foreigners, with potentially profitable business ideas (**positive net present value projects**) but limited financial resources (expenditures > revenues). Lenders or savers include domestic households, businesses, governments, and foreigners with excess funds (revenues > expenditures). The financial system also helps to link risk-averse entities called hedgers to risk-loving ones known as speculators. As Figure 2.1 illustrates, you are probably already deeply embedded in the financial system as both a borrower and a saver.

financial system

A densely interconnected network of financial intermediaries, facilitators, and markets that allocates capital, shares risks, and facilitates intertemporal trade.

positive net present value projects

A project likely to be profitable at a given interest rate after comparing the present values of both expenditures and revenues.

FIGURE 2.1 The financial system at work for you

You might not yet have a mortgage or own stock but you probably have at least one loan or credit account and a deposit account.

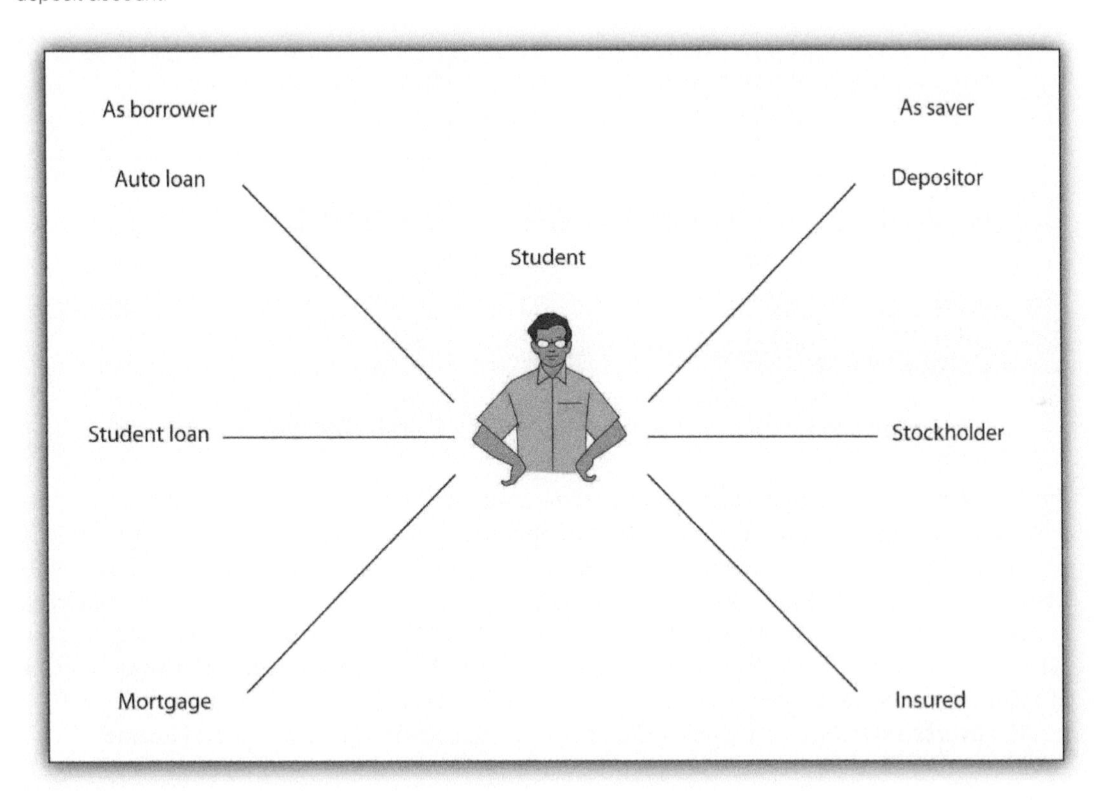

Occasionally, people and companies, especially small businesses or ones that sell into rapidly growing markets, have enough wealth (a stock) and income (a flow) to implement their ideas without outside help by plowing back profits (aka **internal finance**). *Most of the time, however, people and firms with good ideas do not have the savings or cash needed to draw up blueprints, create prototypes, lease office or production space, pay employees, obtain permits and licenses, or suffer the myriad risks of bringing a new or improved good to market.* Without savings, a rich uncle or close friend, or some other form of **external finance**, people remain wannabe entrepreneurs and companies cannot complete their projects. That should concern you because the world is a poorer place for it.[14] It should also concern you because many students need loans in order to afford college and thereby increase their future earnings.

internal finance

Financing that comes from the company itself, the plowing of profits back into the business.

external finance

Obtaining short- or long-term funding from outside sources (those external to the company).

minimum efficient scale

The smallest a business can be and still remain efficient and/or profitable.

Why do we need a financial system? Why can't individuals and companies simply borrow from other individuals and companies when they need to? *Lending, like supplying many other types of goods, is most efficiently and cheaply conducted by specialists, companies that do only one thing (or a couple of related activities) very well because they have much practice doing it and because they tap economies of scale.* The fixed costs of making loans—advertising for borrowers, buying and maintaining computers, leasing suitable office space, writing up contracts, and the like—are fairly substantial. To recoup those fixed costs, to drive them toward insignificance, lenders have to do quite a volume of business. Little guys usually just can't be profitable. This is not to say, however, that bigger is always better, only that to be efficient financial companies must exceed **minimum efficient scale**.

Key Takeaways

- The financial system is a dense network of interrelated markets and intermediaries that allocates capital and shares risks by linking savers to spenders, investors to entrepreneurs, lenders to borrowers, and the risk-averse to risk-takers.
- It also increases gains from trade by providing payment services and facilitating exchange.
- A financial system is necessary because few businesses can rely on internal finance alone.
- Specialized financial firms that have achieved minimum efficient scale are better at connecting investors to entrepreneurs than nonfinancial individuals and companies are.

2.3 Asymmetric Information: The Real Evil

Learning Objective

1. What is asymmetric information, what problems does it cause, and what can mitigate it?

scarcity

The finite availability of resources coupled with the infinite demand for them; the fact that goods are not available in sufficient quantity to satisfy everyone's wants.

adverse selection

The fact that the least desirable borrowers and those who seek insurance most desire loans and insurance policies.

moral hazard

Any postcontractual change in behavior that injures other parties to the contract.

Finance also suffers from a peculiar problem that is not easily overcome by just anybody. Undoubtedly, you've already encountered the concept of opportunity costs, the nasty fact that to obtain X you must give up Y, that you can't have your cake and eat it too. You may not have heard of asymmetric information, another nasty fact that makes life much more complicated. Like **scarcity**, asymmetric information inheres in nature, the devil incarnate. That is but a slight exaggeration. When a seller (borrower, a seller of securities) knows more than a buyer (lender or investor, a buyer of securities), only trouble can result. Like the devil in Dante's *Inferno*,[15] this devil has two big ugly heads, **adverse selection**, which raises Cain before a contract is signed, and **moral hazard**, which entails sinning after contract consummation. (Later, we'll learn about a third head, the principal-agency problem, a special type of moral hazard.)

Due to adverse selection, the fact that the riskiest borrowers are the ones who most strongly desire loans, lenders attract sundry rogues, knaves, thieves, and ne'er-do-wells, like pollen-laden flowers attract bees (or Natty Light[16] attracts frat boys?). *If they are unaware of that selection bias, lenders will find themselves burned so often that they will prefer to keep their savings under their mattresses rather than risk lending it.* Unless recognized and effectively countered, moral hazard will lead to the same suboptimal outcome. *After a loan has been made, even good borrowers sometimes turn into thieves because they realize that they can gamble with other people's money.* So instead of setting up a nice little ice cream shop with the loan as they promised, a disturbing number decide instead to try to get rich quick by taking a quick trip to Vegas or Atlantic City[17] for some potentially lucrative fun at the blackjack table. If they lose, they think it is no biggie because it wasn't their money.

One of the major functions of the financial system is to tangle with those devilish information asymmetries. It never kills asymmetry, but it reduces its influence, affecting intermediaries by screening insurance and credit applicants and monitoring them thereafter, as well as markets by providing price information and analysis. With asymmetric information thus scotched, businesses and other borrowers can obtain funds and insurance cheaply enough to allow them to become more efficient, innovate, invent, and expand into new markets. *By providing relatively inexpensive forms of external finance, financial systems make it possible for entrepreneurs and other firms to test their ideas in the marketplace.* They do so by eliminating, or at least reducing, two major constraints on **liquidity** and **capital**, or the need for short-term cash and long-term dedicated funds. They reduce those constraints in two major ways: directly (though often with the aid of **facilitators**) via **markets** and indirectly via **intermediaries**. Another way to think about that is to realize that the financial system makes it easy to trade intertemporally, or across time. Instead of immediately paying for supplies with cash, companies can use the financial system to acquire what they need today and pay for it tomorrow, next week, next month, or next year, giving them time to produce and distribute their products.

liquidity

The ease, speed, and cost of selling an asset.

capital

In this context, long-term financing.

facilitators

In this context, businesses that help markets to function more efficiently.

markets

Institutions where the quantities and prices of goods are determined.

intermediaries

Businesses that connect investors to entrepreneurs via various financial contracts, like checking accounts and insurance policies.

Stop and Think Box

You might think that you would never stoop so low as to take advantage of a lender or insurer. That may be true, but financial institutions are not worried about you per se; they are worried about the typical reaction to asymmetric information. Besides, you may not be as pristine as you think. Have you ever done any of the following?

- Stolen anything from work?
- Taken a longer break than allowed?
- Deliberately slowed down at work?
- Cheated on a paper or exam?
- Lied to a friend or parent?

If so, you have taken advantage (or merely tried to, if you were caught) of asymmetric information.

Key Takeaways

- Asymmetric information occurs when one party knows more about an economic transaction or asset than the other party does.
- Adverse selection occurs before a transaction takes place. If unmitigated, lenders and insurers will attract the worst risks.
- Moral hazard occurs after a transaction takes place. If unmitigated, borrowers and the insured will take advantage of lenders and insurers.
- Financial systems help to reduce the problems associated with both adverse selection and moral hazard by screening applicants and monitoring borrowers and insureds.

2.4 Financial Instruments

Learning Objectives

1. What are financial instruments or securities?
2. What economic function do financial instruments fulfill?
3. What are the characteristics of different types of financial instruments?

Financial instruments, sometimes called **financial securities**, are legal contracts that detail the obligations of their **makers**, the individuals, governments, or businesses that issue (initially sell) them *and promise to make payment*, and the rights of their **holders**, the individuals, governments, or businesses that currently own them and *expect to receive payment. Their major function is to specify who owes what to whom, when or under what conditions payment is due, and how and where payment should be made.*

Financial instruments come in three major varieties—**debt**, **equity**, and **hybrid**. Debt instruments, such as bonds, indicate a lender–borrower relationship in which the borrower promises to pay a fixed sum and interest to the lender at a specific date or over some period of time. Equity instruments, such as stocks, represent an ownership stake in which the holder of the instrument receives some portion of the **issuer**'s profits. Hybrid instruments, such as preferred stock, have some of the characteristics of both debt and equity instruments. Like a bond, preferred stock instruments promise fixed payments on specific dates but, like a common stock, only if the issuer's profits warrant. Convertible bonds, by contrast, are hybrid instruments because they provide holders with the option of converting debt instruments into equities.

Today, many financial instruments are merely electronic accounting entries—numbers in a spreadsheet linked to a contract. In the past, however, they took corporeal form as in the case of stock certificates, like that pictured in Figure 2.2.

Financial instruments
Contracts for the payment of money; securities.

financial securities
Another term for financial instruments.

makers
The issuers or initial sellers of a financial instrument; the entities promising payment.

holders
The owners or possessors of a financial instrument; the entities entitled to payment.

debt
A financial instrument in which a type of maker called a borrower promises to pay a fixed sum on a fixed date to a holder called a lender (or bondholder).

equity
A financial instrument in which a type of maker called an issuer promises to pay a portion of its profits to a holder called an owner (or stockholder or shareholder).

hybrid
A financial instrument that has some of the characteristics of debt and some of the characteristics of equity.

issuer
The maker or initial seller of a financial instrument.

FIGURE 2.2 Allied Paper stock certificate, 1964

Twenty-five shares owned by Mrs. Pearl Lanoff, one of millions of American women who owned corporate stock by the mid-1960s.

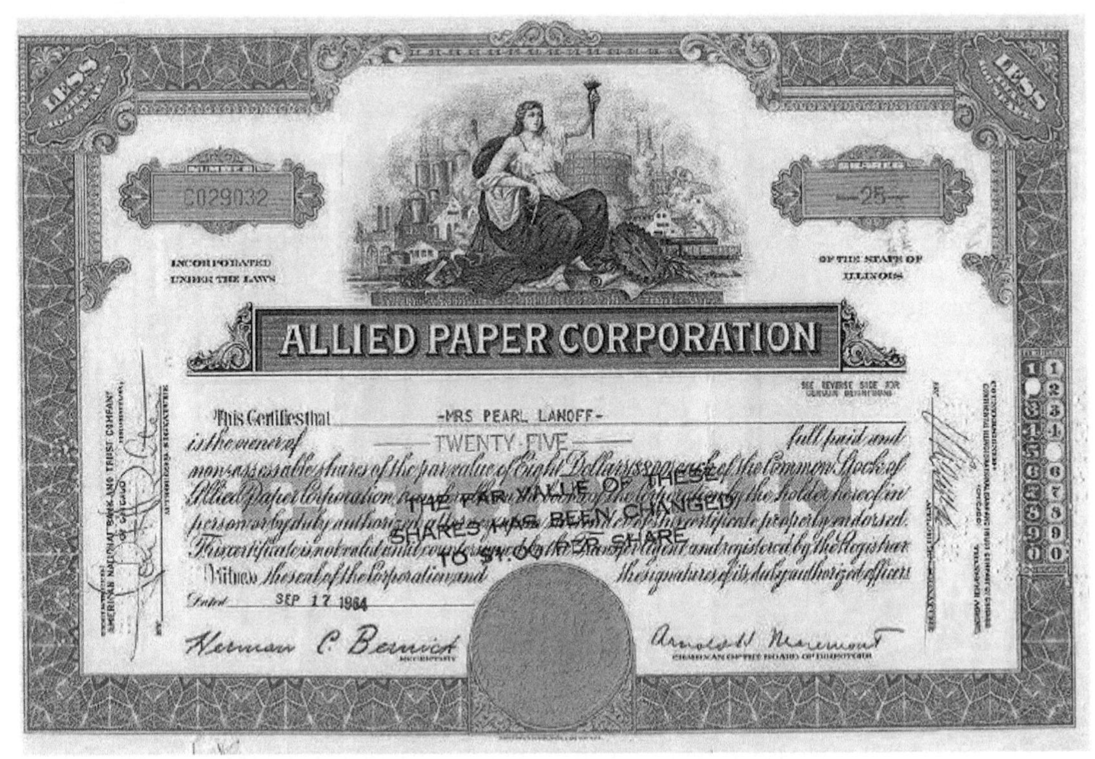

Source: http://wikimediafoundation.org/wiki/File:Allied_Paper_Corporation_Stock_Certificate_1964.jpg.

Stop and Think Box

How would you characterize financial instruments in the following forms?

- I, Joe Schmo, promise to pay to Jane Doe at her home on Mockingbird Lane $100 at the end of the fiscal quarter.
- I, Joe Schmo, promise to pay to Jane Doe at her home on Mockingbird Lane 10 percent of all profits arising from my taco stand at the end of each fiscal quarter.
- I, Joe Schmo, promise to pay to Jane Doe at her home on Mockingbird Lane $100 at the end of each fiscal quarter if my taco stand earns at least that much profit.

The first instrument is a debt because Joe promises to pay Jane a fixed sum on a certain date. Joe is a simple borrower and Jane, his creditor/lender. The second instrument is an equity because Joe promises to pay Jane a percentage of profit, making Jane a part owner of the business. The third instrument is a hybrid because Joe promises to pay Jane a fixed sum but only if his taco stand is profitable. Parallel to the first instrument, Jane will receive a fixed sum on a fixed date (as in a loan), but like the second instrument, payment of the sum is contingent on the taco stand's profits (as in an ownership stake).

Key Takeaways

- Financial instruments, or securities, are contracts that specify who pays whom as well as how, if, when, and where payment is due.
- Debt instruments are for fixed sums on fixed dates and need to be paid in all events.
- Equities are ownership stakes that entitle owners to a portion of profits.
- Hybrid instruments are part debt and part equity or are convertible from one into the other.

2.5 Financial Markets

Learning Objective

1. In what ways can financial markets and instruments be grouped?

Financial markets come in a variety of flavors to accommodate the wide array of financial instruments or securities that have been found beneficial to both borrowers and lenders over the years. Primary markets are where newly created (issued) instruments are sold for the first time. Most securities are negotiable. In other words, they can be sold to other investors at will in what are called secondary markets. Stock exchanges, or secondary markets for ownership stakes in corporations called stocks (aka shares or equities), are the most well-known type, but there are also secondary markets for debt, including bonds (evidences of sums owed, IOUs), mortgages, and **derivatives** and other instruments. Not all secondary markets are organized as exchanges, centralized locations, like the New York Stock Exchange or the Chicago Board of Trade, for the sale of securities. Some are over-the-counter (OTC) markets run by **dealers** connected via various telecom devices (first by post and semaphore [flag signals], then by telegraph, then telephone, and now computer). Completely electronic markets, called electronic communication networks (ECNs), have gained much ground in recent years and now dominate most trading.[18]

derivatives

Derivatives are complex financial instruments, the prices of which are based on the prices of underlying assets, variables, or indices. Some investors use them to hedge (reduce) risks, while others (speculators) use them to increase risks.

dealers

Businesses that buy and sell securities continuously at bid and ask prices, profiting from the difference or spread between the two prices.

Money markets are used to trade instruments with less than a year to maturity (repayment of principal). Examples include the markets for T-bills (Treasury bills or short-term government bonds), commercial paper (short-term corporate bonds), banker's acceptances (guaranteed bank funds, like a cashier's check), negotiable certificates of deposit (large-denomination negotiable CDs, called NCDs), Fed funds (overnight loans of reserves between banks), call loans (overnight loans on the collateral of stock), repurchase agreements (short-term loans on the collateral of T-bills), and foreign exchange (currencies of other countries).

FIGURE 2.3 Nineteenth-century picture of male telegraph operator

Securities with a year or more to maturity trade in capital markets. Some capital market instruments, called perpetuities, never mature or fall due. Equities (ownership claims on the assets and income of corporations) and perpetual interest-only loans are prime examples. (Some interest-only loans mature in fifteen or thirty years with a so-called balloon payment, in which the principal falls due all at once at the end of the loan.) Most capital market instruments, including mortgages (loans on real estate **collateral**), corporate bonds, government bonds, and commercial and consumer loans, have fixed maturities ranging from a year to several hundred years, though most capital market instruments issued today have maturities of thirty years or less. Figure 2.4 briefly summarizes the differences between various types of financial markets.

collateral

Property pledged as security for the repayment of a loan.

FIGURE 2.4 Types of financial markets

Market Type	Characteristics of Securities	Market Structure
Equity vs. debt	Ownership claim on assets and earnings vs. fixed claim on revenues	-
Primary vs. secondary	"new" vs. "used"	-
Exchange vs. OTC	-	Centralized vs. decentralized
Money vs. capital	Short vs. long term to maturity	-

Derivatives contracts trade in a third type of financial market. Derivatives allow investors to spread and share a wide variety of risks, from changes in interest rates and stock market indices[19] to undesirable weather conditions[20] (too sunny for farmers, too rainy for amusement parks, too cold for orange growers, too hot for ski resorts). Financial derivatives are in some ways even more complicated than the derivatives in calculus, so they are discussed in detail in a separate chapter.

Some call financial markets "direct finance," though most admit the term is a misnomer because the functioning of the markets is usually aided by one or more market facilitators, including brokers, dealers, brokerages, and investment banks. Brokers facilitate secondary markets by linking sellers to buyers of securities in exchange for a fee or a commission, a percentage of the sale price. Dealers "make a market" by continuously buying and selling securities, profiting from the spread, or the difference between the sale and purchase prices. (For example, a dealer might buy a certain type of bond at, say, $99 and resell it at $99.125, ten thousand times a day, or even a second in this age of **High Frequency Trading**.) Brokerages engage in both brokering and dealing and usually also provide their clients with advice and information. Investment banks facilitate primary markets by underwriting (buying for resale to investors) stock and bond offerings, including initial public offerings (IPOs) of stocks, and by arranging **direct placement** of bonds. Sometimes investment banks act merely as brokers, introducing securities issuers to investors, usually institutional investors like the financial intermediaries discussed below. Sometimes they act as dealers, buying the securities themselves for later (hopefully soon!) resale to investors. And sometimes they provide advice, usually regarding **merger** and **acquisition**. Investment banks took a beating during the financial crisis that began in 2007. Most of the major ones went bankrupt or merged with large commercial banks. Early reports of the death of investment banking turned out to be premature, but the sector is depressed at present; two large ones and numerous small ones, niche players called boutiques, remain.[21]

High Frequency Trading

High Frequency Trading is done with the aid of computers and trading algorithms that can buy or sell securities in microseconds (millionths of a second). It now accounts for over half of all U.S. equity trading volume.

direct placement

A sale of financial securities, usually bonds, via direct negotiations with buyers, usually large institutional investors like insurance and investment companies.

merger

A merger occurs when two or more extant business firms combine into one through a pooling of interests or through purchase.

acquisition

When one company takes a controlling interest in another; when one business buys another.

Stop and Think Box

In eighteenth-century Pennsylvania and Maryland, people could buy real estate, especially in urban areas, on so-called ground rent, in which they obtained clear title and ownership of the land (and any buildings or other improvements on it) in exchange for the promise to pay some percentage (usually 6) of the purchase price forever. What portion of the financial system did ground rents (some of which are still being paid) inhabit? How else might ground rents be described?

Ground rents were a form of market or direct finance. They were financial instruments or, more specifically, perpetual mortgages akin to interest-only loans.

Financial markets are increasingly international in scope. Integration of transatlantic financial markets began early in the nineteenth century and accelerated after the mid-nineteenth-century introduction of the transoceanic telegraph systems. The process reversed early in the twentieth century due to both world wars and the Cold War; the demise of the gold standard;[22] and the creation of Bretton Woods, a system of fixed exchange rates, discretionary monetary policy, and capital immobility.[23] (We'll explore these topics and a related matter, the so-called trilemma, or impossible trinity, in another chapter.) With the end of the Bretton Woods arrangement in the early 1970s and the Cold War in the late 1980s/early 1990s, financial globalization reversed course once again. Today, governments, corporations, and other securities issuers (borrowers) can sell bonds, called foreign bonds, in a foreign country denominated in that foreign country's currency. (For example, the Mexican government can sell dollar-denominated bonds in U.S. markets.) Issuers can also sell Eurobonds or Eurocurrencies, bonds issued (created and sold) in foreign countries but denominated in the home country's currency. (For example, U.S. companies can sell dollar-denominated bonds in London and U.S. dollars can be deposited in non-U.S. banks. Note that the term *Euro* has nothing to do with the euro, the currency of the European Union, but rather means "outside." A Euro loan, therefore, could be a loan denominated in euro but made in London, New York, Tokyo, or Perth.) It is now also quite easy to invest in foreign stock exchanges,[24] many of which have grown in size and importance in the last few years, even if they struggled through the panic of 2008.

Stop and Think Box

To purchase the Louisiana Territory from Napoleon in 1803, the U.S. government sold long-term, dollar-denominated bonds in Europe. What portion of the financial system did those bonds inhabit? Be as specific as possible.

Those government bonds were Eurobonds because the U.S. government issued them overseas but denominated them in U.S. dollars.

Key Takeaways

- Financial markets can be categorized or grouped by issuance (primary vs. secondary markets), type of instrument (stock, bond, derivative), or market organization (exchange or OTC).
- Financial instruments can be grouped by time to maturity (money vs. capital) or type of obligation (stock, bond, derivative).

2.6 Financial Intermediaries

Learning Objective

1. In what ways can financial intermediaries be classified?

assets

Assets are "things owned" as opposed to liabilities, which are "things owed."

risk

The probability of loss.

return

The percentage gain or loss from an investment.

liabilities

Liabilities are "things owed" to others, as opposed to assets, which are "things owned."

Like financial markets, financial intermediaries are highly specialized. *Sometimes called the indirect method of finance, intermediaries, like markets, link investors/lenders/savers to borrowers/entrepreneurs/spenders but do so in an ingenious way, by transforming* **assets**. Unlike facilitators, which, as we have seen, merely broker or buy and sell the same securities, intermediaries buy and sell instruments with different **risk**, **return**, and/or liquidity characteristics. The easiest example to understand is that of a bank that sells relatively low risk (which is to say, safe), low return, and highly liquid **liabilities**, called demand deposits, to investors called depositors and buys the relatively risky, high return, and nonliquid securities of borrowers in the form of loans, mortgages, and/or bonds. Note, too, that investor–depositors own claims on the bank itself rather than on the bank's borrowers.

Financial intermediaries are sometimes categorized according to the type of asset transformations they undertake. As noted above, depository institutions, including commercial banks, savings banks, and credit unions, issue short-term deposits and buy long-term securities. Traditionally, commercial banks specialized in issuing demand, transaction, or checking deposits and making loans to businesses. Savings banks issued time or savings deposits and made mortgage loans to households and businesses, while credit unions issued time deposits and made consumer loans.

(Finance companies also specialize in consumer loans but are not considered depository institutions because they raise funds by selling commercial paper, bonds, and equities rather than by issuing deposits.)

Due to **deregulation**, *though, the lines between different types of depository institutions have blurred in recent years.* Ownership structure, charter terms, and regulatory agencies now represent the easiest way to distinguish between different types of depository institutions. Almost all commercial and many savings banks are joint-stock corporations. In other words, stockholders own them. Some savings banks and all credit unions are mutual corporations and hence are owned by those who have made deposits with them.

Insurance companies are also divided between mutual and joint-stock corporations. They issue contracts or policies that mature or come due should some contingency occur, which is a mechanism for spreading and sharing risks. Term life insurance policies pay off if the insured dies within the contract period, while life annuities pay off if the insured is still alive. Health insurance pays when an insured needs medical assistance. Property or casualty insurance, such as fire or automobile insurance, comes due in the event of a loss, like a fire or an accident. Liability insurance pays off when someone is sued for a tort (damages). Insurers invest policyholder **premiums** in stocks, corporate and government bonds, and various money market instruments, depending on the nature of the contingencies they insure against. Life insurance companies, for example, invest in longer-term assets than automobile or health insurers because, on average, life insurance claims occur much later than property or health claims. (In the parlance of insurance industry insiders, life insurance has a much longer "tail" than property insurance.)

The third major type of intermediary is the investment company, a category that includes pension and government retirement funds, which transform corporate bonds and stocks into annuities, and mutual funds and money market mutual funds, which transform diverse portfolios of capital and money market instruments, respectively, into **nonnegotiable** *but easily* **redeemable** *"shares."*

As Figure 2.5 *shows, the relative importance of commercial banks and life insurance companies has waned since World War II due to the proliferation of additional investment options.* As Figure 2.6 shows, their decline is relative only; the assets of all major types of intermediaries have grown rapidly over the last decade. The figures are in current dollars, or dollars not adjusted for inflation, and the U.S. economy has grown significantly since the war, in no small part due to the financial system. Nevertheless, as shown in Figure 2.7, the assets of financial intermediaries have grown steadily as a percentage of **GDP** in a process that critics deride as "**financialization.**"

deregulation

Generally, deregulation refers to any industry where regulations are eliminated or significantly reduced. In this context, deregulation refers to a series of regulatory reforms of the financial industry undertaken in the 1980s and 1990s.

premium

In this context, a sum paid for an insurance contract.

nonnegotiable

Nontransferable to third parties.

redeemable

In this context, changeable into cash money by the fund.

GDP

GDP, or gross domestic product, is one of several different measures of aggregate output, the total value of all final goods and services produced in an economy.

financialization

Financialization is a term used by critics of the rapid growth of the financial system. The general notion idea shared by such critics is that the financial system has grown larger to enrich itself at the expense of the real sector of the economy. In other words, financial sector growth, since the mid-1990s if not the early 1980s, has hurt, rather than aided, the non-financial part of the economy.

FIGURE 2.5 Share of total U.S. financial assets, year-end, 1945–2010

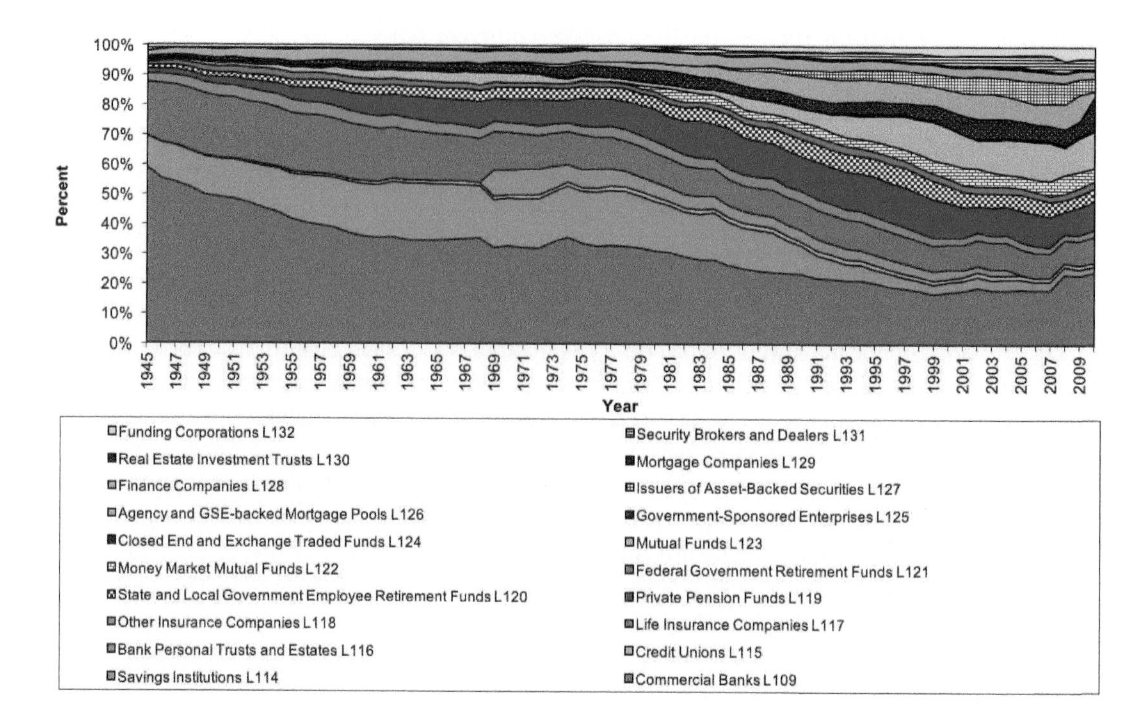

FIGURE 2.6 Assets of financial intermediaries, selected years, 1945–2005

Billions USD (current)	1945	1955	1965	1975	1985	1995	2005
Commercial Banks L109	143.6	187.9	341.6	885.1	2,376.3	4,493.8	9,236.0
Savings Institutions L114	25.6	69.1	187.1	453.4	1,274.9	1,012.8	1,788.7
Credit Unions L115	0.4	2.9	10.8	36.1	134.8	310.7	685.5
Bank Personal Trusts and Estates L116	0.0	0.0	0.0	158.9	358.3	774.9	924.6
Life Insurance Companies L117	43.9	87.9	154.2	297.7	796.1	2,063.6	4,380.7
Other Insurance Companies L118	6.3	19.6	36.8	80.3	298.6	740.3	1,265.4
Private Pension Funds L119	4.1	19.6	80.2	244.3	1226.3	2,888.8	4,613.3
State and Local Government Employee Retirement Funds L120	2.6	10.8	34.1	104.0	398.7	1,308.1	2,721.7
Federal Government Retirement Funds L121	2.9	10.0	19.7	42.1	172.1	541.1	1,075.0
Money Market Mutual Funds L122	0.0	0.0	0.0	3.7	242.4	741.3	2,006.9
Mutual Funds L123	1.2	7.8	35.2	43.0	245.9	1,852.8	6,045.1
Closed End and Exchange Traded Funds L124	1.0	3.5	7.6	9.0	8.3	136.4	270.8
Government-Sponsored Enterprises L125	2.3	5.5	18.9	93.4	324.0	897.4	2,805.1
Agency and GSE-backed Mortgage Pools L126	0.0	0.1	0.9	28.5	367.9	1,570.7	3,677.5
Issuers of Asset-Backed Securities L127	0.0	0.0	0.0	0.0	37.2	762.9	3,059.1
Finance Companies L128	4.3	18.2	44.4	97.2	338.4	672.3	1334.6
Mortgage Companies L129	0.1	1.4	4.5	9.3	24.7	33.0	32.1
Real Estate Investment Trusts L130	0.0	0.0	0.0	7.3	10.4	33.3	354.6
Security Brokers and Dealers L131	5.0	5.9	10.3	21.5	156.0	568.1	2,144.1
Funding Corporations L132	0.0	0.1	0.5	1.3	135.4	383.4	1,488.0
Total Financial Assets	243.3	450.3	986.8	2,616.1	8,926.7	21,785.7	51,913.8

FIGURE 2.7 Financial assets to gross domestic product (GDP), 1945–2015

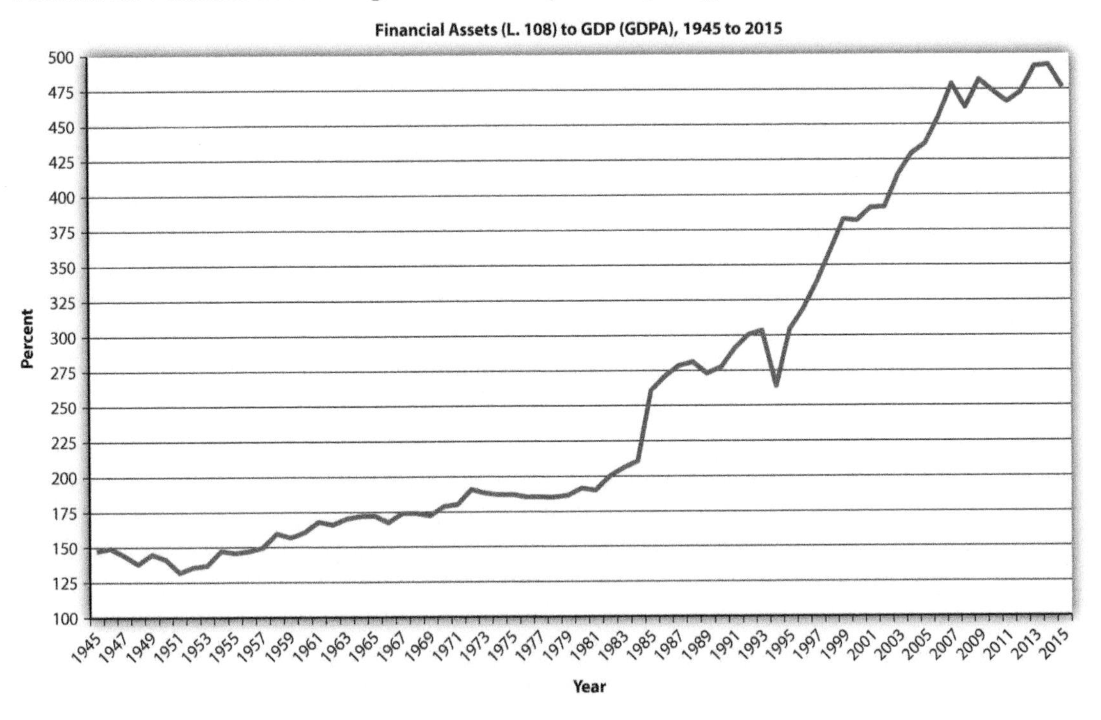

Financial markets have exhibited similar growth. For example, the Dow Jones Industrial Average (DJIA),[25] a mechanism for tracking the prices of the shares of the nation's most important corporations, grew from less than 200 at the end of World War II to just shy of 700 when John F. Kennedy took office in 1961, to around 1,000 when Ronald Reagan became president twenty years later, to over 3,200 in 1992 and over 10,000 by 1999.[26] Trading volumes on the New York Stock Exchange[27] and the NASDAQ[28] have likewise soared. In 1945, daily trading volumes rarely exceeded 2 million shares. By 1975, 10 million shares was considered a slow day. By 2005, over 1 billion shares were regularly traded each day. By 2015, about 10 billion shares traded daily, thanks largely to the rise of High Frequency Trading and ECNs.[29]

Key Takeaway

- Financial intermediaries, including depository institutions (commercial banks, savings banks, credit unions) and insurers (life, health, property, and casualty), can be grouped by the composition of their balance sheets (nature of their assets and liabilities and the asset transformations they undertake) or their ownership structures, the origins of their corporate charters, and/or the identities of their regulators.

2.7 Competition Between Markets and Intermediaries

Learning Objective

1. What trade-offs do investors face? How do borrowers decide whether to use financial markets or intermediaries to obtain the funds they need?

Why do investors (savers) sometimes choose to invest in intermediaries rather than directly in financial markets? Why do borrowers sometimes choose to reduce their liquidity and capital constraints via intermediaries and sometimes via markets? Markets and intermediaries often fulfill the same needs, though in different ways. *Borrowers/securities issuers typically choose the alternative with the lowest overall cost, while investors/savers choose to invest in the markets or intermediaries that provide them with the risk-return-liquidity trade-off that best suits them.*

Return is how much an investor gets from owning an asset. It can be positive (yipee!) or negative (d'oh!). *Risk is variability of return.* A "risky" asset might pay off big or be a big loser. A "safe" asset will probably return something mundane and expected. *Liquidity is the speed with which an asset can be sold at something close to its real market value.* A highly "liquid" asset, like a Federal Reserve note, can be exchanged instantaneously at no cost. A "liquid" asset, like a Treasury bond, can be sold in a few minutes for a minimal fee. An "illiquid" asset, like a house in a depressed neighborhood, may take months or years to sell and cost a significant portion of its value to unload.

ceteris paribus

All else equal.

default

Non- or partial payment of a loan, bond, or other payment obligation.

Risk is a bad thing, while return and liquidity are good things. Therefore, every saver wants to invest in riskless, easily saleable investments that generate high returns. Of course, such opportunities occur infrequently because investors bid up their prices, thus reducing their returns. (As we'll see in another chapter, the higher the price of an investment, the lower its return, **ceteris paribus**.) To keep returns high, some investors will be willing to give up some liquidity or to take on more risk. For example, they might buy securities *not* backed by collateral (assets like buildings, businesses, or safe financial instruments like T-bills that the borrower promises to forfeit in case of **default**). As a result of the competition between investors, and between borrowers, the financial system offers instruments with a wide variety of characteristics, ranging from highly liquid, very safe, but low-return T-bills and demand deposits, to medium-risk, medium-liquidity, medium-return mortgages, to risky but potentially lucrative and easily sold derivatives like put options and foreign exchange futures contracts.

Investors care about more than risk, return, and liquidity, but generally other considerations are secondary. For example, investors will pay more for investments with fixed redemption dates rather than ones that can be called (repaid) at the borrower's option because fixed redemption dates reduce investors' uncertainty. They will also sometimes pay a little more for instruments issued by environmentally or socially conscious companies and countries and less for those issued by dirty, rude ones.

Stop and Think Box

In the fall of 2006, interest rates on conventional thirty-year home mortgages without a prepayment penalty (a fee charged to the borrower if he/she repays the principal early) were about 6.5 percent per year. But mortgages with otherwise identical terms that contained a prepayment penalty for the first seven years of the loan could be had for 6.25 percent per year. Why was that the case?

In addition to risk, return, and liquidity, investors are concerned about the uncertainty of repayment terms. They are willing to receive a lower return (ceteris paribus, of course) in exchange for a guarantee that a loan will not be repaid for a significant period of time.

As noted above, borrowers also compete with each other for the lowest cost methods of meeting their external financing needs. Obviously, borrowers want to pay as little for funds as possible and would like nothing better than to borrow huge sums forever, unconditionally, and at zero interest. Nobody wants to lend on those terms, though, so borrowers compete with each other for funds by offering investors higher returns, less risk, or more liquid instruments. *They use whichever part of the financial system, markets or intermediaries, offers them the best deal.* A company may sell commercial paper in the money market rather than obtain a bank loan, for example, if it is large enough and well-known enough to interest enough investors and market facilitators. A smaller, newer company, though, may find that a bank loan is much easier and cheaper to obtain.

Key Takeaways

- Investors primarily trade off among risk, return, and liquidity, and to a lesser extent they also value the certainty of redemption terms.
- Borrowers want to obtain funds as cheaply as possible and on repayment terms as flexible as possible.

2.8 Regulation

Learning Objective

1. What are the major goals of financial regulation?

Like investors, borrowers are concerned about the total net costs (all costs plus all benefits) of different types of finance. One big consideration is government and self-regulation. *Compared with most other parts of modern capitalist economies, the financial system is relatively heavily regulated.* Regulators like the Securities and Exchange Commission (SEC, which oversees exchanges and OTC markets), the New York Stock Exchange (NYSE, which oversees itself as an SRO or self-regulating organization[30]), and the Commodities Futures Trading Commission (CFTC, which oversees futures market exchanges) monitor and regulate financial markets. Other regulators, including the Office of the Comptroller of the Currency (which oversees federally chartered commercial banks), the Federal Deposit Insurance Corporation (FDIC, which oversees almost all depositories), and sundry state banking and insurance commissions, monitor financial intermediaries. Companies that wish to avoid direct regulatory scrutiny due to its high cost tend to use intermediaries rather than markets. For example, instead of selling shares to the public, which would require following the many rules of the SEC and the NYSE (or other exchange or OTC market), a company might decide that it would be cheaper to obtain a long-term bank loan or sell bonds to life insurers, mutual funds, and other institutional investors in a direct placement.

Regulators serve four major functions. First, they try to reduce asymmetric information by encouraging **transparency**. That usually means requiring both financial market participants and intermediaries to disclose accurate information to investors in a clear and timely manner. A second and closely related goal is to protect consumers from scammers, shysters, and assorted other grifters, as well as from the failure of honest but ill-fated or poorly run institutions. They do the latter by directly limiting the types of assets that various types of financial institutions can hold and by mandating minimum reserve and capitalization levels. Third, they strive to promote financial system competition and efficiency by ensuring that the entry and exit of firms is as easy and cheap as possible, consistent with their first two goals. For example, new banks can form but only after their incorporators (founders) and initial executives have been carefully screened. Insurance companies can go out of business (exit) but only after they have made adequate provision to fulfill their promises to policyholders.

transparency

In general, the opposite of opacity. In this context, transparency means a relatively low degree of asymmetric information.

lender of last resort

During a financial crisis or panic, a lender of last resort makes loans when no one else will.

deposit insurance

Insurance that pays off if a bank defaults on its deposit liabilities.

Great Inflation

Peacetime inflation rates in the United States in the 1970s were higher than any time before or since.

*Finally, regulators also try to ensure the soundness of the financial system by acting as a***lender of last resort**, *mandating***deposit insurance**, *and limiting competition through restrictions on entry and interest rates.* The first two forms of regulation are relatively uncontroversial, although many believe that the lender of last resort function should not be combined with a too big to fail (TBTF) policy, and that deposit insurance can increase risk-taking by bankers. Limiting competition is a highly controversial means of ensuring safety because it extends privileges to existing institutions over new ones. Little surprise, then, that the regulated companies themselves are often the strongest supporters of that type of regulation!

Stop and Think Box

For decades, the Federal Reserve capped the interest rates that banks could pay on checking deposits at zero and the interest rates that they could pay on time or savings deposits at around 6 percent per year. What was the intended economic effect of those restrictions? Why didn't existing banks lobby for their repeal until the Great Inflation of the 1970s?

The restrictions were put in place to limit competition among banks, allowing them to be profitable without assuming too much risk. Existing banks were more than happy to reap relatively riskless profits until inflation exceeded the interest rates that they could legally pay. At that point, disintermediation was rampant. In other words, many people pulled their money out of banks and put them directly into the market, via money market and stock and bond mutual funds.

Key Takeaways

- Regulators attempt to maximize macroeconomic stability and transparency and to minimize investor risk and loss.
- The policies they implement to do so, however, can be controversial and are not always effective.

2.9 Suggested Reading

Barth, James, Gerard Caprio, and Ross Levine. *Rethinking Bank Regulation: Till Angels Govern.* New York: Cambridge University Press, 2008.

Bebczuk, Ricardo. *Asymmetric Information in Financial Markets: Introduction and Applications.* New York: Cambridge University Press, 2003.

Gitman, Lawrence and Chad Zutter, Principles of Managerial Finance. New York: Prentice Hall, 2011.

Landier, Augustin, and Vinay Nair. *Investing for Change: Profit from Responsible Investment.* New York: Oxford University Press, 2008.

Parmeswaran, Sunil. *Fundamentals of Financial Instruments: An Introduction to Stocks, Bonds, Foreign Exchange, and Derivatives.* Hoboken, N.J.: Wiley, 2011.

Tyson, Eric. *Personal Finance for Dummies*, 5th ed. Hoboken, NJ: John Wiley and Sons, 2006.

Endnotes

1. www.amazon.com/Bonfire-Vanities-Tom-Wolfe/dp/0553275976
2. www.imdb.com/title/tt0099165
3. www.imdb.com/name/nm0000362
4. www.imdb.com/name/nm0000060
5. www.imdb.com/title/tt0102609
6. 1987: www.imdb.com/title/tt0094291; 2010: www.imdb.com/title/tt1027718
7. www.imdb.com/title/tt1596363/
8. For a list and description of others, see fortune.com/2015/12/27/big-short-wall-street-movies/
9. www.bibliomania.com/0/6/3/1050/frameset.html
10. www.nndb.com/films/309/000033210
11. www.imdb.com/character/ch0004662/
12. en.wikipedia.org/wiki/The_Smartest_Guys_in_the_Room
13. Will Goetzmann, *Money Changes Everything: How Finance Made Civilization Possible* (Princeton: Princeton University Press, 2016).
14. www.innovation-america.org/archive.php?articleID=79
15. www.fullbooks.com/Dante-s-Inferno.html
16. www.urbandictionary.com/define.php?term=natty+light
17. James Karmel, *Gambling on the American Dream: Atlantic City and the Casino Era* (New York: Routledge, 2008).
18. "Stock Exchanges: The Battle of the Bourses," *The Economist* (31 May 2008), 77–79.
19. quote.yahoo.com/m1?u
20. www.cme.com/trading/prd/weather/index.html
21. "American Finance: And Then There Were None. What the death of the investment bank means for Wall Street," *The Economist* (27 September 2008), 85–86.
22. John H. Wood, "The Demise of the Gold Standard," *Economic Perspectives* (Nov. 1981): 13-23.
23. economics.about.com/od/foreigntrade/a/bretton_woods.htm
24. www.forbes.com/sites/baldwin/2011/06/27/how-to-trade-foreign-stocks/#574be4e25ab9
25. www.djindexes.com/averages/
26. www.measuringworth.com/datasets/DJA/index.php
27. www.nyse.com
28. www.nasdaq.com
29. www.itg.com/trading-volume/quarter/
30. en.wikipedia.org/wiki/Self-regulatory_organization

CHAPTER 3

Money

Chapter Objectives

By the end of this chapter, students should be able to:

1. Define money.
2. Describe the work or economic functions that money performs.
3. Define barter and explain why it is economically inefficient.
4. Explain why some forms of commodity money are better than others.
5. Explain why representative, credit, and fiat money supplanted commodity money.
6. Define the money supply and explain how and why it is measured.

3.1 Of Love, Money, and Transactional Efficiency

Learning Objective

1. What is money and what economic functions does it perform?

Like love, money is ubiquitous, yet few of us feel that we have enough of either. As abstract concepts, money and love are both slippery, yet most of us believe that we know them when we see them. *Despite those similarities, mixing money and love can be dangerous.* The love of money is said to be one of the seven deadly sins; the money of love, despite its hoariness, is illegal in many jurisdictions in the United States and abroad.

Jest and wordplay aside, *money is, perhaps, the most important invention of all time.* Like the other major contenders for the title, indoor plumbing, internal combustion engines, computers, and other modern gadgets of too recent origin to consider; the wheel, which needs no introduction; the hearth, a pit for controlling fire; and the atlatl, a spear thrower similar in concept to a lacrosse stick, money is a force multiplier. In other words, it allows its users to complete much more work in a given amount of time than nonusers can possibly do, just as the wheel let porters move more stuff, the hearth helped cooks prepare more food, and the atlatl allowed hunters (warriors) to kill more prey (enemies).

What work does money do? *It facilitates trade by making it easier to buy and sell goods compared to barter, the exchange of one nonmoney good for another.* (If you've ever traded baseball cards, clothes, beers, phone numbers, homework assignments, or any other nonmoney goods, you've engaged in barter.) This is no minor matter because trade is the one thing that makes us human. As that great eighteenth-century Scottish economist Adam Smith (and others) pointed out, no other animal trades with nonrelatives of the same species. The inherent predisposition to trade may explain why humans have relatively large brains and relatively small digestive tracts. Trade certainly explains why humans have more material comforts by far than any other species on the planet. Each trade that is fairly consummated enriches both the buyer and the seller. The good feeling people get when they buy (sell) a good is what economists call **consumer surplus** (**producer**

consumer surplus

In a standard supply and demand graph, that area above the price line and below the demand curve.

producer surplus

In a standard supply and demand graph, that area below the price line and above the supply curve.

surplus). By making trading relatively easy, money helps to make humanity happier. (Note that this is not the same as claiming that wealth makes people happy. Although sometimes used synonymously with wealth in everyday speech, money is actually a special form of wealth.)

Imagine what life would be like without money. Suppose you try to fill up your automobile's gasoline tank, or take mass transit to school, or acquire *any* good, without using money (or credit, money's close cousin). How would you do it? You would have to find something that the seller desired. That could take a long time and quite possibly forever. If you don't believe me, go to any Craigslist posting,[1] where you will find listings like the one that follows. It's a fun diversion, but what would this person think is a "fair" trade? A lava lamp and a Grateful Dead poster? Would she give you a ball of yarn in change?

Date: 2006-11-30, 2:37 PM EST

Hello Craigslisters,

I recently moved to NYC and I have no use for the six items pictured below. Starting from the upper left going clockwise, I have: a working desk lamp, a hardcover copy of the NY Times best-selling book The Historian, *an unused leather-bound photo album, a giant bouncy-ball that lights up when it bounces, a pair of goofy sunglasses, and a hand-made tribal mask from Mexico.*

Make me any offer for any or all of the items, and if it's fair, we'll trade.

In the lingo of economists, by serving as a means or medium of exchange, *money eliminates one of the major difficulties of barter*, fulfilling this mutual or double coincidence of wants. And it does it quite well as it zips across the country and the entire globe.

Another serious difficulty with barter helps us to see the second major type of work that money does. Suppose that the gas station attendant or bus driver wanted chewing gum and you had some. Exchange may still not take place because a crucial question remains unanswered: how many sticks of gum is a gallon of gas or a bus trip worth? Ascertaining the answer turns out to be an insurmountable barrier in most instances. *In a money economy, the number of prices equals the number of traded goods because each has a money price, the good's cost in terms of the unit of account. In a barter economy, by contrast, the number of prices equals the number of pairs of goods.* So, for example, an economy with just 1,000 goods (a very poor economy indeed) would require 499,500 different prices! Little wonder, then, that barter economies, when they exist, usually produce only ten or so tradable goods, which means about forty-five different prices, each good paired with nine others. By serving as a unit of account, a measuring rod of economic value, money makes price determination much easier.

The unit of account function of money is more abstract than its work as a medium of exchange and hence is less well understood, but that does not mean that it is less important. *To be an effective force multiplier, money has to eliminate both of barter's biggest deficiencies*. In other words, it has to end the double coincidence of wants problem *and* reduce the number of prices, ideally to one per good. It does the former by acting as a medium of exchange, something that people acquire not for its own sake but to trade away to another person for something of use. The latter it does by serving as a unit of account, as a way of *reckoning value*. When functioning as a unit of account, money helps us to answer the question, "How much is that worth?," much like inches help us to answer, "How long is that?" or degrees Fahrenheit or Celsius help us to ascertain, "What is the temperature of that?" By helping us to reckon value, money allows us to easily and quickly compare the economic value of unlike things, to compare apples and oranges, both literally and figuratively.

Stop and Think Box

After the demise of the Soviet Union, inflation reigned supreme as the Russian ruble lost more and more of its value each day. Rubles remained a medium of exchange, but in many places in Russia, prices and debts began to be denominated in "bucks." What were bucks and why did they arise?

Bucks were U.S. dollars, used not just as a physical medium of exchange but also as a unit of account and standard of deferred payment, as a way of reckoning value in a stable unit. Russians could buy goods and services with Federal Reserve Notes, if they had any, or with enough paper rubles to buy the number of U.S. dollars demanded in the spot market. So if it took 100 rubles to buy a "buck," a shopkeeper would want 3,000 rubles for a pair of blue jeans he priced at $30 ($30 x 100 rubles per $1 = 3,000 rubles).

Money also works as a store of value and as a standard of deferred compensation. By store of value, economists mean that money can store purchasing power over time. Of course, many other assets—real estate, financial securities, precious metals, and gems—perform precisely the same function. *Storing value, therefore, is not exclusively a trait of money, and, in fact, fiat monies are usually a very poor store of value.* By standard of deferred compensation, economists mean that money can be used to denominate a debt, an obligation to make a payment in the future.

To help you to see the different functions of money, consider the following transaction:

Customer: How much for a gallon of gasoline? (A)

Attendant: $2.99 (A)

Customer: Great, fill 'er up.

Attendant: Will that be cash (E), check (E), debit (E), or credit (D)?

In the places labeled (A), money is working as a unit of account. The customer is trying to reckon the value of the gasoline, information that the attendant quickly encapsulates by quoting a money price. The customer just as quickly decides that she would rather have the gasoline than the money, or more precisely the other goods that the money could acquire, and requests the trade. The attendant responds by inquiring which medium of exchange (E) the customer wishes to use to pay for the good. Cash refers to physical currency, like **Federal Reserve notes** or Treasury coins. Check refers to a *paper* order for the transfer of money from a bank account. Debit refers to an *electronic* order for a transfer from a bank account or a prepaid declining balance debit card. Credit entails the prearranged transfer of funds from the customer's creditor, a bank or other lender, in exchange for a small service fee from the gas station[2] and the customer's promise to repay the lender (and perhaps interest and a yearly fee). In the case of the credit transaction, money is working as a standard of deferred payment (D) because the customer promises to repay the lender the amount of the loan (purchase price of the gasoline) at some point in the future. (We will speak of credit money below, but students should not allow the lingo to confuse them. Credit cards and other loans are not money per se but rather are ways of obtaining it. The distinction will become clearer as your course of study during the semester unfolds.)

Federal Reserve notes

Fiat paper money issued by America's central bank, the Federal Reserve.

Of course, conversations like the one above rarely occur today. Except in New Jersey and a few other places, people pump their own gas; stations post their prices on big signs for all to see; and in addition to dispensing the product, gas pumps handle credit and debit (and sometimes cash) purchases with ease. Money makes all that possible, *saving humanity untold hours of waste over the trillions of exchanges completed each year.*

Key Takeaways

- Barter entails the exchange of one good for another. It is inefficient because it requires satisfaction of the double coincidence of wants (party one must have what party two desires, and vice versa) and pricing problems (the number of prices of goods equals the number of possible pairs).
- Perhaps the most important invention of all time, money is anything that reduces the transaction costs of barter, anything that is commonly accepted as payment or in exchange.
- Money serves as a medium of exchange (physical means of payment), unit of account (measure of economic value), store of value (method of storing said value over time), and standard of deferred payment (basis upon which debts are repaid).

3.2 Better to Have Had Money and Lost It Than to Have Never Had Money at All

Learning Objective

1. What usually happens when money is absent in an economy?

To further appreciate money's importance, consider what happens when it is absent—*universal distress, followed quickly by money's reintroduction or reinvention*! After World War I, for example, the German government created too much money too quickly. Hyperinflation, a very rapid rise in the prices of all goods, ensued. Prices increased so fast that workers insisted on being paid twice daily so they could run, not walk, to the nearest store to buy food before their hard-earned wages became worthless. Before the hyperinflation, it was said that you could buy a wheelbarrow full of food with a purse full of cash. During the hyperinflation, you needed a wheelbarrow full of cash to purchase a purse full of food. At the end of the debacle, you kept the wheelbarrow at home lest your most valuable asset, the wheelbarrow, be stolen! At the end of the crisis, the German economy was on a barter basis, but only briefly before currency reforms stopped the inflation and restored a money economy.

seigniorage

Profit earned from the issuance of money.

dollarization

Adoption of a foreign currency (not necessarily U.S. dollars despite the term) as both a means of making payments and a means of reckoning value.

Stop and Think Box

During its 2001–2002 financial crisis, Argentina faced a severe shortage of its money, called pesos. Private firms responded by setting up giant flea markets where goods were priced and paid for using the firm's notes, which in most instances were called creditós. The creditós could be used in subsequent flea markets run by the issuing firm but not in markets run by other firms.

Creditós had very limited circulation outside the flea markets. As soon as the peso crisis passed, the firms stopped running flea markets and no longer honored the creditós they had issued. What happened in Argentina?

A new form of private credit money spontaneously arose to fill the vacuum created by the dearth of pesos. Although not as liquid or safe as pesos, creditós were far superior to barter. The end-game default can be interpreted as seigniorage, the profit the issuers of creditós exacted for providing money to local Argentine communities. In other nations, like Ecuador, collapse of the local currency led to dollarization or adoption of a foreign currency (such as U.S. dollars) as both a medium of exchange and unit of account.

In prisons, prisoner-of-war camps, and other settings where money is unavailable, *inmates quickly learn the inadequacies of barter firsthand and adopt the best available commodity as money*—a medium of exchange; unit of account; a store of value; and even, to the limited extent that credit is available in such circumstances, a standard of deferred payment. Packs of cigarettes often emerge as the **commodity money** of choice. (Talk about one's fortune going up in smoke!) There are good economic reasons for this preference. Although not perfect, cigarettes are a serviceable medium of exchange. First and foremost, sealed packs of cigarettes are easily authenticated because it would be extremely difficult to counterfeit or adulterate them, especially under prison conditions. Although they differ somewhat from brand to brand, they are also relatively uniform in quality. If you gave up a bar of soap for two packs, you could rest relatively well assured that you were not being cheated. Second, cigarette packs are divisible, into twenty individual cigarettes, or "loosies," without giving up much of their ease of authentication. (A loosie is *easier* to adulterate than a sealed pack, say, by replacing the tobacco with sawdust, but is still not *easy*.) Divisibility is important because supply and demand might well dictate an equilibrium price that includes a fraction of a pack, just as it often leads to prices that are a fraction of a dollar ($), yen (¥), euro (€), or pound (£). Individual cigarettes are also somewhat divisible but only when filterless or when consumed. One might, for instance, sell a good blanket for four packs, two loosies, and five drags or puffs.

commodity money

Forms of money that have intrinsic value as a commodity.

Cigarettes also have relatively high value-to-weight and value-to-bulk ratios. In other words, they are relatively valuable given their size and weight. That portability is, of course, important to their function as a medium of exchange. Although they eventually go stale and can be ruined if smashed or drenched in water, sealed cigarettes packs are durable enough to also serve as an intermediate term store of value. The elasticity of the supply of cigarette packs is volatile, however, because smokers find it difficult to quit smoking, no matter the price and the fact that the quantity of packs in circulation depends on shipments from the outside world. In modern prisons, this is less of a problem, but in prisoner-of-war (POW) camps, sudden gluts caused the prices of goods (non-cigarettes) to soar (that is, the value of cigarettes plummeted), only to be followed by long periods of deflation (lower prices for noncigarettes) as the supply of cigarettes dried up and each cigarette gained in purchasing power.

Key Takeaways

- Where money is absent, an available commodity with the best combination of ease of authentication, uniformity, divisibility, durability, portability, and elasticity of supply may emerge as money.
- In other instances, as in Argentina, private credit money may emerge.

3.3 A Short History of Moolah

Learning Objective

1. What characteristics does a good medium of exchange possess?

FIGURE 3.1 Cowrie money from early China.

This doesn't look like money to you, but it did to people in early China

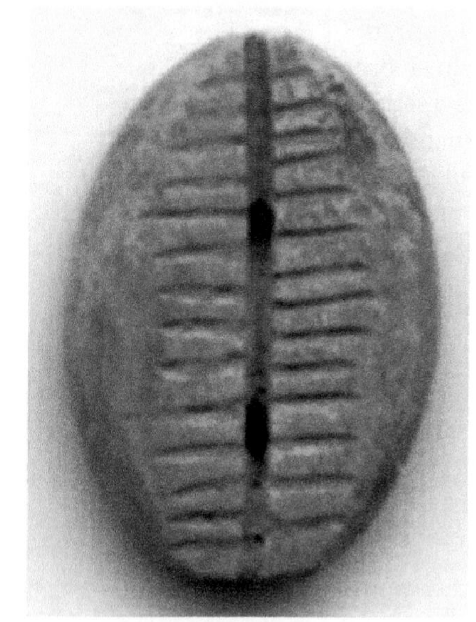

Source: http://www.joelscoins.com

Much stranger commodities than cigarettes have served as money over the ages, and for the most part served well. As storied economist John Kenneth Galbraith once claimed, "More than most things, an understanding of money requires an appreciation of its history," so a brief history lesson is in order here.[3] As Figure 3.1 suggests, various types of live animals, parts of dead animals, grains, metals, rocks, and shells have been money at one time and place or another.[4]

We generally find that, as with the case of prison inmates, *early societies used available commodities that had the best combination of ease of authentication, uniformity, divisibility, durability, portability, and elasticity of supply*. Hay (grassy livestock feed) rarely emerges as money because it is too easy to adulterate with weeds; its low value-to-bulk renders its portability very low due to the trouble and expense of transporting it; and until it is properly baled and stored, a rainstorm can ruin it. Tobacco, by contrast, has served as a commodity money because it is more uniform, durable, portable, and easily authenticated than hay. In colonial Virginia, tobacco was turned into a form of **representative money** when trustworthy and knowledgeable inspectors attested to its quality, stored it in safe warehouses, and issued paper receipts for it. *The receipts, shown in* Figure 3.2, *rather than the tobacco itself, served as an extremely uniform, durable, divisible, portable, and easily authenticated medium of exchange.*

FIGURE 3.2 Eighteenth-century tobacco transfer note

The number, date, and signatures served as anti-counterfeiting measures on this early representative money.

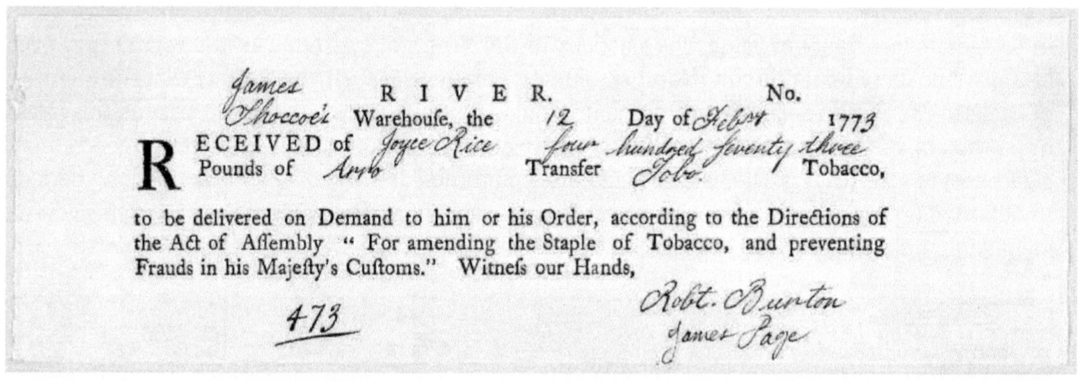

James RIVER. No.
Shoccoe's Warehoufe, the 12 Day of Febry 1773
RECEIVED of Joyce Rice four hundred feventy three
Pounds of Arrb Transfer Tobo. Tobacco,
to be delivered on Demand to him or his Order, according to the Directions of the Act of Affembly "For amending the Staple of Tobacco, and preventing Frauds in his Majefty's Cuftoms." Witnefs our Hands,
473
Robt. Burton
James Page

Courtesy: The Colonial Williamsburg Foundation.

representative money

Intrinsically valueless (or nearly so) tokens that can be exchanged for commodities at a fixed, predetermined rate.

Diamonds, rubies, and other rare gems seldom become money because they are *not uniform in quality and are difficult to authenticate*. One needs expensive specialized training and equipment to value them properly. (See Figure 3.3 for an example.) *Gold*, by contrast, has often served as money because, as an element (symbol = Au; atomic number = 79),[5] it is perfectly uniform in its pure form. It is also easily divisible; relatively highly portable for a commodity; and, though soft for a metal, quite durable. Gold can be adulterated by mixing it with cheaper metals. Even when coined, it can be clipped, sweated, or otherwise adulterated. Relatively easy ways of authenticating gold and other precious metals in their bullion (bar or brick) and coin forms exist, however.[6] Gold's elasticity of supply, traditionally quite low due to its *rarity*, is its biggest shortcoming. *Money must be scarce, meaning that free goods like air and water (where plentiful) will not work as money, but it need not be rare, and in fact, the best forms of money are not rare.*

Many students have no problem seeing how commodities with use value, like food and cigarettes, or rarity value, like gold and silver, can be money. They often wonder, though, about the sanity of people who used common, useless items as money. Before congratulating themselves on their own rationality, however, they ought to peek into their wallets and purses, where they may discover, if they haven't already used it on tuition, books, and entertainment, that they possess some greenish pieces of paper, called Federal Reserve notes, the use value of which is nearly nil.[7] True, those notes are fiat money. In other words, they appear to enjoy the advantage of legal tender status. The face of the notes makes clear that they are "legal tender for all debts, public and private." That means that it is *illegal to refuse them*. That little note on the notes notwithstanding, it is clear[8] that people today accept Federal Reserve notes for the same reason that people in the past accepted clamshells, beads, or other low use-value items, because they know that they can turn around and successfully exchange them for goods. In fact, *many economists define money as anything commonly accepted in exchange*. (So Ron Paul dollars are not money!)[9]

FIGURE 3.3
Is it real?
Answer: No, it's a Cubic Zirconium, a fake diamond. Or is it???

© 2010 Jupiterimages Corporation

Key Takeaways

- The best medium of exchange combines ease of authentication, uniformity, divisibility, durability, portability, and elasticity of supply.
- Gold is not necessarily the best type of money because its supply is relatively inelastic.
- Declaring a medium of exchange as legal tender may help that medium of exchange to circulate, but simply knowing that something is readily accepted in exchange can work just as well.

3.4 Commodity and Credit Monies

Learning Objective

1. How do representative and credit monies compare to commodity monies?

Truth be told, the people who used lion teeth or rocks with holes in them as money might find moderns a bit off their rockers for using money created by the government. The reason is simple: *commodity monies are self-equilibrating, but government fiat monies are not* because they are sometimes subject more to the whims of politicians and bureaucrats than to the forces of supply and demand, as we will see in a later chapter. Commodity money systems can self-equilibrate, or essentially run themselves, because commodities are scarce (but as noted above, not necessarily rare). In other words, the opportunity costs of their acquisition and production are greater than zero. That means that at some point people will find it just as profitable to produce nonmonetary goods as to produce money directly. At that point, money creation naturally ceases until more is needed. One way to see this is to consider the incentives of individuals to produce money or nonmonetary goods in a very simple economy.

Suppose, for example, that clamshells are money and that ten can be found in one hour, on average. Suppose too that people on average can also produce a bow in two hours, an arrow in one hour, and a dead rabbit in three hours. In that situation, an arrow would cost ten clamshells, a bow twenty clamshells, and a rabbit thirty clamshells because at those prices people would be indifferent whether they spent, say, six hours collecting clamshells (6 × 10 = 60), making arrows (6 × 10 = 60), making bows ([6/2 hours per bow] = 3 bows produced in 6 hours; 3 × 20 = 60), or hunting rabbits ([6/3]

= 2; 2 × 30 = 60). If clamshells are somehow removed from circulation (maybe by being traded away), it will be more remunerative to harvest clamshells than to make bows or arrows or to fricassee rabbits until the supply of clamshells is restored, which should not be long. (In fact, if people *expected* the exodus of the clamshells, the adjustment might well be instantaneous.)

Commodity money systems also automatically adjust to structural changes in the economy. If it suddenly became easier to find clamshells, say, twenty in an hour, everybody would harvest clamshells until the clamshell prices of arrows, bows, and rabbits doubled, restoring equilibrium. If clamshell production dropped to five an hour, prices would also drop by half because no one would harvest clamshells when they could earn twice as many clamshells in an hour producing arrows, bows, or rabbits. If clamshell production remained steady but it became easier to produce bows, the only thing that would change would be the price of bows relative to the prices of arrows and rabbits, and not the price level, or all prices. For example, if it was possible to produce bows in 1.5 hours instead of 2, the price of bows would drop to 15 clamshells (when 10 clamshells can be harvested in an hour).

As noted earlier, gold is a very good commodity money in most respects and, like clamshells, its quantity is self-equilibrating. (If you wish, you can reread the previous two paragraphs substituting "grains of gold" for clamshells.) Early in the twentieth century, however, governments shifted away from its use, ostensibly because of competition from superior types of exchange medium and the inelasticity of its supply. When gold became more abundant and output remained constant, the price level increased because there was more money chasing the same amount of goods and services. When the quantity of gold remained constant and output increased, the price level declined because there was no longer enough gold around to maintain the former prices, as in Figure 3.4. By making each ounce of gold more valuable, thus increasing one's ability to purchase more goods and services than formerly, the decline in prices should have triggered an immediate increase in gold production, thereby rendering the deflation, or reduction of the price level, mild and transitory, as in our hypothetical clam case. Due to the difficulty of finding new veins of gold, however, changes in the price level were often prolonged.[10] During the deep economic troubles of the 1930s, many countries experiencing prolonged deflations, including the United States, decided it was better to abandon gold in favor of much more elastic credit and fiat monies.

FIGURE 3.4 Supply and Demand for Gold

Where gold is money, a higher price for gold means a lower price for everything else.

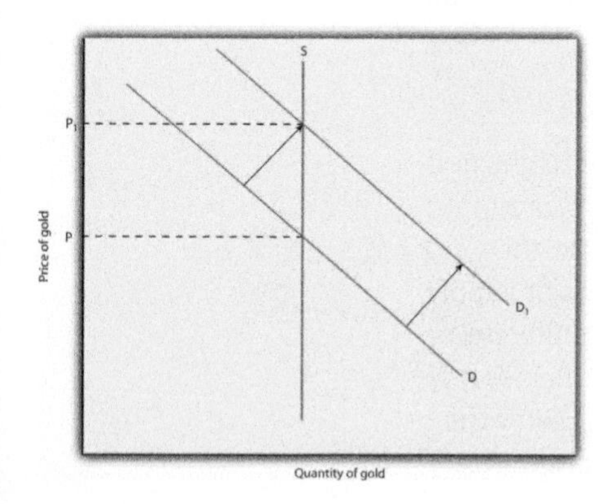

The end of gold's reign was, in a sense, overdue. Gold's monetary life had been extended by the invention and widespread use of credit money, including *banknotes* and *deposits*, because such money essentially rendered the gold supply more elastic. By the late seventeenth century, goldsmiths, skilled artisans who made gold watches and other auric goods, began to safeguard gold for their customers and to issue a form of representative money by issuing receipts to depositors. Like tobacco receipts, the gold receipts could be returned to the issuing goldsmith for gold. People often preferred to hold the receipts rather than the gold itself because they were even more portable and easily authenticated than the metal. So the receipts began to circulate as a medium of exchange. *Credit money was born when the goldsmiths, now protobankers, discovered that due to the public's strong preference for the receipts, they could issue notes to a greater value than the gold they had on physical deposit. They could therefore use the receipts to make loans or buy bonds or other income-generating assets.*

By the eighteenth century, banks in Great Britain, the United States, and a few other places *increased the elasticity of the supply of gold by engaging in just such fractional reserve banking.* Consider the following bank **balance sheet**:

balance sheet

A financial statement showing the sum or stock of an economic entity's assets (things owned) and liabilities (things owed). Assets should equal liabilities, including equity (aka capital or net worth).

Assets:	
Gold	200
Public securities	100
Loans	600
Office and real estate	100
Total	1,000
Liabilities:	
Notes (receipts)	800
Deposits	100
Equity	100
Total	1,000

Because most people preferred to hold notes and deposits instead of gold, the bank could hold only a small reserve of gold to pay to holders of its demand liabilities (notes and deposits) and earn seigniorage, or the profit from the issuance of money, on the rest.[11] Here only 200 (dollars or pounds or whatever) of gold did the work of 900 (the value of receipts or notes in circulation plus deposits). Bankers essentially made gold less rare and also gained some control over its elasticity via the reserve ratio (reserves/monetary liabilities or 200/900), which was relatively unregulated by government at that time. *Bankers could change the ratio as they saw fit, sometimes decreasing and sometimes increasing it, thereby changing the money supply, or the total quantity of money in the economy.*

Stop and Think Box

In Ithaca, New York, and hundreds of other communities worldwide, consortia of businesses issue zero-interest bearer paper notes. The notes are denominated in local units (Hours in Ithaca; Greenbacks, Berkshares, and other names elsewhere)[12] and are designed to circulate as cash, like Federal Reserve notes. In the United States, the issuer must redeem the notes for dollars (unit of account) upon demand at a fixed conversion rate. Each Ithaca Hour, for example, is equal to 10 USD. The community notes are not a legal tender, have no intrinsic value, and generally circulate in an extremely limited geographical area. The issuers often use Marxist rhetoric (workers create all value but get shafted by the "capitalist" political and economic system, etc.), claiming that holding the notes will help the local economy by keeping money invested locally. (For more details, browse www.ithacahours.com). What is really going on in Ithaca and the other community money centers?

The issuers of the notes are interested in earning seigniorage, or profits from the issuance of money. They act like fractional reserve bankers, issuing Hours in exchange for dollars, which they put out to interest. They don't earn much, though, because most people are smart enough to realize their credit money is less liquid and more risky than other forms of credit money, like bank deposits, and much higher risk than fiat money, like Federal Reserve Notes. In fact, there is no good reason to hold such notes unless one believes ("buys into") the dubious Marxist rhetoric that often accompanies them.

automatic transfer from savings (ATS)

An account that automatically moves funds from your savings account if your checking account is depleted. (Of course, such an account doesn't help if you don't have any money in your savings account either.)

sweep accounts

Accounts so-named because, at the close of a bank's business day, a computer program sweeps balances out of checking accounts, invests them overnight, and credits them (and the interest earned) back the next morning just before the bank resumes business.

money market mutual funds

MMMFs are mutual funds that invest in short-term, or money market, instruments. Fund owners earn the going market interest rates, minus management fees, and can draw upon their shares by check but at a cost higher than that of most bank checking accounts.

credit risk

The probability of not being paid a sum due.

Since its invention, *credit money has been extremely successful because it is an almost perfect medium of exchange.* Take, for example, bank deposits. Essentially just an accounting entry crediting so much money (unit of account) to a person or organization, deposits are easily authenticated, perfectly uniform, divisible to fractions of a penny, highly portable via written or electronic orders, and extremely durable. Moreover, their supply is highly elastic because they can be created and destroyed at will. The usefulness of deposits is further extended by varying their characteristics to meet different risk, return, liquidity, and maturity preferences. The most common and familiar type of deposit, called a checking, transaction, or demand deposit account, pays no or relatively low interest, but funds can be withdrawn at any time via teller during banking hours, via ATM 24/7, or with a debit card or check. Other deposits, called time or savings deposits or certificates of deposit, pay relatively high interest but either cannot be withdrawn at all before a prespecified date or can be withdrawn only if the depositor suffers a penalty that wipes out much of the interest earned. Between those two extremes have emerged a variety of hybrids, like **automatic transfer from savings (ATS)**, **sweep accounts**, and **money market mutual funds**. Most forms of electronic or e-money, like sQuidcards[13], are just new forms of credit money.

The biggest problem with credit money is that the issuer may default. Many banking regulations, as we will see in a later chapter, attempt to minimize that risk. Other issuers of credit money are not so closely regulated, however, and hence constitute serious **credit risk** for holders of their liabilities. Due to the inherently risky nature of fractional reserve banking, an issuer of credit money is much more likely to default (be unable to pay as promised) than the issuer of representative money. Like representative and fiat monies, credit money is relatively easy to counterfeit (illegally copy).

As mentioned earlier, fiat money, like Federal Reserve Notes, ostensibly circulates because the government requires market participants to accept it in payment at face value. Ultimately, however, people accept fiat money for the same reason they accept other types of money, because they know other people will take it without complaint or cavil. Fiat money is even more elastic than credit money because governments can create or destroy it at will for very little cost. This tremendous elasticity, however, means governments can cause inflation if they issue more fiat money than the current price level requires. In other words, unlike commodity and representative monies, fiat money is not self-equilibrating. A central bank or other monetary authority must decide how much to circulate at any given time. Monetary authorities choose wisely at times, but other times they do not, either as an honest mistake or quite purposefully.

In short, each major type of money has some advantages and disadvantages. Monetary systems, like everything else in economic life, are subject to trade-offs. What is best for one society may not be best for another and, indeed, may change over time. Table 3.1 reviews the taxonomy of money discussed in this chapter and the relative merits of different types of money.

TABLE 3.1 A Taxonomy of Money

Type	Definition	Examples	Advantage(s)	Disadvantage(s)
Commodity	Physical assets with a relatively high degree of liquidity due to their uniformity, durability, divisibility, portability, and ease of authentication	Clamshells; tobacco; gold	Self-equilibrating	Inelastic supply; storage, transportation, division, wastage, and authentication costs
Representative	Claims on commodities in the actual physical possession of the money issuer	Tobacco notes; gold deposit notes	Easier/cheaper to store, transport, divide, safekeep, and authenticate than the underlying commodity	Default and counterfeiting risk; supply elasticity limited by the underlying commodity
Credit	Claims on the general assets of the money issuer and NOT fully backed by commodity, fiat, or other monies	Bank deposits; banknotes	Supply elasticity limited only by the reserve ratio	Default and counterfeiting risk; some inflation risk
Fiat	Legal tender enforced by government decree	Federal Reserve Notes	Extremely elastic supply	Inflation risk; counterfeiting risk

Key Takeaways

- Representative, fiat, and credit monies are more efficient than commodity money because they are superior media of exchange and units of account. Their quality is more uniform and easily ascertained, they have low weight-to-value ratios, they are more divisible and their divisibility is more flexible, and their supply is more elastic.
- The supply of representative, credit, and especially fiat monies generally does not self-equilibrate the way the supply of commodity money does, which creates inflation risks. Also, all three types of money are more easily counterfeited than commodity monies, and representative and especially credit monies are subject to default risk.

3.5 Measuring Money

Learning Objective

1. What is the money supply and how is it measured?

Due in part to the profusion of different types of credit money, measuring the money supply today is no easy task. The Fed, or Federal Reserve System, America's monetary authority and central bank, has therefore developed a number of monetary aggregates, or different measures of the money supply. The monetary base (MB) is the unweighted total of Federal Reserve notes and Treasury coins in circulation, plus bank reserves (deposits with the Federal Reserve). M0 is MB minus bank reserves. M1 adds to M0 (cash in circulation) travelers' checks, demand deposits, and other deposits upon which checks can be drawn. (Banks other than the Fed no longer issue notes. If they did, they would be considered components of M1.) A broader aggregate, M2, includes M1 as well as time/savings deposits and retail money market mutual fund shares. A yet broader aggregate, M3, includes

M2 as well as institutional time deposits, money market mutual fund shares, repurchase agreements, and Eurodollars, but its publication was discontinued by the Fed in 2006.

The Fed estimates several measures of the money supply because the movements of each estimate are not highly correlated and the appropriate monetary aggregate varies over time and question. As we will see, the money supply helps to determine important macroeconomic variables like inflation, unemployment, and interest rates. Accurately measuring the money supply is so important that monetary economists still search for better ways of doing it. One approach, called *divisia* after its French inventor, François Divisia (1925), weights credit instruments by their liquidity, or in other words, their degree of money-ness, or ease of use as a medium of exchange. The Federal Reserve Bank of Saint Louis tracks the U.S. money supply using various divisia formulas.[14]

Each Friday, the *Wall Street Journal* publishes the M1 and M2 monetary aggregates in its "Federal Reserve Data" column. The data is also available on the Federal Reserve's website: http://www.federalreserve.gov/releases/h6/. *Students are cautioned, however, that the published data are mere estimates; the Fed often revises the figures by as much as 2 or 3 percent*. Other countries' central banks also report their monetary aggregates. Links to the websites of other central banks can be found here: http://www.bis.org/cbanks.htm.

Key Takeaways

- The money supply is the stock of all money in an economy.
- It is measured in a variety of ways to aid in the conduct of monetary policy and in macroeconomic forecasting.

3.6 Suggested Reading

Anderson, Richard G., and Kenneth A. Kavajecz. "A Historical Perspective on the Federal Reserve's Monetary Aggregates: Definition, Construction and Targeting." *Federal Reserve Bank of St. Louis Review* (March/April 1994): 1–31. http://research.stlouisfed.org/publications/review/94/03/9403rg.pdf.

Bernstein, Peter. *A Primer on Money, Banking, and Gold*. Hoboken, NJ: John Wiley and Sons, 2008.

Davies, Glyn. *A History of Money: From Ancient Times to the Present Day*. Cardiff: University of Wales Press, 2002.

Martin, Felix. *Money: The Unauthorized Biography*. New York: Vintage, 2014.

Endnotes

1. newyork.craigslist.org/about/sites
2. Gas stations and other vendors sometimes charge higher prices for credit than for cash sales to compensate them for the transaction fee charged by the credit card companies. Most have given up such policies, however, due to competition for customers who found it convenient to charge purchases at a time before debit cards were widespread and many merchants refused to accept checks due to the high moral hazard. (Too many "bounced," or were returned, unpaid, for insufficient funds in the customer's account.)
3. John Kenneth Galbraith, *Money, Whence It Came, Where It Went* (New York: Houghton Mifflin, 1975).
4. www.ex.ac.uk/~RDavies/arian/amser/chrono.html
5. www.webelements.com
6. If you look through the Gunston Hall probate inventory database here: www.gunstonhall.org/library/probate/, you'll discover that a large percentage of households in Maryland and Virginia in the late eighteenth and early nineteenth centuries owned a set of money scales. People regularly weighed coins to authenticate them and determine their real value.
7. In the past, paper money that lost its value in exchange was used as wallpaper; thumb paper (to keep grimy young hands from dirtying textbooks, which in real terms were even more expensive in the distant past than at present, believe it or not); and tissue paper, for both the nose and the posterior! They were also used to tar and feather dogs and the occasional hated government official.

8. During the American Revolution, Congress declared its paper money, Continental dollars, a legal tender. Despite the proclamation, Continentals soon lost almost all of their value, giving rise to the expression "Not worth a Continental." Other examples of the failure of tender clauses abound.
9. www.youtube.com/watch?v=qMhz_ki_B7o
10. This chart depicts changes in the price level in the United States between 1865 and 1900, when the country's unit of account was defined in gold. Note that prices fell in most years. That deflation led to a series of political upheavals that resulted in the formation of the Populist Party and a prolonged struggle among Silverites, who desired to raise prices by monetizing silver; Greenbackers, who sought to raise prices through the issuance of fiat money; and Gold Bugs, who insisted on maintenance of the status quo. *The Wonderful Wizard of Oz*, a children's book by Frank Baum made legendary by a movie version starring Judy Garland as protagonist Dorothy, is an allegory depicting the major political divisions of the era. Oz is of course the abbreviation for ounce; the yellow brick road refers to the gold standard; the Emerald City symbolizes Greenbacks; and in the book, Dorothy's slippers were silver, not ruby, as they were depicted in the movie.
11. Seigniorage can be earned in several ways. One way is to earn interest on assets acquired with liabilities that pay no interest or, more generally, on the positive spread between return on assets and the cost of monetary liabilities. The Federal Reserve, for example, pays no interest on its notes and very low interest on its deposits but earns interest on the Treasury securities and other assets that it buys with its notes and deposits. Another way to earn seigniorage is to mint coins that have a higher face or nominal value than production cost. Debasing the coinage, or extracting seigniorage by increasing the nominal value of a given sum of gold or silver, was highly profitable and therefore a favorite sport of kings.
12. en.wikipedia.org/wiki/Local_currency#Modern_local_currencies
13. https://www.squidcard.com/products-solutions/emoney-services
14. research.stlouisfed.org/msi; https://research.stlouisfed.org/publications/review/1992/11/01/an-extended-series-of-divisia-monetary-aggregates/

FIGURE 3.5 Changes in the U.S. price level, 1865–1900

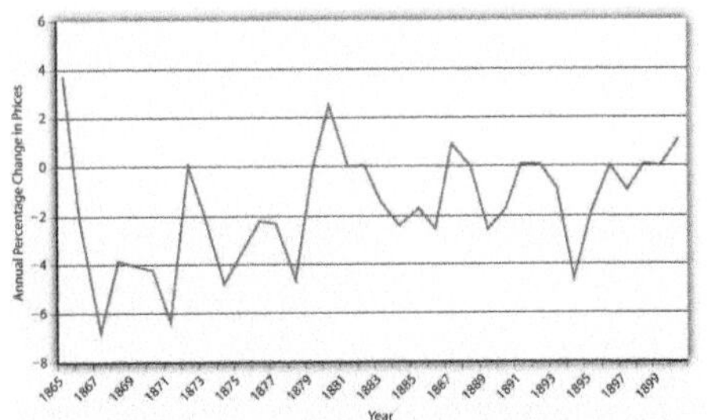

Source: http://www.measuringworth.com/inflation

CHAPTER 4

Interest Rates

Chapter Objectives

By the end of this chapter, students should be able to:

1. Define interest and explain its importance.
2. Write and explain the present value formula.
3. Write and explain the future value formula.
4. Calculate present and future value for multiple periods with annual and more frequent compounding.
5. Define and price major types of debt instruments including discount bonds, simple loans, fixed payment loans, coupon bonds, and perpetuities.
6. Define yield to maturity and identify the types of financial instruments for which it is relatively easy to calculate.
7. Explain why bond prices move inversely to market interest rates.
8. Explain why some bond prices are more volatile than others.
9. Define rate of return and explain how it differs from yield to maturity.
10. Explain the difference between real and nominal interest rates.

4.1 The Interest of Interest

Learning Objective

1. What is interest and why is it important?

Interest, *the opportunity cost of money, is far from mysterious, but it warrants our careful consideration because of its importance.* **Interest rates**, *the price of borrowing money, are crucial determinants of the prices of assets, especially financial instruments like stocks and bonds, and general macroeconomic conditions, including***economic growth**. In fact, ceteris paribus (like your grades!), the probability of you landing a job upon graduation will depend in large part on prevailing interest rates. If rates are low, businesses will be more likely to borrow money, expand production, and hire you. If rates are high, businesses will be less likely to expand or to hire you. Without a job, you'll be forced to move back home. Best to pay attention then!

Interest

The opportunity cost of money.

Interest rates

The price of borrowed money.

economic growth

Real per capita GDP.

yield to maturity (YTM)

The most economically accurate way of measuring interest rates.

present value (PV)

The value of money today.

future value (FV)

The value of money at some point in the future.

Interest can be thought of as the payment it takes to induce a lender to part with his, her, or its money for some period of time, be it a day, week, month, year, decade, or century. To make comparisons between those payments easier, interest is almost always expressed as an annual percentage rate, the number of dollars (or other currency)[1] paid for the use of $100 per year. *Several ways of measuring interest rates exist, but here you'll learn only* **yield to maturity (YTM)**, *the method preferred by economists for its accuracy*. The key is to learn to compare the value of money today, called **present value (PV)** (represented here by the variable PV and aka present discounted value or price), to the value of money tomorrow, called **future value (FV)** (represented here by the variable FV).

Key Takeaways

- Interest is the opportunity cost of lending money or the price of borrowing it and can be thought of as the payment a borrower needs to induce him, her, or it to lend.
- Interest is important because it helps to determine the price of assets, especially financial assets, and to determine various macroeconomic variables, including aggregate output.

4.2 Present and Future Value

Learning Objective

1. What are the formulas for present value and future value, and what types of questions do they help to answer?

inflation

A sustained increase in the price level or average prices.

nominal interest rates

The price of borrowing money as it is usually stated, unadjusted for inflation.

real interest rate

The price of borrowing money adjusted for inflation.

compounding

Earning interest on interest.

compounding period

The amount of time that passes before interest begins to earn interest.

A moment's reflection should convince you that money today is always[2]*worth more than money tomorrow.* If you don't believe me, send me all of your money immediately. I'll return every cent of it—scout's honor—in exactly one year. I won't hold my breath. You'd be foolish indeed to forgo food, clothes, housing, transportation, and entertainment for a year for no remuneration whatsoever. That's why a dollar today is worth more than a dollar tomorrow. (Another reason that a dollar today is worth more than a dollar tomorrow is that, in modern economies based on fiat money, prices tend to rise every year. So $100 tomorrow will buy fewer goods and services than $100 today will. We will discuss the impact of **inflation** on interest rates more at the end of this chapter. For now, we consider only **nominal interest rates**, not the **real interest rate**.) But what if I told you that if you gave me $100 today, I'd give you $1,000 in a year? Most lenders would jump at that offer (provided they thought I would pay as promised and not default), but I wouldn't offer it and neither would most borrowers. In fact, about $110 would be the most I'd be willing to give you in a year for $100 today. That's an interest rate of 10 percent ($10/$100 = .1 or 10%), which, as comedian Adam Sandler might say, is "not too shabby."[3] If we let the loan ride, as they say, capitalizing the interest or, in other words, paying interest on the interest every year, called annually **compounding** interest, your $100 investment would grow in value, as shown in Figure 4.1. (The **compounding period** need not be a year, and it is even possible to compound interest continuously, but unless otherwise noted we will compound annually in this chapter.)

FIGURE 4.1 The fate of $100 invested at 10%, compounded annually

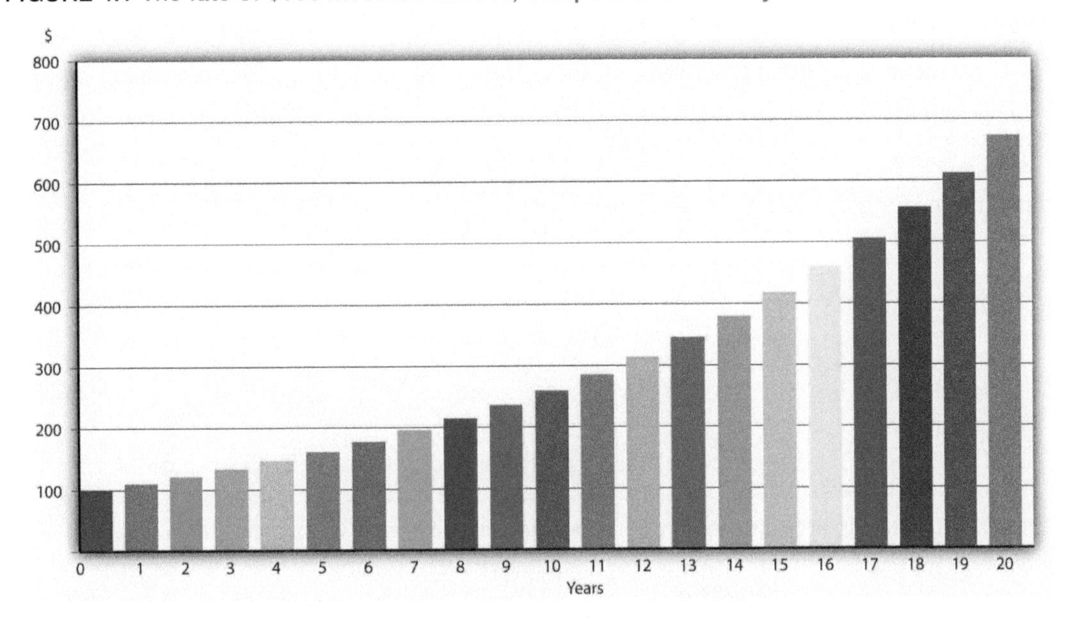

The figures in the table are easily calculated by multiplying the previous year's value by 1.10, 1 representing the principal value and .10 representing the interest rate *expressed as a decimal*. So $100 today (year = 0) is, at 10 percent interest compounded annually, worth $110 in a year (100 × 1.1), $121 after two years (110 × 1.1), $131.10 after three years (121 × 1.1), and so forth. The quick way to calculate this for any year is to use the following formula:

$FV = PV(1 + i)^n$

where

FV = the future value (the value of your investment in the future)

PV = the present value (the amount of your investment today)

$(1 + i)^n$ = the future value factor (aka the present value factor or discount factor in the equation below)

i = interest rate (decimalized, for example, 6% = .06; 25% = .25, 2.763% = .02763, etc.)

n = number of terms (here, years; elsewhere days, months, quarters)

For $100 borrowed today at 10 percent compounded annually, in 100 years I'd owe you $1,378,061 ($FV = 100 \times 1.1^{100}$). (Good luck collecting that one!)

What if someone offers to pay you, say, $1,000 in 5 years? How much would you be willing to pay today for that? Clearly, something less than $1,000. Instead of taking a PV and expanding it via multiplication to determine an FV, here you must do the opposite, or in other words, reduce or "discount" an FV to a PV. You do so by dividing, as in the following formula:

$$PV = FV/(1+i)^n$$
$$\text{or } PV = 1000/(1+i)^5$$

Obviously, we can't solve this equation unless one of the two remaining variables is given. If the interest rate is given as 5 percent, you would pay $783.53 today for $1,000 payable in 5 years ($PV = 1{,}000/1.05^5$). If it is 20 percent, you'd give only $401.88 ($PV = 1{,}000/1.2^5$). If it is 1 percent, you would give $951.47 ($PV = 1{,}000/1.01^5$). *Notice that as the interest rate rises (falls), the present value (price) of the future payment falls (rises). In other words, the price (PV) of some future payment (some FV; generically, a bond) and the rate of interest are inversely related.* You can see this algebraically by noting that the *i* term is in the denominator, so as it gets larger, PV must get smaller (holding FV constant, of course). Economically this makes sense because a higher interest rate means a higher opportunity cost for money, so a sum payable in the future is worth less the more dear money is (the more it costs to borrow it).

If payment of the bond described just above were to be made in ten years instead of five, at 1 percent interest per year, you'd pay $905.29 ($PV = 1{,}000/1.01^{10}$). Note here that, holding the interest rate (and all other factors) constant, you give less today for a payment further in the future ($905.29 < $951.47). That too makes good sense because you're without your money longer and need to be compensated for it by paying a lower price for the bond/promise/IOU today.

Stop and Think Box

Congratulations, you just won the Powerball: $100 million payable in $5 million installments over 20 years! Did you really win $100 million? (*Hint*: Calculate the PV of the final payment with interest at 4 percent.)

No; 5 × 20 = 100, but the money payable next year and in subsequent years is not worth $5 million today if interest rates are above 0, and they almost always are. For example, the last payment, with interest rates at 4 percent compounded annually, has a PV of only $5{,}000{,}000/(1.04)^{20}$ = $2,281,934.73.

This is a great place to stop and drill until calculating present value and future value becomes second nature to you. Work through the following problems until it hurts. Then do them again, standing on your head or on one leg.

Exercises

For all questions in this set, interest compounds annually and there are no transaction fees, defaults, etc.

1. On your seventieth birthday, you learn that your grandma, bless her soul, deposited $50.00 for you on the day of your birth in a savings account bearing 5 percent interest. How much is in the account?
2. You won $1 million in the lottery but unfortunately the money is payable in a year and you want to start spending it right away. If interest is at 8 percent, how much can you receive today in exchange for that $1 million in a year?
3. As a college freshman, you hoped to save $2,500 to "pimp your ride" as a college graduation present to yourself. You put $2,012.98 from your high school graduation haul in the bank at 5 percent interest. Will you meet your goal?
4. You've won a scholarship for your senior year worth $1,500, but it is payable only after graduation, a year hence. If interest is at 15 percent, how much is your scholarship worth today?
5. You determine that you need $1,750,000 saved in order to retire comfortably. When you turn 25, you inherit $350,017. If you invest that sum immediately at 4.42 percent, can you retire at age 65 if you have no other savings?
6. You own two bonds, each with a face, or payoff, value of $1,000. One falls due in exactly one year and the other in exactly three years. If interest is at 2.35 percent, how much are those bonds worth today? What if interest rates jump to 12.25 percent?
7. To purchase a car, you borrowed $10,000 from your brother. You offered to pay him 8 percent interest and to repay the loan in exactly three years. How much will you owe your bro?
8. As part of a lawsuit settlement, a major corporation offers you $75,000 today or $100,000 next year. Which do you choose if interest rates are 5 percent? If they are 13.47886 percent?

9. Exactly 150 years ago, the U.S. government promised to pay a certain Indian tribe $3,500, or 7 percent interest until it did so. Somehow, the account was unpaid. How much does the government owe the tribe for this promise?
10. As part of an insurance settlement, you are offered $100,000 today or $125,000 in five years. If the applicable interest rate is 1 percent, which option do you choose? What if the interest rate is 5 percent?

Key Takeaways

- The present value formula is $PV = FV/(1 + i)^n$ where PV = present value, FV = future value, i = decimalized interest rate, and n = number of periods. It answers questions like, "How much would you pay today for $X at time y in the future, given an interest rate and a compounding period?"
- The future value formula is $FV = PV\times (1 + i)^n$. It answers questions like, "How much will $X invested today at some interest rate and compounding period be worth at time Y?"

4.3 Compounding Periods

Learning Objective

1. If interest compounds other than annually, how does one calculate PV and FV?

Interest does not always compound annually, as assumed in the problems already presented in this chapter. Sometimes it compounds quarterly, monthly, daily, even continuously. The more frequent the compounding period, the more valuable the bond or other instrument, all else constant. The mathematics remains the same (though a little more difficult when compounding is continuous), but you must be careful about what you plug into the equation for i and n. For example, $1,000 invested at 12 percent for a year compounded annually would be worth $\$1{,}000 \times (1.12)^1 = \$1{,}120.00$. But that same sum invested for the same term at the same rate of interest but compounded *monthly* would grow to $\$1{,}000 \times (1.01)^{12} = \$1{,}126.83$ because the interest paid each month is capitalized, earning interest at 12 percent. Note that we represent i as the interest paid *per period* (.12 interest/12 months in a year = .01) and n as the number of periods (12 in a year; 12 × 1 = 12), rather than the number of years.[4] That same sum, and so forth with interest compounded quarterly (4 times a year) would grow to $\$1{,}000 \times (1.03)^4 = \$1{,}125.51$. The differences among annual, monthly, and quarterly compounding here are fairly trivial, amounting to less than $7 all told, but are important for bigger sums, higher interest rates, more frequent compounding periods, and longer terms. One million dollars at 4 percent for a year compounded annually comes to $\$1{,}000{,}000 \times (1.04) = \$1{,}040{,}000$, while on the same terms compounded quarterly, it produces $\$1{,}000{,}000 \times (1.01)^4 = \$1{,}040{,}604.01$. (I'll take the latter sum over the former any day and "invest" the surplus in a very nice dinner and concert tickets.) Likewise, $100 at 300 percent interest for 5 years compounded annually becomes $100 \times (4)^5 = \$102{,}400$. Compounded quarterly, that $100 grows to $\$100 \times (1.75)^{20} = \$7{,}257{,}064.34$! A mere $1 at 6 percent compounded annually for 100 years will be worth $\$1 \times (1.06)^{100} = \$339.30$. The same buck at the same interest compounded monthly swells in a century to $\$1 \times (1.005)^{1200} = \$397.44$. *This all makes good sense because interest is being received sooner than the end of the year and hence is more valuable because, as we know, money now is better than money later.*

Do a few exercises now to make sure you get it.

Exercises

For all questions in this set, interest rates are stated in annual terms, but the interest compounds quarterly (four times a year). Also, assume there are no transaction fees, defaults, etc.

1. On your seventieth birthday, you learn that your grandma, bless her soul, deposited $50.00 for you on the day of your birth in a savings account bearing 5 percent interest. How much is in the account?
2. You won $1 million in the lottery but unfortunately the money is payable in a year and you want to start spending it right away. If interest is at 8 percent, how much can you receive today in exchange for that $1 million in year?
3. As a freshman, you hoped to save $2,500 to "pimp your ride" as a college graduation present to yourself. You put $2,012.98 from your high school graduation haul in the bank at 5 percent interest. Will you meet your goal if you graduate in four years?
4. You've won a scholarship for your senior year worth $1,500, but it is payable only after graduation, a year hence. If interest is at 15 percent, how much is your scholarship worth today?
5. You won the lottery and netted a million bucks, but you need $5 million to buy a little island that you have had your eye on. If interest is at 12 percent, will you be able to buy your island in 30 years, assuming its price is unchanged at that time?

Key Takeaways

- Present and future value can be calculated for any compounding period (except continuously) using the same formulas presented in this chapter.
- Care must be taken, however, to ensure that the i and n terms are adjusted appropriately.

4.4 Pricing Debt Instruments

Learning Objective

1. What are debt instruments and how are they priced?

debt instrument

A bond, IOU, or other contract (like a discount bond, simple loan, fixed payment loan, or coupon bond) promising the payment of money in the future.

Believe it or not, you are now equipped to calculate the price of any **debt instrument** *or contract provided you know the rate of interest, compounding period, and the size and timing of the payments.* Four major types of instruments that you are likely to encounter include discount bonds, simple loans, fixed-payment loans, and coupon bonds.

A **discount bond** (aka a **zero coupon bond** or simply a **zero**) makes only one payment, its face value on its maturity or redemption date, so its price is easily calculated using the present value formula. If the interest rate is 6 percent, the price of a discount bond with a $1,000 face value due in exactly a year would be $943.40 (1,000/1.06). If the interest rate is 12 percent, the same discount bond's price would be only $892.86 (1,000/1.12). If the bond is due in two years at 12 percent, its price would be $797.19 ($1{,}000/(1.12^2)$), and so forth.

A **simple loan** is the name for a loan where the borrower repays the principal and interest at the end of the loan. Use the future value formula to calculate the sum due upon maturity. For example, a simple loan of $1,000 for one year at 3.5 percent would require the borrower to repay $1,035.00 (1,000 × 1.035), while a simple loan at the same rate for two years would require a payment of $1,071.23 ($1{,}000 \times 1.035^2$). (Note that the correct answer is not just $35 doubled due to the effects of compounding or capitalizing the interest due at the end of the first year.)

A **fixed-payment loan** (aka a fully amortized loan) is one in which the borrower periodically (for example, weekly, bimonthly, monthly, quarterly, annually, etc.) repays a portion of the principal along with the interest. With such loans, which include most auto loans and home mortgages, all payments are equal. There is no big balloon or principal payment at the end because the principal shrinks, slowly at first but more rapidly as the final payment grows nearer, as in Figure 4.2.

Principal borrowed: $500,000.00; Annual number of payments: 12; Total number of payments: 360; Annual interest rate: 6.00%; Regular monthly payment amount: $2,997.75.

discount bond

A debt instrument that makes only one payment, its face value on its maturity or redemption date. Also known as a zero coupon bond.

zero coupon bond

See discount bond.

zero

See discount bond.

simple loan

A debt instrument where the borrower repays the principal and interest at the end of the loan.

fixed-payment loan

A debt instrument in which the borrower makes periodic repayments of principal and interest.

FIGURE 4.2 Sample thirty-year amortizing mortgage

Payment No.	Principal	Interest	Cumulative Principal	Cumulative Interest	Principal Balance
1	497.75	2,500.00	497.75	2,500.00	499,502.25
2	500.24	2,497.51	997.99	4,997.51	499,002.01
3	502.74	2,495.01	1,500.73	7,492.52	498,499.27
4	505.25	2,492.50	2,005.98	9,985.02	497,994.02
5	507.78	2,489.97	2,513.76	12,474.99	497,486.24
6	510.32	2,487.43	3,024.08	14,962.42	496,975.92
7	512.87	2,484.88	3,536.95	17,447.30	496,463.05
8	515.43	2,482.32	4,052.38	19,929.62	495,947.62
9	518.01	2,479.74	4,570.39	22,409.36	495,429.61
10	520.60	2,477.15	5,090.99	24,886.51	494,909.01
11	523.20	2,474.55	5,614.19	27,361.06	494,385.81
12	525.82	2,471.93	6,140.01	29,832.99	493,859.99
...	...	...	...	...	...
348	2,809.54	188.21	465,166.83	578,050.17	34,833.17
349	2,823.58	174.17	467,990.41	578,224.34	32,009.59
350	2,837.70	160.05	470,828.11	578,384.39	29,171.89
351	2,851.89	145.86	473,680.00	578,530.25	26,320.00
352	2,866.15	131.60	476,546.15	578,661.85	23,453.85
353	2,880.48	117.27	479,426.63	578,779.12	20,573.37
354	2,894.88	102.87	482,321.51	578,881.99	17,678.49
355	2,909.36	88.39	485,230.87	578,970.38	14,769.13
356	2,923.90	73.85	488,154.77	579,044.23	11,845.23
357	2,938.52	59.23	491,093.29	579,103.46	8,906.71
358	2,953.22	44.53	494,046.51	579,147.99	5,953.49
359	2,967.98	29.77	479,014.49	579,177.76	2,985.51
360	2,985.51	14.93	500,000.00	579,192.69	0.00

Today, such schedules are most easily created using specialized financial software, including websites like http://www.amortization-calc.com/, http://www.yona.com/loan/, or http://www.bankrate.com/. If you wanted to buy this mortgage (in other words, if you wanted to purchase the right to receive the monthly repayments of $2,997.75) from the original lender (there are still secondary markets for mortgages, though they are less active than they were before the financial crisis that began in 2007), you'd simply sum the present value of each of the remaining monthly payments. (Again, a computer is highly recommended here!)

coupon bond

A debt instrument that makes interest payments periodically until its maturity or redemption date, when the final interest payment and the principal are to be paid.

Finally, a **coupon bond** *is so-called because, in the past, owners of the bond received interest payments by clipping one of the coupons and remitting it to the borrower (or its paying agent, usually a bank).* Figure 4.3 is a $1,000 par value coupon bond issued in 1902, with some of the coupons still attached (on the left side of the figure).

FIGURE 4.3 Michigan Central Railroad, 3.5 percent bearer gold bond with coupons attached, 1902.

Museum of American Finance

Even if it no longer uses a physical coupon like the one illustrated in Figure 4.3, a coupon bond makes one or more interest payments periodically (for example, monthly, quarterly, semiannually, annually, etc.) until its maturity or redemption date, when the final interest payment and all of the principal are paid. *The sum of the present values of each future payment will give you the price.* So we can calculate the price today of a $10,000 face or par value coupon bond that pays 5 percent interest annually until its face value is redeemed (its principal is repaid) in exactly five years if the market rate of interest is 6 percent, 4 percent, or any other percent for that matter, simply by summing the present value of each payment:

PV_1 = $500/(1.06) = $471.70 (This is the interest payment after the first year. The $500 is the **coupon** or interest payment, which is calculated by multiplying the bond's face value, in this case, $10,000, by the bond's contractual rate of interest or "coupon rate," in this case, 5 percent. $10,000 × .05 = $500.)

coupon

The interest rate promised to the owner of a coupon bond.

PV_2 = $500 / $(1.06)^2$ = $445.00 (If this doesn't look familiar, you didn't do Exercise 1 enough!)

PV_3 = $500 / $(1.06)^3$ = $419.81

PV_4 = $500 / $(1.06)^4$ = $396.05

PV_5 = $10,500 / $(1.06)^5$ = $7,846.21

($10,500 is the final interest payment of $500 plus the repayment of the bond's face value of $10,000.)

That adds up to $9,578.77. If you are wondering why the bond is worth less than its face value, the key is the difference between the contractual interest or coupon rate it pays, 5 percent, and the market rate of interest, 6 percent. *Because the bond pays at a rate lower than the going market, people are not willing to pay as much for it, so its price sinks below par.* By the same reasoning, people should be willing to pay more than the face value for this bond if interest rates sink below its coupon rate of 5 percent. Indeed, when the market rate of interest is 4 percent, its price is $10,445.18 (give or take a few pennies, depending on rounding):

PV_1 = $500 / (1.04) = $480.77

PV_2 = $500 / $(1.04)^2$ = $462.28

PV_3 = $500 / $(1.04)^3$ = $444.50

PV_4 = $500 / $(1.04)^4$ = $427.40

PV_5 = $10,500 / $(1.04)^5$ = $8,630.23

If the market interest rate is exactly equal to the coupon rate, the bond will sell at its par value, in this case, $10,000.00. Check it out:

PV_1 = $500 / (1.05) = $476.1905

PV_2 = $500 / $(1.05)^2$ = $453.5147

$$PV_3 = \$500 / (1.05)^3 = \$431.9188$$

$$PV_4 = \$500 / (1.05)^4 = \$411.3512$$

$$PV_5 = \$10,500 / (1.05)^5 = \$8,227.0247$$

Calculating the price of a bond that makes quarterly payments over thirty years can become quite tedious because, by the method shown above, that would entail calculating the PV of 120 (30 years times 4 payments a year) payments. Until not too long ago, people used special bond tables to help them make the calculations more quickly. *Today, to speed things up and depending on their needs, most people use financial calculators, specialized financial software, and canned spreadsheet functions like Excel's PRICEDISC or PRICEMAT, custom spreadsheet formulas, or Web-based calculators like* http://www.calculatorweb.com/calculators/bondcalc.shtml or http://www.zenwealth.com/businessfinanceonline/BV/BondCalculator.html.

It's time once again to get a little practice. Don't worry; these are easy enough to work out on your own.

Exercises

Assume no default risks or transaction costs.

1. What is the price of a 10 percent coupon bond, payable annually, with a $100 face value that matures in 3 years if interest rates are 7 percent?
2. What is the price of a 5 percent coupon bond, payable annually, with a $1,000 face value that matures in 5 years if interest rates are 5 percent?
3. If interest rates were 4 percent, how much would you give today for a loan with a $100,000 balloon principal payment due in a year and that will pay $16,000 in interest at the end of each quarter, including the final quarter when the principal falls due?
4. What is the value today of a share of stock that you think will be worth $50 in a year and that throws off $1 in dividends each quarter until then, assuming the market interest rate is 10 percent?
5. What is the value today of a share of stock that you think will be worth $50 in a year and that throws off $1 in dividends each quarter until then if the market interest rate is 1 percent?

Key Takeaways

- Debt instruments—like discount bonds, simple loans, fixed payment loans, and coupon bonds—are contracts that promise payment in the future.
- They are priced by calculating the sum of the present value of the promised payments.

4.5 What's the Yield on That?

Learning Objective

1. What is yield to maturity and for what types of financial instruments is the yield to maturity relatively easy to calculate?

Thus far, we have assumed or been given a market interest rate and then calculated the price (PV) of the instrument. Or, given the PV and an interest rate, we've calculated the FV. *Sometimes it is useful to do the opposite, to calculate the interest rate, or yield to maturity, if given the PV and FV.* Say that you know that someone paid $750 for a zero coupon bond with a face value of $1,000 that will mature in exactly a year and you want to know what interest rate he or she paid. You know that PV = FV/(1 + i). Solving for i:

$$\text{Multiply each side of the equation by } (1+\text{i}): (1+\text{i}) \times \text{PV} = \text{FV}$$

$$\text{Multiply the terms on the left side of the equation: PV} + \text{PVi} = \text{FV}$$

$$\text{Subtract PV from each side of the equation: PVi} = \text{FV} - \text{PV}$$

$$\text{Divide each side of the equation by PV}: \text{i} = (\text{FV} - \text{PV}) / \text{PV}$$

$$\text{So in this case i} = (1000 - 750) / 750 = 250 / 750 = .3333, \text{ or } 33.33 \text{ percent.}$$

You can check your work by reversing the problem—that is, asking how much you'd pay today for $1,000 in a year if interest was at 33.33 percent: PV = 1,000/(1.3333333) = $750. Voilà!

Stop and Think Box

Suppose you have $1,000 to invest for a year and two ways of investing it (each equal in terms of risk and liquidity): a discount bond due in one year with a face value of $1,000 for $912 or a bank account at 6.35 percent compounded annually. Which should you take?

Choose the bond, which will yield 9.65 percent: (1,000 − 912)/912 = .0965. To maximize your haul, invest the $88 left over from the purchase of the bond in the bank account.

Consol

A type of perpetual bond issued by the British government.

*Calculating the yield to maturity for a perpetual debt, one with no maturity or repayment date, like a***Consol***, ground rent, or perpetual interest-only mortgage, is also quite easy.* The price or PV of a perpetuity is equal to the yearly payment—the only FV available from an instrument that by definition will never repay its principal—divided by the going rate of interest:

$$\text{PV} = \text{FV} / \text{i (decimalized)}$$

So a $1,000 ground rent that pays $50 a year (a 5 percent coupon rate) would be worth $1,000 if interest rates were 5 percent, less if rates are higher, more if lower:

$$\text{PV} = 50 / .05 = \$1{,}000$$

$$\text{PV} = 50 / .10 = \$500$$

$$\text{PV} = 50 / .01 = \$5{,}000$$

Calculating the yield to maturity of a perpetuity, if given the PV and FV, is easily done by taking the equation and solving for i:

$$\text{PV} = \text{FV} / \text{i}$$

$$\text{Multiply each side by i}: \text{PVi} = \text{FV}$$

$$\text{Divided by PV}: \text{i} = \text{FV} / \text{PV}$$

So the yield to maturity of a ground rent that pays $60 per year and that currently sells for $600 would be 10 percent: *i* = 60/600 = .10 = 10%.

Stop and Think Box

A ground rent contract consummated in Philadelphia, Pennsylvania, in 1756 is still being paid today. Someone recently paid $455 for the $23.17 annual payment. What is the ground rent's yield to maturity? If the interest rate rises to 10 percent, how much will the ground rent be worth? What if interest falls to 2 percent?

i = C/P so *i* = 23.17/455 = 0.05092 = 5.09%; PV = 23.17/.1 = $231.70; PV = 23.17/.02 = $1,158.50.

Calculating yield to maturity for coupon bonds and fixed-payment loans, however, is mathematically nasty business without a computer or bond table. In the past, people used to estimate the yield to maturity on such instruments by pretending they were perpetuities or engaging in trial-and-error interpolation. In the first method, you use the easy perpetuity equation (*i* = FV/PV) to get a quick estimate called the **current yield**. *Unfortunately, current yield can be wide of the mark, especially for bonds with maturities less than twenty years and bonds whose prices are far from their par value.*[5] In the second method, one backs into the yield to maturity by making successive guesses about *i* and plugging them into the PV formula. Not fun, but you'll eventually get there. Most people today therefore use a financial calculator, spreadsheet, or Web-based utility rather than such erroneous (current yield) or laborious (interpolation) processes. You should be able to calculate the yield to maturity of one-year discount bonds or perpetuities by hand, or at worst with the aid of a simple (nonfinancial) calculator. Here is a little practice.

current yield

A quick (*i* = FV/PV) but flawed method for calculating interest rates of nonperpetual debt.

Exercises

1. A $100 bond payable in a year sells for $97.56. What is the yield to maturity?
2. Sam promises to pay Joe $1,904 in a year if Joe gives him $1,498 today. What interest rate is Sam paying and what interest rate is Joe earning?
3. Every year, the U.S. government pays a certain Indian tribe $10,000 and, by terms of its treaty with that tribe, must do so forever. Mr. Trump offered to purchase the right to receive that stream for a one-time payment of $143,500. What yield to maturity did Trump offer the Indians?
4. What is the yield to maturity of a British Consol paying £400 per year that sold for £27,653?

Key Takeaways

- Yield to maturity is the most economically accurate way of measuring nominal interest rates.
- It is easily calculated for one-year discount bonds *i* = (FV–PV)/PV and perpetuities *i* = C/PV where C is the coupon or annual payment.

4.6 Calculating Returns

Learning Objective

1. What is the rate of return and how does it differ from yield to maturity?

return

A measure of the profitability of an investment that takes into account changes in the value of the bond or other asset.

The information provided in this chapter is not all you need to know about bonds if you were to become a bond trader because the bond market, which in the United States is over 200 years old, has some odd conventions that do not make much economic sense. Most students will not become professional bond traders, so in the interest of sanity, yours and ours, we will not delve into the intricacies here. (If you do become a bond trader, you will quickly and easily pick up on the conventions anyway.) Our goal here is to understand the basics of PV, FV, yield to maturity (YTM), and, finally, **return**. Students sometimes conflate the last two concepts. *The yield to maturity is merely a measure of the interest rate. Return is more a measure of how lucrative an investment is because it accounts for changes in the price of the bond* (or other asset, financial or otherwise) *over some period.* More formally,

$$R = (C + P_{t1} - P_{t0}) / P_{t0}$$

where:

R = return from holding the asset for some time period, t_0 to t_1

P_{t0} = the price at time t_0 (this can also be thought of as the purchase price)

P_{t1} = the price at time t_1 (this can also be thought of as the sale or going market price)

C = coupon (or other) payment

So imagine you purchased a 5 percent coupon bond with a $100 face value that matures in three years when the interest rate is 5 percent. As we learned above, the market price of such a bond would equal its face value, or $100. *We also learned that bond prices and interest rates are inversely related.* As the market interest rate increases, the PV of the bond's future payments decreases and the bond becomes less valuable. As the rate decreases, the PV of future payments increases and the bond becomes more valuable. If the interest rate increased (decreased) to 6 (4) percent, the value of the bond would decrease (increase), so the returns you earned on the bond would not equal the yield to maturity. For example, suppose you purchased the bond for $100 but its price a year hence stood at $103 because interest rates decreased a little. Your return would be R = (5 + 3)/100 = .08, or 8%. But if in the next year, interest rates soared, driving the market price of the bond down to $65, your return (from purchase) would be R = (10 − 35)/100 = −.25 or negative 25%. Yes, negative. *It is quite possible to lose wealth by investing in bonds or other fixed-rate financial instruments, even if there is no default* (i.e., even if payments are punctually made as promised). Similarly, if you purchased $1 million worth of municipal bonds that paid coupons of $50,000 annually, your return would not be a simple 5 percent because the market price of the bonds may have gone up or down in the first year. If the bonds lost $100,000 in market value, your return would be a negative 5 percent: R = (50,000 − 100,000)/1,000,000 = −.05. If they gained $100,000, by contrast, your return would be 15 percent: R = (50,000 + 100,000)/1,000,000 = .15. If the bonds gained $100,000 over two years, the total return would be 20 percent because two coupon payments would have been made too: R = (100,000 + 100,000)/1,000,000 = .20.

Stop and Think Box

As part of its effort to repay the large debts it accrued during the Revolutionary War, the U.S. federal government in the early 1790s issued three types of bonds: a coupon bond that paid 6 percent per year, a coupon bond that paid 3 percent per year, and a zero coupon bond that became a 6 percent coupon bond in 1801. For most of the 1790s and early 1800s, the price of the 6 percent bonds hovered around par. Given that information, what was the yield to maturity on government debt in that period? What, in general terms, were the prices of the 3 percent and zero coupon bonds?

The yield to maturity was about 6 percent because the 6 percent coupon bonds traded at around par. The price of the 3 percent coupon bonds must have been well below par because who would pay $100 to get $3 a year when she could pay $100 and get $6 a year? Finally, the zeroes must have appreciated toward the price of the 6 percent coupon bonds as the conversion date neared.

Note that a capital loss or gain is not, repeat not, predicated on actually selling the bond or other asset. One way to think about this is that the rate of return formula merely calculates the return *if* the bond were to be sold. Another way to think about it is to realize that whether the bond is sold or not, its owner is still poorer (richer) by the amount of the loss (gain) because the value of his assets, and hence his net worth, has shrunk (increased) by that amount. The risk of such loss or gain is known as **interest rate risk** to distinguish it from other types of risks, like **default risk** (the risk of nonpayment). Interest rate risk is higher the longer the maturity of a bond because more FVs are affected by increasing the interest rate, and the most distant ones are the most highly affected. Check this out: The PV of $1,000 in 10 years at 5% compounded annually is $1{,}000/(1.05)^{10}$ = $613.91. At 10% it is $1{,}000/(1.10)^{10}$ = $385.54, a loss of 37.2%. The PV of $1,000 in 30 years at 5% and 10% is $1{,}000/(1.05)^{30}$ = $231.38 and $1{,}000/(1.10)^{30}$ = $57.31, respectively, a loss of 75.23 percent. Duration is a technical measure of interest rate risk that we will not investigate here, where the main point is merely that rising interest rates hurt bond prices (and hence bondholders); falling interest rates help bond prices.

interest rate risk

The risk that the market price of a bond or other debt instrument will decrease due to increases in the interest rate.

default risk

The risk that a bond or other debt instrument will not make the promised payments.

Key Takeaways

- The rate of return accounts for changes in the market price of a bond or other asset while the yield to maturity does not.
- Yield to maturity (YTM) is almost always positive but returns are often negative due to interest rate risk, the risk that interest rates will rise, depressing bond prices.
- When the market interest rate increases, bond prices decrease because the opportunity cost of lending money has increased, making bonds less attractive investments unless their price falls.
- Algebraically, $PV = FV/(1 + i)^n$. The interest rate is in the denominator, so as *i* gets bigger, PV must get smaller.
- Bonds with longer periods to maturity have more volatile prices, ceteris paribus, because the PV of their distant FV shrinks more, to very small sums.

4.7 Inflation and Interest Rates

Learning Objective

1. What is the difference between real and nominal interest rates and why is the distinction important?

You might well ask at this point, What factors change interest rates? One big factor is inflation. As the price level rises, so too do interest rates, or at least what economists call nominal interest rates, the type of rates we've discussed so far. *If nominal rates do not increase (and they often don't, or can't), lenders might receive more nominal dollars than they lent but actually get back less purchasing power.* Imagine, for example, that you lent $100 for one year at 6 percent interest when a loaf of bread, pack of chewing gum, and two-liter bottle of Mountain Dew each cost $1. At the end of the simple loan, you would get back $100 × 1.06 = $106 and be able to enjoy an extra $6 of goods, say, two loaves of bread, two packs of gum, and two bottles of the caffeine and sugar rush known as "Doin' the Dew." But what if prices doubled over that year? Instead of some combination of 106 goodies, you'd be able to buy only fifty-three. Your nominal return would be positive, but your real return, what you could actually buy with the $106, would be steeply negative.

A simple equation, the Fisher Equation, named after Irving Fisher, the early twentieth-century U.S. economist who articulated it,[6]*helps us to understand the relationship between inflation and interest rates more precisely:*

$$i = i_r + \pi \text{ or, rearranging the terms, } i_r = i - \pi \text{ or, again rearranging the terms, } \pi = i - i_r$$

where

i_r = the real interest rate

i = the nominal interest rate (the type of interest rate the first part of this chapter discussed exclusively)

π = inflation (or expected inflation)

FIGURE 4.4 U.S. real ex post interest rate, 1961–2015
Real interest rates calculated after the fact

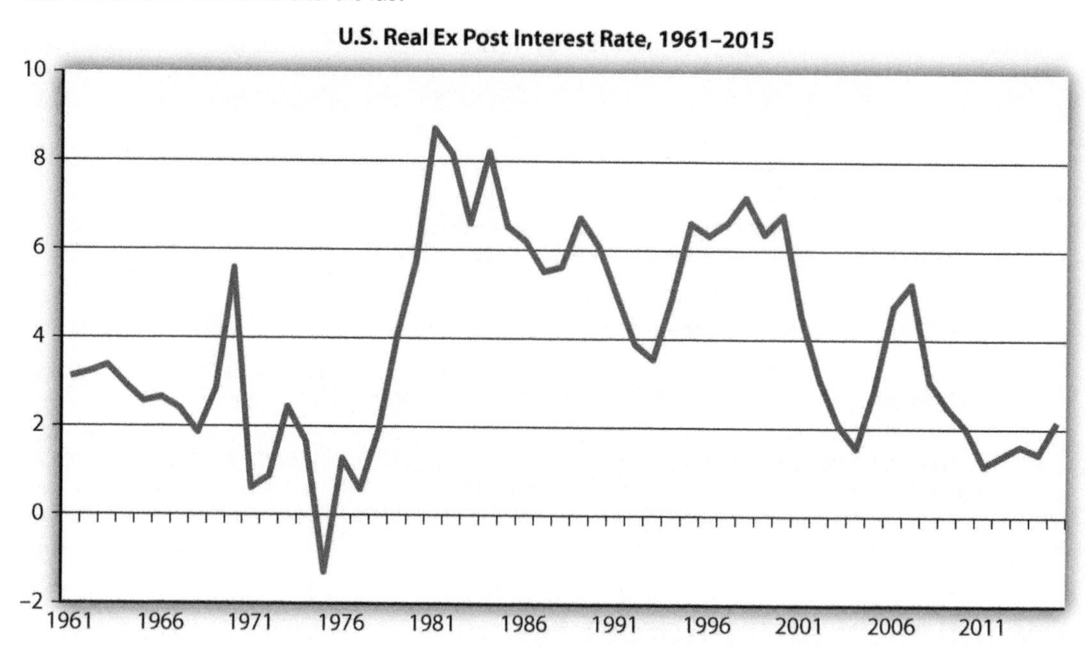

ex post
After the fact.

ex ante
Before the fact.

In plain English, after the fact (**ex post** in economists' lingo), the nominal interest rate is equal to the real interest rate plus actual inflation. Real ex post interest rates in the United States, as calculated by the World Bank, are shown in Figure 4.5. The negative rates in the mid-1970s indicate that actual inflation proved to be higher than what market participants expected.

Before the fact (**ex ante** in economists' lingo), the nominal interest rate is equal to the real interest rate plus the expectation of inflation. Economists are still trying to figure out how to accurately measure inflation expectations so no standard time series of ex ante real interest rates yet exists. Many attempts have shown extended periods of negative real rates, something that is not easily explained by the assumptions of the Fisher Equation. Some economists have challenged the Fisher Equation while others challenge the estimates of inflation expectations.

Stop and Think Box

In early 2007, a man had a wallet returned that he had lost over sixty years earlier in France, during World War II.[7] In addition to his original Social Security card and a picture of his parents, the man received an unspecified sum of cash. Was losing the wallet a good investment? Why or why not?

No, because the risk that it would never be returned was very high. Plus, the dollar lost a significant amount of its purchasing power over the period due to inflation and the money earned no interest. At just 3 percent compounded annually, \$100 would have grown to $100 \times (1.03)^{60} =$ \$589.16 after 60 years. At 6 percent, \$100 would have grown to $100 \times (1.06)^{60} =$ \$3,298.77.

Traditionally, inflation expectations were unobservable so real rates were known only ex post. However, relatively new and special types of bonds indexed to inflation, called Treasury Inflation Protection Securities (TIPS), provide real interest rate information, allowing market participants to observe ex ante inflation expectations. For example, if the yield to maturity on a regular, nonindexed ten-year Treasury bond is 5 percent, and the yield on the ten-year TIPS is 2 percent, the inflation expectation, via the Fisher Equation $\pi = i - i_r$, is 5 −2 = 3 percent. Figure 4.4 shows how inflation expectations have waxed and waned since the introduction of TIPS in 1997.

Key Takeaways

- The difference between the real and the nominal interest rate is literally inflation or inflation expectations.
- According to the Fisher Equation, nominal interest equals real interest plus inflation (or inflation expectations), or real interest equals nominal interest minus inflation (expectations).
- If actual inflation exceeds inflation expectations, real ex post (inflation-adjusted, after the fact) returns on bonds can be negative.

4.8 Suggested Reading

Fisher, Irving. *The Purchasing Power of Money: Its Determination and Relation to Credit Interest and Crises.* New York: Cosimo Classics, 2006.

Thau, Annette. *The Bond Book: Everything Investors Need to Know About Treasuries, Municipals, GNMAs, Corporates, Zeroes, Bond Funds, Money Market Funds, and More.* 3rd Ed. New York: McGraw Hill, 2010.

Wild, Russell. *Bond Investing for Dummies.* Hoboken, NJ: John Wiley and Sons, 2007.

Endnotes

1. fx.sauder.ubc.ca/currency_table.html
2. Certain interest rates occasionally turn very slightly negative. The phenomenon, while more common than usual in recent years, is so rare and minor in the big scheme of things that it need not detain us long here. Basically, some lenders are willing to receive less than they lent in low interest (low inflation) environments in exchange for the convenience and physical safety of investing large sums of cash in a single instrument. The negative interest rate in that case is best thought of as a zero interest rate with an associated fee. Many checking accounts, when fees are taken into account, could be considered negative interest rate investments. Another possibility is that the investor expects deflation, or a decrease in the price level. So while the investor might spend \$1,000 today to receive \$999 in the future, the investor expects that the future \$999 will buy more goods than the \$1,000 today.
3. www.azlyrics.com/lyrics/adamsandler/thechanukahsong.html
4. Technically, this is an approximation. A little more mathematics is required to get the precise answer. Alas, the rise of computers, which do the precise calculations in real business settings, has made us lazy.
5. Current yield is simply the yield to maturity of a perpetuity, so the more like a perpetuity a bond is, the better the current yield will approximate its yield to maturity. The shorter the maturity of a bond, the less like a Consol it is, so the less accurate the current yield formula will be. Similarly, the current yield works better the closer a bond's price is to par because yield to maturity equals the coupon rate when the bond is at par. As the price deviates further from par, the less well the current yield can approximate the yield to maturity.
6. To be frank, Benjamin Franklin and other colonists in eighteenth-century America understood it well.

7. ABC News video, "Wallet Returned, 60 Years Later, A World War II Veteran gets his wallet returned to him sixty years later" (1/9/2007).

CHAPTER 5

The Economics of Interest Rate Fluctuations

Chapter Objectives

By the end of this chapter, students should be able to

1. Describe, at the first level of analysis, the factors that cause changes in the interest rate.
2. List and explain four major factors that determine the quantity demanded of an asset.
3. List and explain three major factors that cause shifts in the bond supply curve.
4. Explain why the Fisher Equation holds; that is, explain why the expectation of higher inflation leads to a higher nominal interest rate.
5. Predict, in a general way, what will happen to the interest rate during an economic expansion or contraction and explain why.
6. Discuss how changes in the money supply may affect interest rates.

5.1 Interest Rate Fluctuations

Learning Objective

1. As a first approximation, what causes the interest rate to change?

*If you followed the gist of*Chapter 4*, you learned (we hope!) about the time value of money, including how to calculate future value (FV), present value (PV), yield to maturity, current yield (the yield to maturity of a perpetuity), rate of return, and real interest rates.* You also learned that a change in the interest rate has a profound effect on the value of assets, especially bonds and other types of loans, but also equities and derivatives. (In this chapter, we'll use the generic term *bonds* throughout.) That might not be a very important insight if interest rates were stable for long periods. The fact is, however, interest rates change monthly, weekly, daily, and even, in some markets, by the nanosecond. Consider Figure 5.1 and Figure 5.2. The first figure shows yields on one-month U.S. Treasury bills from 2001 to 2017, the second shows a zoomed-in view on just March 2008. Clearly, there are long-term secular trends as well as short-term ups and downs.

FIGURE 5.1 Daily yields on one-month U.S. Treasury bills, 2001–2017
These are nominal interest rates of course.

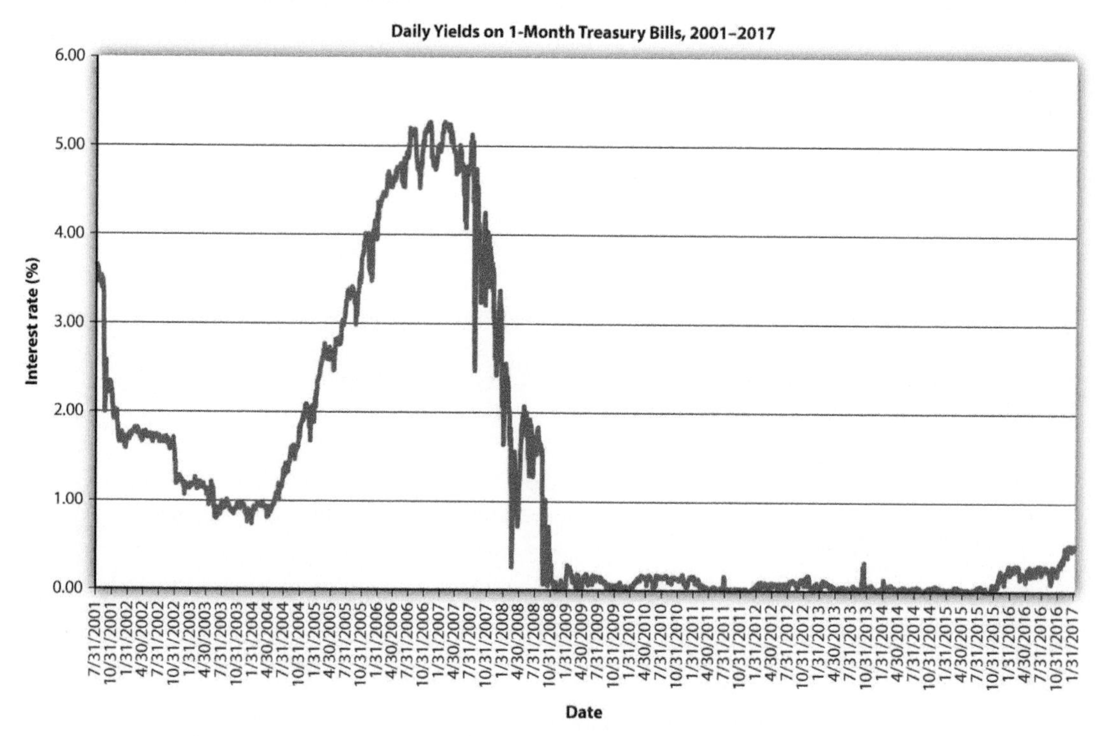

FIGURE 5.2 Daily yields on one-month U.S. Treasury bills, March 2008
This was before the financial panic of 2008 sent rates to almost zero for close to a decade.

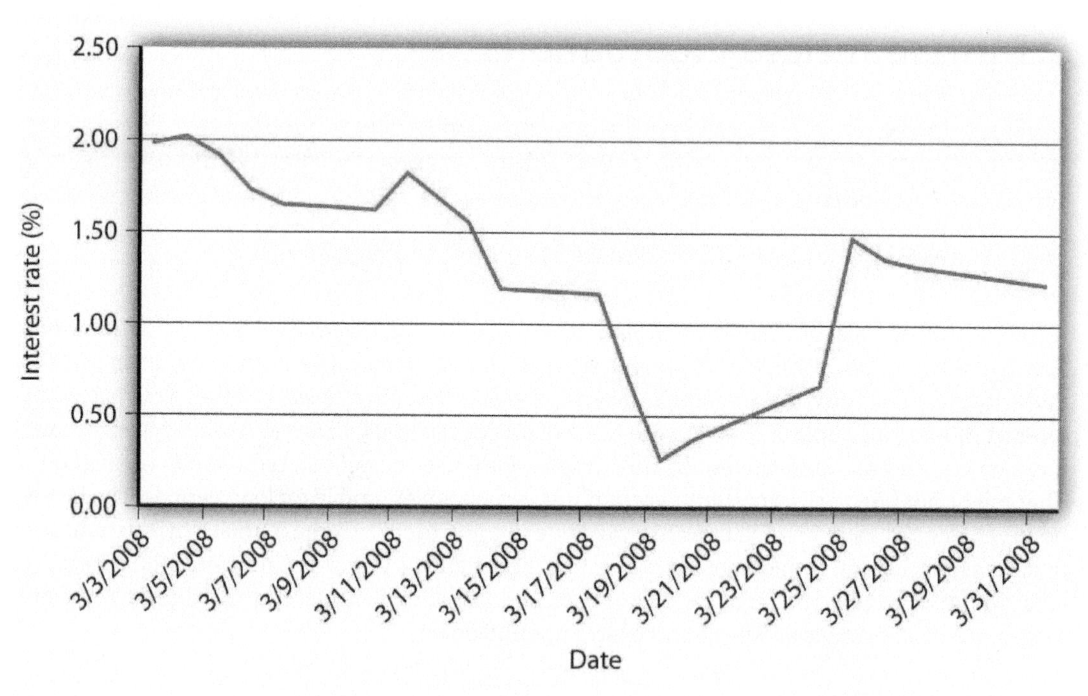

You should now be primed to ask, Why does the interest rate fluctuate? In other words, what causes interest rate movements like those shown above? In this aptly named chapter, we will examine the economic factors that determine the nominal interest rate. We will ignore, until the next chapter, the fact that interest rates differ on different types of securities. *In this chapter we will concern ourselves only with the general level of interest rates, which economists call "the" interest rate.*

As Figure 5.3 and Figure 5.4 show, interest rates tend to track each other, so by focusing on what makes one interest rate move, we have a leg up on making sense of movements in the literally thousands of interest rates out there in the real world.

FIGURE 5.3 The risk structure of interest rates in the United States, 1919–2016
The spreads are due to differences in risk (return volatility)

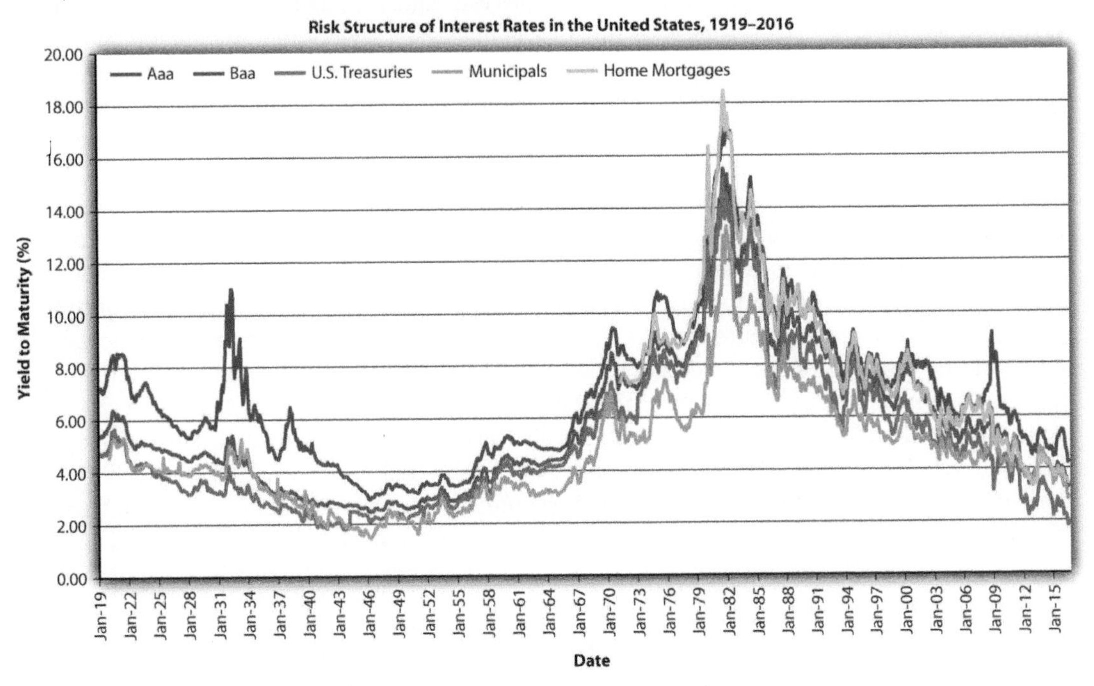

FIGURE 5.4 The term structure of interest rates in the United States, 1960–2016
Note that long term bonds usually have higher yields than short term bonds

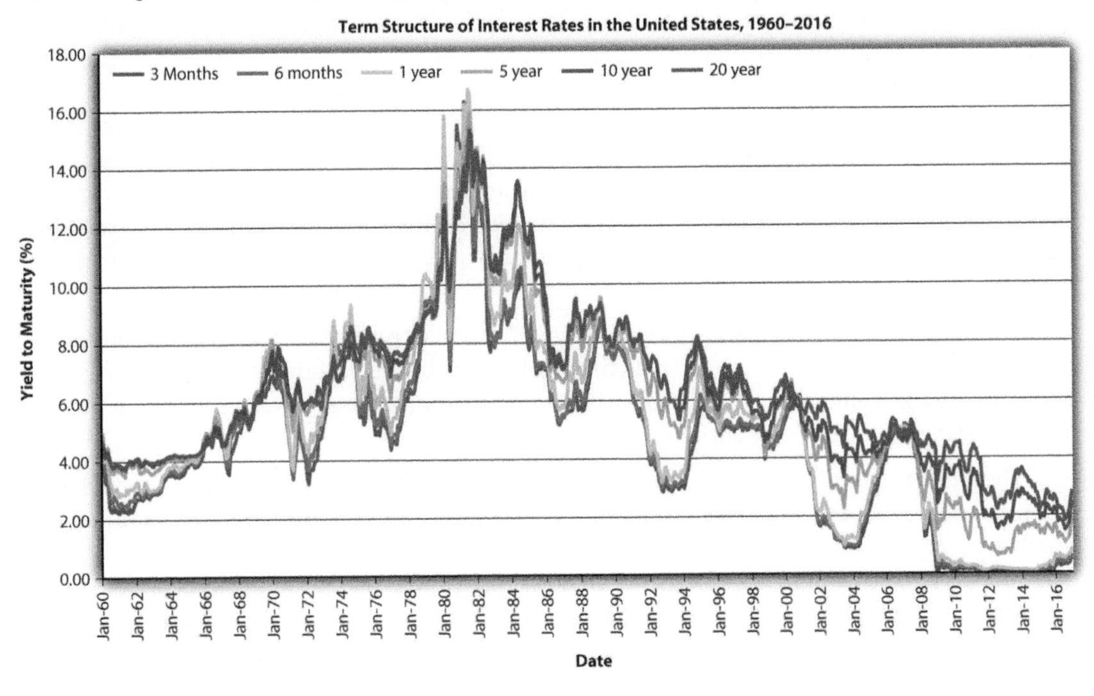

The ability to forecast changes in the interest rate is a rare but profitable gift. Professional interest rate forecasters are seldom right on the mark and often are far astray, and half the time they don't even get the direction (up or down) right.[1] That's what we'd expect if their forecasts were determined by flipping a coin! Therefore, we don't expect you to be able to predict changes in the interest rate, but we do expect you to be able to post-dict them. In other words, you should be able to narrate, in words and appropriate graphs, why past changes occurred. You should also be able to make predictions by invoking the ceteris paribus assumption.

The previous graphs reveal that interest rates generally trended downward from 1920 to 1945, then generally rose until the early 1980s, when they began trending downward again through 2016. During the 1920s, general business conditions were favorable. In other words, taxes and regulations were relatively low, while confidence in public policies was high. President Calvin Coolidge summed this up when he said, "The business of America is business." Therefore, the demand for bonds increased (the demand curve shifted right), pushing prices higher and yields lower. The 1930s witnessed the Great Depression, an economic recession of unprecedented magnitude that dried up profit opportunities for businesses and hence shifted the supply curve of bonds hard left, further increasing bond prices and depressing yields. (If the federal government had not run budget deficits some years during the depression, the interest rate would have dropped even further.) During World War II, the government used monetary policy to keep interest rates low. After the war, that policy came home to roost as inflation began to become, for the first time in American history, a perennial fact of life. Contemporaries called it "creeping inflation." A higher price level, of course, put upward pressure on the interest rate (think Fisher Equation). The unprecedented increase in prices during the 1970s (what some have called the "Great Inflation") drove nominal interest rates higher still. Only in the early 1980s, after the Federal Reserve mended its ways (a topic to which we will return) and brought inflation under control, did the interest rate begin to fall. Positive geopolitical events in the late 1980s and early 1990s, namely, the end of the Cold War and the birth of what we today call "globalization," also helped to reduce interest rates by rendering the general business climate more favorable (thus pushing the demand curve for bonds to the right, bond prices upward, and yields downward). Low levels of inflation and general economic stagnation have kept the interest rate low since the Panic of 2008. Pretty darn neat, eh?

The keys to understanding why "the" interest rate changes over time are simple price theory (supply and demand) and the theory of asset demand. Like other types of goods, bonds and other financial instruments trade in markets. The demand curve for bonds, as for most goods, slopes downward; the supply curve slopes upward in the usual fashion. There is little mystery here. The supply curve slopes upward because, as the price of bonds increases (which is to say, as their yield to maturity decreases), holding the bonds' face values and coupons and the rest of the world constant, borrowers (sellers of securities) will supply a higher quantity, just as producers facing higher prices for their wares will supply more cheese or automobiles. As the price of bonds falls, or as the yield to maturity that sellers and borrowers offer increases, sellers and borrowers will supply fewer bonds. (Why sell 'em if they aren't going to fetch much?) When they can obtain funds cheaply, companies will be eager to borrow to expand because it is more likely that it will be profitable to do so. When funds are dear, companies will not see many "profitable" (i.e., positive present net value) projects to pursue.

The demand curve for bonds slopes downward for similar reasons. When bond prices are high (yields to maturity are low), few will be demanded because investors (buyers) will find other, more lucrative uses of their money. As bond prices fall (bond yields increase), investors will want more of the increasingly good deals (better returns) that they offer.

The market price of a bond and the quantity that will be traded is determined, of course, by the intersection of the supply and demand curves, as in Figure 5.5. The equilibrium price prevails in the market because, if the market price were temporarily greater than p^*, the market would be glutted with bonds. In other words, the quantity of bonds supplied would exceed the quantity demanded, so sellers of bonds would lower their asking price until equilibrium was restored. If the market price temporarily dipped below p^*, excess demand would prevail (the quantity demanded would exceed the quantity supplied), and investors would bid up the price of the bonds to the equilibrium point.

FIGURE 5.5 Equilibrium in the bond market

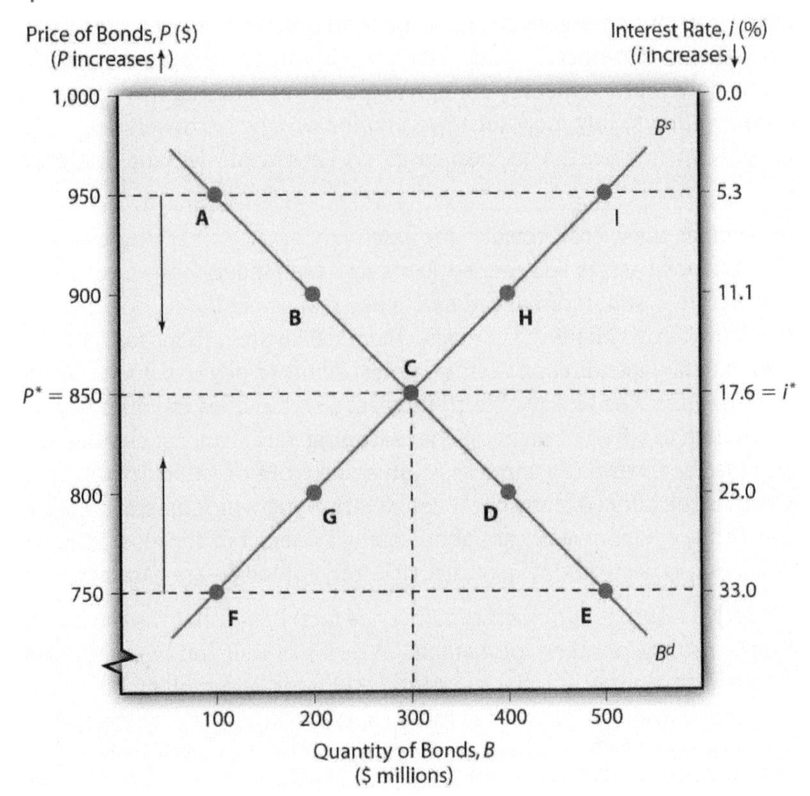

As with other goods, the supply and demand curves for bonds can shift right or left, with results familiar to principles ("Econ 101") students. If the supply of bonds increases (the supply curve shifts right), the market price will decrease (the interest rate will increase) and the quantity of bonds traded will increase. If the supply of bonds decreases (the supply curve shifts left), bond prices increase (the interest rate falls) and the equilibrium quantity decreases. If the demand for bonds falls (the demand curve shifts left), prices and quantities decrease (and the interest rate increases). If demand increases (the demand curve shifts right), prices and quantities rise (and the interest rate falls).

Key Takeaways

- The interest rate changes due to changes in supply and demand for bonds.
- Or, to be more precise, any changes in the slopes or locations of the supply and/or demand curves for bonds (and other financial instruments) lead to changes in the equilibrium point (p^* and q^*) where the supply and demand curves intersect, which is to say, where the quantity demanded equals the quantity supplied.

5.2 Shifts in Supply and Demand for Bonds

Learning Objective

1. What causes the supply and demand for bonds to shift?

Shifting supply and demand curves around can be fun, but figuring out why the curves shift is the interesting part. (Determining the shape and slope of the curves is interesting too, but these details will not detain us here.) Movements along the curve, or why the supply curve slopes upward and the demand curve downward, were easy enough to grasp. Determining why the whole curve moves, why investors are willing to buy more (or fewer) bonds, or why borrowers are willing to sell more (or fewer) bonds *at a given price* is a bit more involved. Let's tackle demand first, then we will move on to supply.

Wealth determines the overall demand for assets. An asset (something owned) is any store of value, including financial assets like money, loans (for the lender), bonds, equities (stocks), and a potpourri of derivatives[2] and nonfinancial assets like real estate (land, buildings), precious metals (gold, silver, platinum), gems (diamonds, rubies, emeralds), hydrocarbons (oil, natural gas), and (to a greater or lesser extent, depending on their qualities) all other physical goods (as opposed to bads, like pollution, or freebies, like air). As wealth increases, so too does the quantity demanded of all types of assets, though to different degrees. The reasoning here is almost circular: if it is to be maintained, wealth must be invested in some asset, in some store of value. In which type of asset to invest new wealth is the difficult decision. When determining *which assets to hold*, most economic entities (people, firms, governments) care about many factors, but for most investors most of the time, three variables—expected relative return, risk, and liquidity—are paramount.

Expected relative return is the ex ante (before the fact) belief that the return on one asset will be higher than the returns of other comparable (in terms of risk and liquidity) assets. *Return is a good thing, of course, so as expected relative return increases, the demand for an asset also increases (the entire demand curve shifts right).* That can happen because the expected return on the asset itself increases, because the expected return on comparables decreases, or because of a combination thereof. Clearly, two major factors will affect return expectations and hence the demand for certain financial assets, like bonds: expected interest rates and, via the Fisher Equation, expected inflation. If the interest rate is expected to increase for any reason (including, but not limited to, expected increases in inflation), bond prices are expected to fall, so the demand will decrease (the entire demand curve will shift left). Conversely, if the interest rate is thought to decrease for any reason (including, but not limited to, the expected taming of inflation), bond prices are expected to rise, so the entire demand curve will shift right.

Overall, though, calculating relative expected returns is sticky business that is best addressed in more specialized financial books and courses. If you want an introduction, investigate the capital asset pricing model (CAPM)[3] and the arbitrage pricing theory (APT).[4] Calculating return is not terribly difficult and neither is comparing returns among a variety of assets. What's tricky is forecasting future returns and making sure that assets are comparable by controlling for risk, among other things. *Risk is the uncertainty of an asset's returns. It comes in a variety of flavors, all of them unsavory, so as it increases, the demand decreases (the entire curve shifts left), ceteris paribus.* Two major types of risk are default risk (aka credit risk), the chance that a financial contract will not be honored, and interest rate risk, the chance that the interest rate will rise and hence decrease a bond or loan's price. An offsetting risk is called reinvestment risk, which bites when the interest rate decreases because coupon or other interest payments have to be reinvested at a lower yield to maturity. *To be willing to take on more risk, whatever its flavor, rational investors must expect a higher relative return.* Investors who require a much higher return for assuming a little bit of risk are called risk-averse. Those who will take on much risk for a little higher return are called risk-loving, risk-seekers, or risk-tolerant. (Investors who take on more risk without compensation are neither risk-averse nor risk-tolerant, but rather irrational.) Risks can be idiosyncratic (pertinent to a particular company), sectoral (pertinent to an entire industry, like trucking or restaurants), or systemic (economy-wide).

investment portfolio

The set of financial and other investments or assets held by an economic entity.

Liquidity risk occurs when an asset cannot be sold as quickly or cheaply as expected, be it for idiosyncratic, sectoral, or systemic reasons. *This, too, is a serious risk because liquidity, or (to be more precise) liquidity relative to other assets, is the third major determinant of asset demand.* Because investors often need to change their **investment portfolio** or dis-save (spend some of their wealth on consumption), liquidity, the ability to sell an asset quickly and cheaply, is a good thing. The more liquid an asset is, therefore, the further right the demand curve for it will shift, all else being equal.

During the financial crisis that began in 2007, the prices of a certain type of bond collateralized by subprime mortgages, long-term loans collateralized with homes and made to relatively risky borrowers, collapsed. In other words, their yields had to increase markedly to induce investors to own them. They dropped in price after investors realized that the bonds, a type of asset-backed security (ABS), had much higher default rates and much lower levels of liquidity than they had previously believed.

Figure 5.6 summarizes the chapter discussion so far.

FIGURE 5.6 Variables that influence demand for bonds
You should fully understand this table before moving on in the text, dontcha think?

Variable	Change in Variable	Change in Quantity Demanded	Shift in Demand Curve
Wealth	Up	Up	Right
Expected relative return	Up	Up	Right
Expected interest rate	Up	Down	Left
Inflation expectations	Up	Down	Left
Relative risk	Up	Down	Left
Relative liquidity	Up	Up	Right

So much for demand. Why does the supply curve for bonds shift to and fro? *There are many reasons, but the three main ones are government budgets, inflation expectations, and general business conditions.* When governments run budget deficits, they often borrow by selling bonds, pushing the supply curve rightward and bond prices down (yields up), ceteris paribus. When governments run surpluses, and they occasionally do, believe it or not, they redeem and/or buy their bonds back on net, pushing the supply curve to the left and bond prices up (yields down), all else being equal. (For historical time series data on the U.S. national debt, which was usually composed mostly of bonds, browse http://www.economagic.com/em-cgi/data.exe/treas/pubdebt.)

Stop and Think Box

You are a copyeditor for *Barron's*. What, if anything, appears wrong in the following sentence? How do you know?

"Recent increases in the profitability of investments, inflation expectations, and government surpluses will surely lead to increased bond supplies in the near future."

Government deficits, not surpluses, lead to increased bond supplies.

The expectation of higher inflation, other factors held constant, will cause borrowers to issue more bonds, driving the supply curve rightward, and bond prices down (and yields up). The Fisher

Equation, $i_r = i - \pi^e$, explains this nicely. If the inflation expectation term π^e increases while nominal interest rate i stays the same, the real interest rate i_r must decrease. *From the perspective of borrowers, the real cost of borrowing falls, which means that borrowing becomes more attractive.* So they sell bonds.

Borrowing also becomes more attractive when general business conditions become more favorable, as when taxes and regulatory costs decrease or the economy expands. Although individuals sometimes try to borrow out of financial weakness or desperation, relatively few such loans are made because they are high risk. Most economic entities borrow out of strength, to finance expansion and engage in new projects they believe will be profitable. So when economic prospects are good, taxes are low, and regulations are not too costly, businesses are eager to borrow, often by selling bonds, shifting the supply curve to the right and bond prices down (yields up).

Figure 5.7 summarizes the chapter discussion so far.

FIGURE 5.7 Variables that determine the supply of bonds
This is another important table to understand before moving on.

Variable	Change in Variable	Change in Quantity Supplied	Shift in Supply Curve
Government budget	Deficit/Surplus	Up/Down	Right/Left
Inflation expectations	Up/Down	Up/Down	Right/Left
General business conditions	Up/Down	Up/Down	Right/Left

As Yoda might say, "Pause here, we must" to make sure we're on track.[5] Try out these questions until you are comfortable. Remember that the ceteris paribus condition holds in each.

Exercises

1. What will happen to bond prices if stock trading commissions decrease? Why?
2. What will happen to bond prices if bond trading commissions increase? Why?
3. What will happen to bond prices if the government implements tax increases? Why?
4. If government revenues drop significantly (and remember all else stays the same, including government expenditures), what will likely happen to bond prices? Why?
5. If the government guaranteed the payment of bonds, what would happen to their prices? Why?
6. What will happen to bond prices if the government implements regulatory reforms that reduce regulatory costs for businesses? Why?
7. If government revenues increase significantly, what will likely happen to bond prices? Why?
8. What will happen to bond prices if terrorism ended and the world's nations unilaterally disarmed and adopted free trade policies? Why?
9. What will happen to bond prices if world peace brought substantially lower government budget deficits?

If you've already figured out that expected inflation will decrease bond prices, and increase bond yields, by both shifting the supply curve to the right and the demand curve to the left, as in Figure 5.8 *, kudos to you!*

FIGURE 5.8 Expected inflation and bond prices
Looks like Fisher was right!

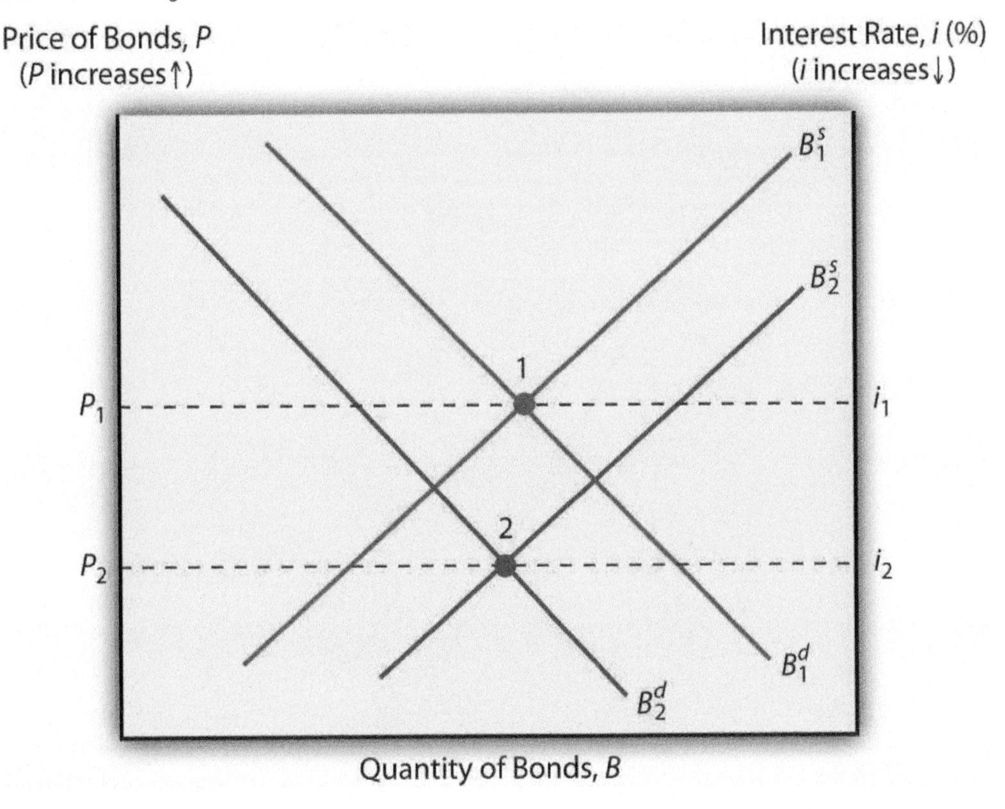

If you noticed that the response of bond prices and yields to a business cycle expansion is indeterminate, booya! As noted above, a boom shifts the bond supply curve to the right by inducing businesses to borrow and thus take advantage of the bonanza. Holding demand constant, that action reduces bond prices (raises the interest rate). But demand does not stay constant because economic expansion increases wealth, which increases demand for bonds (shifts the curve to the right), which in turn increases bond prices (reduces the interest rate). The net effect on the interest rate, therefore, depends on how much each curve shifts, as in Figure 5.9.

FIGURE 5.9 Business cycle expansion and bond prices
Expansions usually cause interest rates to rise (bond prices to fall)

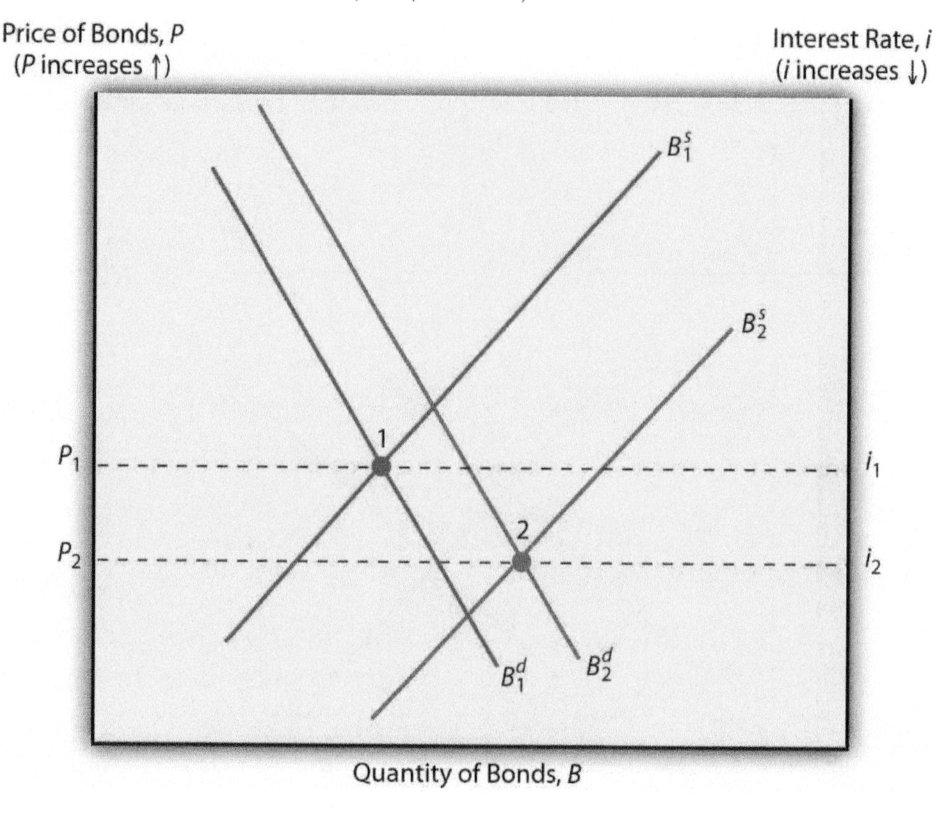

In reality, the interest rate usually rises (bond prices fall) during expansions and the interest rate always falls (bond prices always increase) during recessions. For example, the interest rate fell to very low levels during the Great Depression (an almost worldwide downturn in economic output in the early 1930s) and during Japan's extended economic funk (period of low to no increase in per capita incomes) in the 1990s-2000s.[6] Moreover, as we'll see in later chapters, central bankers do everything they can to reduce interest rates during recessions in an effort to stimulate borrowing and hence, hopefully, the economy.

Key Takeaways

- The demand curve for bonds shifts due to changes in wealth, expected relative returns, risk, and liquidity.
- Wealth, returns, and liquidity are positively related to demand; risk is inversely related to demand.
- Wealth sets the general level of demand. Investors then trade off risk for returns and liquidity.
- The supply curve for bonds shifts due to changes in government budgets, inflation expectations, and general business conditions.
- Deficits cause governments to issue bonds and hence shift the bond supply curve right; surpluses have the opposite effect.
- Expected inflation leads businesses to issue bonds because inflation reduces real borrowing costs, ceteris paribus; decreases in expected inflation or deflation expectations have the opposite effect.
- Expectations of future general business conditions, including tax reductions, regulatory cost reduction, and increased economic growth (economic expansion or boom), induce businesses to borrow (issue bonds), while higher taxes, more costly regulations, and recessions shift the bond supply curve left.

- Theoretically, whether a business expansion leads to higher interest rates or not depends on the degree of the shift in the bond supply and demand curves.
- An expansion will cause the bond supply curve to shift right, which alone will decrease bond prices (increase the interest rate).
- But expansions also cause the demand for bonds to increase (the bond demand curve to shift right), which has the effect of increasing bond prices (and hence lowering bond yields).
- Empirically, the bond supply curve typically shifts much further than the bond demand curve, so the interest rate usually rises during expansions and always falls during recessions.

5.3 Predictions and Effects

Learning Objective

1. How does the interest rate react to changes in the money supply?

We're almost there! At first blush, increasing the money supply would seem to decrease interest rates through what is called a liquidity effect: more money in circulation means more money to lend and hence, like more apples or carrots in a market, lower prices. Reality, however, is not so simple when it comes to the money supply. *Government entities regulate the money supply and have a habit of expanding it because doing so prudently increases economic growth, employment, incomes, and other good stuff. Unfortunately, expanding the money supply also causes prices to rise almost every year, with no reversion to earlier levels.* When the money supply increases, incomes rise, prices increase, and people expect inflation to occur. *Each of those three effects, called the income, price level, and expected inflation effects, respectively, causes the interest rate to rise. Higher incomes mean more demand for bonds and higher prices, and expected inflation means bondholders need to receive a higher interest rate to offset losses in money's purchasing power (the Fisher Effect).* When the money supply increases, the liquidity effect, which lowers the interest rate, battles those three countervailing effects. Sometimes, the liquidity effect wins. When the money supply increases (or increases faster than usual), the liquidity effect overpowers the countervailing effects, and the interest rate declines and stays below the previous level. Sometimes, often in modern industrial economies with **independent central banks**, the liquidity effect prevails at first and the interest rate declines, but then incomes rise, inflation expectations increase, and the price level actually rises, *eventually* causing the interest rate to increase above the original level. Finally, sometimes, as in modern undeveloped countries with weak central banking institutions, the expectation of inflation is so strong and so quick that it overwhelms the liquidity effect, driving up the interest rate immediately. Later, after incomes and the price level increase, the interest rate soars yet higher. Figure 5.10 summarizes this discussion graphically.

independent central bank

A monetary authority that is controlled by public-interested technocrats rather than by self-interested politicians.

FIGURE 5.10 Money supply growth and nominal interest rates
Three possible effects of increasing the money supply on interest rates over time.

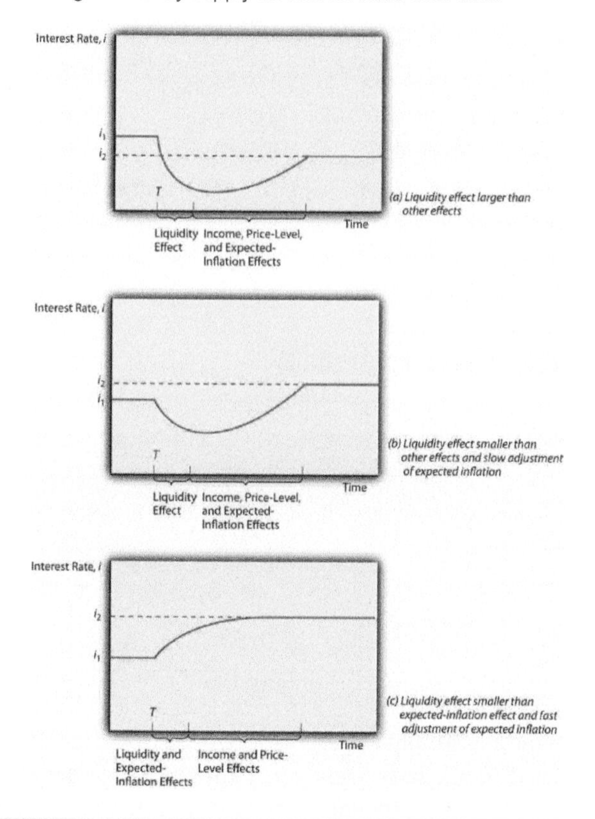

Stop and Think Box

Famed monetary economist and Nobel laureate Milton Friedman[7] was a staunch supporter of free markets and a critic of changes in the price level, particularly the rampant inflation of the 1970s. He argued that government monetary authorities ought to increase the money supply at some known, constant rate. If Friedman was so worried about price level changes, why didn't he advocate permanently fixing the money supply (MS)?

By fixing the MS, the interest rate would have risen higher and higher as the demand for money increased due to higher incomes and even simple population growth. Only deflation (decreases in the price level) could have countered that tendency, but deflation, Friedman knew, was as pernicious as inflation. A constant rate of MS growth, he believed, would keep the price level relatively stable and interest rate fluctuations less frequent or severe.

Key Takeaways

- Intuitively, an increase in the money supply decreases the interest rate and a decrease in the money supply increases it.
- Under a floating or fiat money system like we have today, an increase in the money supply might induce interest rates to rise immediately if inflation expectations were strong or to rise with a lag as actual inflation took place.

5.4 Suggested Reading

Constable, Simon, and Robert E. Wright. *The Wall Street Journal Guide to the 50 Economic Indicators That Really Matter: From Big Macs to "Zombie Banks," the Indicators Smart Investors Watch to Beat the Market.* New York: HarperCollins Business, 2011.

Gilliland, Michael, Len Tashman, and Udo Sglavo. *Business Forecasting: Practical Problems and Solutions.* Hoboken, N.J.: Wiley, 2016.

Friedman, Milton. *The Optimum Quantity of Money.* Piscataway, NJ: Aldine Transaction, 2005.

Endnotes

1. www.finpipe.com/intratgo.htm
2. www.thebalance.com/what-are-derivatives-3305833
3. www.valuebasedmanagement.net/methods_capm.html;www.moneychimp.com/articles/valuation/capm.htm
4. moneyterms.co.uk/apt
5. www.yodaspeak.co.uk/index.php
6. www.economist.com/node/10729998
7. www.econlib.org/library/Enc/bios/Friedman.html

CHAPTER 6

The Economics of Interest-Rate Spreads and Yield Curves

Chapter Objectives

By the end of this chapter, students should be able to:

1. Define the risk structure of interest rates and explain its importance.
2. Explain *flight to quality*.
3. Define the *term structure of interest rates* and explain its importance.
4. Describe a yield curve and explain its economic meaning.

6.1 Interest-Rate Determinants I: The Risk Structure

Learning Objective

1. What is the risk structure of interest rates and flight to quality, and what do they explain?

In this chapter, we're going to figure out, as best we can, why yields on different types of bonds differ. The analysis will help us to understand a couple of stylized facts derived from the history of interest rates and Figure 6.1 and Figure 6.2:

FIGURE 6.1 The risk structure of interest rates in the United States, 1919–2016
The spreads are due to differences in risk (return volatility)

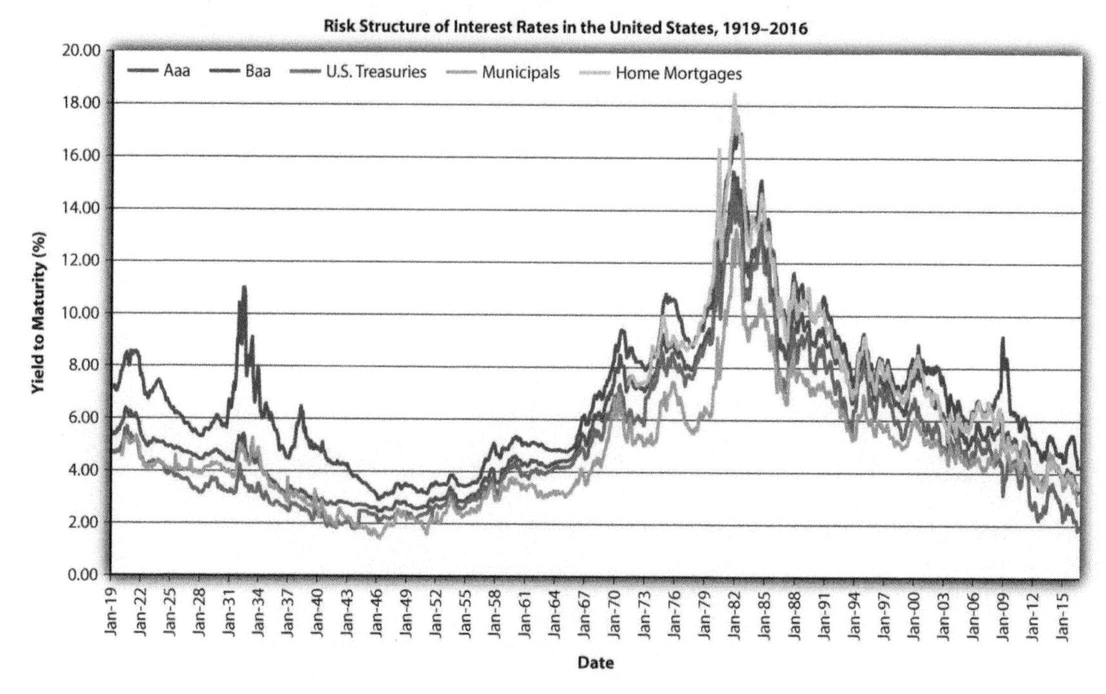

FIGURE 6.2 The term structure of interest rates in the United States, 1960–2016
Note that long term bonds usually have higher yields than short term bonds

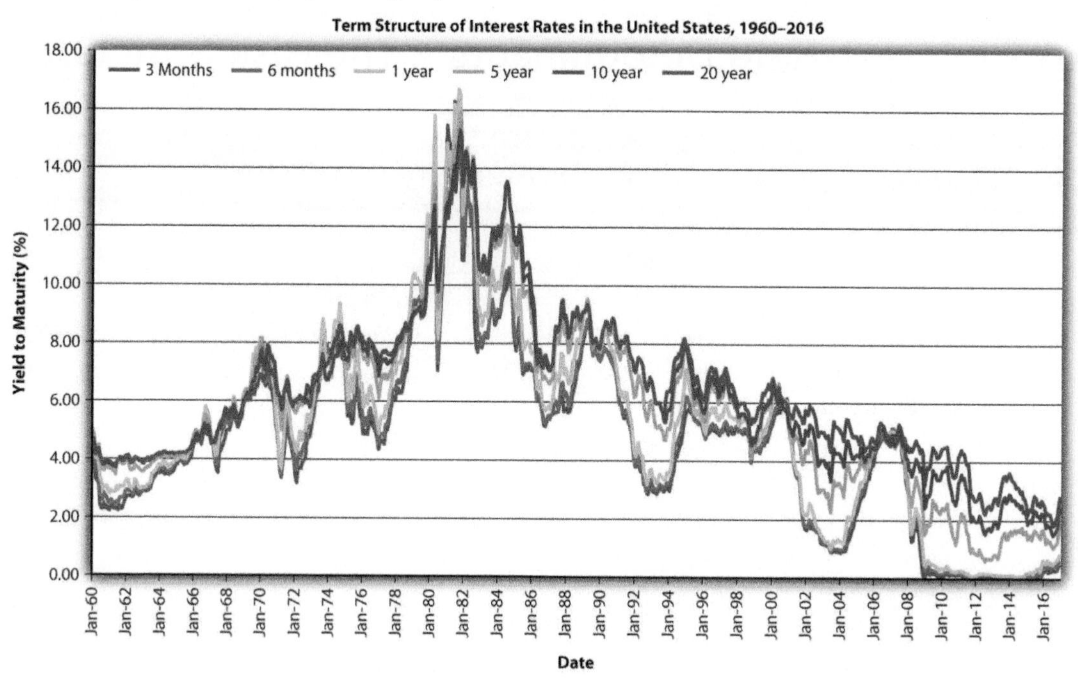

1. Why the yields on Baa corporate bonds are always higher than the yields on Aaa corporate bonds, which in turn are higher than those on Treasury bonds (issued by the federal government), which for a long time have been higher still than those on munis (bonds issued by municipalities, like state and local governments).
2. Why the yields on corporate Baa bonds bucked the trend of lower rates in the early 1930s and why, at one time, municipal bonds yielded more than Treasuries.
3. Why bonds issued by the same economic entity (the U.S. government) with different maturities generally, but not always, have different yields and why the rank ordering changes over time.

Figure 6.1, which holds maturity constant, is the easiest to understand because we've already discussed the major concepts. We'll tackle it, and what economists call the risk structure of interest rates, first. Investors care mostly about three things: risk, return, and liquidity. Because the bonds in Figure 6.1 are all long-term bonds, their expected relative returns might appear at first glance to be identical. *Investors know, however, that bonds issued by different economic entities have very different probabilities of defaulting.* Specifically, they know the following:

1. The U.S. government has never defaulted on its bonds and is extremely unlikely to do so because even if its much-vaunted political stability were to be shattered and its efficient tax administration (that wonderful institution, the Internal Revenue Service [IRS]) were to stumble, it could always meet its nominal obligations by creating money. (That might create inflation, as it has at times in the past. Nevertheless, except for a special type of bond called TIPS, the government and other bond issuers promise to pay a nominal value, not a real [inflation-adjusted] sum, so the government does not technically default when it pays its obligations by printing money.)
2. Municipalities have defaulted on their bonds in the past and could do so again in the future because, although they have the power to tax, they do not have the power to create money at will. (Although in the past, most recently during the Great Depression, some issued money-like—let's call them extralegal—bills of credit, or chits.) Nevertheless, the risk of default on municipal bonds (aka munis) is often quite low, especially for revenue bonds, upon which specific taxes and fees are pledged for interest payments.
3. Interest earned on munis is exempt from most forms of income taxation, while interest earned on Treasuries and corporate bonds is fully taxable.
4. Corporations are more likely to default on their bonds than governments are because they must rely on business conditions and management acumen. They have no power to tax and only a limited ability to create the less-liquid forms of money, a power that decreases in proportion to their need! (I'm thinking of gift cards, declining balance debit cards, trade credit, and so forth.) Some corporations are more likely to default on their bonds than others. Several credit-rating agencies, including Moody's and Standard and Poor's, assess the probability of default and assign grades to each bond. There is quite a bit of grade inflation built in (the highest grade being not A or even A+ but Aaa), the agencies are rife with conflicts of interest, and the market usually senses problems before the agencies do. Nevertheless, bond ratings are a standard proxy for default risk because, as Figure 6.3 shows, lower-rated bonds are indeed more likely to default than higher-rated ones. Like Treasuries, corporate bonds are fully taxable.
5. The most liquid bond markets are usually those for Treasuries. The liquidity of corporate and municipal bonds is usually a function of the size of the issuer and the amount of bonds outstanding. So the bonds of the state of New Jersey might be more liquid than those of a small corporation, but less liquid than the bonds of, say, General Electric.

FIGURE 6.3 Default rates on bonds rated by Moody's from 1983 to 1999

Moody's Rating	One-Year Default Rate from 1983 to 1999 (%)	20-Year Default Rate from 1920–1999 (%)
Aaa	0.0	< 5
Aa1	0.0	< 10
Aa2	0.0	< 10
Aa3	0.1	< 10
A1	0.0	< 10
A2	0.0	< 10
A3	0.0	< 10
Baa1	0.0	c. 15
Baa2	0.1	c. 15
Baa3	0.3	c. 15
Ba1	0.6	c. 30
Ba2	0.5	c. 30
Ba3	2.5	c. 30
B1	3.5	c. 45
B2	6.9	c. 45
B3	12.2	c. 45

Equipped with this knowledge, we can easily understand the reasons for the rank ordering in Figure 6.1.[1] *Corporate Baa bonds have the highest yields because they have the highest default risk (of those graphed), and the markets for their bonds are generally not very liquid. Corporate Aaa bonds are next because they are relatively safer (less default risk) than Baa bonds and they may be relatively liquid, too. U.S. Treasuries are extremely safe and the markets for them are extremely liquid, so their yields are lower than those of corporate bonds.* In other words, investors do not need as high a yield to own Treasuries as they need to own corporates. Another way to put this is that investors place a positive *risk premium* (to be more precise, a credit or default risk, liquidity, and tax premium) on corporate bonds.

Stop and Think Box

Corporate bond ratings go all the way down to C (Moody's) or D (Standard and Poor's). (These used to be called high-yield or junk bonds but are now generally referred to as B.I.G. or below investment grade bonds.) If plotted on Figure 6.1, where would the yields of such bonds land? How do you know?

They would have higher yields and hence would be above the Baa line because they would have a higher default risk, the same tax treatment, and perhaps less liquidity.

The low yield on munis is best explained by their tax exemptions. Before income taxes became important, the yield on munis was higher than that of Treasuries, as we would expect given that Treasuries are more liquid and more likely to be paid as promised. During World War II, investors, especially wealthy individuals, eager for tax-exempt income and convinced that the fiscal problems faced by many municipalities during the depression were over, purchased large quantities of municipal bonds, driving their prices up (and their yields down). *Almost all the time since, tax considerations, which are considerable given our highest income brackets exceed 30 percent, have overcome the relatively high default risk and illiquidity of municipal bonds, rendering them more valuable than Treasuries, ceteris paribus.*

FIGURE 6.4 Risk premiums and bond spreads during the Great Depression, 1929–1939
More default risk, less liquidity, and no tax exemption = higher yields (lower bond price)

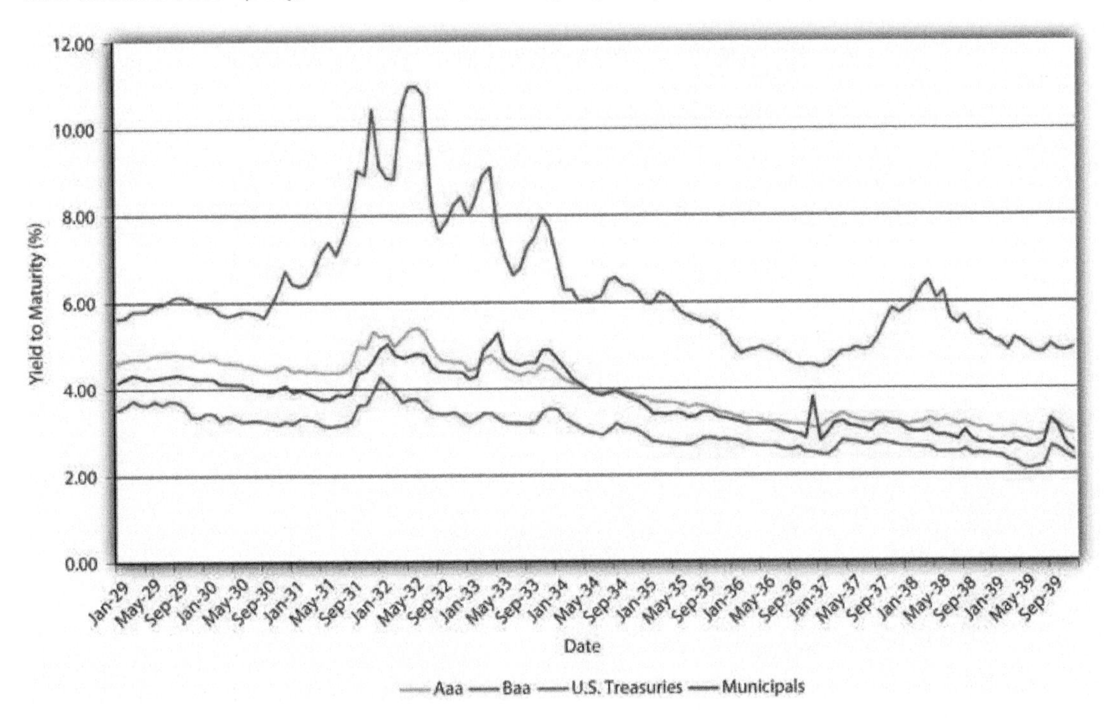

Risk, after-tax returns, and liquidity also help to explain changes in spreads, the difference between yields of bonds of different types (the distance between the lines in Figure 6.1 and Figure 6.4). The big spike in Baa bond yields in the early 1930s, the darkest days of the Great Depression, was due to one simple cause: companies with Baa bond ratings were going belly-up left and right, leaving bondholders hanging. As Figure 6.4 shows, companies that issued Aaa bonds, municipalities, and possibly even the federal government were also more likely to default in that desperate period, but they were not nearly as likely to as weaker companies. Yields on their bonds therefore increased, but only a little, so the spread between Baa corporates and other bonds increased considerably in those troubled years. In better times, the spreads narrowed, only to widen again during the so-called Roosevelt Recession of 1937–1938.

FIGURE 6.5 The flight to quality (Treasuries) and from risk (corporate securities)
As investors sell the riskier asset (left panel) and buy the safer one (right panel), the risk premium increases.

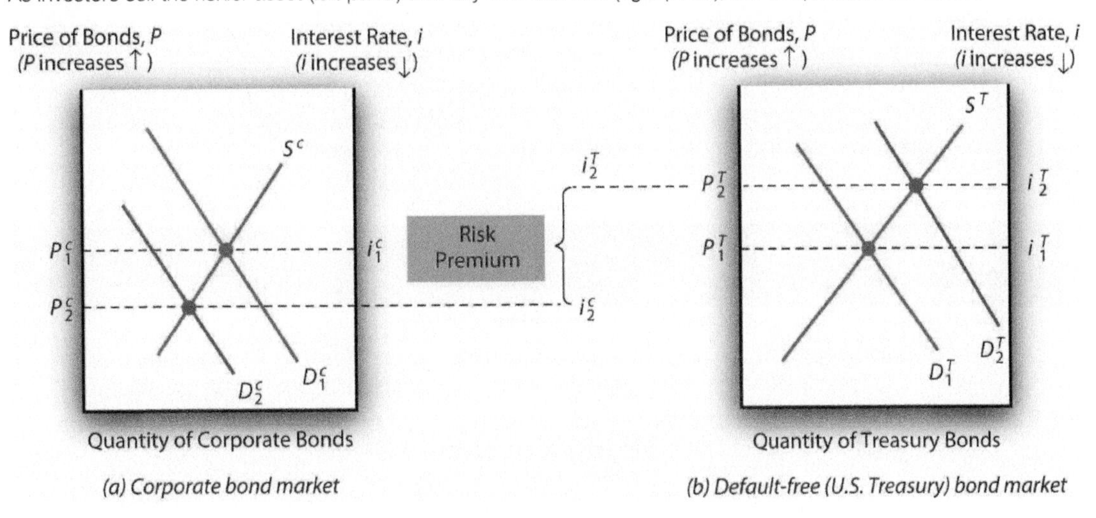

During crises, spreads can quickly soar because investors sell riskier assets, like Baa bonds, driving their prices down, and simultaneously buy safe ones, like Treasuries, driving their prices up. This so-called flight to quality is represented in Figure 6.5.

Stop and Think Box

In the confusion following the terrorist attacks on New York City and Washington, DC, on September 11, 2001, some claimed that people who had prior knowledge of the attacks made huge profits in the financial markets. How would that have been possible?

The most obvious way, given the analyses provided in this chapter, would have been to sell riskier corporate bonds and buy U.S. Treasuries on the eve of the attack in expectation of a flight to quality, the mass exchange of risky assets (and subsequent price decline) for safe ones (and subsequent price increase). Such a flight to quality actually occurred. Look what happened to the yields of 20-year Treasury bonds (recalling that lower yields means higher prices):

Date	Yield %
Sept. 4	5.59
Sept. 5	5.57
Sept. 6	5.50
Sept. 7	5.45
Sept. 10	5.50
Sept. 11	no trading
Sept. 12	no trading
Sept. 13	5.41
Sept. 14	5.38
Sept. 17	5.44

Data from https://fred.stlouisfed.org/series/DGS20

Key Takeaways

- The risk structure of interest rates explains why bonds of the same maturity but issued by different economic entities have different yields (interest rates).
- The three major risks are default, liquidity, and after-tax return.
- By concentrating on the three major risks, you can ascertain why some bonds are more (less) valuable than others, holding their term (repayment date) constant.
- You can also post-dict, if not outright predict, the changes in rank order as well as the spread (or difference in yield) between different types of bonds.
- A flight to quality occurs during a crisis when investors sell risky assets (like below-investment-grade bonds) and buy safe ones (like Treasury bonds or gold).

Exercises

1. What would happen to the spreads between different types of bonds if the federal government made Treasuries tax-exempt and at the same time raised income taxes considerably?
2. If the Supreme Court unexpectedly declared a major source of municipal government tax revenue illegal, what would happen to municipal bond yields?

3. If several important bond brokers reduced the brokerage fee they charge for trading Baa corporate bonds (while keeping their fees for other bonds the same), what would happen to bond spreads?
4. What happened to bond spreads when Enron, a major corporation, collapsed in December 2001?

6.2 The Determinants of Interest Rates II: The Term Structure

Learning Objective

1. What is the term structure of interest rates and the yield curve, and what do they explain?

Now we are going to hold the risk structure of interest rates—default risk, liquidity, and taxes—constant and concentrate on what economists call the term structure of interest rates, the variability of returns due to differing maturities. As Figure 6.2 reveals, even bonds from the same issuer, in this case, the U.S. government, can have yields that vary according to the length of time they have to run before their principals are repaid. Note that the general postwar trend is the same as that in Figure 6.1, a trend upward followed by an equally dramatic slide. Unlike Figure 6.1, however, the ranking of the series here is much less stable. Sometimes short-term Treasuries have lower yields than long-term ones, sometimes they have about the same yield, and sometimes they have higher yields.

To study this phenomenon more closely, economists and market watchers use a tool called a yield curve, which is basically a snapshot of yields of bonds of different maturities at a given moment. Figure 6.6 is what the Treasury yield curve looks like as reported by Reuters. The current yield curve can also be viewed many places online, including Bloomberg, the *Wall Street Journal*, and the U.S. Treasury itself.[2] *What observers have discovered is that the yields of bonds of different maturities (but identical risk structures) tend to move in tandem. They also note that yield curves usually slope upward. In other words, short-term rates are usually lower than long-term rates. Sometimes, however, the yield "curve" is actually flat—yields for bonds of different maturities are identical, or nearly so. Sometimes, particularly when short-term rates are higher than normal, the curve inverts or slopes downward, indicating that the yield on short-term bonds is higher than that on long-term bonds. And sometimes the curve goes up and down, resembling a sideways S (sometimes tilted on its face and sometimes its back) or Z.* What explains this? (Remember, it can't be tax, default, or liquidity risk because those variables are all the same for Treasuries.)

FIGURE 6.6 Treasury yield curve

This is important economic information believe it or not!

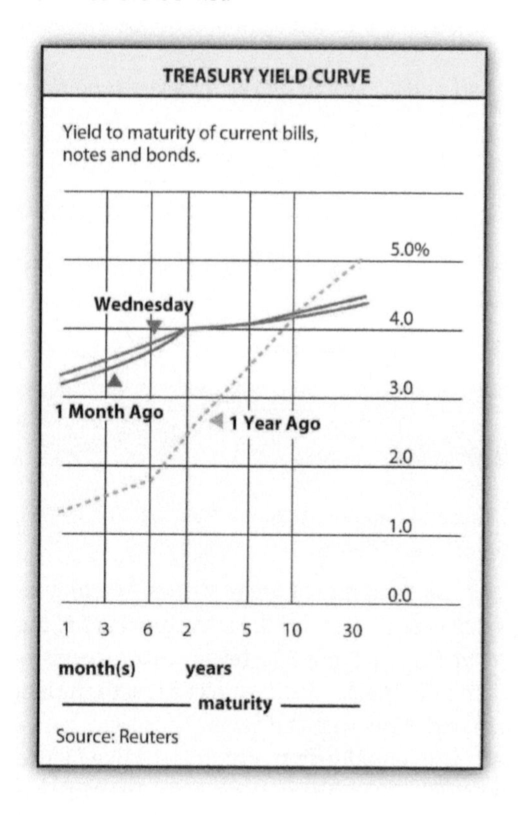

liquidity preference

The name of one of the theories that economists use to explain the yield curve that emphasizes the fact that investors typically prefer more liquid, shorter-term bonds to longer-term ones.

preferred habitat

The name of one of the theories that economists use to explain the yield curve that emphasizes the fact that short- and long-term bonds are partial substitutes; investors' usual preference for short-term bonds can be reversed under some circumstances, like when interest rates are thought to be temporarily high.

Theory and empirical evidence both point to the same conclusion: bonds of different maturities are partial substitutes for each other, not perfect substitutes, but not completely segmented either. Generally, investors prefer short-term bonds to long-term ones, but they reverse their preference if the interest rate goes unusually high. Investors are willing to pay more for short-term bonds, other factors (like "the" interest rate and the risk structure) held constant, because longer-term bonds are more subject to interest rate risk. Or, to put it another way, investors need a premium (in the form of a lower price or higher yield) to hold long-term bonds. (This notion has been called **liquidity preference** because it stresses that investors *prefer* shorter-term or more *liquid* bonds.) Ergo, the yield curve usually slopes upward, as it does in Figure 6.6.

But what about those times when the curve is flat or inverted? Investors give up their preference for short-term bonds when they expect a high interest rate for a short period. (This idea has been called **preferred habitat** because it suggests that short and long term bonds are, to some extent, substitutes, and whichever is *preferred* can change under the right circumstances or in the right *habitat*.) *Investors can think of a long-term bond yield as the average of the yields on shorter-term obligations, so when the interest rate is high by historical norms but expected after a year or so to revert to some long-term mean, they will actually begin to prefer long-term bonds and will buy them at much higher prices (lower yields) than short-term bonds, which is in anticipation of relatively large price increases in long-term bonds when interest rates decrease.* More formally, investors believe that

$$i n = [(i e 0 + i e 1 + i e 2 + i e 3 + ... \ i e (n - 1)) / n] + \rho n$$

where

i_n = interest rate today on a bond that matures in *n* years

i^e_x = expected interest rate at time × (0, 1, 2, 3,...through n)

ρ = the liquidity or term premium for an n-period bond (it is always positive and increases with n)

So the yield today of a bond with 5 years to maturity, if the liquidity premium is .5 percent and the expected interest rate each year is 4, is 4.5:

$i_5 = (4 + 4 + 4 + 4 + 4)/5 + .5 = 20/5 + .5 = 4.5$, implying an upward sloping yield curve because $4 < 4.5$.

If the interest rate is expected to rise over the next 5 years, the yield curve slopes upward yet more steeply:

$i_5 = (4 + 5 + 6 + 7 + 8)/5 + .5 = 30/5 + .5 = 6.5$, again implying an upward sloping curve because $4 < 6.5$.

If, on the other hand, interest rates are expected to fall over the next 5 years, the yield curve will slope downward, as in this example:

$i_5 = (12 + 10 + 8 + 5 + 5)/5 + .5 = 40/5 + .5 = 8.5$, implying an inverted yield curve because $12 > 8.5$.

Investors may also realize that long-term bonds will increase in price when interest rates fall (as they are expected to do in this example and as we learned in Chapter 3), so they are willing to pay more for them now.

Stop and Think Box

In the nineteenth century, the yield curve was usually flat under normal conditions. (It inverted during financial panics.) In other words, short-term and long-term bonds issued by the same economic entity did not often differ much in price. Why might that have been?

One possibility is that there was no liquidity premium then. Then, as now, short-term bonds suffered less interest rate risk than long-term bonds, but investors often complained of extremely high levels of reinvestment risk, of their inability to easily and cheaply reinvest the principal of bonds and mortgages when they were repaid. Often, lenders urged good borrowers not to repay (but to continue to service their obligations, of course). Another not mutually exclusive possibility is that the long-term price level stability engendered by the specie standard made the interest rate less volatile. The expectation was that the interest rate would not long stray from its long-term tendency.

The neat thing about this theory is that it reveals the yield curve as the market's prediction of future short-term interest rates, making it, by extension, an economic forecasting tool. Where the curve slopes sharply upward, the market expects future short-term interest rates to rise. Where it slopes slightly upward, the market expects future short-term rates to remain the same. Where the curve is flat, rates, it is thought, will fall moderately in the future. Inversion of the curve means short-term interest rates should fall sharply, as in the numerical example above. *The simplest way to remember this is to realize that the prediction equals the yield curve minus ρ_n, the term premium.*

Empirical research suggests that the yield curve is a good predictor of future interest rates in the very short term, the next few months, and the long term, but not in between. Part of the difficulty is that ρ_n is not well understood nor is it easily observable. It may change over time and/or not increase much from one maturity to the next on the short end of the curve. Nevertheless, economic forecasters use the yield curve to make predictions about inflation and the business cycle. A flat or inverted curve, for instance, portends lower short-term interest rates in the future, which is consistent with a recession but also with lower inflation rates, as we learned in Chapter 5. A curve sloped steeply upward, by contrast, portends higher future interest rates, which might be brought about by an increase in inflation rates or an economic boom.

Time once again to ensure that we're on the same page, er, website.

Exercises

1. What does the following yield curve tell us?

   Treasury yield curve for January 20, 2006.

Maturity	Yield (%)
1 month	3.95
3 months	4.35
6 months	4.48
1 year	4.44
2 years	4.37
3 years	4.32
5 years	4.31
7 years	4.32
10 years	4.37
20 years	4.59

2. What does the following yield curve predict?

   Treasury yield curve for July 31, 2000.

Maturity	Yield (%)
1 month	
3 months	6.20
6 months	6.35
1 year	
2 years	6.30
3 years	6.30
5 years	6.15
7 years	
10 years	6.03
30 years	5.78

Key Takeaways

- The *term structure of interest rates* explains why bonds issued by the same economic entity but of different maturities sometimes have different yields.
- Plotting yield against maturity produces an important analytical tool called the yield curve.
- The yield curve is a snapshot of the term structure of interest rates created by plotting yield against maturity for a single class of bonds, like Treasuries or munis, which reveals the market's prediction of future short-term interest rates, and thus, by extension, can be used to make inferences about inflation and business cycle expectations.

6.3 Suggested Reading

Choudry, Moorad. *Analysing and Interpreting the Yield Curve.* Hoboken, NJ: John Wiley and Sons, 2004.

Constable, Simon and Robert E. Wright. *The Wall Street Journal Guide to the 50 Economic Indicators That Really Matter: From Big Macs to "Zombie Banks," the Indicators Smart Investors Watch to Beat the Market.* New York: HarperCollins Business, 2011.

Fabozzi, Frank, Steven Mann, and Moorad Choudry. *Measuring and Controlling Interest Rate and Credit Risk.* Hoboken, NJ: John Wiley and Sons, 2003.

Homer, Sidney, and Richard E. Sylla. *A History of Interest Rates*, 4th ed. Hoboken, NJ: John Wiley and Sons, 2005.

Jha, Siddartha. *Interest Rate Markets: A Practical Approach to Fixed Income.* Hoboken, NJ: John Wiley and Sons, 2011.

Endnotes

1. Figure 6.3, by the way, should not be taken as evidence that credit rating agencies provide investors with useful information. Before 1970 or so, they sold ratings to investors and generally did a good job of ranking risks in a competitive market for ratings. Thereafter, however, they formed a government-sanctioned oligopoly and began to charge issuers for ratings. The resulting conflict of interest degraded the quality of ratings to the point that the big three rating agencies failed to predict the crises of 1997–98 in Southeast Asia and 2008 in the United States and Europe. Today, few investors still take their ratings seriously, as evidenced by the fact that Treasury bond prices actually *increased* after U.S. government bonds were downgraded by credit rating agency Standard and Poor's in August 2011.
2. www.bloomberg.com/markets/rates/index.html;
   www.ustreas.gov/offices/domestic-finance/debt-management/interest-rate/yield.shtml

CHAPTER 7

Rational Expectations, Efficient Markets, and the Valuation of Corporate Equities

Chapter Objectives

By the end of this chapter, students should be able to:

1. Explain when expectations are rational and when they are irrational.
2. Explain how corporate equities (stocks, shares of a corporation) are valued.
3. Explain what is meant by the term *market efficiency*.
4. Describe the ways in which financial markets are efficient.
5. Describe the ways in which financial markets are inefficient.

7.1 The Theory of Rational Expectations

Learning Objective

1. When are expectations rational and when are they irrational?

Market volatility

In this context, frequent changes in securities prices.

rational expectations

An economic theory that posits that market participants, in this case investors, input all available relevant information into the best forecasting model available.

economic fundamentals

Key variables in the pricing of assets. They include expected inflation, interest, default, and earnings rates.

investors

Participants in financial markets; purchasers of financial securities.

Market volatility, the constantly changing prices of financial instruments,[1] tricks some people into thinking that financial markets, especially stock markets, are flim-flams or gigantic roulette wheels. Stock prices, they suspect, are at best random and at worst rigged. *In fact, financial markets are typically more efficient, and hence fairer, than other markets*. The direction of price *movements* (up or down) is indeed random, but price *levels* are usually based on the **rational expectations** of a large number of market participants. While financial scams certainly exist, the stock and bond markets are not rigged. Except perhaps for some penny stocks (p* < $1), securities prices are usually based on **economic fundamentals** and are not systematically manipulated by insiders or conspirators. Investing in corporate equities certainly entails risk, but it is not akin to playing the lottery. Luck can play a role in investing, as in anything in life, but unlike a Powerball drawing, Lady Luck is not the whole of the game by a long shot. Far from being gamblers, **investors** are switches in the most advanced computing devices in the history of the world, financial markets. Prices in those markets help to determine what gets made and what doesn't, how much gets produced and how, and where and how those goods are sold.

Financial markets, in the world's most economically advanced countries anyway, have been rational and efficient decision-making machines for several centuries. In 1688, a broker in Amsterdam, Netherlands, named Joseph de la Vega, left posterity with vivid descriptions of the Dutch securities market.[2] The market, he claimed, was just a game of misinformation and spin management that pitted bulls (those who profited from an increase in prices) against bears (those who profited from a decrease in prices):

> *"The bulls are like the giraffe which is scared by nothing. . . . They love everything, they praise everything, they exaggerate everything. . . . The bulls make the public believe that their tricks signify wealth and that crops grow on graves. When attacked by serpents, they . . . regard them as both a delicate and a delicious meal. . . . They are not impressed by a fire nor perturbed by a debacle. . . . The bears, on the contrary, are completely ruled by fear, trepidation, and nervousness. Rabbits become elephants, brawls in a tavern become rebellions, faint shadows appear to them as signs of chaos. . . . What is there miraculous about the likelihood that every dwarf will become a giant in the eyes of the bears?"*[3]

Joseph de la Vega went on to detail a dozen different ways in which cabals of bears and herds of bulls tried to influence securities prices. The net effect of such machinations, though, was unclear. Sometimes the bulls won, sometimes the bears won, but their activities often canceled each other out. "Numerous brokers are inexhaustible in inventing involved maneuvers," de la Vega explained, "but for just this reason do not achieve their purposes." Systematic manipulation of the market was impossible because the bulls and bears competed against each other, each tugging at the price, but ultimately in vain. Also, as rational investors learned the tricks of trading, they came to expect hyperbole, false rumors, sham sales, and the like. So, in the final analysis, market fundamentals, not the whims of nefarious individuals, determined prices. Exactly the same could be said of most of today's securities markets. *Generally speaking, stock and other securities prices fluctuate due to genuine changes in supply or demand, not because of the machinations of bulls and bears.*

Joseph de la Vega's 300+-year-old description of what was then the world's most advanced securities market also made clear that *expectations, rather than actualities, moved prices*. "The expectation of an event," he noted, "creates a much deeper impression upon the exchange than the event itself." As noted in the preceding chapters, expectations are still paramount today. People invest based on what they believe the future will bring, not on what the present brings or the past has wrought, though they often look to the present and past (sometimes even the distant past) for clues about the future.

Rational expectations theory posits that investor expectations will be the best guess of the future using all available information. Expectations do not have to be correct to be rational; they just have to make logical sense given what is known at any particular moment. An expectation would be irrational if it did not logically follow from what is known or if it ignored available information. For the former reason, investors expend considerable sums on schooling, books, lectures, seminars, and the like, to learn the best ways to reason correctly given certain types of information. (This textbook and course are a good start, but competition for the best **model** is keen. Investment models and strategies constantly morph, adapting to changes in the real world.) For the latter reason, investors update their expectations, or forecasts, with great frequency, as new information becomes available, which occurs basically 24/7/365.

If everyone's expectations are rational, then why don't investors agree on how much assets are worth? One investor may think **gold** a steal at $900/ounce, while another wouldn't touch the stuff for a penny over $750. One investor might think $943.40 just right for a **zero coupon bond**, but another might think it a good deal only at $942.51. One may think that XYZ stock is overpriced at $22.57 a share, while another would buy a small quantity of it at that price, and yet another would buy all she could at that price. *Such differences in valuation are important because they allow trades to occur by inducing some investors to sell and others to buy.*

As it turns out, *investors sometimes have different sets of information available to them*. Some investors may have **inside information**, news that is unknown outside a small circle. Others may lack certain types of information because they think it is too costly to obtain. Other times, *investors think of the information they know in common differently because their utility functions (their goals and aspirations, if you will) differ*. So they have different time horizons, different holding periods, and different sensitivities to risk.

At yet other times, investors use different **valuation models**, different theories of how to predict fundamentals most accurately and how those fundamentals determine securities prices. For example, some investors foresee long causal chains more clearly than other investors do. Recall from Chapter 5 that the demand for asset X is partly a function of its expected return relative to all assets not-X. So investors must consider information directly related to asset X *and all other assets*. A new piece of information half a world away that alters expectations about a nation's ability to repay its debts, a sector's future prospects, or a single company's profits regularly ripples through the entire financial world. Ripple indeed evokes the right metaphor. Like throwing a pebble into a pond, the disruption is greatest at the epicenter, the spot where the rock hits the water, but it dissipates over time and space. The bigger the pebble (the bigger the news), the bigger the splash and the larger and longer lasting the disruption. Most days, the world's financial pond is pelted with millions of little pebbles, little pieces of news that cause prices to jiggle up and down. Every now and again, a big stone, even a boulder, hits the pond, causing significant price changes throughout the pond for quite a long time. (Economists call such boulders shocks, and they include financial crises like that of 2007–2008. Financial crises almost always follow **asset bubbles**, which we will discuss in more detail below.)

Some investors understand the effect of some ripples more quickly and clearly than others. This shouldn't be taken to mean that some investors are smarter than others, only that they understand the types of ripples particular pebbles will make better than others do. The roles could reverse with the next pebble, with the next bit of news. Moreover, investors constantly strive to improve their understanding of the ways that certain types of news affect securities prices. They emulate successful people and develop new models and theories of their own, not for the joy of learning but for the clink of cold hard cash. For example, investors who understood that oil prices hitting $50 per barrel would increase the share price of home insulation manufacturers merely stayed up with the crowd. It's pretty obvious that higher home heating costs would induce people to buy insulation. The investors who quickly figured out that the share price of a Canadian shingle manufacturer would jump too were the ones that earned above-market returns. (High oil prices made it profitable to extract oil from Canada's oil sand fields, but not enough people lived in the area around Fort McMurray, Alberta, to meet labor demands. People flocking to the region to work needed new homes, the roofs of which needed shingles, lots of them.[4])

model

In this context, a theory about the most accurate way to price securities or to estimate the value of future variables such as interest rates, risk, earnings, and other fundamentals.

gold

At one time, gold was money, that is, the unit of account against which the value of all goods was measured. It is now just a precious metal that trades on world markets like other commodities, its price rising and falling with shifts in supply and demand.

zero coupon bond

A discount bond that pays no coupon or interest. The interest is earned by the difference between the bond's face or par value and the price at which it is sold.

inside information

Information relevant to the valuation of stock or other security and known only to a small group of people.

valuation models

Theories of securities prices and their determinants.

asset bubble

In this context, a rapid increase in asset prices that is not easily justified by fundamentals like expected earnings, interest rates, and the like.

For all those reasons, investors often have a wide variety of opinions about the value of different assets. More mechanically, investors might have different opinions about bond valuations because they must have different views about the applicable discount or interest rate. To review,

$$PV = FV / (1 + i)^n$$

If this is a one-year zero coupon bond, FV = $1,000, and *i* = 6%, then the bond price = ($1,000/1.06) = $943.40. But if one believes *i* = 6.01, then the bond price = ($1,000/1.0601) = $942.51. To understand how investors can value the same stock differently, we must investigate how they value corporate equities.

Key Takeaways

- Expectations are rational when they logically follow from all available relevant information.
- Expectations are irrational if some available pertinent information is ignored or if conclusions do not flow logically from available information.

7.2 Valuing Corporate Equities

Learning Objective

1. How are corporate equities valued?

A corporate equity, or stock, is sometimes called a share because it is just that, a share in the ownership of a joint-stock corporation. Ownership entitles investors to a say in how the corporation is run. Today that usually means one vote per share in corporate elections for the board of directors, a group of people who direct, oversee, and monitor the corporation's professional managers. *Ownership also means that investors are residual claimants, entitling them to a proportionate share of the corporation's net earnings (profits), its cash flows, and its assets once all other claims against it have been settled.*

stockholders (or shareholders)

Owners of corporate equities. Generally, they are entitled to one vote per share in corporate elections for directors and a proportionate share of the corporation's profits.

dividends

In this context, cash distributions of corporate earnings to shareholders.

In exchange for their investment, **stockholders** may receive a flow of cash payments, usually made quarterly, called **dividends**. Dividends differ from bond coupons in important ways. Unlike coupons, they are not fixed. They may go up or down over time. Also, if a company fails to pay dividends on its stock, it is not considered in default. (We speak here of common stock. Another type of financial instrument, a preferred share [preference shares in the United Kingdom], promises to pay a fixed dividend. Such instruments are a type of equity-debt hybrid and are priced more like coupon bonds.) In fact, many corporations today do not pay any dividends, and for good reasons. Small, rapidly growing companies, it is widely believed, should plow their profits back into their businesses rather than return money to shareholders. *That is not cheating the stockholders, because profits left with the company instead of paid out as dividends raise the share price.* The company has more cash than it otherwise would, after all, and stockholders own the profits whether they are left with the company or put into their pockets. Plus, it is generally thought that growing companies put the money to more profitable use than stockholders could.

Internal Revenue Service (IRS)

The tax collector of the U.S. federal government.

There is a tax benefit to retaining earnings, too. Taxes on dividends, which the **Internal Revenue Service (IRS)** considers income, are usually higher than taxes on share appreciation, which the IRS considers capital gains.[5] Also, dividends are taxed in the year they are paid, which may be inconvenient for stockholders, but capital gains taxes are incurred only when the stockholders sell their shares, so they have more control over their tax liabilities. Similarly, companies that have stopped growing will sometimes buy their own stock in the market rather than pay dividends. Fewer shares outstanding means that each share is worth more (the price per share equals the total value of the company divided by the number of shares, so as the denominator declines, the price per share increases), so stockholders are "paid" with a higher stock price. Nevertheless, some corporations continue to pay dividends. *The point here is that what really matters when valuing corporate equities is earnings or profits because, as noted above, they belong to the stockholders whether they are divided, kept as cash, or used to repurchase shares.*

The simplest stock valuation method, the one-period valuation model, simply calculates the discounted present value of dividends and selling price over a one-year holding period:

$$P = E / (1 + k) + P_1 / (1 + k)$$

where:

P = price now

E = yearly dividends

k = required rate of return (this can be thought of as a risk-free return plus a risk premium)

P_1 = expected price at year's end

So if a company is expected to pay no dividends, its share price is expected to be $75 at the end of the year, and the **required rate of return (or k)** (a sort of risk-adjusted interest rate) on investments in its risk class is 10 percent, an investor would buy the stock if its market price was at or below P = 0/1.10 + 75/1.10 = $68.18. Another investor might also require a 10 percent return but think the stock will be worth $104 at the end of the year. He'd pay P = 0/1.10 + 104/1.1 = $94.55 for the stock today! A third investor might agree with the first that the stock will be worth $75 in a year, but she might need a 12 percent return. She'd pay only up to P = 0/1.12 + 75/1.12 = $66.96 per share. Yet another investor might also require a 12 percent return to hold the stock and think $75 a reasonable price a year from now, but he might also think earnings of $1 per share is in the offing. He'd pay P = 1/1.12 + 75/1.12 = .89 + 66.96 = $67.85 per share.

required rate of return (or k)

Serves the same purpose as *i* in present value calculations. In other words, it measures the opportunity cost of making an investment; *k* is influenced by *i* but also by default and other risks.

For longer holding periods, one can use the generalized dividend valuation model, which discounts expected future earnings to their present value. That can be done mechanically, as we did for coupon bonds in Chapter 4, or with a little fancier math:

$$P = t = 1 \infty E t / 1 + k t$$

That sideways 8 means infinity. So this equation basically says that the price of a share now is the sum (σ) of the discounted present values of the expected earnings between now and infinity. The neat thing about this equation is that the expected future sales price of the stock drops out of the equation because the present value of any sum at any decent required rate of return quickly becomes negligible. (For example, the present value of an asset expected to be worth $10 in 20 years at 15 percent interest is only PV = $10/(1.15)^{20}$ = $0.61 today.) So for all intents and purposes in this model, called the Gordon Growth model, *a corporate equity is worth the discounted present value of its expected future earnings stream.*

$$P = E(1 + g) / (k - g)$$

where

P= price today

E = most recent earnings

k = required return

g = constant growth rate

So the price of a stock today that recently earned $1 per share and has expected earnings growth of 5 percent would be $21.00 if the required return was 10 percent (P = 1.05/.05). If another investor estimates either *k* or *g* differently, perhaps because he knows more (or less) about a country, industry, or company's future prospects, P will of course change, perhaps radically. For a little practice, complete the following exercises now.

Exercises

1. Use the one-period valuation model $P = E/(1 + k) + P1/(1 + k)$ to price the following stocks (remember to decimalize percentages).

Dividends (E = $)	Required return (k = %)	Expected price next year (P1 = $)	Answer: price today (P = $)
1.00	10	20	19.10
1.00	15	20	18.26
1.00	20	20	17.50
0	5	20	19.05
0	5	30	28.57
0	5	40	38.10
1.00	10	50	46.36
1.50	10	50	46.82
2.00	10	50	47.27
0	10	1	0.91

2. Use the Gordon growth model $P = E \times (1 + g)/(k - g)$ to value the following stocks (remember to decimalize percentages).

Earnings (E = $)	Required return (k = %)	Expected earnings growth rate (g = %)	Answer: price today (P = $)
1	10	5	20.00
1	15	5	10.00
1	20	5	6.67
1	10	5	20.00
2	10	5	40.00
3	10	5	60.00
1	30	5	4.00
1	30	10	10.00
1	30	15	20.00
100	20	10	1,000.00

Stop and Think Box

Stock prices plummeted after the terrorist attacks on 9/11. Use the Gordon growth model to explain why.

Stock prices plummeted after 9/11 because risks increased, raising *k*, and because expectations of corporate profits dropped, decreasing *g*. So the numerator of the Gordon growth model decreased and the denominator increased, both of which caused P to decrease.

Key Takeaways

- In general, corporate equities are valued the same way that any financial security is, by discounting expected future cash flows.
- With stocks, corporate earnings replace actual cash payments because shareholders own profits, whether they receive them as cash dividends or not.
- The formula for valuing a stock to be held one year, called the one-period valuation model, is $P = E/(1 + k) + P_1/(1 + k)$, where E is dividends, P_1 is the expected sales price of the stock next year, and k is the return required to hold the stock given its risk and liquidity characteristics. It can be thought of as a risk-free rate plus a risk premium.
- In the Gordon growth model, earnings are assumed to grow at a constant rate forever, so stock values can be estimated without guessing the future sales price by using the following formula: $P = E(1 + g)/(k - g)$, where E = the most recent earnings, g = the rate of earnings growth, and k = the required return where $k > g$.

7.3 Financial Market Efficiency

Learning Objectives

1. In what senses can financial markets be efficient or inefficient?
2. What is portfolio diversification and sectoral asset allocation, and how do they help investors to earn market returns?

Now here is the freaky thing. While at any given moment, most investors' valuations are wrong (too low or too high), the market's valuation, *given the information available at that moment*, is always correct, though in a tautological or circular way only. You may recall from your principles course that markets "discover" prices and quantities. If the market price of anything differs from the equilibrium price (where the supply and demand curves intersect), market participants will bid the market price up or down until equilibrium is achieved. In other words, a good, including a financial security, is worth precisely what the market says it is worth.

At any given time, some people expect the future market price of an asset will move higher or that it is currently underpriced, a value or bargain, so to speak. They want to buy. Others believe it will move lower, that it is currently overpriced. They want to sell. Sometimes the buyers are right and sometimes the sellers are, but that is beside the point, at least from the viewpoint of economic efficiency. The key is that the investor who values the asset most highly will come to own it because he'll be willing to pay the most for it. Financial markets are therefore *allocationally efficient. In other words, where free markets reign, assets are put to their most highly valued use, even if most market participants don't know what that use or value is.* That's really remarkable when you think about it and goes a long way to explaining why many economists grow hot under the collar when governments create barriers that restrict information flows or asset transfers.

Financial markets are also efficient in the sense of being highly integrated. In other words, prices of similar securities track each other closely over time and prices of the same security trading in different markets are identical, or nearly so. Were they not, *arbitrage, or the riskless profit opportunity that arises when the same security at the same time has different prices in different markets,* would take place. By buying in the lower market and immediately selling in the higher market, an investor could make easy money. Unsurprisingly, as soon as an arbitrage opportunity appears, it is immediately exploited until it is no longer profitable. (Buying in the lower market raises the price there, while selling in the higher market decreases the price there.) Therefore, only slight price differences that do not exceed transaction costs (brokerage fees, bid-ask spreads, etc.) persist.

The size of those price differences and the speed with which arbitrage opportunities are closed depend on the available technology. Today, institutional investors can complete international financial market trades in just microseconds and for just a few hundredths or even thousandths of a percent. In the early nineteenth century, U.S.-London arbitrageurs (investors who engage in arbitrage) confronted lags of several weeks and transaction costs of several percent. Little wonder that price differentials were larger and more persistent in the early nineteenth century. But the early markets were still rational because they were as efficient as they could be at the time. (Perhaps in the future, new technology will make microseconds and hundredths of a percent look pitifully archaic.)

Arbitrage, or the lack thereof, has been the source of numerous jokes and gags, including a two-part episode of the 1990s comedy sitcom *Seinfeld*. In the episodes, Cosmo Kramer and his friend Newman (the postal worker) decide to try to arbitrage the deposit on cans and bottles of soda, which is 5 cents in New York, where Seinfeld and his goofy friends live, and 10 cents in Michigan. The two friends load up Newman's postal truck with cans and head west, only to discover that the transaction costs (fuel, tolls, hotels, and what not) are too high, especially given the fact that Kramer is easily sidetracked.[6] *High transaction costs also explain why people don't arbitrage the international price differentials of Big Macs and many other physical things.*[7] Online sites like eBay, however, have made arbitrage in nonperishables more possible than ever by greatly reducing transaction costs.

In another joke (at least I hope it's a joke!), two economics professors think they see an arbitrage opportunity in wheat. After carefully studying all the transaction costs—freight, insurance, brokerage, weighing fees, foreign exchange volatility, weight lost in transit, even the interest on money over the expected shipping time—they conclude that they can make a bundle buying low in Chicago and selling high in London. They go for it, but when the wheat arrives in London, they learn that a British ton (long ton, or 2,240 pounds) and a U.S. ton (short ton, or 2,000 pounds) are not the same thing. *The price of wheat only appeared to be lower in Chicago because a smaller quantity was being priced.*

Some economists believe financial markets are so efficient that unexploited profit opportunities like arbitrage are virtually impossible. Such extreme views have also become the butt of jokes, like the one where a young, untenured assistant professor of economics bends over to pick up a $20 bill off the sidewalk, only to be chided by an older, ostensibly wiser, and indubitably tenured colleague who advises him that if the object on the ground were real money, somebody else would have already have picked it up.[8] But we all know that money is sometimes lost and that somebody else is lucky enough to pocket it. At the same time, however, some people stick their hands into toilets to retrieve authentic-looking $20 bills, so we also know that things are not always what they seem. Arbitrage and other unexploited profit opportunities are not unicorns. *They do exist on occasion*. But especially in financial markets, they are so fleeting that they might best be compared to kaons or baryons, rare and short-lived subatomic particles.

In an efficient market, *all unexploited profit opportunities, not just arbitrage opportunities, will be eliminated as quickly as the current technology set allows*. Say, for example, the rate of return on a stock is 10 percent but the optimal forecast or best guess rate of return, due to a change in information or in a valuation model, was 15 percent. Investors would quickly bid up the price of the stock, thereby reducing its return. Remember that $R = (C + P_{t1} - P_{t0})/P_{t0}$. As P_{t0}, the price now, increases, R must decrease. Conversely, if the rate of return on a stock is currently 10 percent but the optimal forecast rate of return dropped to 5 percent, investors would sell the stock until its price decreased enough to increase the return to 10 percent. *In other words, in an efficient market, the optimal forecast return and the current equilibrium return are one and the same.*

Financial market efficiency means that it is difficult or impossible to earn abnormally high returns at any given level of risk. (Remember, returns increase with risk.) Yes, an investor who invests 100 percent in **hedge funds** will likely garner a higher return than one who buys only short-dated Treasury notes. Holding risk (and liquidity) constant, though, returns should be the same, especially over long periods. In fact, creating a stock portfolio by throwing darts at a dartboard covered with ticker symbols returns as much, on average, as the choices of experienced stock pickers choosing from the same set of companies. Chimpanzees and orangutans have also done as well as the darts and the experts. Many studies have shown that *actively managed mutual funds do not systematically outperform (provide higher returns than) the market*. In any given period, some funds beat the market handily, but others lag it considerably. Over time, some stellar performers turn into dogs, and vice versa. (That is why regulators force financial firms to remind investors that past performance is not a guarantee of future returns.)

hedge fund

A type of relatively unregulated mutual fund that engages in sophisticated trading strategies. Only wealthy individuals and institutional investors are allowed to invest directly in such funds.

That is not to say, however, that you shouldn't invest in mutual funds. In fact, mutual funds are much less risky (have lower return variability) than individual stocks or any set of stocks you are likely to pick on your own. **Portfolio diversification**, the investment strategy often described as not putting all of your eggs (money) in one basket (asset), is a crucial concept. So-called indexed mutual funds provide diversification by passively or automatically buying a broad sample of stocks in a particular market (e.g., the Dow or NASDAQ) and almost invariably charge investors relatively low fees. ETFs, or exchange-traded funds, also track various market indices, have extremely low fees, and trade on exchanges just like corporate shares.

Portfolio diversification

Entails investing in a relatively large number of issuers within an asset class, such as buying the shares of hundreds of corporations rather than just one or a few in order to reduce return risk. Some of the investments will go sour, others will flourish, and most will fall in between.

Sectoral asset allocation is another important concept for investors. A basic strategy is to invest heavily in stocks and other risky assets when young but to shift into less volatile assets, like short-term bonds, as one nears retirement or other cash-out event. *Proper diversification and allocation strategies will not help investors to "beat the market," but they will definitely help the market from beating them.* In other words, those strategies provide guidelines that help investors to earn average market returns safely and over the long term. With luck, pluck, and years of patience, modest wealth can be accumulated, but a complete bust will be unlikely.

sectoral asset allocation

Entails investing in a variety of different asset classes (e.g., some bonds, some stocks, and some commodities) consistent with the investor's goals and lifecycle stage.

Stop and Think Box

I once received the following hot tip in my e-mail:

> *Saturday, March 17, 2007*
>
> *Dear Friend:*
>
> *If you give me permission...I will show you how to make money in a high-profit sector, starting with just $300–$600. The profits are enormous. You can start with as little as $300. And what's more, there is absolutely no risk because you will "Test Drive" the system before you shell out any money. So what is this "secret" high-profit sector that you can get in on with just $300–$600 or less??? Dear Friend, it's called "penny stocks"—stocks that cost less than $5 per share. Don't laugh—at one time Wal-Mart was a "penny stock." So was Microsoft. And a few years ago, America Online was selling for just .59 cents a share, and Yahoo was only a $2 stock. These are not rare and isolated examples. Every month people buy penny stocks at bargain prices and make a small fortune within a short time.*
>
> *Very recently, these three-penny stocks made huge profits. In January, ARGON Corp. was at $2.69. Our indicators picked up the beginning of the upward move of this stock. Within three months the stock shot up to $28.94 a share, turning a $300 investment into $3,238 in just three months. In November, Immugen (IMGN) was at $2.76 a share. We followed the decline of this stock from $13 to as little as $1.75 a share. But our technicals were showing an upward move. Stock went up to $34.10 a share. An investment of $500 would have a net gain of $5,677. RF Micro Devices was at $1.75 in August 1999. It exploded to $65.09 a share by April 2000. An investment of only $500 in this stock would have a net profit of $18,097. In fact, the profits are huge in penny stocks. And smart investors who picked these so-called penny stocks made huge profits. They watched their money double seemingly day after day, week after week, month after month. Double, triple, quadruple, and more.*

Should I buy? Why or why not?

I did not invest, and you shouldn't either if confronted with a similar scenario. If the individual who sent the message really knows that the stock is going to appreciate, why should he tell anyone? Shouldn't he buy the shares himself, borrowing to the hilt if necessary to do so? So why would he try to entice me to buy this stock? He probably owns a few (hundred, thousand, million) shares and wants to drive their price up by finding suckers and fools to buy it so he can sell. This is called "pumping and dumping"[9] and it runs afoul of any number of laws, rules, and regulations, so you shouldn't think about sending such e-mails yourself, unless you want to spend some time in Martha Stewart's prison.[10] And don't think you can free-ride on the game, either. One quirky fellow named Joshua Cyr actually tracks the prices of the hot stock tips he has received, pretending to buy 1,000 shares of each. On one day in March 2007, his website claimed that his pretend investment of $70,987.00 was then worth a whopping $9,483.10, a net gain of –$61,503.90. Even if he had bought and sold almost immediately, he would have still lost money because most stocks experienced very modest and short-lived "pops" followed by quick declines. A few of us are idiots, but most are not (or we are too poor or too lazy to act on the tips). Learning this, the scammers started to pretend that they were sending the message to a close friend to make it seem as though the recipient stumbled upon important inside information. Beware, because their ruses are likely to grow increasingly sophisticated.

In some ways, darts and apes are better stock pickers than people because the fees and transaction costs associated with actively managed funds often erase any superior performance they provide. For this reason, *many economists urge investors to buy passively managed mutual funds or exchange traded funds (ETFs) indexed to broad markets, like the S&P or the Dow Jones Indus-*

trial Average, because they tend to have the lowest fees, taxes, and trading costs. Such funds "win" by not losing, providing investors with an inexpensive way of diversifying risk and earning the market rate of return, whatever that happens to be over a given holding period (time frame).

Key Takeaways

- Markets are efficient if they allocate resources to their most highly valued use and if excess profit opportunities are rare and quickly extinguished.
- Financial markets are usually allocationally efficient. In other words, they ensure that resources are allocated to their most highly valued uses, and outsized risk-adjusted profits (as through arbitrage, the instantaneous purchase and sale of the same security in two different markets to take advantage of price differentials) are uncommon and disappear rapidly.
- Portfolio diversification and sectoral asset allocation help investors to earn average market returns by spreading risks over numerous assets and by steering investors toward assets consistent with their age and financial goals.

7.4 Evidence of Market Efficiency

Learning Objective

1. How efficient are our markets?

Sophisticated statistical analyses of stock and other securities prices indicate that they follow a "random walk." That is why stock charts often look like the path of a drunk staggering home after a party, just as in Figure 7.1. As noted at the beginning of this chapter, securities prices in efficient markets are *not* random. They are determined by fundamentals, particularly interest rate, inflation, and profit expectations. What is random is their direction, up or down, in the next period. That's because relevant news cannot be systematically predicted. (If it could, it wouldn't be news.) So-called technical analysis, the attempt to predict future stock prices based on their past behavior, is therefore largely a chimera. On average, technical analysts do not outperform the market. Some technical analysts do, but others do not. The differences are largely a function of luck. (The fact that technical analysts and actively managed funds persist, however, suggests that financial markets are still far short of perfect efficiency.)

FIGURE 7.1 Sample random series

Up or down, which way will she move? Nobody knows!

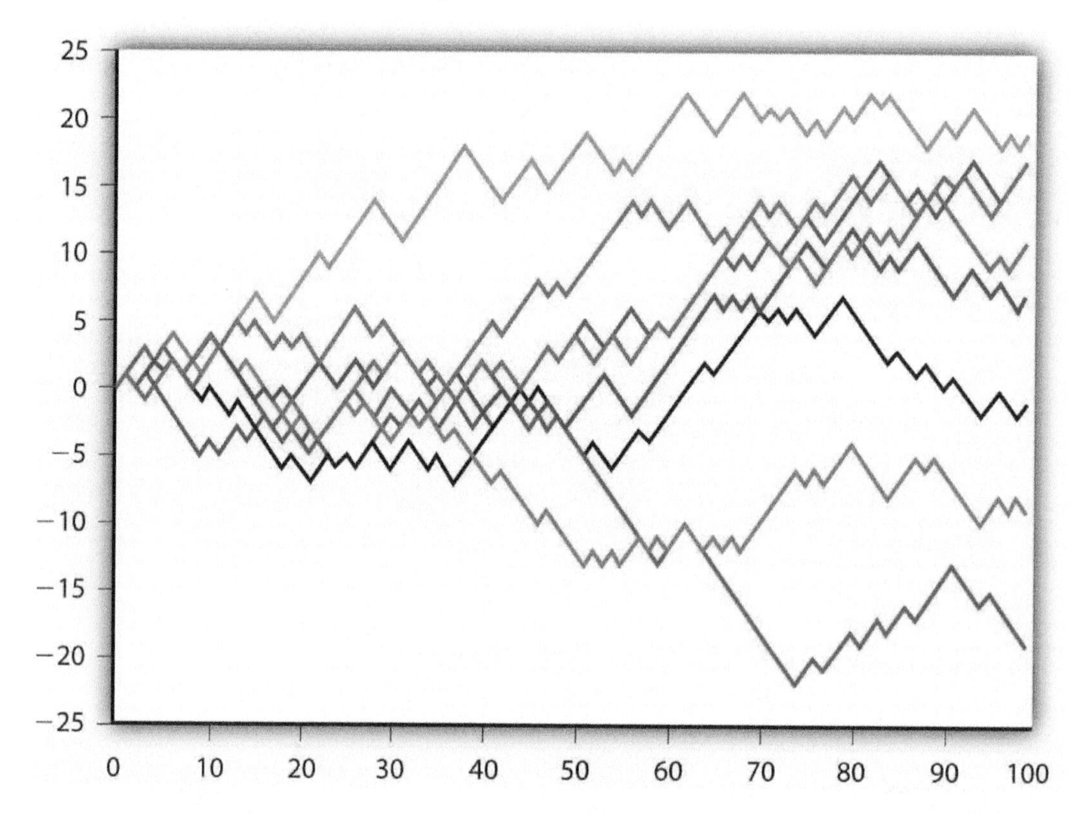

In fact, *in addition to allocational efficiency, economists talk about three types of market efficiency: weak, semistrong, and strong.* These terms are described in Figure 7.2. Today, most financial markets appear to be semistrong at best. As it turns out, that's pretty good.

FIGURE 7.2 Types of efficiency

Most modern financial markets appear to be semi-strong form efficient

Type of Efficiency	Distinguishing Characteristics
Allocational	Resources are put to their most highly valued use.
Weak form	All past market prices and data are fully reflected in prices, rendering technical analysis useless.
Semi-strong form	All *publicly available* information is fully reflected in price, rendering fundamental analysis useless.
Strong form	*All* information is fully reflected in prices, rendering inside information useless.

Some markets are more efficient than others. Thanks to technology improvements, today's financial markets are more efficient (though not necessarily more rational) than those of yore. In every age, financial markets tend to be more efficient than real estate markets, which in turn tend to be more efficient than commodities markets and labor and many services markets. That's because financial instruments tend to have a very high value compared to their weight (indeed they have no weight whatsoever today), are of uniform quality (a given share of Microsoft is the same as any other share[11]), and are little subject to wastage (you could lose bearer bonds or cash, but most other financial instruments are registered, meaning a record of your ownership is kept apart from physical possession of the instruments themselves). Most commodities are relatively bulky, are not always uniform in quality, and deteriorate over time. In fact, futures markets have arisen to make commodities markets (for gold, wheat, orange juice, and many others) more efficient. Financial markets, particularly mortgage markets, also help to improve the efficiency of real estate markets. Nevertheless, considerable inefficiencies persist. As the *Wall Street Journal* reported in March 2007, it was possible to make outsized profits by purchasing homes sold at foreclosure, tax, and other auctions, then selling them at a hefty profit, accounting for transaction costs, without even going through the trouble or expense of fixing them up. That is nothing short of real estate arbitrage![12]

Labor and services markets are the least efficient of all. People won't or can't move to their highest valued uses; they adapt very slowly to technology changes; and myriad regulations, some imposed by government and others by labor unions, limit their flexibility on the job. Some improvements have been made in recent years thanks to global outsourcing, but it is clear that the number of unexploited profit opportunities in labor markets far exceeds those in the financial markets. Finally, markets for education,[13] health care,[14] and custom construction services[15] are also highly inefficient, probably due to high levels of asymmetric information.

Stop and Think Box

A friend urges you to subscribe to a certain reputable investment report. Should you buy? Another friend brags about the huge returns she has made by buying and selling stocks frequently. Should you emulate her trading strategies?

Buying an investment report makes more sense than following the unsolicited hot stock tip discussed above, but it still may not be a good idea. Many legitimate companies try to sell information and advice to investors. The value of that information and advice, however, may be limited. The information may be tainted by conflicts of interest. Even if the research is unbiased and good, by the time the newsletter reaches you, even if it is electronic, the market has probably already priced the information, so there will be no above-market profit opportunities remaining to exploit. In fact, only one investment advice newsletter, *Value Line Survey (VLS)*, has consistently provided advice that leads to abnormally high risk-adjusted returns. It isn't clear if *VLS* has deeper insights into the market, if it has simply gotten lucky, or if its mystique has made its predictions a self-fulfilling prophecy: investors believe that it picks super stocks, so they buy its recommendations, driving prices up, just as it predicted! The three explanations are not, in fact, mutually exclusive. Luck and skill may have created the mystique underlying *VLS*'s continued success.

As far as emulating your friend's trading strategies, you should investigate the matter more thoroughly first. For starters, people tend to brag about their gains and forget about their losses. Even if your friend is genuinely successful at picking stocks, she is likely just getting lucky. Her luck could turn just as your money gets in the game. To the extent that markets are efficient, investors are better off choosing the level of risk they are comfortable with and earning the market return. That usually entails buying and holding a diverse portfolio via an indexed mutual fund or ETF, which minimizes taxes and brokerage fees, both of which can add up. Long-term index investors also waste less time tracking stocks and worrying about market gyrations.

As noted above, none of this should be taken to mean that financial markets are perfectly efficient. *Researchers have uncovered certain anomalies, situations where it is or was possible to outperform the market, holding risk and liquidity constant.* I say *was* because exposing an anomaly will often induce investors to exploit it until it is eliminated. One such anomaly was the so-called January Effect, a predictable rise in stock prices that for many years occurred each January until its existence was recognized and publicized. Similarly, stock prices in the past tended to display mean reversion. In other words, stocks with low returns in one period tended to have high returns in the next, and vice versa. The phenomenon appears to have disappeared, however, with the advent of trading strategies like the Dogs of the Dow, where investors buy beaten-down stocks in the knowledge that they can only go up (though a few will go to zero and stay there).[16]

Other anomalies, though, appear to persist. The prices of many financial securities, including stocks, tend to overshoot when there is unexpected bad news. After a huge initial drop, the price often meanders back upward over a period of several weeks. This suggests that investors should buy soon after bad news hits, then sell at a higher price a few weeks later. Sometimes, prices seem to adjust only slowly to news, even highly specific announcements about corporate profit expectations. That suggests that investors could earn above-market returns by buying immediately on good news and selling after a few weeks when the price catches up to the news.

Some anomalies may be due to deficiencies in our understanding of risk and liquidity rather than market inefficiency. One of these is the small-firm effect. Returns on smaller companies, *apparently* holding risk and liquidity constant, are abnormally large. Why then don't investors flock to such companies, driving their stock prices up until the outsized returns disappear? Some suspect that the companies are riskier, or at least appear riskier to investors, than researchers believe. Others believe the root issues are asymmetric information, the fact that the quality and quantity of information about smaller firms is inferior to that of larger ones, and inaccurate measurement of liquidity. Similarly, some researchers believe that stock prices are more volatile than they should be given changes in underlying fundamentals. That finding too might stem from the fact that researchers aren't as prescient as the market.

The most important example of financial market inefficiencies are so-called asset bubbles or manias. Periodically, market prices soar far beyond what the fundamentals suggest they should. During stock market manias, like the dot-com bubble of the late 1990s, investors apparently popped sanguine values for g into models like the Gordon growth model or, given the large run-up in prices, large P_1 values into the one-period valuation model. In any event, starting in March 2000, the valuations for most of the shares were discovered to be too high, so share prices rapidly dropped. *Bubbles are not necessarily irrational, but they are certainly inefficient to the extent that they lead to the misallocation of resources when prices are rising and unexploited profit opportunitieswhen prices head south.*

Asset bubbles are very common affairs. Literally thousands of bubbles have arisen throughout human history, typically when assets

1. can be purchased with cheap, borrowed money;
2. attract the attention of numerous, inexperienced traders;
3. cannot be easily "**sold short**" (when nobody can profit from a declining price);
4. are subject to high levels of moral hazard due to the expectation of a bailout (rescue funds provided by the government or other entity);
5. are subject to high agency costs (e.g., poorly aligned incentives between investors and intermediaries or market facilitators).

sold short

The process of short selling, of profiting from the *decline* of an asset's price.

Agricultural commodities (e.g., tulips, tea, sheep, and sugar beets) have experienced bubbles most frequently but the precious metals (gold and silver), real estate, equities, bonds, and derivatives have also witnessed bubble activity. Most bubbles caused relatively little economic damage, but a real estate bubble in the early 1760s helped to foment the American Revolution, one in Treasury bonds helped to form the two party system in the 1790s, and one in stocks exacerbated the Great Depression. Since the tech bubble burst in 2000, we've already experienced another, in housing and home mortgages.

Recurrent investor euphoria may be rooted in the deepest recesses of the human mind. Whether we evolved from the great apes or were created by some Divine Being, one thing is clear: *our brains are pretty scrambled, especially when it comes to probabilities and percentages.* For example, a study[17] published in *Review of Finance* showed that investors, even sophisticated ones, expect less change in future stock prices when asked to state their forecasts in currency (so many dollars or euros per share) than when asked to state them as returns (a percentage gain or loss).[18] In South Dakota in 2016, a large majority voted to outlaw interest charges above 36 percent on small, short-term loans because they thought a 37 percent rate was "too high" or "predatory" even though it generated fees of just pennies.[19] Even non-profits and charities, it turns out, cannot afford to lend small sums for short terms for a mere 36 percent.[20]

Behavioral finance uses insights from evolutionary psychology, anthropology, sociology, the neurosciences, and psychology to try to unravel how the human brain functions in areas related to finance.[21] For example, many people are averse to **short selling**, selling (or borrowing and then selling) a stock that appears overvalued with the expectation of buying it back later at a lower price. (Short sellers profit by owning more shares of the stock, or the same number of shares and a sum of cash, depending on how they go about it.) A dearth of short selling may allow stock prices to spiral too high, leading to asset bubbles. Another human foible is that we tend to be overly confident in our own judgments. Many actually believe that they are smarter than the markets in which they trade! (As noted above, many researchers appear to fall into the same trap.) People also tend to herd. They will, like the common misconception about lemmings, run with the crowd, seemingly oblivious to the cliff looming just ahead.

Behavioral finance

A new interdisciplinary subject matter that tries to understand the limits of human rationality, especially as it applies to financial markets.

short selling

Selling a stock or other asset at a high price and buying it back later at a lower price. It is the logical equivalent of buying low and selling high, but many investors don't attempt it.

Many people also fail the so-called Linda Problem. When asked if a twenty-seven-year-old philosophy major concerned about social issues is more likely to be either (a) a bank teller or (b) a bank teller active in a local community activist organization, most choose the latter. The former, however, is the logical choice because *b* is a subset of *a*. The St. Petersburg Paradox also points to humanity's less-than-logical brain: most people will pay $1 for a one-in-a-million chance to win $1 million dollars but they will not receive $1 for a one-in-a-million chance of losing $1 million dollars, although the two transactions, as opposite sides of the same bet, are mathematically equivalent.[22] Most people, it seems, are naturally but irrationally risk averse.

Finally, as noted above, another source of inefficiency in financial (and nonfinancial) markets is asymmetric information, when one party to a transaction has better information than the other. Usually, the asymmetry arises due to inside information as when the seller, for instance, knows the company is weak but the buyer does not. Regulators try to reduce information asymmetries by outlawing outright fraud and by encouraging timely and full disclosure of pertinent information to the public. In short, they try to promote what economists call **transparency**. Some markets, however, remain quite opaque.[23]

transparency

In general, the opposite of opacity. In this context, transparency means a relatively low degree of asymmetric information.

In short, our financial markets appear to be semistrong form efficient. Greater transparency and more fervent attempts to overcome the natural limitations of human rationality would help to move the markets closer to strong form efficiency.

Key Takeaways

- Beyond allocational efficiency, markets may be classed as weak, semistrong, or strong form efficient.
- If the market is weak form efficient, technical analysis is useless because securities prices already reflect past prices.
- If the market is semistrong form efficient, fundamental analysis is also useless because prices reflect all publicly available information.
- If the market is strong form efficient, inside information is useless too because prices reflect *all* information.
- Securities prices tend to track each other closely over time and in fact usually display random walk behavior, moving up and down unpredictably.
- Neither technical analysis nor fundamental analysis outperforms the market on average, but inside information apparently does, so most financial markets today are at best semistrong form efficient.
- Although more efficient than commodities, labor, and services markets, financial markets are not completely efficient.
- Various anomalies, like the January and small-firm effects, market overreaction and volatility, mean reversion, and asset bubbles, suggest that securities markets sometimes yield out-

sized gains to the quick and the smart, people who overcome the mushy, often illogical brains all humans are apparently born with. But the quest is a never-ending one; no strategy works for long.

7.5 Suggested Reading

Bernstein, Peter. *Against the Gods: The Remarkable Story of Risk*. Hoboken, NJ: John Wiley and Sons, 1998.

Burnham, Terry. *Mean Markets and Lizard Brains: How to Profit from the New Science of Irrationality*. Hoboken, NJ: John Wiley and Sons, 2008.

Damodaran, Aswath. *The Little Book of Valuation: How to Value a Company, Pick a Stock, and Profit*. Hoboken, NJ: John Wiley and Sons, 2011.

Mackay, Charles, and Joseph de la Vega. *Extraordinary Popular Delusions and the Madness of Crowds and Confusion de Confusiones*. Hoboken, NJ: John Wiley and Sons, 1995.

Malkiel, Burton. *A Random Walk Down Wall Street: The Time-Tested Strategy for Successful Investing*, 9th ed. New York: W. W. Norton, 2007.

Endnotes

1. www.cboe.com/micro/vix/introduction.aspx
2. en.wikipedia.org/wiki/Joseph_Penso
3. Joseph de la Vega, *Confusion de Confusiones*.
4. www.npr.org/templates/story/story.php?storyId=6098557
5. www.irs.gov/
6. en.wikipedia.org/wiki/The_Bottle_Deposit,_Part_1
7. www.economist.com/markets/Bigmac/Index.cfm
8. http://www.economistsdoitwithmodels.com/2012/01/01/an-economist-finds-a-10-bill-and-a-lesson-on-efficient-markets/ and http://www.barrypopik.com/index.php/new_york_city/entry/if_it_were_a_real_20_bill
9. www.fool.com/foolu/askfoolu/2002/askfoolu020107.htm
10. www.csmonitor.com/2004/1008/p01s01-usju.html
11. Any share of the same class, that is. As noted, some corporations issue preferred shares, which differ from the common shares discussed in this chapter. Other corporations issue shares, usually denominated Class A or Class B, that have different voting rights.
12. James R. Hagerty, "Foreclosure Rise Brings Business to One Investor," *Wall Street Journal*, March 14, 2007, A1.
13. www.forbes.com/columnists/2005/12/29/higher-education-partnerships-cx_rw_1230college.html
14. www.amazon.com/Fubarnomics-Lighthearted-Serious-Americas-Economic/dp/1616141913/ref=ntt_at_ep_dpi_3
15. www.amazon.com/Broken-Buildings-Busted-Budgets-Trillion-Dollar/dp/0226472671/ref=sr_1_1/002-2618567-2654432?ie
16. www.dogsofthedow.com
17. Markus Glaser, Thomas Langer, Jens Reynders, and Martin Weber, "Framing Effects in Stock Market Forecasts: The Differences Between Asking for Prices and Asking for Returns," *Review of Finance* (2007) 11:325–357.
18. This is a new example of the well-known framing effect. Predict the future stock price of a stock that goes from \$35 to \$37 to \$39 to \$41 to \$43 to \$45. Now predict the future stock price of a stock whose returns are +\$2, +\$2, +\$2, +\$2, +\$2, and +\$2. If you are like most people, your answer to the first will be less than \$45 but your answer to the second will be +\$2 even though both series provide precisely the same information. In other words, the way a problem is set up or framed influences the way people respond to it.
19. https://www.americanbanker.com/news/south-dakota-approves-36-rate-cap-on-payday-lenders; https://ballotpedia.org/South_Dakota_Payday_Lending_Initiative,_Initiated_Measure_21_(2016)
20. Robert Mayer, *Quick Cash: The Story of the Loan Shark* (DeKalb: Northern Illinois University Press, 2010), 225.
21. www.behaviouralfinance.net
22. Not even lottery or raffle organizations make such a bet. Instead, they promise to pay the winner only a percentage of total ticket sales and pocket the rest. That is a major reason why lotteries and other forms of gambling are closely regulated.
23. www.sec.gov/news/press/2011/2011-83.htm

CHAPTER 8

Financial Structure, Transaction Costs, and Asymmetric Information

Chapter Objectives

By the end of this chapter, students should be able to:

1. Describe how nonfinancial companies meet their external financing needs.
2. Explain why bonds play a relatively large role in the external financing of U.S. companies.
3. Explain why most external finance is channeled through financial intermediaries.
4. Define transaction costs and explain their importance.
5. Define and describe asymmetric information and its importance.
6. Define and explain adverse selection, moral hazard, and agency problems.
7. Explain why the financial system is heavily regulated.

8.1 The Sources of External Finance

Learning Objective

1. How can companies meet their external financing needs?

Thus far, we have spent a lot of time discussing financial markets and learning how to calculate the prices of various types of financial securities, including stocks and bonds. Securities markets *are* important, especially in the U.S. economy. But you may recall from Chapter 2 that the *financial system connects savers to spenders or investors to entrepreneurs in two ways, via markets and via financial intermediaries*. It turns out that the latter channel is larger than the former. That's right, in dollar terms, banks, insurance companies, and other intermediaries are more important than the stock and bond markets. The markets tend to garner more media attention because they are relatively transparent. Most of the real action, however, takes place behind closed doors in banks and other institutional lenders.

trade credit

Credit granted in the course of trade, as when suppliers ship their wares, then bill net 15 or 30, or when customers, like libraries for academic journals, pay for goods or services before they are provided.

Not convinced? Check out Figure 8.1, which shows the sources of external funds for nonfinancial businesses in four of the world's most advanced economies: the United States, Germany, Japan, and Canada. In none of those countries does the stock market (i.e., equities) supply more than 12 percent of external finance. *Loans, from banks and nonbank financial companies, supply the vast bulk of external finance in three of those countries and a majority in the fourth, the United States.* The bond market supplies the rest, around 10 percent or so of total external finance (excluding **trade credit**), except in the United States, where bonds supply about a third of the external finance of nonfinancial businesses. (As we'll learn later, U.S. banking has been relatively weak historically, which helps to explain why the bond market and loans from nonbank financial companies are relatively important in the United States. In short, more companies found it worthwhile to borrow from life insurance companies or to sell bonds than to obtain bank loans.)

FIGURE 8.1 Sources of external finance for nonfinancial companies in four financially and economically developed countries

Intermediaries rule!

Country	Bank Loans (%)	Loans from Non-bank Financial Firms (%)	Bonds (%)	Equities (%)
United States	18	38	32	11
Canada	56	18	15	12
Germany	76	10	7	8
Japan	78	8	9	5

As noted above, the numbers in Figure 8.1 do not include trade credit. Most companies are small and most small companies finance most of their activities by borrowing from their suppliers or, sometimes, their customers. Most such financing, however, ultimately comes from loans, bonds, or stock. In other words, *companies that extend trade credit act, in a sense, as nonbank intermediaries*, channeling equity, bonds, and loans to small companies. This makes sense because suppliers usually know more about small companies than banks or individual investors do. And information, we'll see, is key.

Also note that the equity figures are somewhat misleading given that, once sold, a share provides financing forever, or at least until the company folds or buys it back. The figures above do not account for that, so a $1,000 year-long bank loan renewed each year for 20 years would count as $20,000 of bank loans, while the sale of $1,000 of equities would count only as $1,000. Despite that bias in the methodology, *it is clear that most external finance does not, in fact, come from the sale of stocks or bonds*. Moreover, in less economically and financially developed countries, an even higher percentage of external financing comes to nonfinancial companies via intermediaries rather than markets.

collateralize

To pledge some asset, like land or financial securities, for the repayment of a loan.

*What explains the facts highlighted in*Figure 8.1? Why are bank and other loans more important sources of external finance than stocks and bonds? Why does indirect finance, via intermediaries, trump direct finance, via markets? For that matter, why are most of those loans **collateralized**? Why are loan contracts so complex? Why are only the largest companies able to raise funds directly by selling stocks and bonds? Finally, why are financial systems worldwide one of the most heavily regulated economic sectors?

Those questions can be answered in three ways: transaction costs, asymmetric information, and the free-rider problem. Explaining what those three terms mean, however, will take a little doing.

Key Takeaways

- To meet their external financing needs, companies can sell equity (stock) and commercial paper and longer-term bonds and they can obtain loans from banks and nonbank financial institutions.
- They can also obtain trade credit from suppliers and customers, but most of those funds ultimately come from loans, bonds, or equity.
- Most external financing comes from loans, with bonds and equities a distant second, except in the United States, where bonds provide about a third of external financing for nonfinancial companies.
- Bonds play a relatively larger role in the external financing of U.S. companies because the U.S. banking system has been weak historically. That weakness induced companies to obtain more loans from nonbank financial institutions like life insurance companies and also to issue more bonds.

8.2 Transaction Costs, Asymmetric Information, and the Free-Rider Problem

Learning Objective

1. Why is most external finance channeled through financial intermediaries?

minimum efficient scale

The smallest a business can be and still remain efficient and/or profitable.

Minimum efficient scale in finance is larger than most individuals can invest. Somebody with $100, $1,000, $10,000, even $100,000 to invest would have a hard time making any profit at all, let alone the going risk-adjusted return. That is because *most of his or her profits would be eaten up in transaction costs like banking and brokerage fees, dealer spreads, attorney fees, and the opportunity cost of his or her time, and liquidity and diversification losses.* Many types of bonds come in $10,000 increments and so are out of the question for many small investors. A single share of some companies, like Berkshire Hathaway, costs thousands or tens of thousands of dollars and so is also out of reach.[1] Most shares cost far less, but transaction fees, even after the online trading revolution of the early 2000s, are still quite high, especially if an investor were to try to diversify by buying only a few shares of many companies. Financial markets are efficient enough that arbitrage opportunities are rare and fleeting. Those who make a living engaging in arbitrage, like hedge fund D. E. Shaw, do so mainly by exploiting scale economies. They need superfast (read "expensive") computers and nerdy (read "expensive") employees to operate custom (read "expensive") programs on them. They also need to engage in large-scale transactions because of high fixed costs. With a flat brokerage fee of $50, for example, you won't profit making .001 percent on a $1,000 trade, but you will on a $1,000,000,000 one.

What about making loans directly to entrepreneurs or other borrowers? Fuggeddaboutit! The time, trouble, and cash (e.g., for advertisements like that excerpted below) it would take to find a suitable borrower would likely wipe out any profits from interest. The legal fees alone would swamp you! (It helps if you can be your own lawyer, like John C. Knapp.) *And, as we'll learn below, making loans isn't all that easy.* You'll still occasionally see advertisements like those that used to appear in the eighteenth century, but they are rare and might in fact be placed by predators, people who are more interested in robbing you (or worse) than lending to you. A small investor might be able to find a relative, co-religionist, colleague, or other acquaintance to lend to relatively cheaply. But how could the investor know if the borrower was the best one, given the interest rate charged? What is the best rate, anyway? To answer those questions even haphazardly would cost relatively big bucks. And here is another hint: friends and relatives often think that a "loan" is actually a "gift," if you catch my "drift."

Scrivener's Office, &c.

Cash solicited as usual on good real or personal Security, whether Mortgage, Bond, Note, Bills, &c. The New Hampshire Sterling Bills, the Amount, of One Thousand Pounds York Currency, (heretofore advertised) still to be Let on approved Security. . . .

—*John C. Knapp, Attorney at Law*[2]

peer-to-peer banking

In this new type of banking, a facilitator links lenders to borrowers, acting more like a securities broker than a bank.

A new type of banking, called **peer-to-peer banking**, might reduce some of those transaction costs. In peer-to-peer banking, a financial facilitator, like Zopa.com or Prosper.com, reduces transaction costs by electronically matching individual borrowers and lenders. Most peer-to-peer facilitators screen loan applicants in at least a rudimentary fashion and also provide diversification services, distributing lenders' funds to numerous borrowers to reduce the negative impact of any defaults.[3] Although the infant industry is currently growing, *the peer-to-peer concept is still unproven and there are powerful reasons to doubt its success.* Even if the concept succeeds (and it might given its Thomas Friedman–*The World Is Flat*ishness[4]), it will only reinforce the point made here about the inability of most individuals to invest profitably without help.

Financial intermediaries clearly can provide such help. They have been doing so for at least a millennium (yep, a thousand years, maybe more). *One key to their success is their ability to keep credit information that they have created a secret.* Bankers have incentives to discover who the best borrowers are because it is difficult for others to steal that information. Insurers cannot simply wait for another insurer to discern good from bad risks and then exploit the information. Free riding, in other words, is minimal in traditional financial intermediation.

Another key is the ability of financial intermediaries to achieve minimum efficient scale. Banks, insurers, and other intermediaries pool the resources of many investors. That allows them to diversify cheaply because instead of buying 10 shares of XYZ's $10 stock and paying $7 for the privilege (7/100 = .07) they can buy 1,000,000 shares for a brokerage fee of maybe $1,000 ($1,000/1,000,000 = .001). In addition, financial intermediaries do not have to sell assets as frequently as individuals (ceteris paribus, of course) because they can usually make payments out of inflows like deposits or premium payments. Their cash flow, in other words, reduces their liquidity costs. Individual investors, on the other hand, often find it necessary to sell assets (and incur the costs associated therewith) to pay their bills.

As specialists, financial intermediaries are also experts at what they do. That does not mean that they are perfect—far from it, as we learned during the financial crisis that began in 2007—but they are certainly more efficient at accepting deposits, making loans, or insuring risks than you or I will ever be (unless we work for a financial intermediary, in which case we'll likely become incredibly efficient in one or at most a handful of functions). That expertise covers many areas, from database management to telecommunications. *But it is most important in the reduction of asymmetric information.*

Asymmetric information is the devil incarnate, a scourge of humanity second only to scarcity. Seriously, it is a crucial concept to grasp if you want to understand why the financial system exists, and why it is, for the most part, heavily regulated. *Asymmetric information makes our markets, financial and otherwise, less efficient than they otherwise would be by allowing the party with superior information to take advantage of the party with inferior information.* Where asymmetric information is high, resources are not put to their most highly valued uses, and it is possible to make outsized profits by cheating others. Asymmetric information helps to give markets, including financial markets, the bad rep they have acquired in some circles.

FIGURE 8.2 Adverse selection, moral hazard, and agency problems incarnate
I would NOT want to run into that pooch in a dark alley!

Financial intermediaries and markets can reduce or mitigate asymmetric information, but they can no more eliminate it than they can end scarcity. Financial markets are more transparent than ever before, yet dark corners remain.[5] The government and market participants can, and have, forced companies to reveal important information about their revenues, expenses, and the like, and even follow certain accounting standards.[6] As a CEO in a famous *Wall Street Journal* cartoon once put it, "All these regulations take the fun out of capitalism." But at the edges of every rule and regulation there is ample room for shysters to play.[7] When managers found that they could not easily manipulate earnings forecasts (and hence stock prices, as we learned in Chapter 7), for example, they began to backdate **stock options** to enrich themselves at the expense of stockholders and other corporate stakeholders.

stock options

In this context, a form of compensation given to executives, managers, and sometimes other employees to reward them for increasing their company's stock price. By backdating the options, managers were able to profit from their stock options, although stock prices declined (or did not rise very much).

What is the precise nature of this great asymmetric evil? *Turns out this devil, this Cerberus, has three heads: adverse selection, moral hazard, and the principal-agent problem.* Let's lop off each head in turn.

Key Takeaways

- Transaction costs, asymmetric information, and the free-rider problem explain why most external finance is channeled through intermediaries.
- Most individuals do not control enough funds to invest profitably given the fact that fixed costs are high and variable costs are low in most areas of finance. In other words, it costs almost as much to buy 10 shares as it does to buy 10,000.
- Also, individuals do not engage in enough transactions to be proficient or expert at it.
- Financial intermediaries, by contrast, achieve minimum efficient scale and become quite expert at what they do, though they remain far from perfect.
- Transaction costs are any and all costs associated with completing an exchange.

- Transaction costs include, but are not limited to, broker commissions; dealer spreads; bank fees; legal fees; search, selection, and monitoring costs; and the opportunity cost of time devoted to investment-related activities.
- They are important because they detract from bottom-line profits, eliminating or greatly reducing them in the case of individuals and firms that have not achieved minimum efficient scale.
- Transaction costs are one reason why institutional intermediaries dominate external finance.

8.3 Adverse Selection

Learning Objective

1. What problems do asymmetric information and, more specifically, adverse selection cause and how can they be mitigated?

Adverse selection is precontractual asymmetric information. It occurs because the riskiest potential borrowers and insureds have the greatest incentive to obtain a loan or insurance.

The classic case of adverse selection, the one that brought the phenomenon back[8]*to the attention of economists in 1970, is the market for "lemons," which is to say, breakdown-prone automobiles.* The lemons story, with appropriate changes, applies to everything from horses to bonds, to lemons (the fruit), to construction services. That is because the lemons story is a simple but powerful one. People who offer lemons for sale know that their cars stink. Most people looking to buy cars, though, can't tell that a car is prone to breakdown. They might kick the tires, take it for a short spin, look under the hood, etc., all without discovering the truth. The seller has superior information and indeed has an incentive to increase the asymmetry by putting a Band-Aid over any obvious problems. (He might, for example, warm the car up thoroughly before showing it, put top-quality gasoline in the tank, clean up the oil spots in the driveway, and so forth.) He may even explain that the car was owned by his poor deceased grandmother, who used it only to drive to church on Sundays (for services) and Wednesdays (for bingo), and that she took meticulous care of it. The hapless buyer, the story goes, offers the average price for used cars of the particular make, model, year, and mileage for sale. *The seller happily (and greedily if you want to be moralistic about it) accepts. A day, week, month, or year later, the buyers learns that he has overpaid, that the automobile he purchased is a lemon.* He complains to his relatives, friends, and neighbors, many of whom tell similar horror stories. A consensus emerges that all used cars are lemons.

Of course, some used cars are actually "peaches," very reliable means of personal transportation. The problem is that owners of peaches can't credibly inform buyers of the car's quality. Oh, she can say, truthfully, that the car was owned by her poor deceased grandmother who used it only to drive to church on Sundays (for services) and Wednesdays (for bingo) and that she took meticulous care of it. But that sounds a lot like what the owner of the lemon says too. (In fact, I just copied and pasted it from above!) So the asymmetric information remains and the hapless buyer offers the average price for used cars of the particular make, model, year, and mileage for sale. (Another copy and paste job!) *But this time the seller, instead of accepting the offer, gets offended and storms off (or at least declines).* So the buyer's relatives, friends, and neighbors are half right—not all the used cars for sale are lemons, but those that are bought are!

Now appears our hero, the used car dealer, who is literally a dealer in the same sense a securities dealer is: he buys from sellers at one (bid) price and then sells to buyers at a higher (ask) price. *He earns his profits or spread by facilitating the market process by reducing asymmetric information.* Relative to the common person, he is an expert at assessing the true value of used automobiles. (Or his operation is large enough that he can hire such people and afford to pay them.

See the transaction costs section above.) So he pays more for peaches than lemons (ceteris paribus, of course) and the used car market begins to function at a much higher level of efficiency. Why is it, then, that the stereotype of the used car salesman is not very complimentary? That the guy in Figure 8.3 seems more typical than the guy in Figure 8.4?

Several explanations come to mind. The market for used car dealers may be too competitive, leading to many failures, which gives dealers incentives to engage in rent seeking (ripping off customers) and disincentives to establish long-term relationships. Or the market may not be competitive enough, perhaps due to high barriers to entry. Because sellers and buyers have few choices, dealers find that they can engage in sharp business practices[9] and still attract customers as long as they remain better than the alternative, the nonfacilitated market. I think the latter more likely because *in recent years, many used car salesmen have cleaned up their acts in the face of national competition* from the likes of AutoNation and similar companies.[10] Moreover, CarFax.com and similar companies have reduced asymmetric information by tracking vehicle damage using each car's unique vehicle identification number (VIN), making it easier for buyers to reduce asymmetric information without the aid of a dealer.

FIGURE 8.3 Shady used car salesman

The double thumbs up, the smile, the sunglasses, the hair. Individually they are fine but put them all in one place and . . . ugh!

What does this have to do with the financial system? Plenty, as it turns out. As noted above, adverse selection applies to a wide variety of markets and products, including financial ones. Let's suppose that, like our friend Mr. Knapp, you have some money to lend and the response to your advertisement is overwhelming. Many borrowers are in the market. Information is asymmetric—you can't really tell who the safest borrowers are. So you decide to ration the credit as if it were apples, by lowering the price you are willing to give for their bonds (raising the interest rate on the loan). Big mistake! As the interest rate increases (the sum that the borrower/securities seller will accept for his IOU decreases), the best borrowers drop out of the bidding. After all, they know that their projects are safe, that they are the equivalent of an automotive peach. *People with riskier business projects continue bidding until they too find the cost of borrowing too high and bow out, leaving you to lend to some knave, to some human lemon, at a very high rate of interest.* That, my friend, is adverse selection.

FIGURE 8.4 Not-so-shady used car salesman

I'd trust this guy with my kids!

Adverse selection also afflicts the market for insurance. Safe risks are not willing to pay much for insurance because they know that the likelihood that they will suffer a loss and make a claim is low. Risky people and companies, by contrast, will pay very high rates for insurance because they know that they will probably suffer a loss. Anyone offering insurance on the basis of premium alone will end up with the stinky end of the stick, just as the lender who rations on price alone will.

Like used car dealers, financial facilitators and intermediaries seek to profit by reducing adverse selection. They do so by specializing in discerning good from bad credit and insurance risks. *Their main weapon here is called screening and it's what all those forms and questions are about when you apply for a loan or insurance policy.* Potential lenders want to know if you pay your bills on time, if your income minus expenses is large and stable enough to service the loan, if you have any collateral that might protect them from loss, and the like. Potential insurers want to know if you have filed many insurance claims in the past because that may indicate that you are clumsy; not very careful with your possessions; or worse, a shyster who makes a living filing insurance claims. They also want to know more about the insured property so they don't insure it for too much, a sure inducement to start a fire or cause an accident. They also need to figure out how much risk is involved, how likely a certain type of car is to be totaled if involved in an accident,[11] the probability of a wood-frame house burning to the ground in a given area,[12] the chance of a Rolex watch being stolen, and so forth.

Stop and Think Box

Credit-protection insurance policies promise to make payments to people who find themselves unemployed or incapacitated. Whenever solicited to buy such insurance, I always ask how the insurer overcomes adverse selection because there are never any applications or premium schedules, just one fixed rate. Why do I care?

I care because I'm a peach of a person. I know that if I lived a more dangerous lifestyle or was employed in a more volatile industry that I'd snap the policy right up. Given my current situation, however, I don't think it very likely that I will become unemployed or incapacitated, so I don't feel much urgency to buy such a policy at the same rate as some guy or gal who's about to go sky-diving instead of going to work. I don't want to subsidize them or to deal with a company that doesn't know the first thing about insurance.

Financial intermediaries are not perfect screeners. They often make mistakes. Insurers like State Farm, for example, underestimated the likelihood of a massive storm like Katrina striking the Gulf Coast. And subprime mortgage lenders, companies that lend to risky borrowers on the collateral of their homes, grossly miscalculated the likelihood that their borrowers would default. Competition between lenders and insurers induces them to lower their screening standards to make the sale. (In a famous cartoon in the *Wall Street Journal*, a clearly nonplussed father asks a concerned mom how their son's imaginary friend got preapproved for a credit card.) At some point, though, adverse selection always rears its ugly head, forcing lenders and insurance providers to improve their screening procedures and tighten their standards once again. And, on average, they do much better than you or I acting alone could do.

free-rider problem

Trying to hop a ride without paying for it. More technically, it is any behavior where a party takes more than his or her fair share of the benefits, or does not pay his or her fair share of the costs, of some activity.

Another way of reducing adverse selection is the private production and sale of information. Before the 1970s, companies like Standard and Poor's, Bests, Duff and Phelps, Fitch's, and Moody's compiled and analyzed data on companies, rated the riskiness of their bonds, and then sold that information to investors in huge books. The **free-rider problem**, though, killed off that business model. Specifically, the advent of cheap photocopying induced people to buy the books, photocopy them, and sell them at a fraction of the price that the bond-rating agencies could charge. (The free riders had to pay only the variable costs of publication; the rating agencies had to pay the large fixed costs of compiling and analyzing the data.) So in the mid-1970s, the bond-rating agencies began to give their ratings away to investors and instead charged bond issuers for the privilege of being rated. The new model greatly decreased the effectiveness of the ratings because the new arrangement quickly led to rating inflation similar to grade inflation. (Pleasure flows with the cash. Instead of pleasing investors, the agencies started to please the issuers.) After every major financial crisis, including the subprime mortgage mess of 2007, academics and former government regulators lambaste credit-rating agencies for their poor performance relative to markets and point out the incentive flaws built into their business model. Thus far, little has changed, but encrypted databases might allow a return to the investor-pay model. But then another form of free riding would arise as investors who did not subscribe to the database would observe and mimic the trades of those investors known to have subscriptions. *Due to the free-rider problem inherent in markets, banks and other financial intermediaries have incentives to create private information about borrowers and people who are insured. This helps to explain why they trump bond and stock markets.*

Adverse selection can also be reduced by contracting with groups instead of individuals. Insurers, for example, offer group health and life insurance policies to employers because doing so reduces adverse selection. Chronically or terminally ill people usually do not seek employment, so the riskiest part of the population is excluded from the insurance pool. Moreover, it is easier for insurers to predict how many claims a group of people will submit over some period of time than to predict the probability that a specific individual will make a claim. Life expectancy tables, for example, accurately predict how many people will die in a given year but not which particular individuals will perish.[13]

Governments can no more legislate away adverse selection than they can end scarcity by decree. They can, however, give markets and intermediaries a helping hand. In the United States, for example, the Securities and Exchange Commission (SEC) tries to ensure that corporations provide market participants with accurate and timely information about themselves, reducing the information asymmetry between themselves and potential bond- and stockholders.[14] Like sellers of lemons, however, bad companies often outfox the SEC (and similar regulators in other countries) and investors, especially when said investors place too much confidence in government regulators. In 2001, for example, a high-flying energy trading company named Enron suddenly encountered insurmountable financial difficulties and was forced to file for bankruptcy, the largest in American history at that time. Few saw Enron's implosion coming because the company hid its debt and losses in a maze of offshore shell companies and other accounting smokescreens. Some dumbfounded investors hadn't bothered watching the energy giant because they believed the government was doing it for them. It wasn't.

Key Takeaways

- Asymmetric information decreases the efficiency of financial markets, thereby reducing the flow of funds to entrepreneurs and injuring the real economy.
- Adverse selection is precontractual asymmetric information.
- It can be mitigated by screening out high-risk members of the applicant pool.
- Financial market facilitators can also become expert specialists and attain minimum efficient scale, but financial markets are hampered by the free-rider problem.
- In short, few firms find it profitable to produce information because it is easy for others to copy and profit from it. Banks and other intermediaries, by contrast, create proprietary information about their borrowers and people they insure.

8.4 Moral Hazard

Learning Objective

1. What is moral hazard and how can it be mitigated?

Moral hazard is postcontractual asymmetric information. It occurs whenever a borrower or insured entity (an approved borrower or policyholder, not a mere applicant) engages in behaviors that are not in the best interest of the lender or insurer. If a borrower uses a bank loan to buy lottery tickets instead of Treasuries, as agreed upon with the lender, that's moral hazard. If an insured person leaves the door of his or her home or car unlocked or lets candles burn all night unattended, that's moral hazard. It's also moral hazard if a borrower fails to repay a loan when he or she has the wherewithal to do so, or if an insured driver fakes an accident.

We call such behavior moral hazard because it was long thought to indicate a lack of morals or character and in a sense it does. But thinking about the problem in those terms does not help to mitigate it. We all have a price. How high that price is can't be easily determined and may indeed change, but offered enough money, every human being (except maybe Gandhi, prophets, and saints) will engage in immoral activities for personal gain *if given the chance.* It's tempting indeed to put other people's money at risk. As we've learned, the more risk, the more reward. Why not borrow money to put to risk? If the rewards come, the principal and interest are easily repaid. If the rewards don't come, the borrower defaults and suffers but little. Back in the day, as they say, borrowers who didn't repay their loans were thrown into jail until they paid up. Three problems eventually ended that practice. First, it is difficult to earn money to repay the loan when you're imprisoned! (The original assumption was that the borrower had the money but wouldn't cough it up.) Second, not everyone defaults on a loan due to moral hazard. Bad luck, a soft economy, and/or poor execution can turn the best business plan to mush. Third, lenders are almost as culpable as the borrowers for moral hazard if they don't take steps to try to mitigate it. A locked door, an old adage goes, keeps an honest man honest. Don't tempt people, in other words, and most won't rob you. There are locks against moral hazard. They are not foolproof but they get the job done most of the time.

Stop and Think Box

Investment banks engage in many activities, two of which, research and underwriting, have created conflicts of interest. The customers of ibanks' research activities, investors, want unbiased information. The customers of ibanks' underwriting activities, bond issuers, want optimistic reports. A few years back, problems arose when the interests of bond issuers, who provided ibanks with most of their profits, began to supersede the interests of investors. Specifically, ibank managers forced their research departments to avoid making negative or controversial comments about clients. The situation grew worse during the Internet stock mania of the late 1990s, when ibank research analysts like Jack Grubman (a Dickensian name but true!) of Citigroup (then Salomon Smith Barney) made outrageous claims about the value of high-tech companies. That in itself wasn't evil because everyone makes mistakes. What raised hackles was that the private e-mails of those same analysts indicated that they thought the companies they were hyping were extremely weak. And most were. What sort of problem does this particular conflict of interest represent? How does it injure the economy? What can be done to rectify the problem?

This is an example of asymmetric information and, more specifically, moral hazard. Investors contracted with the ibanks for unbiased investment research but instead received extremely biased advice that induced them to pay too much for securities, particularly the equities of weak tech companies. As a result, the efficiency of our financial markets decreased as resources went to firms that did not deserve them and could not put them to their most highly valued use. That, of course, injured economic growth. One way to solve this problem would be to allow ibanks to engage in securities underwriting or research, but not both. That would make ibanks less profitable, though, as doing both creates economies of scope. (That's why ibanks got into the business of selling research in the first place.) Another solution is to create a "Chinese wall" within each ibank between their research and underwriting departments. This apparent reference to the Great Wall of China, which despite its grandeur was repeatedly breached by "barbarian" invaders with help from insiders, also belies that strategy's weakness.[15] If the wall is so high that it is impenetrable, then the economies of scope are diminished to the vanishing point. If the wall is low or porous, then the conflict of interest can again arise. Rational expectations and transparency could help here. Investors now know (or at least could/should know) that ibanks can provide biased research reports and hence should remain wary. Government regulations could help here by mandating that ibanks completely and accurately disclose their interests in the companies that they research and evaluate. That extra transparency would then allow investors to discount rosy prognostications that appear to be driven by ibanks' underwriting interests. The Global Legal Settlement of 2002, which was brokered by Eliot Spitzer (then New York State Attorney General and New York's governor until he ran into a little moral hazard problem himself!), bans spinning, requires investment banks to sever the links between underwriting and research, and slapped a $1.4 billion fine on the ten largest ibanks.

restrictive covenants

Clauses in loan contracts that restrict the uses to which borrowed funds can be put and otherwise direct borrower behavior.

The main weapon against moral hazard is monitoring, which is just a fancy term for paying attention! No matter how well they have screened (reduced adverse selection), lenders and insurers cannot contract and forget. They have to make sure that their customers do not use the superior information inherent in their situation to take advantage. Banks have a particularly easy and powerful way of doing this: watching checking accounts. Banks rarely provide cash loans because the temptation of running off with the money, the moral hazard, would be too high. Instead, they credit the amount of the loan to a checking account upon which the borrower can draw funds. (This procedure has a second positive feature for banks called compensatory balances. A loan for, say, $1 million does not leave the bank at once but does so only gradually. That raises the effective interest rate because the borrower pays interest on the total sum, not just that drawn out of the bank.) The bank can then watch to ensure that the borrower is using the funds appropriately. *Most loans contain***restrictive covenants**, *clauses that specify in great detail how the loan is to be used and how the borrower is to behave.* If the borrower breaks one or more covenants, the entire loan may fall due immediately. Covenants may require that the borrower obtain life insurance, that he or she keep collateral in good condition, or that various business ratios be kept within certain parameters.[16] Often, loans will contain covenants requiring borrowers to provide lenders with various types of information, including audited financial reports, thus minimizing the lender's monitoring costs.

Another powerful way of reducing moral hazard is to align incentives. That can be done by making sure the borrower or insured has some skin in the game, that he, she, or it will suffer if a loan goes bad or a loss is incurred.[17] That will induce the borrower or insured to behave in the lender's or insurer's best interest. *Collateral, property pledged for the repayment of a loan, is a good way to reduce moral hazard.* Borrowers don't take kindly to losing, say, their homes. Also, the more equity they have—in their home or business or investment portfolio—the harder they will fight to keep from losing it. Some will still default, but not purposely. In other words, the higher one's net worth (market value of assets minus market value of liabilities), the less likely one is to default, which could trigger bankruptcy proceedings that would reduce or even wipe out the borrower's net worth. This is why, by the way, it is sometimes alleged that you have to have money to borrow money. That isn't literally true, of course. What is true is that owning assets free and clear of debt makes it much easier to borrow.

Similarly, insurers long ago learned that they should insure only a part of the value of a ship, car, home, or life. *That is why they insist on deductibles or co-insurance.* If you will lose nothing if you total your car, you might attempt that late-night trip on icy roads or sign up for a demolition derby. If an accident will cost you $500 (deductible) or 20 percent of the costs of the damage (co-insurance), you will think twice or thrice before doing something risky with your car.

When it comes to reducing moral hazard, financial intermediaries have advantages over individuals. *Monitoring is not cheap. Indeed, economists sometimes refer to it as "costly state verification."* Economies of scale give intermediaries an upper hand. Monitoring is also not easy, so specialization and expertise also render financial intermediaries more efficient than individuals at reducing moral hazard. If nothing else, financial intermediaries can afford to hire the best legal talent to frighten the devil out of would-be scammers. Borrowers can no longer be imprisoned for defaulting, but they can go to prison for fraud. Statutes against fraud are one way that the government helps to chop at the second head of the asymmetric information Cerberus.

Financial intermediaries also have monitoring advantages over markets. Bondholder A will try to free-ride on Bondholder B, who will gladly let Bondholder C suffer the costs of state verification, and all of them hope that the government will do the dirty work. In the end, nobody may monitor the bond issuer.

Key Takeaways

- Moral hazard is postcontractual asymmetric information.
- Moral hazard can be mitigated by monitoring counterparties after contracting.

8.5 Agency Problems

Learning Objective

1. What are agency problems and how can they be mitigated?

The principal-agent problem is an important subcategory of moral hazard that involves postcontractual asymmetric information of a specific type. In many, nay, most instances, principals (owners) must appoint agents (employees) to conduct some or all of their business affairs on their behalf. Stockholders in joint-stock corporations, for example, hire professional managers to run their businesses. Those managers in turn hire other managers, who in turn hire supervisors, who then hire employees (depending on how hierarchical the company is). The principal-agent problem arises when any of those agents does not act in the best interest of the principal, for example, when employees and/or managers steal, slack off, act rudely toward customers, or otherwise cheat the company's owners. If you've ever held a job, you've probably been guilty of such activities yourself. (I admit I have, but it's best not to get into the details!) If you've ever been a boss, or better yet an owner, you've probably been the victim of agency problems. (I have been on this end too, like when I was eight years old and my brother told him me that our lemonade stand had revenues of only $1.50 when in fact it brought in $10.75. Hey, that was *a lot* of money back then!)

Stop and Think Box

As the author of this textbook[18] and many others have pointed out, investment banks often underprice stock initial public offerings (IPOs). In other words, they offer the shares of early-stage companies that decide to go public for too little money, as evidenced by the large first day "pops" or "bumps" in the stock price in the aftermarket (the secondary market). Pricing the shares of a new company is tricky business, but the underpricing was too prevalent to have been honest errors, which one would think would be too high about half of the time and too low the other half. All sorts of reasons were proffered for the systematic underpricing, including the fact that many shares could not be "flipped" or resold for some weeks or months after the IPO. Upon investigation, however, a major cause of underpricing turned out to be a conflict of interest called spinning: ibanks often purposely underpriced IPOs so that there would be excess demand, so that investors would demand a larger quantity of shares than were being offered. Whenever that occurs, shares must be rationed by nonprice mechanisms. The ibanks could then dole out the hot shares to friends or family, and, in return for future business, the executives of other companies! Who does spinning hurt? Help? Be as specific as possible.

Spinning hurts the owners of the company going public because they do not receive as much from the IPO as they could have if the shares were priced closer to the market rate. It may also hurt investors in the companies whose executives received the underpriced shares who, in reciprocation for the hot shares, might not use the best ibank when their companies later issue bonds or stock or attempt a merger or acquisition. Spinning helps the ibank by giving it a tool to acquire more business. It also aids whoever gets the underpriced shares.

efficiency wages

Wages higher than the equilibrium or market clearing rate. Employers offer them to reduce agency problems, hoping employees will value their jobs so much they will try to please owners by behaving in the owners' interest.

Monitoring helps to mitigate the principal-agent problem. That's what supervisors, cameras, and corporate snitches are for. *Another, often more powerful way of reducing agency problems is to try to align the incentives of employees with those of owners by paying* **efficiency wages**, *commissions, bonuses, stock options, and the like.* Caution is the watchword here, though, because people will do *precisely* what they have incentive to do. Failure to recognize that apparently universal human trait has had adverse consequences for some organizations, a point made in business schools through easily understood case stories. In one story, a major ice cream retailer decided to help out its employees by allowing them to consume, free of charge, any mistakes they might make in the course of serving customers. *What was meant to be an environmentally sensitive (no waste) little perk turned into a major problem as employee waistlines bulged and profits shrank because hungry employees found it easy to make delicious frozen mistakes.* ("Oh, you said chocolate. I thought you said *my* favorite flavor, mint chocolate chip. Excuse me because I am now on break. I have to eat this mint chocolate chip treat before it melts.")

In another story, a debt collection agency reduced its efficiency and profitability by agreeing to a change in the way that it compensated its collectors. Initially, collectors received bonuses based on the dollars collected divided by the dollars assigned to be collected. So, for example, a collector who brought in $250,000 of the $1 million due on his accounts would receive a bigger bonus than a collector who collected only $100,000 of the same denominator (250/1,000 = .25 > 100/1,000 =

.10). Collectors complained, however, that it was not fair to them if one or more of their accounts went bankrupt, rendering collection impossible. The managers of the collection agency agreed and began to deduct the value of bankrupt accounts from the collectors' denominators. Under the new incentive scheme, a collector who brought in $100,000 would receive a bigger bonus than his colleague if, say, $800,000 of his accounts claimed bankruptcy (100/[1,000 – 800 = 200] = .5, which is > 250/1,000 = .25). Soon, the collectors transformed themselves into bankruptcy counselors! The new scheme inadvertently created a perverse incentive, that is, one diametrically opposed to the collection agency's interest, which was to collect as many dollars as possible, not to help debtors file for bankruptcy.

In a competitive market, pressure from competitors and the incentives of managers would soon rectify such mishaps. But when the incentive structure of management is out of kilter, bigger and deeper problems often appear. When managers are paid with stock options, for instance, they are given an incentive to increase stock prices, which they almost invariably do, sometimes by making their companies' more efficient but sometimes, as investors in the U.S. stock market in the late 1990s learned, through accounting legerdemain. *Therefore, corporate governance looms large and requires constant attention from shareholders, business consulting firms, and government regulators.*

A free-rider problem, however, makes it difficult to coordinate the monitoring activities that keep agents in line. If Stockholder A watches management, then Stockholder B doesn't have to but he will still reap the benefits of the monitoring. Ditto with Stockholder C, who sits around hoping Stockholder D will do the dirty and costly work of monitoring executive pay and perks, and the like. Often, nobody ends up monitoring managers, who raise their salaries to obscene levels, slack off work, go empire-building, or all three![19] This governance conundrum helps to explain why the sale of stocks is such a relatively unimportant form of external finance worldwide.

Governance becomes less problematic when the equity owner is actively involved in management. That is why investment banker J. P. Morgan used to put "his people" (principals in J. P. Morgan and Company) on the boards of companies in which Morgan had large stakes. A similar approach has long been used by Warren Buffett's Berkshire Hathaway. Venture capital firms also insist on taking some management control and have the added advantage that the equity of startup firms does not, indeed cannot, trade. (It does only after it holds an **IPO** or direct public offering [**DPO**]). So other investors cannot free-ride on its costly state verification. The recent interest in private equity, funds invested in privately owned (versus publicly traded) companies, stems from this dynamic as well as the desire to avoid costly regulations like Sarbanes-Oxley.[20]

initial public offering (IPO)

Offering of stock to investors with the aid of an investment bank.

direct public offering (DPO)

Offering of stock to investors without the aid of an investment bank.

Stop and Think Box

Investment banks are not the only financial services firms that have recently suffered from conflicts of interest. Accounting firms that both audit (confirm the accuracy and appropriateness of) corporate financial statements and provide tax, business strategy, and other consulting services found it difficult to reconcile the conflicts inherent in being both the creator and the inspector of businesses. Auditors were too soft in the hopes of winning or keeping consulting business because they could not very well criticize the plans put in place by their own consultants. One of the big five accounting firms, Arthur Andersen, actually collapsed after the market and the SEC discovered that its auditing procedures had been compromised. How could this type of conflict of interest be reduced?

In this case, simply informing investors of the problem would probably not work. Financial statements have to be correct; the free-rider problem ensures that no investor would have an incentive to verify them him- or herself. The traditional solution to this problem was the auditor and no better one has yet been found. But the question is, how to ensure that auditors do their jobs? One answer, enacted in the Sarbanes-Oxley Act of 2002 (aka SOX and Sarbox), is to establish a new regulator, the Public Company Accounting Oversight Board (PCAOB) to oversee the activities of auditors.[21] The law also increased the SEC's budget (but it's still tiny compared to the grand scheme of things), made it illegal for accounting firms to offer audit and nonaudit services simultaneously, and increased criminal charges for white-collar crimes. The most controversial provision in SOX requires corporate executive officers (CEOs) and corporate financial officers (CFOs) to certify the accuracy of corporate financial statements and requires corporate boards to establish unpaid audit committees composed of outside directors, that is, directors who are not members of management. The jury is still out on SOX. The consensus so far appears to be that it is overkill: that it costs too much given the benefits it provides.

Government regulators try to reduce asymmetric information. Sometimes they succeed. Often, however, they do not. Asymmetric information is such a major problem, however, that their efforts will likely continue, whether all businesses like it or not.

Key Takeaways

- Agency problems are a special form of moral hazard involving employers and employees or other principal-agent relationships.
- Agency problems can be mitigated by closely aligning the incentives of the agents (employees) with those of the principal (employer).
- Regulations are essentially attempts by the government to subdue the Cerberus of asymmetric information.
- Some government regulations, like laws against fraud, are clearly necessary and highly effective.
- Others, though, like parts of Sarbanes-Oxley, may add to the costs of doing business without much corresponding gain.

8.6 Suggested Reading

Allen, Franklin, and Douglas Gale. *Comparing Financial Systems.* Cambridge, MA: MIT Press, 2001.

Demirguc-Kunt, Asli, and Ross Levine. *Financial Structure and Economic Growth: A Cross-Country Comparison of Banks, Markets, and Development.* Cambridge, MA: MIT Press, 2004.

Laffont, Jean-Jacques, and David Martimort. *The Theory of Incentives: The Principal-Agent Model.* Princeton, NJ: Princeton University Press, 2001.

Endnotes

1. www.berkshirehathaway.com
2. From Early American Newspapers, an Archive of Americana Collection, published by Readex (Readex.com), a division of NewsBank, Inc.
3. For details, see "Options Grow for Investors to Lend Online," *Wall Street Journal*, July 18, 2007.
4. en.wikipedia.org/wiki/The_World_is_Flat
5. www.investopedia.com/articles/00/100900.asp
6. www.fasb.org
7. knowledge.wharton.upenn.edu/article.cfm?articleid=585&CFID=4138806&CFTOKEN=88010645
8. Classical economists like Adam Smith recognized adverse selection and asymmetric information more generally, but they did not label or stress the concepts.
9. www.m-w.com/dictionary/sharp
10. en.wikipedia.org/wiki/AutoNation
11. www.edmunds.com/ownership/safety/articles/43804/article.html
12. www.usfa.dhs.gov/statistics/national/residential.shtm
13. https://www.ssa.gov/oact/STATS/table4c6.html
14. www.sec.gov
15. en.wikipedia.org/wiki/Great_Wall_of_China
16. http://www.investinganswers.com/financial-dictionary/debt-bankruptcy/restrictive-covenant-5339
17. https://en.wikipedia.org/wiki/Skin_in_the_game_(phrase)

18. ideas.repec.org/a/taf/acbsfi/v12y2002i3p419-437.html
19. www.investopedia.com/terms/e/empirebuilding.asp
20. www.sec.gov/info/smallbus/pnealis.pdf
21. www.pcaobus.org

CHAPTER 9

Bank Management

Chapter Objectives

By the end of this chapter, students should be able to:

1. Explain what a balance sheet and a T-account are.
2. Explain what banks do in five words and also at length.
3. Describe how bankers manage their banks' balance sheets.
4. Explain why regulators mandate minimum reserve and capital ratios.
5. Describe how bankers manage credit risk.
6. Describe how bankers manage interest rate risk.
7. Describe off-balance sheet activities and explain their importance.

9.1 The Balance Sheet

Learning Objective

1. What is a balance sheet and what are the major types of bank assets and liabilities?

Thus far, we've studied financial markets and institutions from 30,000 feet. We're finally ready to "dive down to the deck" and learn how banks and other financial intermediaries are actually managed. We start with the balance sheet, a financial statement that takes a snapshot of what a company owns (assets) and owes (liabilities) at a given moment. *The key equation here is a simple one:*

ASSETS (aka uses of funds) = LIABILITIES (aka sources of funds) + EQUITY (aka net worth or capital).

Liabilities are monies that companies borrow in order to buy assets, which is why liabilities are sometimes called "sources of funds" and assets, "uses of funds." The hope is that the liabilities will cost less than the assets will earn, that a bank, for example, will borrow at 2 percent and lend at 5 percent or more. The difference between the two, called the **gross spread**, is the most important aspect of bank profitability. (The bank's expenses and taxes, its cost of doing business, is the other major factor in its profitability.)

gross spread

The difference between what a bank earns on its assets and what it pays for its liabilities. Profit before taxes, expenses, and other (non-interest related) costs of doing business.

The equity, net worth, or capital variable is a residual that makes the two sides of the equation balance or equal each other. This is because a company's owners (stockholders in the case of a joint stock corporation, depositors or policyholders in the case of a mutual) are "junior" to the company's creditors. If the company shuts down, holders of the company's liabilities (its creditors) get paid out of the proceeds of the assets first. Anything left after the sale of the assets is then divided among the owners.

If a company is economically viable, the value of what it owns will exceed the value of what it owes. Equity, therefore, will be positive and the company will be a going concern (will continue operating). If a company is not viable, the value of what it owes will exceed what it owns. Equity, therefore, will be negative, and the company will be economically bankrupt. (This does not mean, however, that it will cease operating at that time. Regulators, stockholders, or creditors may force a shutdown well before equity becomes zero, or they may allow the company to continue operating "in the red" in the hope that its assets will increase and/or its liabilities decrease enough to return equity to positive territory.)

The value of assets and liabilities (and, hence, equity) fluctuates due to changes in interest rates and asset prices. How to account for those changes is a difficult yet crucial subject because accounting rules will affect the residual equity and perceptions of a company's value and viability. Sometimes, it is most appropriate to account for assets according to historical cost—how much the company paid to acquire it. Other times, it is most appropriate to account for assets according to their current market value, a process called "marking to market." Often, a blend of the two extremes makes the best sense. For instance, a bank might be allowed to hold a bond at its historical cost unless the issuer defaults or is downgraded by a rating agency.

FIGURE 9.1 Bank assets and liabilities
This balance sheet has been simplified for easier comprehension.

Assets (Things Owned, Uses of Funds)	Description	Liabilities (Things Owed, Sources of Funds)	Description
Reserves	Cash in the vault and deposits with the central bank	Transaction Deposits (a.k.a. checkable deposits)	Deposits that can be withdrawn immediately in person at the bank, at an ATM, via debit card, or by check
Securities (a.k.a. secondary reserves)	Government, agency, and other liquid bonds	Nontransaction Deposits (a.k.a. time or savings deposits)	Deposits that can be withdrawn without penalty only after the passage of a predetermined amount of time or that are not accessible by check. They come in retail and institutional (large denomination) varieties, including passbook savings, CDs, and NCDs.
Loans	Loan to other banks, securities dealers, nonbank businesses, and consumers. Some loans are collateralized with accounts receivable, real estate, or securities.	Borrowings	Loans from the central bank or other banks (called, confusingly, federal funds)
Other Assets	Physical capital like branches and computer systems	Equity (a.k.a. net worth or capital)	The residual that makes A = L. The book value of the bank.

FIGURE 9.2 Assets and liabilities of U.S. commercial banks, February 15, 2017
Even this is somewhat simplified.

Assets and liabilities of U.S. commercial banks, 15 February 2017					
Assets	Billions USD	Percent of Total	Liabilities	Billions USD	Percent of Total
Reserves	2,343.8	14.54	Deposits	11,529.3	71.54
Secondary Reserves	3,348.6	20.78	Borrowings	2,013.2	12.49
Loans	9,132.5	56.66	Other liabilities	796.3	4.94
Other assets	1,292.1	8.02	Bank capital	1,778.2	11.03
	16,117.0	100.00		16,117.0	100.00

Figure 9.1 lists and describes the major types of bank assets and liabilities, and Figure 9.2 shows the combined balance sheet of all U.S. commercial banks on February 15, 2017. For the most recent figures, browse www.federalreserve.gov/releases/h8/current.

reserves

In this context, cash funds that bankers maintain to meet deposit outflows and other payments.

required reserves

A minimum amount of cash funds that banks are required by regulators to hold.

secondary reserves

Noncash, liquid assets, like government bonds, that bankers can quickly sell to obtain cash.

Stop and Think Box

In the first half of the nineteenth century, bank reserves in the United States consisted solely of full-bodied specie (gold or silver coins). Banks pledged to pay specie for both their notes and deposits immediately upon demand. The government did not mandate minimum reserve ratios. What level of reserves do you think those banks kept? (Higher or lower than today's required reserves?) Why?

With some notorious exceptions known as wildcat banks, which were basically financial scams, banks kept reserves in the range of 20 to 30 percent, much higher than today's required reserves. They did so for several reasons. First, unlike today, there was no fast, easy, cheap way for banks to borrow from the government or other banks. They occasionally did so, but getting what was needed in time was far from assured. So basically borrowing was closed to them. Banks in major cities like Boston, New York, and Philadelphia could keep secondary reserves, but before the advent of the telegraph, banks in the hinterland could not be certain that they could sell the volume of bonds they needed to into thin local markets. In those areas, which included most banks (by number), secondary reserves were of little use. And the potential for large net outflows was higher than it is today because early bankers sometimes collected the liabilities of rival banks, then presented them all at once in the hopes of catching the other guy with inadequate specie reserves. Also, runs by depositors were much more frequent then. There was only one thing for a prudent early banker to do: keep his or her vaults brimming with coins.

Key Takeaways

- A balance sheet is a financial statement that lists what a company owns (its assets or uses of funds) and what it owes (its liabilities or sources of funds).
- Major bank assets include reserves, secondary reserves, loans, and other assets.
- Major bank liabilities include deposits, borrowings, and shareholder equity.

9.2 Assets, Liabilities, and T-Accounts

Learning Objectives

1. In five words, what do banks do?
2. Without a word limitation, how would you describe what functions they fulfill?

As Figure 9.1 and Figure 9.2 show, commercial banks own reserves of cash and deposits with the Fed; secondary reserves of government and other liquid securities; loans to businesses, consumers, and other banks; and other assets, including buildings, computer systems, and other physical stuff. *Each of those assets plays an important role in the bank's overall business strategy.* A bank's physical assets are needed to conduct its business, whether it be a traditional brick-and-mortar bank, a full e-commerce bank (there are servers and a headquarters someplace), or a hybrid click-and-mortar institution. Reserves allow banks to pay their transaction deposits and other liabilities. In many countries, regulators mandate a minimum level of reserves, called required reserves. When banks hold more than the reserve requirement, the extra reserves are called excess reserves. When reserves paid zero interest, as they did until recently, U.S. bankers usually kept excess reserves to a minimum, preferring instead to hold secondary reserves like Treasuries and other safe, liquid, interest-earning securities. Banks' bread-and-butter asset is, of course, their loans. They derive most of their income from loans, so they must be very careful who they lend to and on what terms. Banks lend to other banks via the federal funds market, but also in the process of clearing checks, which are called "cash items in process of collection." Most of their loans, however, go to nonbanks. Some loans are uncollateralized, but many are backed by real estate (in which case the loans are called mortgages), accounts receivable (factorage), or securities (call loans).

Stop and Think Box

Savings banks, a type of bank that issues only savings deposits, and life insurance companies hold significantly fewer reserves than commercial banks do. Why?

Savings banks and life insurance companies do not suffer large net outflows very often. People do draw down their savings by withdrawing money from their savings accounts, cashing in their life insurance, or taking out policy loans, but remember that one of the advantages of relatively large intermediaries is that they can often meet outflows from inflows. In other words, savings banks and life insurance companies can usually pay customer A's withdrawal (policy loan or surrender) from customer B's deposit (premium payment). Therefore, they have no need to carry large reserves, which are expensive in terms of opportunity costs.

Where do banks get the wherewithal to purchase those assets? *The right-hand side of the balance sheet lists a bank's liabilities or the sources of its funds.* Transaction deposits include negotiable order of withdrawal accounts (NOW) and money market deposit accounts (MMDAs), in addition to good old checkable deposits. Banks like transaction deposits because they can avoid paying much, if any, interest on them. Some depositors find the liquidity that transaction accounts provide so convenient they even pay for the privilege of keeping their money in the bank via various fees, of which more anon. Banks justify the fees by pointing out that it is costly to keep the books, transfer money, and maintain sufficient cash reserves to meet withdrawals.

bank holding company

A corporate entity than owns one or more banks and banking-related subsidiaries.

The administrative costs of nontransaction deposits are lower so banks pay interest for those funds. Nontransaction deposits range from the traditional passbook savings account to negotiable certificates of deposit (NCDs) with denominations greater than $100,000. Checks cannot be drawn on passbook savings accounts, but depositors can withdraw from or add to the account at will. Because they are more liquid, they pay lower rates of interest than time deposits (aka certificates of deposit), which impose stiff penalties for early withdrawals. *Banks also borrow outright from other banks overnight* via what is called the federal funds market (whether the banks are borrowing to satisfy Federal Reserve requirements or for general liquidity purposes), and directly from the Federal Reserve via discount loans (aka advances). They can also borrow from corporations, including their parent companies if they are part of a **bank holding company**.

That leaves only bank net worth, the difference between the value of a bank's assets and its liabilities. Equity originally comes from stockholders when they pay for shares in the bank's initial public offering (IPO) or direct public offering (DPO). Later, it comes mostly from retained earnings, but sometimes banks make a seasoned offering of additional stock. Regulators watch bank capital closely because the more equity a bank has, the less likely it is that it will fail. Today, having learned this lesson the hard way, U.S. regulators will close a bank down well before its equity reaches zero. Provided, that is, they catch it first. Even well-capitalized banks can fail very quickly, especially if they trade in the derivatives market, of which more below.

At the broadest level, banks and other financial intermediaries engage in asset transformation. In other words, *they sell liabilities with certain liquidity, risk, return, and denominational characteristics and use those funds to buy assets with a different set of characteristics.* Intermediaries link investors (purchasers of banks' liabilities) to entrepreneurs (sellers of banks' assets) in a more sophisticated way than mere market facilitators like dealer-brokers and peer-to-peer bankers do.

More specifically, banks (aka depository institutions) engage in three types of asset transformation, each of which creates a type of risk. First, banks turn short-term deposits into long-term loans. In other words, they *borrow short and lend long*. This creates interest rate risk. Second, banks turn relatively liquid liabilities (e.g., demand deposits) into relatively illiquid assets like mortgages, thus creating liquidity risk. Third, banks issue relatively safe debt (e.g., insured deposits) and use it to fund relatively risky assets, like loans, and thereby create credit risk.

Other financial intermediaries transform assets in other ways. Finance companies borrow long and lend short, rendering their management much easier than that of a bank. Life insurance companies sell contracts (called policies) that pay off when or if (during the policy period of a term policy) the insured party dies. Property and casualty companies sell policies that pay if some exigency, like an automobile crash, occurs during the policy period. The liabilities of insurance companies are said to be contingent because they come due if an event happens rather than after a specified period of time.

Asset transformation and balance sheets provide us with only a snapshot view of a financial intermediary's business. That's useful, but, of course, intermediaries, like banks, are dynamic places where changes constantly occur. *The easiest way to analyze that dynamism is via so-called T-accounts, simplified balance sheets that list only changes in liabilities and assets.* By the way, they are called T-accounts because they look like a T. Sort of. Note in the T-accounts below the horizontal and vertical rules that cross each other, sort of like a T.

Suppose somebody deposits $17.52 in cash in a checking account. The T-account for the bank accepting the deposit would be the following:

Some Bank	
Assets	Liabilities
Reserves +$17.52	Transaction deposits +$17.52

If another person deposits in her checking account in Some Bank a check for $4,419.19 drawn on Another Bank,[1] the initial T-account for that transaction would be the following:

Some Bank	
Assets	Liabilities
Cash in collection +$4,419.19	Transaction deposits +$4,419.19

Once collected in a few days, the T-account for Some Bank would be the following:

Some Bank	
Assets	Liabilities
Cash in collection −$4,419.19	
Reserves +$4,419.19	

The T-account for Another Bank would be the following:

Another Bank	
Assets	Liabilities
Reserves −$4,419.19	
Transaction deposits +$4,419.19	

Gain some practice using T-accounts by completing the exercises, keeping in mind that each side (assets and liabilities) of a T-account should balance (equal each other) as in the examples above.

Exercises

Write out the T-accounts for the following transactions.

1. Larry closes his $73,500.88 account with JPMC Bank, spends $500.88 of that money on consumption goods, then places the rest in W Bank.
2. Suppose regulators tell W Bank that it needs to hold only 5 percent of those transaction deposits in reserve.
3. W Bank decides that it needs to hold no excess reserves but needs to bolster its secondary reserves.
4. A depositor in W bank decides to move $7,000 from her checking account to a CD in W Bank.
5. W Bank sells $500,000 of Treasuries and uses the proceeds to fund two $200,000 mortgages and the purchase of $100,000 of municipal bonds.

   (*Note*: This is net. The bank merely moved $100,000 from one type of security to another.)

Key Takeaways

- In five words, banks lend (1) long (2) and (3) borrow (4) short (5).
- Like other financial intermediaries, banks are in the business of transforming assets, of issuing liabilities with one set of characteristics to investors and of buying the liabilities of borrowers with another set of characteristics.
- Generally, banks issue short-term liabilities but buy long-term assets.
- This raises specific types of management problems that bankers must be proficient at solving if they are to succeed.

9.3 Bank Management Principles

Learning Objective

1. What are the major problems facing bank managers and why is bank management closely regulated?

Bankers must manage their assets and liabilities to ensure three conditions:

1. *Their bank has enough reserves on hand to pay for any deposit outflows* (net decreases in deposits) *but not so many as to render the bank unprofitable*. This tricky trade-off is called **liquidity management**.
2. *Their bank earns profits*. To do so, the bank must own a diverse portfolio of remunerative assets. This is known as **asset management**. It must also obtain its funds as cheaply as possible, which is known as **liability management**.
3. *Their bank has sufficient net worth or equity capital to maintain a cushion against bankruptcy or regulatory attention but not so much that the bank is unprofitable*. This second tricky trade-off is called **capital adequacy management**.

In their quest to earn profits and manage liquidity and capital, banks face two major risks: credit risk, the risk of borrowers defaulting on the loans and securities it owns, and interest rate risk, the risk that interest rate changes will decrease the returns on its assets and/or increase the cost of its liabilities. The financial panic of 2008 reminded bankers that they also can face liability and capital adequacy risks if financial markets become less liquid or seize up completely (trading is greatly reduced or completely stops; q* approaches 0).

liquidity management

Ensuring that the bank has just the right amount of reserves—not too little, which would endanger the bank's solvency, nor too much, which would decrease its profitability.

asset management

Ensuring that the bank's assets have the right combination of liquidity, safety, and return.

liability management

Attracting enough deposits or borrowing enough to ensure that the bank can make the loans or purchase the assets it wants.

capital adequacy management

Ensuring that the bank has enough capital, equity, or net worth to remain in operation while maintaining bank profitability as measured by return on equity (ROE).

Stop and Think Box

What's wrong with the following bank balance sheet?

Flower City Bank Balance Sheet	June 31, 2019 (Thousands USD)
Liabilities	Assets
Reserves $10	Transaction deposits $20
Security $10	Nontransaction deposits $50
Lones $70	Borrowings (-$15)
Other assets $5	Capitol worth $10
Totals $100	$100

There are only 30 days in June. It can't be in thousands of dollars because this bank would be well below efficient minimum scale. The A-L labels are reversed but the entries are okay. By convention, assets go on the left and liabilities on the right. Borrowings can be 0 but not negative. Only equity capital can be negative. What is "Capitol worth?" A does not equal L. Indeed, the columns do not sum to the purported "totals." It is Loans (not Lones) and Securities (not Security). Thankfully, assets is not abbreviated!

Let's turn first to liquidity management. Big Apple Bank has the following balance sheet:

Big Apple Bank	Balance Sheet (Millions USD)
Assets	Liabilities
Reserves $10	Transaction deposits $30
Securities $10	Nontransaction deposits $55
Loans $70	Borrowings $5
Other assets $10	Capital $10
Totals $100	$100

Suppose the bank then experiences a net transaction deposit outflow of $5 million. The bank's balance sheet (we could also use T-accounts here but we won't) is now like this:

Big Apple Bank	Balance Sheet (Millions USD)
Assets	Liabilities
Reserves $5	Transaction deposits $25
Securities $10	Nontransaction deposits $55
Loans $70	Borrowings $5
Other assets $10	Capital $10
Totals $95	$95

The bank's reserve ratio (reserves/transaction deposits) has dropped from 10/30 = .3334 to 5/25 = .2000. That's still pretty good. But if another $5 million flows out of the bank on net (maybe $10 million is deposited but $15 million is withdrawn), the balance sheet will look like this:

Big Apple Bank	Balance Sheet (Millions USD)
Assets	Liabilities
Reserves $0	Transaction deposits $20
Securities $10	Nontransaction deposits $55
Loans $70	Borrowings $5
Other assets $10	Capital $10
Totals $90	$90

The bank's reserve ratio now drops to 0/20 = .0000. That's bound to be below the reserve ratio required by regulators and in any event is very dangerous for the bank. What to do? *To manage this liquidity problem, bankers will increase reserves by the least expensive means at their disposal.* That almost certainly will not entail selling off real estate or calling in or selling loans. Real estate takes a long time to sell, but, more importantly, the bank needs it to conduct business! Calling in loans (not renewing them as they come due and literally calling in any that happen to have a call feature) will likely antagonize borrowers. (Loans can also be sold to other lenders, but they may not pay much for them because adverse selection is high. Banks that sell loans have an incentive to sell off the ones to the worst borrowers. If a bank reduces that risk by promising to buy back any loans that default, that bank risks losing the borrower's future business.) The bank might be willing to sell its securities, which are also called secondary reserves for a reason. If the bankers decide that is the best path, the balance sheet will look like this:

Big Apple Bank	Balance Sheet (Millions USD)
Assets	Liabilities
Reserves $10	Transaction deposits $20
Securities $0	Nontransaction deposits $55
Loans $70	Borrowings $5
Other assets $10	Capital $10
Totals $90	$90

The reserve ratio is now .5000, which is high but prudent if the bank's managers believe that more net deposit outflows are likely. Excess reserves are insurance against further outflows, but keeping them is costly because the bank is no longer earning interest on the $10 million of securities it sold. Of course, the bank could sell just, say, $2, $3, or $4 million of securities if it thought the net deposit outflow was likely to stop.

The bankers might also decide to try to lure depositors back by offering a higher rate of interest, lower fees, and/or better service. That might take some time, though, so in the meantime they might decide to borrow $5 million from the Fed or from other banks in the federal funds market. In that case, the bank's balance sheet would change to the following:

Big Apple Bank	Balance Sheet (Millions USD)
Assets	Liabilities
Reserves $5	Transaction deposits $20
Securities $10	Nontransaction deposits $55
Loans $70	Borrowings $10
Other assets $10	Capital $10
Totals $95	$95

Notice how changes in liabilities drive the bank's size, which shrank from $100 to $90 million when deposits shrank, which stayed the same size when assets were manipulated, but which grew when $5 million was borrowed. That is why a bank's liabilities are sometimes called its "sources of funds."

Now try your hand at liquidity management in the exercises.

Exercises

Manage the liquidity of the Timberlake Bank given the following scenarios. The legal reserve requirement is 5 percent. Use this initial balance sheet to answer each question:

Timberlake Bank	Balance Sheet (Millions USD)
Assets	Liabilities
Reserves $5	Transaction deposits $100
Securities $10	Nontransaction deposits $250
Loans $385	Borrowings $50
Other assets $100	Capital $100
Totals $500	$500

1. Deposits outflows of $3.5 and inflows of $3.5.
2. Deposit outflows of $4.2 and inflows of $5.8.
3. Deposit outflows of $3.7 and inflows of $0.2.
4. A large depositor says that she needs $1.5 million from her checking account, but just for two days. Otherwise, net outflows are expected to be about zero.
5. Net transaction deposit outflows are zero, but there is a $5 million net outflow from nontransaction deposits.

Asset management entails the usual trade-off between risk and return. Bankers want to make safe, high-interest rate loans but, of course, few of those are to be found. So they must choose between giving up some interest or suffering higher default rates. Bankers must also be careful to diversify, to make loans to a variety of different types of borrowers, preferably in different geographic regions. That is because sometimes entire sectors or regions go bust and the bank will too if most of its loans were made in a depressed region or to the struggling group. Finally, bankers must bear in mind that they need some secondary reserves, some assets that can be quickly and cheaply sold to bolster reserves if need be.

Today, bankers' decisions about how many excess and secondary reserves to hold is partly a function of their ability to manage their liabilities. Historically, bankers did not try to manage their liabilities. They took deposit levels as given and worked from there. Since the 1960s, however, banks, especially big ones in New York, Chicago, and San Francisco (the so-called money centers), began to actively manage their liabilities by

a. actively trying to attract deposits;
b. selling large denomination NCDs to institutional investors;
c. borrowing from other banks in the overnight federal funds market.

Recent regulatory reforms have made it easier for banks to actively manage their liabilities. In typical times today, if a bank has a profitable loan opportunity, it will not hesitate to raise the funds by borrowing from another bank, attracting deposits with higher interest rates, or selling an NCD.

That leaves us with capital adequacy management. Like reserves, banks would hold capital without regulatory prodding because equity or net worth buffers banks (and other companies) from temporary losses, downturns, and setbacks. However, like reserves, capital is costly. The more there is of it, holding profits constant, the less each dollar of it earns. So capital, like reserves, is now subject to minimums called capital requirements.

Consider the balance sheet of Safety Bank:

Safety Bank	Balance Sheet (Billions USD)
Assets	Liabilities
Reserves $1	Transaction deposits $10
Securities $5	Nontransaction deposits $75
Loans $90	Borrowings $5
Other assets $4	Capital $10
Totals $100	$100

If $5 billion of its loans went bad and had to be completely written off, Safety Bank would still be in operation:

Safety Bank	Balance Sheet (Billions USD)
Assets	Liabilities
Reserves $1	Transaction deposits $10
Securities $5	Nontransaction deposits $75
Loans $85	Borrowings $5
Other assets $4	Capital $5
Totals $95	$95

Now, consider Shaky Bank:

Shaky Bank	Balance Sheet (Billions USD)
Assets	Liabilities
Reserves $1	Transaction deposits $10
Securities $5	Nontransaction deposits $80
Loans $90	Borrowings $9
Other assets $4	Capital $1
Totals $100	$100

If $5 billion of its loans go bad, so too does Shaky.

Shaky Bank	Balance Sheet (Billions USD)
Assets	Liabilities
Reserves $1	Transaction deposits $10
Securities $5	Nontransaction deposits $80
Loans $85	Borrowings $9
Other assets $4	Capital (-$4)
Totals $95	$95

You don't need to be a certified public accountant (CPA) to know that red numbers and negative signs are not good news. Shaky Bank is a now a new kind of bank, bank*rupt*.

Why would a banker manage capital like Shaky Bank instead of like Safety Bank? In a word, profitability. There are two major ways of measuring profitability: return on assets (ROA) and return on equity (ROE).

ROA = net after-tax profit/assets

ROE = net after-tax profit/equity (capital, net worth)

Suppose that, before the loan debacle, both Safety and Shaky Bank had $10 billion in profits. The ROA of both would be 10/100 = .10. *But Shaky Bank's ROE, what shareholders care about most, would leave Safety Bank in the dust because Shaky Bank is more highly leveraged (more assets per dollar of equity).*

Shaky Bank ROE = 10/1 = 10

Safety Bank ROE = 10/10 = 1

This, of course, is nothing more than the standard risk-return trade-off applied to banking. *Regulators in many countries have therefore found it prudent to mandate capital adequacy standards to ensure that some bankers are not taking on high levels of risk in the pursuit of high profits.*

Bankers manage bank capital in several ways:

a. By buying (selling) their own bank's stock in the open market. That reduces (increases) the number of shares outstanding, raising (decreasing) capital and ROE, ceteris paribus
b. By paying (withholding) dividends, which decreases (increases) capital, increasing (decreasing) ROE, all else equal
c. By increasing (decreasing) the bank's assets, which, with capital held constant, increases (decreases) ROE

These same concepts and principles—asset, liability, capital, and liquidity management, and capital-liquidity and capital-profitability trade-offs—apply to other types of financial intermediaries as well, though the details, of course, differ.

Key Takeaways

- Bankers must manage their bank's liquidity (reserves, for regulatory reasons and to conduct business effectively), capital (for regulatory reasons and to buffer against negative shocks), assets, and liabilities.
- There is an opportunity cost to holding reserves, which pay no interest, and capital, which must share the profits of the business.
- Left to their own judgment, bankers would hold reserves > 0 and capital > 0, but they might not hold enough to prevent bank failures at what the government or a country's citizens deem an acceptably low rate.
- That induces government regulators to create and monitor minimum requirements.

9.4 Credit Risk

Learning Objective

1. What is credit risk and how do bankers manage it?

As noted above, loans are banks' bread and butter. *No matter how good bankers are at asset, liability, and capital adequacy management, they will be failures if they cannot manage credit risk.* Keeping defaults to a minimum requires bankers to be keen students of asymmetric information (adverse selection and moral hazard) and techniques for reducing them.

Bankers and insurers, like computer folks, know about GIGO—garbage in, garbage out. If they lend to or insure risky people and companies, they are going to suffer. So they carefully screen applicants for loans and insurance. In other words, *to reduce asymmetric information, financial intermediaries create information about applicants.* One way they do so is to ask applicants a wide variety of questions.

Financial intermediaries use the application only as a starting point. *Because risky applicants might stretch the truth or even outright lie on the application, intermediaries typically do two things: (1) make the application a binding part of the financial contract, and (2) verify the information with disinterested third parties.* The first allows them to void contracts if applications are fraudulent. If someone applied for life insurance but did not disclose that he or she was suffering from a terminal disease, the life insurance company would not pay, though it might return any premiums. (That may sound cruel to you, but it isn't. In the process of protecting its profits, the insurance company is also protecting its policyholders.) In other situations, the intermediary might not catch a falsehood in an application until it is too late, so it also verifies important information by calling employers (Is John Doe really the Supreme Commander of XYZ Corporation?), conducting medical examinations (Is Jane Smith really in perfect health despite being 3' 6" tall and weighing 567 pounds?), hiring appraisers (Is a one-bedroom, half-bath house on the wrong side of the tracks really worth $1.2 million?), and so forth. Financial intermediaries can also buy credit reports from third-party report providers like Equifax, Experian, or Trans Union. Similarly, insurance companies regularly share information with each other so that risky applicants can't take advantage of them easily.

To help improve their screening acumen, many financial intermediaries specialize. By making loans to only one or a few types of borrowers, by insuring automobiles in a handful of states, by insuring farms but not factories, intermediaries get very good at discerning risky applicants from the rest. Specialization also helps to keep monitoring costs to a minimum. Remember that, to reduce moral hazard (postcontractual asymmetric information), intermediaries have to pay attention to what borrowers and people who are insured do. By specializing, intermediaries know what sort of restrictive covenants (aka loan covenants) to build into their contracts. Loan covenants include the frequency of providing financial reports, the types of information to be provided in said reports, working capital requirements, permission for onsite inspections, limitations on account withdrawals, and call options if business performance deteriorates as measured by specific business ratios. Insurance companies also build covenants into their contracts. You can't turn your home into a brothel, it turns out, and retain your insurance coverage. To reduce moral hazard further, insurers also investigate claims that seem fishy. If you wrap your car around a tree the day after insuring it or increasing your coverage, the insurer's claims adjuster is probably going to take a very close look at the alleged accident. Like everything else in life, however, specialization has its costs. Some companies overspecialize, hurting their asset management by making too many loans or issuing too many policies in one place or to one group. *While credit risks decrease due to specialization, systemic risk to assets increases, requiring bankers (and other financiers) to make difficult decisions regarding how much to specialize.*

Forging long-term relationships with customers can also help financial intermediaries to manage their credit risks. Bankers, for instance, can lend with better assurance if they can study the checking and savings accounts of applicants over a period of years or decades. Repayment records of applicants who had previously obtained loans can be checked easily and cheaply. Moreover, the expectation (there's that word again) of a long-term relationship changes the borrower's calculations. The game, if you will, is to play nice so that loans will be forthcoming in the future.

One way that lenders create long-term relationships with businesses is by providing loan commitments, promises to lend $x at y interest (or y plus some market rate) for z years. Such arrangements are so beneficial for both lenders and borrowers that most commercial loans in fact originate in loan commitments. Such commitments are sometimes called lines of credit, particularly when extended to consumers. Because lines of credit can be revoked under specific circumstances, they act to reduce risky behavior on the part of borrowers.

Bankers also often insist on collateral—assets pledged by the borrower for repayment of a loan. When those assets are cash left in the bank, the collateral is called compensating or compensatory balances. *Another powerful tool to combat asymmetric information is credit rationing, refusing to make a loan at any interest rate (to reduce adverse selection) or lending less than the sum requested (to reduce moral hazard).* Insurers also engage in both types of rationing, and for the same reasons: people willing to pay high rates or premiums must be risky, and the more that is lent or insured (ceteris paribus) the higher the likelihood that the customer will abscond, cheat, or set aflame, as the case may be.

nonperforming loan

A loan that is in default, where the borrower is not making stipulated payments of interest or principal.

As the world learned to its chagrin in 2007–2008, banks and other lenders are not perfect screeners. Sometimes, under competitive pressure, they lend to borrowers they should not have. Sometimes, individual bankers profit handsomely by lending to very risky borrowers, even though their actions endanger their banks' very existence. Other times, external political or societal pressures induce bankers to make loans they normally wouldn't. Such excesses are always reversed eventually because the lenders suffer from high levels of **nonperforming loans**.

Stop and Think Box

In the first quarter of 2007, banks and other intermediaries specializing in originating home mortgages (called mortgage companies) experienced a major setback in the so-called subprime market, the segment of the market that caters to high-risk borrowers, because default rates soared much higher than expected. Losses were so extensive that many people feared, correctly as it turned out, that they could trigger a financial crisis. To stave off such a potentially dangerous outcome, why didn't the government immediately intervene by guaranteeing the subprime mortgages?

The government must be careful to try to support the financial system without giving succor to those who have screwed up. Directly bailing out the subprime lenders by guaranteeing mortgage payments would cause moral hazard to skyrocket, it realized. Borrowers might be more likely to default by rationalizing that the crime is a victimless one (though, in fact, all taxpayers would suffer—recall that there is no such thing as a free lunch in economics). Lenders would learn that they can make crazy loans to anyone because good ol' Uncle Sam will cushion, or even prevent, their fall.

Key Takeaways

- Credit risk is the chance that a borrower will default on a loan by not fully meeting stipulated payments on time.
- Bankers manage credit risk by screening applicants (taking applications and verifying the information they contain), monitoring loan recipients, requiring collateral like real estate and compensatory balances, and including a variety of restrictive covenants in loans.
- They also manage credit risk by trading off between the costs and benefits of specialization and portfolio diversification.

9.5 Interest-Rate Risk

Learning Objective

1. What is interest rate risk and how do bankers manage it?

Financial intermediaries can also be brought low by changes in interest rates. Consider the situation of Some Bank, which like most depository institutions borrows short and lends long:

Some Bank	(Billions USD)
Assets	Liabilities
Interest-rate-sensitive assets like variable rate and short-term loans and short-term securities $10	Interest-rate-sensitive liabilities like variable rate CDs and MMDAs $20
Fixed-rate assets like reserves, long-term loans and securities $50	Fixed-rate liabilities like checkable deposits, CDs, equity capital $40

If interest rates increase, Some Bank's gross profits, the difference between what it pays for its liabilities and earns on its assets, will decline (assuming the spread stays the same) because the value of its rate-sensitive liabilities (short-term and variable-rate time deposits) exceeds that of its rate-sensitive assets (short-term and variable- rate loans and securities). Say, for instance, it today pays 3 percent for its rate-sensitive liabilities and receives 7 percent on its rate-sensitive assets. That means it is paying 20 × .03 = $.6 billion to earn 10 × .07 = $.7 billion. (Not bad work if you can get it.) If interest rates increase 1 percent on each side of the balance sheet, Some Bank will be paying 20 × .04 = $.8 billion to earn 10 × .08 = $.8 billion. (No profits there.) If rates increase another 1 percent, it will have to pay 20 × .05 = $1 billion to earn 10 × .09 = $.9 billion, a total loss of $.2 billion (from a $.1 billion profit to a $.1 billion loss).

Stop and Think Box

Inflation was unexpectedly high in the 1970s. Given what you learned about the relationship between inflation and nominal interest rates (as inflation increases, so too must nominal interest rates, all else equal), and between interest rates and bank profitability in this chapter, what happened in the 1980s?

Bank profitability sank to the point that many banks, the infamous savings and loans (S&Ls), went under. Inflation (via the Fisher Equation) caused nominal interest rates to increase, which hurt banks' profitability because they were earning low rates on long-term assets (like thirty-year bonds) while having to pay high rates on their short-term liabilities. Mounting losses induced many bankers to take on added risks, including risks in the derivatives markets. A few restored their banks to profitability, but others destroyed all of their bank's capital and then some.

Of course, if the value of its risk-sensitive assets exceeded that of its liabilities, the bank would profit from interest rate increases. It would suffer, though, if interest rates decreased. Imagine Some Bank has $10 billion in interest rate-sensitive assets at 8 percent and only $1 billion in interest rate-sensitive liabilities at 5 percent. It is earning 10 × .08 = $.8 billion while paying 1 × .05 = $.05 billion. If interest rates decreased, it might earn only 10 × .05 = $.5 billion while paying 1 × .02 = $.02 billion; thus, ceteris paribus, its gross profits would decline from .8 - .05 = $.75 billion to .5 - .02 = $.48 billion, a loss of $.27 billion. More formally, this type of calculation, called basic gap analysis, is

$$C_p = (A_r - L_r) \times \Delta i$$

where:

C_p = changes in profitability

A_r = risk-sensitive assets

L_r = risk-sensitive liabilities

Δi = change in interest rates

So, returning to our first example,

$$C_p = (10 - 20) \times .02 = -10 \times .02 = -\$.2 \text{ billion},$$

and the example above,

$$C_p = (10 - 1) - (-.03) = -\$.27 \text{ billion}.$$

Complete the exercise to get comfortable conducting basic gap analysis.

Exercise

1. Use the basic gap analysis formula to estimate Some Bank's loss or gain under the following scenarios.

$$C_? = (A_r - L_r) \times \Delta i$$

Risk Sensitive Assets (Millions USD)	Risk Sensitive Liabilities (Millions USD)	Change in Interest Rates (%)	Answer: CP (Millions USD)
100	100	100	0
100	200	10	−10
100	200	−10	10
199	200	10	-0.1
199	200	−10	0.1
200	100	10	10
200	100	−10	−10
200	199	10	0.1
200	199	−10	-0.1
1,000	0	1	10
0	1,000	1	-10

$$C\rho = (A_r - L_r) \times \Delta i$$

Now, take a look at Figure 9.3, which summarizes, in a 2 × 2 matrix, what happens to bank profits when the gap is positive ($A_r > L_r$) or negative ($A_r < L_r$) when interest rates fall or rise. Basically, *bankers want to have more interest-sensitive assets than liabilities if they think that interest rates are likely to rise and they want to have more interest rate-sensitive liabilities than assets if they think that interest rates are likely to decline.*

FIGURE 9.3 Basic gap analysis matrix
+ = good; - = bad

Bank Profits	Interest Rates Go Up	Interest Rates Go Down
+ GAP = $A_r > L_r$	+/+ = +	+/− = −
− GAP = $A_r < L_r$	−/+ = −	−/− = +

Of course, not all rate-sensitive liabilities and assets have the same maturities, so to assess their interest rate risk exposure bankers usually engage in more sophisticated analyses like the maturity bucket approach, standardized gap analysis, or duration analysis. Duration, also known as Macaulay's Duration, measures the average length of a security's stream of payments. In this context, *duration is used to estimate the sensitivity of a security's or a portfolio's market value to interest rate changes via this formula:*

$$\Delta\%P = -\Delta\%i \times d$$

$\Delta\%P$ = percentage change in market value

Δi = change in interest (*not* decimalized, i.e., represent 5% as 5, not .05. Also note the negative sign. The sign is negative because interest rates and prices are inversely related.)

d = duration (years)

So, if interest rates increase 2 percent and the average duration of a bank's $100 million of assets is 3 years, the value of those assets will fall approximately -2 × 3 = -6%, or $6 million. If the value of that bank's liabilities (excluding equity) is $95 million, and the duration is also 3 years, the value of the liabilities will also fall, 95 × .06 = $5.7 million, effectively reducing the bank's equity (6 - 5.7=) $.3 million. If the duration of the bank's liabilities is only 1 year, then its liabilities will fall -2 × 1 = -2% or 95 × .02 = $1.9 million, and the bank will suffer an even larger loss (6 - 1.9 =) of $4.1 million. If, on the other hand, the duration of the bank's liabilities is 10 years, its liabilities will decrease -2 × 10 = -20% or $19 million and the bank will profit from the interest rate rise.

A basic interest rate risk reduction strategy when interest rates are expected to fall is to keep the duration of liabilities short and the duration of assets long. That way, the bank continues to earn the old, higher rate on its assets but benefits from the new lower rates on its deposits, CDs, and other liabilities. *As noted above, borrowing short and lending long is second nature for banks, which tend to thrive when interest rates go down.* When interest rates increase, banks would like to keep the duration of assets short and the duration of liabilities long. That way, the bank earns the new, higher rate on its assets and keeps its liabilities locked in at the older, lower rates. *But banks can only go so far in this direction because it runs against their nature*; few people want to borrow if the loans are callable and fewer still want long-term checkable deposits!

Key Takeaways

- Interest rate risk is the chance that interest rates may increase, decreasing the value of bank assets.
- Bankers manage interest rate risk by performing analyses like basic gap analysis, which compares a bank's interest rate risk-sensitive assets and liabilities, and duration analysis, which accounts for the fact that bank assets and liabilities have different maturities.
- Such analyses, combined with interest rate predictions, tell bankers when to increase or decrease their rate-sensitive assets or liabilities, and whether to shorten or lengthen the duration of their assets or liabilities.

9.6 Off the Balance Sheet

Learning Objective

1. What are off-balance-sheet activities and why do bankers engage in them?

To protect themselves against interest rate increases, banks go off road, engaging in activities that do not appear on their balance sheets.[2]*Banks charge customers all sorts of fees, and not just the little ones that they sometimes slap on retail checking depositors*. They also charge fees for loan guarantees, backup lines of credit, letters of credit, and foreign exchange transactions. Banks also now sell some of their loans to investors. Banks usually make about .15 percent when they sell a loan, which can be thought of as their fee for originating the loan, for, in other words, finding and screening the borrower. So, for example, a bank might discount the $100,000 note of XYZ Corp. for 1 year at 8 percent. We know from the present value formula that on the day it is made, said loan is worth PV = FV/(1 + i) = 100,000/1.08 = $92,592.59. The bank might sell it for 100,000/1.0785 = $92,721.37 and pocket the difference. Such activities are not without risks, however. Loan guarantees can become very costly if the guaranteed party defaults. Similarly, banks often sell loans with a guarantee or stipulation that they will buy them back if the borrower defaults. (If they didn't do so, as noted above, investors would not pay much for them because they would fear adverse selection, that is, the bank pawning off their worse loans on unsuspecting third parties.) Although loans and fees can help keep up bank revenues and profits in the face of rising interest rates, they do not absolve the bank of the necessity of carefully managing its credit risks.

Banks (and other financial intermediaries) also take off-balance-sheet positions in derivatives markets, including futures and interest rate swaps. *They sometimes use derivatives to hedge their risks; that is, they try to earn income should the bank's main business suffer a decline if, say, interest rates rise*. For example, bankers sell futures contracts on U.S. Treasuries at the Chicago Board of Trade. If interest rates increase, the price of bonds, we know, will decrease. The bank can then effectively buy bonds in the open market at less than the contract price, make good on the contract, and pocket the difference, helping to offset the damage the interest rate increase will cause the bank's balance sheet.

Bankers can also hedge their bank's interest rate risk by engaging in interest rate swaps. A bank might agree to pay a finance company a fixed 6 percent on a $100 million notational principal (or $6 million) every year for ten years in exchange for the finance company's promise to pay to the bank a market rate like the federal funds rate or London Interbank Offering Rate (LIBOR) plus 3 percent. If the market rate increases from 3 percent (which initially would entail a wash because 6 fixed = 3 LIBOR plus 3 contractual) to 5 percent, the finance company will pay the net due to the bank, (3 + 5 = 8 − 6 = 2% on $100 million = $2 million), which the bank can use to cover the damage to its balance sheet brought about by the higher rates. If interest rates later fall to 2 percent, the bank will have to start paying the finance company (6 − [3 + 2] = 1% on $100 million) $1 million per year but will well be able to afford it.

Banks and other financial intermediaries also sometimes speculate in derivatives and the foreign exchange markets, hoping to make a big killing. Of course, with the potential for high returns comes high levels of risk. Several hoary banks have gone bankrupt because they assumed too much off-balance-sheet risk. In some cases, the failures were due to the principal-agent problem: rogue traders bet their jobs, and their banks, and lost. In other cases, traders were mere scapegoats, instructed to behave as they did by the bank's managers or owners. In either case, it is difficult to have much sympathy for the bankers, who were either deliberate risk-takers or incompetent. There are some very basic internal controls that can prevent traders from risking too much of the capital of the banks they trade for, as well as techniques, called value at risk and stress testing,[3] that allow bankers to assess their bank's derivative risk exposure.

Key Takeaways

- Off-balance-sheet activities like fees, loan sales, and derivatives trading help banks to manage their interest rate risk by providing them with income that is not based on assets (and hence is off the balance sheet).
- Derivatives trading can be used to hedge or reduce interest rate risks but can also be used by risky bankers or rogue traders to increase risk to the point of endangering a bank's capital cushion and hence its economic existence.

9.7 Suggested Reading

Bessis, Joel. *Risk Management in Banking*. Hoboken, NJ: John Wiley and Sons, 2011.

Choudhry, Moorad. *Bank Asset and Liability Management: Strategy, Trading, Analysis*. Hoboken, NJ: John Wiley and Sons, 2007.

Dermine, Jean, and Youssef Bissada. *Asset and Liability Management: A Guide to Value Creation and Risk Control*. New York: Prentice Hall, 2002.

Koch, Timothy W. and S. Scott Macdonald. *Bank Management*. New York: Cengage, 2014.

Endnotes

1. If that check were drawn on Some Bank, there would be no need for a T-account because the bank would merely subtract the amount from the account of the payer, or in other words, the check maker, and add it to the account of the payee or check recipient.
2. This is not to say that these activities are not accounted for. It isn't illegal or even slimy. These activities will appear on revenue statements, cash flow analyses, etc. They do not, however, appear on the balance sheet, on the list of the bank's assets and liabilities.
3. financial-dictionary.thefreedictionary.com/Stress+Testing

CHAPTER 10

Innovation and Structure in Banking and Finance

Chapter Objectives

By the end of this chapter, students should be able to:

1. Explain why bankers and other financiers innovate.
2. Explain how widespread unit banking in the United States affected financial innovation.
3. Explain how the Great Inflation of the 1970s affected banks and banking.
4. Define loophole mining and lobbying and explain their importance.
5. Describe how technology changed the banking industry after World War II.
6. Define traditional banking and describe the causes of its demise.
7. Define industry consolidation and explain how it is measured.
8. Define financial conglomeration and explain its importance.
9. Define industry concentration and explain how it is measured.

10.1 Early Financial Innovations

Learning Objective

1. Why do bankers and other financiers innovate in the face of branching restrictions and other regulations?

Banking today is much the same everywhere. And, at the broadest level, today's banks are not much different from banks hundreds of years ago. Philadelphian Thomas Willing, America's first banker and life insurer, and a marine insurance pioneer, would likely understand the functioning of today's largest, most complex banks and insurance companies with little trouble.[1] (He'd certainly understand interest-only mortgages because he used them extensively as early as the 1760s.) Despite broad similarities, banking and other aspects of the financial system vary in detail over time and place, thanks in large part to innovations: new ideas, products, and markets. Innovation, in turn, is driven by changes in the financial environment, specifically in macroeconomic volatility, technology, competition, and regulation. (I discuss the economics of regulation in detail elsewhere. Here, I'll simply mention regulations that have helped to spur innovation.)

The first U.S. commercial bank, the Bank of North America, began operations in early 1782. For the next two centuries or so, banking innovation in the United States was rather glacial because regulations were relatively light, pertinent technological changes were few, and competition was sparse. Before the Civil War, all but a few of America's incorporated banks were chartered by one of the state governments rather than the national government (and only two of those were important). *Most states forbade intrastate branching; interstate branching was all but unheard of,* except when conducted by relatively small private (unincorporated) banks. During the Civil War, Congress passed a law authorizing the establishment of *national banks*, but the term referred only to the fact that the national government chartered and regulated them. Despite their name, the banks that came into existence under the national banking acts could not branch across state lines, and their ability to branch within their state of domicile depended on the branching rules imposed by that state. As before the war, most states forbade branching. Moreover, state governments continued to charter banks too. The national government tried to dissuade them from doing so by taxing state bank notes heavily, but the banks responded nimbly, issuing deposits instead. *Unlike most countries, which developed a few, large banks with extensive systems of branches, the United States was home to hundreds, then thousands, then tens of thousands of tiny branchless, or unit, banks.*

Most of those unit banks were spread evenly throughout the country. Because banking was essentially a local retail business, most unit banks enjoyed near-monopolies. If you didn't like the local bank, you were free to do your banking elsewhere, but that might require putting one's money in a bank over hill and over dale, a full day's trek away by horse. Most people were reluctant to do that, so the local bank got their business, even if its terms were not particularly good. Little regulated and lightly pressed by competitors, American banks became stodgy affairs, the stuff of WaMu commercials.[2] *Spreads between sources of funds and uses of funds were large and stable, leading to the infamous 3-6-3 rule: borrow at 3 percent, lend at 6 percent, and golf at 3 p.m.* Reforming the system proved difficult because the owners and managers of small banks enjoyed significant local political clout.[3]

Near-monopoly in banking, however, led to innovation in the financial markets. Instead of depositing money in the local bank, some investors looked for higher returns by lending directly to entrepreneurs. Instead of paying high rates at the bank, some entrepreneurs sought cheaper funds by selling bonds directly into the market. As a result, the United States developed the world's largest, most efficient, and most innovative financial markets. The United States gave birth to large, liquid markets for commercial paper (short-dated business IOUs) and junk bonds (aka BIG, or below investment grade, bonds), which are high-yielding but risky bonds issued by relatively small or weak companies. Markets suffer from higher levels of asymmetric information and more free-rider problems than financial intermediaries do, however, so along with innovative securities markets came instances of fraud, of people issuing overvalued or fraudulent securities. And that led to several layers of securities regulation and, inevitably, yet more innovation.

Stop and Think Box

Unlike banks, U.S. life insurance companies could establish branches or agencies wherever they pleased, including foreign countries. Life insurers must maintain massive accumulations of assets so that they will certainly be able to pay claims when an insured person dies. From the late nineteenth century until the middle of the twentieth, therefore, America's largest financial institutions were not its banks, but its life insurers, and competition among the biggest ones—Massachusetts Mutual, MetLife, Prudential, New York Life, and the Equitable—was fierce. Given that information, what do you think innovation in life insurance was like compared to commercial banking?

Innovation in life insurance should have been more rapid because competition was more intense. Data-processing innovations, like the use of punch-card-tabulating machines,[4] automated mechanical mailing address machines,[5] and mainframe computers,[6] occurred in life insurers before they did in most banks.

Key Takeaways

- Bankers and financiers innovate to continue to earn profits despite a rapidly evolving financial environment, including changes in competition, regulation, technology, and the macroeconomy.

- Unit banks enjoyed local monopolies and were lightly regulated, so there was little incentive for them to innovate but plenty of reason for investors and borrowers to meet directly via the second major conduit of external finance, markets.
- Unit banking dampened banking innovation but spurred financial market innovation.
- Traditionally, bankers earned profits from the spread between the cost of their liabilities and the earnings on their assets. It was a staid business characterized by the 3-6-3 rule.

10.2 Innovations Galore

Learning Objective

1. Why did the Great Inflation spur financial innovation?

Competition keeps gross spreads (the difference between what borrowers pay for loans and what depositors receive) down, but it is also important because it drives bankers to adopt new technologies and search for ways to reduce the negative effects of volatility. It is not surprising, therefore, that as changing regulations, globalization, computerization, and unprecendented macroeconomic volatility rendered the U.S. financial system more competitive in the 1970s and 1980s, the pace of financial innovation increased dramatically. As Figure 10.1 shows, beginning in the late 1960s, inflation rose steadily and grew increasingly erratic. Not surprisingly, nominal interest rates rose as well, via the Fisher Equation. Interest rate risk, particularly rising interest rates, is one of the things that keeps bankers awake at night. They could not have slept much during the Great Inflation of 1968 to 1982, when the aggregate price level rose over 110 percent all told, more than any fifteen-year period before or since.

FIGURE 10.1 U.S. inflation rates, 1950–1989
The 1970s weren't just about disco dancing.

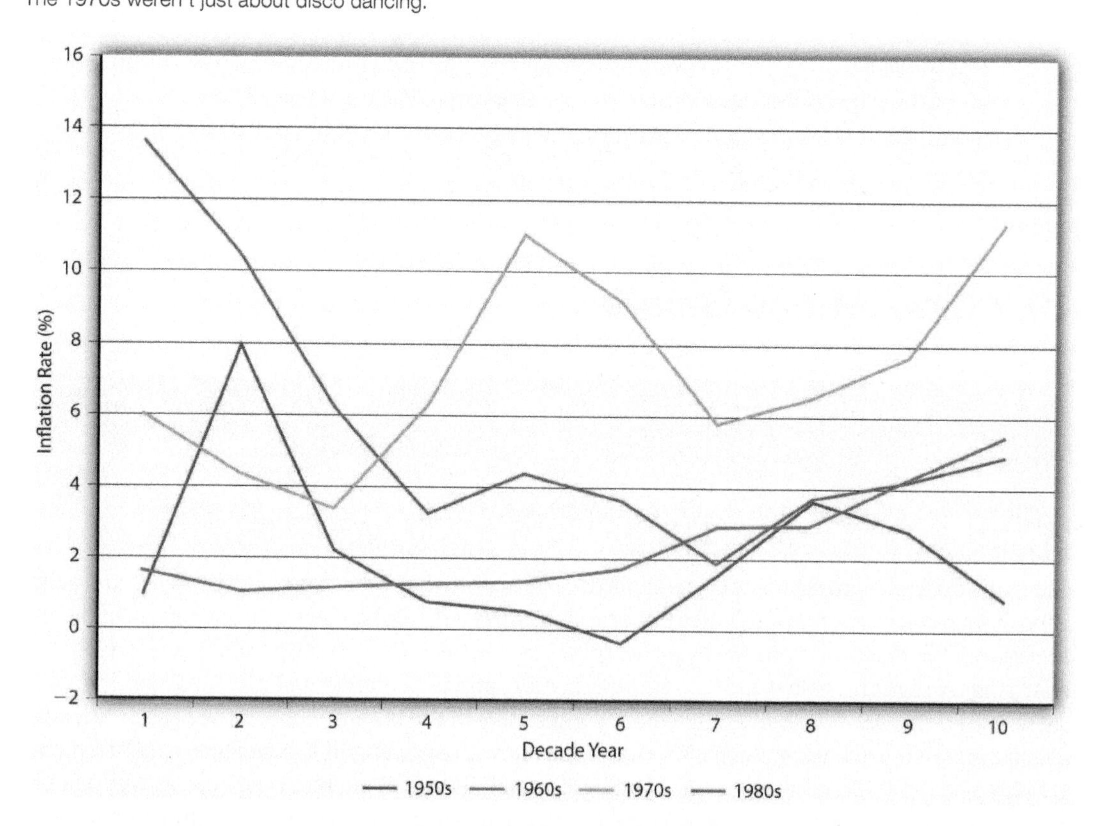

Bankers responded to the increased interest rate risk by inducing others to assume it. Bankers can use financial derivatives, like options, futures, and swaps, to hedge their interest rate risks. It is no coincidence that the modern revival of such markets occurred during the 1970s. Also in the 1970s, bankers began to make adjustable-rate mortgage loans. Traditionally, mortgages had been fixed rate. The borrower promised to pay, say, 6 percent over the entire fifteen-, twenty-, or thirty-year term of the loan. Fixed-rate loans were great for banks when interest rates declined (or stayed the same). But when rates rose, banks got stuck with long-term assets that earned well below what they had to pay for their short-term liabilities. One solution was to get borrowers to take on the risk by inducing them to promise to pay some market rate, like the six-month Treasury rate, plus 2, 3, 4, or 5 percent. That way, when interest rates rise, the borrower has to pay more to the bank, helping it with its gap problem. Of course, when rates decrease, the borrower pays less to the bank. The key is to realize that with adjustable-rate loans, interest rate risk, as well as reward, falls on the borrower, rather than the bank. To induce borrowers to take on that risk, banks must offer them a more attractive (lower) interest rate than on fixed-rate mortgages. Fixed-rate mortgages remain popular, however, because many people don't like the risk of possibly paying higher rates in the future. Furthermore, if their mortgages contain no prepayment penalty clause (and most don't), borrowers know that they can take advantage of lower interest rates by refinancing—getting a new loan at the current, lower rate and using the proceeds to pay off the higher-rate loan. Due to the high transaction costs ("closing costs" like loan application fees, appraisal costs, title insurance, and so forth) associated with home mortgage re-fis, however, interest rates must decline more than a little bit before it is worthwhile to re-finance.[7]

Bankers also responded to increased competition and disintermediation (removal of funds by depositors looking for better returns) by finding new and improved ways to connect to customers. ATMs (automated teller machines), for example, increased the liquidity of deposits by making it easier for depositors to make deposits and withdrawals during off hours and at locations remote from their neighborhood branch.

Stop and Think Box

In the 1970s and 1980s, life insurance companies sought regulatory approval for a number of innovations, including adjustable-rate policy loans and variable annuities. Why? *Hint*: Policy loans are loans that whole life insurance policyholders can take out against the cash value of their policies. Most policies stipulated a 5 or 6 percent fixed rate. Annuities, annual payments made during the life of the annuitant, were also traditionally fixed.

Life insurance companies, like banks, were adversely affected by disintermediation during the Great Inflation. (In other words, policyholders, like bank depositors, reduced the amount that they lent to insurers.) Policyholders astutely borrowed the cash values of their life insurance policies at 5 or 6 percent, then re-lent the money to others at the going market rate, which was often in the double digits. By making the policy loans variable, life insurers could adjust them upward when rates increased to limit such arbitrage. Similarly, fixed annuities were a difficult sell during the Great Inflation because annuitants saw the real value (the purchasing power) of their annual payments decrease dramatically. By promising to pay annuitants more when interest rates and inflation were high, variable-rate annuities helped insurers to attract customers.

Key Takeaways

- By increasing macroeconomic instability, nominal interest rates, and competition between banks and financial markets, the Great Inflation forced bankers and other financiers to innovate.
- Bankers innovated by introducing new products, like adjustable-rate mortgages and sweep accounts; new techniques, like derivatives and other off-balance-sheet activities; and new technologies, including credit card payment systems and automated and online banking facilities.

10.3 Loophole Mining and Lobbying

Learning Objective

1. What are loophole mining and lobbying, and why are they important?

Competition for profits also drives bankers and other financiers to look for regulatory loopholes, a process sometimes called loophole mining. Loophole mining is both legal and ethical and works better in nations, like the United States, with a **permissive regulatory system** rather than a restrictive one, or, in other words, in places where anything is allowed unless it is explicitly forbidden.[8] During the Great Inflation, banks could not legally pay any interest on checking deposits or more than about 6 percent on time deposits, both far less than going market rates. Banks tried to lure depositors by giving them toasters and other gifts, attempting desperately to skirt the interest rate caps by sweetening the pot. Few depositors bit. Massive **disintermediation** ensued because depositors pulled their money out of banks to buy assets that could provide a market rate of return. Financiers responded by developing money market mutual funds (MMMFs), which offered checking account–like liquidity while paying interest at market rates, and by investing in short-term, high-grade assets like Treasury Bills and AAA-rated corporate commercial paper. (The growth of MMMFs in turn aided the growth and development of the commercial paper markets.)

permissive regulatory system

A system that allows financiers to engage in any activities they wish that are not explicitly forbidden. It is easier for financial innovation than a restrictive regulatory system.

disintermediation

The opposite of intermediation, when investors pull money out of banks and other financial intermediaries.

Stop and Think Box

To work around regulations against interstate banking, some banks, particularly in markets that transcended state lines, established so-called nonbank banks. Because the law defined banks as institutions that "accept deposits *and* make loans," banks surmised, correctly, that they could establish de facto branches that did one function or the other, but not both. What is this type of behavior called and why is it important?

This is loophole mining leading to financial innovation. Unfortunately, this particular innovation was much less economically efficient than establishing real branches would have been. The banks that created nonbank banks likely profited, but not as much as they would have if they had not had to resort to such a technicality. Moreover, the nonbank bank's customers would have been less inconvenienced!

Bankers also used loophole mining by creating so-called sweep accounts, checking accounts that were invested each night in ("swept" into) overnight loans. The interest earned on those loans was credited to the account the next morning, allowing banks to pay rates above the official deposit rate ceilings. Sweep accounts also allowed banks to do the end around on reserve requirements, legal minimums of cash and Federal Reserve deposits. Recall that banks earn limited interest on reserves, so they often wish that they could hold fewer reserves than regulators require, particularly when interest rates are high. *By using computers to sweep checking accounts at the close of business each day, banks reduced their de jure deposits and thus their reserve requirements to the point that reserve regulations today are largely moot, a point to which we shall return.*

Bank holding companies (BHCs), parent companies that own multiple banks and banking-related service companies, offered bankers another way to use loophole mining because regulation of BHCs was, for a long time, more liberal than unit bank regulation. In particular, BHCs could circumvent restrictive branching regulations and earn extra profits by providing investment advice, data processing, and credit card services. Today, bank holding companies own almost all of the big U.S. banks. J. P. Morgan Chase, Bank of America, and Citigroup are all BHCs.[9]

Not all regulations can be circumvented cost effectively via loophole mining, however, so sometimes bankers and other financiers have to push for regulatory reforms. The Great Inflation and the decline of traditional banking, we'll learn below, induced bankers to lobby to change the regulatory regime they faced. Like loophole mining, lobbying in and of itself is legal and ethical so long as the laws and social mores related to such activities are not violated. The bankers largely succeeded, aided in part by a banking crisis.

Key Takeaways

- Loophole mining is a legal and ethical type of innovation where bankers and other financiers look for creative ways of circumventing regulations.
- Lobbying is a legal and ethical type of innovation where bankers and other financiers try to change regulations.
- The Great Inflation also induced bankers to use loophole mining (for example, by using bank holding companies). When that was too costly, bankers lobbied to change the regulatory system, generally to make it less restrictive.

10.4 Banking on Technology

Learning Objective

1. How has technology aided financial innovation?

Proliferation of the telegraph and the telephone in the nineteenth century did little to change banking. Bankers in remote places could place orders with securities brokers more quickly and cheaply than before, customers could perform certain limited transactions by talking with a teller by phone rather than in person, and mechanical computers made certain types of data storage and number crunching faster. The widespread use of automobiles led to the adoption of drive-up teller windows in the 1950s. None of those technologies, however, transformed the face of the business. *The advent of cheap electronic computing and digital telecommunications after World War II, however, did eventually spur significant innovation.*

Retail-level credit has always been a major component of the American economy, but it began to get crimped in the late nineteenth and early twentieth centuries in large urban areas where people no longer knew their neighbors and clerks left for new jobs with alarming frequency. Some stores began to issue credit cards to their customers. These credit cards were literally identification cards that let the clerks know that the customer had a credit account with the store. The system was inefficient because consumers needed a different card for each store in which they shopped. Moreover, screening good borrowers from bad isn't easy and minimum efficient scale is quite high, so even large department store chains were not very efficient at issuing the cards. Observers realized that economies of scale could be exploited if one company decided who was creditworthy and provided a payment system that allowed participation by a large percentage of retailers.

After World War II, Diners Club applied the idea to restaurants, essentially telling restaurateurs that it would pay their customers' bills. (Diners Club later collected from the customers.) The service was very costly, however, so new credit card systems did not spread successfully until the late 1960s, *when improvements in computer technology and telecommunications made it possible for machines to conduct the transactions at both the point of sale and card issuer sides of the transaction.* Since then, several major credit card networks have arisen, and thousands of institutions, including many nonbanks, now issue credit cards.

Basically, Visa and MasterCard have created private payment systems that are win-win-win. Retailers win because they are assured of getting paid (checks sometimes bounce days after the fact, but credit and debit cards can be verified before goods are given or services are rendered). Retailers pay a small fixed fee (that's why a shopkeeper might not let you charge a 50 cent pack of gum) and a few percentage points for each transaction because they believe that their customers like to pay by credit card. Indeed many do. Carrying a credit card is much easier and safer than carrying around cash. By law, cardholders are liable for no more than $50 if their card is lost or stolen, provided they report it in a timely manner. Credit cards are small and light, especially compared to large sums of cash, and they eliminate the need for small change. They also allow consumers to smooth their consumption over time by allowing them to tap a line of credit on demand. Although interest rates on credit cards are generally high, the cardholder can avoid interest charges by paying the bill in full each month. Finally, banks and other card issuers win because of the fees they receive from vendors. Some also charge cardholders an annual fee. Competition, however, has largely ended the annual fee card and indeed driven issuers to refund some of the fees they collect from retailers to cardholders to induce people to pay with their cards rather than with cash, checks, or competitors' cards. That's what all of the business about cash back, rewards, frequent flier points, and the like, is about.

Debit cards look like credit cards but actually tap into the cardholder's checking account much like an instantaneous check. Retailers like them better than checks, though, because a debit card can't bounce, or be returned for insufficient funds days after the customer has walked off with the store owner's property. Consumers who find it difficult to control their spending find debit cards useful because it gives them firm budget constraints, that is, the sums in their respective checking accounts. If a debit card is lost or stolen, however, the cardholder's liability is generally much higher than it is with a credit card. Today, many debit cards are also automatic teller machine (ATM) cards, cards that allow customers to withdraw cash from ATMs. That makes sense because, like debit cards, ATM cards are linked directly to each cardholder's checking (and sometimes savings) accounts. *ATMs are much smaller, cheaper, and more convenient than full-service branches, so many banks established networks of them instead of branches.* Before bank branching restrictions were lifted, ATMs also received more favorable regulatory treatment than branches. There are more than 250,000 ATMs in the United States today, all linked to bank databases via the miraculous telecom devices developed in the late twentieth century.

FIGURE 10.2 Banque Nationale du Canada

Yeah, I'd bank there!

Further technological advances have led to the creation of automated banking machines (ABMs); online banking, home banking, or e-banking; and virtual banks. ABMs are combinations of ATMs, websites, and dedicated customer service telephone lines that allow customers to make deposits, transfer funds between accounts, or engage in even more sophisticated banking transactions without stepping foot in the bank. Online banking allows customers to bank from their home or work computers. *Banks have found online banking so much cheaper than traditional in-bank methods that some have encouraged depositors and other customers to bank from home or via machines by charging them fees for the privilege of talking to a teller!* A few banks are completely virtual, having no physical branches. So-called click-and-mortar, or hybrid, banks appear more viable than completely virtual banks at present, however, because virtual banks seem a little too ephemeral, a little too like the wild cat banks of old. As during the good old days, a grand edifice still inspires confidence in depositors and policyholders. The bank in Figure 10.2, for some reason, evokes more confidence than the bank in Figure 10.3.

FIGURE 10.3 An actual bank in a trailer

I might prefer to keep my money under my mattress.

Technological improvements also made possible the rise of **securitization**, *the process of transforming illiquid financial assets like mortgages, automobile loans, and accounts receivable into marketable securities.* Computers make it relatively easy and cheap to bundle loans together, sell them to investors, and pass the payments through to the new owner. Because they are composed of bundles of smaller loans, the securitized loans are diversified against default risk and are sold in the large round sums that institutional investors crave. Securitization allows bankers to specialize in originating loans rather than in holding assets. They can improve their balance sheets by securitizing and selling loans, using the cash to fund new loans. As we'll see shortly, however, securitization has also opened the door to smaller competitors.

securitization

The process of combining multiple mortgages or other loans into a single instrument, usually for resale to institutional investors such as hedge funds or investment banks.

Key Takeaways

- Technology, particularly digital electronic computers and telecommunication devices, made possible sweep accounts, securitization, credit and debit card networks, ATMs, ABMs, and online banking.
- ATMs, ABMs, and online banking reduced a bank's expenses.
- Sweep accounts reduced the cost of required reserves.
- Securitization allows banks to specialize in making loans, as opposed to holding assets.
- Credit card issuance is often lucrative.

10.5 Banking Industry Profitability and Structure

Learning Objective

1. What role does market structure (concentration, consolidation, conglomeration) play in the banking industry's profitability?

Despite their best innovation efforts, banks have been steadily losing market share as sources of loans to nonfinancial borrowers. In the 1970s, commercial banks and other depository institutions (the so-called thrifts—credit unions, savings and loans, savings banks) controlled over 60 percent of that market. Today, they have only about a third. The market for loans to nonfinancial borrowers grew very quickly over the last quarter century, however, so that decline is a relative one only. Banks are still extremely profitable, so much so that before the financial catastrophe of 2007–2009 many new banks tried to form each year. *But bankers have to work harder than ever for those profits; the good old days of traditional banking and the 3-6-3 rule are long gone.* Fees and other off-balance-sheet activities now account for almost half of bank income, up from about 7 percent in 1980. The traditional source of profit, the spread between the cost of liabilities and the returns on assets, has steadily eroded from both ends.

As noted, the interest rates that banks could pay on deposits were capped (under so-called Regulation Q) at 0 for checking deposits and about 6 percent on time deposits. (The hope was that, if they faced limited competition for funds, banks would be safer.) Until the Great Inflation, bankers loved the caps because they limited competition for deposits. When interest rates rose enough to cause disintermediation, to cause funds to flow out of banks to higher-yielding investments like money market mutual funds, bankers lobbied for an end to the interest rate restrictions and their request was granted in the 1980s. Since then, banks have had to compete with each other as well as with money market mutual funds for deposits. *Unsurprisingly, banks' gross spreads have eroded, and deposits have become relatively less important as sources of funds.*

On the asset side, banks can't charge as much for loans, ceteris paribus, as they once did because they face increasingly stiff competition from the commercial paper and bond markets, especially the so-called junk bond market. Now, instead of having to cozy up to a bank, smaller and riskier companies can sell bonds directly to investors. Issuing bonds incurs costs besides interest charges—namely, mandatory information disclosure and constant feedback from investors on the issuing firm's performance via its bond prices—but companies are willing to bear those costs if they can get a better interest rate than banks offer.

As mentioned, securitization has also hurt banks by giving rise to numerous small lenders that basically sell every loan they originate. Such companies can be efficient at smaller scale because they do not have to attract and retain deposits or engage in more sophisticated asset and liability management techniques. All they have to do is originate loans and sell them to investors, using the proceeds to make new loans. Finance companies especially have eaten into banks' market share in commercial lending, and a slew of specialized mortgage lenders made major inroads into the home mortgage market. What is good for the goose, as they say, is good for the gander.[10]

As a result of those competitive pressures, many banks exited the business, some by going bankrupt, others by merging with larger institutions. The banking crisis of the 1980s enabled bankers and regulators to make further reforms, including greatly easing restrictions on branch banking and investment banking (securities) activities. In 1933, at the nadir of the Great Depression, commercial (receiving deposits and making loans) and investment banking activities (underwriting securities offerings) were strictly separated by legislation usually called Glass-Steagall, after the congressional members who cooked it up. The gradual de facto erosion of Glass-Steagall in the late 1980s and 1990s (by means of bank holding companies and a sympathetic Federal Reserve) and its de jure elimination in 1999 allowed investment and commercial banks to merge and to engage in each other's activities. Due to those and other regulatory changes, usually called deregulation, and the decline of traditional banking, banks began to merge in large numbers, a process called consolidation, and began to enter into nonbanking financial activities, like insurance, a process called conglomeration.

*As*Figure 10.4 and Figure 10.5*show, consolidation and conglomeration have left the nation with fewer but larger and more profitable (and ostensibly more efficient) banks.* Due to the demise of Glass-Steagall, conglomerate banks can now more easily tap economies of scope, the ability to use a single resource to supply numerous products or services. For example, banks can now use the information they create about borrowers to offer loans or securities underwriting and can use branches to schlep insurance. Consolidation has also allowed banks to diversify their risks geographically and to tap economies of scale. That is important because minimum efficient scale may have increased in recent decades due to the high initial costs of employing the latest and greatest computer and telecommunications technologies. Larger banks may be safer than smaller ones, ceteris paribus, because they have more diversified loan portfolios and more stable deposit bases. Unlike most small banks, large ones are not reliant on the economic fortunes of one city or company, or even one country or economic sector.

FIGURE 10.4 Number of FDIC commercial banks, year-end, 1980–2016
Where will it all end?

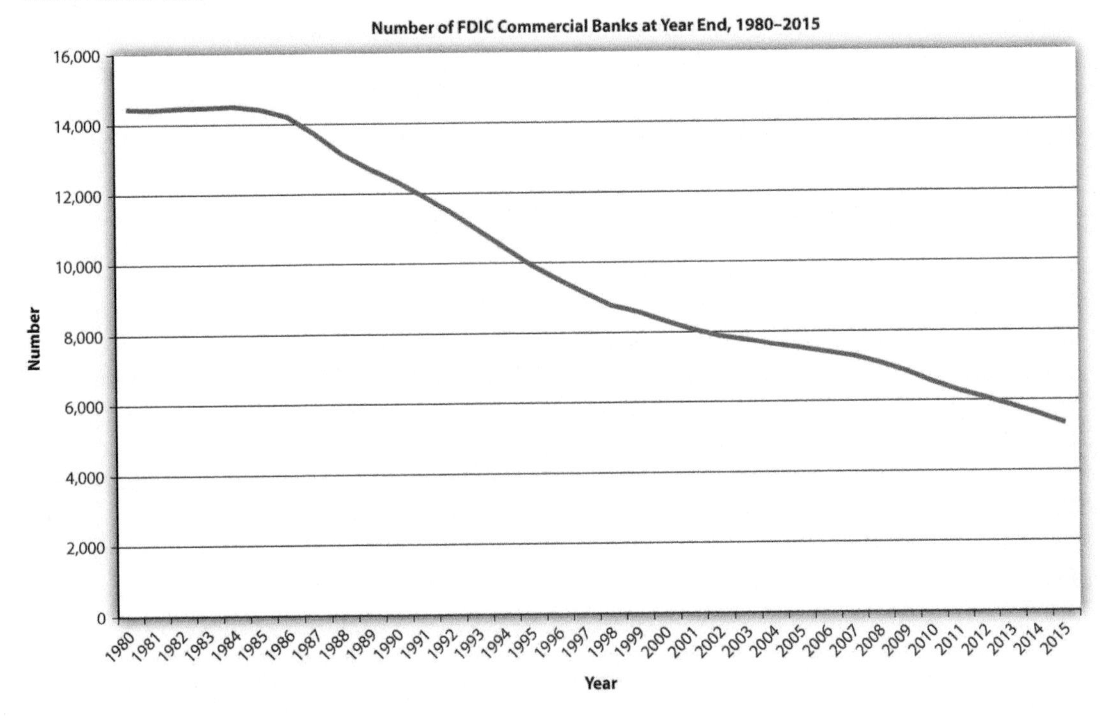

FIGURE 10.5 U.S. banks: return on equity, 1935–2016
Up and down but mostly up.

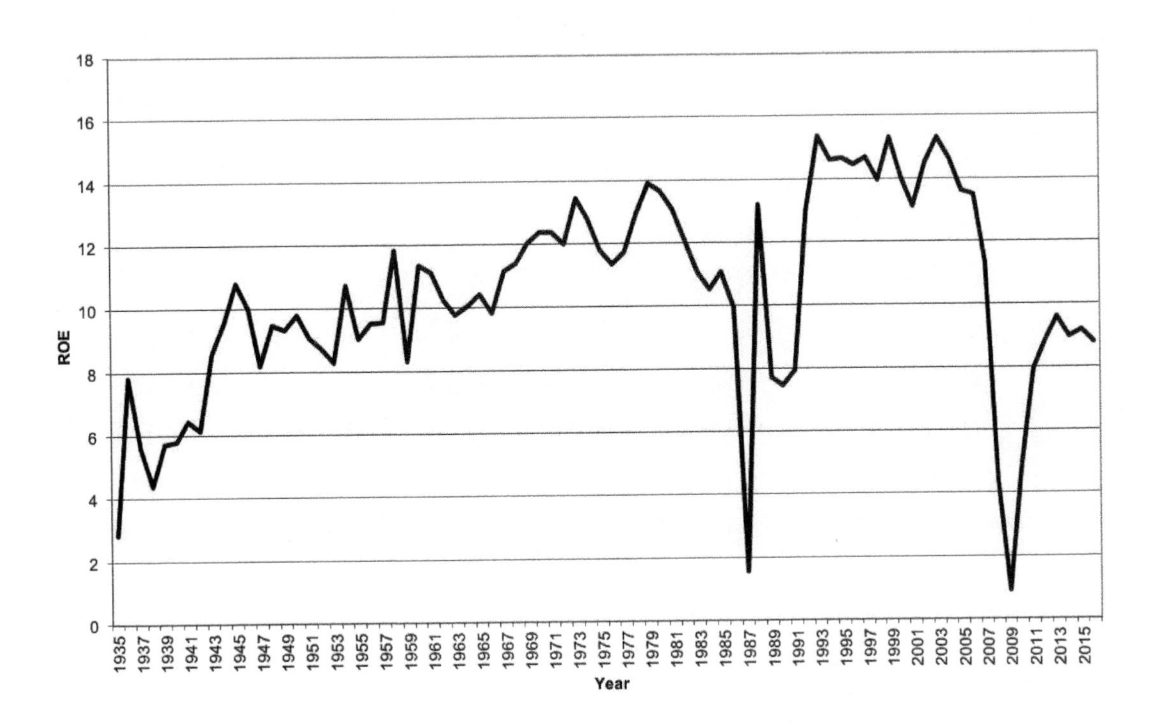

The Federal Reserve labels the entities that have arisen from the recent wave of mergers large, complex banking organizations (LCBOs) or large, complex financial institutions (LCFIs). Those names, though, also point to the costs of the new regime. *Consolidation may have made banks and other financial institutions too big, complex, and politically potent to regulate effectively. Also, to justify their merger activities to shareholders, many banks have increased their profitability, not by becoming more efficient, but by taking on higher levels of risk.* Finally, conglomerates may be able to engage in many different activities, thereby diversifying their revenues and risks, but they may not do any of them very well, thereby actually increasing the risk of failure. A combination of consolidation, conglomeration, and concentration helped to trigger a systemic financial crisis acute enough to negatively affect the national and world economies.

Herfindahl index

A measure of market concentration calculated by summing the square of the market shares of the companies operating in a given market.

Today, the U.S. banking industry is far more concentrated than during most of its past. In other words, a few large banks have a larger share of assets, deposits, and capital than ever before. That may in turn give those banks considerable market power, the ability to charge more for loans and to pay less for deposits. Figure 10.6 shows the increase in the industry's **Herfindahl index**, which is a measure of market concentration calculated by taking the sum of the squares of the market shares of each firm in a particular industry. Whether scaled between 0 and 1 or 0 and 10,000, the Herfindahl index is low (near zero) if an industry is composed of numerous small firms, and it is high (near 1 or 10,000) the closer an industry is to monopoly (1 × 1 = 1; 100 × 100 = 10,000). While the Herfindahl index of the U.S. banking sector has increased markedly in recent years, thousands of small banks keep the national index from reaching 1,800, the magic number that triggers greater antitrust scrutiny by the Justice Department. At the end of 2006, for example, 3,246 of the nation's 7,402 commercial banks had assets of less than $100 million. Another 3,662 banks had assets greater than $100 million but less than $1 billion, leaving only 494 banks with assets over $1 billion.

FIGURE 10.6 Concentration in the U.S. banking sector, 2005–2016

That's more concentrated than my orange juice!

Year	H-Assets	H-Deposits	H-Equity
2005	392	269	240
2006	337	302	253
2007	364	333	267
2008	412	379	318
2009	423	381	357
2010	451	414	381
2011	468	435	401
2012	469	434	398
2013	473	447	416
2014	486	460	433
2015	451	428	422
2016	465	439	419

Those 500 or so big banks, however, control the vast bulk of the industry's assets (and hence liabilities and capital too). As Figure 10.7 shows, the nation's ten largest banks are rapidly gaining market share. *Nevertheless, U.S. banking is still far less concentrated than the banking sectors of most other countries.* In Canada, for example, the commercial bank Herfindahl index hovers around 1,600, and in Colombia and Chile, the biggest five banks make more than 60 percent of all loans. The United States is such a large country and banking, despite the changes wrought by the Information Revolution, is still such a local business that certain regions have levels of concentration high enough that some fear that banks there are earning quasi-monopoly rents, the high profits associated with oligopolistic and monopolistic market structures. The good news is that bank entry is fairly easy, so if banks become too profitable in some regions, new banks will form to compete with them, bringing the Herfindahl index, n-firm concentration ratios, and ultimately bank profits back in line. Since the mid-1980s, scores to hundreds of new banks, called de novo banks, began operation in the United States each year. After a lull following the financial crisis of 2007–2009, the number of new banks trying to form began to increase again starting in 2016.

FIGURE 10.7 Shares of top ten U.S. banks, 2005–2016

Yep, more concentrated any way you slice it.

Year	Assets	Deposits	Equity
2005	43	42	37
2006	45	43	40
2007	47	44	41
2008	48	47	40
2009	49	48	44
2010	50	48	46
2011	51	51	47
2012	52	51	48
2013	53	52	49
2014	53	52	50
2015	52	51	49
2016	52	51	49

Stop and Think Box

In 2003, Canada was home to the banks (and a handful of small ones that can be safely ignored) listed in the following chart. How concentrated was the Canadian banking sector as measured by the five-firm concentration ratio? The Herfindahl index?

FIGURE 10.8 Canadian bank assets, 2003

Bank Name	Assets $C Millions
Scotiabank	211,473
Royal Bank of Canada	300,894
Canadian Imperial	206,114
Bank of Montreal	190,106
Toronto-Dominion	202,233
Desjardins Group	73,237
National Bank of Canada	59,930
HSBC Bank Canada	26,510
Laurentian Bank	12,505
VanCity	6,968
Total	1,289,970

The five-firm concentration ratio is calculated simply by summing the market shares of the five largest banks:

FIGURE 10.9 Five-firm concentration ratio

Bank Name	Assets $C Millions	Market Share
Scotiabank	211,473	16.39364
Royal Bank of Canada	300,894	23.32566
Canadian Imperial	206,114	15.9782
Bank of Montreal	190,106	14.73724
Toronto-Dominion	202,233	15.67734
Total		86.11208

So the five-bank concentration ratio (for assets) in Canada in 2003 was 86 percent.

The Herfindahl index is calculated by summing the squares of the market shares of each bank:

FIGURE 10.10 Herfindahl index

Bank Name	Assets $C Millions	Market Share	Squared
Scotiabank	211,473	16.39364	268.7513361
Royal Bank of Canada	300,894	23.32566	544.0863555
Canadian Imperial	206,114	15.9782	255.3029086
Bank of Montreal	190,106	14.73724	217.1863003
Toronto-Dominion	202,233	15.67734	245.7790313
Desjardins Group	73,237	5.677419	32.23308485
National Bank of Canada	59,930	4.645844	21.5838709
HSBC Bank Canada	26,510	2.055087	4.223380738
Laurentian	12,505	0.969402	0.939740992

So the Herfindahl index for bank assets in Canada in 2003 was 1,590.

Starting a new bank is not as difficult as it sounds. About twenty or so incorporators need to put about $50,000 each at risk for the year or two it takes to gain regulatory approval. They must then subscribe at least the same amount in a private placement of stock that provides the bank with some of its capital. The new bank can then begin operations, usually with two branches, one in an asset-rich area, the other in a deposit-rich one. Consultants like Dan Hudson of NuBank.com help new banks to form and begin operations.[11] Due to the ease of creating new banks and regulations that effectively cap the size of megabanks, and the handful of U.S. banks with over $1 trillion of assets, many observers think that the U.S. banking sector will remain competitive, composed of numerous small banks, a few (dozen, even score) megabanks, and hundreds of large regional players. The small and regional banks will survive by exploiting geographical and specialized niches, like catering to depositors who enjoy interacting with live people instead of machines. Small banks also tend to lend to small businesses, of which America has many. Despite funny television commercials to the contrary, large banks will also lend to small businesses, but smaller, community banks are often better at it because they know more about local markets and borrowers and hence can better assess their business plans.[12]

The United States also allows individuals to establish other types of depository institutions, including savings and loan associations, mutual savings banks, and credit unions. Few new savings banks are created, and many existing ones have taken commercial bank charters or merged with commercial banks, but new credit union formation is fairly brisk. Credit unions are mutual (that is, owned by depositors rather than shareholders) depository institutions organized around a group of people who share a common bond, like the same employer. They are tax-exempt and historically quite small. Recently, regulators have allowed them to expand so that they can maintain minimum efficient scale and diversify their asset portfolios more widely.

The U.S. banking industry is also increasingly international in scope. Thus, *foreign banks can enter the U.S. market relatively easily*. Today, foreign banks hold more than 10 percent of total U.S. bank assets and make more than 16 percent of loans to U.S. corporations. Foreign banks can buy U.S. banks or they can simply establish branches in the United States. Foreign banks used to be subject to less stringent regulations than domestic banks, but that was changed in 1978. Increasingly, bank regulations worldwide have converged.

The internationalization of banking also means that U.S. banks can operate in other countries. To date, about 100 U.S. banks have branches abroad, up from just eight in 1960. International banking has grown along with international trade and foreign direct investment. International banking is also a way to diversify assets, tap markets where spreads are larger than in the United States, and get a piece of the Eurodollar market. Eurodollars are dollar-denominated deposits in foreign banks that help international businesses to conduct trade and banks to avoid reserve requirements and other taxing regulations and capital controls. London, Singapore, and the Cayman Islands are the main centers for Eurodollars and, not surprisingly, favorite locations for U.S. banks to establish overseas branches. To help finance trade, U.S. banks also have a strong presence elsewhere, particularly in East Asia and in Latin America.

The nature of banking in the United States and abroad is changing, apparently converging on the European, specifically the British, model. In some countries in continental Europe, like Germany and Switzerland, so-called universal banks that offer commercial and investment banking services and insurance prevail. In other countries, like Great Britain and its commonwealth members, full-blown financial conglomerates are less common, but most banks engage in both commercial and investment banking activities. Meanwhile, foreign securities markets are modeling themselves after American markets, growing larger and more sophisticated. Increasingly, the world's financial system is becoming one. That should make it more efficient, but it also raises fears of financial catastrophe, a point to which we shall return.

Key Takeaways

- Industry consolidation is measured by the number of banks in existence at a given time.
- As the number of banks declines (because mergers and bankruptcies exceed new bank formation), the industry is said to become more consolidated. It is important because a more consolidated industry may be safer and more profitable as smaller, weaker institutions are swallowed up by larger, stronger ones.
- However, consolidation can also lead to higher costs for consumers and borrowers and poorer service.
- Bigger banks are likely to be more diversified than smaller ones, but they might also take on higher levels of risk, thereby threatening the stability of the financial system.
- Conglomeration refers to the scope of activities that a bank or other financial intermediary is allowed to engage in.
- Traditionally, U.S. banks could engage in commercial banking activities or investment banking activities, but not both, and they could not sell or underwrite insurance. Due to recent regulatory changes, however, banks and other financial intermediaries and facilitators like brokerages can now merge into the same company or exist under the same holding company umbrella.
- This deregulation may increase competition for financial intermediaries, thereby driving innovation. It could also lead, however, to the creation of financial conglomerates that are too large and complex to regulate adequately.
- Industry concentration is a proxy for competition and is measured by the n-firm concentration of assets (revenues, capital, etc., where *n* is 1, 3, 5, 10, 25, 50, etc.) or by the Herfindahl index, the sum of the square of the market shares (again for assets, deposits, revenues, capital, etc.) of each company in the industry or in a given city, state, or region.

- Concentration is important because a highly concentrated industry may be less competitive, leading to less innovation, higher costs for borrowers, outsized profits for suppliers (in this case banks), and a more fragile (prone to systemic crisis) banking system.
- On the other hand, as banking has grown more concentrated, individual banks have become more geographically diversified, which may help them to better weather economic downturns.

10.6 Suggested Reading

Anderloni, Luisa, David Llewellyn, and Reinhard Schmidt. *Financial Innovation in Retail and Corporate Banking*. Northampton, MA: Edward Elgar, 2009.

Banner, Stuart. *Anglo-American Securities Regulation: Cultural and Political Roots, 1690–1860*. New York: Cambridge University Press, 2002.

Freedman, Roy. *Introduction to Financial Technology*. New York: Academic Press, 2006.

Shiller, Robert. *The New Financial Order: Risk in the 21st Century*. Princeton, NJ: Princeton University Press, 2004.

Wright, Robert E. *The Wealth of Nations Rediscovered: Integration and Expansion in American Financial Markets, 1780–1850*. New York: Cambridge University Press, 2002.

Wright, Robert E., and David J. Cowen. *Financial Founding Fathers: The Men Who Made America Rich*. Chicago, IL: Chicago University Press, 2006.

Wright, Robert E., and George D. Smith. *Mutually Beneficial: The Guardian and Life Insurance in America*. New York: New York University Press, 2004.

Endnotes

1. www.augie.edu/academics/areas-study/nef-family-chair-political-economy/thomas-willing-institute
2. www.youtube.com/watch?v=BJ7EIKbnnkw
3. Raghuram Ragan and Rodney Ramcharan, "Constituencies and Legislation: Fight Over the McFadden Act of 1927," NBER Working Paper No. w17266 (August 2011). papers.ssrn.com/sol3/papers.cfm?abstract_id=1905859.
4. www.officemuseum.com/IMagesWWW/Tabulating_Machine_Co_card_punch_left_end.JPG
5. www.officemuseum.com/IMagesWWW/1904_1912_Graphotype_Addressograph_Co_Chicago_OM.JPG
6. ccs.mit.edu/papers/CCSWP196.html
7. www.bankrate.com/brm/calc_vml/refi/refi.asp
8. Doug Arner, *Financial Stability, Economic Growth, and the Role of Law* (New York: Cambridge University Press, 2007), 263.
9. https://www.ffiec.gov/nicpubweb/nicweb/HCSGreaterThan10B.aspx
10. https://en.wiktionary.org/wiki/what's_good_for_the_goose_is_good_for_the_gander
11. www.nubank.com
12. https://ilsr.org/banks-and-small-business-lending/

CHAPTER 11

The Economics of Financial Regulation

Chapter Objectives

By the end of this chapter, students should be able to:

1. Explain why the government can't simply legislate bad things out of existence.
2. Describe the public interest and private interest models of government and explain why they are important.
3. Explain how asymmetric information interferes with regulatory efforts.
4. Describe how government regulators exacerbated the Great Depression.
5. Describe how government regulators made the Savings and Loan Crisis worse.
6. Assess recent regulatory reforms in the United States and both Basel accords.

11.1 Market Failures and Public Choice

Learning Objectives

1. Why can't the government legislate bad things out of existence?
2. Which model of government, public interest or private interest, is the most accurate depiction of reality?

market failures

The inefficient allocation of resources by a free market caused by asymmetric information, externalities (costs or benefits not reflected in market prices), natural monopolies or other forms of excessive market power, and public goods (goods like national defense that cannot be profitably supplied by non-government entities due to free-rider problems).

loophole mining

The search for ways around regulations.

lobbying

Attempts to change regulations.

unintended consequences

Events (usually negative) caused by regulations that lawmakers did not foresee.

public interest model

A model of government developed by political scientists that posits that politicians, bureaucrats, and other government workers serve the public in lieu of themselves.

public choice

See private interest model.

private interest model

A model of government developed by economists that posits that politicians, bureaucrats, and other government workers serve themselves in lieu of the citizens or public.

Some regulations are clearly salubrious and should be retained. The main justifications for financial system regulation—**market failures**—do occur, and government regulations can, and sometimes have, helped to mitigate them. Like everything else in life, however, regulations are costly (not gratis) and hence entail trade-offs. As detailed in another chapter, they induce perfectly legal but bureaucratically disruptive **loophole mining** and **lobbying** activities. They can also lead to severely twisted, **unintended consequences**, like banks purposely making bad loans.

The goal of this chapter is not to bash all regulation but rather to critique specific financial regulations in the hopes of creating better regulatory policies in the (hopefully near) future. The place to start, I believe, is to think about what regulators and regulations cannot do, and that is fix the world by decree. *Simply making an activity illegal does not mean that it will stop.* Because the government faces a budget constraint and opportunity costs, it can't afford to monitor everyone all the time. What's bad for some is often good for others, so many people willingly supply illegal goods or activities. As a result, many illegal activities are commonplace; in no particular order, sodomy, drug use, reckless use of automobiles, and music piracy come to mind. This may seem like a simple point, but many people believe that regulation can really work if only regulations, and the regulators charged with enforcing them, are strengthened. If regulations failed in the past, they believe that means regulators needed more money or authority, or both.

The problem with this view, however, is that government officials may not be the angels many people assume they are. If you believe that government is infallible, it's not your fault. Especially if you went through the U.S. public school system, you likely learned an interpretation of government called the public interest model. As its name suggests, *the***public interest model***posits that government officials work in the interests of the public, of "the people," if you will.* It's the sort of thing Abraham Lincoln had in mind in his famous Gettysburg Address when he said "that government of the people, by the people, for the people, shall not perish from the earth."[1] That's outstanding political rhetoric, better than anything current spin artists concoct, but is it a fair representation of reality?

Many economists think not. They believe that private interest prevails, even in the government. *According to their model, called the* **public choice** *or, less confusingly, the* **private interest model***, politicians and bureaucrats often behave in their own interests rather than those of the public.* Of course, they don't go around saying that they need law X or regulation Y "to help me to get rich via bribes, to bailout my brother-in-law, or to ensure that I soon receive a cushy job in the private sector." Rather, they say that society needs law X or regulation Y to protect widows and orphans, to stymie the efforts of bad guys, or to make the rich pay for their success.

In many countries, the ones we will call "predatory" in the context of the Growth Diamond model, the private interest model clearly holds sway. In rich countries, the public interest model becomes more plausible. Nevertheless, many economic regulations, though clothed in public interest rhetoric, appear on close inspection to conform to the private interest model. As University of Chicago economist and Nobel Laureate George Stigler[2] pointed out decades ago, regulators are often "captured"[3] by the industry they regulate. *In other words, the industry establishes regulations for itself by influencing the decisions of regulators.* Financial regulators, as we'll see, are no exception.

Regardless of regulators' and politicians' motivations, another very sticky question arises: *could regulators stop bad activities, events, and people even if they wanted to? The answer in many contexts appears to be an unequivocal "No!"* The reason is our old nemesis, asymmetric information, which, readers should recall, inheres in nature and pervades all. It flummoxes governments as much as markets and intermediaries. The implications of this insight are devastating for the effectiveness of regulators and their regulations, as Figure 11.1 makes clear.

FIGURE 11.1 Asymmetric information and regulation

Round and round we go, where the cycle stops, nobody knows!

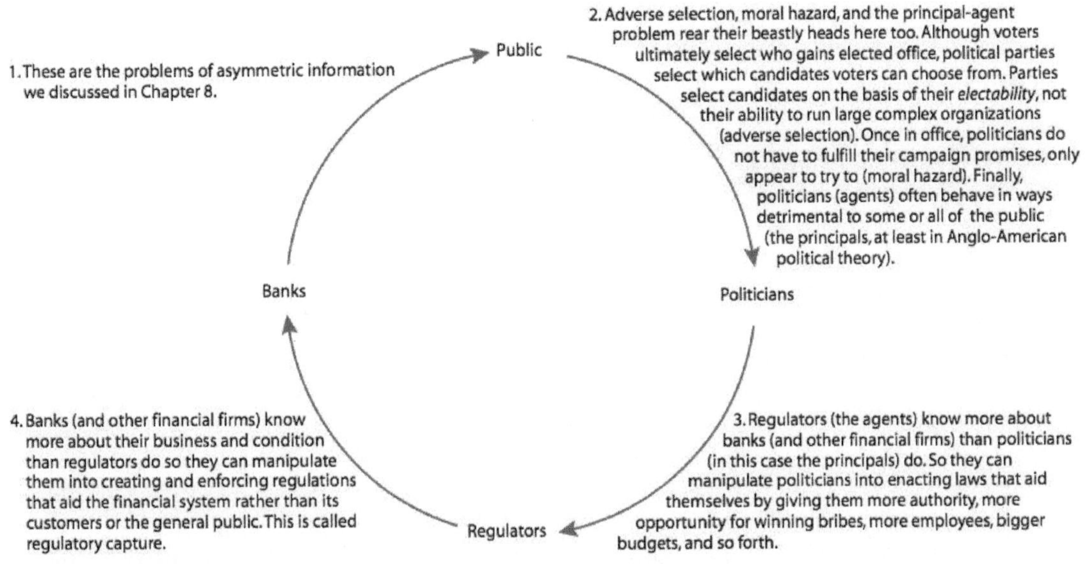

Source: Adapted from James R. Barth, Gerard Caprio, Jr., and Ross Levine, *Rethinking Bank Regulation: Til Angels Govern* (New York: Cambridge University Press, 2006), 6.

Although Figure 11.1 is aesthetically pleasing (great job, guys!) it does not paint a pretty picture. *Due to multiple levels of nearly intractable problems of asymmetric information,* **democracy** *is no guarantee that government will serve the public interest.* Matters are even worse in societies still plagued by **predatory government**, where corruption further fouls up the works by giving politicians, regulators, and bankers (and other financiers) incentives to perpetuate the current system, no matter how suboptimal it may be from the public's point of view.

democracy

A type of government that is of, for, and by the people because it allows citizens to choose candidates and policies via elections.

predatory government

A type of government that is of, for, and by the ruling elite and that fails to supply basic public goods like life, liberty, and property.

And if you really want to get your head spinning, consider this: agency problems within the government, within regulatory bureaucracies, and within banks abound. Within banks, traders and loan officers want to keep their jobs, earn promotions, and bring home large bonuses. They can do the latter two by taking large risks, and sometimes they choose to do so. Sometimes shareholders want to take on much larger risks than managers or depositors or other debt holders do. Sometimes it's the managers who have incentives to place big bets, to get their stock options "in the money."[4] Within bureaucracies, regulators have incentives to hide their mistakes and to take credit for good outcomes, even if they had little or nothing to do with them. The same is true for the government, where the legislature may try to discredit the executive's policies, or vice versa, and withhold information or even spread disinformation to "prove" its case.

Stop and Think Box

In the 1910s and early 1920s, a majority of U.S. states passed securities regulations called Blue Sky Laws that ostensibly sought to prevent slimy securities dealers from selling nothing but the blue sky to poor, defenseless widows and orphans. Can you figure out what was really going on? (*Hint*: Recall that this was a period of traditional banking, unit banks, the 3-6-3 rule, and all that. Recall, too, that securities markets are an alternative method of linking investors to borrowers.)

We probably gave it away with that last hint. Blue Sky Laws, scholars now realize, were veiled attempts to protect the monopolies of unit bankers upset about losing business to the securities markets. Unable to garner public sympathy for their plight, the bankers instead spoke in terms of public interest, of defrauded widows and orphans. There were certainly some scams about, but not enough to warrant the more virulent Blue Sky Laws, which actually gave state officials the power to forbid issuance of securities they didn't like, and in some states, that was most of them!

It's okay if you feel a bit uneasy with these new ideas. I think that as adults you can handle straight talk. It'll be better for everyone—you, me, our children and grandchildren—if you learn to look at the government's actions with a critical eye. *Regulators have failed in the past and will do so again unless we align the interests of all the major parties depicted in* Figure 11.1 *more closely, empowering market forces to do most of the heavy lifting.*

Key Takeaways

- The government can't legislate bad things away because it can't be every place at once. Like the rest of us, government faces budget constraints and opportunity costs. Therefore, it cannot stop activities that some people enjoy or find profitable.
- According to the public interest model, government tries to enact laws, regulations, and policies that benefit the public.
- The private interest (or public choice) model, by contrast, suggests that government officials enact laws that are in their own private interest.
- It is important to know which model is a more accurate description of reality because the models have very different implications for our attitudes toward regulation.
- If one believes the public interest model is usually correct, then one will be more likely to call for government regulation, even if one admits that regulatory goals may in fact be difficult to achieve regardless of the intentions of politicians and bureaucrats.
- If one believes the private interest model is a more accurate depiction of the real world, one will be more skeptical of government regulation.
- Asymmetric information creates a principal-agent problem between the public and elected officials, another principal-agent problem between those officials and regulators, and yet another principal-agent problem between regulators and banks (and other financial firms) because in each case, one party (politicians, regulators, banks) knows more than the other (public, politicians, regulators).
- So there are at least three places where the public's interest can be stymied: in political elections, in the interaction between Congress and the president and regulatory agencies, and in the interaction between regulators and the regulated. And that's ignoring the often extensive agency problems found *within* governments, regulatory agencies, and financial institutions!

11.2 The Great Depression as Regulatory Failure

Learning Objectives

1. How did the government exacerbate the Great Depression?

externalities

Costs or benefits of an economic activity that are not included in the price, that are not internalized by the buyer and/or seller. Negative externalities, like pollution, impose costs on society; positive externalities, like education, provide societal benefits.

Time and time again, government regulators have either failed to stop financial crises or have exacerbated them. Examples are too numerous to discuss in detail here, so we will address only two of the more egregious cases, the Great Depression of the 1930s and, in the next section, the Savings and Loan (S&L) Crisis of the 1980s. Generally, when economic matters go FUBAR (**F**ouled **U**p **B**eyond **A**ll **R**ecognition in polite circles), observers blame either "market failures" like asymmetric information and **externalities**, or they blame the government. Reality is rarely that simple. *Most major economic foul-ups stem from a combination of market and government failures, what I like to call hybrid failures.* So while it would be an exaggeration to claim that government policies were the only causes of the Great Depression or the Savings and Loan Crisis, it is fair to say that they made matters worse, much worse.

The stock market crash of 1929 did not start the Great Depression, but it did give the economy a strong push downhill.[5] A precipitous decline in stock prices like that of 1929 can cause uncertainty to increase and balance sheets to deteriorate, worsening asymmetric information problems and leading to a decline in economic activity. That, in turn, can cause bank panics, further increases in asymmetric information, and yet further declines in economic activity followed by an unanticipated decline in the price level. *As* Figure 11.2 *shows, that is precisely what happened during the Great Depression—per capita gross domestic product (GDP) shrank, the number of bankruptcies soared, M1 and M2 (measures of the money supply) declined, and so did the price level.*

FIGURE 11.2 Major macro variables during the Great Depression
The Great Depression was great as in big, not as in good.

Year	Nominal Per Capita GDP ($)	Price Level (%)	Bank Failures (#)	M1 ($ billions)	M2 ($ billions)
1928	808	-1.38	498	26.4	46.4
1929	851	0.00	659	26.6	46.6
1930	741	-2.51	1,350	25.8	45.7
1931	617	-8.80	2,293	24.1	42.7
1932	470	-10.31	1,453	21.1	36.1
1933	449	-5.12	4,000	19.9	32.2
1934	522	3.32	55	21.9	34.4
1935	576	2.54	28	25.9	39.1
1936	654	0.95	73	29.6	43.5
1937	713	3.61	78	30.9	45.7

Weren't evil financiers completely responsible for this mess, as nine out of ten people thought at the time? Absolutely not. For starters, very few financiers benefited from the depression and they did not have the ability to cause such a mess. Most would have stopped the downward spiral if it was in their power to do so, as J. P. Morgan did when panic seized the financial system in 1907.[6] In fact, only the government had the resources and institutions to stop the Great Depression and it failed to do so. *Mistake number one occurred during the 1920s, when the government allowed stock and real estate prices to rise to dizzying heights.* (The Dow Jones Industrial Average started the decade at 108.76, dropped to around 60, then began a slow climb to 200 by the end of 1927. It hit 300 by the end of 1928 and 350 by August 1929.)[7] By slowly raising interest rates beginning in, say, mid-1928, the Federal Reserve (Fed) could have deflated the stock market **bubble** before it grew to enormous proportions and burst in 1929.

bubble

Occurs when the price of an asset rises significantly above its rational range, with its price based on fundamentals like interest rates, profitability, and so forth.

lender of last resort (LLR)

A clearinghouse, central bank, or government that lends during crises, usually by following some variant of Bagehot's Rule/ Hamilton's Rule.

Bagehot's/Hamilton's Rule

A policy, described first by Alexander Hamilton and later by Walter Bagehot, in which, during a crisis, a lender of last resort lends freely at a penalty rate to all borrowers who can post sufficient collateral.

clearinghouses

Support institutions that help banks to clear sums due to each other arising from checks, notes, loans, and other banking activities. Prior to 1914, clearinghouses also acted as lenders of last resort during panics.

Mistake number two occurred after the crash, in late 1929 and 1930, when the Federal Reserve raised interest rates. A much better policy response at that point would have been to lower interest rates in order to help troubled banks and stimulate business investment and hence private job growth. In addition, the Federal Reserve did not behave like a **lender of last resort (LLR)** during the crisis and follow **Bagehot's/Hamilton's Rule**. Before the Fed began operations in the fall of 1914, regional **clearinghouses** had acted as LLRs, but during the Depression they assumed, wrongly as it turned out, that the Fed had relieved them of that responsibility. They were, accordingly, unprepared to thwart major bank runs.[8]

The government's third mistake was its banking policy. *The United States was home to tens of thousands of tiny unit banks that simply were not large or diversified enough to ride out the depression.* If a factory or other major employer succumbed, the local bank too was doomed. Depositors understood this, so at the first sign of trouble they ran on their banks, pulling out their deposits before they went under. Their actions guaranteed that their banks would indeed fail. Meanwhile, across the border in Canada, which was home to a few large and highly diversified banks, few bank disturbances took place. California also weathered the Great Depression relatively well, in part because its banks, which freely branched throughout the large state, enjoyed relatively well-diversified assets and hence avoided the worst of the bank crises.

The government's fourth failure was to raise tariffs in a misguided attempt to "beggar thy neighbor."[9] Detailed analysis of this failure, which falls outside the bailiwick of finance, I'll leave to your international economics textbook and a case elsewhere in this book. Here, we'll just paraphrase Mr. Mackey from South Park: "Tariffs are bad, mmmkay?"[10]

But what about Franklin Delano Roosevelt (FDR)[11] and his New Deal?[12] Didn't the new administration stop the Great Depression, particularly via deposit insurance, Glass-Steagall, securities market reforms, and reassuring speeches about having nothing to fear but fear itself?[13] The United States did suffer its most acute banking crisis in March 1933, just as FDR took office on March 4.[14] (The Twentieth Amendment, ratified in 1938, changed the presidential inauguration date to January 20, which it is to this day.) But many suspect that FDR himself brought the crisis on by increasing uncertainty about the new administration's policy path. *Whatever the cause of the crisis, it shattered confidence in the banking system. FDR's creation of a deposit insurance scheme under the aegis of a new federal agency, the Federal Deposit Insurance Corporation (FDIC), did restore confidence, inducing people to stop running on the banks and thereby stopping the economy's death spiral.* Since then, bank runs have been rare occurrences directed at specific shaky banks and not system-wide disturbances as during the Great Depression and earlier banking crises.

But as with everything in life, deposit insurance is far from cost-free. In fact, the latest research suggests it is a wash. Deposit insurance does prevent bank runs because depositors know the insurance fund will repay them if their bank goes belly up. (Today, it insures $250,000 per depositor per insured bank. For details, browse https://www.fdic.gov/deposit/deposits/.) However, insurance also reduces depositor monitoring, which allows bankers to take on added risk. In the nineteenth century, depositors disciplined banks that took on too much risk by withdrawing their deposits. As we've seen, that decreases the size of the bank and reduces reserves, forcing bankers to decrease their risk profile. With deposit insurance, depositors (quite rationally) blithely ignore the adverse selection problem and shift their funds to wherever they will fetch the most interest. They don't ask how Shaky Bank is able to pay 15 percent for six-month certificates of deposit (CDs) when other banks pay only 5 percent. Who cares, they reason, my deposits are insured! Indeed, but as we'll learn below, taxpayers insure the insurer.

Another New Deal financial reform, Glass-Steagall, in no way helped the U.S. economy or financial system and may have hurt both. For over half a century, Glass-Steagall prevented U.S. banks from simultaneously engaging in commercial (taking deposits and making loans) and investment banking (underwriting securities and advising on mergers) activities. Only two groups clearly gained from the legislation, politicians who could thump their chests on the campaign stump and claim to have saved the country from greedy financiers and, ironically enough, big investment banks. The latter, it turns out, wrote the act and did so in such a way that it protected their oligopoly from the competition of commercial banks and smaller, more retail-oriented investment banks.

The act was clearly unnecessary from an economic standpoint because most countries had no such legislation and suffered no ill effects because of its absence. (The Dodd-Frank Act's Volcker Rule represents a better approach because it outlaws various dubious *practices*, like proprietary trading, not valid organizational *forms*).

The Security and Exchange Commission's (SEC) genesis is almost as tawdry and its record almost as bad. The SEC's stated goal, to increase the transparency of America's financial markets, was a laudable one. Unfortunately, the SEC simply does not do its job very well. As the late, great, free-market proponent Milton Friedman put it:

> *"You are not free to raise funds on the capital markets[15] unless you fill out the numerous pages of forms the SEC requires and unless you satisfy the SEC that the prospectus you propose to issue presents such a bleak picture of your prospects that no investor in his right mind would invest in your project if he took the prospectus literally.[16] And getting SEC approval may cost upwards of $100,000—which certainly discourages the small firms our government professes to help."[17]*

Stop and Think Box

As noted above, the FDIC insures bank deposits up to $250,000 *per depositor per insured bank*. What if an investor wants to deposit $1 million or $1 billion? Must the investor put most of her money at risk?

Depositors can loophole mine as well as anyone. And they did, or, to be more precise, intermediaries known as deposit brokers did. Deposit brokers chopped up big deposits into insured-sized chunks, then spread them all over creation. The telecommunications revolution made this relatively easy and cheap to do, and the S&L crisis created many a zombie bank willing to pay high interest for deposits.

Key Takeaway

- In addition to imposing high tariffs, the government exacerbated the Great Depression by (1) allowing the asset bubble of the late 1920s to continue; (2) responding to the crash inappropriately by raising the interest rate and restricting M1 and M2; and (3) passing reforms of dubious long-term efficacy, including deposit insurance, Glass-Steagall, and the SEC.

11.3 The Savings and Loan Regulatory Debacle

Learning Objective

1. How did regulators exacerbate the Savings and Loan Crisis of the 1980s?

3-6-3 rule

Tongue-in-cheek rule of thumb for heavily regulated banks that took deposits at 3 percent, made loans at 6 percent, and allowed their managers to leave at 3 p.m. to play golf.

Although the economy improved after 1933, regulatory regimes did not. Ever fearful of a repeat of the Great Depression, U.S. regulators sought to make banks highly safe and highly profitable so none would ever dare to fail. Basically, the government regulated the interest rate, assuring banks a nice profit—that's what the **3-6-3 rule** was all about. Regulators also made it difficult to start a new bank to keep competition levels down, all in the name of stability. *The game worked well until the late 1960s, then went to hell in a handbasket as technological breakthroughs and the Great Inflation conspired to destroy traditional banking.*

Here's where things get interesting. *Savings and loan associations were particularly hard hit by the changed financial environment because their gaps were huge.* The sources of their funds were savings accounts and their uses were mortgages, most of them for thirty years at fixed rates. Like this:

Typical Savings and Loan Bank Balance Sheet (Millions USD)	
Assets	Liabilities
Reserves $10	Deposits $130
Securities $10	Borrowings $15
Mortgages $130	Capital $15
Other assets $10	
Totals $160	$160

Along comes the Great Inflation and there go the deposits. Then S&L's balance sheets looked like this:

Typical Savings and Loan Bank Balance Sheet (Millions USD)	
Assets	Liabilities
Reserves $1	Deposits $100
Securities $1	Borrowings $30
Mortgages $130	Capital $10
Other assets $8	
Totals $140	$140

This bank is clearly in deep doodoo. Were it alone, it soon would have lost its remaining capital and failed. But there were some 750 of them in like situation. So they went to the regulators and asked for help. The regulators were happy to oblige because they did not want to have a bunch of failed banks on their hands, especially given that the deposits of those banks were insured. *So regulators eliminated the interest rate caps and allowed S&Ls to engage in a variety of new activities, like making commercial real estate loans and buying junk bonds, hitherto forbidden. Given the demise of traditional banking, that was a reasonable response. The problem was that most S&L bankers didn't have a clue about how to do anything other than traditional banking. Most of them got chewed.* Their balance sheets then began to resemble a train wreck:

Typical Savings and Loan Bank Balance Sheet (Millions USD)	
Assets	Liabilities
Reserves $1	Deposits $120
Securities $1	Borrowings $22
Mortgages $130	Capital $0
Other assets $10	
Totals $142	$142

Now comes the most egregious part. *Fearful of losing their jobs, regulators kept these economically dead (capital < $0) banks alive. Instead of shutting them down, they engaged in what is called* **regulatory forbearance**. Specifically, they allowed S&Ls to add "goodwill" to the asset side of their balance sheets, restoring them to life—on paper. (Technically, they allowed the banks to switch from generally accepted accounting principles [GAAP] to regulatory accounting principles [RAP].) Seems like a cool thing for the regulators to do, right? Wrong! A teacher can pass a kid who can't read, but the kid still can't read. Similarly, a regulator can pass a bank with no capital, but still can't make the bank viable. In fact, the bank situation is worse because the kid has other chances to learn to read. By contrast, zombie banks, as these S&Ls were called, have little hope of recovery. Regulators should have shot them in the head instead, which as any zombie-movie fan knows is the only way to stop the undead dead in their tracks.[18]

regulatory forbearance

Whenever regulators, for whatever reason, consciously decide not to enforce one or more regulations.

Recall that if somebody has no capital, no skin in the game, to borrow Warren Buffett's phrase again, moral hazard will be extremely high because the person is playing only with other people's money. In this case, the money wasn't even that of depositors but rather of the deposit insurer, a government agency. *The managers of the S&Ls did what anyone in the same situation would do: they rolled the dice, engaging in highly risky investments funded with deposits and borrowings for which they paid a hefty premium.* In other words, they borrowed from depositors and other lenders at high rates and invested in highly risky loans. A few got lucky and pulled their banks out of the red. Most of the risky loans, however, quickly turned sour. When the whole thing was over, their balance sheets looked like this:

Typical Savings and Loan Bank Balance Sheet (Millions USD)	
Assets	Liabilities
Reserves $10	Deposits $200
Securities $10	Borrowings $100
Mortgages $100	Capital –$60
Goodwill $30	
Crazy, risky loans $70	
Other assets $20	
Totals $240	$240

The regulators could no longer forbear. *The insurance fund could not meet the deposit liabilities of the thousands of failed S&Ls, so the bill ended up in the lap of U.S. taxpayers.*

Stop and Think Box

In the 1980s, in response to the Great Inflation and the technological revolution, regulators in Scandinavia (Sweden, Norway, and Finland) deregulated their heavily regulated banking systems. Bankers who usually lent only to the best borrowers at government mandated rates suddenly found themselves competing for both depositors and borrowers. What happened?

Scandinavia suffered from worse banking crises than the United States. In particular, Scandinavian bankers were not very good at screening good from bad borrowers because they had long been accustomed to lending to just the best. They inevitably made many mistakes, which led to defaults and ultimately asset and capital write-downs.

The most depressing aspect of this story is that the United States has unusually *good* regulators. As Figure 11.3 shows, other countries have suffered through far worse banking crises and losses. Note that at 3 percent of U.S. GDP, the S&L crisis was no picnic, but it pales in comparison to the losses in Argentina, Indonesia, China, Jamaica, and elsewhere.

FIGURE 11.3 Banking crises around the globe through 2002
Most of the white nations had no Western-style banks to fail!

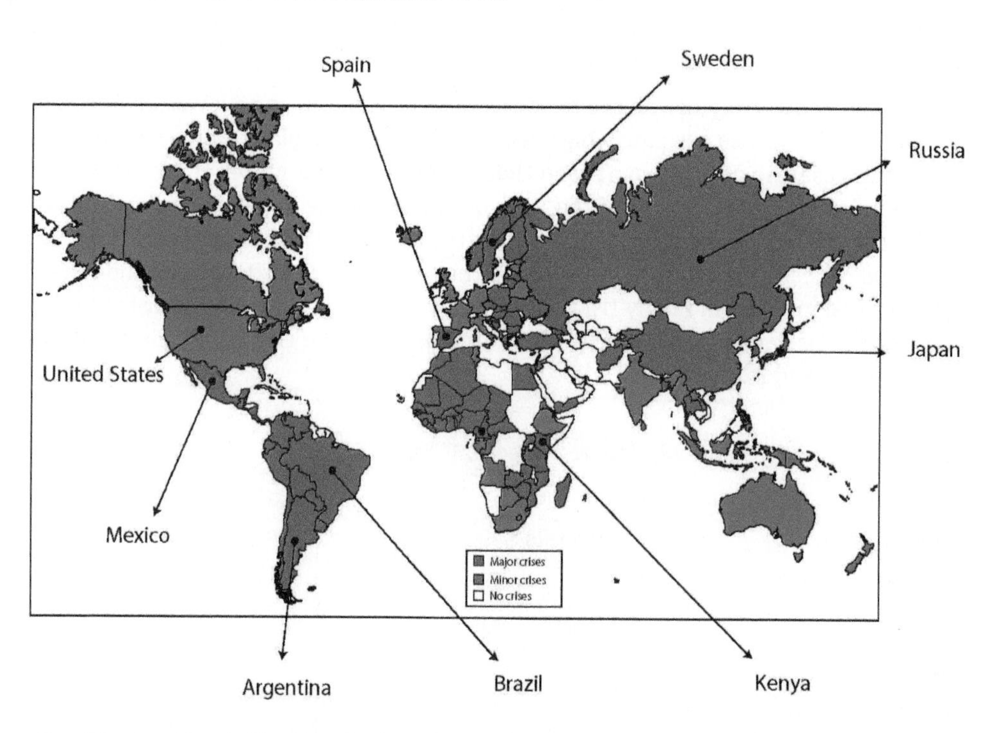

Data from Gerard Caprio and Daniela Klingebiel, Episodes of Systemic and Borderline Financial Crises (World Bank, January 2003)

Key Takeaways

- First, regulators were too slow to realize that traditional banking—the 3-6-3 rule and easy profitable banking—was dying due to the Great Inflation and technological improvements.
- Second, they allowed the institutions most vulnerable to the rapidly changing financial environment, savings and loan associations, too much latitude to engage in new, more sophisticated banking techniques, like liability management, without sufficient experience or training.
- Third, regulators engaged in forbearance, allowing essentially bankrupt companies to continue operations without realizing that the end result, due to very high levels of moral hazard, would be further losses.

11.4 Better but Still Not Good: U.S. Regulatory Reforms

Learning Objective

1. Have regulatory reforms and changes in market structure made the U.S. banking industry safer?

The S&L crisis and the failure of a few big commercial banks induced a series of regulatory reforms in the United States. The first such act, the Financial Institutions Reform, Recovery, and Enforcement Act (FIRREA), became law in August 1989. That act canned the old S&L regulators, created new regulatory agencies, and bailed out the bankrupt insurance fund. In the end, U.S. taxpayers reimbursed depositors at the failed S&Ls. FIRREA also re-regulated S&Ls, increasing their capital requirements and imposing the same risk-based capital standards that commercial banks are subject to. Since passage of the act, many S&Ls have converted to commercial banks and few new S&Ls have been formed.

In 1991, the government enacted further reforms in the Federal Deposit Insurance Corporation Improvement Act (FDICIA), which continued the bailout of the S&Ls and the deposit insurance fund, raised deposit insurance premiums, and forced the FDIC to close failed banks using the least costly method. (Failed banks can be dismembered and their pieces sold off one by one. That often entails selling assets at a discount. Or an entire bank can be sold to a healthy bank, which, of course, wants a little sugar [read, "cash"] to induce it to embrace a zombie!) The act also forced the FDIC to charge risk-based insurance premiums instead of a flat fee. The system it developed, however, resulted in 90 percent of banks, accounting for 95 percent of all deposits, paying the same premium. The original idea of taxing risky banks and rewarding safe ones was therefore subverted.

FDICIA's crowning glory is that it requires regulators to intervene earlier and more stridently when banks first get into trouble, well before losses eat away their capital. The idea is to close banks before they go broke, and certainly before they arise from the dead. See Figure 11.4 for details. Of course, banks can go under, *have gone under*, in a matter of hours, well before regulators can act or even know what is happening. Regulators do not and, of course, cannot monitor banks 24/7/365. And despite the law, regulators might still forbear, just like your neighbor might still smoke pot, even though it's illegal.

FIGURE 11.4 Regulation of bank capitalization
Less capital = more reward but also more risk. Duh!

Group Number	Title	Regulatory Action	Rationale
1	Well capitalized	Securities underwriting allowed.	Reward banks for holding extra capital
2	Adequately capitalized	None.	Goldilocks and the Three Bears "Just Right"
3	Undercapitalized	Must submit a capital restoration plan, restrict asset growth, and get approval for new branches and activities.	The bank needs more capital and should have a plan for it. Restrictions are designed to keep the bank from assuming too much risk.
4	Significantly undercapitalized	Cannot pay a higher rate than average for deposits.	This is to prevent banks in this category from attracting insured deposits at high rates that will force it to undertake risky activities.
5	Critically undercapitalized	Must be closed down.	No more zombies!

too-big-to-fail (TBTF) policy

The explicit or implicit promise of regulators that they will not allow a given financial institution to fail because to do so would cause too large of a shock for the financial system to handle. While that sounds reassuring and noble, the policy increases moral hazard, encouraging large financial institutions to take on large risks.

*The other problem with FDICIA is that it weakened but ultimately maintained the*thetoo-big-to-fail (TBTF) policy. Regulators cooked up TBTF during the 1980s to justify bailing out a big shaky bank called Continental Illinois. Like deposit insurance, TBTF was ostensibly a noble notion. If a really big bank failed and owed large sums to lots of other banks and nonbank financial institutions, it could cause a domino effect that could topple numerous companies very quickly. That, in turn, would cause asymmetric information and uncertainty to rise, risk premia on bonds to jump, stock prices to fall...you get the picture.[19]*The problem is that if a bank thinks it is too big to be allowed to fail, it has an incentive to take on a lot of risk, confident that the government will have its back if it gets into trouble.* (Banks in this respect are little different from drunken frat boys, or so I've heard.) Financier Henry Kaufman has termed this problem the Bigness Dilemma[20] and long feared that it could lead to a catastrophic economic meltdown, a political crisis, or a major economic slump. His fears came to fruition during the financial crisis of 2007–2008, of which we will learn more in another chapter. Similarly some analysts believe that Japan's TBTF policy was a leading cause of its recent fifteen-year economic funk. So like most other regulations, TBTF imposes costs that may exceed its benefits, depending on the details of how each are tallied. Such tallies, unfortunately, are often suffused with partisan ideological assumptions.

In 1994, the Riegle-Neal Interstate Banking and Branching Efficiency Act finally overturned most prohibitions on interstate banking. That law led to considerable consolidation, the effects of which are still unclear. Nevertheless, the act was long overdue, as was the Gramm-Leach-Bliley Financial Services Modernization Act of 1999, which repealed Glass-Steagall, allowing the same institutions to engage in both commercial and investment banking activities. The act has led to some conglomeration, but not as much as many observers expected. Again, it may be some time before the overall effects of the reform become clear. So far, both acts appear to have strengthened the financial system by making banks more profitable and diversified. Some large complex banking organizations and large complex financial institutions (LCBOs and LCFIs, respectively) held up well in the face of the subprime mortgage crisis, but others went bankrupt. The recent crisis appears to have been rooted in more fundamental issues, like TBTF and a dearth of internal incentive alignment within financial institutions, big and small, than in the regulatory reforms of the 1990s.

Key Takeaways

- To some extent, it is too early to tell what the effects of financial consolidation, concentration, and conglomeration will be.
- Overall, it appears that the U.S. financial reforms of the 1990s range from salutary (repeal of branching restrictions and Glass-Steagall) to destabilizing (retention of the too-big-to-fail policy).

11.5 Basel II, Basel III, and Dodd-Frank

Learning Objective

1. Will Basel II render the banking industry safe? If not, what might?

Due to the prevalence of banking crises worldwide and the financial system's increasingly global and integrated nature, international regulators, especially the Bank for International Settlements in Basel, Switzerland, have also been busy. Their recommendations are not binding on sovereign nations, but to date they have obtained significant buy-in worldwide. America's financial reforms in the 1990s, for example, were influenced by the so-called Basel I recommendations of 1988. Almost all countries have complied, on paper anyway, with Basel I rules on minimum and risk-weighted capitalization. *Risk-weighting was indeed an improvement over the older capitalization requirements, which were simply a minimum leverage ratio:*

$$\frac{\text{Capital}}{\text{assets}}$$

So the leverage ratio of the following bank would be 6 percent (6/100 = .06, or 6%), which in the past was generally considered adequate.

Some Bank Balance Sheet (Millions USD)	
Assets	Liabilities
Reserves $10	Deposits $80
Securities $10	Borrowings $14
Loans $70	Capital $6
Other assets $10	
Totals $100	$100

Of course, leverage ratios are much too simplistic because a bank with a leverage ratio of only 4 percent but with a diversified portfolio of very safe loans would be much safer than one with a leverage ratio of 10 percent but whose assets were invested entirely in lottery tickets!

The concept of weighting risks is therefore a solid one. A bank holding nothing but reserves would need very little capital compared to one holding mostly high-risk loans to biotech and nanotech startups. *Bankers, however, consider the Basel I weights too arbitrary and too broad.* For example, Basel I suggested weighting sovereign bonds at zero. That's great for developed countries, but plenty of poorer nations regularly default on their bonds. Some types of assets received a weighting of .5, others 1, others 1.5, and so forth, as the asset grew riskier. So, for example, the following assets would be weighted according to their risk before being put into a leverage ratio:

Reserves	$100,000,000 × 0 = 0
Governments	$50,000,000 × 0 = 0
Commercial loans	$600,000,000 × 1 = 600,000,000
Mortgages	$100,000,000 × 1.5 = 150,000,000

And so forth. But the weights were arbitrary. Are mortgages exactly half again as risky as commercial loans? Basel I basically encouraged banks to decrease their holdings of assets that the regulations overweighted and to stock up on assets that it underweighted. Not a pretty sight.

In response to such criticism, the Basel Committee on Banking Supervision announced in June 2004 a new set of guidelines, called Basel II, initially slated for implementation in 2008 and 2009 in the G10 countries. Basel II contains three pillars: capital, supervisory review process, and market discipline. According to the latest and greatest research, *Rethinking Bank Regulation* by James Barth, Gerard Caprio, and Ross Levine, the first two pillars are not very useful ways of regulating banks. The new risk weighting is an improvement, but it still grossly oversimplifies risk management and is not holistic enough. Moreover, supervisors cannot monitor every aspect of every bank all the time. Banks have to make periodic call reports on their balance sheets, income, and dividends but, like homeowners selling their homes, they pretty up the place before the prospective buyers arrive. In more developed countries, regulators also conduct surprise on-site examinations during which the examiners rate banks according to the so-called CAMELS formulation:

C = capital adequacy

A = asset quality

M = management

E = earnings

L = liquidity (reserves)

S = sensitivity to market risk.

A, M, and S are even more difficult to ascertain than C, E, and L and, as noted above, any or all of the variables can change very rapidly. Moreover, *much banking activity these days takes place off the balance sheet, where it is even more difficult for regulators to find and accurately assess.* Finally, in many jurisdictions, examiners are incorrecty compensated and hence do not do a very thorough job.

corporate governance

Guidelines concerning how an incorporated business should be ruled, including the number of directors and the process by which they are selected.

Barth, Caprio, and Levine argue that the third pillar of Basel II, financial market monitoring, is different. In aggregate, market participants can and in fact do monitor banks and bankers much more often and much more astutely than regulators can because they have much more at stake than a relatively low-paying job. *Barth, Caprio, and Levine argue persuasively that instead of conceiving of themselves as police officers, judges, and juries, bank regulators should see themselves as aides, as helping bank depositors (and other creditors of the bank) and stockholders to keep the bankers in line.* After all, nobody gains from a bank's failure. The key, they believe, is to ensure that debt and equity holders have incentives and opportunities to monitor bank management to ensure that they are not taking on too much risk. That means reducing asymmetric information by ensuring reliable information disclosure and urging that **corporate governance** best practices be followed.[21]

Regulators can also provide banks with incentives to keep their asset bases sufficiently diversified and to prevent them from engaging in inappropriate activities, like building rocket ships or running water treatment plants. Screening new banks and bankers, if regulators do it to reduce adverse selection (omit shysters or inexperienced people) rather than to aid existing banks (by blocking all or most new entrants and hence limiting competition) or to line their own pockets (via bribes), is another area where regulators can be effective. By focusing on a few key reachable goals, regulators can concentrate their limited resources and get the job done, the job of letting people look after their own property themselves. The market-based approach, scholars note, is most important in less-developed countries where regulators are more likely to be on the take (to enact and enforce regulations simply to augment their incomes via bribes).

U.S. implementation of Basel II was disrupted by the worst financial dislocation in 80 years. Intense lobbying pressure combined with the uncertainties created by the 2008 crisis led to numerous changes and implementation delays. Basel II, Basel II.5, and Basel III are slowly being implement in the U.S.[22] but the situation became confused when President Donald J. Trump announced his intention to repeal all or parts of Dodd-Frank.[23]

In July 2010, the U.S. government attempted to make the financial system less fragile by passing the Dodd-Frank Wall Street Reform and Protection Act. The law mandated the creation of a new:

- Financial Stability Oversight Council;
- Office of Financial Research;
- Consumer Financial Protection Bureau;
- advanced warning system that will attempt to identify and address systemic risks before they threaten financial institutions and markets.

It also called for:

- more stringent capital and liquidity requirements for LCFIs;
- tougher regulation of systemically important non-bank financial companies;
- the breakup of LCFIs, if necessary;
- tougher restrictions on bailouts;
- more transparency for asset-backed securities and other "exotic" financial instruments;
- improved corporate governance rules designed to give shareholders more say over the structure of executive compensation.

Despite the sweeping nature of those reforms, many scholars and financiers remained skeptical of the new law because it has not clearly eliminated the problems associated with TBTF policy, bailouts, and other causes of the financial crisis of 2007–2009. Its future under a Trump presidency is uncertain but a group of economists at New York University have backed an intriguing compromise called the CHOICE Act, which allows banks to hold higher capital ratios in exchange for exemptions from Dodd-Frank.[24]

Key Takeaways

- Basel I and II have provided regulators with more sophisticated ways of analyzing the adequacy of bank capital.
- Nevertheless, it appears that regulators lag behind banks and their bankers, in part because of agency problems within regulatory bureaucracies and in part because of the gulf of asymmetric information separating banks and regulators, particularly when it comes to the quality of assets and the extent and risk of off-balance-sheet activities.
- If scholars like Barth, Caprio, and Levine are correct, regulators ought to think of ways of helping financial markets, particularly bank debt and equity holders, to monitor banks.
- They should also improve their screening of new bank applicants without unduly restricting entry, and set and enforce broad guidelines for portfolio diversification and admissible activities.

11.6 Suggested Reading

Acharya, Viral et al, eds. *Regulating Wall Street: The Dodd-Frank Act and the New Architecture of Global Finance*. Hoboken, NJ: John Wiley and Sons, 2011.

Arner, Douglas. *Financial Stability, Economic Growth, and the Role of Law*. New York: Cambridge University Press, 2007.

Barth, James, Gerard Caprio, and Ross Levine. *Rethinking Bank Regulation*. New York: Cambridge University Press, 2006.

Barth, James, S. Trimbath, and Glenn Yago. *The Savings and Loan Crisis: Lessons from a Regulatory Failure*. New York: Springer, 2004.

Benston, George. *Regulating Financial Markets: A Critique and Some Proposals*. Washington, DC: AEI Press, 1999.

Bernanke, Ben S. *Essays on the Great Depression*. Princeton, NJ: Princeton University Press, 2000.

Gup, Benton. *Too Big to Fail: Policies and Practices in Government Bailouts*. Westport, CT: Praeger, 2004.

Stern, Gary, and Ron Feldman. *Too Big to Fail: The Hazards of Bank Bailouts*. Washington, DC: Brookings Institution Press, 2004.

Tullock, Gordon, Arthur Seldon, and Gordon Brady. *Government Failure: A Primer in Public Choice*. Washington, DC: Cato Institute, 2002.

Winston, Clifford. *Government Failure Versus Market Failure: Microeconomics Policy Research and Government Performance*. Washington, DC: AEI-Brookings Joint Center for Regulatory Studies, 2006.

Endnotes

1. showcase.netins.net/web/creative/lincoln/speeches/gettysburg.htm
2. www.econlib.org/LIBRARY/Enc/bios/Stigler.html
3. en.wikipedia.org/wiki/Regulatory_capture
4. http://www.investopedia.com/terms/i/inthemoney.asp
5. stocks.fundamentalfinance.com/stock-market-crash-of-1929.php
6. www.bos.frb.org/about/pubs/panicof1.pdf
7. measuringworth.com/datasets/DJA
8. Michael Bordo and David Wheelock, "The Promise and Performance of the Federal Reserve as Lender of Last Resort," Norges Bank Working Paper 201 (20 January 2011). papers.ssrn.com/sol3/papers.cfm?abstract_id=1847472
9. https://en.wikipedia.org/wiki/Beggar_thy_neighbour
10. en.wikipedia.org/wiki/List_of_staff_at_South_Park_Elementary#Mr._Mackey
11. https://www.whitehouse.gov/1600/presidents/franklindroosevelt
12. newdeal.feri.org
13. historymatters.gmu.edu/d/5057
14. www.bartleby.com/124/pres49.html
15. This part is inaccurate. Financiers went loophole mining and found a real doozy called a private placement. As opposed to a public offering, in a private placement securities issuers can avoid SEC disclosure requirements by selling directly to institutional investors like life insurance companies and other "accredited investors" (legalese for "rich people").
16. This part is all too true. Check out the prospectus of Internet giant Google at www.sec.gov/Archives/edgar/data/1288776/000119312504142742/ds1a.htm. If you don't dig Google, check out any company you like via Edgar, the SEC's filing database, at www.sec.gov/edgar.shtml.
17. Milton Friedman and Rose Friedman, *Free to Choose: A Personal Statement* (New York: Harcourt, 1980), 66.
18. http://www.monstersandcritics.com/lists/humor/top-10-ways-to-kill-a-zombie/
19. If not, read an article that influenced policymakers: Ben Bernanke, "Nonmonetary Effects of the Financial Crisis in the Propagation of the Great Depression," *American Economic Review* 73 (June 1983): 257–76.
20. The dilemma is that big banks in other regards are stabilizing rather than destabilizing because they have clearly achieved efficient scale and maintain a diversified portfolio of assets.
21. Frederick D. Lipman, *Corporate Governance Best Practices: Strategies for Public, Private, and Not-for-Profit Organizations* (Hoboken, N.J.: Wiley, 2006).
22. https://fas.org/sgp/crs/misc/R42744.pdf
23. https://www.nytimes.com/2017/02/03/business/dealbook/trump-congress-financial-regulations.html?_r=0
24. Matthew P. Richardson, Kermit L. Schoenholtz, Bruce Tuckman, and Lawrence J. White, eds. *Regulating Wall Street: CHOICE Act vs. Dodd-Frank* (New York: New York University, 2017).

CHAPTER 12

Financial Derivatives

Chapter Objectives

By the end of this chapter, students should be able to:

1. Define financial derivative and explain the economic functions that financial derivatives fulfill.
2. Define and describe the four major types of derivatives: forwards, futures, options, and swaps.
3. Explain the economic functions of hedging and speculating.

12.1 Derivatives and Their Functions

Learning Objective

1. What are financial derivatives and what economic needs do they fulfill?

Financial derivatives are special types of financial instruments, the prices of which are ultimately *derived from* the price or performance of some underlying asset. While some derivatives contracts may require physical delivery of the underlying asset, most do not. In other words, physical delivery is not a necessary attribute of derivatives and that helps to differentiate them from corporate shares, bonds, and asset backed securities. Investors use derivatives to hedge (*decrease* **return volatility**) or to speculate (*increase the volatility of returns*) so ultimately they care about monetary compensation for changes in the price in the underlying asset, not the underlying asset itself.

return volatility

The statistical dispersion of financial returns on an investment.

Although often derided in the press and movies, *derivatives are inherently neither good nor bad, they are merely tools used to limit losses (hedge) or to multiply gains and losses (speculate).* Speculation has a bad rep but in fact it makes hedging possible because *hedgers cannot always find another hedger to serve as a counterparty*. Speculators, in other words, add liquidity to derivatives markets.

Ultimately, the prices of derivatives are a *function of supply and demand*, both of which are subject to valuation models too mathematically complex to address here. The basic forms and functions of the four main types of derivatives—*forwards, futures, options, and swaps*—are easily narrated and understood, however, and form the basis of this chapter.

Figure 12.1 is a generalized representation of the four major types of derivatives, forwards, futures, options, and swaps. Over time, the market price of some asset, the underlying asset, changes. Those (hedger or speculator) interested in the long or buy position are therefore hurt as the price rises from the current or some desired price, so the derivative contract aids them. Those (hedger or speculator) interested in the short or sell position are hurt as the price drops, so in that case the derivative contract aids them. The precise type of aid varies depending on the type of derivative used, the subject to which we now turn.

FIGURE 12.1 Stylized derivative contract

The details depend on whether the counterparties are using a forward, futures, option, or swap.

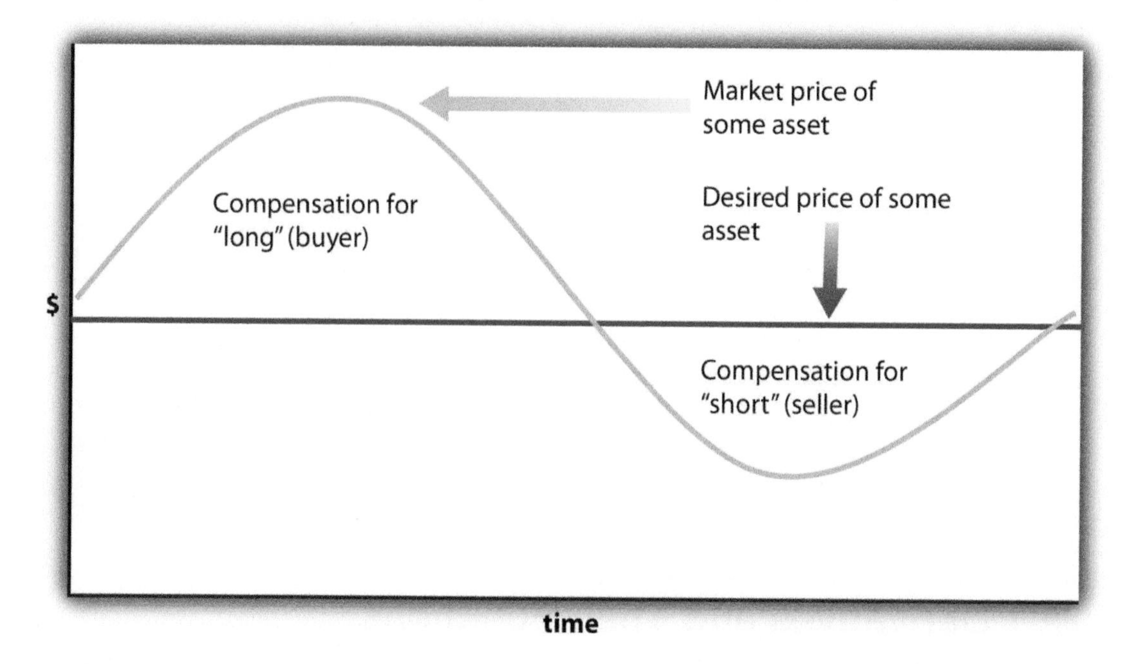

Stop and Think Box

If you could, would you receive a guaranteed grade of B for this course? Or would you rather have a chance of receiving an A even if that meant that you might fail the course?

If you take the guaranteed B, you are hedging or reducing your return (grade) variability. If you are willing to accept an A or an F, you are acting like a speculator and may end up on the dean's list or on academic probation. Neither choice is wrong or bad but is merely a tool by which you can achieve your preferences.

Key Takeaways

- Derivatives are instruments, the price of which derives from the price or performance of some underlying asset.
- Derivatives can be used to hedge (reduce risk) or to speculate (increase risk).
- Derivatives are just tools that investors can use to increase or decrease return volatility and hence are not inherently bad. Speculation is the obverse of hedging, which would be impossible to do without speculators serving as counterparties.

12.2 Forwards and Futures

Learning Objectives

1. What is a forward contract and what is it used for?
2. What is a futures contract and what is its economic purpose?

Imagine you want to throw a party at the end of the semester and have a budget of $100 for beer. (If you are underage or a teetotaler think about root beer instead.) You know your buddies will drink up any (root) beer you bring into the house before the party so you have to wait until the day of the event to make your purchases. The problem is that the price of your favorite beer jumps around. Sometimes it costs $20 per case but other times it is $30. Having 5 cases of the good stuff would mean an awesome party but having 3 cases of the good stuff and a case of (insert your favorite word for bad $10/case beer here) would be...like totally lame. What to do?

Buyers naturally fear increases in the prices of the things they want to own in the future. Sellers, by contrast, fear price decreases. Those mutual fears can lead to the creation of a financial instrument known as a forward. In a forward contract, a buyer and a seller agree *today* on the price of an asset to be purchased and delivered in the future. That way, the buyer knows precisely how much he will have to pay and the seller knows precisely how much she will receive. You could sign a forward contract with your beer distributor pegging the price of your favorite beer at $25 per case and thus ensure that you will have 4 cases of the good stuff at your end of semester bash. Similarly, a farmer and a grocer could contract at planting to fix the price of watermelons, corn, and so forth at harvest time.

Agricultural forward contracts like that just described have been used for centuries if not millennia. Their use is limited by three major problems with forward contracts: (1) it is often costly/difficult to find a willing counterparty; (2) the market for forwards is illiquid due to their idiosyncratic nature so they are not easily sold to other parties if desired; (3) one party usually has an incentive to break the agreement. Imagine, for example, that the price of your favorite beer dropped to only $15 per case. You might feel cheated at having to pay $25 and renege on your promise. Conversely, if your beer went to $40 per case the distributor might tell you to get lost when you tried to pay $25 under the forward contract.

Exchanges like the Chicago Board Options Exchange (CBOE), Chicago Mercantile Exchange (CME), Chicago Board of Trade (CBOT), and Minneapolis Grain Exchange (MGEX) developed futures to obviate the difficulties with forward contracts by: (1) efficiently linking buyers and sellers; (2) developing standardized weights, definitions, standards, and expiration dates for widely traded commodities, currencies, and other assets; (3) enforcing contracts between counterparties. Each contract specifies the underlying asset (which ranges from bonds to currencies, butter to orange juice, ethanol to oil, and gold to uranium), its amount and quality grade, and the type (cash or physical) and date of settlement or contract expiration. CME, for example, offers a futures contract on copper in which physical settlement of 25,000 pounds of copper is due on any of the last three business days of the delivery month.[1] In many contracts, especially for financial assets, physical delivery is not desired or demanded. Instead, a cash settlement representing the difference between the contract price and the spot market price on the expiration date is made. (Note that even in cases where physical delivery is required, the parties would do just as well to settle differences in cash so long as the underlying commodity was easily purchased elsewhere. Delivery is for the *convenience* of both parties but economically unnecessary to the core concept of derivatives.)

To lock in the price that it will have to *pay* for an asset in the future, a business should *purchase a futures contract*, thereby committing another party to supply it at the contract price. To lock in the price it will *receive* for an asset in the future, a business should *sell a futures contract*, thereby committing a buyer to purchase it at the contract price.

Here is a concrete example of how a futures contract can be used to hedge against price movements in an underlying asset: If you wanted to hedge the sale of 1 million barrels of crude oil you could sell a 3-month futures contract for $100 per barrel. If the market price of crude was $90 per barrel at the expiration date, you would get $10 per barrel from the buyer of the contract plus the market price ($90), or $100 per barrel. If the market price of crude was $110 at the end of the contract, by contrast, you would have to pay $10 per barrel to the buyer of the contract. Again, you would net $100 per barrel, $110 in the market minus the $10 paid to the contract counterparty.

margin accounts

Accounts in which a futures trader deposits cash equal to the difference between the value of the futures contract and the underlying asset.

To ensure that you would not renege in the latter case by not paying $10 per barrel to the counterparty, futures exchanges require **margin accounts** and other safeguards. As the contract and market prices diverge, the incentive to default increases and exchanges know it. So they require investors to post bonds or to increase the deposits in their margin accounts or they will pay the money in the margin account to the counterparty and close the contract.

Stop and Think Box

Could a futures contract price ever be lower than the current market price? If not, why not? If so, how?

Futures contract prices will be lower than current market prices if market participants anticipate lower future prices due to deflation, changes in relative prices, or changes in supply or demand conditions. Cold weather in Florida, for example, can make orange juice futures soar on the expectation of a damaged crop (decreased supply) but unexpectedly mild weather in climatically marginal groves can have the opposite effect. Similarly, the expected completion of a new refinery might make gasoline futures decline.

Key Takeaways

- Buyers and sellers can hedge or lock in the price they will pay/receive for assets in the future by contracting for the price today.
- Such contracts, called forwards, are costly to consummate, illiquid, and subject to high levels of default risk.
- Standardized forward contracts, called futures, were developed by exchanges to reduce the problems associated with forwards and have proliferated widely across asset classes.

12.3 Options and Swaps

Learning Objectives

1. What are options and how can they be used to hedge and speculate?
2. What are swaps and how are they used to hedge and speculate?

Options are aptly named financial derivatives that give their holders the option (which is to say the right, but not the obligation) to purchase (call) or sell (put) an underlying asset at a predetermined strike price, on (if a so-called European option) or before (if a so-called American option) a predetermined expiration date. Options are most often written on stocks (equities) but can be linked to other types of assets as well. To induce investors to issue an option and thereby obligate themselves to make a disadvantageous trade, option holders must pay a premium to the option issuer based on the option type, strike price, expiration date, interest rates, and volatility of the underlying asset. (The most famous option valuation model is called Black-Scholes.[2] It is rather complicated, but various online calculators will painlessly compute the option premium for users who input the values of the key variables.)[3]

Options can be used to hedge or speculate in various ways. An investor might buy a call option on a stock in the hopes that the stock price will rise above the strike price, allowing her to buy the stock at the strike price (e.g., $90) and immediately resell it at the higher market price (e.g., $100). Or an investor might buy a put option to minimize his losses. If the stock fell from $100 to $50 per share, for example, a put option at $75 would be profitable or "in the money" because the investor could buy the stock in the market at $50 and then exercise his option to sell the stock to the option issuer at $75 for a gross profit of $25 per share.

Buying and selling calls and puts can be combined to create a variety of investment strategies with colorful names like bear put spreads and bull collars. Do yourself a favor and study the subject more thoroughly before dabbling in options, especially before selling them. The purchaser of an option can never lose more than the premium paid because the worst case scenario is that the option remains "out of the money." For example, if the market price of a share on which you hold a European call option is below the option's strike price on the expiration date the option would expire valueless. (If the market price was $15 you would not want to exercise your right to buy at $20.) Similarly, if the market price (e.g., $25 to $30 range) of an American put option remains above the strike price (e.g., $15) for the entire term of the contract, the option would be out of the money. (Why exercise your right to sell something for $15 that you could sell for $25 plus?!) The seller of an option, by contrast, can lose a large sum if an option goes a long way into the money. For example, the seller of a call option with a strike price of $50 would lose $950 per share if the price of the underlying share soared to $1,000. (The holder of the option would exercise its right to call or buy the shares from the option issuer at $50.) Such large movements are rare, of course, but it would only take one instance to ruin most individual option issuers.

Stop and Think Box

All else equal, what should cost more to purchase, an American or a European option? Why?

American options are more valuable than European options, ceteris paribus, because the American option is more likely to be valuable or "in the money" as it can be exercised on numerous days, not just one.

Swaps are very different from options (though they can be combined to form a derivative called a swaption, or an option to enter into a swap). As the name implies, swaps are exchanges of one asset for another on a predetermined, typically repeated basis. A savings bank, for example, might agree to give $50,000 per year to a finance company in exchange for the finance company's promise to pay the savings bank $1 million times a variable interest rate such as **LIBOR**. Such an agreement, called an interest rate swap, would buffer the bank against rising interest rates while protecting the finance company from lower ones, as in the following table:

LIBOR

The London Interbank Offered Rate, or the variable interest rate at which banks lend to each other overnight in the London wholesale money market.

TABLE 12.1 Payments Under an Interest Rate Swap

Year	Savings bank owes ($)	LIBOR (%)	Finance company owes ($)	Net payment to/ from bank ($)	Net payment to/from finance company ($)
1	50,000	5.00	50,000	0	0
2	50,000	6.00	60,000	10,000	−10,000
3	50,000	4.00	40,000	−10,000	10,000
4	50,000	1.25	12,500	-37,500	37,500

A credit default swap (CDS) is a type of swap used to create an unregulated form of insurance against a default by a bond issuer such as a country or corporation. In a CDS, the holder of bonds promises to make a relatively small payment (similar to an insurance premium) to a counterparty in exchange for a large payment if the bond issuer does not pay principal or interest on its bonds as promised. CDSs exacerbated the financial crisis of 2008 because many counterparties failed to make good on their promise to indemnify bondholders in case of default. CDSs are still largely unregulated and present systemic risks that most other derivatives do not.

Key Takeaways

- Options are financial derivatives that in exchange for a premium provide holders with the option (the right but not the obligation) to buy or sell a stock or other underlying asset at a predetermined price up to or on a predetermined date.
- Option holders/buyers can never lose more than the premium paid for the option, the value of which is a function of interest rates, the strike price, the expiration date, and the volatility of the underlying asset.
- Swaps are derivatives in which two parties agree to swap or exchange one asset for another at one or more future dates. Like options, they can be used to hedge or speculate.
- Credit Default Swaps are a special form of swap akin to an insurance policy on bonds. Despite their ability to increase systemic volatility, they remain largely unregulated.

12.4 Suggested Reading

Durbin, Michael. *All About Derivatives*. 2nd ed. New York: McGraw-Hill, 2010.

Gottesman, Aron. *Derivatives Essentials: An Introduction to Forwards, Futures, Options, and Swaps*. New York: Wiley, 2016.

Thomsett, Michael. *The Mathematics of Options: Quantifying Derivative Price, Payoff, Probability, and Risk*. New York: Palgrave Macmillan, 2017.

Endnotes

1. www.cmegroup.com/trading/metals/base/copper_contract_specifications.html
2. en.wikipedia.org/wiki/Black–Scholes
3. www.money-zine.com/Calculators/Investment-Calculators/Black-Scholes-Calculator

CHAPTER 13

Financial Crises: Causes and Consequences

Learning Objectives

By the end of this chapter, students should be able to:

1. Define financial crisis and differentiate between systemic and nonsystemic crises.
2. Describe a generic asset bubble.
3. Define leverage and explain its role in asset bubble formation.
4. Explain why bubbles burst, causing financial panics.
5. Define and explain the importance of lender of last resort.
6. Define and explain the importance of bailouts.
7. Narrate the causes and consequences of the financial crisis that began in 2007.
8. Describe the major features of Islamic finance and assess its ability to reduce financial instability.

13.1 Financial Crisis Taxonomies

Learning Objectives

1. What is a financial crisis?
2. How do financial shocks and crises affect the real economy?

A **financial crisis** occurs when one or more financial markets or intermediaries cease functioning or function only erratically and inefficiently. A **nonsystemic crisis** involves only one or a few markets or sectors, like the Savings and Loan Crisis. A **systemic crisis** involves all, or almost all, of the financial system to some extent, as during the Great Depression and the crisis of 2008.

Financial crises are neither new nor unusual. Thousands of crises, including the infamous Tulip Mania and South Sea Company episodes, have rocked financial systems throughout the world in the past five hundred years. Two such crises, in 1764–1768 and 1773, helped lead to the American Revolution.[1] After its independence, the United States suffered systemic crises in 1792, 1818–1819, 1837–1839, 1857, 1873, 1884, 1893–1895, 1907, 1929–1933, and 2008. Nonsystemic crises have been even more numerous and include the credit crunch of 1966, stock market crashes in 1973–1974 (when the Dow dropped from a 1,039 close on January 12, 1973, to a 788 close on December 5, 1973, to a 578 close on December 6, 1974) and 1987, not to mention the "Flash Crash" of May 6, 2010, the failure of Long-Term Capital Management in 1998, the dot-com troubles of 2000, the dramatic events following the terrorist attacks in 2001, and the subprime mortgage debacle of 2007. Sometimes, nonsystemic crises burn out or are brought under control before they spread to other parts of the financial system. Other times, as in 1929 and 2007, nonsystemic crises spread like a wildfire until they threaten to burn the entire system.

financial crisis

The functioning of one or more financial markets or intermediaries becomes erratic or ceases altogether.

nonsystemic crisis

A particular market or intermediary functions erratically or inefficiently.

systemic crisis

The functioning of all, or nearly all, of the financial system degrades.

shocks

In economics, sudden, unexpected changes. Shocks usually have adverse consequences, but some can be salutary. The ones discussed here are all bad for the financial system and hence the economy.

Financial crises can be classified in other ways as well. Some affect banks but not other parts of the financial system. Others mostly involve government debt and/or currency, as in bouts of inflation or rapid depreciation in foreign exchange markets. All types can spread to the other types and even to other nations via balance sheet deterioration and increases in asymmetric information. *Five* **shocks**, *alone or in combination, have a strong propensity to initiate financial crises.*

Increases in uncertainty. When companies cannot plan for the future and when investors feel they cannot estimate future corporate earnings or interest, inflation, or default rates, they tend to play it safe. They hold cash instead of investing in a new factory or equipment. That, of course, reduces aggregate economic activity.

Increases in interest rates. Higher interest rates make business projects less profitable and hence less likely to be completed, a direct blow to gross domestic product (GDP). Also, higher interest rates tend to exacerbate adverse selection by discouraging better borrowers but having little or no effect on the borrowing decisions of riskier companies and individuals. As a result, lenders are saddled with higher default rates in high interest-rate environments. So, contrary to what one would think, high rates reduce their desire to lend. To the extent that businesses own government or other bonds, higher interest rates decrease their net worth, leading to balance sheet deterioration, of which we will soon learn more. Finally, higher interest rates hurt cash flow (receipts minus expenditures), rendering firms more likely to default.

Government fiscal problems. Governments that expend more than they take in via taxes and other revenues have to borrow. The more they borrow, the harder it is for them to service their loans, raising fears of a default, which decreases the market price of their bonds. This hurts the balance sheets of firms that invest in government bonds and may lead to an exchange rate crisis as investors sell assets denominated in the local currency in a flight to safety. Precipitous declines in the value of local currency cause enormous difficulties for firms that have borrowed in foreign currencies, such as dollars, sterling, euro, or yen, because they have to pay more units of local currency than expected for each unit of foreign currency. Many are unable to do so and they default, increasing uncertainty and asymmetric information.

Balance sheet deterioration. Whenever a firm's balance sheet deteriorates, which is to say, whenever its net worth falls because the value of its assets decreases and/or the value of its liabilities increases, or because stock market participants value the firm less highly, the Cerberus of asymmetric information rears its trio of ugly, fang-infested faces. The company now has less at stake, so it might engage in riskier activities, exacerbating adverse selection. As its net worth declines, moral hazard increases because it grows more likely to default on existing obligations, in turn because it has less at stake. Finally, agency problems become more prevalent as employee bonuses shrink and stock options become valueless. As employees begin to shirk, steal, and look for other work on company time, productivity plummets, and further declines in profitability cannot be far behind. The same negative cycle can also be jump-started by an unanticipated deflation, a decrease in the aggregate price level, because that will make the firm's liabilities (debts) more onerous in real terms (i.e., adjusted for lower prices).

Banking problems and panics. If anything hurts banks' balance sheets (like higher than expected default rates on loans they have made), banks will reduce their lending to avoid going bankrupt and/or incurring the wrath of regulators. As we have seen, banks are the most important source of external finance in most countries, so their decision to curtail will negatively affect the economy by reducing the flow of funds between investors and entrepreneurs. If bank balance sheets are hurt badly enough, some may fail. That may trigger the failure of yet more banks for two reasons. First, banks often owe each other considerable sums. If a big bank that owes much too many smaller banks were to fail, it could endanger the solvency of the creditor banks. Second, the failure of a few banks may induce the holders of banks' monetary liabilities (today mostly deposits, but in the past, as we've seen, also bank notes) to run on the bank, to pull their funds out en masse because they can't tell if their bank is a good one or not. The tragic thing about this is that, because all banks engage in fractional reserve banking (which is to say that no bank keeps enough cash on hand to meet all of its monetary liabilities), runs often become self-fulfilling prophecies, destroying even solvent institutions in a matter of days or even hours. Banking panics and the dead banks they leave in their wake cause uncertainty, higher interest rates, and balance sheet deterioration, all of which, as we've seen, hurt aggregate economic activity.

A downward spiral often ensues. Interest rate increases, stock market declines, uncertainty, balance sheet deterioration, and fiscal imbalances all tend to increase asymmetric information. That, in turn, causes economic activity to decline, triggering more crises, including bank panics and/or foreign exchange crises, which increase asymmetric information yet further. Economic activity again declines, perhaps triggering more crises or an unanticipated decline in the price level. That is the point, traditionally, where recessions turn into depressions, unusually long and steep economic downturns.

Stop and Think Box

In early 1792, U.S. banks curtailed their lending. This caused a securities speculator and shyster by the name of William Duer to go bankrupt, owing large sums of money to hundreds of investors. The uncertainty caused by Duer's sudden failure caused people to panic, inducing them to sell securities, even government bonds, for cash. By midsummer, though, the economy was again humming along nicely. In 1819, banks again curtailed lending, leading to a rash of mercantile failures. People again panicked, this time running on banks (but clutching their government bonds for dear life). Many banks failed and unemployment soared. Economic activity shrank, and it took years to recover. Why did the economy right itself quickly in 1792 but only slowly in 1819?

In 1792, America's central bank (then the Secretary of the Treasury, Alexander Hamilton, working in conjunction with the Bank of the United States [1791-1811]) acted as a lender of last resort. By adding liquidity to the economy, the central bank calmed fears, reduced uncertainty and asymmetric information, and kept interest rates from spiking and balance sheets from deteriorating further. In 1819, the central bank (with a new Treasury secretary and a new bank, the "Second" Bank of the United States [1816-1836]) crawled under a rock, allowing the initial crisis to increase asymmetric information, reduce aggregate output, and ultimately cause an unexpected debt deflation. Since 1819, the United States has suffered from financial crises on numerous occasions. Sometimes they have ended quickly and quietly, as when Alan Greenspan stymied the stock market crash of 1987. Other times, like after the stock market crash of 1929, the economy did not fare well at all.[2]

Assuming their vital human capital and market infrastructure have not been destroyed by the depression, economies will eventually reverse themselves after many companies have gone bankrupt, the balance sheets of surviving firms improve, and uncertainty, asymmetric information, and interest rates decrease. *It is better for everyone, however, if financial crises can be nipped in the bud before they turn ugly.* This is one of the major functions of central banks like the European Central Bank (ECB) and the Fed. Generally, all that the central bank needs to do at the outset of a crisis is to restore confidence, reduce uncertainty, and keep interest rates in line by adding liquidity (cash) to the economy by acting as a lender of last resort, helping out banks and other financial intermediaries with loans and buying government bonds in the open market. Sometimes a bailout, a transfer of wealth from taxpayers to the financial system, becomes necessary. Figure 13.1 summarizes this discussion of the ill consequences of financial shocks.

But in case you didn't get the memo, nothing is ever really free. (Well, except for free goods.)[3] When central banks stop financial panics, especially when they do so by bailing out failed companies, they risk creating moral hazard by teaching market participants that they will shield them from risks. That is why some economists, like Allan Meltzer, said "Let 'Em Fail," in the op-ed pages of the *Wall Street Journal*[4] when some hedge funds ran into trouble due to the unexpected deterioration of the subprime mortgage market in 2007. Hamilton's Law (née Bagehot's Law, which urges lenders of last resort to lend freely at a penalty rate on good security) is powerful precisely because it minimizes moral hazard by providing relief only to the more prudent and solvent firms while allowing the riskiest ones to go under.

FIGURE 13.1 Anatomy of a financial crisis and economic decline

Note: At any point the downward spiral can be stopped by adequate central bank intervention.

Triggers	Which lead to	Which causes	Which leads to	Which causes	And finally
Uncertainty	Caution and declines in economic activity	Increases in asymmetric information	Generalized panic	Further increases in asymmetric information and further declines in economic activity	Debt deflation and further increase in asymmetrical information and declines in economic activity
Increases in Interest Rates	Fewer profitable business projects; balance sheet deterioration; cash flow problems; increase in asymmetric information	"	Stagnation and bankruptcies	"	"
Stock Market Decline	Balance sheet deterioration	"		"	"
Bank Problems	Loan curtailments; increases in interest rates and uncertainty	"	Bank runs	Bank failures	"
Fiscal Imbalances	Expectations of government default; balance sheet deterioration	"	Exchange Rate Crisis	"	"

Stop and Think Box

"While we ridicule ancient superstition we have an implicit faith in the bubbles of banking, and yet it is difficult to discover a greater absurdity, in ascribing omnipotence to bulls, cats and onions, than for a man to carry about a thousand acres of land...in his pocket book....This gross bubble is practiced every day, even upon the infidelity of avarice itself....So we see wise and honest Americans, of the nineteenth century, embracing phantoms for realities, and running mad in schemes of refinement, tastes, pleasures, wealth and power, by the soul [sic] aid of this *hocus pocus*."—*Cause of, and Cure for, Hard Times*.[5] When were these words penned? How do you know?

This was undoubtedly penned during one of the nineteenth century U.S. financial crises mentioned previously. Note the negative tone, the allusion to Americans, and the reference to the nineteenth century. In fact, the pamphlet appeared in 1818. For a kick, compare/contrast it to blogs bemoaning the crisis that began in 2007:

http://cartledged.blogspot.com/2007/09/greedy-bastards-club.html

http://www.washingtonmonthly.com/archives/individual/2008_03/013339.php

http://thedefenestrators.blogspot.com/2008/10/death-to-bankers.html

Both systemic and nonsystemic crises damage the real economy by preventing the normal flow of credit from savers to entrepreneurs and other businesses and by making it more difficult or expensive to spread risks. Given the damage financial crises can cause, scholars and policymakers are keenly interested in their causes and consequences. You should be, too.

Key Takeaways

- Throughout history, systemic (widespread) and nonsystemic (confined to a few industries) financial crises have damaged the real economy by disrupting the normal flow of credit and insurance.
- Understanding the causes and consequences of financial crises is therefore important.
- Financial shocks and crises affect the real economy by increasing asymmetric information.
- Increased asymmetric information, in turn, reduces the amount of funds channeled from investors to entrepreneurs.
- Starved of external finance, businesses cut back production, decreasing aggregate economic activity.
- The conduits include rapidly rising interest rates, foreign exchange crises, and bank panics.

13.2 Asset Bubbles

Learning Objective

1. What are asset bubbles and what role does leverage play in their creation?

Asset bubbles *are increases in the value of some assets, like bonds, commodities (cotton, gold, oil, tulips), equities, or real estate, above their rational or fundamental level.* Some combination of low interest rates, new technology, unprecedented increases in demand for the asset, and leverage typically create bubbles.

Asset bubbles

The price of some class of asset, like stocks or real estate, increases more rapidly than economic fundamentals.

Low interest rates can cause bubbles by lowering the total cost of asset ownership. Recall that interest rates and bond prices are inversely related. Algebraically, the *i* term is in the denominator of the PV formula—$PV = FV/(1 + i)^n$—so as it gets smaller, PV must get larger (holding FV constant, of course).

Stop and Think Box

In colonial New York in the 1740s and 1750s, interest rates on mortgages were generally 8 percent. In the late 1750s and early 1760s, they fell to about 4 percent, and expected revenues from land ownership increased by about 50 percent. What happened to real estate prices? Why?

They rose significantly because it was cheaper to borrow money, thus lowering the total cost of real estate ownership, and because the land was expected to create higher revenues. Thinking of the land as a perpetuity and FV as the expected revenues arising from it:

$$PV = FV / i$$

$$PV = £100 / .08 = £1,250$$

$$PV = £100 / .04 = £2,500$$

And that is just the interest rate effect. Increasing FV by £50 leads to the following:

$$PV = £150 / .04 = £3,750, \text{ or a tripling of prices.}$$

In 1762, Benjamin Franklin reported that the "Rent of old Houses, and Value of Lands,...are trebled in the last Six Years."[6] Unfortunately for the colonists, increases in FV proved transient, and interest rates soon soared past 8 percent.

The effect of new technology can be thought of as increasing FV, leading, of course, to a higher PV. Or, in the case of equities, low interest rates decrease *k* (required return) and new inventions increase *g* (constant growth rate) in the Gordon growth model—$P = E \times (1 + g)/(k - g)$—both of which lead to a higher price. During bubbles, investors overestimate the likely effects of new technology and place unreasonably high estimates on FV and *g*.

Large increases in the demand for an asset occur for a variety of reasons. *Demand can be increased merely by investors' expectations of higher prices in the future, as in the one period valuation model*—$P = E/(1 + k) + P_1/(1 + k)$. If many investors believe that P_1 must be greater than P a year (or any other period) hence, demand for the asset will increase and the expectation of a higher P_1 will be vindicated. That sometimes leads investors to believe that P_2 will be higher than P_1, leading to a self-fulfilling cycle that repeats through P_3 to P_X. At some point, the value of the asset becomes detached from fundamental reality, driven solely by expectations of yet higher future prices. *In fact, some scholars verify the existence of an asset bubble when news about the price of an asset affects the economy, rather than the economy affecting the price of the asset.*

To increase their returns, investors often employ leverage, or borrowing. Compare three investors, one who buys asset X entirely with his own money, one who borrows half of the price of asset X, and one who borrows 90 percent of the price of asset X. Their returns (not including the cost of borrowing, which as noted above is usually low during bubbles) will be equal to those calculated in Figure 13.2.

FIGURE 13.2 The effects of leverage on returns in a rising market

Leverage increases returns but also risks!

Period	Asset Price	Cumulative Return, No Leverage (%)	Cumulative Return, 50% Leverage (%)	Cumulative Return, 90% Leverage (%)
0	100	--	--	--
1	110	10	60	100
2	120	20	70	110
3	130	30	80	120

The figures were calculated using the rate of return formula: $R = (C + P_{t1} - P_{to})/P_{to}$. Here, coupons are zero and hence drop out so that $R = (P_{t1} - P_{to})/P_{to}$.

In this example, returns for the unleveraged investor are great:

$$110 - 100/100 = .1 \text{ (rendered as 10\% in the figure)}$$

$$120 - 100/100 = .2$$

$$130 - 100/100 = .3$$

But the returns are not as high as the investor who borrowed half the cash, in essence paying only $50 of his own money for the $100 asset at the outset:

$$110 - 50/100 = .6$$

$$120 - 50/100 = .7$$

$$130 - 50/100 = .8$$

But even he looks like a chump compared to the investor who borrowed most of the money to finance the original purchase, putting up only $10 of his own money:

$$110 - 10/100 = 1$$

$$120 - 10 = 1.1$$

$$130 - 10 = 1.2$$

If you are thinking the most highly leveraged investor is the smart one, recall that a trade-off between risk and return exists before continuing.

Key Takeaways

- Asset bubbles occur when the prices of some asset, like stocks or real estate, increase rapidly due to some combination of low interest rates, high leverage, new technology, and large, often self-fulfilling shifts in demand.
- The expectation of higher prices in the future, combined with high levels of borrowing, allow asset prices to detach from their underlying economic fundamentals.

13.3 Financial Panics

Learning Objective

1. What are financial panics and what causes them?

A**financial panic***occurs when leveraged financial intermediaries and other investors must sell assets quickly in order to meet lenders'***calls**. Lenders call loans, or ask for repayment, when interest rates increase and/or when the value of collateral pledged to repay the loan sinks below the amount the borrower owes. Calls are a normal part of everyday business, but during a panic, they all come en masse due to some shock, often the **bursting** of an asset bubble. Bubbles, like people, are bound to die but nobody knows in advance when they will do so. A burst is sometimes triggered by an obvious shock, like a natural catastrophe or the failure of an important company, but sometimes something as seemingly innocuous as a large sell order can touch them off.

During a panic, almost everybody must sell and few can or want to buy, so prices plummet, triggering additional calls, and yet more selling. Invariably, some investors, usually the most highly leveraged ones, cannot sell assets quickly enough, or for a high enough price, to "meet the call" and repay their loans. Banks and other lenders begin to suffer defaults. Their lenders (other banks, depositors, holders of commercial paper), in turn, begin to wonder if they are still creditworthy. Asymmetric information and uncertainty reign supreme, inducing lenders to restrict credit. *At some point, investors' emotions take over, and they literally go into a panic, one that makes Tony Soprano's panic attacks seem like a stroll in the park.*[7]

financial panic

Panicked selling occurs during the rapid de-leveraging of the financial system following the bursting of an asset bubble.

calls

A lender asks a borrower to repay, usually because interest rates have increased and/or the value of collateral has declined.

bursting

When an asset bubble rapidly deflates (i.e., the price of the asset rapidly decreases).

de-leveraging

Lenders force borrowers to invest more of their own equity in assets.

credit crunch

The volume of loans decreases dramatically, usually in response to the bursting of an asset bubble during a financial crisis.

negative bubble

A bubble characterized by prices that are far below their rational value.

Panics often cause the rapid **de-leveraging** *of the financial system, a period when interest rates for riskier types of loans and securities increase and/or when a* **credit crunch**, *or a large decrease in the volume of lending, takes place.* Such conditions often usher in a **negative bubble**, a period when high interest rates, tight credit, and expectations of lower asset prices in the future cause asset values to trend downward, sometimes well below the values indicated by underlying economic fundamentals. *During de-leveraging, the forces that drove asset prices up now conspire to drag them lower.*

Stop and Think Box

In New York in 1764, interest rates spiked from 6 to 12 percent and expected revenues from land plummeted by about 25 percent. What happened to real estate prices and why?

They dropped significantly because it was more expensive to borrow money, thus increasing the total cost of real estate ownership, and because the land was expected to yield lower revenues. Thinking of the land as a perpetuity and FV as the expected revenues arising from it:

$$PV = FV / i$$

$$PV = £100 / .06 = £1{,}666.66$$

$$PV = £100 / .12 = £833.33$$

And that is just the interest rate effect. Decreasing FV by £25 leads to the following:

$$PV = £75 / .12 = £625, \text{ or a decrease of about two-thirds.}$$

"I know of sundry Estates [farms and other landed property] that has been taken by Execution [foreclosed upon]," a New York merchant reported late in 1766, "and sold for not more than one third of their value owing to the scarcity of money."[8]

As shown in Figure 13.3, the most highly leveraged investor suffers most of all.

FIGURE 13.3 The effects of leverage on returns in a falling market

Leverage doesn't look so cool now, does it!

Period	Asset Price	Cumulative Return, No Leverage (%)	Cumulative Return, 50% Leverage (%)	Cumulative Return, 90% Leverage (%)
0	100	–	–	–
1	90	−10	−10+	−10+
2	80	−20	−20+	−20+
3	70	−30	−30+	−30+

Again, I used the rate of return formula, but coupons are zero so that $R = (P_{t1} - P_{to})/P_{to}$. As the price of the asset falls, the unleveraged investor suffers negative returns:

$$90 - 100 / 100 = -.1$$

$$80 - 100 / 100 = -.2$$

$$70 - 100 / 100 = -.3$$

The leveraged investors lose the same percentage and must now pay a high interest rate for their loans, or put up the equity themselves, at a time when the opportunity cost of doing so is substantial:

$$(90 - 50 + 50) / 100 = -.1 + \text{interest on } \$50$$

$$(80 - 50 + 50)/100 = -.2 + \text{interest on } \$50$$

$$(70 - 50 + 50) / 100 = -.3 + \text{interest on } \$50$$

The higher the leverage, the larger the sum that must be borrowed at high rates.

$$(90 - 90 + 90) / 100 = -.1 + \text{interest on } \$90$$

$$(80 - 90 + 90) / 100 = -.2 + \text{interest on } \$90$$

$$(70 - 90 + 90) / 100 = -.3 + \text{interest on } \$90$$

Also, the higher the leverage, the smaller the price change needs to be to trigger a call. At 50 percent leverage, a $100 asset could drop to $50 before the lender must call. At 90 percent leverage, a $100 asset need lose only $10 to induce a call.

Key Takeaways

- The bursting of an asset bubble, or the rapidly declining prices of an asset class, usually leads to a financial panic, reductions in the quantity of available credit, and the de-leveraging of the financial system.
- The most highly leveraged investors suffer most.

13.4 Lender of Last Resort (LLR)

Learning Objective

1. What is a lender of last resort and what does it do?

As noted, financial panics and the de-leveraging that often occurs after them can wreak havoc on the real economy by decreasing the volume of loans, insurance contracts, and other beneficial financial products. That, in turn, can cause firms to reduce output and employment. *Lenders of last resort try to stop panics and de-leveraging by adding liquidity to the financial system and/or attempting to restore investor confidence.* They add liquidity by increasing the money supply, reducing interest rates, and making loans to worthy borrowers who find themselves shut off from their normal sources of external finance. They try to restore investor confidence by making upbeat statements about the overall health of the economy and/or financial system and by implementing policies that investors are likely to find beneficial. After a stock market crash in 1987, for example, the Federal Reserve stopped a panic *merely by promising to loan liberally to temporarily strapped banks.*

Stop and Think Box

In a single day, October 19, 1987, the S&P fell by 20 percent. What caused such a rapid decline? Why did the panic not result in de-leveraging or recession?

According to a short history of the event by Mark Carlson ("A Brief History of the 1987 Stock Market Crash with a Discussion of the Federal Reserve Response"),[9] "During the years prior to the crash, equity markets had been posting strong gains. . . . There had been an influx of new investors. . . . Equities were also boosted by some favorable tax treatments given to the financing of corporate buyouts. . . . The macroeconomic outlook during the months leading up to the crash had become somewhat less certain. . . . Interest rates were rising globally. . . . A growing U.S. trade deficit and decline in the value of the dollar were leading to concerns about inflation and the need for higher interest rates in the United States as well." On the day of the crash, investors learned that deficits were higher than expected and that the favorable tax rules might change. As prices dropped, "record margin calls" were made, fueling further selling. The panic did not proceed further because Federal Reserve Chairman Alan Greenspan restored confidence in the stock market by promising to make large loans to banks exposed to brokers hurt by the steep decline in stock prices. Specifically, the Fed made it known that "The Federal Reserve, consistent with its responsibilities as the Nation's central bank, affirmed today its readiness to serve as a source of liquidity to support the economic and financial system."

Lenders of last resort partially emulate three rules first promulgated by U.S. Treasury Secretary Alexander Hamilton (1789–1795) but popularized by *Economist* editor Walter Bagehot in his 1873 book *Lombard Street*. As Bagehot put it, during a banking panic an LLR should make loans:

> *at a very high rate of interest. This will operate as a heavy fine on unreasonable timidity, and will prevent the greatest number of applications by persons who do not require it. The rate should be raised early in the panic, so that the fine may be paid early; that no one may borrow out of idle precaution without paying well for it; that the Banking reserve may be protected as far as possible. Secondly. That at this rate these advances should be made on all good banking securities, and as largely as the public ask for them. The reason is plain. The object is to stay alarm, and nothing therefore should be done to cause alarm. But the way to cause alarm is to refuse some one who has good security to offer . . . No advances indeed need be made by which the Bank will ultimately lose. The amount of bad business in commercial countries is an infinitesimally small fraction of the whole business . . . The great majority, the majority to be protected, are the 'sound' people, the people who have good security to offer. If it is known that the Bank of England [the LLR in Bagehot's time and country] is freely advancing on what in ordinary times is reckoned a good security—on what is then commonly pledged and easily convertible—the alarm of the solvent merchants and bankers will be stayed. But if securities, really good and usually convertible, are refused by the Bank, the alarm will not abate, the other loans made will fail in obtaining their end, and the panic will become worse and worse.*

This is usually translated as LLRs lending freely on good security at a penalty rate. Today, central banks acting as LLR usually lend freely on good collateral but only to banks, not the public. Moreover, they typically reduce interest rates in order to stimulate the economy. The unfortunate result of the latter change is to increase moral hazard, or risk taking on the part of banks that "bank on" cheap loans from the LLR should they run into difficulties.

The most common form of lender of last resort today is the government central bank, like the European Central Bank (ECB) or the Federal Reserve. The International Monetary Fund (IMF) sometimes tries to act as a sort of international lender of last resort, but it has been largely unsuccessful in that role. In the past, wealthy individuals like J. P. Morgan and private entities like bank clearinghouses tried to act as lenders of last resort, with mixed success. Most individuals did not have enough wealth or influence to thwart a panic, and bank clearinghouses were at most regional in nature.

Key Takeaway

- A lender of last resort is an individual, a private institution, or, more commonly, a government central bank that attempts to stop a financial panic and/or postpanic de-leveraging by increasing the money supply, decreasing interest rates, making loans, and/or restoring investor confidence.

13.5 Bailouts and Resolutions

Learning Objective

1. What is a bailout and how does it differ from the actions of a lender of last resort?
2. What is a resolution, and how does it differ from a bailout?

As noted above, lenders of last resort provide liquidity, loans, and confidence. They make loans to solvent institutions facing temporary solvency problems due to the crisis, not inevitable bankruptcy.[10] **Bailouts**, *by contrast, restore the losses suffered by one or more economic agents, usually with taxpayer money*. The restoration can come in the form of outright grants or the purchase of equity but often takes the form of subsidized or government-guaranteed loans. Unsurprisingly, bailouts are often politically controversial because they can appear to be unfair and because they increase moral hazard, or risk-taking on the part of entities that expect to be bailed out if they encounter difficulties. *Nevertheless, if the lender of last resort cannot stop the formation of a negative bubble or massive de-leveraging, bailouts can be an effective way of mitigating further declines in economic activity.*

bailout

When taxpayer money is used to restore losses suffered by economic agents.

During the Great Depression, for example, the federal government used $500 million of taxpayer money to capitalize the Reconstruction Finance Corporation (RFC). In its initial phase, the RFC made some $2 billion in low-interest loans to troubled banks, railroads, and other businesses. *Though at first deprecated as welfare for the rich, the RFC, most observers now concede, helped the economy to recover by keeping important companies afloat.* Also during the depression, the Home Owners Loan Corporation (HOLC), seeded with $200 million of taxpayer dollars, bailed out homeowners, many of whom had **negative equity** in their homes, by refinancing mortgages on terms favorable to the borrowers.

negative equity

The market price of an asset is less than the sum borrowed to acquire it. Also known as being "in the bucket" or "under water."

In a resolution, by contrast, a government agency, like the Federal Deposit Insurance Corporation (FDIC), disposes of a failed bank's assets (one at a time or in bulk to an acquiring institution) and uses the proceeds to repay the bank's creditors and owners according to their seniority, a predetermined order depending on their class (depositor, bondholder, stockholder). The line between resolutions and bailouts sometimes blurs. In the aftermath of the Savings and Loan Crisis, for example, the Resolution Trust Corporation (RTC) closed 747 thrifts with total assets of almost $400 billion. The RTC cost taxpayers only $125 billion while staving off a more severe systemic crisis.

Stop and Think Box

The 1979 bailout of automaker Chrysler, which entailed a government guarantee of its debt, saved the troubled corporation from bankruptcy. It quickly paid off its debt, and the U.S. Treasury, and hence taxpayers, were actually the richer for it. Was this bailout successful?

At the time, many observers thought so. Chrysler creditors, who received 30 cents for every dollar the troubled automaker owed them, did not think so, however, arguing that they had been fleeced to protect Chrysler stockholders. Workers who lost their jobs or were forced to accept reductions in pay and benefits were also skeptical. After Chrysler and the other U.S. carmakers fell into serious financial trouble after the Panic of 2008, some scholars suggested that the bailout was a disaster in the long term because it fooled Detroit executives into thinking they could continue business as usual. In retrospect, it may have been better to allow Chrysler to fail and a new, leaner, meaner company to emerge like a Phoenix from its ashes. Chastened Ford and GM executives would have worked harder and smarter, too, knowing that they would not be bailed out if they ran into difficulties.

Key Takeaways

- Bailouts usually occur after the actions of a lender of last resort, such as a central bank, have proven inadequate to stop negative effects on the real economy.
- Unlike resolutions, where assets are sold off to compensate creditors and owners according to their seniority, bailouts usually entail restoring losses to one or more economic agents using taxpayer funds.
- Although politically controversial, bailouts can stop negative bubbles from leading to excessive de-leveraging, debt deflation, and economic depression.

13.6 The Crisis of 2007–2009

Learning Objectives

1. What factors led to the financial crisis of 2007–2009?

subprime mortgages

Loans to risky borrowers collateralized with real estate, usually primary residences but sometimes vacation homes.

The most recent financial crisis began in 2007 as a nonsystemic crisis linked to **subprime mortgages**, *or risky loans to homeowners. In 2008, the failure of several major financial services companies turned it into the most severe systemic crisis in the United States since the Great Depression.*

The troubles began with a major housing asset bubble. As shown in Figure 13.4, between January 2000 and 2006, a major index of housing prices in the United States more than doubled. (Prices went up more in some areas than in others because real estate is a local asset.) Home prices rose rapidly for several reasons. As shown in Figure 13.5, mortgage rates were quite low, to a large extent because the Federal Reserve kept the federal funds rate, the rate at which banks lend to each other overnight, very low.

FIGURE 13.4 Case-Shiller U.S. Home Price Composite Index, 2000–2010

Up, up, but not away!

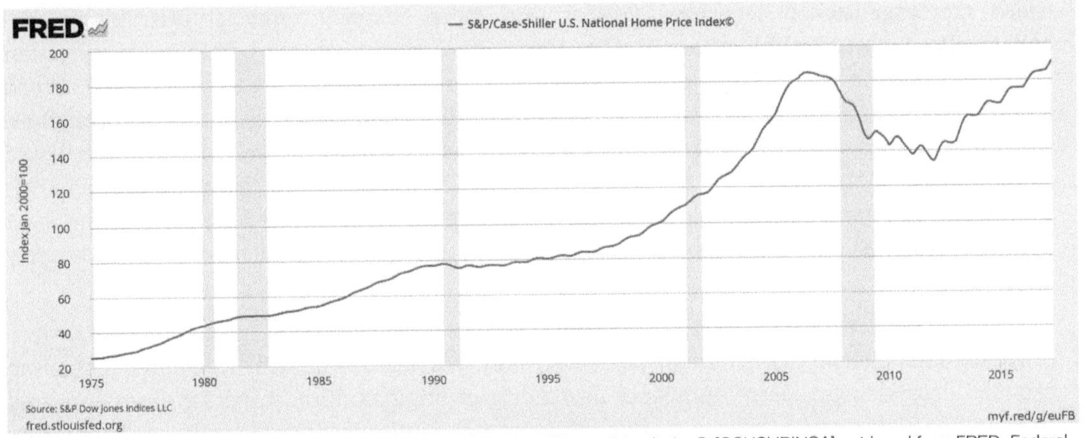

Source: S&P Dow Jones Indices LLC, S&P/Case-Shiller U.S. National Home Price Index© [CSUSHPINSA], retrieved from FRED, Federal Reserve Bank of St. Louis; https://fred.stlouisfed.org/series/CSUSHPINSA, August 27, 2017.

FIGURE 13.5 U.S. interest rates, 2000–2010

Remember, low interest means high price (and vice versa).

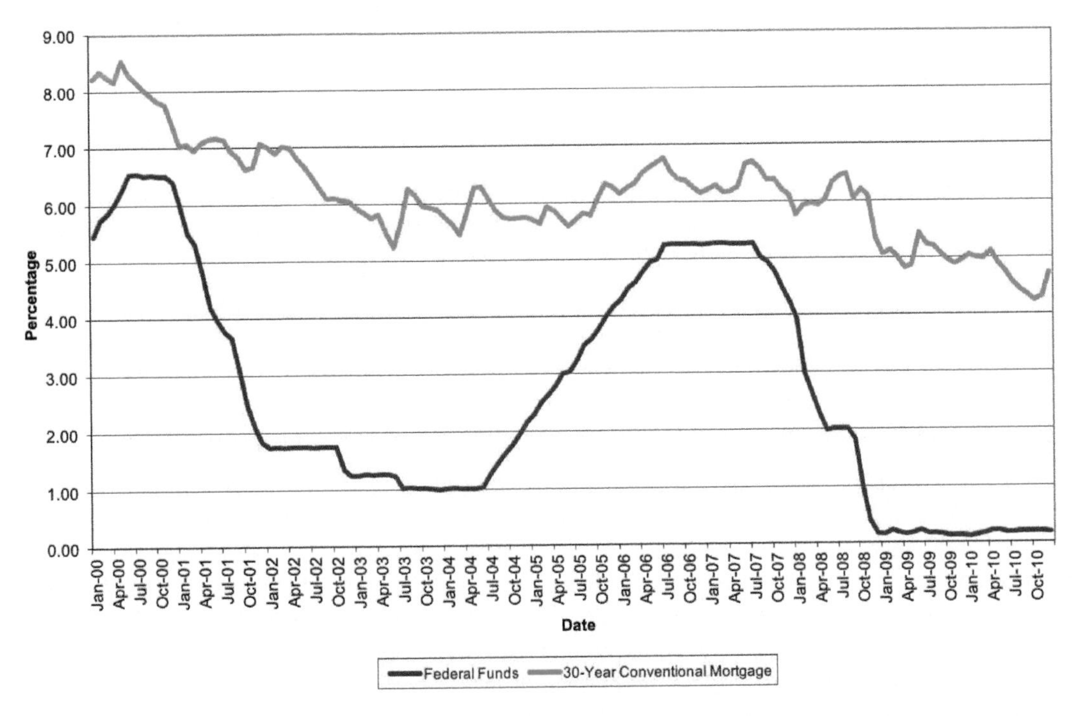

Mortgages also became much easier to obtain. Traditionally, mortgage lenders held mortgage loans on their own balance sheets. If a homeowner defaulted, the lender, usually a bank or life insurance company, suffered the loss. Lenders were therefore understandably cautious about whom they lent to and on what terms. To shield themselves from loss, lenders insisted that borrowers contribute a substantial percentage of the home's value as a down payment. The down payment ensured that the borrower had some equity at stake, some reason to work hard and not to default. It also provided lenders with a buffer if housing prices declined. Traditionally, lenders also verified that borrowers were employed or had other means of income from investments or other sources.

financial engineer

A person who engages in financial engineering, the process of creating new, hopefully improved, financial products by redesigning or repackaging existing financial instruments.

mortgage-backed securities

A bundle of home mortgages.

collateralized mortgage obligations

A type of derivative formed by financial engineering mortgage-backed securities into tranches with different risk-return characteristics.

tranches

French for "slice." Part of a structured finance instrument such as a collateralized mortgage obligation.

All that changed with the widespread advent of securitization, the practice of bundling and selling mortgages to institutional investors. Banks also began to "**financial engineer**" those bundles, called **mortgage-backed securities** (MBSs), into more complex financial instruments like **collateralized mortgage obligations** (CMOs). MBSs afforded investors the portfolio diversification benefits of holding a large number of mortgages; CMOs allowed investors to pick the risk-return profile they desired. They did so by slicing a group of MBSs into derivative securities (aka **tranches**) with credit ratings ranging from AAA, which would be the last to suffer losses, to BBB, which would suffer from the first defaults. The AAA tranches, of course, enjoyed a higher price (lower yield) than the lower-rated tranches. The holders of the lowest-rated tranches, those who took on the most risks, suffered most during the subprime maelstrom but ultimately all MBS holders were adversely affected.

Securitization allowed mortgage lenders to specialize in making loans, turning them more into originators than lenders. Origination was much easier than lending because it required little or no capital. Unsurprisingly, a large number of new mortgage originators, most mere brokers, appeared on the scene. *Paid a commission at closing, originators had little incentive to screen good borrowers from bad and much more incentive to sign up anyone with a pulse.* A race to the bottom occurred as originators competed for business by reducing screening and other credit standards. At the height of the bubble, loans to no income, no job or assets (NINJA) borrowers were common. So-called liars' loans for hundreds of thousands of dollars were made to borrowers without documenting their income or assets. Instead of insisting on a substantial down payment, many originators cajoled homeowners into *borrowing 125 percent of the value of the home* because it increased their commissions. They also aggressively pushed adjustable rate mortgages (ARMs) that offered low initial teaser rates that later reset at much higher levels.

Regulators allowed, and even condoned, such practices in the name of "affordable housing," even though six earlier U.S. mortgage securitization schemes had ended badly.[11] Regulators also allowed Fannie Mae and Freddie Mac, two giant stockholder-owned mortgage securitization companies whose debt was effectively guaranteed by the federal government, to take on excessive risks and leverage themselves to the hilt. They also allowed credit-rating agencies to give investment-grade ratings to complicated mortgage-backed securities of dubious quality.

Observers, including Yale's Robert Shiller[12] and NYU Stern's Nouriel Roubini,[13] warned about the impending crisis, but few listened. *As long as housing prices kept rising, shoddy underwriting, weak regulatory oversight, and overrated securities were not problems because borrowers who got into trouble could easily refinance or sell the house for a profit.* Indeed, many people began to purchase houses with the intention of "flipping" them a month later for a quick buck.

In June 2006, however, housing prices peaked, and by the end of that year it was clear that the bubble had gone bye-bye. By summer 2007, prices were falling quickly. Defaults mounted as the sale/refinance option disappeared, and borrowers wondered why they should continue paying a $300,000 mortgage on a house worth only $250,000, especially at a time when a nasty increase in fuel costs and a minor bout of inflation strained personal budgets. Highly leveraged subprime mortgage lenders, like Countrywide and Indymac, suffered large enough losses to erode their narrow base of equity capital, necessitating their bankruptcy or sale to stronger entities. By early 2008, investment bank Bear Stearns, which was deeply involved in subprime securitization products, teetered on the edge of bankruptcy before being purchased by J. P. Morgan for a mere $10 per share.

FIGURE 13.6 Delinquency rate on U.S. residential mortgages, 2000–2011
Good times, bad times, you know we've had our share. Note: Shaded areas indicate U.S. recessions.

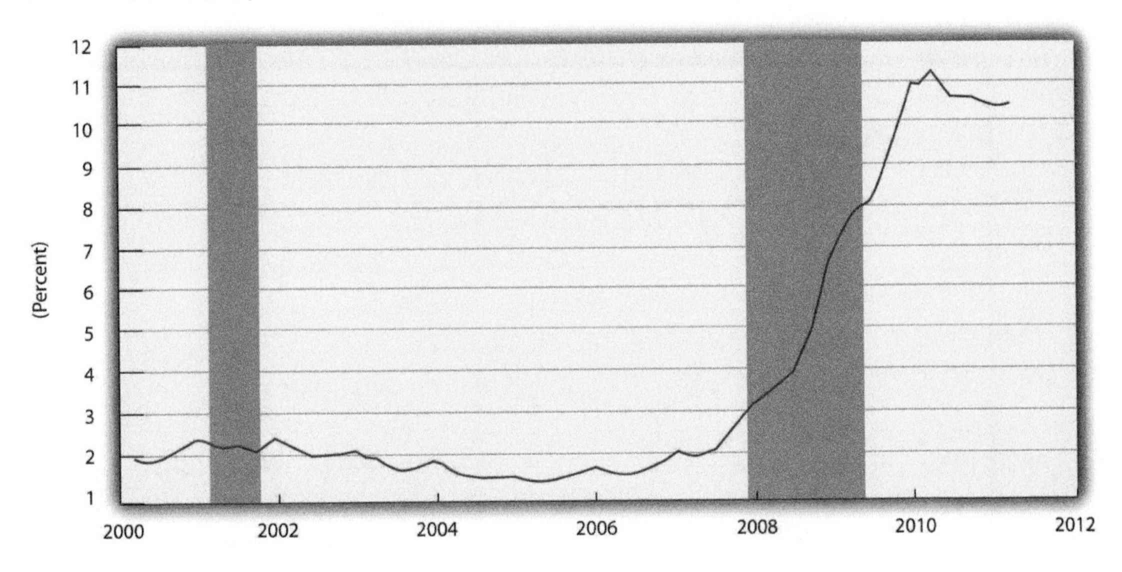

Data from: Board of Governors of the Federal Reserve System. 2011 research.stlouisfed.org.

As the crisis worsened, becoming more systemic in nature as asymmetric information intensified, the Federal Reserve responded as a lender of last resort by cutting its federal funds target from about 5 to less than 2 percent between August 2007 and August 2008. It also made massive loans directly to distressed financial institutions. Mortgage rates decreased from a high of 6.7 percent in July 2007 to 5.76 percent in January 2008, but later rebounded to almost 6.5 percent in August 2008. *Moreover, housing prices continued to slide, from an index score of 216 in July 2007 to just 178 a year later. Defaults on subprime mortgages continued to climb, endangering the solvency of other highly leveraged financial institutions, including Fannie Mae and Freddie Mac, which the government had to nationalize (take over and run).* The government also arranged for the purchase of Merrill Lynch by Bank of America for $50 billion in stock. But it decided, probably due to criticism that its actions were creating moral hazard, to allow Lehman Brothers to go bankrupt. That policy quickly backfired, however, because Lehman dragged one of its major counterparties, AIG, down with it. Once bitten, twice shy, the government stepped in with a massive bailout for AIG to keep it from bankrupting yet other large institutions as it toppled.

FIGURE 13.7 Daily closing value of the Dow Jones Industrial Average, September–October 2008

Oh Dow, where art thou?

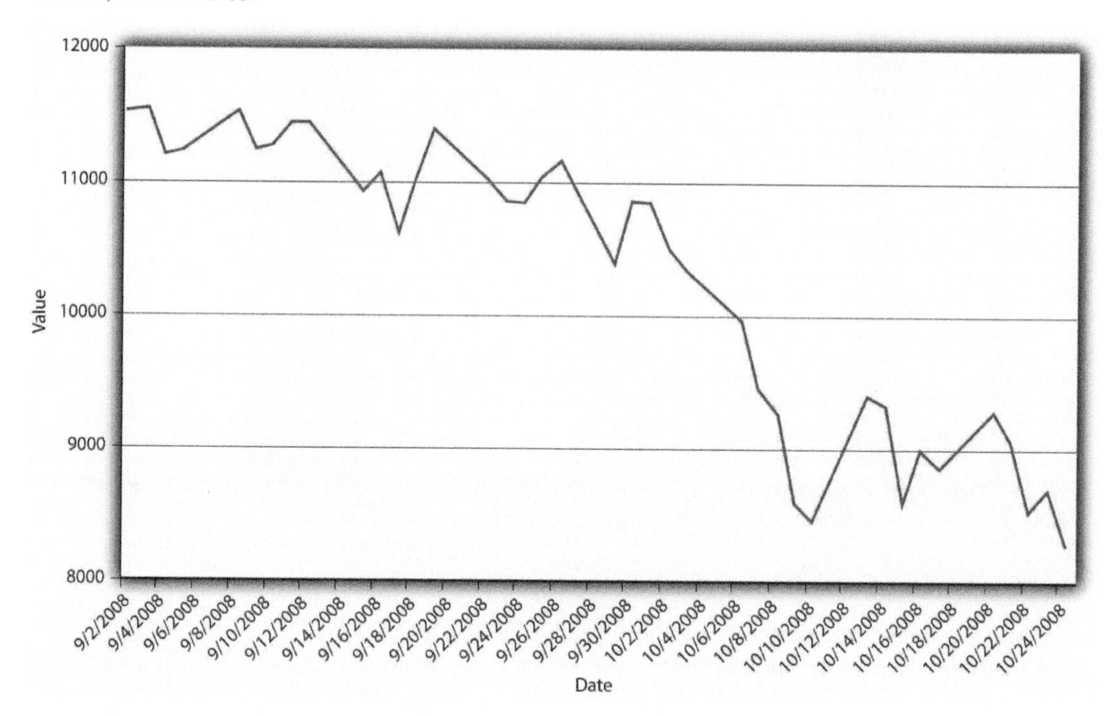

FIGURE 13.8 Bond yields, September–October 2008

Note the increase in spreads.

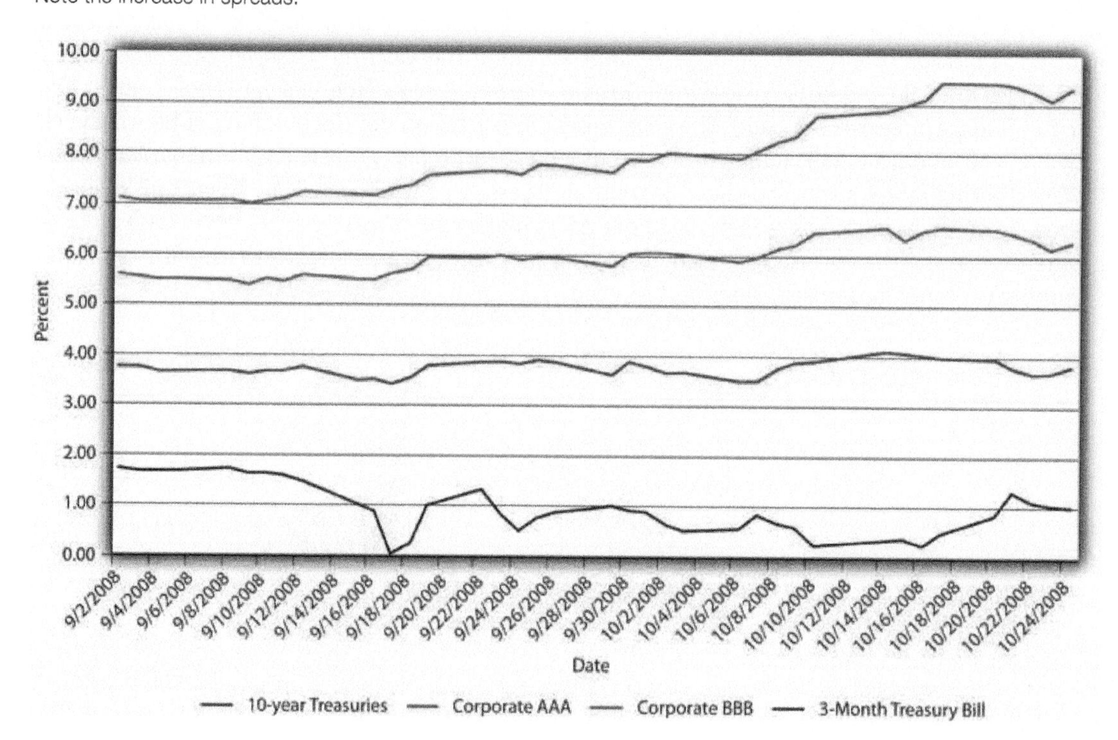

The damage, however, had been done and panic overtook both the credit and stock markets in September and October 2008. With each passing day, asymmetric information grew more intense. With Treasury bonds the only clear safe haven, investors fled other markets thereby causing significant disruptions and failures. The entire asset-backed commercial paper market shut down, money market withdrawals soared after one of the largest of those staid institutions reported losses ("broke the buck," a very rare event indeed), and mortgage and bond insurers dropped like flies hit with a can of Raid. Figure 13.7 and Figure 13.8 graphically portray the resulting carnage in the stock and bond markets.

Stop and Think Box

What is happening in Figure 13.8?

Investors sold corporate bonds, especially the riskier Baa ones, forcing their prices down and yields up. In a classic flight to quality, they bought Treasuries, especially short-dated ones, the yields of which dropped from 1.69 percent on September 1 to .03 percent on September 17.

With an economic recession and major elections looming, politicians worked feverishly to develop a bailout plan. The Bush administration's plan, which offered some $700 billion to large financial institutions, initially met defeat in the House of Representatives. After various amendments, including the addition of a large sum of pork barrel sweeteners, the bill passed the Senate and the House. The plan empowered the Treasury to purchase distressed assets and to inject capital directly into banks. Combined with the $300 billion Hope for Homeowners plan, a bailout for some distressed subprime borrowers, and the direct bailout of AIG, the government's bailout effort became the largest, in percentage of GDP terms, since the Great Depression. The Treasury later decided that buying so-called toxic assets, assets of uncertain and possibly no value, was not economically or politically prudent. Instead, it purchased preferred shares in most major banks, *even those that did not desire any assistance.* That raised fear of government ownership of banks, which has a dubious history because many governments have found the temptation to direct loans to political favorites, instead of the best borrowers, irresistible.[14]

Economists and policymakers are now busy trying to prevent a repeat performance, or at least mitigate the scale of the next bubble. One approach is to educate people about bubbles in the hope that they will be more cautious investors. Another is to encourage bank regulators to use their powers to keep leverage to a minimum. A third approach is to use monetary policy—higher interest rates or tighter money supply growth—to deflate bubbles before they grow large enough to endanger the entire financial system. Each approach has its strengths and weaknesses. Education might make investors afraid to take on any risk. Tighter regulation and monetary policy might squelch legitimate, wealth-creating industries and sectors. A combination of better education, more watchful regulators, and less accommodative monetary policy may serve us best.

The Dodd-Frank Wall Street Reform and Consumer Protection Act, a massive regulatory reform passed in July 2010 in direct response to the crisis, may be a step in that direction, but critics note that the legislation is complex, unwieldy, and "does not incorporate a clear or consistent approach to the problem of regulating the financial sector."[15] Like other regulations passed in the wake of panics, it may stop an exact repeat of the 2008 crisis but probably will not prevent a different set of institutions, instruments, derivatives, and bubbles from causing another crisis in the future. Instead of creating new approaches to regulation, like a proposed tax on banks that pose systemic risks, the Dodd-Frank Act establishes new tools like **resolution plans** as well as new agencies like the Financial Stability Oversight Council, which is charged with monitoring and reducing systemic risk. The act also simultaneously increases and decreases the powers of others, including the Federal Reserve, which must now enforce stiffer capital, liquidity, leverage, and risk management requirements. The future of Dodd-Frank is uncertain as the Donald J. Trump administration has signaled that it would like to see the act repealed or at least heavily revised and has made considerable progress towards its goals.

resolution plans

So-called "living wills" that banks have to create under Federal Reserve supervision that, it is hoped, will enable regulators like the FDIC to more easily, quickly, and cheaply wind down the affairs of impaired or failed banks.

In the final section, we describe simple financial regulations over a millennium old and assess the extent to which they may help to make the global financial system safer and even fairer.

Key Takeaways

- Low interest rates, indifferent regulators, unrealistic credit ratings for complex mortgage derivatives, and poor incentives for mortgage originators led to a housing bubble that burst in 2006.
- As housing prices fell, homeowners with dubious credit and negative equity began to default in unexpectedly high numbers.
- Highly leveraged financial institutions could not absorb the losses and had to shut down or be absorbed by stronger institutions.
- Despite the Fed's efforts as lender of last resort, the nonsystemic crisis became systemic in September 2008 following the failure of Lehman Brothers and AIG.
- The government responded with huge bailouts of subprime mortgage holders and major financial institutions.

13.7 Islamic Banking and Financial Stability

Learning Objectives

1. Describe the major features of Islamic finance and assess its ability to reduce financial instability.

Several scholars claim that *the 1997–1998 financial crisis* (exchange rate crises, mostly in East Asia, after the Russian bond default and the LTCM failure) and the *2008 fiasco did not hurt Islamic banks.*[16] If those claims are true, Western regulators would do well to consider reforms along Islamic lines.

Before we can assess such claims, however, we need to learn more about Islamic finance, especially Islamic banking. Insurance, financial instruments, and financial practices are considered Islamic if they are *halal*, or in other words if Muslim scholars consider them in line with Quranic or *Shari'a* law, and more specifically Islamic rules on transactions, or *Fiqh al-Muamalat*. Everyone acknowledges that the *Quran* (2:274) forbids the taking or receiving of interest: "God has made buying and selling lawful and *riba* unlawful." *Riba* includes interest but also, and this is very important, *any increase not shared with a counterparty*.[17]

Banking without interest seems unlikely at best but experience proves otherwise. From a single bank in Egypt in 1963, the number of Islamic banks in operation had risen to more than 300, across 75 countries, by 2010. By 2012, the total assets of Islamic banks exceeded $1.2 trillion, with growth averaging an astonishing 15 to 20 percent per year.[18]

Islamic insurance also thrives in the form of *takaful* or joint guarantee, a close analog of Western mutual assurance wherein participants contribute to a common fund, invested of course in *Shari'a* compliant ways, from which claims are settled. Although Western-style insurance is *haram* (prohibited) because of its reliance on *riba* and its countenance of *maisir* (gambling), *takaful* meets all the religious tests and has found a major market in Malaysia and other southeast Asian Muslim nations.[19]

Islamic banks (IBs) invest in assets that do not pay explicit interest. Some (*Musharakah/Mudarabah*) are based on Profit and Loss Sharing (PLS), while others (*Murabahah, Ijarah*) are essentially Fixed Income instruments. *Ijarah* are leasing arrangements whereby an IB purchases an asset and then leases it to the customer for a fixed period and price. *Murabahah* resemble conventional bonds and hence are sometimes considered *haram* even though they are safer than PLS and constitute a majority of IBs' assets. Instead of lending $1,000 to a borrower at

10 percent for a year and collecting $1,100 to fund the purchase of, say, a refrigerator, an IB will buy the refrigerator for $1,000 and sell it to its customer for $1,100, with payment due in a year. On the surface, IBs have simply engaged in loophole mining (*hilah* or subterfuge, artifice, or stratagem) and have discovered yet another way to avoid a usury cap (this one set at zero).[20] If the sum due were not paid, however, a conventional bank would charge the borrower additional interest *and* repossess the refrigerator. The IB, by contrast, would allow its customer more time to pay at no charge, even if it eventually had to repossess the collateral due to non-payment.[21] So while the Western bank's return is fixed by law, that of the IB is not, rendering the transaction more like an equity stake than a loan.

As their name implies, PLSs are more clearly *equity investments* and hence readily accepted by most Islamic authorities as *halal*.[22] Closely analogous to conventional venture capital funding, *Mudarabah* contracts are profit-sharing arrangements whereby an IB profits only if the entrepreneur does as well and shared losses are a distinct possibility. *Musharakah* are joint ventures and hence also based on equity-ownership and a partnership relationship rather than loans and a debtor-creditor relationship.[23]

IBs cannot pay interest, either, so they cannot actively manage their liabilities as easily as modern Western banks do. That means their growth is based largely on deposits, which are structured as *Wadiah* or a trusteeship. While IBs can pay depositors *hibah* (a gift), the payment is entirely discretionary and hence not *riba*. Borrowing through short-term loans, like NCDs, is, however, *haram*, unless it takes the form of a *sukuk*, or a bond rendered *halal* (at least in the eyes of some) by the fact that the issuer also serves as trustee. So while IBs can experience depositor runs, they can stop them with a promise of *hibah*. In addition, they do not face gap risks as serious as those faced by conventional banks because they pay for most of their sources of funds on a strictly voluntary basis.[24]

IBs may also be better governed than Western banks as traditional checks and balances at the latter deteriorated over the twentieth century.[25] Better governance, *ceteris paribus*, should enhance safety and stability, especially when combined with the higher capital ratios (less leverage) and higher reserve ratios (more liquidity) maintained by IBs.[26] But adherence to *Shari'a* law comes at an inevitable cost. Islamic banks suffer from lower productivity, even after accounting for a wide range of factors like scale and country of origin.[27] Similarly, IBs in Pakistan consistently post lower average ROA and ROE than Pakistan's conventional banks do.[28] Of course the finding that lower-risk banks produce lower returns should not come as a surprise.

Islamic finance's biggest contribution to stability might be its treatment of all exploitative behavior as *riba*. Western finance, particularly investment banking, often becomes a battle for bucks where the exploitation of *clients* is not only allowed but celebrated with calls to "rip someone's face off" or "blow someone up."[29] Muslim scholars instead encourage fair trading, where buyers and sellers look for ways to share the surplus created by trading (all that area below the demand curve and above the supply curve). For Muslims, profits are simply a means to an end, and not an end in and of themselves, so sharing surplus is not only moral, it is logical. Fair trading and stability reduce incentives to exact *riba*, which further stabilizes the economy by reducing the failures and other extreme outcomes that commonly occur when one party uses information or other advantages to expropriate counterparties.[30]

Of course, as noted elsewhere in this book, not all non-Muslims are wild-eyed capitalists like Montgomery C. Burns. Venture capitalist funds, mutual insurers, and credit unions embody many of the key aspects of Islamic finance without abandoning interest as a key tool for compensating economic entities for the opportunity cost of their money. To reduce the likelihood of another financial crisis, then, perhaps regulators should try to reduce non-interest forms of *riba*, or exploitative practices like financial predation and undisclosed conflicts of interest.[31]

Key Takeaways

- Islamic banks perform better than conventional ones during financial crises because they take on less risk thanks to higher levels of reserves and capitalization, which may stem from superior governance.
- Riba, or the taking of interest or other exploitative actions, is haram, or prohibited under the Quran. That restriction has not prevented the explosive growth of Islamic finance, including banking and insurance.
- Islamic financial instruments often resemble Western financial arrangements in many particulars but usually contain key, if subtle, differences that render them halal, or acceptable under Shari'a law.
- Regulators interested in reducing financial system fragility who do not wish to adopt Islamic banking in total may still learn from Islamic financial principles, including when it is appropriate to favor mutuality, equity partnerships instead of debtor-creditor relationships, and higher levels of capital and liquidity.

13.8 Suggested Reading

Acharya, Viral, Thomas Cooley, Matthew Richardson, and Ingo Walter. *Regulating Wall Street: The Dodd-Frank Act and the New Architecture of Global Finance.* Hoboken, NJ: John Wiley and Sons, 2011.

Barwell, Richard. *Macroeconomic Policy After the Crash: Issues in Microprudential and Macroprudential Policy.* New York: Palgrave Macmillan, 2017.

Claessens, Stijn, M. Ayan Kose, Luc Laeven, and Fabian Valencia. *Financial Crises: Causes, Consequences, and Policy Responses.* International Monetary Fund, 2014.

Kindleberger, Charles, and Robert Aliber. *Manias, Panics, and Crashes: A History of Financial Crises*, 5th ed. Hoboken, NJ: John Wiley and Sons, 2005.

Reinhart, Carmen, and Kenneth Rogoff. *This Time Is Different: Eight Centuries of Financial Folly.* Princeton: Princeton University Press, 2009.

Roubini, Nouriel, and Brad Stetser. *Bailouts or Bail-ins: Responding to Financial Crises in Emerging Markets.* New York: Peterson Institute, 2004.

Skrabec, Quentin. *The 100 Most Important American Financial Crises.* New York: Greenwood, 2014.

Sprague, Irvine. *Bailout: An Insider's Account of Bank Failures and Rescues.* New York: Beard Books, 2000.

Wright, Robert E., ed. *Bailouts: Public Money, Private Profit.* New York: Columbia University Press, 2010.

Endnotes

1. Tim Arango, "The Housing-Bubble and the American Revolution," *New York Times* (29 November 2008), WK5. www.nytimes.com/2008/11/30/weekinreview/30arango .html?_r=2&pagewanted=1&ref=weekinreview
2. www.amatecon.com/gd/gdcandc.html
3. en.wikipedia.org/wiki/Free_good
4. July 21, 2007. online.wsj.com/article/SB118498744630073854.html
5. *Cause of, and Cure for, Hard Times* (Anonymous, 1818)
6. For more on the crisis, see Tim Arango, "The Housing-Bubble Revolution," *New York Times* (30 November 2008), WK 5. www.nytimes.com/2008/11/30 / weekinreview/30arango.html?_r=2&pagewanted=1&ref=weekinreview
7. www.menshealth.com/health/when-panic-attacks
8. Robert E. Wright, *Fubarnomics: A Lighthearted, Serious Look at America's Economic Ills* (Amherst, NY. Prometheus, 2010), 44.

9. www.federalreserve.gov/Pubs/feds/2007/200713/200713pap.pdf
10. Doug Arner, *Financial Stability, Economic Growth, and the Role of Law* (New York: Cambridge University Press, 2007), 139–140.
11. Kenneth Snowden, "Mortgage Securitization in the United States: Twentieth Century Developments in Historical Perspective," in Michael Bordo and Richard Sylla, eds., *Anglo-American Financial Systems: Institutions and Markets in the Twentieth Century* (Burr Ridge, IL: Irwin Professional Publishing, 1995), 261–298.
12. www.econ.yale.edu/~shiller
13. pages.stern.nyu.edu/~nroubini
14. "Leaving Las Vegas: No Dire Mistakes so Far, but Governments Will Find Exiting Banks Far Harder Than Entering Them," *The Economist* (22 November 2008), 22.
15. Viral Acharya, Thomas Cooley, Matthew Richardson, and Ingo Walter, *Regulating Wall Street: The Dodd-Frank Act and the New Architecture of Global Finance* (Hoboken: John Wiley and Sons, 2011), 45.
16. Nor Hayati Bt Ahmad and Mohamad Akbar Noor Bin Mohamad Noor, "The Impact of 1998 and 2008 Financial Crises on Profitability of Islamic Banks," *Bangladesh Development Studies* 34, 1 (March 2011): 1–22; Shumi Akhtar and Maria Jahromi, "Impact of the Global Financial Crisis on Islamic and Conventional Stocks and Bonds," *Accounting and Finance* (May 2015): 1-33; Thorsten Beck, Asli Demirguc-Kunt, and Ouarda Merrouche, "Islamic vs. Conventional Banking: Business Model, Efficiency and Stability," World Bank, Policy Research Working Paper 5446 (October 2010).
17. Madiha Khan, "Islamic Banking Practices: Islamic Law and Prohibition of Riba," *Islamic Studies* 50, 3/4 (Autumn-Winter 2011): 413-22.
18. Bashar H. Malkawi, "Shari'ah Board in the Governance Structure of Islamic Financial Institutions," *American Journal of Comparative Law* 61, 3 (Summer 2013): 539-77.
19. Mohit Anand, "Islamic Insurance in Malaysia: Insights for the Indian Insurance Industry," *Singapore Journal of Legal Studies* (July 2014): 1-23.
20. Muhammad Tahir Mansoori, "Is 'Islamic Banking' Islamic?: Analysis of Current Debate on Shari'ah Legitimacy of Islamic Banking and Finance," *Islamic Studies* 50, 3/4 (Autumn-Winter 2011): 383-411.
21. Muhammad Ali Shaikh, "Contemporary Islamic Banking: The Issue of Murabahah," *Islamic Studies* 50, 3/4 (Autumn-Winter 2011): 435-48.
22. Zafar Eqbal, "Relevance of Islamic Banking System in the Present Economic Scenario," *Journal of the Indian Law Institute* 53, 2 (April-June 2011): 356-361.
23. Shahzad Q. Qadri, "Islamic Banking: An Introduction," *Business Law Today* 17, 6 (July/ August 2008): 58-61.
24. Shahzad Q. Qadri, "Islamic Banking: An Introduction," *Business Law Today* 17, 6 (July/August 2008): 58-61.
25. Robert E. Wright, *Corporation Nation* (Philadelphia: University of Pennsylvania Press, 2014); Bashar H. Malkawi, "Shari'ah Board in the Governance Structure of Islamic Financial Institutions," *American Journal of Comparative Law* 61, 3 (Summer 2013): 539-77.
26. Thorsten Beck, Asli Demirguc-Kunt, and Ouarda Merrouche, "Islamic vs. Conventional Banking: Business Model, Efficiency and Stability," World Bank, Policy Research Working Paper 5446 (October 2010).
27. Mariani Abdul-Majid, David S. Saal, and Giuliana Battisti, "Efficiency in Islamic and Conventional Banking: An International Comparison," *Journal of Productivity Analysis* 34, 1 (August 2010): 25-43.
28. Ramiz ur Rehmans and Inayat Ullah Mangla, "Corporate Governance and Performance of Financial Institutions in Pakistan: A Comparison between Conventional and Islamic Banks in Pakistan," *Pakistan Development Review* 49, 4 (Winter 2010): 461-75.
29. Frank Partnoy, *FIASCO: The Inside Story of a Wall Street Trader* (New York: Penguin, 1997), 14.
30. Asad Zaman, "Islamic Economics: A Survey of the Literature," *Islamic Studies* 49, 1 (Spring 2010): 37-63.
31. Robert E. Wright, *From Jim Crow Finance to Subprime Shenanigans: Expunging Financial Exclusion, Discrimination, and Predation from America* (New York: Columbia University Press, 2018).

CHAPTER 14

Central Bank Form and Function

Chapter Objectives

By the end of this chapter, students should be able to:

1. Define *central bank* and explain the importance of central banking.
2. Briefly sketch the history of U.S. central banking.
3. Explain when and how a country can do without a central bank.
4. Briefly sketch the structure of the Federal Reserve System.
5. Explain how other central banks compare to the Fed.
6. Define central bank independence and explain its importance.
7. Explain why independent central bankers prefer lower inflation rates than government officials do.

14.1 America's Central Banks

Learning Objectives

1. What is a central bank?
2. Why is central banking important?
3. How can a country manage without a central bank?
4. What is the history of central banking in the United States?

A **central bank** is a bank under some degree of government control that is generally charged with

- controlling the money supply (to a greater or lesser degree);
- providing price stability (influencing the price level);
- attaining economic output and employment goals;
- regulating commercial banks (and perhaps other depository and nondepository financial institutions);
- stabilizing the macroeconomy (proactively and/or by acting as a lender of last resort during financial crises);
- providing a payments system (check clearing and long-distance payments).

central bank

A bank that regulates the money supply, interest rates, and/or other financial institutions on behalf of the government.

Central banks also often act as the national government's banker by holding its deposits and making payments on its behalf. *During its 200-plus-year existence, the United States has had three different central banks and two periods, one short and one extremely long, with no central bank.*

base money

The most elementary form of money in a given society at a given time. The only type of money that can compose a bank's primary reserve.

Chartered by the federal government in 1791, the Bank of the United States (BUS) worked in conjunction with the U.S. Treasury secretary to act as a lender of last resort and a regulator of commercial banks. Specifically, it helped Alexander Hamilton, America's first Secretary of the Treasury,[1] to stymie the Panic of 1792. *It also returned the notes of commercial banks for redemption into gold and silver (the era's* ***base money****), thereby regulating commercial banks' reserve ratios and hence the money supply.* Owned by private shareholders, *the BUS was quite independent, a good trait for a central bank to have, as we'll see.* Its very independence and power to regulate commercial banks, however, made it unpopular in some influential political circles. Its charter was not renewed when it expired in 1811. The government's difficulties financing the War of 1812 (aka the Second War for Independence) convinced many that the country needed a new central bank. As a result, the government chartered the Bank of the United States (informally called the Second Bank or SBUS) in 1816. Insufficiently independent of the government at first, the SBUS, which like the BUS was headquartered in Philadelphia but had more numerous branches, stumbled by allowing commercial banks to increase their lending too much. It also suffered from internal agency problems, particularly at its branch in Baltimore. When a financial panic struck in late 1818 and early 1819, it failed to prevent a recession and debt deflation. Private stockholders reasserted control over the bank, placing it under the able direction of Nicholas Biddle, who successfully prevented the British economic meltdown of 1825 from spreading to America. Under Biddle, the SBUS also became an effective regulator of the nation's commercial banks, which by the 1820s numbered in the hundreds. Like the BUS before it, the SBUS paid for its diligence with its life. Aided by many commercial bankers, particularly those in Philadelphia's financial rival Manhattan, and America's traditional distaste for powerful institutions, Andrew Jackson vetoed the act rechartering it. (The SBUS continued its corporate life under a Pennsylvania charter, but it no longer had nationwide branches and was no longer the nation's central bank. It went bankrupt a few years later.)

From 1837 until late 1914, the United States had no central bank. Private institutions cropped up to clear checks and transfer funds over long distances. The Treasury kept its funds in commercial banks and in the hands of its tax collectors and left bank regulation to the market (deposit and note holders and stockholders) and state governments. The monetary base (gold and silver) it left largely to the whims of international trade. It could do so because the United States and most of the world's other major economies were on a gold and/or silver standard, meaning that their respective units of account were fixed in terms of so many grains of the precious stuff and hence fixed against each other.[2] The system was self-equilibrating. In other words, discretionary monetary policy was unnecessary because gold and silver flowed into or out of economies automatically, as needed. (The price level could move up or down in the short-term but eventually reverted to the long-term mean because deflation [inflation] created incentives [disincentives] to bring more gold and silver to market.) Nations today that maintain fixed exchange rates also find no need for a central bank, but instead use a simpler institution called a currency board. Countries that use a foreign currency as their own, a process called dollarization, need nothing at all because they essentially outsource their monetary policy to the central bank of the nation whose currency they use. (That is often the United States, hence the term *dollarization.*) Other central banking functions, like clearing checks and regulating financial institutions, can be performed by other entities, public and private. The function of lender of last resort typically cannot be fulfilled, however, by anything other than a central bank.

Indeed, the biggest problem with the U.S. arrangement was that there was no official systemwide lender of last resort, nobody to increase the money supply or lower interest rates in the face of a shock. As a result, the United States suffered from banking crises and financial panics of increasing ferocity beginning soon after the Second Bank's demise: 1837, 1839, 1857, 1873, 1884, 1893, and 1907. Most of those panics were followed by recessions and debt deflation because there was no institution wealthy enough to stop the death spiral (a shock, increased asymmetric information, decline in economic activity, bank panic, increased asymmetric information, decline in economic activity, unanticipated decline in the price level). In 1907, J. P. Morgan (the man, with help from his bank and web of business associates) mitigated, but did not prevent, a serious recession by acting as a lender of last resort. The episode convinced many Americans that the time had come to create a new central bank lest private financiers come to wield too much power. Anyone with the power to stop a panic, they reasoned, had the power to start one. Americans still feared powerful government institutions too, however, so it took another six years (1913) to agree on the new bank's structure, which was highly decentralized geographically and chock full of checks and balances. It took another year (1914) to get the bank, often called simply the Fed or the Federal Reserve, into operation.

Key Takeaways

- A central bank is a bank under some degree of government control that is responsible for influencing the money supply, interest rates, inflation, and other macroeconomic outcomes like output and employment. A central bank is usually the lender of last resort, the institution that can (and should) add liquidity and confidence to the financial system at the outbreak of panics and crises. On a quotidian basis, central banks also may clear checks, regulate banks and/or other financial institutions, and serve as the national government's bank.
- Early in its history, the United States was home to two privately owned central banks, the Bank of the United States and the Second Bank, that acted as a lender of last resort and regulated commercial banks by returning their notes to them for redemption in base money (then gold and silver). Although economically effective, both were politically unpopular so when their twenty-year charters expired, they were not renewed. From 1837 until the end of 1914, the United States had no central bank, but the Treasury Department fulfilled some of its functions.
- A country can do without a central bank if it is on fixed exchange rates, such as the gold standard, or otherwise gives up discretionary monetary policy, as when countries dollarize or adopt a foreign currency as their own. In such cases, other institutions fulfill central banking functions: government departments regulate financial institutions, commercial banks safeguard the government's deposits, a currency board administers the fixed exchange rate mechanism, clearinghouses established by banks clear checks, and so forth.
- The Treasury Department did not act as a lender of last resort, however, so recurrent banking crises and financial panics plagued the economy. When J. P. Morgan acted as a lender of last resort during the Panic of 1907, political sentiments shifted and the Federal Reserve system emerged out of a series of political compromises six years later.

14.2 The Federal Reserve System's Structure

Learning Objective

1. What is the structure of the Federal Reserve system?

The Federal Reserve is composed of twelve numbered districts, each with its own Federal Reserve Bank: Boston (1), New York (2), Philadelphia (3), Cleveland (4), Richmond (5), Atlanta (6), Chicago (7), St. Louis (8), Minneapolis (9), Kansas City (10), Dallas (11), and San Francisco (12). Except for regions 1 and 3, each of those **district banks** also operates one or more branches. For example, the Federal Reserve Bank of New York (FRBNY) maintains a branch in Buffalo; the Atlanta Fed has branches in Nashville, Birmingham, New Orleans, Jacksonville, and Miami. The Fed's headquarters is located in Washington, DC.[3]

district banks

One of the twelve banks comprising the Federal Reserve system.

Missouri is the only state with two federal reserve district banks. This was thought necessary to secure the votes of Missouri congressional representatives for the bill. (So much for public interest!) *The districts don't seem to be evenly balanced economically.* They were, more or less, when the legislation was passed before World War I, but since then, the West Coast, Southwest, and Southeast (Sunbelt) have grown in economic importance relative to the Northeast and old Midwest (Rustbelt). (District 3 encompasses only southern New Jersey and eastern Pennsylvania, an area that is no longer the economic powerhouse it once was.) Rather than redistrict, the Fed has simply shifted resources over the years toward the larger and economically more potent districts.

Each Federal Reserve bank is owned (but not entirely controlled) by the commercial banks in its district, and they are members of the system. Those banks, which include all nationally chartered banks and any state banks that choose to join, own restricted[4] shares in the Fed, which they use to elect six district bank directors, three of whom have to be professional bankers and three of whom have to be nonbank business leaders. The Board of Governors in Washington selects another three directors, who are supposed to represent the public interest and are not allowed to work for or own stock in any bank. The nine directors, with the consent of the board, then appoint a president.

The twelve district banks do mostly grunt work:

- Issue new Federal Reserve notes (FRNs) in place of worn currency
- Clear checks
- Lend to banks within their districts
- Act as a liaison between the Fed and the business community
- Collect data on regional business and economic conditions
- Conduct monetary policy research
- Evaluate bank merger and new activities applications
- Examine bank holding companies and state-chartered member banks[5]

The FRBNY is the most important of the district banks because, in addition to the tasks listed above, it also conducts so-called open market operations, buying and selling government bonds (and occasionally other assets) on behalf of the Federal Reserve system and at the behest of headquarters in Washington. Moreover, the FRBNY is a member of the Bank for International Settlements (BIS)[6] and safeguards over $100 billion in gold owned by the world's major central banks. Finally, the FRBNY's president is the only permanent member of the Federal Open Market Committee (FOMC).

The FOMC is composed of the seven members of the Board of Governors, the president of the FRBNY, and the presidents of the other district banks, though only four of the last-mentioned group can vote (on a rotating basis). The FOMC meets every six weeks or so to decide on monetary policy, specifically on the rate of growth of the money supply or the federal funds target rate, an important interest rate, both of which are controlled via so-called open market operations. Until recently, the Fed had only two other tools for implementing monetary policy, the discount rate at which district banks lend directly to member banks and reserve requirements. Prior to the crisis of 2007–2008, neither was an effective tool for a long time, so the market and the media naturally concentrated on the FOMC and have even taken to calling it "the Fed," although technically it is only one part of the central bank. *The head of the Fed is the Board of Governors, which is composed of a chairperson, currently Janet Yellen, and six governors.*[7] All seven are appointed by the president of the United States and confirmed by the U.S. Senate. The governors must come from different Federal Reserve districts and serve a single fourteen-year term. The chairperson is selected from among the governors and serves a four-year, renewable term. The chairperson is the most powerful member of the Fed because he or she controls the board, which controls the FOMC, which controls the FRBNY's open market operations, which influences the money supply or a key interest rate. The chairperson also effectively controls reserve requirements and the discount rate. He or she (Yellen was the first, but not likely the last, female chairperson) is also the Fed's public face and its major liaison to the national government. Although de jure power within the Fed is diffused by the checks and balances discussed above, today de facto power is concentrated in the chairperson. That allows the Fed to be effective but ensures that a rogue chairperson cannot abuse his or her power.

Historically, some chairpersons have made nebbishes look effective, while others, including most recently Alan Greenspan, have been considered, if not infallible demigods, then at least erudite gurus. *Neither extreme view is accurate because all chairpersons have relied heavily on the advice and consent of the other governors, the district banks' presidents, and the Fed's research staff of economists, which is the world's largest.* The researchers provide the chairperson and the entire FOMC with new data, qualitative assessments of economic trends, and quantitative output from the latest and greatest macroeconomic models. They also examine the global economy and analyze the foreign exchange market, on the lookout for possible shocks from abroad. Fed economists also help the district banks to do their jobs by investigating market and competition conditions and engaging in educational and other public outreach programs.

Key Takeaways

- The Fed is composed of a Washington-based headquarters and twelve district banks and their branches.
- The district banks, which are owned by the member banks, fulfill the Fed's quotidian duties like clearing checks and conducting economic research.
- The most important of the district banks is the Federal Reserve Bank of New York (FRBNY), which conducts open market operations, the buying and selling of bonds that influences the money supply and interest rates.
- It also safeguards much of the world's gold and has a permanent seat on the Federal Open Market Committee (FOMC), the Fed's most important policymaking body.
- Composed of the Board of Governors and the presidents of the district banks, the FOMC meets every six weeks or so to decide whether monetary policy should be tightened (interest rates increased), loosened (interest rates decreased), or maintained.
- The Fed is full of checks and balances, but is clearly led by the chairperson of the Board of Governors.
- The chairperson often personifies the Fed, as he or she is the bank's public face.
- Nevertheless, a large number of people, from common businesspeople to the Fed's research economists, influence his or her decisions through the data, opinions, and analysis they present.

14.3 Other Important Central Banks

Learning Objective

1. How do other central banks compare to the Fed?

The Fed is the world's most important central bank because the United States has been the world's most important economy since at least World War II. *But the Maastricht Treaty created a contender:*[8] *the European Central Bank (ECB),*[9] *the central bank of the euro area, the seventeen major countries that have adopted the euro as their unit of account:* Austria, Belgium, Cyprus, Estonia, Finland, France, Germany, Greece, Ireland, Italy, Luxembourg, Malta, the Netherlands, Portugal, Slovakia, Slovenia and Spain (see Figure 14.1).

FIGURE 14.1 The Eurozone

If you plan to visit any of these countries, be prepared to see prices stated in Euro.

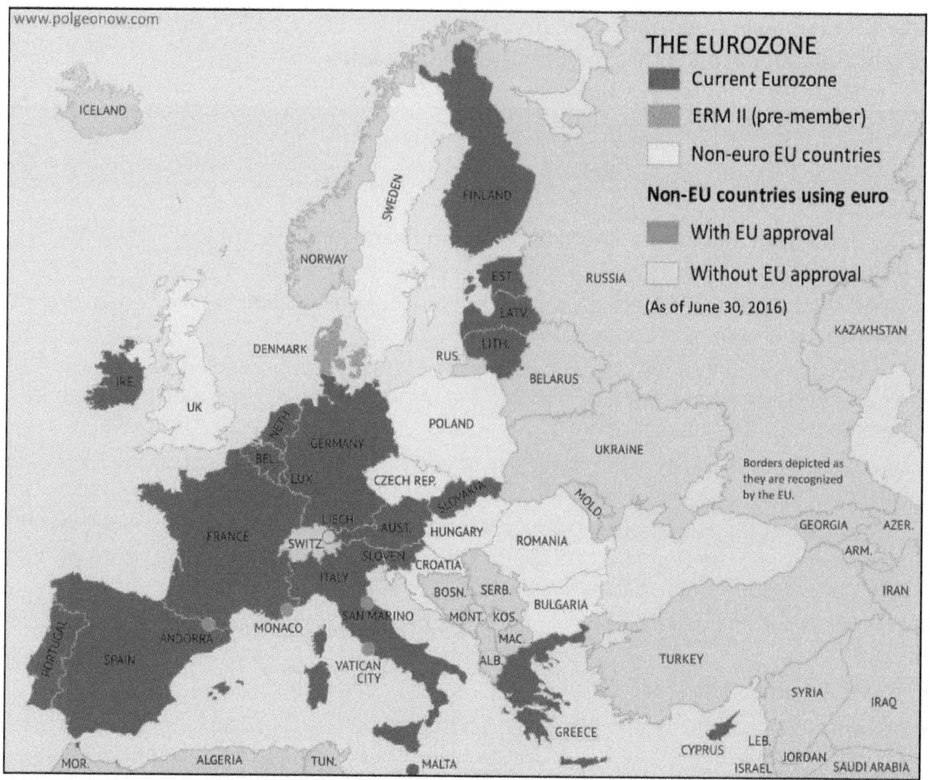

Source: The Eurozone, European Union, and other countries using the euro. Map by Evan Centanni, from blank map by Ssolbergj. License: CC BY-SA; http://www.polgeonow.com/

The ECB is part of a larger system, the European System of Central Banks (ESCB), some of the countries of which (Bulgaria, Czech Republic, Denmark, Estonia, Cyprus, Latvia, Lithuania, Hungary, Malta, Poland, Romania, Slovakia, and Sweden) are part of the European Union but have opted out of the currency union. (At the time of writing, the U.K. was still part of the EU but negotiating its exit. Part of the U.K., Scotland, was considering leaving the U.K. and staying in the EU.) Other countries in the ESCB, including Bulgaria, Denmark, Latvia, and Lithuania, currently link their national currencies to the euro.

The ECB or Eurosystem was consciously modeled on the Fed, so it is not surprising that their structures are similar. Each nation is like a Federal Reserve district headed by its national central bank (NCB). At its headquarters in Frankfurt sits the ECB's Executive Board, the structural equivalent of the Fed's Board of Governors, and the Governing Council, which like the Fed's FOMC makes monetary policy decisions. The ECB is more decentralized than the Fed, however, because the NCBs control their own budgets and conduct their own open market operations. Also unlike the Fed, the ECB does not regulate financial institutions, a task left to each individual country's government. The two central banks, of course, also differ in many matters of detail. The ECB was led by Frenchman Jean-Claude Trichet from 2003 until November 2011, when he was replaced by Italian economist and central banker Mario Draghi.[10] Unless he resigns, like the ECB's first president, Dutchman Wim Duisenberg did (1998–2003), Draghi will serve a single 8-year term. Like the other presidents, he was appointed by the European Council, which is comprised of the heads of state of the EU member states, the president of the European Commission, and the president of the European Council.

Three other important central banks, the Bank of England, the Bank of Japan, and the Bank of Canada, look nothing like the Fed or the ECB because they are unitary institutions with no districts. *Although they are more independent from their respective governments than in the past, most are not as independent as the Fed or the ECB.* Despite their structural differences and relative dearth of independence, unit central banks like the Bank of Japan implement monetary policy in ways very similar to the Fed and ECB.[11]

Key Takeaway

- The European Central Bank (ECB), the central bank of the nations that have adopted the euro, and the larger European System of Central Banks (ECSB), of which it is a part, are modeled after the Fed. Nevertheless, numerous differences of detail can be detected. The ECB's national central banks (NCBs), for example, are much more powerful than the Fed's district banks because they control their own budgets and conduct open market operations. Most of the world's other central banks are structured differently than the ECB and the Fed because they are unit banks without districts or branches. Most are less independent than the Fed and ECB but conduct monetary policy in the same ways.

14.4 Central Bank Independence

Learning Objective

1. What is central bank independence, why is it important, and why do independent central bankers prefer lower inflation rates than government officials usually do?

What exactly is central bank **independence** (sometimes referred to as **autonomy**) and why is it important? *Independence means just that, independence from the dictates of government, the freedom to conduct monetary policy as central bankers (and not politicians) wish.* Why does it matter whether a central bank is independent or not? Figure 14.2, the results of a classic study, reveals all.

independence

In this context, a central bank is independent to the degree that it need not follow the dictates of the government that created it.

autonomy

Central bank autonomy is largely synonymous with central bank independence.

FIGURE 14.2 Central bank independence and inflation
Mo' independence means less inflation.

Country	Independence	Average Inflation, 1973–1988
New Zealand	1	12.2
Spain	1.5	12.4
Italy	1.75	12.5
Australia	2	9.5
Belgium	2	6.0
France	2	8.2
Norway	2	8.2
Sweden	2	8.3
United Kingdom	2	6.7
Canada	2.5	7.2
Denmark	2.5	8.6
Japan	2.5	4.5
Netherlands	2.5	4.3
United States	3.5	6.4
Germany	4	3.4
Switzerland	4	3.1

Note that as a country's central bank becomes more independent (as its independence score increases from 1 to 4), its average inflation rate drops. The negative relationship is quite pronounced, producing a correlation coefficient of -.7976. The correlation is so strong, in fact, that many believe that independence *causes* low inflation. (Correlation alone cannot establish causation, but a strong correlation coefficient is a necessary first step in establishing causation.) Some scholars have argued, however, that the results were rigged, that researchers simply assigned central banks with a good record on inflation with a high independence score. (If this is true, it would destroy the causal implications of the study.) While it is true that rating a central bank's independence is something of an art, there are clear rules to follow. Where there is no rule of law, as in dictatorships, there can be no independence. The central banker must do as he or she is instructed or be sacked or possibly shot. Little wonder, then, that many Latin American and African countries had very high rates of inflation when they were ruled by dictators.

In nations with rule of law, like those in Figure 14.2, it's best to follow the purse. *If a central bank has control of its own budget, as the Fed and ECB (and some of its predecessors, like the Bundesbank of Germany) do, then the bank is quite independent because it is beholden to no one.* The Fed is slightly less independent than the ECB, however, because its existence is not constitutionally guaranteed. (Indeed, as we learned above, the United States had a nasty habit of dispatching its early central banks.) Congress could change or abolish the Fed simply by passing a law and getting the president to sign it or it could override his veto. The ECB, by contrast, was formed by an international treaty, changes to which must be ratified by all the signatories, a chore and a half to achieve, to be sure! *Finally, central banks led by people who are appointed are more independent than those led by popularly elected officials. Long, nonrenewable terms are better for independence than short, renewable ones, which tend to induce bankers to curry the favor of whoever decides their fate when their term expires.*

None of this is to say, however, that determining a central bank's independence is easy, particularly when de jure and de facto realities differ. The Bank of Canada's independence is limited by the fact that the Bank Act of 1967 made the government ultimately responsible for Canada's monetary policy. But, in fact, the Canadian government has allowed its central bank to run the money show. The same could be said of the Bank of England. The Bank of Japan's independence was strengthened in 1998 but the Ministry of Finance, a government agency, still controls part of its budget and can request delays in monetary policy decisions. The current de facto independence of those banks could be undermined and quite quickly at that.

Stop and Think Box

"Bank of Japan Faces Test of Independence," *Wall Street Journal*, August 10, 2000. "The political storm over a possible interest rate increase by the Bank of Japan is shaping up to be the biggest challenge to the central bank's independence since it gained autonomy two years ago. Members of the ruling Liberal Democratic Party stepped up pressure on the bank to leave the country's interest rates where they are now." Why does the Liberal Democratic Party (LDP) want to influence the Bank of Japan's (BoJ's) interest rate policy? Why was the issue important enough to warrant a major article in a major business newspaper?

The LDP wanted to influence the BoJ's interest rate policy for political reasons, namely, to keep the economy from slowing, a potential threat to its rule. This was an important story because the de facto "independence" of the BoJ was at stake and hence the market's perception of the Japanese central bank's ability to raise interest rates to stop inflation in the face of political pressure.

Why, when left to their own devices, are central bankers tougher on inflation than governments, politicians, or the general populace? Partly because they represent bank, business, and creditor interests, all of which are hurt if prices rise quickly and unexpectedly. Banks are naturally uncomfortable in rising interest rate environments, and inflation invariably brings with it higher rates. Net creditors—economic entities that are owed more than they owe—also dislike inflation because it erodes the real value of the money owed them. Finally, businesses tend to dislike inflation because it increases uncertainty, reduces the effectiveness of price signals (i.e., clouds the extent to which higher prices mean higher product demand), and makes long-term planning difficult. Central bankers also know the damage that inflation can do to an economy, so a public interest motivation drives them as well.

People and the politicians they elect to office, on the other hand, sometimes desire inflation. Many households are net debtors, meaning that they owe more money than is owed to them. Inflation, they know, will decrease the real burden of their debts. In addition, most members of the public do not want the higher interest rates that are sometimes necessary to combat inflation because it will cost them money and perhaps even their jobs. They would rather suffer from some inflation, in other words, rather than deal with the pain of keeping prices in check.

Politicians know voter preferences, so they, too, tend to err on the side of higher rather than lower inflation. Politicians also know that monetary stimulus—increasing the money supply at a faster rate than usual or lowering the interest rate—can stimulate a short burst of economic growth that will make people happy with the status quo and ready to return incumbents to office. If inflation ensues and the economy turns sour for a while after the election, that is okay because matters will likely sort out before the next election, when politicians will be again inclined to pump out money. *Some evidence of just such a political business cycle in the postwar United States has been found.*[12] Politicians might also want to print money simply to avoid raising direct taxes. The resultant inflation acts like a tax on cash balances (which lose value each day) and blame can be cast on the central bankers.

All in all, then, it is a good idea to have a central bank with a good deal of independence, though some liberals complain that independent central banks aren't sufficiently "democratic." But who says everything should be democratic? Would you want the armed forces run by majority vote? Your company? Your household? Have you heard about the tyranny of the majority?[13] That's when two wolves and a sheep vote on what's for dinner. Central bank independence is not just about inflation but about how well the overall economy performs. There is no indication that the inflation fighting done by independent central banks in any way harms economic growth or employment in the long run. Keeping the lid on inflation, which can seriously injure national economies, is therefore a very good policy indeed.

Another knock against independent central banks is that they are not very transparent. The Fed, for example, has long been infamous for its secrecy. When forced by law to disclose more information about its actions sooner, it turned to obfuscation. To this day, decoding the FOMC's press releases is an interesting game of semantics. For all its unclear language, the Fed is more open than the ECB, which will not make the minutes of its policy meetings public until twenty years after they take place. The Fed also now, like many central banks, publishes some of its economic forecasts and its inflation rate target. Theory suggests that central banks should be transparent when trying to stop inflation but opaque when trying to stimulate the economy.

Key Takeaways

- Central bank independence is a measure of how free from government influence central bankers are. Independence increases as a central bank controls its own budget; it cannot be destroyed or modified by mere legislation (or, worse, executive fiat), and it is enhanced when central banks are composed of people serving long, nonrenewable terms. Independence is important because researchers have found that the more independent a central bank is, the lower the inflation it allows without injuring growth and employment goals.

- When unanticipated, inflation redistributes resources from net creditors to net debtors, creates uncertainty, and raises nominal interest rates, hurting economic growth.
- Independent central bankers represent bank, business, and net creditor interests that are hurt by high levels of inflation. Elected officials represent voters, many of whom are net debtors, and hence beneficiaries of debt-eroding inflationary measures.
- They also know that well-timed monetary stimulus can help them obtain re-election by inducing economic growth in the months leading up to the election. The inflation that follows will bring some pain, but there will be time for correction before the next election. Governments where officials are not elected, as in dictatorships, often have difficulty collecting taxes, so they use the central bank as a source of revenue, simply printing money (creating bank deposits) to make payments. High levels of inflation act as a sort of currency tax, a tax on cash balances that lose some of their purchasing power each day.

14.5 Suggested Reading

Bernanke, Ben Shalom. *The Courage to Act: A Memoir of a Crisis and Its Aftermath*. New York: Norton, 2015.

Bremner, Robert. *Chairman of the Fed: William McChesney Martin Jr. and the Creation of the American Financial System*. New Haven, CT: Yale University Press, 2004.

Bruner, Robert, and Sean Carr. *The Panic of 1907: Lessons Learned from the Market's Perfect Storm*. Hoboken, NJ: John Wiley and Sons, 2007.

Clark, William Roberts. *Capitalism, Not Globalism: Capital Mobility, Central Bank Independence, and the Political Control of the Economy*. Ann Arbor, MI: University of Michigan Press, 2005.

Meltzer, Allan. *A History of the Federal Reserve, Volume 1: 1913–1951*. Chicago, IL: University of Chicago Press, 2003.

Silber, William. *Volcker: The Triumph of Persistence*. New York: Bloomsbury, 2012.

Timberlake, Richard. *Monetary Policy in the United States: An Intellectual and Institutional History*. Chicago, IL: University of Chicago Press, 1993.

Endnotes

1. www.treasury.gov/about/history/Pages/ahamilton.aspx
2. This does not mean that the exchange rate didn't change, merely that it stayed within a narrow band of transaction costs.
3. For an interactive map of the system, browse www.federalreserve.gov/otherfrb.htm.
4. The Fed's stock is not traded in public markets and pays an annual dividend no higher than 6 percent.
5. The Comptroller of the Currency is the primary regulator of federally chartered banks. State regulators and the FDIC regulate state banks that are not members of the Federal Reserve system.
6. www.bis.org
7. https://www.federalreserve.gov/aboutthefed/bios/board/yellen.htm
8. https://europa.eu/european-union/sites/europaeu/files/docs/body/treaty_on_european_union_en.pdf
9. www.ecb.int/home/html/index.en.html
10. https://en.wikipedia.org/wiki/Mario_Draghi
11. Dieter Gerdesmeier, Francesco Mongelli, and Barbara Roffia, "The Eurosystem, the US Federal Reserve and the Bank of Japan: Similarities and Differences," ECB Working Paper Series No. 742 (March 2007).
12. See, for example, Jac Heckelman, "Historical Political Business Cycles in the United States," EH.Net Encyclopedia (2001). http://eh.net/encyclopedia/historical-political-business-cycles-in-the-united-states/. The clearest evidence implicates Richard Nixon. See Burton Abrams and James Butkiewicz, "The Political Business cycle: New Evidence from the Nixon Tapes," https://jmcb.osu.edu/sites/jmcb.osu.edu/files/papers-political-business-10293_0.pdf
13. xroads.virginia.edu/~hyper/detoc/1_ch15.htm

CHAPTER 15

The Money Supply Process and the Money Multipliers

Chapter Objectives

By the end of this chapter, students should be able to:

1. Describe who determines the money supply.
2. Explain how the central bank's balance sheet differs from the balance sheets of commercial banks and other depository institutions.
3. Define the monetary base and explain its importance.
4. Define open market operations and explain how they affect the monetary base.
5. Describe the multiple deposit creation process.
6. Define the simple deposit multiplier and explain its information content.
7. List and explain the two major limitations or assumptions of the simple deposit multiplier.
8. Compare and contrast the simple money multiplier and the m1 and m2 multipliers.
9. Write the equation that helps us to understand how changes in the monetary base affect the money supply.
10. Explain why the M2 multiplier is almost always larger than the m1 multiplier.
11. Explain why the required reserve ratio, the excess reserve ratio, and the currency ratio are in the denominator of the m1 and m2 money multipliers.
12. Explain why the currency, time deposit, and money market mutual fund ratios are in the numerator of the M2 money multiplier.
13. Describe how central banks influence the money supply.
14. Describe how banks, borrowers, and depositors influence the money supply.

15.1 The Central Bank's Balance Sheet

Learning Objectives

1. Who determines the money supply?
2. How does the central bank's balance sheet differ from the balance sheets of other banks?
3. What is the monetary base?

In most countries today, a central bank or other monetary authority is charged with issuing domestic currency. That is an important charge because the supply of money greatly influences interest and inflation rates and, ultimately, aggregate output. If the central bank's monetary policy is good, if it creates just the right amount of money, the economy will hum, and interest and inflation rates will be low. If it creates too much money too quickly, prices will increase rapidly and wipe out people's savings until even the poorest people are nominal billionaires (as in Zimbabwe recently).[1] If it creates too little money too slowly, prices will fall, wiping out debtors and making it nearly impossible to earn profits in business (as in the Great Depression). But even less extreme errors can have serious negative consequences for the economy and hence your wallets, careers, and dreams. This chapter is a little involved, but it is worth thoroughly understanding the money supply process and money multipliers if you want you and yours to be healthy and happy.

Ultimately, the money supply is determined by the interaction of four groups: commercial banks and other depositories, depositors, borrowers, and the central bank. Like any bank, the central bank's balance sheet is composed of assets and liabilities. Its assets are similar to those of common banks and include government securities[2] and discount loans. The former provide the central bank with income and a liquid asset that it can easily and cheaply buy and sell to alter its balance sheet. The latter are generally loans made to commercial banks. So far, so good. *The central bank's liabilities, however, differ fundamentally from those of common banks.* Its most important liabilities are currency in circulation and reserves.

It may seem strange to see currency and reserves listed as liabilities of the central bank because those things are the *assets* of commercial banks. *In fact, for everyone but the central bank, the central bank's notes, Federal Reserve notes (FRN) in the United States, are assets or things owned. But for the central bank, its notes are things owed (liabilities).* Every financial asset is somebody else's liability, of course. A promissory note (IOU) that you signed would be your liability, but it would be an asset for the note's holder or owner. Similarly, a bank deposit is a liability for the bank but an asset for the depositor. In like fashion, commercial banks own their deposits in the Fed (reserves), so they count them as assets. The Fed owes that money to commercial banks, so it must count them as liabilities. The same goes for FRN: the public *owns* them, but the Fed, as their issuer, *owes* them. (Don't be confused by the fact that what the Fed owes to holders is nothing more than the right to use the notes to pay sums the holders owe to the government for taxes and the like.)

monetary base

The most basic, powerful types of money in a given monetary system, that is, gold and silver under the gold standard, FRN, and reserves (Federal Reserve deposits) today.

Currency in circulation (C) and reserves (R) compose the **monetary base** *(MB, aka high-powered money), the most basic building blocks of the money supply.* Basically, MB = C + R, an equation you'll want to internalize. In the United States, C includes FRN and coins issued by the U.S. Treasury. We can ignore the latter because it is a relatively small percentage of the MB, and the Treasury cannot legally manage the volume of coinage in circulation in an active fashion, but rather only meets the demand for each denomination, currently: .01, .05, .10, .25, .50, and 1.00 coins. (The Fed also supplies the $1.00 unit, and for some reason Americans prefer $1 notes to coins. In most countries, coins fill demand for the single currency unit denomination.) C includes only FRN and coins in the hands of nonbanks. Any FRN in banks is called vault cash and is included in R, which also includes bank deposits with the Fed. Reserves are of two types: those required or mandated by the central bank (RR), and any additional or excess reserves (ER) that banks voluntarily hold. The latter are usually small, but they can grow substantially during panics like that of September–October 2008.

Central banks, of course, are highly profitable institutions because their assets earn interest but their liabilities are costless, or nearly so. Printing money en masse with modern technology is pretty cheap, and reserves are nothing more than accounting entries. Many central banks, including the Federal Reserve, now pay interest on reserves, but of course any interest paid is composed of cheap notes or, more likely, even cheaper accounting entries. Central banks, therefore, have no gap problems, and liquidity management is a snap because they can always print more notes or create more reserves. Central banks anachronistically own prodigious quantities of gold, but some have begun to sell off their holdings because they no longer convert their notes into gold or anything else for that matter.[3] Gold is no longer part of the MB but is rather just a commodity with unusually good monetary characteristics (high value-to-weight ratio, divisible, easily authenticated, and so forth).

Key Takeaways

- It is important to understand the money supply process because having too much or too little money will lead to negative economic outcomes including high(er) inflation and low(er) total output.
- The central bank, depository institutions of every stripe, borrowers, and depositors all help to determine the money supply.
- The central bank helps to determine the money supply by controlling the monetary base (MB), aka high-powered money or its monetary liabilities.
- The central bank's balance sheet differs from those of other banks because its monetary liabilities, currency in circulation (C), and reserves (R), are everyone else's assets.
- The monetary base or MB = C + R, where C = currency in circulation (not in the central bank or any bank); R = reserves = bank vault cash and deposits with the central bank.

15.2 Open Market Operations

Learning Objective

1. What are open market operations and how do they affect the monetary base?

open market operations

The purchase or sale of assets by a central bank in order to adjust the money supply. *See monetary base.*

We are now ready to understand how the central bank influences the money supply (MS) with the aid of T-accounts—accounts that show only the changes in balance sheets. Like regular balance sheets, however, T-accounts must balance (asset changes must equal liability changes). *Central banks like the Fed influence the MS via the MB. They control their monetary liabilities, MB, by buying and selling securities, a process called* **open market operations**. If a central bank wants to increase the MB, it need only buy a security. (Any asset will do, but securities, especially government bonds, are generally best because there is little default risk, liquidity is high, and they pay interest.) If a central bank bought a $10,000 bond from a bank, the following would occur:

Banking System	
Assets	Liabilities
Securities −$10,000	
Reserves +$10,000	

The banking system would lose $10,000 worth of securities but gain $10,000 of reserves (probably a credit in its account with the central bank but, as noted above, FRN or other forms of cash also count as reserves).

Central Bank	
Assets	Liabilities
Securities +$10,000	Reserves +$10,000

The central bank would gain $10,000 of securities essentially by creating $10,000 of reserves. Notice that the item transferred, securities, has opposite signs, negative for the banking system and positive for the central bank. That makes good sense if you think about it because one party is selling (giving up) and the other is buying (receiving). Note also that the central bank's liability has the same sign as the banking system's asset. That too makes sense because, as noted above, the central bank's liabilities are everyone else's assets. So if the central bank's liabilities increase or decrease, everyone else's assets should do likewise.

If the central bank happens to buy a bond from the public (any nonbank), and that entity deposits the proceeds in its bank, precisely the same outcome would occur, though via a slightly more circuitous route:

Some Dude	
Assets	Liabilities
Securities –$10,000	
Checkable deposits +$10,000	

Banking System	
Assets	Liabilities
Reserves +$10,000	Checkable deposits +$10,000

Central Bank	
Assets	Liabilities
Securities +$10,000	Reserves +$10,000

If the nonbank seller of the security keeps the proceeds as cash (FRN), however, the outcome is slightly different:

Some Dude	
Assets	Liabilities
Securities –$10,000	
Currency +$10,000	

Central Bank	
Assets	Liabilities
Securities +$10,000	Currency in circulation +$10,000

Note that in either case, however, the MB increases by the amount of the purchase because either C or R increases by the amount of the purchase. Keep in mind that currency in circulation means cash (like FRN) no longer in the central bank. An IOU in the hands of its maker is no liability; cash in the hands of its issuer is not a liability. So although the money existed physically before Some Dude sold his bond, it did not exist economically as money until it left its papa (mama?), the central bank. If the transaction were reversed and Some Dude bought a bond from the central bank with currency, the notes he paid would cease to be money, and currency in circulation would decrease by $10,000.

In fact, whenever the central bank *sells* an asset, the exact opposite of the above T-accounts occurs: *the MB shrinks because C (and/or R) decreases along with the central bank's securities holdings, and banks or the nonbank public own more securities but less C or R.*

The nonbank public can influence the relative share of C and R but not the MB. Say that you had $55.50 in your bank account but wanted $30 in cash to take your significant other to the carnival. Your T-account would look like the following because you turned $30 of deposits into $30 of FRN:

Your T-Account	
Assets	Liabilities
Checkable deposits −$30.00	
Currency +$30.00	

Your bank's T-account would look like the following because it lost $30 of deposits and $30 of reserves, the $30 you walked off with:

Your Bank	
Assets	Liabilities
Reserves −$30.00	Checkable deposits −$30.00

The central bank's T-account would look like the following because the nonbank public (you!) would hold $30 and your bank's reserves would decrease accordingly (as noted above):

Central Bank	
Assets	Liabilities
	Currency in circulation +$30.00
	Reserves −$30.00

The central bank can also control the monetary base by making loans to banks and receiving their loan repayments. A loan increases the MB and a repayment decreases it. A $1 million loan and repayment a week later looks like this:

Central Bank		
Assets	Liabilities	Date
Loans +$1,000,000	Reserves +$1,000,000	January 1, 2020
Loans −$1,000,000	Reserves −$1,000,000	January 8, 2020

Banking System		
Assets	Liabilities	Date
Reserves +$1,000,000	Borrowings +$1,000,000	January 1, 2020
Reserves −$1,000,000	Borrowings −$1,000,000	January 8, 2020

Take time now to practice deciphering the effects of open market operations and central bank loans and repayments via T-accounts in Exercise 1. You'll be glad you did.

Exercises

Use T-accounts to describe what happens in the following instances:

1. The Bank of Japan **sells** ¥10 billion of securities to banks.
2. The Bank of England **buys** £97 million of securities from banks.
3. Banks **borrow** €897 million from the ECB.
4. Banks **repay** $C80 million of loans to the Bank of Canada.
5. The Fed **buys** $75 billion of securities from the nonbank public, which deposits $70 billion and keeps $5 billion in cash.

Key Takeaways

- MB is important because an increase (decrease) in it will increase (decrease) the money supply (M1—currency plus checkable deposits, M2—M1 plus time deposits and retail money market deposit accounts, etc.) by some multiple (hence the "high-powered" nickname).
- Open market operations occur whenever a central bank buys or sells assets, usually government bonds.
- By purchasing bonds (or anything else for that matter), the central bank increases the monetary base and hence, by some multiple, the money supply. (Picture the central bank giving up some money to acquire the bond, thereby putting FRN or reserves into circulation.)
- By selling bonds, the central bank decreases the monetary base and hence the money supply by some multiple. (Picture the central bank giving up a bond and receiving money for it, removing FRN or reserves from circulation.)
- Similarly, the MB and MS increase whenever the Fed makes a loan, and they decrease whenever a borrower repays the Fed.

15.3 A Simple Model of Multiple Deposit Creation

Learning Objectives

1. What is the multiple deposit creation process?
2. What is the money multiplier?
3. What are the major limitations of the simple deposit multiplier?

The central bank pretty much controls the size of the monetary base. (The check clearing process and the government's banking activities can cause some short-term flutter, but generally the central bank can anticipate such fluctuations and respond accordingly.) *That does not mean, however, that the central bank controls the money supply, which consists of more than just MB.* (M1, for example, also includes checkable deposits.) The reason is that each $1 (or €1, etc.) of additional MB creates some multiple, generally > 1, of new deposits in a process called multiple deposit creation.

Suppose Some Bank wants to decrease its holding of securities and increase its lending. It could sell $1 million of its securities to the central bank. The T-accounts would be:

Some Bank	
Assets	Liabilities
Securities −$1 million	
Reserves +$1 million	

Central Bank	
Assets	Liabilities
Securities +$1 million	Reserves +$1 million

Some Bank suddenly has $1 million in excess reserves. (Its deposits are unchanged, but it has $1 million more in cash.) The bank can now make more loans. So its T-account will be the following:

Some Bank	
Assets	Liabilities
Loans +$1 million	Deposits +$1 million

Deposits are created in the process of making the loan, so the bank has effectively increased M1 by $1 million. The borrower will not leave the proceeds of the loan in the bank for long but instead will use it, within the guidelines set by the loan's covenants, to make payments. As the deposits flow out of Some Bank, its excess reserves decline until finally Some Bank has essentially swapped securities for loans:

Some Bank	
Assets	Liabilities
Securities -$1 million	
Loans +$1 million	

But now there is another $1 million of checkable deposits out there and they rarely rest. Suppose, for simplicity's sake, they all end up at Another Bank. Its T-account would be the following:

Another Bank	
Assets Bank	Liabilities
Reserves +$1 million	Checkable deposits +$1 million

If the required reserve ratio (rr) is 10 percent, Another Bank can, and likely will, use those deposits to fund a loan, making its T-account:

Another Bank	
Assets	Liabilities
Reserves +$.1 million	Checkable Deposits +$1 million
Loans +$.9 million	

That loan will also eventually be paid out to others and deposited into other banks, which in turn will lend 90 percent of them (1/rr) to other borrowers. Even if a bank decides to invest in securities instead of loans, as long as it buys the bonds from anyone but the central bank, the multiple deposit creation expansion will continue, as in Figure 15.1.

FIGURE 15.1 Multiple deposit creation, with an increase in reserves of $1 million, if rr = .10
The equation is quite a bit easier, eh!

Bank	Increase in Deposits ($)	Increase in Loans ($)	Increase in Reserves ($)
Some	0	1,000,000	0
Another	1,000,000	900,000	100,000
Yet Another	900,000	810,000	90,000
Still Another	810,000	729,000	81,000
You Get the Picture	729,000	656,100	72,900
...	...	...	...
Totals	$10 million	$10 million	$1 million

Notice that the increase in deposits is the same as the increase in loans from the previous bank. The increase in reserves is the increase in deposits times the required reserve ratio of .10, and the increase in loans is the increase in deposits times the remainder, .90. Rather than working through this rather clunky process every time, you can calculate the effects of increasing reserves with the so-called *simple deposit multiplier formula*:

$$\triangle D = (1/rr) \times \triangle R$$

where:

•D = change in deposits

•R = change in reserves

rr = required reserve ratio

$$1/.1 \times 1 \text{ million} = 10 \text{ million, just as in Figure 15.1}$$

Practice calculating the simple deposit multiplier in Exercise 2.

Exercise

1. Use the simple deposit multiplier $\triangle D = (1/rr) \times \triangle R$ to calculate the change in deposits given the following conditions:

Required Reserve Ratio	Change in Reserves	Answer: Change in Deposits
.1	10	100
.5	10	20
1	10	10
.1	−10	−100
.1	100	1,000
0	43.5	ERROR—cannot divide by 0

Stop and Think Box

Suppose the Federal Reserve wants to increase the amount of checkable deposits by \$1,000,000 by conducting open market operations. Using the simple model of multiple deposit creation, determine what value of securities the Fed should purchase, assuming a required reserve ratio of 5 percent. What two major assumptions does the simple model of multiple deposit creation make? Show the appropriate equation and work.

The Fed should purchase \$50,000 worth of securities. The simple model of multiple deposit creation is $\Delta D = (1/rr) \times \Delta R$, which of course is the same as $\Delta R = \Delta D/(1/rr)$. So for this problem 1,000,000/(1/.05) = \$50,000 worth of securities should be purchased. This model assumes that money is not held as cash and that banks do not hold excess reserves.

Pretty easy, eh? *Too bad the simple deposit multiplier isn't very accurate.* It provides an upper bound to the deposit creation process. The model simply isn't very realistic. Sometimes banks hold excess reserves, and people sometimes prefer to hold cash instead of deposits, thereby stopping the multiple deposit creation process cold. If the original borrower, for example, had taken cash and paid it out to people who also preferred cash over deposits no expansion of the money supply would have occurred. Ditto if Some Bank had decided that it was too risky to make new loans and had simply exchanged its securities for reserves. Or if no one was willing to borrow. Those are extreme examples, but anywhere along the process leaks into cash or excess reserves sap the deposit multiplier. That is why, at the beginning of the chapter, we said that depositors, borrowers, and banks were also important players in the money supply determination process. In the next section, we'll take their decisions into account.

Key Takeaways

- The multiple deposit creation process works like this: say that the central bank buys \$100 of securities from Bank 1, which lends the \$100 in cash it receives to some borrower. Said borrower writes checks against the \$100 in deposits created by the loan until all the money rests in Bank 2. Its deposits and reserves increased by \$100, Bank 2 lends as much as it can, say (1 − rr = .9) or \$90, to another borrower, who writes checks against it until it winds up in Bank 3, which also lends 90 percent of it. Bank 4 lends 90 percent of that, Bank 5 lends 90 percent of that, and so on, until a \$100 initial increase in reserves has led to a \$1,000 increase in deposits (and loans).
- The simple deposit multiplier is $\Delta D = (1/rr) \times \Delta R$, where ΔD = change in deposits; ΔR = change in reserves; rr = required reserve ratio.
- The simple deposit multiplier assumes that banks hold no excess reserves and that the public holds no currency. We all know what happens when we assume or ass|u|*me*. These assumptions mean that the simple deposit multiplier overestimates the multiple deposit creation process, providing us with an upper-bound estimate.

15.4 A More Sophisticated Money Multiplier for M1

Learning Objectives

1. How do the simple money multiplier and the more sophisticated one developed here contrast and compare?
2. What equation helps us to understand how changes in the monetary base affect the money supply?

M1

M1 is a measure of the money supply that includes currency in circulation plus checkable deposits.

M2

M2 is a measure of the money supply that includes M1 plus time deposits and noninstitutional (retail) money market funds.

To review, an increase (decrease) in the monetary base (MB, which = C + R) generally leads to an even greater increase (decrease) in the money supply (MS, such as **M1** or **M2**) due to the multiple deposit creation process. In the previous section, you also learned a simple but unrealistic upper-bound formula for estimating the change that assumed that banks hold no excess reserves and that the public holds no currency.

Stop and Think Box

You are a research associate for Moody's subsidiary, High Frequency Economics, in West Chester, Pennsylvania. A client wants you to project changes in M1 given likely increases in the monetary base. Because of a glitch in the Federal Reserve's computer systems, currency, deposit, and excess reserve figures will not be available for at least one week. A private firm, however, can provide you with good estimates of changes in banking system reserves, and of course the required reserve ratio is well known. What equation can you use to help your client? What are the equation's assumptions and limitations?

You cannot use the more complex M1 money multiplier this week because of the Fed's computer glitch, so you should use the simple deposit multiplier from Chapter 15: $\Delta D = (1/rr) \times \Delta R$. The equation provides an upper-bound estimate for changes in deposits. It assumes that the public will hold no more currency and that banks will hold no increased excess reserves.

To get a more realistic estimate, we'll have to do a little more work. *We start with the observation that we can consider the money supply to be a function of the monetary base times some money multiplier (m):*

$$\Delta MS = m \times \Delta MB$$

This is basically a broader version of the simple multiplier formula discussed in the previous section, except that instead of calculating the change in deposits (ΔD) brought about by the change in reserves (ΔR), we will now calculate the change in the money supply (ΔMS) brought about by the change in the monetary base (ΔMB). *Furthermore, instead of using the reciprocal of the required reserve ratio (1/rr) as the multiplier, we will use a more sophisticated one (m_1, and later m_2) that doesn't assume away cash and excess reserves.*

*We can add currency and excess reserves to the equation by algebraically describing their relationship to***checkable deposits***in the form of a ratio:*

C/D = currency ratio

ER/D = excess reserves ratio

Recall that required reserves are equal to checkable deposits (D) times the required reserve ratio (rr). Total reserves equal required reserves plus excess reserves:

checkable deposits

Deposits that can easily, cheaply, and quickly be drawn upon by check in order to make payments. Also known as transaction deposits.

$$R = rrD + ER$$

So we can render MB = C + R as MB = C + rrD + ER. Note that we have successfully removed C and ER from the multiple deposit expansion process by separating them from rrD. After further algebraic manipulations of the above equation and the reciprocal of the reserve ratio (1/rr) concept embedded in the simple deposit multiplier, we're left with a more sophisticated, more realistic money multiplier:

$$m_1 = 1 + (C / D) / [rr + (ER / D) + (C / D)]$$

So if

Required reserve ratio (rr) = .2

Currency in circulation = $100 billion

Deposits = $400 billion

Excess reserves = $10 billion

$$m_1 = 1 + (100 / 400) / (.2 + (10 / 400) + (100 / 400))$$

$$m_1 = 1.25 / (.2 + .025 + .25)$$

$$m_1 = 1.25 / .475 = 2.6316$$

Practice calculating the money multiplier in Exercise 1.

Exercises

1. Given the following, calculate the M1 money multiplier using the formula m1 = 1 + (C/D)/[rr + (ER/D) + (C/D)].

Currency	Deposits	Excess Reserves	Required Reserve Ratio	Answer: m1
100	100	10	.1	1.67
100	100	10	.2	1.54
100	1,000	10	.2	3.55
1,000	100	10	.2	1.07
1,000	100	50	.2	1.02
100	1,000	50	.2	3.14
100	1,000	0	1	1

Once you have m, plug it into the formula *ΔMS* = *m* × *ΔMB*. So if m1 = 2.6316 and the monetary base increases by $100,000, the money supply will increase by $263,160. If m1 = 4.5 and MB decreases by $1 million, the money supply will decrease by $4.5 million, and so forth. Practice this in Exercise 2.

2. Calculate the change in the money supply given the following:

Change in MB	m1	Answer: Change in MS
100	2	200
100	4	400
−100	2	−200
−100	4	−400
1,000	2	2,000
−1,000	2	−2,000
10,000	1	10,000
−10,000	1	−10,000

Stop and Think Box

Explain Figure 15.2 in light of Figure 15.3, Figure 15.4, and Figure 15.5.

FIGURE 15.2 U.S. MB and M1, 1959–2010
Notice the effect of the financial crisis on the MB!

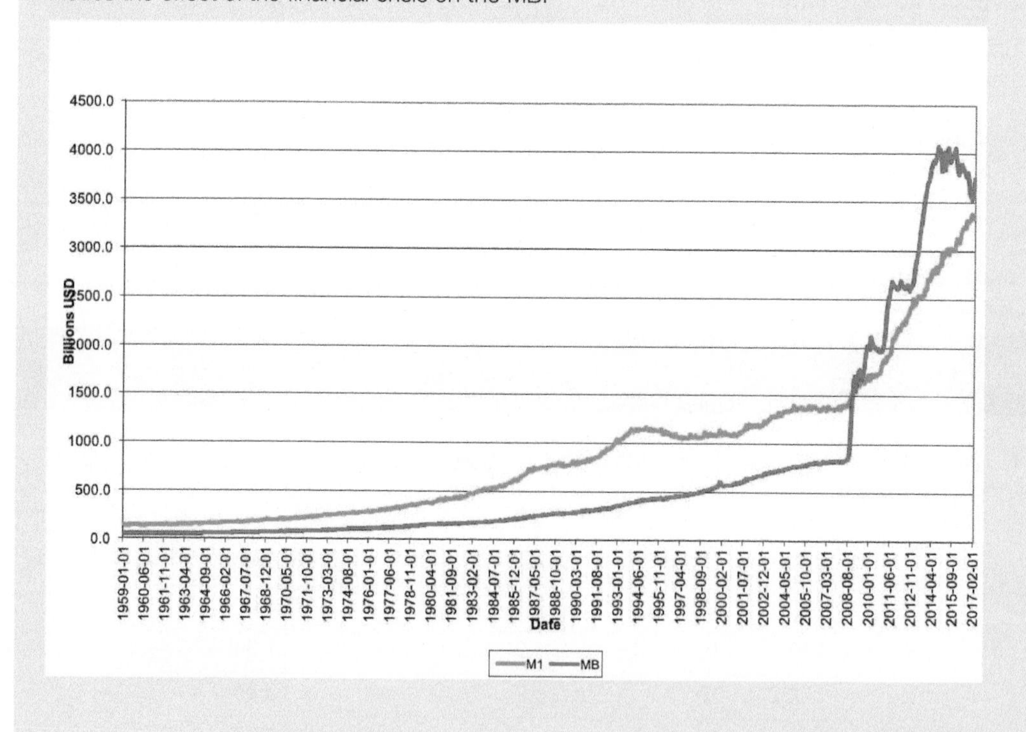

FIGURE 15.3 U.S. m_1, 1959–2010.
Notice the secular drop, due to technology, and the big drop due to the financial crisis of 2008.

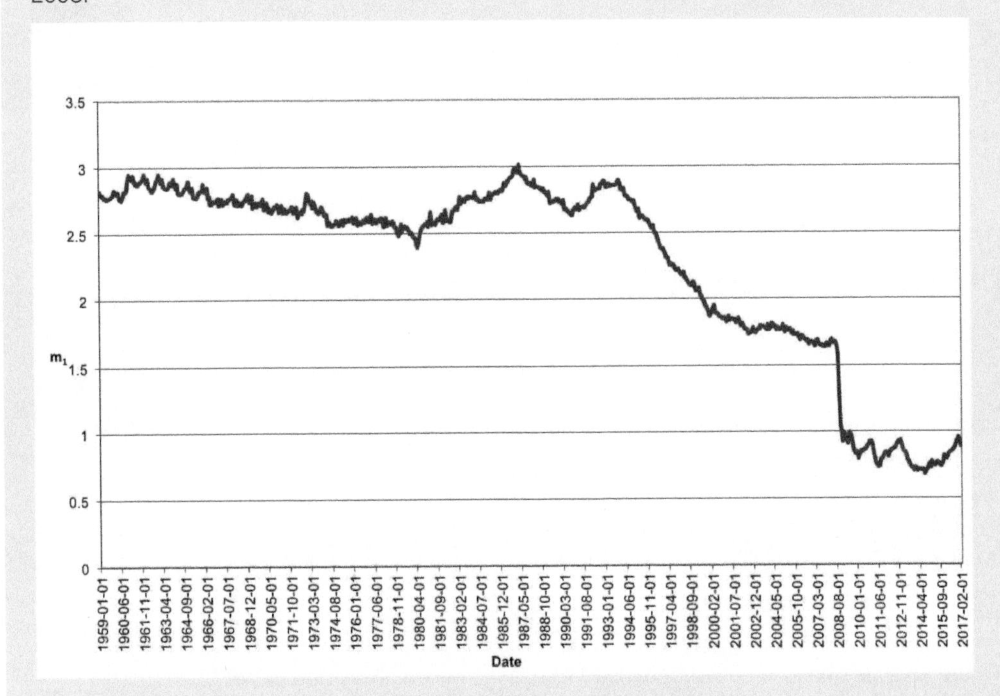

FIGURE 15.4 U.S. currency and checkable deposits, 1959–2010
Up, up, and away!

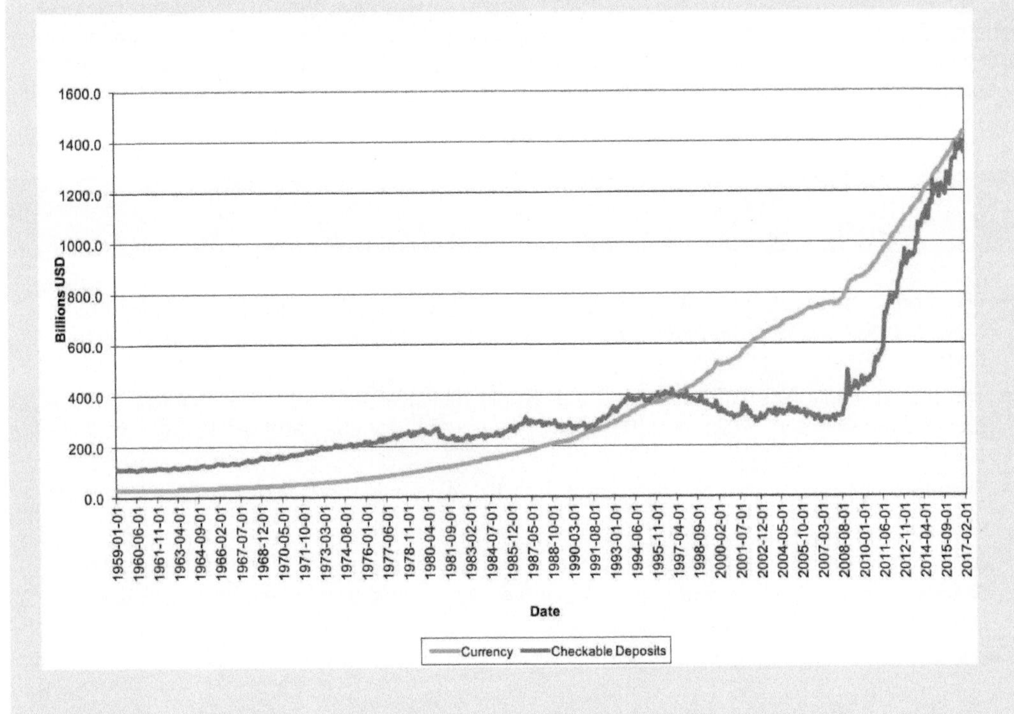

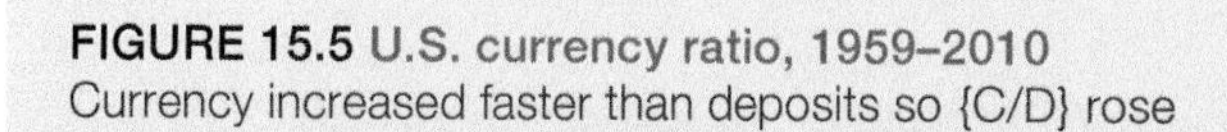

FIGURE 15.5 U.S. currency ratio, 1959–2010
Currency increased faster than deposits so {C/D} rose

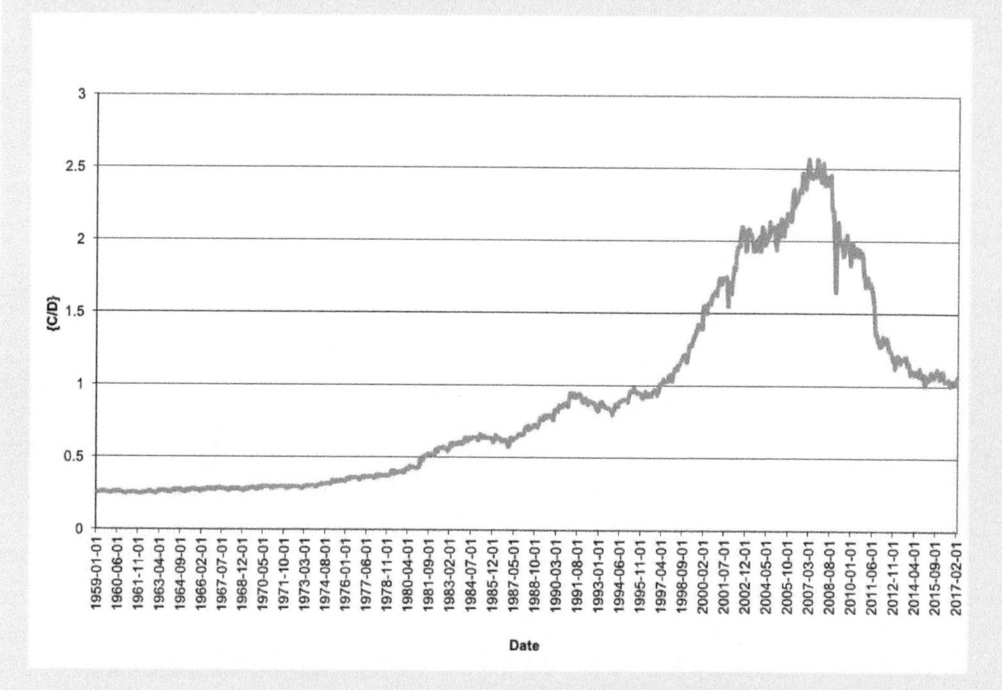

In Figure 15.2, M1 has increased because MB has increased, likely due to net open market purchases by the Fed. Apparently, m_1 has changed rather markedly since the early 1990s. In Figure 15.3, the M1 money multiplier m_1 has indeed dropped considerably since about 1995. That could be caused by an increase in rr, C/D, or ER/D. Figure 15.4 shows that m decreased primarily because C/D increased. It also shows that the increase in C/D was due largely to the stagnation in D coupled with the continued growth of C. The stagnation in D is likely due to the advent of sweep accounts. Figure 15.5 isolates C/D for closer study.

Key Takeaways

- The more sophisticated money multipliers are similar to the simple deposit multiplier in that they equate changes in the money supply to changes in the monetary base times some multiplier.
- The money multipliers differ because the simple multiplier is merely the reciprocal of the required reserve ratio, while the other multipliers account for cash and excess reserve leakages.
- Therefore, m_1 and m_2 are always smaller than 1/rr (except in the rare case where C and ER both = 0).
- $\Delta MS = m \times \Delta MB$, where ΔMS = change in the money supply; m = the money multiplier; ΔMB = change in the monetary base. A positive sign means an increase in the MS; a negative sign means a decrease.

15.5 The M2 Money Multiplier

Learning Objectives

1. Why is the M2 multiplier almost always larger than the M1 multiplier?
2. Why are the required reserve ratio, the excess reserve ratio, and the currency ratio in the denominator of the m_1 and m_2 money multipliers?
3. Why are the currency, time deposit, and money market mutual fund ratios in the numerator of the m_2 money multiplier?

Note that m_1 is the M1 money multiplier. With a little bit more work, one can also calculate the M2 money multiplier (m_2). We want to do this because M2 is a more accurate measure of the money supply than M1, as it is usually a better indicator of changes in prices, interest rates, inflation, and, ultimately, aggregate output. (And hence whether you and your family live in a nice place with a 3D HDTV, three big refrigerators, etc., or if you live in "a van down by the river.")[4]

Recall from Chapter 3 that M2 = C + D + T + MMF, where T = time and savings deposits and MMF = money market funds, money market deposit accounts, and overnight loans. We account for the extra types of deposits in the same way as we accounted for currency and excess reserves, by expressing them as ratios against checkable deposits:

(T/D) = time deposit ratio

(MMF/D) = money market ratio

which leads to the following equation:

$$m_2 = 1 + (C / D) + (T / D) + (MMF / D) / [rr + (ER / D) + (C / D)]$$

Once you calculate m_2, multiply it by the change in MB to calculate the change in the MS, specifically in M2, just as you did in Exercise 2. Notice that the denominator of the m_2 equation is the same as the m_1 equation but that we have added the time and money market ratios to the numerator. *So M2 is always*[5] *> m_1, ceteris paribus, which makes sense when you recall that M2 is composed of M1 plus other forms of money.* To verify this, recall that we calculated m_1 as 2.6316 when

Required reserves (rr) = .2

Currency in circulation = $100 million

Deposits = $400 million

Excess reserves = $10 million

We'll now add time deposits of $900 million and money market funds of $800 million and calculate M2:

$$m_2 = 1 + (C / D) + (T / D) + (MMF / D) / [rr + (ER / D) + (C / D)]$$

$$m_2 = 1 + (100 / 400) + (900 / 400) + (800 / 400) / [.2 + (10 / 400) + (100 / 400)]$$

$$m_2 = 1 + .25 + 2.25 + 2/(.2 + .025 + .25)$$

$$m_2 = 5.5/0.475 = 11.5789$$

This is quite a bit higher than m_1 because time deposits and money market funds are not subject to reserve requirements, so they can expand more than checkable deposits because there is less drag on them during the multiple expansion process.

Practice calculating the m_2 money multiplier on your own in the exercise.

Exercise

1. Calculate the M2 money multiplier using the following formula: M2 = 1 + (C/D) + (T/D) + (MMF/D)/[rr + (ER/D) + (C/D)].

Currency	Deposits	Excess Reserves	Required Reserve Ratio	Time Deposits	Money Market Funds	Answer: M2
100	100	10	0.1	1,000	1,000	18.33
100	100	10	0.2	1,000	100	10
100	100	10	0.2	100	1,000	10
1,000	100	10	0.2	1,000	1,000	3.01
1,000	100	50	0.2	1,000	1,000	2.90
100	1,000	50	0.2	1,000	1,000	8.86
100	1,000	0	1	1,000	1,000	2.82
100	1	10	0.1	1,000	1,000	19.08

Key Takeaways

- Because M1 is part of M2, m_2 is always > m_1 (except in the rare case where time deposits and money market funds = 0, in which case $m_1 = m_2$).
- That fact is reflected in the inclusion of the time deposit and money market fund ratios in the numerator of the M2 multiplier equation.
- Moreover, no reserves are required for time and money market funds, so they will have more multiple expansion than checkable deposits will.
- The required reserve ratio, the excess reserve ratio, and the currency ratio appear in the denominator of the m_1 and m_2 money multipliers because all three slow the multiple deposit creation process. The higher the reserve ratios (required and excess), the smaller the sum available to make loans from a given deposit. The more cash, the smaller the deposit.
- The currency, time deposit, and money market mutual fund ratios are in the numerator of the m_2 money multiplier because M2 is composed of currency, checkable deposits, time deposits, and money market mutual funds.

15.6 Summary and Explanation

Learning Objective

1. How do central banks, banks, depositors, and borrowers influence the money supply?

By way of summary, Figure 15.6 explains why each of the major variables influences m_1 and m_2 in the ways implied by the equations presented above.

FIGURE 15.6 Major influences on m_1 and m_2
Yoda might say "Memorize this for the test you should."

Variable	Change	MS Response	Rationale
rr	Up	Down	Less multiple deposit expansion
(ER/D)	Up	Down	Less multiple deposit expansion
(C/D)	Up	Down	Less multiple deposit expansion
(T/D)	Up	Up	More multiple deposit expansion
(MMF/D)	Up	Up	More multiple deposit expansion

As we saw at the beginning of this chapter, currency holdings, excess reserves, and required reserves slow down the multiple deposit creation process by removing funds from it. The bigger rr and ER/D are, the less each bank lends of the new deposits it receives. *The bigger C/D is, the less money is deposited in the first place.* For those reasons, we place those variables in the denominator. The larger the denominator, holding the numerator constant, the smaller m_1 or m_2 will be, of course. *The appropriate money supply components compose the numerator-currency, and checkable deposits for m_1, and currency, checkable deposits, time deposits, and money market mutual funds compose the numerator for m_2.*

This leaves us to consider why C/D, rr, and ER/D change over time. *Short term, the currency ratio varies directly with the interest rate and the stability of the banking system.* As the interest rate increases, the opportunity cost of keeping cash increases, so people are less anxious to hold it. People are also less anxious to hold currency if the banking system is stable because their money is safer in a checking deposit. If interest rates are extremely low or people believe the banks might be shaky, they naturally want to hold more physical cash. *Longer term, C/D may be influenced by technology and loophole mining, encouraging bankers and depositors to eschew traditional checkable deposits in favor of sweep accounts.*

The required reserve ratio is mandated by the central bank but, as noted in Chapter 10, loophole mining and technology have rendered it less important in recent years because sweep accounts allow banks to minimize the de jure level of their checkable deposits. *In many places, rr is no longer a binding constraint on banks so, as we'll see, most central banks no longer consider changing it as an effective monetary policy tool.* (This in no way affects the money multiplier, which would provide the same figure for m_1 or m_2 whether we calculate them as above or replace rr and ER/D with R/D, where R = total reserves.)

Stop and Think Box

Prove the assertion made above: "This in no way affects the money multiplier, which would provide the same figure for m1 or m2 whether we calculate them as above or replace rr and ER/D with R/D, where R = total reserves." Suppose that C = 100, R = 200, and D = 500 and that R is composed of required reserves of 100 and excess reserves of 100. That means that rr must equal .2(100/500).

Under the formula provided in the text,

$$m_1 = 1 + (C / D) / [rr + (ER / D) + (C / D)]$$

$$m_1 = 1 + .2 / .2 + .2 + .2 = 1.2 / .6 = 2.0$$

Under the formula suggested above,

$$m_1 = 1 + (C / D) / [(R / D) + (C / D)]$$

$$m_1 = 1.2 / .4 + 2 = 2.0$$

Excess reserves (or just reserves in a system without required reserves) are inversely related to the interest rate. In the early 1960s and early 2000s, when the interest rate was well less than 5 percent, ER/D was high, at .003 to .004. In the 1970s and 1980s, when interest rates were 10 percent and higher, ER/D dropped to .001 to .002. As we learned in Chapter 9, *expected deposit outflows directly affect excess reserve levels as banks stock up on reserves to meet the outflows.* When uncertainty is high or a banking crisis is in progress or appears imminent, bankers will increase ER to protect their banks.

In summary, the central bank influences the money supply by controlling the monetary base and, to a far lesser extent, the required reserve ratio. Depositors, banks, and borrowers influence the money supply by influencing m_1 and m_2, specifically by determining the money multiplier, with depositors largely in control of C/D; depositors and banks interacting via deposit outflow expectations to determine ER/D; and borrowers, depositors, banks, and the central bank interacting to determine interest rates and hence to some extent both C/D and ER/D.

Key Takeaways

- Central banks control MB and rr, and affect interest rates, which in turn affect C/D and ER/D.
- Depositors determine C/D by deciding how much cash versus deposits to hold. They also influence interest rates.
- Banks influence interest rates and determine ER/D by deciding how many excess reserves to hold in the face of expected deposit outflows and interest rates.
- Borrowers influence the interest rate and hence to some extent C/D and ER/D.

15.7 Suggested Reading

Hummel, William. *Money: What It Is, How It Works* 2nd ed. Bloomington, IN: iUniverse, 2006.

Mayes, David, and Jan Toporowski. *Open Market Operations and Financial Markets*. New York: Routledge, 2007.

Endnotes

1. https://qz.com/426925/i-was-a-quadrillionaire-in-zimbabwe-but-could-barely-afford-to-buy-bread/; binscorner.com/pages/z/zimbabwe-the-land-of-poor-millionaires.html
2. Students sometimes become confused about this because they think the central bank *is* the government. At most, it is part of the government, and not the part that issues the bonds. Sometimes, as in the case of the BUS and SBUS, it is not part of the government at all.
3. news.goldseek.com/GoldSeek/1177619058.php
4. www.youtube.com/watch?v=3nhgfjrKI0o; https://memegenerator.net/instance/46230001/chris-farley-troll-in-a-van-down-by-the-river

5. M2 would equal m_1 iff T = 0 and MMF = 0, which is highly unlikely. Note: iff means if and only if.

CHAPTER 16

Monetary Policy Tools

Chapter Objectives

By the end of this chapter, students should be able to:

1. List and assess the strengths and weaknesses of the three primary monetary policy tools that central banks have at their disposal.
2. Describe the federal funds market and explain its importance.
3. Explain how the Fed influences the equilibrium fed funds rate to move toward its target rate.
4. Explain the purpose of the Fed's discount window and other lending facilities.
5. List and describe the functioning of additional policy tools in the central banker's toolkit.

16.1 The Federal Funds Market and Reserves

Learning Objectives

1. What three monetary policy tools do central banks have at their disposal?
2. What are the strengths and weaknesses of each? What is the federal funds market and why is it important?

Central banks have three primary tools for influencing the money supply: the reserve requirement, discount loans, and open market operations. The first works through the money multiplier, constraining multiple deposit expansion the larger it becomes. Central banks today rarely use it because most now pay interest on reserves and banks work around reserve requirements. (That is not to say that reserve requirements are not enforced, merely that they are not adjusted to influence MS. Currently, the reserve requirement in the U.S. is 10 percent on transaction account deposits [demand, ATS, NOW, and share draft] greater than $115.1 million and lower amounts on smaller sums.[1]) The second and third tools influence the monetary base (MB = C + R). Discount loans depend on banks (or nonbank borrowers, where applicable) first borrowing from, then repaying loans to, the central bank, which therefore does not have precise control over MB. Open market operations (OMO) are generally preferred as a policy tool because the central bank can easily expand or contract MB to a precise level. Using OMO, central banks can also reverse mistakes quickly.

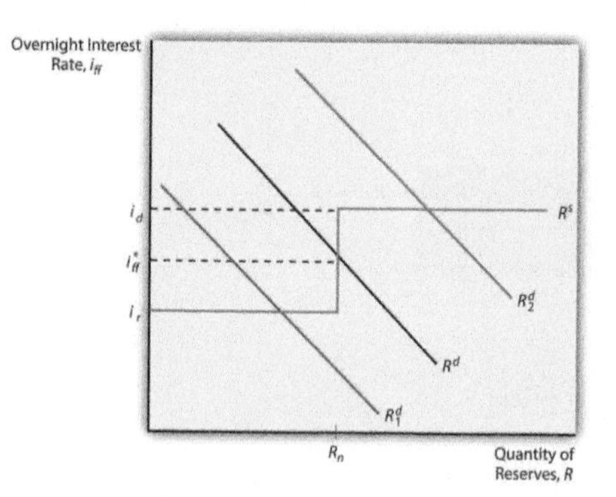

FIGURE 16.1 Equilibrium in the fed funds market

Yeah, the reserve supply and demand curves are unusual. See the text for details.

In the United States, under typical conditions, the Fed conducts monetary policy primarily through the federal funds (fed funds) market, an overnight market where banks that need reserves can borrow them from banks that hold reserves they don't need. Banks can also borrow their reserves directly from the Fed, but, except during crises, most prefer not to because the Fed's discount rate is generally higher than the federal funds rate. Also, borrowing too much, too often from the Fed can induce increased regulatory scrutiny. So usually banks get their overnight funds from the fed funds market, which, as Figure 16.1 shows, pretty much works like any other market.

The downward slope of the demand curve for reserves is easily explained. *Like anything else, as the price of reserves (in this case, the interest rate paid for them) increases, the quantity demanded decreases.* As reserves get cheaper, banks will want more of them because the opportunity cost of that added protection, of that added liquidity, is lower. The R_d curve becomes flat (infinitely elastic), however, at i_r, the interest rate that the Fed pays on banks' reserve balances. That is because no bank would accept less than i_r to lend its reserves in the market (to a bank with a default risk > 0 no less). The Fed currently pays 1 percent on reserves (required and excess), up from the 0.25 percent it paid on reserves when it initially began paying reserves in late 2008.[2]

The reserve supply curve, R_S, is also kinked. Note that the curve takes a hard right (becomes infinitely elastic) at the discount rate. That's because if the federal funds rate ever exceeded the discount rate, banks' thirst for Fed discount loans would be unquenchable as a clear arbitrage opportunity would exist: borrow at the discount rate and relend at the higher market rate. Below that point, the reserve supply curve is vertical (perfectly inelastic).

The intersection of the supply and demand curves is the equilibrium or market rate, the actual or "effective" federal funds rate, ff*. *When the Fed makes open market purchases, the supply of reserves shifts right, lowering ff* (ceteris paribus). When it sells, it moves the reserve supply curve left, increasing ff*, all else constant.* In most circumstances, the discount and reserve rates effectively channel the market federal funds rate into a range.

FIGURE 16.2 Fed funds targeting, 2000–2010
Note how paying interest on reserves after 2008 made it much easier to target the fed funds rate

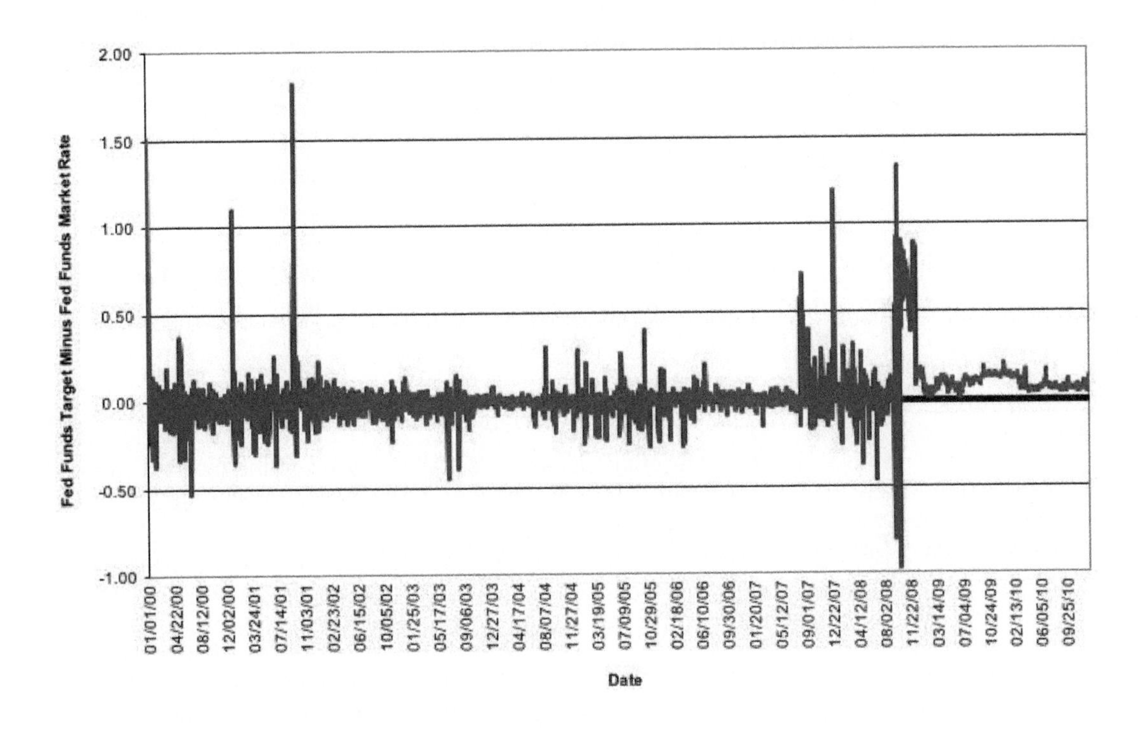

FIGURE 16.3 Fed funds targeting, 2008
Note the jump in volatility as the crisis took hold late in the year.

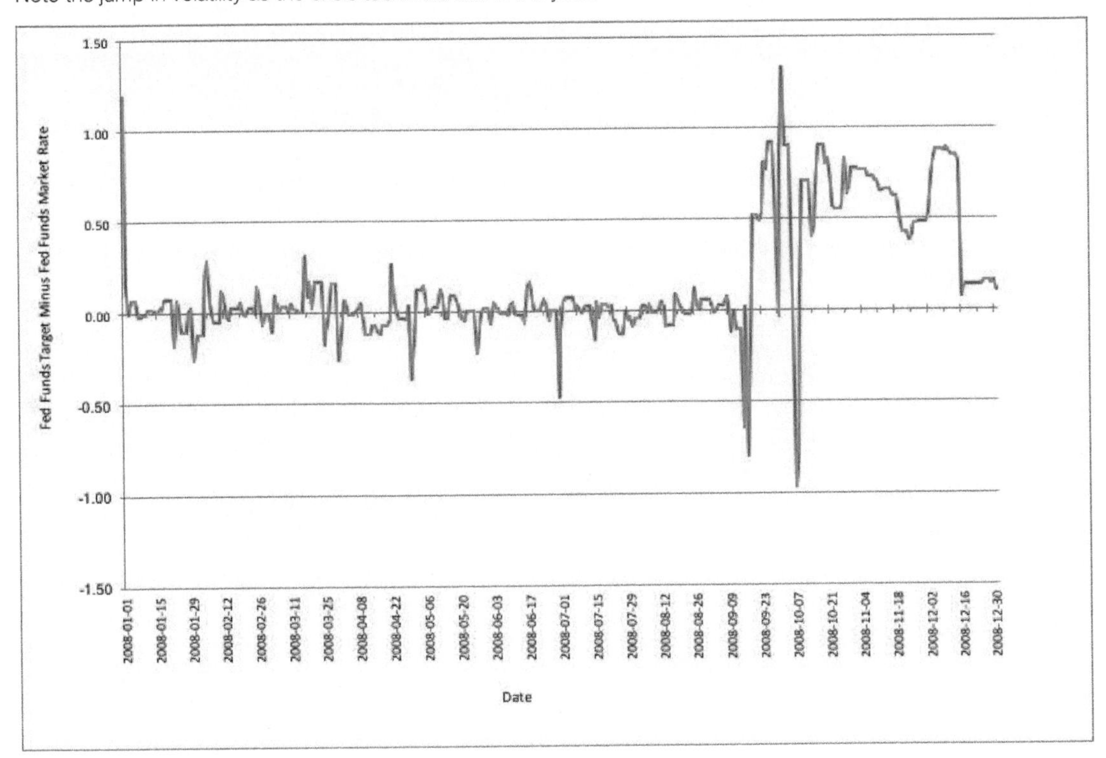

Theoretically, the Fed could also directly affect the demand for reserves by changing the reserve requirement. *If it increased (decreased) rr, demand for reserves would shift up (down), increasing (decreasing) ff**. As noted above, however, banks these days can so easily sidestep required reserves that the Fed's ability to influence the demand for reserves is extremely limited.

Demand for reserves (excess reserves that is) can also shift right or left due to bank liquidity management activities, increasing (decreasing) as expectations of net deposit outflows increase (decrease). The Fed tries to anticipate such shifts and generally has done a good job of counteracting changes in excess reserves through OMO. Going into holidays, for example, banks often hold a little extra vault cash (a form of reserves). Knowing this, the Fed counteracts the rightward shift in demand (which would increase ff*) by shifting the reserve supply curve to the right by buying bonds (thereby decreasing ff* by an offsetting amount). Although there have been days when ff* differed from the target by several percentage points (several hundred basis points), between 1982 and 2007, the fed funds target was, on average, only .0340 of a percent lower than ff*. Between 2000 and the subprime mortgage uproar in the summer of 2007, the Fed did an even better job of moving ff* to its target, as Figure 16.2 shows. During the crises of 2007 and 2008, however, the Fed often missed its target by a long way, as shown in Figure 16.3. So in December 2008, it stopped publishing a feds fund target and instead began to publish the upper limit it was willing to tolerate.

Stop and Think Box

America's first central banks, the Bank of the United States (1791-1811) and the "Second" Bank of the United States (1816-1836), controlled commercial bank reserve levels by varying the speed and intensity by which it redeemed convertible bank liabilities (notes and deposits) for reserves (gold and silver). Can you model that system?

Kudos if you can! I'd plot quantity of reserves along the horizontal axis and interest rate along the vertical axis. The reserve supply curve was probably highly but not perfectly inelastic and the reserve demand curve sloped downward, of course. When the BUS or SBUS wanted to tighten monetary policy, it would return commercial bank monetary liabilities in a great rush, pushing the reserve demand curve to the right, thereby raising the interest rate. When it wanted to soften, it would dawdle before redeeming notes for gold and so forth, allowing the demand for reserves to move left, thereby decreasing the interest rate.

Key Takeaways

- Central banks can influence the money multiplier (simple, m1, m2, etc.) via reserve requirements.
- That tool is somewhat limited these days given the introduction of sweep accounts and other reserve requirement loopholes.
- Central banks can also influence MB via loans to banks and open market operations.
- For day-to-day policy implementation, open market operations are preferable because they are more precise and immediate and almost completely under the control of the central bank, which means it can reverse mistakes quickly.
- Discount loans depend on banks borrowing and repaying loans, so the central bank has less control over MB if it relies on loans alone.
- Discount loans are therefore used now primarily to set a ceiling on the overnight interbank rate and to provide liquidity during crises.
- The federal funds market is the name of the overnight interbank lending market, basically the market where banks borrow and lend bank reserves, in the United States.
- It is important because the Fed uses open market operations (OMO) to move the equilibrium rate ff* toward the target established by the Federal Open Market Committee (FOMC).

16.2 Open Market Operations and the Discount Window

Learning Objectives

1. How does the Fed influence the equilibrium fed funds rate to move toward its target rate?
2. What purpose does the Fed's discount window now serve?

In practical terms, the Fed engages in two types of OMO, dynamic and defensive. As those names imply, it uses dynamic OMO to change the level of the MB, and defensive OMO to offset movements in other factors affecting MB, with an eye toward maintaining the federal funds target rate determined by the Federal Open Market Committee (FOMC) at its most recent meeting. If it wanted to increase the money supply, for example, it would buy bonds "dynamically." If it wanted to keep the money supply stable but knew that a bank was going to repay a large discount loan (which has the effect of decreasing the MB), it would buy bonds "defensively."

The responsibility for actually buying and selling government bonds devolves upon the Federal Reserve Bank of New York (FRBNY). Each trading day, FRBNY staff members look at the level of reserves, the fed funds target, the actual market fed funds rate, expectations regarding float, and Treasury activities. They also garner information about Treasury market conditions through conversations with so-called primary dealers, specialized firms and banks that **make a market** in Treasuries. With the input and consent of the Monetary Affairs Division of the Board of Governors, the FRBNY determines how much to buy or sell and places the appropriate order on the Trading Room Automated Processing System (TRAPS) computer system that links all the primary dealers. The FRBNY then selects the best offers up to the amount it wants to buy or sell. It enters into two types of trades, so-called outright ones, where the bonds permanently join or leave the Fed's balance sheet, and temporary ones, called repos and reverse repos. In a repo (aka a repurchase agreement), the Fed purchases government bonds with the guarantee that the sellers will repurchase them from the Fed, generally one to fifteen days hence. In a reverse repo (aka a matched sale-purchase transaction), the Fed sells securities and the buyer agrees to sell them to the Fed again in the near future. The availability of such self-reversing contracts and the liquidity of the government bond market render open market operations a precise tool for implementing the Fed's monetary policy.

make a market

Buying securities from all comers at a bid price and reselling them to all comers at a slightly higher ask price.

The so-called discount window, where banks come to borrow reserves from the Federal district banks, is today primarily a backup facility used during crises, when the federal funds market might not function effectively. As noted above, the discount rate puts an effective cap on ff* by providing banks with an alternative source of reserves (see Figure 16.4). Note that no matter how far the reserve demand curve shifts to the right, once it reaches the discount rate, it merely slides along it. (I left off the flat portion of the R_d curves as they are unimportant here.)

FIGURE 16.4 The discount window sets an upper bound on overnight interest rates

Why would any bank borrow in the market at a higher rate than it could borrow directly from the Fed?

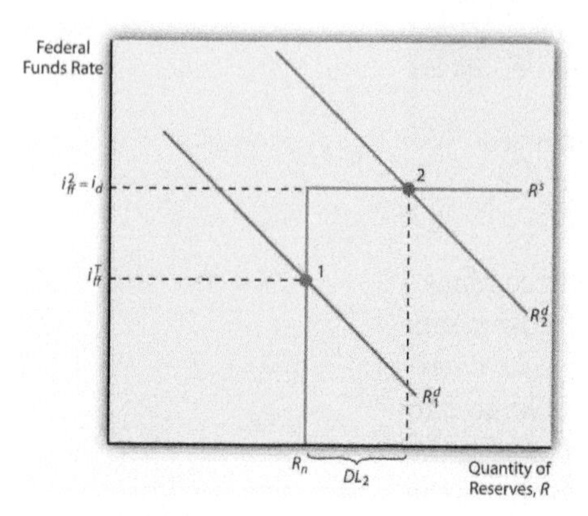

As lender of last resort, the Fed has a responsibility to ensure that banks can obtain as much as they want to borrow provided they can post what in normal times would be considered good collateral security. So that banks do not rely too heavily on the discount window, the discount rate is usually set a full percentage point above ff*, a "penalty" of 100 basis points. (This policy is usually known as Bagehot's Law, but the insight actually originated with Alexander Hamilton, America's first Treasury secretary, so I like to call it Hamilton's Law.) On several occasions (including the 1984 failure of Continental Illinois, a large commercial bank; the stock market crash of 1987; and the subprime mortgage debacle of 2007), the discount window added the liquidity (reserves) and confidence necessary to stave off more serious disruptions to the economy.

Only depository institutions can borrow from the Fed's discount window. *During the financial crisis of 2008, however, many other types of financial institutions, including broker-dealers and money market funds, also encountered significant difficulties due to the breakdown of many credit markets. The Federal Reserve responded by invoking its emergency powers to create additional lending powers and programs*, including the following:[3]

special-purpose vehicle (SPV)

An organizational entity created to perform a specific, or special, task.

1. Term Auction Facility (TAF), a "credit facility" that allows depository institutions to bid for short term funds at a rate established by auction.
2. Primary Dealer Credit Facility (PDCF), which provides overnight loans to primary dealers at the discount rate.
3. Term Securities Lending Facility (TSLF), which also helps primary dealers by exchanging Treasuries for riskier collateral for twenty-eight-day periods.
4. Asset-Backed Commercial Paper Money Market Mutual Liquidity Facility, which helps money market mutual funds to meet redemptions without having to sell their assets into distressed markets.
5. Commercial Paper Funding Facility (CPFF), which allows the FRBNY, through a **special-purpose vehicle** (SPV), to purchase commercial paper (short-term bonds) issued by nonfinancial corporations.
6. Money Market Investor Funding Facility (MMIFF), which is another lending program designed to help the money markets (markets for short-term bonds) return to normal.

Most of these programs[4] phased out as credit conditions returned to normal. (The Bank of England and other central banks have implemented similar programs.[5])

The financial crisis also induced the Fed to engage in several rounds of "quantitative easing" or Large Scale Asset Purchases (LSAP), the goals of which appear to be to increase the prices of (decrease the yields of) Treasury bonds and the other financial assets purchased and to influence the money supply directly. Due to LSAP, the Fed's balance sheet swelled from less than a trillion dollars in early 2008 to almost 3 trillion by August 2011.

Stop and Think Box

What in Sam Hill (https://en.wikipedia.org/wiki/Sam_Hill_) happened in Figure 16.5? (*Hint*: The dates are important.)

FIGURE 16.5 Total bank borrowings from the Federal Reserve System, 2001

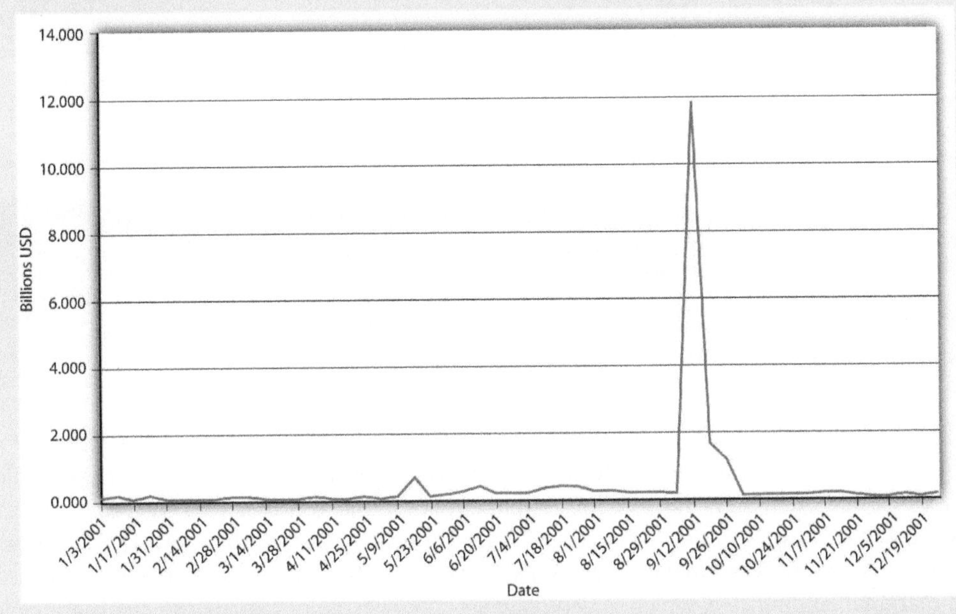

Terrorists attacked New York City and Washington, DC, with hijacked airplanes, shutting down the nation and parts of the financial system for the better part of a week. Some primary dealers were destroyed in the attacks, which also brought on widespread fears of bankruptcies and bank runs. Banks beefed up reserves by selling bonds to the Fed and by borrowing from its discount window. (Excess reserves jumped from a long-term average of around $1 billion to $19 billion.) This is an excellent example of the discount window providing lender-of-last-resort services to the economy.

The discount window is also used to provide moderately shaky banks a longer-term source of credit at an even higher penalty rate .5 percentage (50 basis) points above the regular discount rate. Finally, the Fed will also lend to a small number of banks in vacation and agricultural areas that experience large deposit fluctuations over the course of a year. Increasingly, however, such banks are becoming part of larger banks with more stable deposit profiles, or they handle their liquidity management using the market for negotiable certificates of deposit NCDs or other market borrowings.

Key Takeaways

- The Fed can move the equilibrium fed funds rate toward its target by changing the demand for reserves by changing the required reserve ratio. However, it rarely does so anymore.
- It can also shift the supply curve to the right (add reserves to the system) by buying assets (almost always Treasury bonds) or shift it to the left (remove reserves from the system) by selling assets.

- The discount window caps ff* because if ff* were to rise above the Fed's discount rate, banks would borrow reserves from the Fed (technically its district banks) instead of borrowing them from other banks in the fed funds market.
- Because the Fed typically sets the discount rate a full percentage point (100 basis points) above its feds fund target, ff* rises above the discount rate only in a crisis, as in the aftermath of the 1987 stock market crash and the 2007 subprime mortgage debacle.

16.3 Additional Policy Tools

Learning Objectives

1. What other policy tools can central banks employ other than OMO and discount loans?
2. How do those other tools work?

best practice

Policies generally considered to be state of the art in a given industry, to be something that nonconforming organizations ought to emulate.

The European Central Bank (ECB) also uses open market operations to move the market for overnight interbank lending toward its target. It too uses repos and reverse repos for reversible, defensive OMO, and outright purchases for permanent additions to MB. Unlike the Fed, however, the ECB spreads the love around, conducting OMO in multiple cities throughout the European Union. The ECB's national central banks (NCBs,) like the Fed's district banks, also lend to banks at a so-called marginal lending rate, which is generally set 100 basis points above the overnight cash rate. The ECB pays interest on reserves, a central bank **best practice** the Fed took up only in 2008. Moreover, banks subject to the ECB's regulation have a much more difficult time sidestepping reserve requirements, which the ECB bases on all liabilities, not just transaction deposits.[6] Canada, New Zealand, and Australia also pay interest on reserves but have eliminated reserve requirements, relying instead on what is called the channel, or corridor, system like that used by the Fed and described in Section 16.1.

All of those central banks have additional policy tools, sometimes called "unconventional tools" because traditionally they have been rarely used, at their disposal. These tools are most important when the central bank hits the zero interest rate lower bound. Although central bankers cannot lower nominal interest rates below zero (which critics sometimes call a "liquidity trap" or describe as being as useful as "pushing on a string"), that does not mean that they are powerless to further stimulate the economy.

forward guidance

Forward guidance is an unconventional monetary policy tool whereby the central bank simply reveals its future plans to market participants.

The first unconventional tool, called **forward guidance**, is deceptively simple but potentially powerful. When employing forward guidance, a central bank simply informs market participants of its future intentions regarding monetary policy. It might explicitly state, for example, that it has no intention of raising interest rates for x periods (e.g., 2 years) or it might commit to not raising interest rates until some condition y, perhaps a combination of inflation or unemployment or output, occurs. Both types of announcement can help to reduce long term interest rates by lowering the expected future rates of which they are composed. If market participants believe the bank, forward guidance can be a powerful tool for setting expectations, so responsible central bankers must use it with caution.

quantitative easing

Quantitative easing occurs when a central bank expands bank reserves beyond that necessary to maintain its policy interest rate (e.g., zero).

The second unconventional tool is called **quantitative easing**, or QE for short. With QE, central bankers keep buying assets in order to increase reserves even after the policy interest rate (like ff*) has been achieved. While QE cannot lower the policy interest rate below zero because banks would rather hold zero interest cash than lend at a negative rate, it can affect inflation expectations and hence, through the Fisher Effect, real interest rates. QE can also work to make the central bank's forward guidance more credible because it is putting its money where its mouth is, so to speak. But if forward guidance alone is powerful, adding QE on top of it threatens price level stability, especially given that central bankers do not have much experience with either tool. Three bouts of QE (ingeniously called QE 1, 2, and 3) boosted the Fed's balance sheet from $.9 trillion in 2008 to over $4 trillion by October 2014, when the Fed ceased QE operations.

FIGURE 16.6

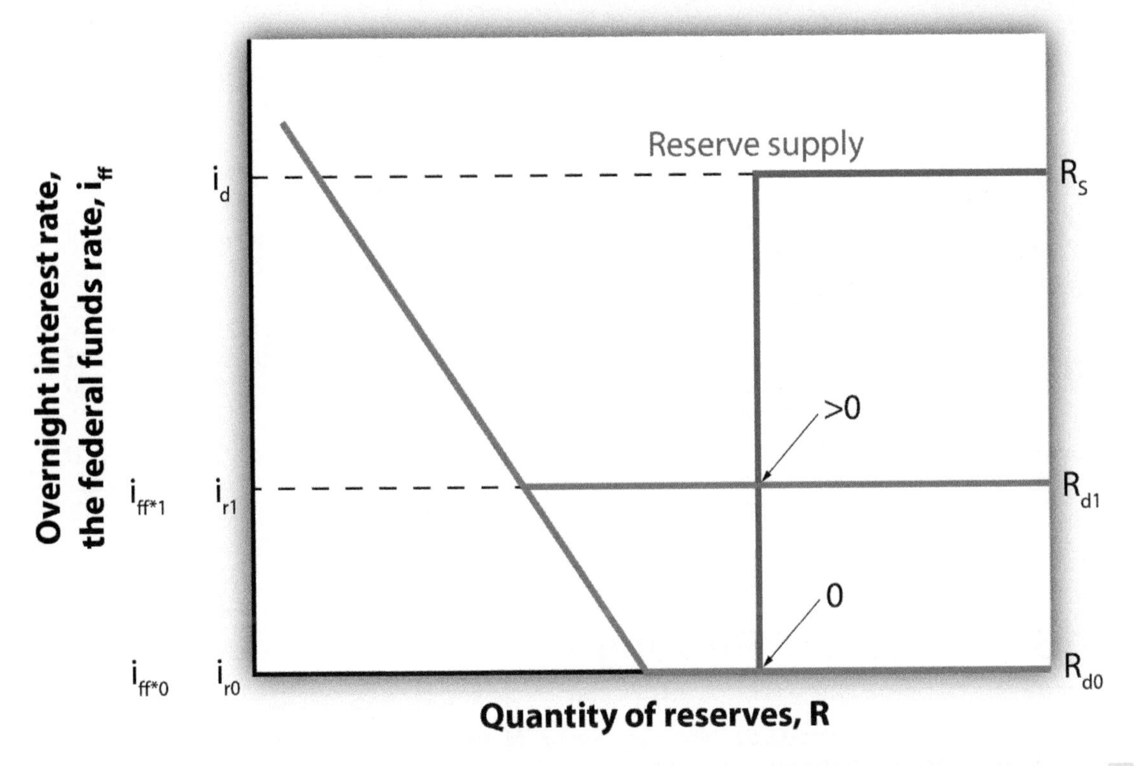

The third and final unconventional monetary policy tool is called **targeted asset purchases**, or TAP for short. With TAP, central bankers do not increase the size of their balance sheets but rather re-jigger the composition of their assets in order to favor one asset, or class of assets, over another. In the aftermath of the Panic of 2008, for example, the Fed replaced Treasuries with large sums of MBS (mortgage-backed securities) in order to bolster mortgage markets (higher prices and greater liquidity). Central bankers will also try to affect the slope of the yield curve by buying longer-dated government bonds or, in the case of the ECB, the bonds of struggling member nations. Central bankers do not like using TAP to "pick winners and losers," however, lest they set off political forces that may seek to reduce their independence.

targeted asset purchases

Targeted asset purchase (TAP) is an unconventional monetary policy tool that occurs when central bankers change the composition of the asset side of their balance sheets in favor of one or more specific assets or classes of assets.

Forward guidance, QE, and TAP did not lead to inflation because the economy (aggregate demand, AD) was so weak for so long after the financial conflagration of 2008. The general presumption is that they staved off deflation and hence another Depression but in so doing created a large inflation overhang. As the economy occasionally showed signs of life (increased AD), most recently in 2017, some observers worried that the Fed, ECB, and other central banks would have to shrink their balance sheets before they could raise interest rates to combat inflation.[7] In fact, the Fed can simply raise the interest rate it pays on deposits, thereby setting a floor on the effective federal funds rate. In other words, central banks using the corridor system are the most powerful monopolists in the universe because they can control both price and quantity simultaneously, as in Figure 16.6, which starts with both the policy interest rate (i_{ff^*0}) and the interest rate paid on reserves (i_{r0}) at 0. Note that the reserve supply, R_s, is greater than (to the right of) the initial reserve demand curve, R_{d0}, due to QE. Without selling assets (shifting R_s left), the Fed can raise the policy interest rate, i_{ff^*1}, by also raising the rate it pays on reserves to i_{r1}, which has the effect of lifting the reserve demand curve to R_{d1}.

Banks that can receive a riskless positive return simply by keeping deposits with the central bank will be less likely to lend those resources to businesses, thus slowing down economic activity and dampening inflation. (In fact, in the limit central banks could raise the rate they pay on their reserves to the point that banks would not lend to private parties at all, but that would be unpopular because it would effectively pay banks to say no to borrowers.)

Key Takeaways

- Most central banks now use OMO instead of discount loans or reserve requirement adjustments for conducting day-to-day monetary policy.
- Some central banks, including those of the euro zone and the British Commonwealth (Canada, Australia, and New Zealand), have developed an ingenious new method called the channel or corridor system.
- Under that system, the market rate is capped at both ends: on the upper end by the discount rate, and at the lower end by the reserve rate, the interest rate the central bank pays to banks for holding reserves.
- The payment of interest on reserves is what will allow central bankers to exit gracefully from the unconventional monetary policy tools, forward guidance, quantitative easing (QE), and targeted asset purchases (TAP) they used after the Panic of 2008, when their policy rate (e.g., the federal funds rate) hit zero.
- Forward guidance promised that policy rates would remain low for an extended period and QE helped to bolster the credibility of those promises. TAP allowed central bankers to influence long term interest rates and to stabilize the prices of important asset classes, like MBS.

16.4 Suggested Reading

Antalik, Norbert. *The ECB's Monetary Policy: Monetary Policy, Instruments, Shortcomings, Analysis.* LAP LAMBERT Academic Publishing, 2013.

Axilrod, Stephen H. *Inside the Fed: Monetary Policy and Its Management, Martin Through Greenspan to Bernanke.* Cambridge, MA: MIT Press, 2009.

Cordella, Tito and Pablo Federico. *Reserve Requirements in the Brave New Macroprudential World.* New York: World Bank Studies, 2014.

de Haan, Jakob and Helge Berger (eds.) *The European Central Bank at Ten.* New York: Springer, 2010.

Hetzel, Robert L. *The Monetary Policy of the Federal Reserve: A History.* New York: Cambridge University Press, 2008.

Mishkin, Frederic S. *Monetary Policy Strategy.* Cambridge, MA: MIT Press, 2007.

Endnotes

1. www.federalreserve.gov/monetarypolicy/reservereq.htm#table1
2. https://www.federalreserve.gov/monetarypolicy/reqresbalances.htm
3. https://www.federalreserve.gov/monetarypolicy/expiredtools.htm
4. blogs.wsj.com/economics/2011/08/09/a-look-inside-the-feds-balance-sheet-12/tab/interactive
5. "Credit Markets: A Lifeline for Banks. The Bank of England's Bold Initiative Should Calm Frayed Financial Nerves," *The Economist*, April 26, 2008, 74–75.
6. https://www.ecb.europa.eu/explainers/tell-me/html/minimum_reserve_req.en.html
7. https://www.forbes.com/sites/timworstall/2017/01/27/ben-bernanke-reveals-how-the-fed-will-unravel-quantitative-easing-after-rate-rises-not-before/#2820af7c269d

CHAPTER 17

Monetary Policy Targets and Goals

Chapter Objectives

By the end of this chapter, students should be able to:

1. Explain why the Fed was generally so ineffective before the late 1980s.
2. Explain why macroeconomic volatility declined from the late 1980s until 2008.
3. List the trade-offs that central banks face and describe how they confront them.
4. Define monetary targeting and explain why it succeeded in some countries and failed in others.
5. Define inflation targeting and explain its importance.
6. Provide and use the Taylor Rule and explain its importance.

17.1 A Short History of Fed Blunders

Learning Objectives

1. Why was the Fed generally so ineffective before the late 1980s?
2. Why has macroeconomic volatility declined since the late 1980s?

The long and at first seemingly salutary reign of Alan Greenspan ("The Great," 1987–2006)[1] and the auspicious beginning of the rule of Ben Bernanke ("The Bald," 2006–2014)[2] temporarily provided the Fed with something it has rarely enjoyed in its nearly century-long existence, the halo of success and widespread approbation. While it would be an exaggeration to call Federal Reserve Board members the Keystone Kops of monetary policy, the Fed's history is more sour than sweet.

Central bankers use tools like open market operations, the buying and selling of assets in the open market, to influence the money supply and interest rates. If they decrease rates, businesses and people will want to borrow more to build factories and offices, buy automobiles, and so forth, thus stimulating the economy. If they increase rates, the opposite will occur as businesses and people find it too costly to purchase big ticket items like houses, boats, and cars. Unlike communist central planners, central bankers do not try to directly run the economy or the various economic entities that compose it, but they do try to steer aggregate behavior toward higher levels of output. *In that sense, central banks are the last bastions of central planning in otherwise free market economies*. And central planning,[3] as the Communists and the Austrian economists who critiqued them discovered, is darn difficult.[4]

This is not a history textbook, but the past can often shed light on the present. History warns us to beware claims of infallibility. In this case, however, it also provides us with a clear reason to be optimistic. *Between 1985 or so and 2007, the U.S. macroeconomy, particularly output, was much less volatile than previously*. That was a happy development for the Fed because it, like some other central banks, is charged with stabilizing the macroeconomy, among other things. The Fed in particular owes its genesis to the desire of Americans to be shielded from financial panics and economic crises.

The Fed itself took credit for almost 60 percent of the reduction in volatility. (Is anyone surprised by this? Don't we all embrace responsibility for good outcomes, but eschew it when things turn ugly?) Skeptics point to other causes for the Great Calm, including dumb luck; less volatile oil prices (the 1970s were a difficult time in this regard);[5] less volatile total factor productivity growth;[6] and improvements in management, especially just-in-time inventory techniques, which has helped to reduce the inventory gluts of yore.[7] *Those factors all played roles, but it also appears that the Fed's monetary policies actually improved.* Before Paul Volcker (1979–1987), the Fed engaged in pro-cyclical monetary policies. Since then, it has tried to engage in anti-cyclical policies. And that, as poet Robert Frost wrote in "The Road Not Taken," has made all the difference.[8]

For reasons that are still not clearly understood, economies have a tendency to cycle through periods of boom and bust, of expansion and contraction. *The Fed used to exacerbate this cycle by making the highs of the business cycle higher and the lows lower than they would otherwise have been.* Yes, that ran directly counter to one of its major missions. Debates rage whether it was simply ineffective or if it purposely made mistakes. It was probably a mixture of both that changed over time. In any event, we needn't "go there" because a simple narrative will suffice.

The Fed was conceived in peace but born in war. As William Silber[9] points out in his book *When Washington Shut Down Wall Street*, the Federal Reserve was rushed into operation to help the U.S. financial system, which had been terribly shocked, economically as well as politically, by the outbreak of the Great War (1914–1918) in Europe.[10] At first, the Fed influenced the monetary base (MB) through its *rediscounts*—it literally discounted again business commercial paper already discounted by commercial banks. A wholesaler would take a bill owed by one of its customers, say, a department store like Wanamaker's, to its bank. The bank might give $9,950 for a $10,000 bill due in sixty days. If, say, thirty days later the bank needed to boost its reserves, it would take the bill to the Fed, which would rediscount it by giving the bank, say, $9,975 in cash for it. The Fed would then collect the $10,000 when it fell due. In the context of World War I, *this policy was inflationary*, leading to double-digit price increases in 1919 and 1920. *The Fed responded by raising the discount rate from 4.75 to 7 percent, setting off a sharp recession.*

The postwar recession hurt the Fed's revenues because the volume of rediscounts shrank precipitously. *It responded by investing in securities and, in so doing, accidentally stumbled upon open market operations.* The Fed fed the speculative asset bubble of the late 1920s, then sat on its hands while the economy crashed and burned in the early 1930s. Here's another tidbit: it also exacerbated the so-called Roosevelt Recession of 1937–1938 by playing with fire, by raising the reserve requirement, a new policy tool placed in its hands by FDR and his New Dealers in the Banking Act of 1935.

During World War II, the Fed became the Treasury's lapdog. Okay, that is an exaggeration, but not much of one. *The Treasury said thou shalt purchase our bonds to keep the prices up (and yields down) and the Fed did, basically monetizing the national debt. In short, the Fed wasn't very independent in this period.* Increases in the supply of some items, coupled with price controls and quantity rationing, kept the lid on inflation during the titanic conflict against Fascism, but after the war the floodgates of inflation opened. Over the course of just three years, 1946, 1947, and 1948, the price level jumped some 30 percent. There was no net change in prices in 1949 and 1950, but the start of the Korean War sent prices up another almost 8 percent in 1951, and the Fed finally got some backbone and stopped pegging interest rates. As the analysis of central bank independence suggests, inflation dropped big time, to 2.19 percent in 1952, and to less than 1 percent in 1953 and 1954. In 1955, prices actually dropped slightly, on average.

This is not to say, however, that the Fed was a fully competent central bank because it continued to exacerbate the business cycle instead of ameliorating it. *Basically, in booms (recessions) business borrowing and the supply of bonds would increase (decrease), driving rates up (down). (For a review of this, see Chapter 5.) The Fed, hoping to keep interest rates at a specific rate, would respond by buying (selling) bonds in order to drive interest rates back down (up), thus increasing (decreas-*

ing) MB and the money supply (MS). So when the economy was naturally expanding, the Fed stoked its fires and when it was contracting, the Fed put its foot on its head. Worse, if interest rates rose (bond prices declined) due to an increase in inflation (think Fisher Equation), the Fed would also buy bonds to support their prices, thereby increasing the MS and causing yet further inflation. This, as much as oil price hikes, caused the Great Inflation of the 1970s. *Throughout the crises of the 1970s and 1980s, the Fed toyed around with various targets (M1, M2, fed funds rate), but none of it mattered much because its pro-cyclical bias remained.*

Stop and Think Box

Another blunder made by the Fed was Reg Q, which capped the interest rates that banks could pay on deposits. When the Great Inflation began in the late 1960s, nominal interest rates rose (think Fisher Equation) above those set by the Fed. What horror *directly* resulted? What Fed goal was thereby impeded?

Shortages known as credit crunches resulted. Whenever $p^* >$ preg, shortages result because the quantity demanded exceeds the quantity supplied by the market. Banks couldn't make loans because they couldn't attract the deposits they needed to fund them. That created much the same effect as high interest rates—entrepreneurs couldn't obtain financing for good business ideas, so they wallowed, decreasing economic activity. In response, banks engaged in loophole mining.

By the late 1980s, the Fed, under Alan Greenspan, finally began to engage in anti-cyclical policies, to "lean into the wind" by raising the federal funds rate before inflation became a problem and by lowering the federal funds rate at the first sign of recession. Since the implementation of this crucial insight, the natural swings of the macroeconomy have been much more docile than hitherto, until the crisis of 2007–2008, that is. The United States experienced two recessions (July 1990–March 1991 and March 2001–November 2001)[11] but they were so-called soft landings, that is, short and shallow. Expansions have been longer than usual and not so intense. Again, some of this might be due to dumb luck (no major wars, low real oil prices [until summer 2008 that is]) and better technology, but there is little doubt the Fed played an important role in the stabilization.

Of course, past performance is no guarantee of future performance. (Just look at the NBA's New York Knicks.) As the crisis of 2007–2008 approached, the Fed resembled a fawn trapped in the headlights of an oncoming eighteen-wheeler, too afraid to continue on its path of raising interest rates and equally frightened of reversing course. The result was an economy that looked like road kill. Being a central banker is a bit like being Goldilocks. It's important to get monetary policy just right, lest we wake up staring down the gullets of three hungry bears. (I don't mean Stephen Colbert's bears[12] here, but rather bear markets.)

Key Takeaways

- The Fed was generally ineffective before the late 1980s because it engaged in pro-cyclical monetary policies, expanding the MS and lowering interest rates during expansions and constricting the MS and raising interest rates during recessions, the exact opposite of what it should have done.
- The Fed was also ineffective because it did not know about open market operations (OMO) at first, because it did not realize the damage its toying with rr could cause after New Dealers gave it control of reserve requirements, and because it gave up its independence to the Treasury during World War II.
- The Fed's switch from pro-cyclical to anti-cyclical monetary policy, where it leans into the wind rather than running with it, played an important role in decreased macroeconomic volatility, although it perhaps cannot take all of the credit because changes in technology,

particularly inventory control, and other lucky events conspired to help improve macro stability over the same period.

- Future events will reveal if central banking has truly and permanently improved.

17.2 Central Bank Goal Trade-offs

Learning Objective

1. What trade-offs do central banks face and how do they confront them?

Central banks worldwide often find themselves between a rock and a hard place. The rock is price stability (inflation control) and the hard place is economic growth and employment. *Although in the long run the two goals are perfectly compatible, in the short run, they sometimes are not. In those instances, the central bank has a difficult decision to make. Should it raise interest rates or slow or even stop MS growth to stave off inflation, or should it decrease interest rates or speed up MS growth to induce companies and consumers to borrow, thereby stoking employment and growth?* In some places, like the European Union, the central bank is instructed by its charter to stop inflation. "The primary objective of the European System of Central Banks," the Maastricht Treaty clearly states, "shall be to maintain price stability. Without prejudice to the objective of price stability, the ESCB shall support the general economic policies in the Community" including high employment and economic growth. The Fed's charter and the Dodd-Frank Act of 2010, by contrast, instruct the Fed to ensure price stability, maximum employment, **and** financial stability. Little wonder that the Fed has not held the line on inflation as well as the European Central Bank (ECB), but unemployment rates in the United States are generally well below those of most European nations. (There are additional reasons for that difference that are not germane to the discussion here.)

Do note that almost nobody wants 100 percent employment, when everyone who wants a job has one. A little unemployment, called frictional unemployment, is a good thing because it allows the labor market to function more smoothly. So-called structural unemployment, when workers' skills do not match job requirements, is not such a good thing, but is probably inevitable in a dynamic economy saddled with a weak educational system. (As structural unemployment increased in the United States, education improved somewhat, but not enough to ensure that all new jobs the economy created could be filled with domestic laborers.) *So the Fed shoots for what is called the natural rate of unemployment. Nobody is quite sure what that rate is, but it is thought to be around 5 percent, give or take.*

Key Takeaways

- The main trade-off that central banks face is a short-term one between inflation, which calls for tighter policy (higher interest rates, slower money growth), and employment and output, which call for looser policy (lower interest rates, faster money growth).
- Some central banks confront trade-offs by explicitly stating that one goal, usually price stability (controlling inflation), is of paramount concern.
- Others, including the Fed, confront the trade-off on an ad hoc, case-by-case basis.

17.3 Central Bank Targets

Learning Objectives

1. What is monetary targeting and why did it succeed in some countries and fail in others?
2. What is inflation targeting and why is it important?

Once a central bank has decided whether it wants to hold the line (no change [Δ]), tighten (increase i, decrease or slow the growth of MS), or ease (lower i, increase MS), it has to figure out how best to do so. Quite a gulf exists between the central bank's goals (low inflation, high employment) and its tools or instruments (OMO, discount loans, changing rr). So it sometimes creates a target between the two, some intermediate goal that it shoots for with its tools, with the expectation that hitting the target's bull's-eye would lead to goal satisfaction:

TOOLS→TARGET→GOAL

In the past, *many central banks targeted monetary aggregates like M1 or M2*. Some, like Germany's Bundesbank and Switzerland's central bank, did so successfully. Others, like the Fed, the Bank of Japan, and the Bank of England, failed miserably. Their failure is partly explained by what economists call the time inconsistency problem, the inability over *time* to follow a good plan *consistently*. (Weight-loss diets suffer from the time inconsistency problem, too, and every form of procrastination is essentially time inconsistent.) Basically, like a wayward dieter or a lazy student (rare animals to be sure), they overshot their targets time and time again, preferring pleasure now at the cost of pain later.

Another major problem was that monetary targets did not always equate to the central banks' goals in any clear way. Long lags between policy implementation and real-world effects made it difficult to know to what degree a policy was working—or not. Worse, the importance of specific aggregates as a determinant of interest rates and the price level waxed and waned over time in ways that proved difficult to predict. Finally, many central banks experienced a disjoint between their tools or operating instruments, which were often interest rates like the federal funds, and their monetary targets. *It turns out that one can't control both an interest rate and a monetary aggregate at the same time.* To see why, study Figure 17.1. Note that if the central bank leaves the supply of money fixed, changes in the demand for money will make the interest rate jiggle up and down. It can only keep *i* fixed by changing the money supply. Because open market operations are the easiest way to conduct monetary policy, most central banks, as we've seen, eventually changed reserves to maintain an interest rate target. With the monetary supply moving round and round, up and down, it became difficult to hit monetary targets.

FIGURE 17.1 Central banks cannot control the MS and interest rates simultaneously

And you thought central banks were omnipotent!

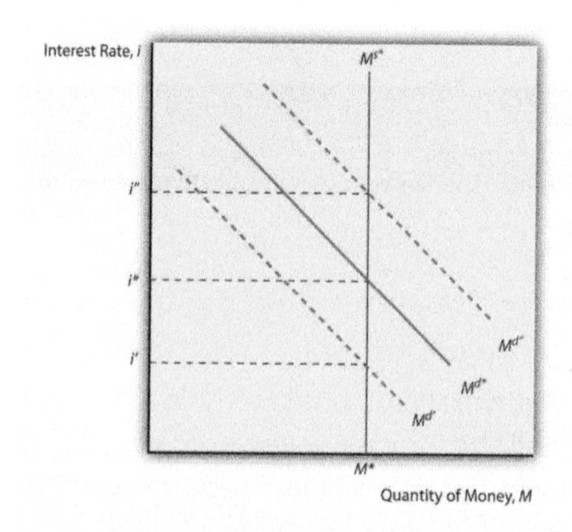

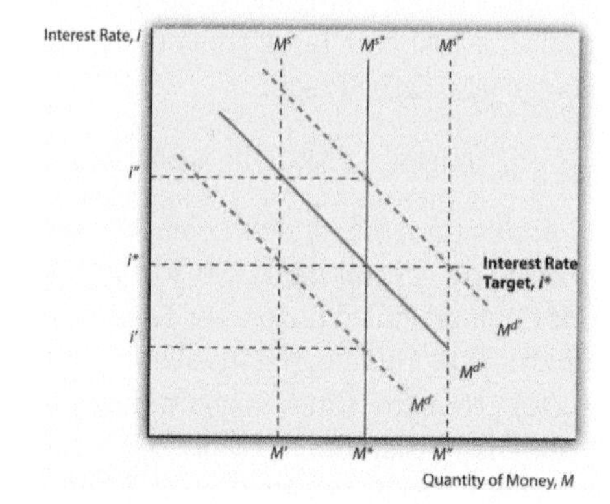

In response to all this, several leading central banks, beginning with New Zealand in 1990, have adopted explicit inflation targets. The result everywhere has been more or less the same: lower employment and output in the short run as inflation expectations are wrung out of the economy, followed by an extended period of prosperity and high employment. As long as it remains somewhat flexible, inflation targeting frees central bankers to do whatever it takes to keep prices in check, to use all available information and not just monetary statistics. Inflation targeting makes them more accountable because the public can easily monitor their success or failure. (New Zealand took this concept a step further, enacting legislation that tied the central banker's job to keeping inflation within the target range.)

Stop and Think Box

What do you think of New Zealand's law that allows the legislature to oust a central banker who allows too much inflation?

Well, it makes the central bank less independent. Of course, independence is valuable to the public only as a means of keeping inflation in check. The policy is only as good as the legislature. If it uses the punishment only to oust incompetent or corrupt central bankers, it should be salutary. If it ousts good central bankers caught in a tough situation (for example, an oil supply shock or war), the law may serve only to keep good people from taking the job. If the central banker's salary is very high relative to what he or she would earn in alternative employment, the law might also induce him or her to try to distort the official inflation figures on which his or her job depends.

The Fed has not yet adopted explicit inflation targeting, though a debate currently rages about whether it should. And under Ben Bernanke, it moved to what some have called inflation targeting-lite, with a new policy of communicating with the public more frequently about its forecasts, which now run to three years instead of the traditional two.[13] As noted above, the Fed is not very transparent, and that has the effect of roiling the financial markets when expectations about its monetary policy turn out to be incorrect. It also induces people to waste a lot of time engaging in "Fed watching," looking for clues about monetary policy. Reporters actually used to comment on the thickness of Greenspan's briefcase when he went into Federal Open Market Committee (FOMC) meetings. No joke![14]

Why doesn't the Fed, which is charged with maintaining financial market and price stability, adopt explicit targets? It may be that it does not want to be held accountable for its performance. It probably wants to protect its independence, but maybe more for its private interest (power) rather than for the public interest (low inflation). *It may also be that the Fed has found the holy grail of monetary policy, a flexible rule that helps it to determine the appropriate federal funds target.*

Key Takeaways

- Monetary targeting entails setting and attempting to meet growth rates of monetary aggregates such as M1 or M2.
- It succeeded in countries like Germany and Switzerland, where the central bank was committed to keeping inflation in check.
- In other countries, like the United States and the United Kingdom, where price stability was not the paramount goal of the central bank, the time inconsistency problem eroded the effectiveness of the targets.
- In short, like a dieter who can't resist that extra helping at dinner and two desserts, the central banks could not stick to a good long-term plan day to day.
- Also, the connection between increases in particular aggregates and the price level broke down, but it took a long time for central bankers to realize it because the lag between policy implementation and real-world outcome was often many months and sometimes years.
- Inflation targeting entails keeping increases in the price level within a predetermined range (e.g., 1 and 2 percent per year).
- Countries whose central banks embraced inflation targeting often suffered a recession and high unemployment at first, but in the long run were able to achieve both price level stability and economic expansion and high employment.
- Inflation targeting makes use of all available information, not just monetary aggregates, and increases the accountability of central banks and bankers. That reduces their independence but not at the expense of higher inflation because inflation targeting, in a sense, is a substitute for independence.

17.4 The Taylor Rule

Learning Objective

1. What is the Taylor Rule and why is it important?

Many observers suspect that since Greenspan the Fed has followed the so-called Taylor Rule, named after the Stanford University economist, John Taylor, who developed it. The **rule** states that the federal funds target should be set according to the following equation:

$$ff^t = \pi + ff^{*r} + \tfrac{1}{2}(\pi \text{ gap}) + \tfrac{1}{2}(\text{Y gap})$$

where

ff^t = federal funds target

π = inflation

ff^{*r} = the real equilibrium fed funds rate

rule

In this context, a monetary policy rule, an equation that tells central bankers what interest rate policies they should put in place given employment, output, inflation, and perhaps other macroeconomic variables.

π gap = inflation gap ($\pi - \pi$ target)

Y gap = output gap (actual output [e.g. GDP] - output potential)

So if the inflation target was 2 percent, actual inflation was 3 percent, output was at its potential, and the real federal funds rate was 2 percent, the Taylor Rule suggests that the fed funds target should be

$$ff^t = \pi + ff^{*r} + ½(\pi \text{ gap}) + ½(\text{Y gap})$$

$$ff^t = 3 + 2 + ½(1) + ½(0)$$

$$ff^t = 5.5$$

If the economy began running a percentage point below its potential, the Taylor Rule would suggest easing monetary policy by lowering the fed funds target to 5 percent:

$$ff^t = 3 + 2 + ½(1) + ½(-1)$$

$$ff^t = 3 + 2 + .5 + -.5 = 5$$

If inflation started to heat up to 4 percent, the Fed should respond by raising the fed funds target to 6.5:

$$ff^t = 4 + 2 + ½(2) + ½(-1) = 6.5$$

Practice calculating the fed funds target on your own in Exercise 1.

Exercise

1. Use the Taylor Rule—$ff^t = \pi + ff^{*r} + ½(\pi \text{ gap}) + ½(\text{Y gap})$—to determine what the federal funds target should be if:

Inflation	Equilibrium Real Fed Funds Rate	Inflation Target	Output	Output Potential	Answer: Fed Funds Target
0	2	1	3	3	1.5
1	2	1	3	3	3
2	2	1	3	3	4.5
3	2	1	3	3	6
1	2	1	2	3	2.5
1	2	1	1	3	2
1	2	1	4	3	3.5
1	2	1	5	3	4
1	2	1	6	3	4.5
7	2	1	7	3	14

Notice that as actual inflation exceeds the target, the Taylor Rule suggests raising the fed funds rate (tightening monetary policy). Notice too that as output falls relative to its potential, the rule suggests decreasing the fed funds rate (easier monetary policy). As output exceeds its potential, however, the rule suggests putting on the brakes by raising rates. Finally, if inflation and output are both screaming, the rule requires that the fed funds target soar quite high indeed, as it did in the early 1980s. In short, *the Taylor Rule is countercyclical and accounts for two important Federal Reserve goals: price stability and employment/output.*

The Taylor Rule nicely explains U.S. macroeconomic history since 1960. In the early 1960s, the two were matched: inflation was low, and growth was strong. In the latter part of the 1960s, the 1970s, and the early 1980s, actual ff* was generally well below what the Taylor Rule said it should be. In that period, inflation was so high we refer to the period as the Great Inflation. In the latter part of the 1980s, ff* was higher than what the Taylor Rule suggested. That was a period of weak growth but decreasing inflation. From 1990 or so until the early 2000s, a period of low inflation and high growth, the Taylor Rule and ff* were very closely matched. In the middle years of the first decade of the new millennium, however, the Fed kept ff* well below the Rule and thereby fueled the housing bubble that led to the 2007–8 crisis. Since then, the economy has been weak and little wonder: the Fed lowered rates to zero, but that was still well above the negative 7 percent or so called for by the rule. Figure 17.2 graphs the latter portion of the story.

FIGURE 17.2 The Fed's feds fund target and the Taylor Rule since 1987
Following the Taylor Rule may bring forth macroeconomic happiness!

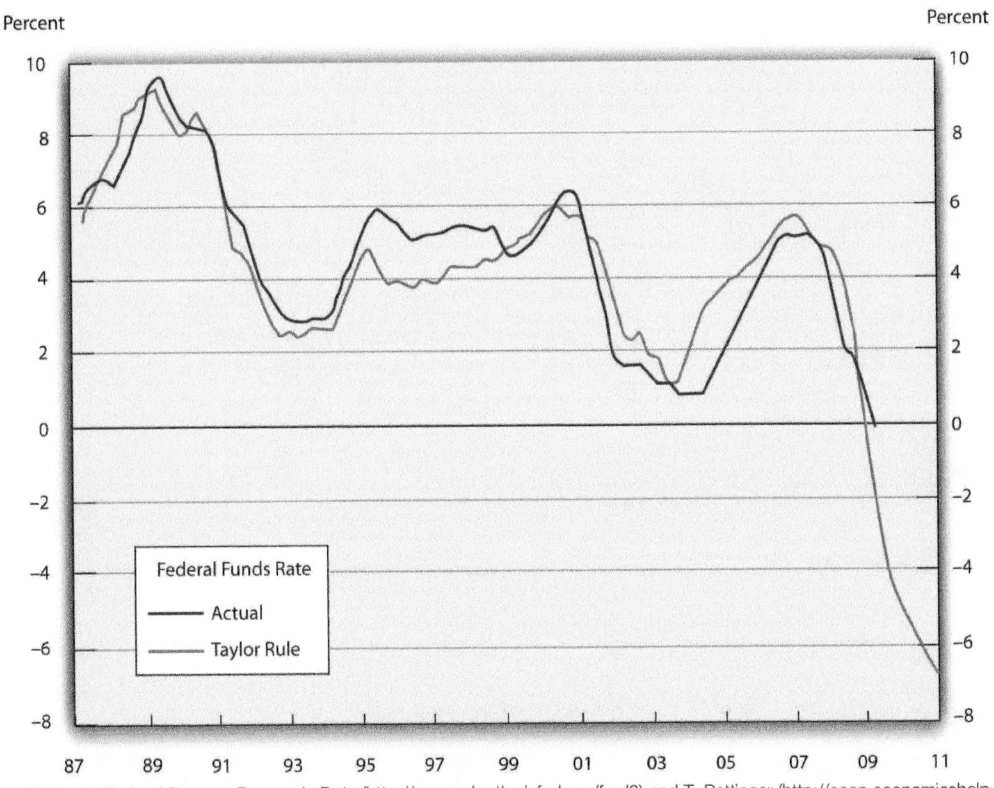

Source: St. Louis Federal Reserve Economic Data (http://research.stlouisfed.org/fred2) and T. Pettinger (http://econ.economicshelp.org/2009/05/taylor-rule-and-interest-rates.html).

Stop and Think Box

Examine Figure 17.3 and Figure 17.4 carefully. Assuming the Fed uses the Taylor Rule, what happened to inflation and output from mid-2003 until mid-2006? Then what happened?

FIGURE 17.3 The Fed's fund target, 2003–2010
Maybe the Fed was too slow to raise, and then lower, interest rates?

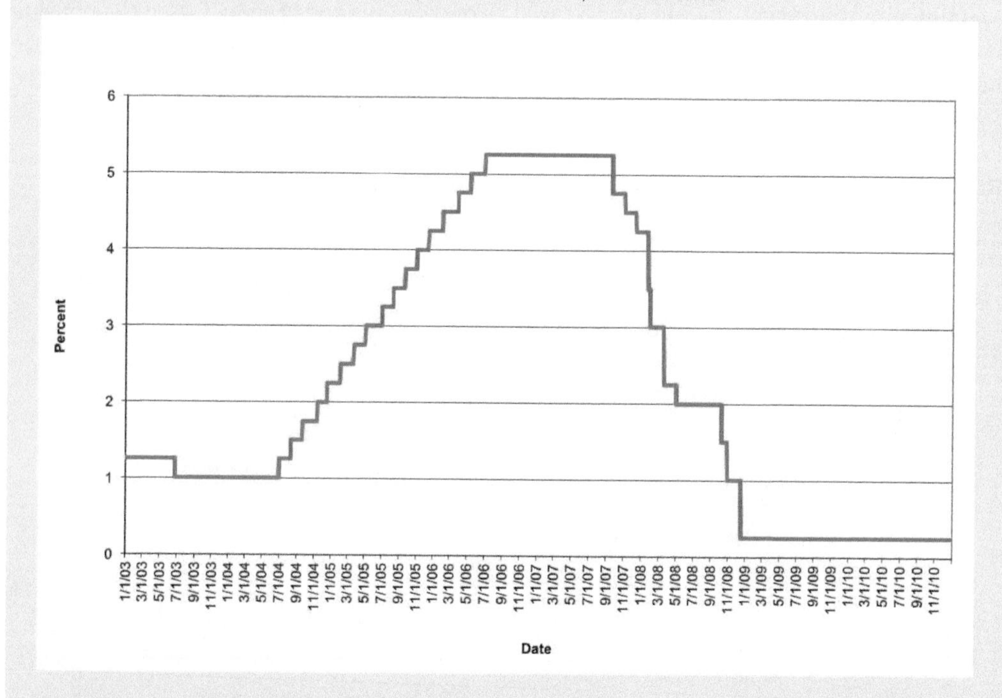

FIGURE 17.4 Inflation and per capita gross domestic product (GDP), 2003–2006
See, inflation was up but growth was a bit down.

Year	Inflation Rate	Per Capita GDP Growth Rate
2003	2.28	2.76
2004	2.66	3.92
2005	3.39	3.31
2006	3.23	3.64

Assuming that the Fed's inflation target, the real equilibrium federal funds rate, and the economy's output potential were unchanged in this period (not bad assumptions), increases in actual inflation and increases in actual output would induce the Fed, via the Taylor Rule, to increase its feds fund target. Both were at play but were moderating by the end of 2006, freezing the funds target at 5.25 percent, as shown in Figure 17.3. Then the subprime mortgage crisis, recession, and Panic of 2008 struck, inducing the Fed quickly to lower its target to 3, then 2, then 1, then almost to zero.

None of this means, however, that the Fed will continue to use the Taylor Rule, if indeed it does so.[15] Nor does it mean that the Taylor Rule will provide the right policy prescriptions in the future. Richard Fisher and W. Michael Cox, the president and chief economist of the Dallas Fed, respectively, believe that globalization makes it increasingly important for the Fed and other central banks to look at world inflation and output levels in order to get domestic monetary policy right.[16]

Stop and Think Box

Foreign exchange rates can also flummox central bankers and their policies. Specifically, increasing (decreasing) interest rates will, ceteris paribus, cause a currency to appreciate (depreciate) in world currency markets. Why is that important?

The value of a currency directly affects foreign trade. When a currency is strong relative to other currencies (when each unit of it can purchase many units of foreign currencies), imports will be stimulated because foreign goods will be cheap. Exports will be hurt, however, because domestic goods will look expensive to foreigners, who will have to give up many units of their local currency. Countries with economies heavily dependent on foreign trade must be extremely careful about the value of their currencies; almost every country is becoming more dependent on foreign trade, making exchange rate policy an increasingly important one for central banks worldwide to consider.

Key Takeaways

- The Taylor Rule is a simple equation—$ff^{t} = \pi + ff^{*r} + ½(\pi \text{ gap}) + ½(Y \text{ gap})$—that allows central bankers to determine what their overnight interbank lending rate target ought to be given actual inflation, an inflation target, actual output, the economy's potential output, and an estimate of the equilibrium real fed funds rate.
- When the Fed has maintained the fed funds rate near that prescribed by the Taylor Rule, the economy has thrived; when it has not, the economy has been plagued by inflation (when the fed funds rate was set below the Taylor rate) or low output (when the fed funds rate was set above the Taylor rate).

17.5 Suggested Reading

Blinder, Alan. *Central Banking in Theory and Practice*. Cambridge, MA: MIT Press, 1999.

Silber, William. *When Washington Shut Down Wall Street: The Great Financial Crisis of 1914 and the Origins of America's Monetary Supremacy*. Princeton, NJ: Princeton University Press, 2007.

Taylor, John B. *Monetary Policy Rules*. Chicago, IL: University of Chicago Press, 2001.

Endnotes

1. wohlstetter.typepad.com/letterfromthecapitol/2006/02/greenspan_the_g.html
2. www.princeton.edu/pr/pictures/a-f/bernanke/bernanke-03-high.jpg
3. en.wikipedia.org/wiki/Planned_economy
4. en.wikipedia.org/wiki/Austrian_School
5. www.imf.org/external/pubs/ft/fandd/2001/12/davis.htm
6. en.wikipedia.org/wiki/Total_factor_productivity
7. http://en.wikipedia.org/wiki/Just-in-time_(business)
8. www.bartleby.com/119/1.html
9. In the interest of full disclosure, Silber was once my colleague, but he is also the co-author of a competing, and storied, money and banking textbook.
10. www.pbs.org/greatwar
11. www.nber.org/cycles/cyclesmain.html
12. www.youtube.com/watch?v=KsTVK9Cv9U8
13. "The Federal Reserve: Letting Light In," *The Economist* (17 November 2007), 88–89.

14. www.amazon.com/Inside-Greenspans-Briefcase-Investment-Strategies/dp/007138913X
15. www.frbsf.org/education/activities/drecon/9803.html
16. See Richard W. Fisher and W. Michael Cox, "The New Inflation Equation," *Wall Street Journal*, April 6, 2007, A11.

CHAPTER 18

Foreign Exchange

Chapter Objectives

By the end of this chapter, students should be able to:

1. Define foreign exchange and explain its importance.
2. Describe the market for foreign exchange.
3. Explain why countries shouldn't be proud that it takes many units of foreign currencies to purchase a single unit of their currency.
4. Define purchasing power parity and explain its importance.
5. List and explain the long-run determinants of exchange rates.
6. List and explain the short-run determinants of exchange rates.
7. Define the interest parity condition and explain when and why it holds.

18.1 The Economic Importance of Currency Markets

Learning Objective

1. What is foreign exchange and why is it important?

Before we turn to monetary theory (gulp!), there is one more real-world financial market we need to investigate in this and the next chapter, the market for foreign currencies or foreign exchange, where the relative prices of national units of account or exchange rates are determined. Why should you care how many U.S. dollars (USD) it takes to buy a euro or a yen, a pound (sterling) or a dollar (of Canada or Australia, respectively)? If you plan to travel to any of those places, you'll want to know so you can evaluate prices. Is €1,000 a good price for a hotel room? How about ¥1,000?[1] *But even if you remain your entire life in a small village in Alaska, one of Hawaii's outer islands, Michigan's Upper Peninsula, or the northern reaches of Maine, the value of USD will affect your life deeply, whether you know it or not.* Come again? How could that possibly be?

Every nation in the world trades with other nations. Some trade more than others (little islands like Iceland, Mauritius, and Ireland lead the way, in percentage of gross domestic product [GDP] terms anyway) but all do it, even illicitly, when the United Nations says that they can't because they've been bad.[2] Conducting trade via barter isn't practical in most circumstances. So we use money. *But what happens when people who want to trade use different types of money, when their units of account are not the same? There are several solutions to that problem.* The most frequent solution today is for one party, usually the buyer, to exchange the money of his or her country for the money of the seller's country, then to consummate the transaction.

How does this affect you? Well, when the unit of account of your country, say, U.S. dollars (USD or plain $), is strong, when it can buy many units of a foreign currency, say, Canadian dollars (C$), Canadian goods look cheap to you. And we all know what happens when goods are cheap. So you stop drinking Bud and start drinking Moosehead. Instead of going to Manhattan to shop, you go to Toronto, and check out some Maple Leafs, Raptors, and Blue Jays games while you're at it. (You go in April, that magical month for sports fans.) When the Blue Jays game gets snowed out, you go instead to the Canadian ballet. (Do you have any sense of humor at all?) You might even consider buying a Canadian snorkel or surf board. (Okay, let's not get crazy.) *The point is you and your fellow Americans import more from Canada.*

The Canadians are very happy about this, but they are not so thrilled with American goods, which look dreadfully expensive to them because they have to give up many of their dear loonies to buy USD. So they too eschew Manhattan for Toronto and drink Moosehead rather than Bud. *In other words, U.S. exports to Canada fall.* And because Canada is a major U.S. trading partner, that does not bode well for the U.S. economy overall, or U.S. residents, even those in remote villages. If USD were to continue to appreciate (strengthen, buy yet more C$), the situation would grow increasingly worse. *Were the dollar to depreciate (weaken, buy fewer C$), the situation would ameliorate and eventually reverse, and you'd go back to Bud, Manhattan shopping sprees, and the Yankees, Mets, Knicks, Nets, Islanders, and Rangers.*

Stop and Think Box

A chain of pizza parlors in the southwestern part of the United States accepts Mexican pesos in payment for its pizzas. Many U.S. retail stores located near the Canadian border accept Canadian currency. (Many Canadian businesses accept U.S. dollars, too.) Why do these businesses accept payment in a foreign currency?

Well, maybe they are good folks who want to help out others and maybe some of them need foreign currencies to purchase supplies. But those are at best ulterior motives in most instances because the exchange rate offered usually heavily favors the retailer. For example, the pizza parlor's exchange rate was 12 pesos to the dollar when the market exchange rate was closer to 11. So a $10 pizza costs 120 pesos (10 × 12) instead of 110 pesos (10 × 11). In short, it makes a tidy and largely riskless profit from the offer.

Or imagine you don't have many assets or a high income, but you need an automobile. You see a commercial that says that there are three V-dubs (German-made Volkswagen automobile models) under $17,000. You think you can afford that and begin to make arrangements to buy a Rabbit. But look in Figure 18.1 at what happens to the dollar price of a Rabbit when the exchange rate changes. Say that the Rabbit of your dreams costs €17,000. When the dollar and the euro are at parity (1 to 1), the Rabbit costs $17,000. If the dollar depreciates (buys fewer euro, and more USD are needed to buy €1), the Rabbit grows increasingly costly to you. If the dollar appreciates (buys more euro, and fewer USD are needed to buy €1), that cool automotive bunny gets very cheap indeed!

FIGURE 18.1 **The dollar price of a €17,000 Rabbit and the euro price of a $10 computer fan**
Whether the dollar is strong or weak, somebody's ox is getting gored!

	USD/€	€/USD	Dollar Price of a Rabbit V-Dub (€17,000)	Euro Price of Each of Your Computer Fans ($10.00)
Strong Dollar	$.80	€1.25	$13,600.00	€12.50
	$.90	€1.11	$15,300.00	€11.11
	$1.00	€1.00	$17,000.00	€10.00
	$1.10	€.91	$18,700.00	€9.09
	$1.20	€.83	$20,400.00	€8.33
	$1.30	€.77	$22,100.00	€7.69
	$1.40	€.71	$23,800.00	€7.14
Weak Dollar	$1.50	€.67	$25,500.00	€6.67

Now imagine that in your remote little town you make fans for French computers that you can sell profitably for $10.00. The dollar's movements will affect you as a producer, but in precisely the opposite way as it affected you as a consumer. When the dollar appreciates against the euro, your computer fans grow more expensive in France (and indeed the entire euro zone), which will undoubtedly cut into sales and maybe your salary or your job. When the dollar depreciates, the euro price of your fans plummet, sales become increasingly brisk, and you think about buying a Cadillac (a more expensive American car).

Key Takeaways

- Foreign exchange is the trading of different national currencies or units of account.
- It is important because the exchange rate, the price of one currency in terms of another, helps to determine a nation's economic health and hence the well-being of all the people residing in it.
- The exchange rate is also important because it can help or hurt specific interests within a country: exporters tend to be helped (hurt) by a weak (strong) domestic currency because they will sell more (less) abroad, while consumers are hurt (helped) by a strong currency because imported goods will be more (less) expensive for them.

18.2 Determining the Exchange Rate

Learning Objectives

1. What is the structure of the foreign exchange market?
2. Why shouldn't countries be proud that it takes many units of foreign currencies to purchase a single unit of their currency?

We can't teach you how to predict future exchange rates because the markets are highly efficient (free floating exchange rates follow a random walk) and because many exchange rates are more or less heavily influenced by monetary authorities. Some countries try to maintain fixed exchange rates by pegging their respective currencies to gold or some other currency, like the U.S. dollar, euro, or Swiss franc. Many others allow exchange rates to float within a range or band, some of which are broader than others. Other countries allow the value of their currencies to freely float, determined solely by supply and demand. Nations that fix their exchange rates or engage in a so-called dirty float (within bands) find it necessary to make periodic adjustments to both the width and range of the bands over time. So trying to make a living predicting exchange rate changes is difficult indeed. That said, *you should be able to post-dict why floating exchange rates changed or, in other words, to narrate plausible reasons why past changes, like those depicted in*Figure 18.2*and*Figure 18.3, *may have occurred.* (This is similar to what we did with interest rates.)

FIGURE 18.2 How many USD did it take to buy 1 Canadian dollar?
Note the long term trends as well as the tremendous short term volatility.

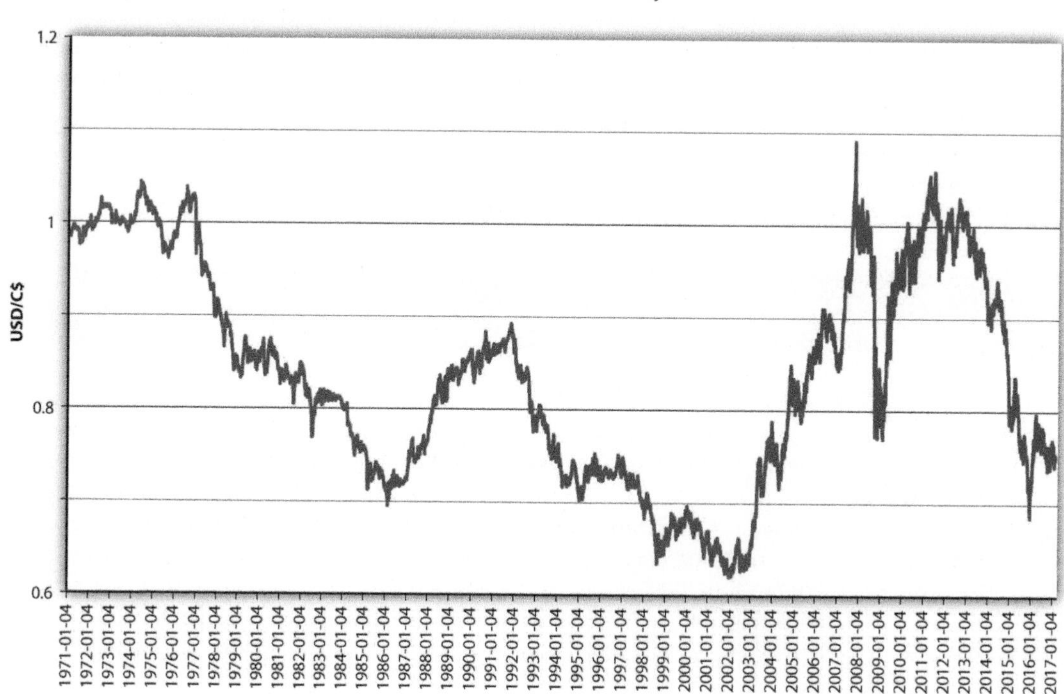

FIGURE 18.3 How many Canadian dollars did it take to buy 1 USD?

This just plots the mathematical reciprocal of Figure 18.1.

*The figures, like the exchange rates in*Figure 18.1, *are mathematical reciprocals of each other. Both express the exchange rate but from different perspectives.* Figure 18.2 asks how many USD it took to buy $C1, or mathematically USD/C$. Figure 18.3 asks how many $C it took to buy 1 USD, or C$/USD. In Figure 18.2, USD weakens as the line moves up the chart because it takes more USD to buy $C1. The dollar strengthens as it moves down the chart because it takes fewer USD to buy $C1. Everything is reversed in Figure 18.3, where upward movements indicate a strengthening of USD (a weakening of $C) because it takes more $C to buy 1 USD, and downward movements indicate a weakening of USD (a strengthening of $C) because it takes fewer $C to buy 1 USD. Again, the figures tell the same story: *USD strengthened vis-à-vis the Canadian dollar from the early 1970s until the late 1980s, weakened from then until the early 1990s, then strengthened until early 2003. Thereafter, USD weakened considerably, experiencing many ups and downs along the way due to relative differences in inflation, interest, and productivity rates in each country. For a short period, it took more than 1 USD to purchase a Canadian dollar butUSD appreciated during the financial crisis in an apparent "flight to quality."* It weakened again during the 2010 recovery, bringing it back to close parity with the Looney until 2013. Ever since, USD has remained strong against the Canadian dollar, in large part due to low oil prices (Canada is a major oil exporter). We could do the same exercise ad nauseam (Latin for "until we vomit") with every pair of currencies in the world. But we won't because the mode of analysis would be precisely the same.

spot exchange rate

The price of one currency in terms of another today.

forward exchange rate

The price of one currency in terms of another in the future.

We'll concentrate on the **spot exchange rate**, the price of one currency in terms of another today, and currencies that are allowed to float freely or at least within wide bands. The **forward exchange rate**, the price today of future exchanges of foreign currencies, is also important but follows the same general principles as the spot market. *Both types of trading are conducted on a wholesale (large-scale) basis by a few score-big international banks in an over-the-counter (OTC) market.* Investors and travelers can buy foreign currencies in a variety of ways, via everything from brokerage accounts to airport kiosks, to their credit cards. Retail purchasers give up more of their domestic currency to receive a given number of units of a foreign currency than the wholesale banks do. (To put the same idea another way, they receive fewer units of the foreign currency for each unit of their domestic currency.) That's partly why the big banks are in the business. The big boys also try to earn profits via speculation, buying (selling) a currency when it is low (high), and selling (buying) it when it is high (low). (They also seek out arbitrage opportunities, but those are rare and fleeting.) Each day, over $1 trillion of wholesale-level ($1 million plus per transaction) foreign exchange transactions take place.

Before we go any further, a few words of caution. Students sometimes think that a strong currency is always better than a weak one. That undoubtedly stems from the fact that *strong* sounds good and *weak* sounds bad. As noted above, however, a strong (weak) currency is neither good nor bad but rather advantageous (disadvantageous) for imports/consumers and disadvantageous (advantageous) for exports/producers of exportable goods and services. Another thing: *no need to thump your chest patriotically because it takes many units of foreign currencies to buy 1 USD.* That would be like proclaiming that you are "hot" because your temperature is 98.6 degrees Fahrenheit instead of 37 degrees Centigrade (that's the same temperature, measured two different ways) or that you are 175 centimeters tall instead of 68.9 inches (another equivalent). Most countries have a very small unit of account compared to the United States, that is all. Other countries, like Great Britain, have units of account that are larger than the USD, so it usually takes more than 1 USD to buy a unit of those currencies. The nominal level of the exchange rate in no way means that one country or economy is better than another. *Changes in exchange rates, by contrast, have profound consequences, as we have seen. They also have profound causes.*

Key Takeaways

- At the wholesale level, the market for foreign exchange is conducted by a few score large international players in huge (> $1 trillion per day) over-the-counter spot and forward markets.
- Those markets appear to be efficient in the sense that exchange rates follow a random walk and arbitrage opportunities, which appear infrequently, are quickly eliminated.
- In the retail segment of the market, tourists, business travelers, and small-scale investors buy and sell foreign currencies, including physical media of exchange (paper notes and coins), where appropriate.
- Compared to the wholesale ($1 million plus per transaction) players, retail purchasers of a foreign currency obtain fewer units of the foreign currency, and retail sellers of a foreign currency receive fewer units of their domestic currency.
- The nominal level of exchange rates is essentially arbitrary. Some countries simply chose a smaller unit of account, a smaller amount of value. That's why it often takes over ¥100 to buy 1 USD. But if the United States had chosen a smaller unit of account, like a cent, or if Japan had chosen a larger one (like ¥100 = ¥1), the yen and USD (and the euro, as it turns out) would be roughly at parity.
- A strong currency is not necessarily a good thing because it promotes imports over exports (because it makes foreign goods look so cheap and domestic goods look so expensive to foreigners).
- A weak currency, despite the loser-sound to it, means strong exports because domestic goods now look cheap both at home and abroad. Imports will decrease, too, because foreign goods will look more expensive to domestic consumers and businesses.

18.3 Long-Run Determinants of Exchange Rates

Learning Objectives

1. What is purchasing power parity?
2. What are the other long-run determinants of exchange rates?

If transaction costs are zero, identical goods should have the same price no matter what unit of account that price is expressed in. Or so says the law of one price. The reason is clear: if they did not, arbitrageurs would buy where the good was cheapest and sell where it was highest until the prices were equalized. Where transaction costs are nontrivial or goods are similar but not identical, we don't expect a single price, but rather a band or range of prices. So if product X cost $100 in Country Y and $110 in Country Z, and it costs $10 to transport X from Y to Z, there would be no arbitrage opportunity and the price differential could persist. If the price of X rose in Z to $120, we'd expect it to increase in Y to at least $110, or arbitrageurs would start buying it in Y and selling it in Z until the prices were within $10 of each other. Similarly, Japanese-style beer is not the same as U.S.-style beer. But it is close enough that we would not expect the prices to vary widely or otherwise consumers would dump Bud, Miller, and Coors in favor of Kirin and Sapporo (or vice versa, as the case may be).

This sort of analysis has led economists to apply the law of one price to entire economies in what they call the theory of *purchasing power parity (PPP), which predicts that, in the long run, exchange rates will reflect price level changes.* In other words, higher rates of inflation in Country A compared to Country B will cause Country A's currency to depreciate vis-à-vis Country B's currency in the long run. In the short run, however, matters are quite different, as Figure 18.4 shows. If PPP held in the short run, USD should have appreciated against the pound (the blue line should be above zero) every year in which inflation in the United Kingdom exceeded inflation in the United States (the red line is above zero), and vice versa. Clearly, that was not the case. *But PPP has the long-run right, in sign but not quite in magnitude.* Between 1975 and 2005, prices rose in Great Britain a shade under 205 percent all told. In that same period, they rose just under 142 percent in the United States. In other words, prices rose about 44 percent ([205 - 142]/142) more in Britain than in the United States. Over that same period, the pound sterling depreciated 22 percent against USD (from £.4505 to £.5495 per USD or from $2.22 to $1.82 per £1), just as PPP theory predicts it should have. But why did the pound weaken only 22 percent against the dollar?

FIGURE 18.4 Purchasing power parity, United Kingdom and United States, 1975–2005
PPP: Great in the long run but no so hot in the short.

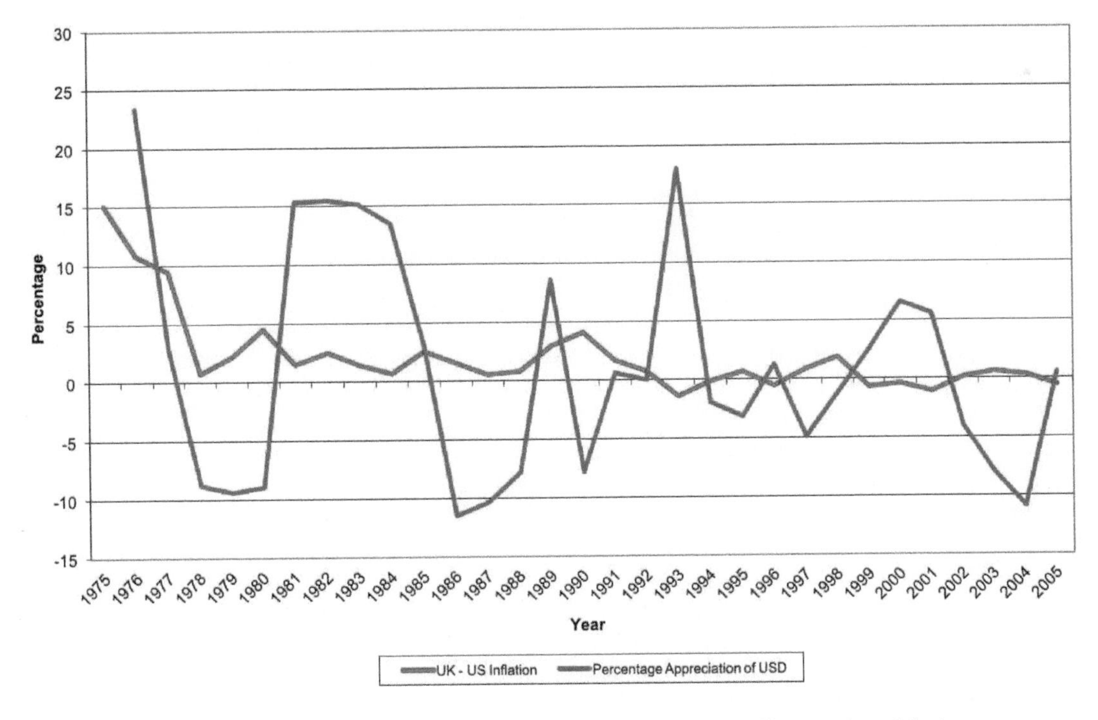

For starters, not all goods and services are traded internationally. Land and haircuts come immediately to mind, but many other things as well when you think about it hard enough. There is no reason for prices of those goods to be the same or even similar in different countries. Arbitrageurs cannot buy low in one place and sell high in another because transaction costs are simply too high. (For example, you could get a great haircut in Malaysia for fifty cents but it would cost several thousand dollars and several days to get there and back.)

In addition, three other factors affect exchange rates in the long run: relative trade barriers, differential preferences for domestic and foreign goods, and differences in productivity. Tariffs (taxes on imported goods), quotas (caps on the quantity of imported goods), and sundry nontariff barriers (NTBs) to trade[3] increase demand for domestic over foreign goods, thereby allowing the domestic currency to appreciate without injuring sales of domestic goods. Preferences for domestic goods have the same effect; preferences for foreign goods (French wine, German beer, Japanese automobiles) have the opposite effect, depreciating the domestic currency by maintaining demand for foreign goods even in the face of higher prices. Finally, as a country becomes relatively more productive than other countries, the price of its wares tends to fall. Its currency, therefore, appreciates because it can do so without injuring exports. If a country's productivity lags that of other countries, by contrast, its currency will depreciate. Of course, this is all ceteris paribus. Figure 18.5 summarizes the discussion.

FIGURE 18.5 Determinants of exchange rates in the long run

If productivity, trade barriers, and demand for exports increase, the domestic currency can appreciate without injuring foreign sales of its goods.

Variable (Domestic/Foreign)	Change	Domestic Currency
Relative Price Level	Up	Depreciate
Relative Productivity	Up	Appreciate
Relative Trade Barriers	Up	Appreciate
Relative Import Demand	Up	Depreciate
Relative Export Demand	Up	Appreciate

Key Takeaways

- Purchasing power parity (PPP) is the application of the law of one price to entire economies.
- It predicts that exchange rates will adjust to relative price level changes, to differential inflation rates between two countries. They indeed do, but only in the long run and not to precisely the same degree.
- In the long run, exchange rates are determined by PPP (as described) and relative differences in productivity, trade barriers, and import and export demand.
- As Country A's price level and import demand increase, and as Country A's productivity, trade barriers, and export demand decrease vis-à-vis another Country B, Country A's currency depreciates and Country B's appreciates.
- Basically, anything that lowers demand for Country A's goods, services, and currency induces the currency to depreciate; anything that increases demand for Country A's stuff induces the currency to appreciate in response.
- Higher inflation relative to Country B makes Country A's stuff look more expensive, lowering demand and inducing depreciation.
- If economic actors in Country A take a fancy to Country B's stuff, they will import it even if Country A's currency weakens, making Country B's stuff more expensive. Reductions in trade barriers (lower tariffs, higher quotas, fewer NTBs) will exacerbate that.

- If, for whatever reason, economic actors in Country B don't like Country A's stuff as much as they used to, they'll buy less of it unless Country A's currency depreciates, making it cheaper.
- Finally, if Country A's productivity slips relative to Country B's, Country A's goods and services will get more expensive than Country B's so it will sell in Country B only if its currency depreciates.

18.4 Short-Run Determinants of Exchange Rates

Learning Objectives

1. What are the short-run determinants of exchange rates?
2. What is the interest parity condition and when and why does it hold?

As Figure 18.6 shows, exchange rates can be very volatile. In a single month (June 2006), the South African rand depreciated from about 6.6 to 7.4 rand to 1 USD, with various ups and downs along the way. The rand then reversed course and appreciated toward 7.1 rand/USD. Such fluctuations are by no means unusual. Why do exchange rates undergo such gyrations? Figure 18.7 summarizes the major factors affecting exchange rates in the short run. *Note that it looks very much like* Figure 18.5 *but with three key differences*. First, instead of actual relative price levels, trade barriers, exports, imports, and productivity driving changes, *expectations of their future direction drive changes*. This should not be surprising given the basic rationality of most financial markets. Second, two additional variables have entered the equation: foreign and domestic interest rates. The intuition behind the first variables is the same as those discussed above, but in the short run, the mere expectation of a change in a variable moves the market. The intuition behind the interest rates is also straightforward. *If something increases demand for the domestic currency, like domestic interest rates increasing or foreign interest rates decreasing, it will appreciate*. If something reduces demand for the domestic currency, like domestic interest rates decreasing or foreign interest rates increasing, it will depreciate. Because expectations and interest rates change frequently, so, too, do exchange rates under the current floating rate regime.

FIGURE 18.6 South Africa-United States exchange rate, June 2006

Up and down, up and down, all in a month.

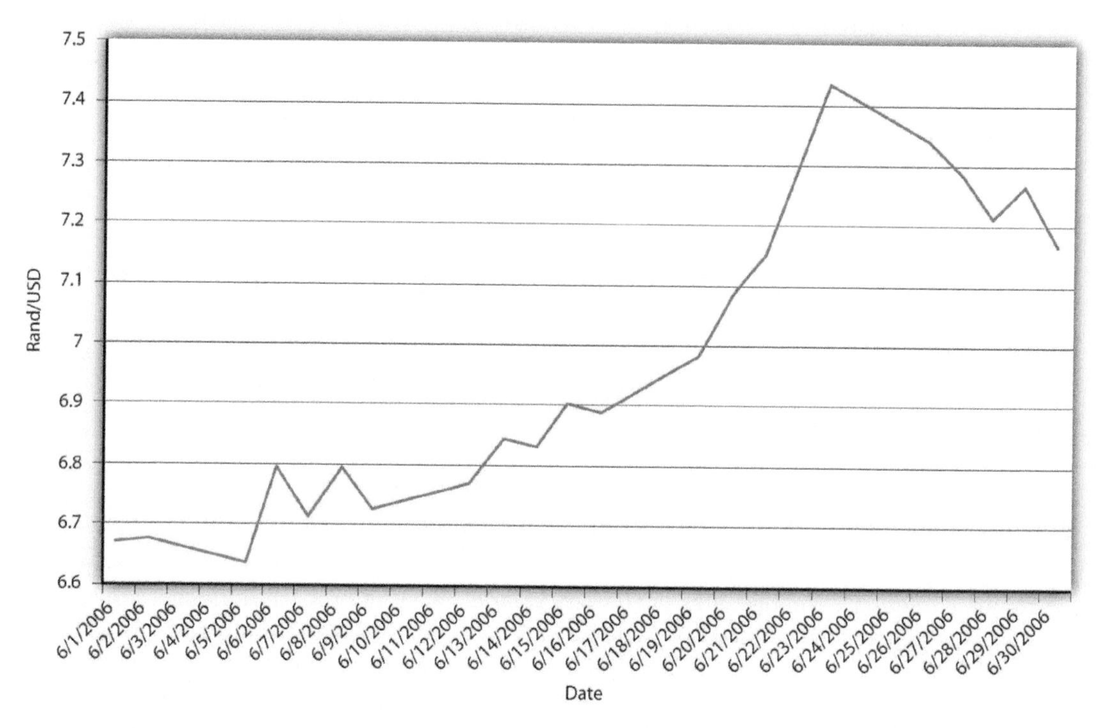

FIGURE 18.7 Determinants of exchange rates in the short run

Yes, expectations regarding interest rates will move FX rates too, smarty pants!

Variable (Domestic/Foreign)	Change	Domestic Currency
Relative Expected Price Level	Up	Depreciate
Relative Expected Productivity	Up	Appreciate
Relative Expected Trade Barriers	Up	Appreciate
Relative Expected Import Demand	Up	Depreciate
Relative Expected Export Demand	Up	Appreciate
Domestic interest rate	Up	Appreciate
Foreign interest rate	Up	Depreciate
Expected future exchange rate	Up	Appreciate

Stop and Think Box

There is an important distinction between real and nominal interest rates. Through the Fisher Equation, we know that the nominal interest rate equals the real interest rate plus inflation expectations. Is that distinction important when considering foreign exchange markets?

Absolutely, and here is why. An increase in nominal interest rates caused by *a rise in the real interest rate* would leave expectations about future exchange rates unchanged and hence *would cause the domestic currency to appreciate*. An increase in nominal interest rates caused *solely by an increase in inflation expectations*, by contrast, would cause the expected future exchange rate to decrease through the expected and actual price level effects. *So the domestic currency would depreciate instead.*

The third difference between the long and short terms is that, in the short term, the expectation of the future direction of the exchange rate plays an important role. The easiest way to see this is to compare two investments with a one-year time horizon: a domestic (say, USD-denominated) bank account that pays 5 percent per year and a foreign (say, pound-sterling-denominated) account paying 6 percent per year. Before you jump for the sterling (6 > 5), you need to consider that, in a year, you're going to want dollars again because you reside in the United States and need USD to buy lunch, pay the rent, and so forth. If the dollar appreciates more than 1 percent over the course of the year, you'd be better off with the dollar deposit. Say that you invest $10,000 in sterling when the exchange rate is $1.50/£1 or, in other words, £.6667/$1. Your investment today would buy 10,000 × .6667 = £6,667. Multiply that by the interest on the sterling deposit (1.06) and you get £7,067.02 in a year. If the exchange rate is unchanged, you're cool because you'll have 7,067.02 × 1.50 = $10,600.53, which is greater than $10,000 invested at 5 percent, which equals 10,000 × 1.05 = $10,500.00. But what if, over the course of that year, the dollar appreciated strongly, to $1.25 per pound? Then your £7,067.02 would buy you only 7,067.02 × 1.25 = $8,833.78. You just took a bath, and not the good kind, because you should have invested in the dollar deposit! Of course, if the dollar depreciated to, say, $1.75, you'll be pheeling phat at 7,067.02 × 1.75 = $12,367.29.

Stop and Think Box

Increases in the growth rate of the money supply will eventually cause the price level to increase, but its effect on nominal interest rates in the short term can vary: rates can dip strongly, then rebound but remain permanently lower than the previous level, decrease temporarily before increasing permanently, or increase immediately. What does this mean for the market for foreign exchange?

The fact that a major short-run determinant of the exchange rate, foreign and domestic interest rates, moves around a lot helps to explain why the foreign exchange market is volatile. That market is also volatile because expectations of many things, including future differential price levels, productivity, and trading levels, will affect it via the expected future exchange rate (the E^{ef} variable in the equation introduced below).

As noted, the markets for foreign exchange and bonds/deposits are highly competitive and efficient, so we wouldn't expect discrepancies in returns to last long. *The law of one price, of course, applies most stringently to financial markets in which international capital mobility is allowed because huge sums of money (deposits) can be sent hither and thither almost immediately and cost-free, ideal conditions for the law of one price to prevail.* So what economists call the interest parity condition often holds (is true). More formally,

$$i^D = i^F - (E^{ef} - E^t) / E^t$$

where:

i^D = domestic interest rate

i^F = foreign interest rate

E^{ef} = expected future exchange rate

E^t = exchange rate today

(Note: express all variables as decimals, e.g. 6% = .06; 5 = 500%.)

In plain English, if the so-called interest parity condition holds, *the domestic interest rate should equal the foreign interest rate minus the expected appreciation of the domestic currency*. If i^F is > i^D, the domestic currency must be expected to appreciate; otherwise, everyone would sell their domestic deposits to buy the foreign ones. If i^F is < i^D, the domestic currency must be expected to depreciate (have a negative sign, two of which make a positive, augmenting i^F); otherwise, everyone would sell the foreign deposits and buy the domestic ones. If you find this confusing, there is another, more intuitive way of stating it: the domestic interest rate must equal the foreign interest rate plus the expected appreciation of the foreign currency. If i^F is < i^D, the expected appreciation of the foreign currency compensates for the lower interest rate, allowing equilibrium. You can practice calculating interest parity in the following Exercise.

Exercise

1. Use the interest parity formula ($i^D = i^F - (E^{ef} - E^t)/E^t$) to calculate the following:

Foreign Interest Rate	Expected Future Exchange Rate	Exchange Rate Today	Answer: Domestic Interest Rate
0.05	1	1	0.05
0.05	1.01	1	0.04
0.05	1.02	1	0.03
0.05	1.03	1	0.02
0.05	0.9	1	0.15
0.05	0.8	1	0.25
0.05	0.7	1	0.35
0.06	1	1	0.06
0.06	1	1.1	0.15
0.06	1	1.2	0.23
0.06	1	1.3	0.29
0.06	1	0.99	0.05
0.06	1	0.95	0.01
0.1	1	0.95	0.05
0.15	1	1	0.15
0.15	1.1	1	0.05
0.15	1	10	1.05

Expected Future Exchange Rate	Exchange Rate Today	Domestic Interest Rate	Answer: Foreign Interest Rate
1	1	0.02	0.02
1.1	1	0.02	0.12
1.2	1	0.02	0.22
1.3	1	0.02	0.32
0.9	1	0.11	0.01
0.8	1	0.21	0.01
0.7	1	0.31	0.01
1	1	0.1	0.10
1	1.1	0.1	0.01
1	1.2	0.2	0.03
1	1.3	0.25	0.02
1	0.9	0.1	0.21
1	0.8	0.1	0.35
1	0.7	0.1	0.53
1	1	0	0.00
10	1	0	9.00
1	5	1	0.20

Key Takeaways

- Because foreign exchange markets are efficient, in the short run, the mere expectation of changes in relative inflation, exports, imports, trade barriers, and productivity moves the markets.
- Also in the short run, differences in interest rates and expectations of the future exchange rate play key roles in exchange rate determination.
- The interest parity condition equates the domestic interest rate to the foreign interest rate minus the appreciation of the domestic currency. (Or, by rearranging the terms, it equates the foreign interest rate to the domestic interest rate plus the expected appreciation of the domestic currency.)
- The interest parity condition holds whenever there is capital mobility, whenever deposits (units of account) can move freely and cheaply from one country to another.
- It holds under those conditions because if it didn't, an arbitrage condition would exist, inducing arbitrageurs to sell the overvalued deposit (side of the equation) and buy the undervalued one until the equation held.

18.5 Modeling the Market for Foreign Exchange

Learning Objective

1. How can the market for foreign exchange be modeled?

*Like other markets, the market for foreign exchange can be graphically modeled to help us visualize the action, as in*Figure 18.8. There are a number of ways to do this, but perhaps the easiest is to plot the quantity of dollars on the horizontal axis and the exchange rate, stated in terms of foreign divided by domestic (say, yen or ¥/USD) on the vertical axis. The supply of dollar assets will be perfectly vertical, unchanged at every exchange rate. The demand for dollars, by contrast, will have the usual downward slope because, at higher exchange rates, fewer dollar assets will be demanded than at lower exchange rates. So at ¥120 to 1 USD, relatively few dollar-denominated assets will be demanded compared to only ¥100 or ¥80 per dollar. The intersection of the supply and demand curves will determine E*, which in this case is ¥100/$, and q*, which in this case is $100 billion.

FIGURE 18.8 Equilibrium in the market for USD

So if you increase demand for dollars, the dollar appreciates (more yen are need to purchase a buck), and vice versa. Ceteris paribus of course.

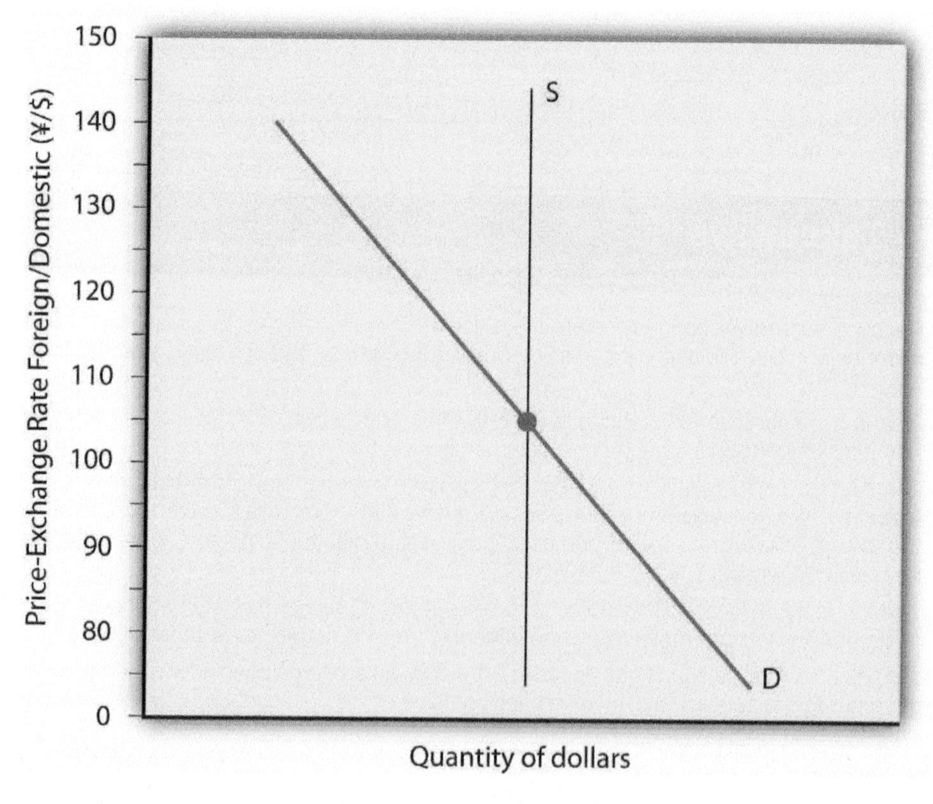

We can immediately see that, holding all else constant, anything that increases demand for dollar-denominated assets (shifts the demand curve to the right), including an increase in the domestic interest rate, a decrease in the foreign interest rate, or an increase in E^{ef} (for any reason, including the variables in Figure 18.5), will cause the dollar to appreciate (E* to increase when stated in terms of foreign/domestic or in this case ¥/$). Anything that causes demand for dollar-denominated assets, including a decrease in the domestic interest rate, an increase in the foreign interest rate, or a decrease in E^{ef}, to decrease (shift the demand curve to the left) will cause the dollar to depreciate (E* to decrease when stated in terms of foreign/domestic).

Stop and Think Box

Post-dict Figure 18.9 using Figure 18.10 and Figure 18.11.

FIGURE 18.9 Euro-dollar exchange rate, 2000–2007
The euro weakened at first, but then strengthened.

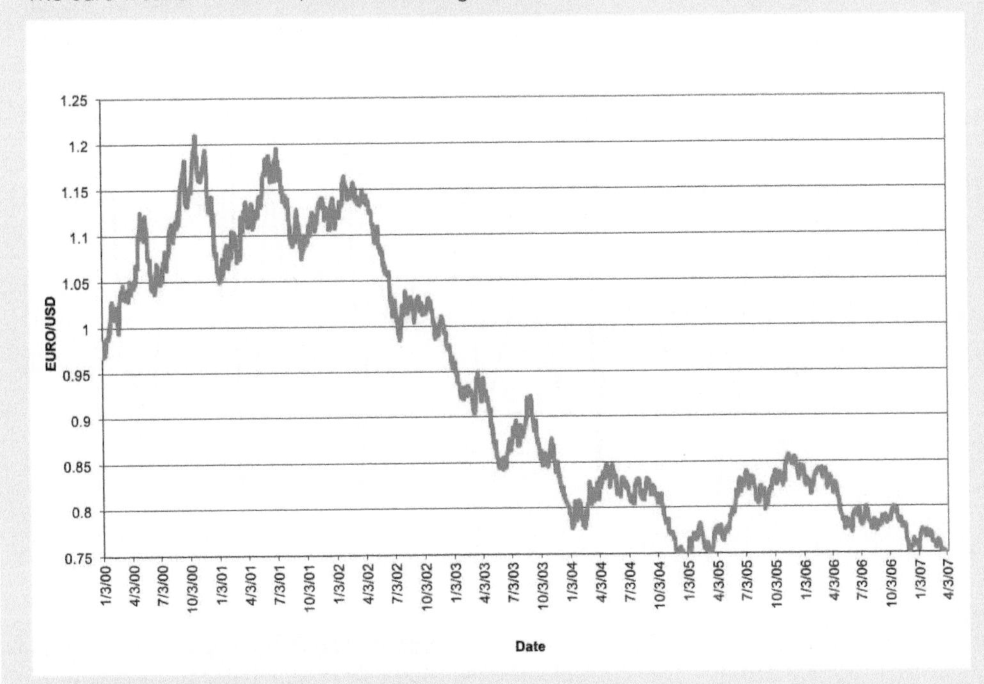

FIGURE 18.10 Interest rates in Europe and the United States, 2000–2007
European interest rates were lower first, then higher, then lower again.

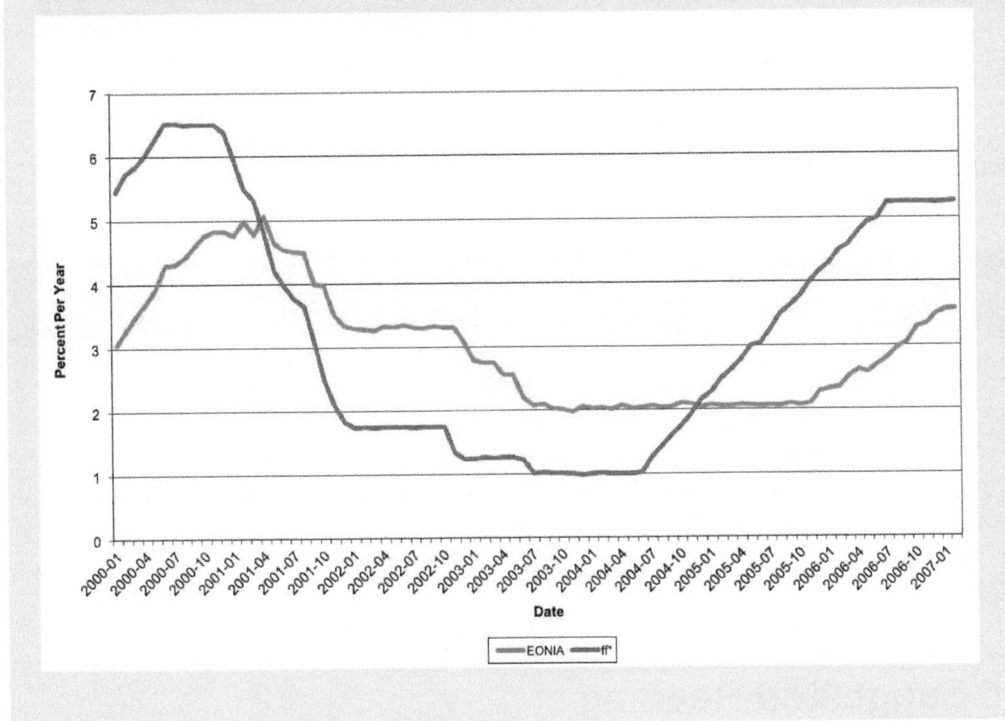

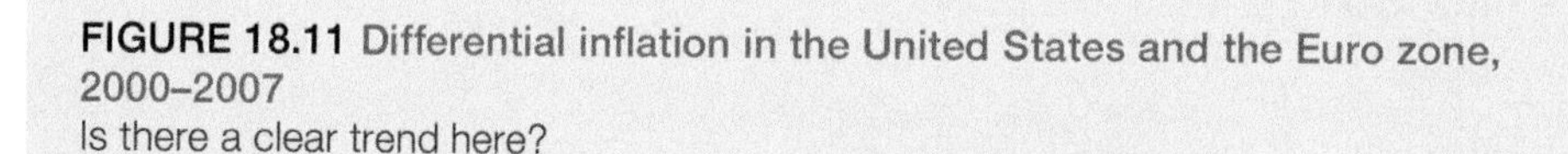

FIGURE 18.11 Differential inflation in the United States and the Euro zone, 2000–2007

Is there a clear trend here?

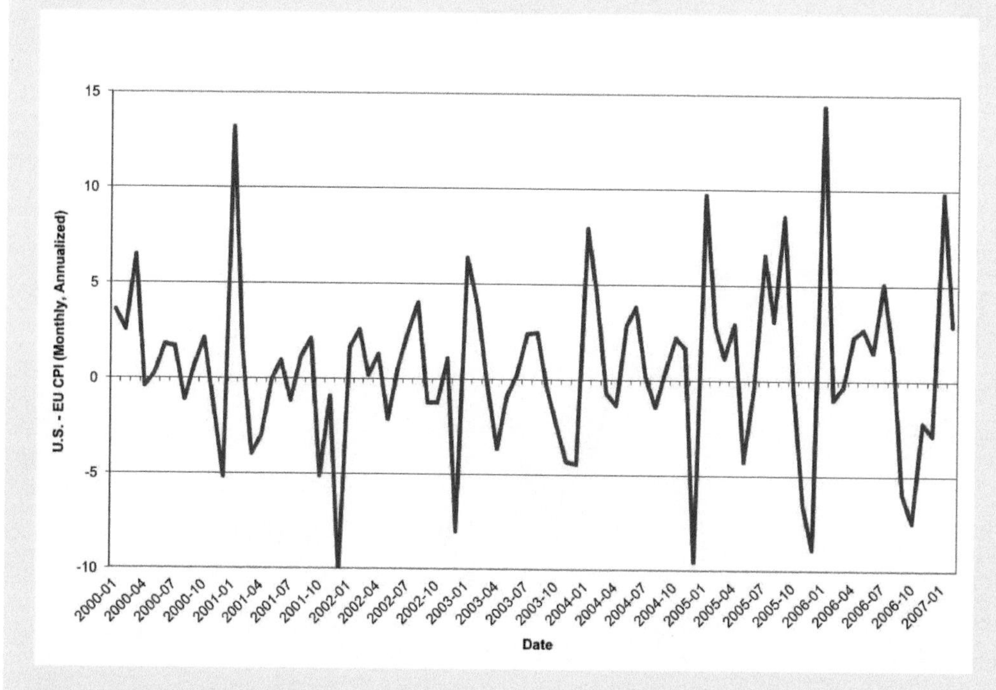

From the beginning of 2000 until early 2002, the dollar appreciated against the euro, moving from rough parity (1 to 1) to €1.10 to €1.20 per USD. This isn't surprising given that U.S. interest rates (proxied here by the fed funds rate ff*) were higher than euro zone interest rates (proxied here by EONIA, the ECB's fed funds equivalent). Moreover, except for the spike in early 2001, the price level in the United States did not rise appreciably faster than prices in the euro zone did. Since mid-2002, prices in the United States have risen faster than prices in the euro zone. (There are more periods when the consumer price index [CPI] in the United States was > the CPI in the euro zone, for example, when the red line is above zero.) After mid-2004, interest rates rose more quickly in the United States than in the euro zone, but not enough to offset the higher U.S. inflation rate. Fears of a recession in the United States and slowing U.S. productivity also dragged on the dollar in the period leading up to the financial crisis.

Key Takeaways

- The market for foreign exchange can be modeled in many different ways.
- The easiest way, perhaps, is to think of the price of a domestic currency, say, USD.
- There is a given quantity of USD that is insensitive to the exchange rate.
- Demand for the domestic currency slopes downward for the usual reasons that economic actors demand more of an asset when it is cheaper.
- The intersection of the two lines determines the exchange rate.

18.6 Suggested Reading

Lien, Kathy. *The Little Book of Currency Trading*. Hoboken, NJ: John Wiley and Sons, 2010.

Peters, Jelle. *Forex for Ambitious Beginners: A Guide to Successful Currency Trading*. New York: Odyssea Publishing, 2012.

Weithers, Tim. *Foreign Exchange: A Practical Guide to the FX Markets*. Hoboken, NJ: John Wiley and Sons, 2011.

Endnotes

1. The symbol for the euro, the currency of the European Union, is €. The symbol for the Japanese yen is ¥.
2. www.cfr.org/sanctions/economic-sanctions/p36259
3. www.wto.org/english/thewto_e/whatis_e/tif_e/agrm9_e.htm

CHAPTER 19

International Monetary Regimes

Chapter Objectives

By the end of this chapter, students should be able to:

1. Define the impossible trinity, or trilemma, and explain its importance.
2. Identify the four major types of international monetary regimes and describe how they differ.
3. Explain how central banks manage the foreign exchange (FX) rate.
4. Explain the benefits of fixing the FX rate, or keeping it within a narrow band.
5. Explain the costs of fixing the FX rate, or keeping it in a narrow band.

19.1 The Trilemma, or Impossible Trinity

Learning Objectives

1. What is the impossible trinity, or trilemma, and why is it important?
2. What are the four major types of international monetary regimes and how do they differ?

The foreign exchange (**foreign exchange rate (FX or forex)**) market described in Chapter 18 is called the free floating regime because monetary authorities allow world markets (via interest rates, and expectations about relative price, productivity, and trade levels) to determine the prices of different currencies in terms of one another. The free float, as we learned, was characterized by tremendous exchange rate volatility and unfettered international capital mobility. It is also characterized by national central banks with tremendous discretion over domestic monetary policy. *The free float is not, however, the only possible international monetary regime. In fact, it has pervaded the world economy only since the early 1970s, and many nations even today do not embrace it.* Between World War II and the early 1970s, much of the world (the so-called first, or free, world) was on a managed, fixed-FX regime called the **Bretton Woods System (BWS)**. Before that, many nations were on the **gold standard (GS)**, as summarized in Figure 19.1.

foreign exchange rate (FX or forex)

The price of one currency in terms of another.

Bretton Woods System (BWS)

A system of fixed exchange rates based on gold and the USD used by most of the world's free (noncommunist) countries in the quarter century after World War II.

gold standard (GS)

A fixed exchange rate regime based on gold.

FIGURE 19.1 The trilemma, or impossible trinity, of international monetary regimes
None of these are "right" or "wrong" but rather each comes with its own distinct (dis)advantages.

International Monetary Regime	Fixed Exchange Rates?	Domestic Discretionary Monetary Policy?	Capital Mobility?
Specie Standard (from ? to World War I) and Gold Exchange Standard (between the world wars)	Yes	No	Yes
Bretton Woods System (World War II to 1971-73)	Yes	Yes	No
Free Float (1973-present)	No	Yes	Yes
Managed Float (1973-present)	Sometimes	Sometimes	Yes

Note that those were the prevailing regimes. Because nations determine their monetary relationship with the rest of the world individually, some countries have always remained outside the prevailing system, often for strategic reasons. In the nineteenth century, for example, some countries chose a silver rather than a gold standard. Some allowed their currencies to float in wartime. Today, some countries maintain fixed exchange rates (usually against USD) or manage their currencies so their exchange rates stay within a band or range. *But just as no country can do away with scarcity or asymmetric information, none can escape the trilemma (a dilemma with three components), also known as the impossible trinity.*

In an ideal world, nations would like to have fixed exchange rates, capital mobility, and monetary policy discretion at the same time in order to reap their respective benefits: exchange rate stability for importers and exporters, liquid securities markets that allocate resources to their best uses globally, and the ability to change interest rates in response to foreign and domestic shocks. *In the real world, however, trade-offs exist. If a nation lowers its domestic interest rate to stave off a recession, for example, its currency (ceteris paribus) will depreciate and hence exchange rate stability will be lost. If the government firmly fixes the exchange rate, capital will emigrate to places where it can earn a higher return unless capital flows are restricted/capital mobility is sacrificed.*

FIGURE 19.2 Strengths and weaknesses of international monetary regimes
Remember, there is no such thing as a free lunch!

Regime	Strength	Weakness
Specie Standard	FX rate stability	Susceptible to domestic shocks due to the lack of domestic monetary discretion
Managed Fixed Exchange Rate System (Bretton Woods)	FX rate stability	Capital immobility; sudden FX rate devaluations/revaluations
Free Float	Free flow of capital and domestic monetary policy flexibility	FX rate instability; susceptibility to international shocks
Managed Float	Free flow of capital and the ability to switch between domestic monetary policy discretion and fixed FX as desired	Sudden FX rate depreciation, appreciation; loss of international reserves; accumulation of too many such reserves

As Figure 19.1 shows, only two of the three holy grails of international monetary policy, fixed exchange rates, international financial capital mobility, and domestic monetary policy discretion, have been simultaneously satisfied. Countries can adroitly change regimes when it suits them, but they cannot enjoy capital mobility, fixed exchange rates, and discretionary monetary policy all at once. That is because to maintain a fixed exchange rate, a monetary authority (like a central bank) has to make that rate its sole consideration (thus giving up on domestic goals like inflation or employment/gross domestic product [GDP]), or it has to seal off the nation from the international financial system by cutting off capital flows. Each component of the trilemma comes laden with costs and benefits, so each major international policy regime has strengths and weaknesses, as outlined in Figure 19.2.

specie standard

A fixed exchange rate regime based on specie (i.e., gold and/or silver).

Stop and Think Box

From 1797 until 1820 or so, Great Britain abandoned the specie standard it had maintained for as long as anyone could remember and allowed the pound sterling to float quite freely. That was a period of almost nonstop warfare known as the Napoleonic Wars. The United States also abandoned its specie standard from 1775 until 1781, from 1814 until 1817, and from 1862 until essentially 1873. Why?

Those were also periods of warfare and their immediate aftermath in the United States—the Revolution, War of 1812, and Civil War, respectively. Apparently during wartime, both countries found the specie standard costly and preferred instead to float with free mobility of financial capital. That allowed them to borrow abroad while simultaneously gaining discretion over domestic monetary policy, essentially allowing them to fund part of the cost of the wars with a currency tax, which is to say, inflation.

Key Takeaways

- The impossible trinity, or trilemma, is one of those aspects of the nature of things, like scarcity and asymmetric information, that makes life difficult.
- Specifically, the trilemma means that a country can follow only two of three policies at once: international capital mobility, fixed exchange rates, and discretionary domestic monetary policy.
- To keep exchange rates fixed, the central bank must either restrict capital flows or give up its control over the domestic money supply, interest rates, and price level.
- This means that a country must make difficult decisions about which variables it wants to control and which it wants to give up to outside forces.
- The four major types of international monetary regime are specie standard, managed fixed exchange rate, free float, and managed float.
- They differ in their solution, so to speak, of the impossible trinity.
- Specie standards, like the classical GS, maintained fixed exchange rates and allowed the free flow of financial capital internationally, rendering it impossible to alter domestic money supplies, interest rates, or inflation rates.
- Managed fixed exchange rate regimes like BWS allowed central banks discretion and fixed exchange rates at the cost of restricting international capital flows.
- Under a free float, free capital flows are again allowed, as is domestic discretionary monetary policy, but at the expense of the security and stability of fixed exchange rates.
- With a managed float, that same solution prevails until the FX rate moves to the top or bottom of the desired band, at which point the central bank gives up its domestic discretion so it can concentrate on appreciating or depreciating its currency.

19.2 Two Systems of Fixed Exchange Rates

Learning Objective

1. What were the two major types of fixed exchange rate regimes and how did they differ?

Under the gold standard, nations defined their respective domestic units of account in terms of so much gold (by weight and fineness or purity) and allowed gold and international checks (known as bills of exchange) to flow between nations unfettered. Thanks to arbitrageurs, the spot exchange rate, the market price of bills of exchange, could not stray very far from the exchange rate implied by the definition of each nation's unit of account. For example, the United States and Great Britain defined their units of account roughly as follows: 1 oz. gold = $20.00; 1 oz. gold = £4. Thus, the implied exchange rate was roughly $5 = £1 (or £.20 = $1). It was not costless to send gold across the Atlantic, so Americans who had payments to make in Britain were willing to buy sterling-denominated bills of exchange for something more than $5 per pound and Americans who owned sterling bills would accept something less than $5 per pound, as the supply and demand conditions in the sterling bills market dictated. If the dollar depreciated too far, however, people would stop buying bills of exchange and would ship gold to Britain instead. That would decrease the U.S. money supply and appreciate the dollar. If the dollar appreciated too much, people would stop selling bills of exchange and would order gold shipped from Britain instead. That increased the U.S. money supply and depreciated the dollar. *The GS system was self-equilibrating, functioning without government intervention (after their initial definition of the domestic unit of account).*

FIGURE 19.3 Dollar-sterling exchange during the classical gold standard
No need to worry or hedge!

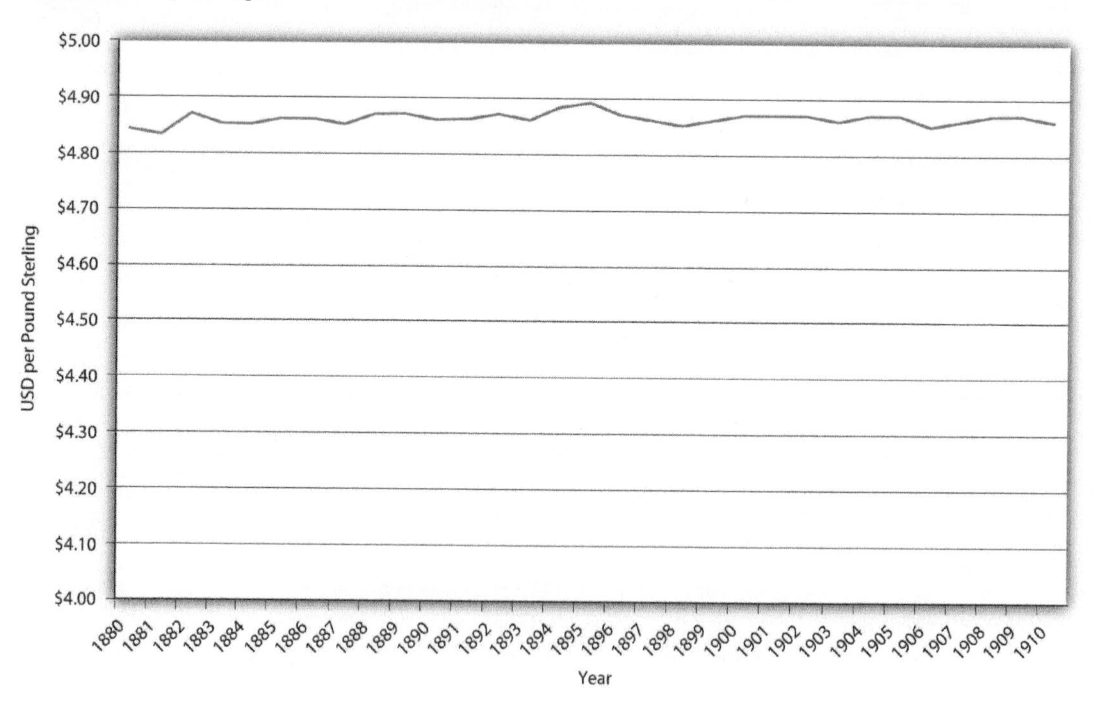

As noted in Figure 19.2 and shown in Figure 19.3, *the great strength of the GS was exchange rate stability*. One weakness of the system was that the United States had so *little control of its domestic monetary policy* that it did not need, or indeed have, a central bank. Other GS countries, too, suffered from their inability to adjust to domestic shocks. Another weakness of the GS was the annoying fact that *gold supplies were rarely in sync with the world economy* (more technically, aggregate demand), sometimes lagging it, thereby *causing deflation*, and sometimes exceeding it, hence *inducing inflation*.

Stop and Think Box

Why did the United States find it prudent to have a central bank (the B.U.S. [1791–1811] and the S.B.U.S. [1816–1836]) during the late eighteenth and early nineteenth centuries, when it was on a specie standard, but not later in the nineteenth century? (*Hint*: Transatlantic transportation technology improved dramatically beginning in the 1810s.)

As discussed in earlier chapters, the B.U.S. and S.B.U.S. had some control over the domestic money supply by regulating commercial bank reserves via the alacrity of its note and deposit redemption policy. Although the United States was on a de facto specie standard (legally bimetallic but de facto silver, then gold) at the time, the exchange rate bands were quite wide because transportation costs (insurance, freight, interest lost in transit) were so large compared to later in the century that the U.S. monetary regime was more akin to a modern managed float. In other words, the central bank had discretion to change the money supply and exchange rates within the wide band that the costly state of technology created and perpetuated until the development of steam packet ships, transatlantic telegraph cables, and so forth.

The Bretton Woods System adopted by the first world countries in the final stages of World War II *was designed to overcome the flaws of the GS while maintaining the stability of fixed exchange rates. By making the dollar the free world's reserve currency (basically substituting USD for gold), it ensured a more elastic supply of international reserves and also allowed the United States to earn seigniorage to help offset the costs it incurred fighting World War II, the Korean War, and the Cold War*. The U.S. government promised to convert USD into gold at a fixed rate ($35 per oz.), essentially rendering the United States the banker to more than half of the world's economy. The other countries in the system maintained fixed exchange rates with the dollar and allowed for domestic monetary policy discretion, so the BWS had to restrict international capital flows, which it did via taxes and restrictions on international financial instrument transactions.[1] Little wonder that the period after World War II witnessed a massive shrinkage of the international financial system.

Under the BWS, if a country could no longer defend its fixed rate with the dollar, it was allowed to devalue its currency, or in other words, to set a newer, weaker exchange rate. As Figure 19.4 reveals, Great Britain devalued several times, as did other members of the BWS. But what ultimately destroyed the system was the fact that the banker, the United States, kept issuing more USD without increasing its reserve of gold. The international equivalent of a bank run ensued because major countries, led by France, exchanged their USD for gold. Attempts to maintain the BWS in the early 1970s failed. Thereafter, Europe created its own fixed exchange rate system called the exchange rate mechanism (ERM), with the German mark as the reserve currency. That system morphed into the European currency union and adopted a common currency called the euro.

FIGURE 19.4 Dollar–sterling exchange under BWS
No worries, except for devaluations now and again!

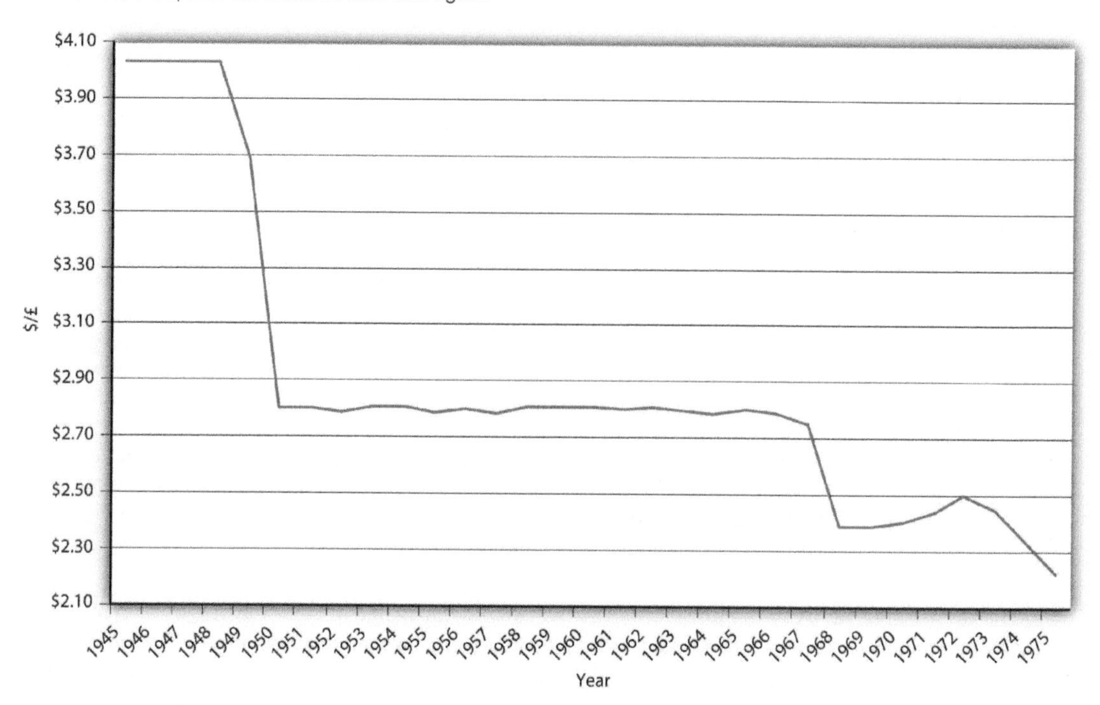

Most countries today allow their currencies to float freely or employ a managed float strategy. With international capital mobility restored in many places after the demise of the BWS, the international financial system has waxed ever stronger since the early 1970s.

Key Takeaways

- The two major types of fixed exchange rate regimes were the gold standard and Bretton Woods.
- The gold standard relied on retail convertibility of gold, while the BWS relied on central bank management where the USD stood as a sort of substitute for gold.

19.3 The Managed or Dirty Float

Learning Objective

1. How can central banks manage the FX rate?

The so-called managed float (aka dirty float) is perhaps the most interesting attempt to, if not eliminate the impossible trinity, at least to blunt its most pernicious characteristic, that of locking countries into the disadvantages outlined in Figure 19.2. *Under a managed float, the central bank allows market forces to determine second-to-second (day-to-day) fluctuations in exchange rates but intervenes if the currency grows too weak or too strong.* In other words, it tries to keep the exchange rate range bound, ostensibly to protect domestic economic interests (exporters, consumers) who would be hurt by rapid exchange rate movements. Those ranges or bands can vary in size from very wide to very narrow and can change levels over time.

Central banks intervene in the foreign exchange markets by exchanging international reserves—assets denominated in foreign currencies, gold, and special drawing rights (**SDRs**)*—for domestic currency.* Consider the case of Central Bank selling $10 billion of international reserves, thereby soaking up $10 billion of MB (the monetary base, or currency in circulation and/or reserves). The T-account would be:

SDRs

Liabilities of the International Monetary Fund (IMF), an institution established as part of the BWS.

Central Bank	
Assets	Liabilities
International reserves –$10 billion	Currency in circulation or reserves –$10 billion

If it were to buy $100 million of international reserves, both MB and its holdings of foreign assets would increase:

Central Bank	
Assets	Liabilities
International reserves +$100 million	Monetary base +$100 million

Such transactions are known in the biz as *unsterilized foreign exchange interventions and they influence the FX rate via changes in MB.* Recall that increasing the money supply (MS) causes the domestic currency to depreciate, while decreasing the MS causes it to appreciate. It does so by influencing both the domestic interest rate (nominal) and expectations about E^{ef}, the future exchange rate, via price level (inflation) expectations. (There is also a direct effect on the MS, but it is too small in most instances to be detectable and so it can be safely ignored. Intuitively, however, increasing the money supply leaves each unit of currency less valuable, while decreasing it renders each unit more valuable.)

Central banks also sometimes engage in so-called sterilized foreign exchange interventions when they offset the purchase or sale of international reserves with a domestic sale or purchase. For example, a central bank might offset or sterilize the purchase of $100 million of international reserves by selling $100 million of domestic government bonds, or vice versa. In terms of a T-account:

Central Bank	
Assets	Liabilities
International reserves +$100 million	Monetary base +$100 million
Government bonds –$100 million	Monetary base –$100 million

Because there is no net change in MB, a sterilized intervention should have no long-term impact on the exchange rate. Apparently, central bankers engage in sterilized interventions as a short-term ruse (where central banks are not transparent, considerable asymmetric information exists between them and the markets) or to signal their desire to the market. *Neither go very far, so for the most part central banks that wish to manage their nation's exchange rate must do so via unsterilized interventions, buying international reserves with domestic currency when they want to depreciate the domestic currency, and selling international reserves for domestic currency when they want the domestic currency to appreciate.*

The degree of float management can range from a hard peg, where a country tries to keep its currency fixed to another, so-called anchor currency, to such wide bands that intervention is rarely undertaken. Figure 19.5 clearly shows that Thailand used to maintain a hard peg against the dollar but gave it up during the Southeast Asian financial crisis of 1997. That big spike was not pleasant for Thailand, especially for economic agents within it that had debts denominated in foreign currencies, which suddenly became much more difficult to repay. (In June 1997, it took only about 25 baht to purchase a dollar. By the end of that year, it took over 50 baht to do so.) Clearly, a major downside of maintaining a hard peg or even a tight band is that it simply is not always possible for the central bank to maintain or defend the peg or band. It can run out of international reserves in a fruitless attempt to prevent a depreciation (cause an appreciation). Or maintenance of the peg might require increasing or decreasing the MB counter to the needs of the domestic economy.

FIGURE 19.5 Thai bhat–USD exchange rate, 1981–2017
That big jump (depreciation) severely hurt Thailand's economy.

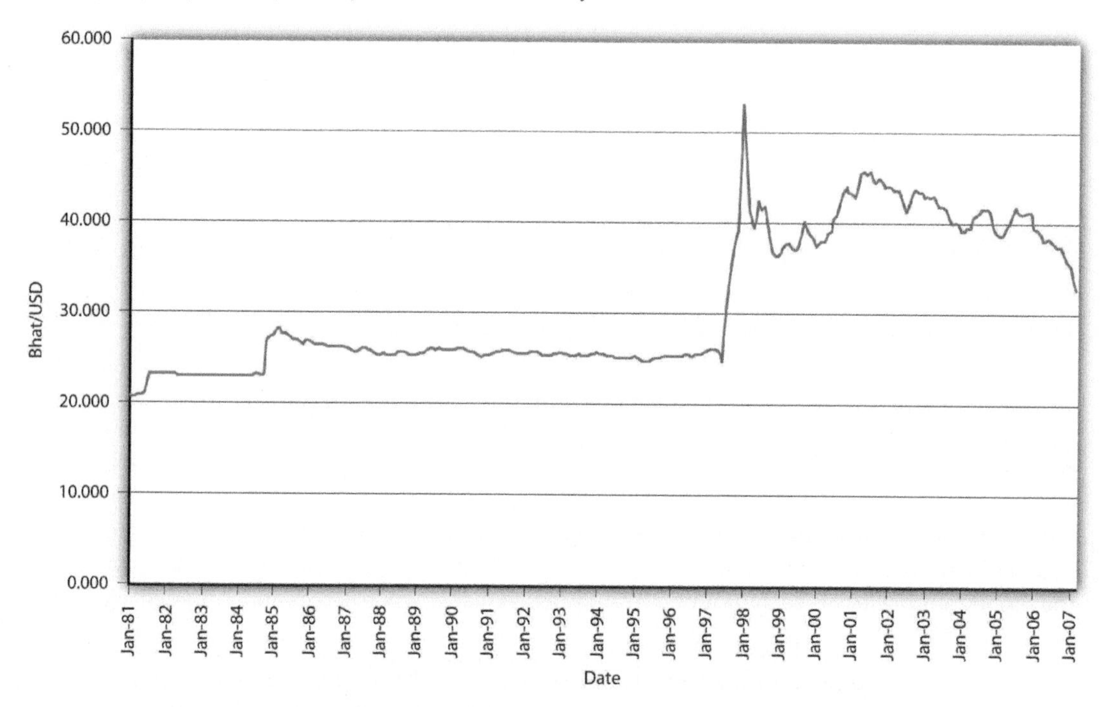

FIGURE 19.6 Intervening in the FX market under a fixed exchange rate regime
When the market exchange rate strays from the peg, costly interventions become necessary.

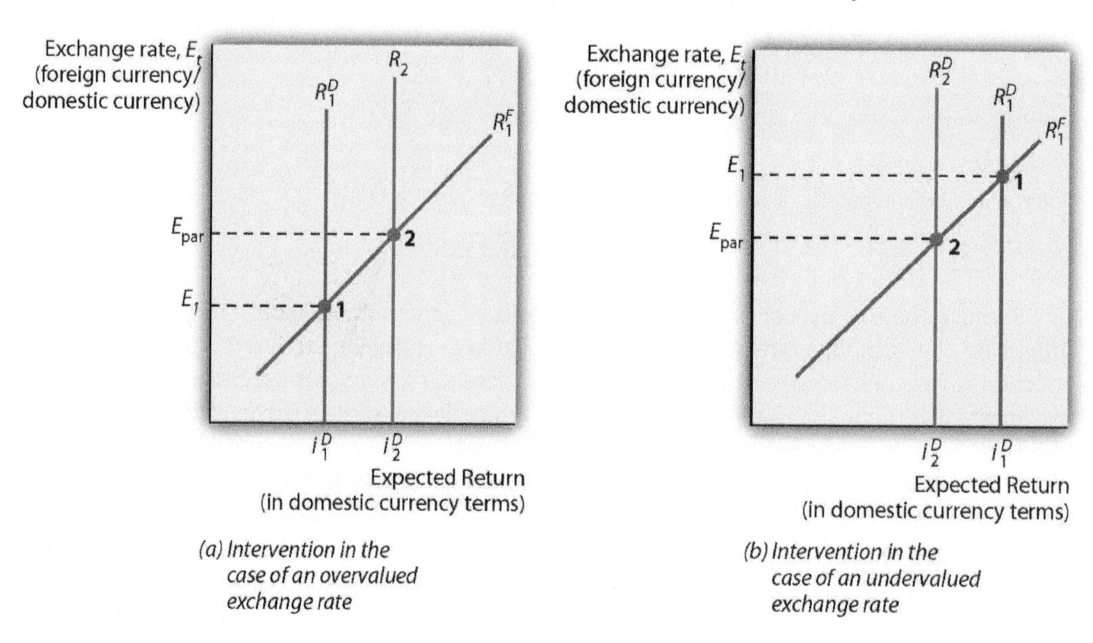

A graph, like the one in Figure 19.6, might be useful here. When the market exchange rate (E_1) is equal to the fixed, pegged, or desired central bank rate (E_{peg}) everything is hunky dory. When a currency is overvalued (by the central bank), which is to say that E_1 is less than E_{peg} (measuring E as foreign currency/domestic currency), the central bank must soak up domestic currency by selling international reserves (foreign assets), that is, raise interest rates to induce appreciation). When a currency is undervalued (by the central bank), which is to say that when E_1 is higher than E_{peg}, the central bank must sell domestic currency (lower interest rates to induce depreciation), thereby gaining international reserves.

Stop and Think Box

In 1990, interest rates rose in Germany due to West Germany's reunification with formerly communist East Germany. (When exchange rates are fixed, the interest parity condition collapses to $i^D = i^F$ because $E^{ef} = E^t$.) Therefore, interest rates also rose in the other countries in the ERM, including France, leading to a slowing of economic growth there. The same problem could recur in the new European currency union or euro zone if part of the zone needs a high interest rate to stave off inflation while another needs a low interest rate to stoke employment and growth. What does this analysis mean for the likelihood of creating a single world currency?

It means that the creation of a world currency is not likely anytime soon. As the European Union has discovered, a common currency has certain advantages, like the savings from not having to convert one currency into another or worry about the current or future exchange rate (because there is none). At the same time, however, the currency union has reminded the world that there is no such thing as a free lunch, that every benefit comes with a cost. The cost in this case is that the larger the common currency area becomes, the more difficult it is for the central bank to implement policies beneficial to the entire currency union. It was for that very reason that Great Britain opted out of the euro.

Key Takeaways

- Central banks influence the FX rate via unsterilized foreign exchange interventions or, more specifically, by buying or selling international reserves (foreign assets) with domestic currency.
- When central banks buy international reserves, they increase MB and hence depreciate their respective currencies by increasing inflation expectations.
- When central banks sell international reserves, they decrease MB and hence appreciate their respective currencies by decreasing inflation expectations.

19.4 The Choice of International Policy Regime

Learning Objective

1. What are the costs and benefits of fixing the FX rate or keeping it within a narrow band?

Problems ensue when the central bank runs out of reserves, as it did in Thailand in 1997. The International Monetary Fund (IMF) often provides loans to countries attempting to defend the value of their currencies. It doesn't really act as an international lender of last resort, however, because it doesn't follow Hamilton's née Bagehot's Law. It simply has no mechanism for adding liquidity quickly, and the longer one waits, the bigger the eventual bill. Moreover, the IMF often forces borrowers to undergo fiscal austerity programs (high government taxes, decreased expenditures, high domestic interest rates, and so forth) that can create as much economic pain as a rapid depreciation would. Finally, it has created a major moral hazard problem, repeatedly lending to the same few countries, which quickly learned that they need not engage in responsible policies in the long run because the IMF would be sure to help out if they got into trouble. Sometimes the medicine is indeed worse than the disease!

Trouble can also arise when a central bank no longer wants to accumulate international reserves (or indeed any assets) because it wants to squelch domestic inflation, as was the case with Germany in 1990–1992. Many fear that China, which currently owns over $2 trillion in international reserves (mostly USD), will find itself in this conundrum soon. The Chinese government accumulated such a huge amount of reserves by fixing its currency (which confusingly goes by two names, the yuan and the renminbi, but one symbol, CNY) at the rate of CNY8.28 per USD. Due to the growth of the Chinese economy relative to the U.S. economy, E* exceeded E_{peg}, inducing the Chinese, per the analysis in Section 19.3, to sell CNY for international reserves to keep the yuan permanently weak, or undervalued relative to the value the market would have assigned it.

Recall that undervaluing the yuan helps Chinese exports by making them appear cheap to foreigners. (If you don't believe me, walk into any Wal-Mart, Target, or other discount store.) *Many people think that China's peg is unfair, a monetary form of dirty pool.* Such folks need to realize that there is no such thing as a free lunch. To maintain its peg, the Chinese government has severely restricted international capital mobility via currency controls, thereby injuring the efficiency of Chinese financial markets, limiting foreign direct investment, and encouraging mass loophole mining. It is also stuck with trillions of relatively low-yielding international reserves that will decline in value when the yuan floats (and probably appreciates strongly), as it eventually must. In other words, *China is setting itself up for the exact opposite of the Southeast Asian Crisis of 1997–1998, where the value of its assets will plummet instead of the value of its liabilities skyrocketing.*

In China's defense, many developing countries find it advantageous to peg their exchange rates to the dollar, the yen, the euro, the pound sterling, or a basket of such important currencies. *The peg, which can be thought of as a monetary policy target similar to an inflation or money supply target, allows the developing nation's central bank to figure out whether to increase or decrease MB and by how much. A hard peg or narrow band effectively ties the domestic inflation rate to that of the anchor country,*[2] *instilling confidence in the developing country's macroeconomic performance.*

Indeed, in extreme cases, some countries have given up their central bank altogether and have dollarized, adopting USD or other currencies (though the process is still called dollarization) as their own. No international law prevents this, and indeed the country whose currency is adopted earns seigniorage and hence has little grounds for complaint. Countries that want to completely outsource their monetary policy but maintain seigniorage revenue (the profits from the issuance of money) adopt a currency board that issues domestic currency but backs it 100 percent with assets denominated in the anchor currency. (The board invests the reserves in interest-bearing assets, the source of the seigniorage.) Argentina benefited from just such a board during the 1990s, when it pegged its peso one-to-one with the dollar, because it finally got inflation, which often ran over 100 percent per year, under control.

Fixed exchange rates not based on commodities like gold or silver are notoriously fragile, however, because relative macroeconomic changes in interest rates, trade, price levels, and productivity can create persistent imbalances over time between the developing and the anchor currencies. Moreover, speculators can force countries to devalue (move E_{peg} down) or revalue (move E_{peg} up) when they hit the bottom or top of a band. They do so by using the derivatives markets to place big bets on the future exchange rate. Unlike most bets, these are one-sided because the speculators lose little money if the central bank successfully defends the peg, but they win a lot if it fails to. Speculator George Soros, for example, is reported to have made $1 billion speculating against the pound sterling during the ERM balance of payments crisis in September 1992. Such crises can cause tremendous economic pain, as when Argentina found it necessary to abandon its currency board and one-to-one peg with the dollar in 2001–2002 due to speculative pressures and fundamental macroeconomic misalignment between the Argentine and U.S. economies. (Basically, the United States was booming and Argentina was in a recession. The former needed higher interest rates/slower money growth and the latter needed lower interest rates/higher money growth but it got the former because of the hard peg to the dollar.)

Developing countries may be best off maintaining what is called a crawling target or crawling peg. Generally, this entails the developing country's central bank allowing its domestic currency to depreciate or appreciate over time, as general macroeconomic conditions (the variables discussed in Chapter 18) dictate. A similar strategy is to recognize imbalances as they occur and change the peg on an ad hoc basis accordingly, perhaps first by allowing the band to widen before permanently moving it. In those ways, developing countries can maintain some FX rate stability, keep inflation in check (though perhaps higher than in the anchor country), and hopefully avoid exchange rate crises.

Stop and Think Box

What sort of international monetary regimes are consistent with Figure 19.7 and Figure 19.8?

FIGURE 19.7 Dollar-yen exchange rate, 1997–2007
Upsies and downsies.

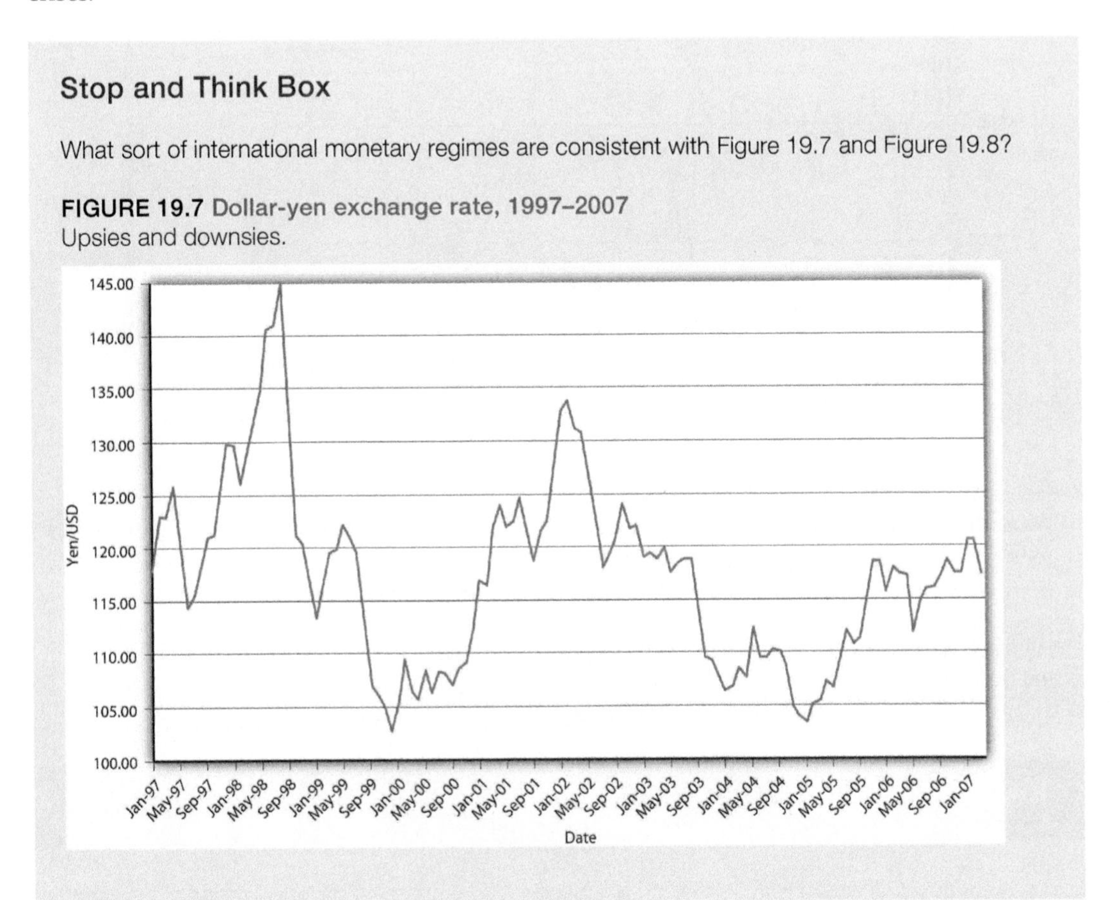

FIGURE 19.8 Hong Kong–USD exchange rate, 1984–2007
Note the scale!

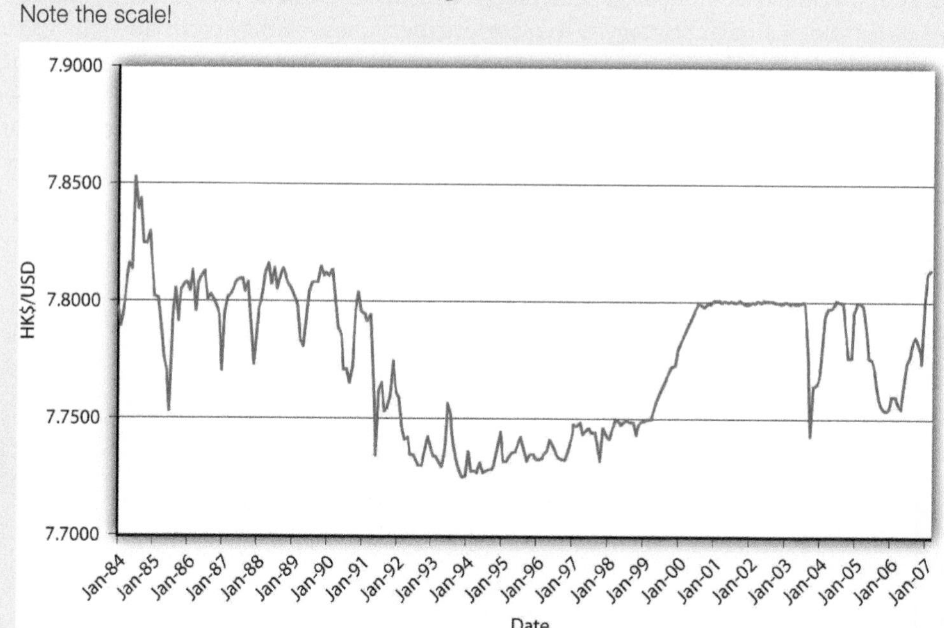

Figure 19.7 certainly is not a fixed exchange rate regime, or a managed float with a tight band. It could be consistent with a fully free float, but it might also represent a managed float with wide bands between about ¥100 to ¥145 per dollar.

It appears highly likely from Figure 19.8 that Hong Kong's monetary authority for most of the period from 1984 to 2007 engaged in a managed float within fairly tight bands bounded by about HK7.725 and HK7.80 to the dollar. Also, for three years early in the new millennium, it pegged the dollar at HK7.80 before returning to a looser but still tight band in 2004.

Key Takeaways

- A country with weak institutions (e.g., a dependent central bank that allows rampant inflation) can essentially free-ride on the monetary policy of a developed country by fixing or pegging its currency to the dollar, euro, yen, pound sterling, or other anchoring currency to a greater or lesser degree.
- In fact, in the limit, a country can simply adopt another country's currency as its own in a process called dollarization.
- If it wants to continue earning seigniorage (profits from the issuance of money), it can create a currency board, the function of which is to maintain 100 percent reserves and full convertibility between the domestic currency and the anchor currency.
- At the other extreme, it can create a crawling peg with wide bands, allowing its currency to appreciate or depreciate day to day according to the interaction of supply and demand, slowly adjusting the band and peg in the long term as macroeconomic conditions dictate.
- When a currency is overvalued, which is to say, when the central bank sets E_{peg} higher than E* (when E is expressed as foreign currency/domestic currency), the central bank must appreciate the currency by selling international reserves for its domestic currency.
- It may run out of reserves before doing so, however, sparking a rapid depreciation that could trigger a financial crisis by rapidly increasing the real value of debts owed by domestic residents but denominated in foreign currencies.
- When a currency is undervalued, which is to say, when the central bank sets E_{peg} below E*, the central bank must depreciate its domestic currency by exchanging it for international reserves. It may accumulate too many such reserves, which often have low yields and which

could quickly lose value if the domestic currency suddenly appreciates, perhaps with the aid of a good push by currency speculators making big one-sided bets.

19.5 Suggested Reading

Bordo, Michael, and Barry Eichengreen. *A Retrospective on the Bretton Woods System: Lessons for International Monetary Reform*. Chicago, IL: University of Chicago Press, 1993.

Chown, John. *A History of Monetary Unions*. New York: Routledge, 2010.

Eichengreen, Barry. *Globalizing Capital: A History of the International Monetary System*. Princeton, NJ: Princeton University Press, 2008.

Moosa, Imad. *Exchange Rate Regimes: Fixed, Flexible or Something in Between*. New York: Palgrave Macmillan, 2005.

Rickards, James. *The New Case for Gold*. New York: Portfolio, 2016.

Salin, Pascal. *The International Monetary System and the Theory of Monetary Systems*. New York: Edward Elgar, 2016.

Endnotes

1. For additional details, see Christopher Neely, "An Introduction to Capital Controls," *Federal Reserve Bank of St. Louis Review* (Nov./Dec. 1999): 13–30. research.stlouisfed.org/publications/review/99/11/9911cn.pdf
2. As noted in Chapter 18, however, not all goods and services are traded internationally, so the rates will not be exactly equal.

CHAPTER 20
Money Demand

Chapter Objectives

By the end of this chapter, students should be able to:

1. Describe Friedman's modern quantity theory of money.
2. Describe the classical quantity theory.
3. Describe Keynes's liquidity preference theory and its improvements.
4. Contrast the modern quantity theory with the liquidity preference theory.

20.1 The Simple Quantity Theory and the Liquidity Preference Theory of Keynes

Learning Objective

1. What is the liquidity preference theory, and how has it been improved?

The rest of this book is about *monetary theory*, a daunting-sounding term. It's not the easiest aspect of money and banking, but it isn't terribly taxing either so there is no need to freak out. We're going to take it nice and slow. *And here's a big hint: you already know most of the outcomes because we've discussed them already in more intuitive terms. In the chapters that follow, we're simply going to provide you with more formal ways of thinking about how the money supply determines output (Y*) and the price level (P*).*

Intuitively, people want to hold a certain amount of cash because it is by definition the most liquid asset in the economy. It can be exchanged for goods at no cost other than the opportunity cost of holding a less liquid income–generating asset instead. When interest rates are low (high), so is the opportunity cost, so people hold more (less) cash. Similarly, when inflation is low (high), people are more (less) likely to hold assets, like cash, that lose purchasing power. Think about it: would you be more likely to keep $100 in your pocket if you believed that prices were constant and your bank pays you .00005% interest, or if you thought that the prices of the things you buy (like gasoline and food) were going up soon and your bank pays depositors 20% interest? (I would hope the former. If the latter, I have some derivative bridge securities to sell you.)

We'll start our theorizing with the demand for money, specifically the simple quantity theory of money, then discuss John Maynard Keynes's improvement on it, called the liquidity preference theory, and end with Milton Friedman's improvement on Keynes' theory, the modern quantity theory of money.

John Maynard Keynes (to distinguish him from his father, economist John Neville Keynes) developed the liquidity preference theory in response to the *pre-Friedman quantity theory of money, which was simply an assumption-laden identity called the equation of exchange:*

$$MV = PY$$

where

M = money supply

V = velocity

P = price level

Y = output

Nobody doubted the equation itself, which, as an identity (like x = x), is undeniable. *But many doubted the way that classical quantity theorists used the equation of exchange as a causal statement—increases in the money supply lead to proportional increases in the price level—although in the long term it was highly predictive. The classical quantity theory also suffered by assuming that money velocity, the number of times per year a unit of currency was spent, was constant.* Although a good first approximation of reality, the classical quantity theory, which critics derided as the "naïve quantity theory of money," was hardly the entire story. In particular, it could not explain why velocity was pro-cyclical (i.e., why it increased during business expansions and decreased during recessions).

To find a better theory, Keynes took a different point of departure, asking in effect, "Why do economic agents hold money?" He came up with three reasons:

1. Transactions: Economic agents need money to make payments. As their incomes rise, so, too, do the number and value of those payments, so *this part of money demand is proportional to income.*
2. Precautions: *S—t happens* was a catch phrase of the 1980s, recalled perhaps most famously in the hit movie *Forrest Gump*. Way back in the 1930s, Keynes already knew that bad stuff happens—and that one defense against it was to keep some spare cash lying around *as a precaution*. It, too, is *directly proportional to income*, Keynes believed.
3. Speculations: People will hold more bonds than money when interest rates are high for two reasons. The opportunity cost of holding money (which Keynes assumed has zero return) is higher, and the expectation is that interest rates will fall, raising the price of bonds. When interest rates are low, the opportunity cost of holding money is low, and the expectation is that rates will rise, decreasing the price of bonds. So people hold larger money balances when rates are low. *Overall, then, money demand and interest rates are inversely related.*

More formally, Keynes's ideas can be stated as

$$Md / P = f(i<->,\ Y<+>)$$

where

M_d/P = demand for real money balances

f means "function of" (this simplifies the mathematics)

i = interest rate

Y = output (income)

<+> = increases in

<-> = decreases in

An increase in interest rates induces people to decrease real money balances for a given income level, implying that velocity must be higher. *So Keynes's view was superior to the classical quantity theory of money because he showed that velocity is not constant but rather is positively related to interest rates, thereby explaining its pro-cyclical nature.* (Recall that interest rates rise during expansions and fall during recessions.) *Keynes's theory was also fruitful because it induced other scholars to elaborate on it further.*

In the early 1950s, for example, a young Will Baumol[1] and James Tobin[2] independently showed that money balances, *held for transaction purposes* (not just speculative ones), were sensitive to interest rates, *even if the return on money was zero.* That is because people can hold bonds or other interest-bearing securities until they need to make a payment. When interest rates are high, people will hold as little money for transaction purposes as possible because it will be worth the time and trouble of investing in bonds and then liquidating them when needed. When rates are low, by contrast, people will hold more money for transaction purposes because it isn't worth the hassle and brokerage fees to play with bonds very often. *So transaction demand for money is negatively related to interest rates.* A similar trade-off applies also to precautionary balances. The lure of high interest rates offsets the fear of bad events occurring. When rates are low, better to play it safe and hold more dough. *So the precautionary demand for money is also negatively related to interest rates.* And both transaction and precautionary demand are closely linked to technology: the faster, cheaper, and more easily bonds and money can be exchanged for each other, the more money-like bonds will be and the lower the demand for cash instruments will be, ceteris paribus.

Key Takeaways

- Before Friedman, the quantity theory of money was a much simpler affair based on the so-called equation of exchange—money times velocity equals the price level times output (MV = PY)—plus the assumptions that changes in the money supply cause changes in output and prices and that velocity changes so slowly it can be safely treated as a constant. Note that the interest rate is not considered at all in this so-called naïve version.
- Keynes and his followers knew that interest rates were important to money demand and that velocity wasn't a constant, so they created a theory whereby economic actors demand money to engage in transactions (buy and sell goods), as a precaution against unexpected negative shocks, and as a speculation.
- Due to the first two motivations, real money balances increase directly with output.
- Due to the speculative motive, real money balances and interest rates are inversely related. When interest rates are high, so is the opportunity cost of holding money.
- Throw in the expectation that rates will likely fall, causing bond prices to rise, and people are induced to hold less money and more bonds.
- When interest rates are low, by contrast, people expect them to rise, which will hurt bond prices. Moreover, the opportunity cost of holding money to make transactions or as a precaution against shocks is low when interest rates are low, so people will hold more money and fewer bonds when interest rates are low.

20.2 Friedman's Modern Quantity Theory of Money

Learning Objective

1. What is the quantity theory of money, and how was it improved by Milton Friedman?

Building on the work of earlier scholars, including Irving Fisher of Fisher Equation fame, Milton Friedman improved on Keynes's liquidity preference theory by treating money like any other asset. He concluded that economic agents (individuals, firms, governments) want to hold a certain quantity of real, as opposed to nominal, money balances. If inflation erodes the purchasing power of the unit of account, economic agents will want to hold higher nominal balances to compensate, to keep their real money balances constant. The level of those real balances, Friedman argued, was a function of permanent income (the present discounted value of all expected future income), the relative expected return on bonds and stocks versus money, and expected inflation.

More formally,

$$Md/P: f(Yp<+>, rb-rm<->, rs-rm<->, \pi e-rm<->)$$

where

M_d/P = demand for real money balances (M_d = money demand; P = price level)

f means "function of" (not equal to)

Y_p = permanent income

$r_b - r_m$ = the expected return on bonds minus the expected return on money

$r_s - r_m$ = the expected return on stocks (equities) minus the expected return on money

$\pi^e - r_m$ = expected inflation minus the expected return on money

$<+>$ = increases in

$<->$ = decreases in

So the demand for real money balances, according to Friedman, increases when permanent income increases and declines when the expected returns on bonds, stocks, or goods increases versus the expected returns on money, which includes both the interest paid on deposits and the services banks provide to depositors.

Stop and Think Box

As noted in the text, money demand is where the action is these days because, as we learned in previous chapters, the central bank determines what the money supply will be, so we can model it as a vertical line. Earlier monetary theorists, however, had no such luxury because, under a specie standard, money was supplied exogenously. What did the supply curve look like before the rise of modern central banking in the twentieth century?

The supply curve sloped upward, as most do. You can think of this in two ways, first, by thinking of interest on the vertical axis. Interest is literally the price of money. When interest is high, more people want to supply money to the system because seigniorage is higher. So more people want to form banks or find other ways of issuing money, extant bankers want to issue more money (notes and/or deposits), and so forth. You can also think of this in terms of the price of gold. When its price is low, there is not much incentive to go out and find more of it because you can earn just as much making cheesecake or whatever. When the price of gold is high, however, everybody wants to go out and prospect for new veins or for new ways of extracting gold atoms from what looks like plain old dirt. The point is that early monetary theorists did not have the luxury of concentrating on the nature of money demand; they also had to worry about the nature of money supply.

This all makes perfectly good sense when you think about it. If people suspect they are permanently more wealthy, they are going to want to hold more money, in real terms, so they can buy caviar and fancy golf clubs and what not. If the return on financial investments decreases vis-à-vis money, they will want to hold more money because its opportunity cost is lower. If inflation expectations increase, but the return on money doesn't, people will want to hold less money, ceteris paribus, because the relative return on goods (land, gold, turnips) will increase. (In other words, expected inflation here proxies the expected return on nonfinancial goods.)

The modern quantity theory is generally thought superior to Keynes's liquidity preference theory because it is more complex, specifying three types of assets (bonds, equities, goods) instead of just one (bonds). It also does not assume that the return on money is zero, or even a constant. In Friedman's theory, velocity is no longer a constant; instead, it is highly predictable and, as in reality and Keynes's formulation, pro-cyclical, rising during expansions and falling during recessions. *Finally, unlike the liquidity preference theory, Friedman's modern quantity theory predicts that interest rate changes should have little effect on money demand.* The reason for this is that Friedman believed that the return on bonds, stocks, goods, and money would be positively correlated, leading to little change in $r_b - r_m$, $r_s - r_m$, or $\pi^e - r_m$ because both sides would rise or fall about the same amount. That insight essentially reduces the modern quantity theory to $M_d/P = f(Y_p <+>)$.

Key Takeaways

- According to Milton Friedman, demand for real money balances (M_d/P) is directly related to permanent income (Y_p)—the discounted present value of expected future income—and indirectly related to the expected differential returns from bonds, stocks (equities), and goods vis-à-vis money ($r_b - r_m$, $r_s - r_m$, $\pi^e - r_m$), where inflation (π) proxies the return on goods.
- Because he believed that the return on money would increase (decrease) as returns on bonds, stocks, and goods increased (decreased), Friedman did not think that interest rate changes mattered much.
- Friedman's modern quantity theory proved itself superior to Keynes's liquidity preference theory because it was more complex, accounting for equities and goods as well as bonds.
- Friedman allowed the return on money to vary and to increase above zero, making it more realistic than Keynes's assumption of zero return.

20.3 The Policy Failure of the Modern Quantity Theory of Money

Learning Objective

1. When, how, and why did Friedman's modern quantity theory of money prove an inadequate guide to policy?

Until the 1970s, Friedman was more or less correct. Interest rates did not strongly affect the demand for money, so velocity was predictable and the quantity of money was closely linked to aggregate output. Except when nominal interest rates hit zero (as in Japan), the demand for money was somewhat sensitive to interest rates, so there was no so-called liquidity trap (where money demand is perfectly horizontal, leaving central bankers impotent). *During the 1970s, however, money demand became more sensitive to interest rate changes, and velocity, output, and inflation became harder to predict.* That's one reason why central banks in the 1970s found that targeting monetary aggregates did not help them to meet their inflation or output goals.

Stop and Think Box

Stare at Figure 20.1 for a spell. How is it related to the discussion in this chapter? Then take a gander at Figure 20.2. In addition to giving us a new perspective on Figure 20.1, it shows that the velocity of money (velocity = GDP/M1 because MV = PY can be solved for V: V = PY/M) has increased considerably since the late 1950s. Why might that be?

FIGURE 20.1 The quarterly volatility of velocity, 1959–2016
Notice how much less stable V became.

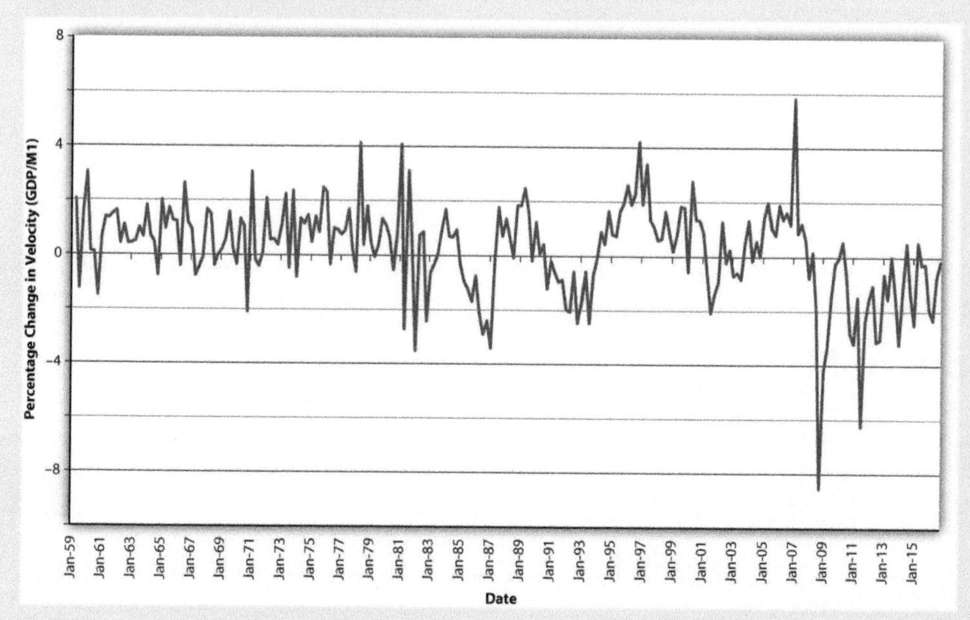

The chapter makes the point that velocity became much less stable and much less predictable in the 1970s and thereafter. Figure 20.1 shows that by measuring the quarterly change in velocity. Before 1970, velocity went up and down between −1 and 3 percent in pretty regular cycles. Thereafter, the variance increased to between over −8 and almost 6 percent, and the pattern has become much less regular. This is important because it shows why Friedman's modern quantity theory of money lost much of its explanatory power in the 1970s, leading to changes in central bank targeting and monetary theory.

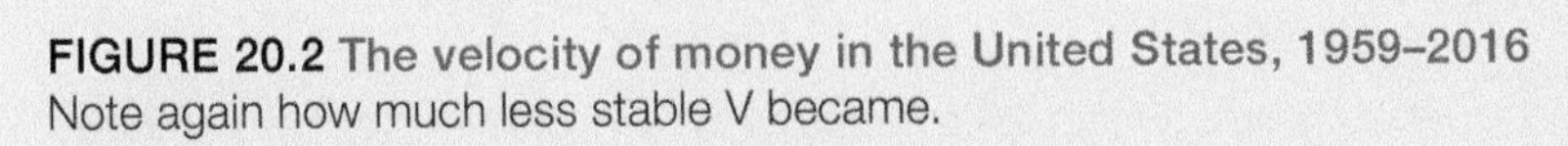

FIGURE 20.2 The velocity of money in the United States, 1959–2016
Note again how much less stable V became.

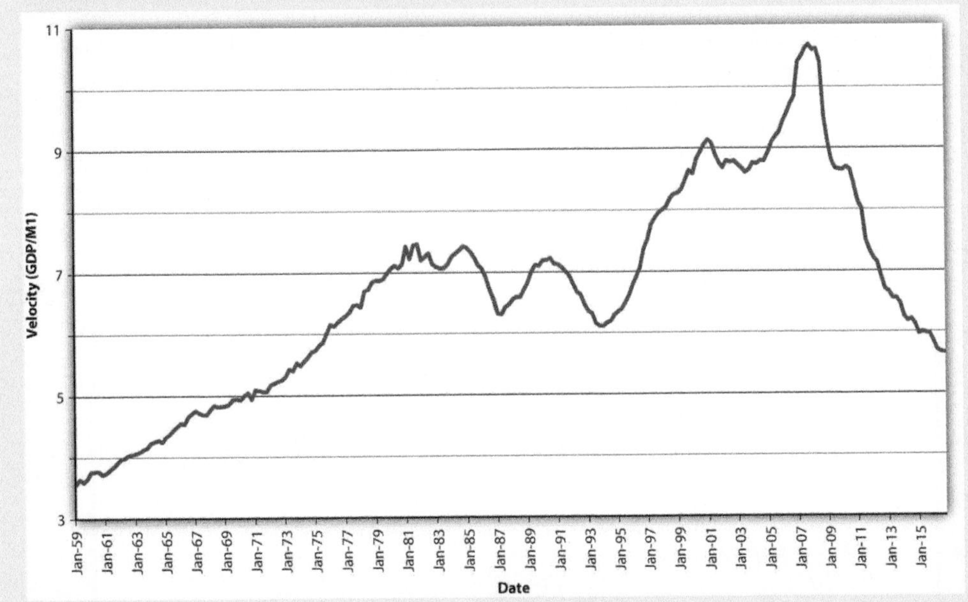

Figure 20.2 suggests that velocity likely increased in the latter half of the twentieth century due to technological improvements that allowed each unit of currency to be used in more transactions over the course of a year. More efficient payment systems (electronic funds transfer), increased use of credit, lower transaction costs, and financial innovations like cash management accounts have all helped to increase V, to help each dollar move through more hands or the same number of hands in less time. Velocity soared to almost 11 during the financial crisis, only to plummet afterwards to below 6.

The breakdown of the quantity theory in the 1970s had severe repercussions for central banking, central bankers, and monetary theorists. That was bad news for them (and for people like myself who grew up in that awful decade), and it is bad news for us because our exploration of monetary theory must continue. Monetary economists have learned a lot over the last few decades by constantly testing, critiquing, and improving models like those of Keynes and Friedman, and we're all going to follow along so you'll know precisely where monetary theory and policy stand at present.

Stop and Think Box

Examine Figure 20.3, Figure 20.4, and Figure 20.5 carefully. Why might velocity have trended upward until approximately 1815 and then fallen? *Hint*: Alexander Hamilton argued in the early 1790s that "in countries in which the national debt is properly funded, and an object of established confidence, it answers most of the purposes of money. Transfers of stock or public debt are there equivalent to payments in specie; or in other words, stock, in the principal transactions of business, passes current as specie. The same thing would, in all probability happen here, under the like circumstances"—if his funding plan was adopted. It was, and interest rates fell dramatically as a result and thereafter remained at around 6 percent in peacetime.

FIGURE 20.3 Velocity of money, 1790–1860
From America's founding to its civil war.

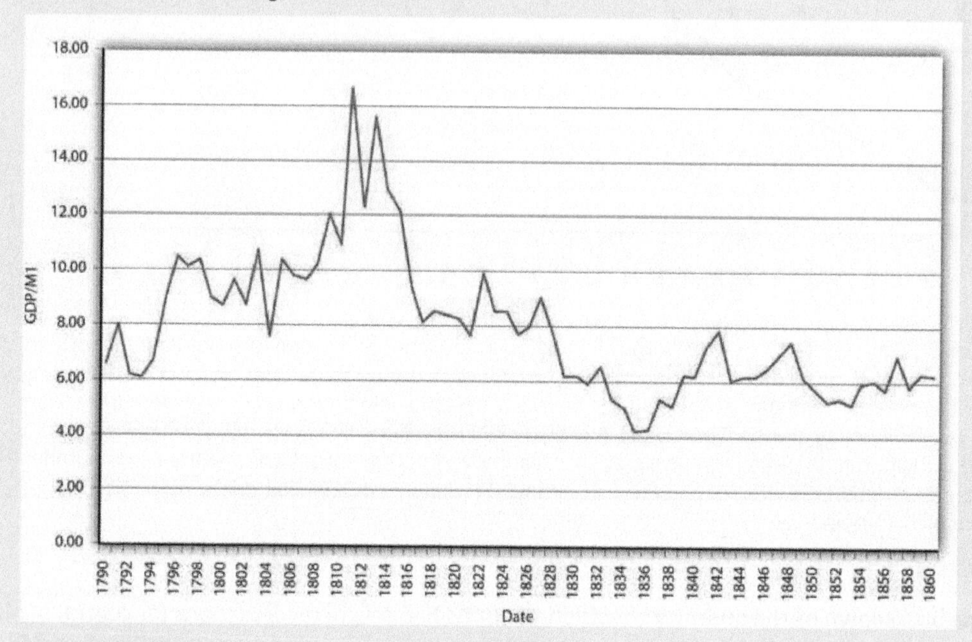

FIGURE 20.4 U.S. national debt, 1790–1860
Total nominal sum owed by the U.S. government from its founding to its civil war.

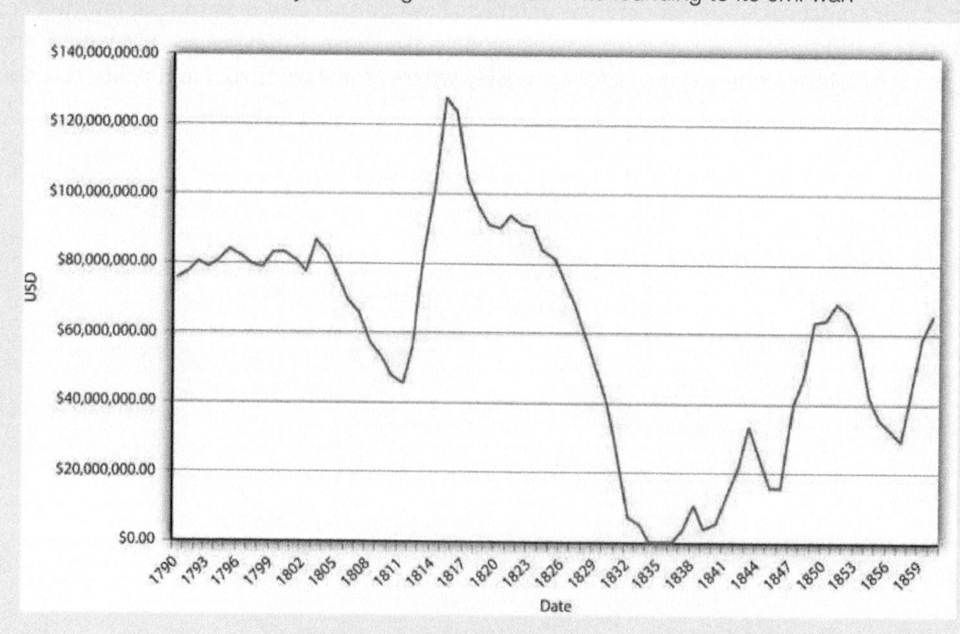

FIGURE 20.5 Volume of public securities trading in select U.S. markets, by year, 1790–1834

This is a prime example of "capta," or numbers seized by researchers, in this case my RA.

Year	Total Volume of Trades ($)	Total No. of Trades
1790	$447,857.92	246
1791	7,846,219.00	5,566
1792	7,171,626.47	7,077
1793	2,593,669.39	2,556
1794	1,936,077.64	2,074
1795	2,224,321.83	3,228
1796	1,585,086.93	2,108
1797	1,080,420.78	1,247
1798	1,061,315.79	950
1799	1,019,449.19	1,069
1800	2,970,559.22	2,186
1801	4,176,301.01	2,866
1802	4,353,652.96	3,052
1803	3,934,689.85	2,168
1804	4,194,508.92	2,190
1805	2,968,683.77	1,688
1806	4,381,071.57	2,303
1807	6,453,146.54	2,311
1808	8,933,783.61	1,904
1809	6,065,009.24	2,191
1810–1819	49,503,929.71	9,915
1820–1834	3,316,642.50	1,345
TOTALS	$128,218,023.84	60,240

Velocity rises when there are money substitutes, highly liquid assets that allow economic agents to earn interest. Apparently Hamilton was right—the national debt answered most of the purposes of money. Ergo, not as much M1 was needed to support the gross domestic product (GDP) and price level, so velocity rose during the period that the debt was large. It then dropped as the government paid off the debt, requiring the use of more M1.

Key Takeaways

- Money demand was indeed somewhat sensitive to interest rates but velocity, while not constant, was predictable, making the link between money and prices that Friedman predicted a close one.
- Friedman's reformulation of the quantity theory held up well only until the 1970s, when it cracked asunder because money demand became more sensitive to interest rate changes, thus causing velocity to vacillate unpredictably and breaking the close link between the quantity of money and output and inflation.

20.4 Suggested Reading

Friedman, Milton. *Money Mischief: Episodes in Monetary History*. New York: Harvest, 1994.

Friedman, Milton, and Anna Jacobson. *A Monetary History of the United States, 1867–1960*. Princeton, NJ: Princeton University Press, 1971.

Kindleberger, Charles. *Keynesianism vs. Monetarism and Other Essays in Financial History*. London: George Allen & Unwin, 1985.

Minsky, Hyman. *John Maynard Keynes*. New York: McGraw-Hill, 2008.

Serletis, Apostolos. *The Demand for Money: Theoretical and Empirical Approaches*. New York: Springer, 2007.

Endnotes

1. pages.stern.nyu.edu/~wbaumol
2. nobelprize.org/nobel_prizes/economics/laureates/1981/tobin-autobio.html

CHAPTER 21

IS-LM

Chapter Objectives

By the end of this chapter, students should be able to:

1. Explain this equation: $Y = Y_{ad} = C + I + G + NX$.
2. Provide the equation for C and explain its importance.
3. Describe the Keynesian cross diagram and explain its use.
4. Describe the investment-savings (IS) curve and its characteristics.
5. Describe the liquidity preference–money (LM) curve and its characteristics.
6. Explain why equilibrium is achieved in the markets for goods and money.
7. Explain the IS-LM model's biggest drawback.

21.1 Aggregate Output and Keynesian Cross Diagrams

Learning Objectives

1. What does this equation mean: $Y = Y_{ad} = C + I + G + NX$?
2. Why is this equation important?
3. What is the equation for C and why is it important?
4. What is the Keynesian cross diagram and what does it help us to do?

Developed in 1937 by economist and Keynes disciple John Hicks, the IS-LM model is still used today to model aggregate output (gross domestic product [GDP], gross national product [GNP], etc.) and interest rates in the short run.[1] It begins with John Maynard Keynes's recognition that

$$Y = Y_{ad} = C + I + G + NX$$

where:

Y = aggregate output (supplied)

Y_{ad} = aggregate demand

C = consumer expenditure

I = investment (on new physical capital like computers and factories, and planned inventory)

G = government spending

NX = net exports (exports minus imports)

Keynes further explained that $C = a + (mpc \times Y_d)$

where:

Y_d = disposable income, all that income above a

a = autonomous consumer expenditure (food, clothing, shelter, and other necessaries)

mpc = marginal propensity to consume (change in consumer expenditure from an extra dollar of income or "disposable income;" it is a constant bounded by 0 and 1)

Practice calculating C in Exercise 1.

Exercise

1. Calculate consumer expenditure using the formula $C = a + (mpc \times Y_d)$.

Autonomous Consumer Expenditure	Marginal Propensity to Consume	Disposable Income	Answer: C
200	0.5	0	200
400	0.5	0	400
200	0.5	200	300
200	0.5	300	350
300	0.5	300	450
300	0.75	300	525
300	0.25	300	375
300	0.01	300	303
300	1	300	600
100	0.5	1000	600
100	0.75	1000	850

consumption function

A mathematical equation thought to express the level of consumer spending.

You can plot a **consumption function** *by drawing a graph,* as in Figure 21.1, *with consumer expenditure on the vertical axis and disposable income on the horizontal.* (Autonomous consumer expenditure a will be the intercept and mpc × Y_d will be the slope.)

FIGURE 21.1 A consumption function

Of course a can be higher or lower and the slope of the line can vary.

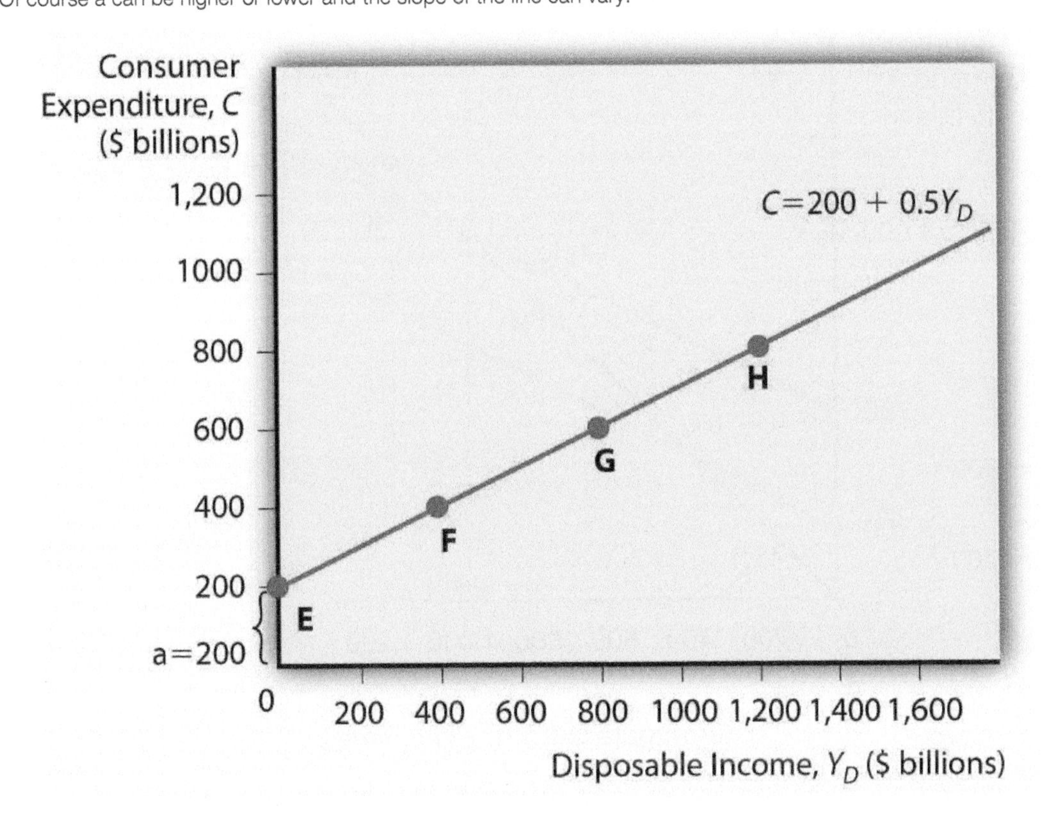

We can go further by adding I, or Investment, which is composed of so-called fixed investment on equipment and structures and planned inventory investment in raw materials, parts, or finished goods. For the present, we will ignore G and NX and, following Keynes, changes in the price level. (Remember, we are talking about the short term here. Remember, too, that Keynes wrote in the context of the gold standard, not an inflationary free floating regime, so he was not concerned with price level changes.) *The simple model that results, called a Keynesian cross diagram, looks like the diagram in*Figure 21.2.

FIGURE 21.2 A Keynesian cross diagram
So Y* = where C + I crosses the 45 degree line.

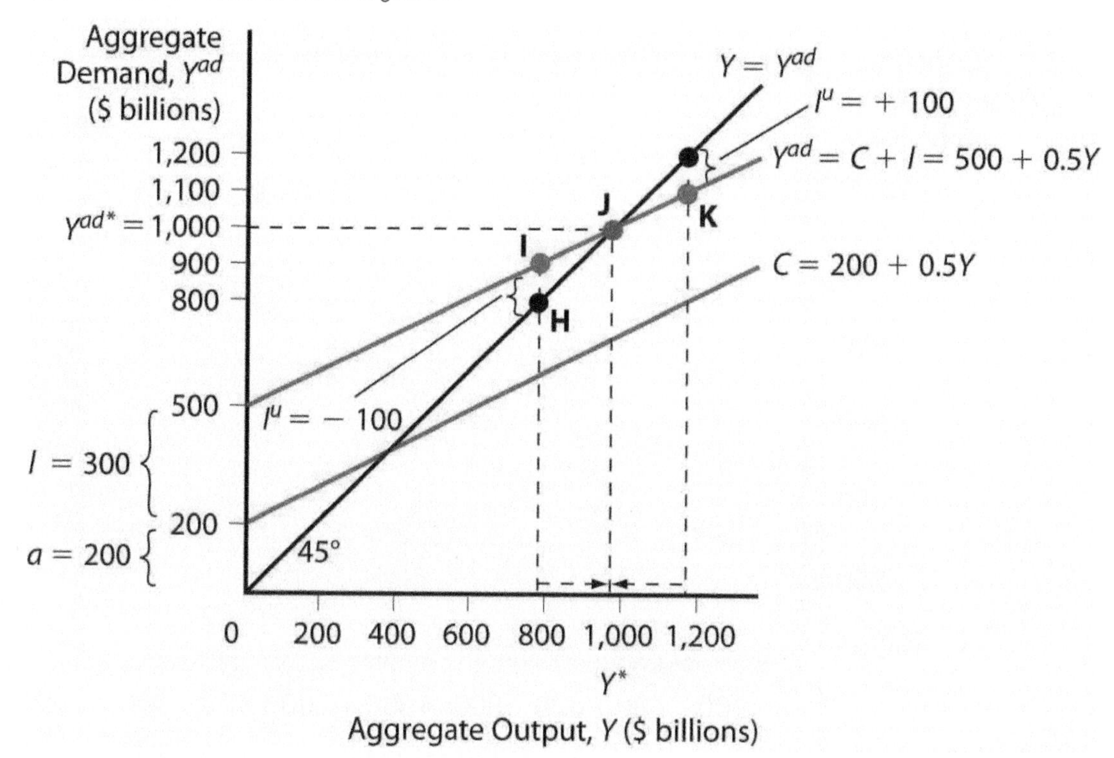

The 45-degree line simply represents the equilibrium Y = Y_{ad}. *The other line, the aggregate demand function, is the consumption function line plus planned investment spending I.* Equilibrium is reached via inventories (part of I). If Y > Y_{ad}, inventory levels will be higher than firms want, so they'll cut production. If Y < Y_{ad}, inventories will shrink below desired levels and firms will increase production. We can now predict changes in aggregate output given changes in the level of I and C and the marginal propensity to consume (the slope of the C component of Y_{ad}).

Suppose I increases. Due to the upward slope of Y_{ad}, aggregate output will increase more than the increase in I. *This is called the expenditure multiplier and it is summed up by the following equation:*

$$Y = (a + I) \times 1 / (1 - mpc)$$

So if *a* is 200 billion, *I* is 400 billion, and *mpc* is .5, *Y* will be

$$Y = 600 \times 1/.5 = 600 \times 2 = 1{,}200\text{USD billion}$$

If I increases to $600 billion, Y = 800 × 2 = $1,600 billion.

If the marginal propensity to consume were to increase to .75, Y would increase to

Y = 800 × 1/.25 = 800 × 4 = $3,200 billion because Y_{ad} would have a much steeper slope. A decline in mpc to .25, by contrast, would flatten Y_{ad} and lead to a lower equilibrium:

$$Y = 800 \times 1/.75 = 800 \times 1.333 = 1{,}066.67\text{USD billion}$$

Practice calculating aggregate output in Exercise 2.

Exercise

1. Calculate aggregate output with the formula: Y = (a + I) × 1/(1 - mpc)

Autonomous Spending	Marginal Propensity to Consume	Investment	Answer: Aggregate Output
200	0.5	500	1400
300	0.5	500	1600
400	0.5	500	1800
500	0.5	500	2000
500	0.6	500	2500
200	0.7	500	2333.33
200	0.8	500	3500
200	0.4	500	1166.67
200	0.3	500	1000
200	0.5	600	1600
200	0.5	700	1800
200	0.5	800	2000
200	0.5	400	1200
200	0.5	300	1000
200	0.5	200	800

Stop and Think Box

During the Great Depression, investment (I) fell from \$232 billion to \$38 billion (in 2000 USD). What happened to aggregate output? How do you know?

Aggregate output fell by more than \$232 billion − \$38 billion = \$194 billion. We know that because investment fell and the marginal propensity to consume was > 0, so the fall was more than \$194 billion, as expressed by the equation $Y = (a + I) \times 1/(1 - mpc)$.

To make the model more realistic, we can easily add NX to the equation. An increase in exports over imports will increase aggregate output Y by the increase in NX times the expenditure multiplier. Likewise, an increase in imports over exports (a decrease in NX) will decrease Y by the decrease in NX times the multiplier.

Government spending (G) also increases Y. We must realize, however, that some government spending comes from taxes, which consumers view as a reduction in income. With taxation, the consumption function becomes the following:

$$C = a + mpc \times (Y_d - T)$$

T means taxes. The effect of G is always larger than that of T because G expands by the multiplier, which is always > 1, while T is multiplied by MPC, which never exceeds 1. So increasing G, even if it is totally funded by T, will increase Y. (Remember, this is a short-run analysis.) *Nevertheless, Keynes argued that, to help a country out of recession, government should cut taxes because that will cause Y_d to rise, ceteris paribus. Or, in more extreme cases, it should borrow and spend (rather than tax and spend) so that it can increase G without increasing T and thus decreasing C.*

Stop and Think Box

Many governments, including that of the United States, responded to the Great Depression by increasing tariffs in what was called a beggar-thy-neighbor policy. Today we know that such policies beggared everyone. What were policymakers thinking?

They were thinking that tariffs would decrease imports and thereby increase NX (exports minus imports) and Y. That would make their trading partner's NX decrease, thus beggaring them by decreasing their Y. It was a simple idea on paper, but in reality it was dead wrong. For starters, other countries retaliated with tariffs of their own. But even if they did not, it was a losing strategy because by making neighbors (trading partners) poorer, the policy limited their ability to import (i.e., decreased the first country's exports) and thus led to no significant long-term change in NX.

Figure 21.3 *sums up the discussion of aggregate demand.*

FIGURE 21.3 The determinants of aggregate demand
See why people hate more T and bigger imports?

Variable	Change in Variable	Change in Y
a	Up	Up
I	Up	Up
NX	Up	Up
G	Up	Up
T	Up	Down
Imports	Up	Down
Exports	Up	Up
mpc	Up	Up

Key Takeaways

- The equation $Y = Y_{ad} = C + I + G + NX$ tells us that aggregate output (or aggregate income) is equal to aggregate demand, which in turn is equal to consumer expenditure plus investment (planned, physical stuff) plus government spending plus net exports (exports – imports).
- It is important because it allows economists to model aggregate output (to discern why, for example, GDP changes).
- In a taxless Eden, like the Gulf Cooperation Council countries, consumer expenditure equals autonomous consumer expenditure (spending on necessaries) (a) plus the marginal propensity to consume (mpc) times disposable income (Y_d), income above a.
- In the rest of the world, $C = a + mpc \times (Y_d - T)$, where T = taxes.

- C, particularly the marginal propensity to consume variable, is important because it gives the aggregate demand curve in a Keynesian cross diagram its upward slope.
- A Keynesian cross diagram is a graph with aggregate demand (Y_{ad}) on the vertical axis and aggregate output (Y) on the horizontal.
- It consists of a 45-degree line where $Y = Y_{ad}$ and a Y_{ad} curve, which plots C + I + G + NX with the slope given by the expenditure multiplier, which is the reciprocal of 1 minus the marginal propensity to consume: $Y = (a + I + NX + G) \times 1/(1 - mpc)$.
- The diagram helps us to see that aggregate output is directly related to a, I, exports, G, and mpc, and indirectly related to T and imports.

21.2 The IS-LM Model

Learning Objectives

1. What are the IS and LM curves?
2. What are their characteristics?
3. What do we learn when we combine the IS and the LM curves on one graph?
4. Why is equilibrium achieved?
5. What is the IS-LM model's biggest drawback?

The Keynesian cross diagram framework is great, as far as it goes. Note that it has nothing to say about interest rates or money, a major shortcoming for us students of money, banking, and monetary policy! It does, however, help us to build a more powerful model that examines equilibrium in the markets for goods and money, the IS (investment-savings) and the LM (liquidity preference–money) curves, respectively (hence the name of the model).

Interest rates are negatively related to I and to NX. The reasoning here is straightforward. When interest rates (*i*) are high, companies would rather invest in bonds than in physical plant (because fewer projects are positive net present value or **+NPV**) or inventory (because it has a high opportunity cost), so I (investment) is low. When rates are low, new physical plant and inventories look cheap and many more projects are +NPV (*i* has come down in the denominator of the present value formula), so I is high. Similarly, when *i* is low the domestic currency will be weak, all else equal. Exports will be facilitated and imports will decline because foreign goods will look expensive. Thus, NX will be high (exports > imports). When *i* is high, by contrast, the domestic currency will be in demand and hence strong. That will hurt exports and increase imports, so NX will drop and perhaps become negative (exports < imports).

+NPV

See *positive net present value*.

Now think of Y_{ad} on a Keynesian cross diagram. As we saw above, aggregate output will rise as I and NX do. So we know that as *i* increases, Y_{ad} decreases, ceteris paribus. *Plotting the interest rate on the vertical axis against aggregate output on the horizontal axis, as below, gives us a downward sloping curve. That's the IS curve!* For each interest rate, it tells us at what point the market for goods (I and NX, get it?) is in equilibrium—holding autonomous consumption, fiscal policy, and other determinants of aggregate demand constant. For all points to the right of the curve, there is an excess supply of goods for that interest rate, which causes firms to decrease inventories, leading to a fall in output toward the curve. For all points to the left of the IS curve, an excess demand for goods persists, which induces firms to increase inventories, leading to increased output toward the curve.

Obviously, the IS curve alone is as insufficient to determine *i* or Y as demand alone is to determine prices or quantities in the standard supply and demand microeconomic price model. We need another curve, one that slopes the other way, which is to say, upward. *That curve is called the LM curve and it represents equilibrium points in the market for money.* The demand for money is positively related to income because more income means more transactions and because more income means more assets, and money is one of those assets. So we can immediately plot an upward sloping LM curve, a curve that holds the money supply constant. To the left of the LM curve there is an excess supply of money given the interest rate and the amount of output. That'll cause people to use their money to buy bonds, thus driving bond prices up, and hence *i* down to the LM curve. To the right of the LM curve, there is an excess demand for money, inducing people to sell bonds for cash, which drives bond prices down and hence *i* up to the LM curve.

FIGURE 21.4 IS-LM diagram: equilibrium in the markets for money and goods
The IS-LM model has nothing to do with Islam per se.

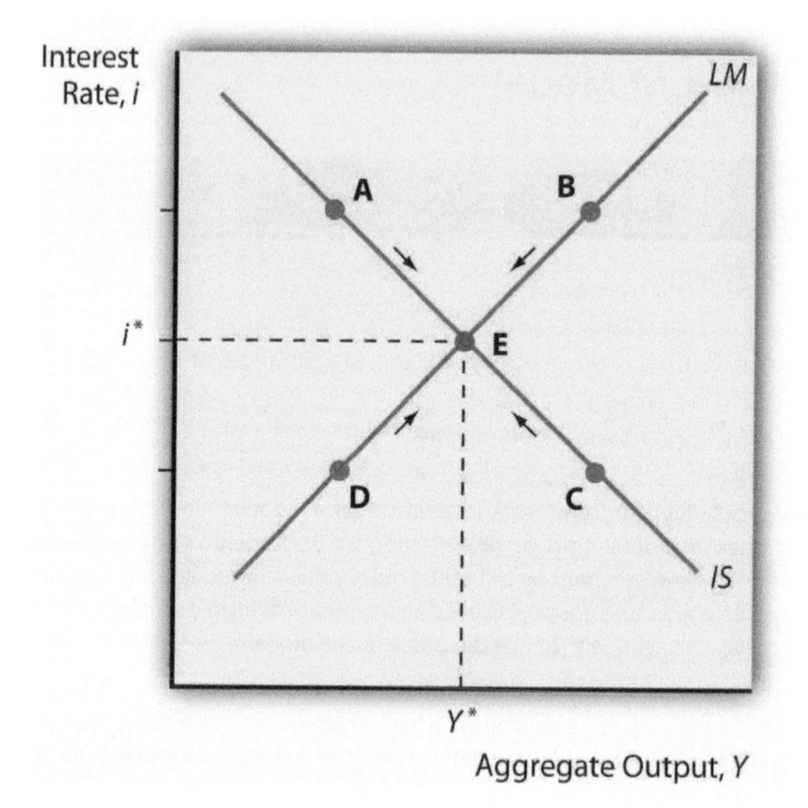

*When we put the IS and LM curves on the graph at the same time, as in*Figure 21.4, *we immediately see that there is only one point, their intersection, where the markets for both goods and money are in equilibrium.* Both the interest rate and aggregate output are determined by that intersection. We can then shift the IS and LM curves around to see how they affect interest rates and output, i* and Y*. In the next chapter, we'll see how policymakers manipulate those curves to increase output. *But we still won't be done because, as mentioned above, the IS-LM model has one major drawback: it works only in the short term or when the price level is otherwise fixed.*

Stop and Think Box

Does Figure 21.5 make sense? Why or why not? What does Figure 21.6 mean? Why is Figure 21.7 not a good representation of G?

FIGURE 21.5 Real Gross Private Domestic Investment (GPDICA), 1929–2017
What happens to I during recessions?

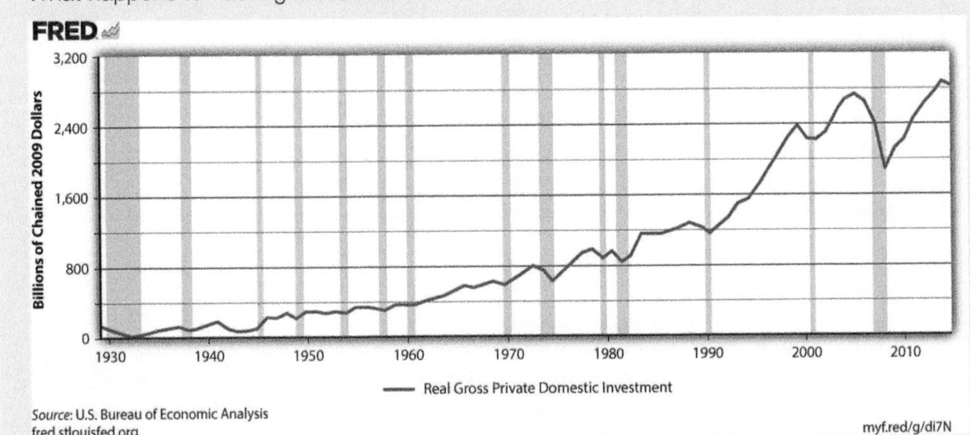

Source: U.S. Department of Commerce, Bureau of Economic Analysis

FIGURE 21.6 Net Export of Goods and Services (NETEXP), 1947–2017
What happens to NX during recessions?

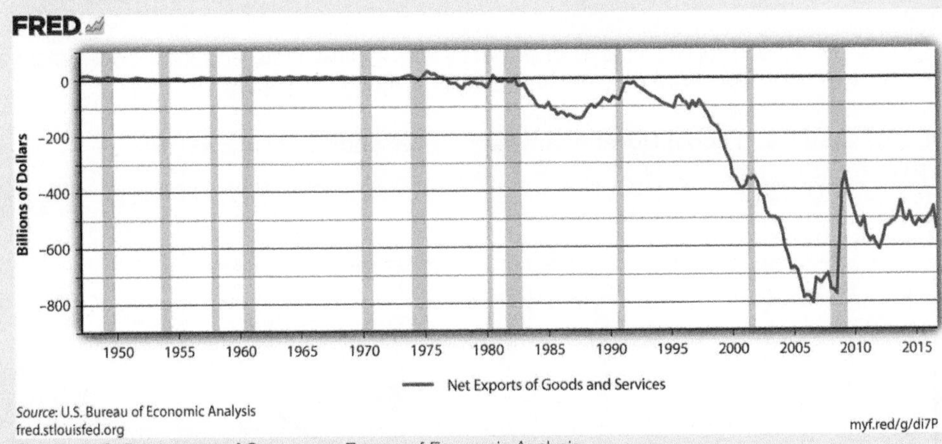

Source: U.S. Department of Commerce, Bureua of Economic Analysis

FIGURE 21.7 Federal Government Current Expenditures (FGEXPND), 1947–2017

Is this all of G?

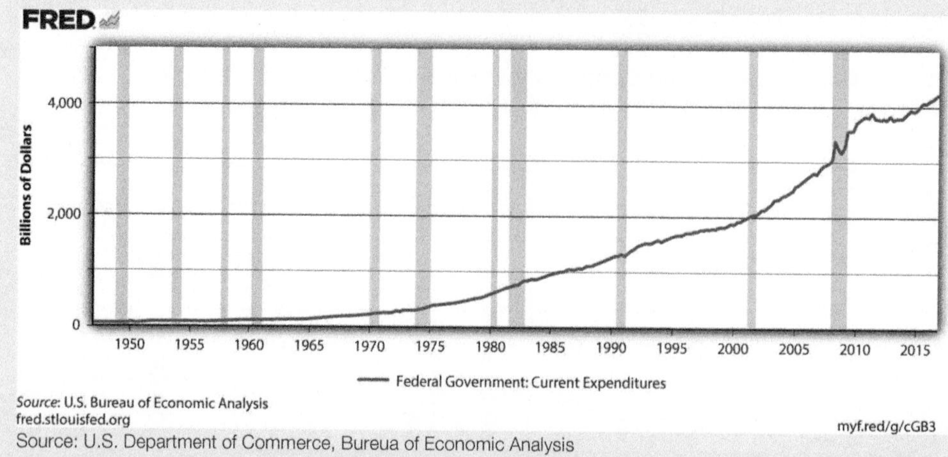

Source: U.S. Department of Commerce, Bureua of Economic Analysis

Figure 21.5 makes perfectly good sense because it depicts I in the equation $Y = Y_{ad} = C + I + G + NX$, and the shaded areas represent recessions, that is, decreases in Y. Note that before almost every recession in the twentieth century, I dropped.

Figure 21.6 means that NX in the United States is considerably negative, that exports < imports by a large margin, creating a significant drain on Y (GDP). Note that NX improved (became less negative) during the crisis and resulting recession but dipped downward again during the 2010 recovery.

Figure 21.7 is not a good representation of G because it ignores state and local government expenditures, which are significant in the United States, as Figure 21.8 shows.

FIGURE 21.8 States and Local Government Current Expenditures (SLEXPND), 1947–2017

Yet more G, and where is T?

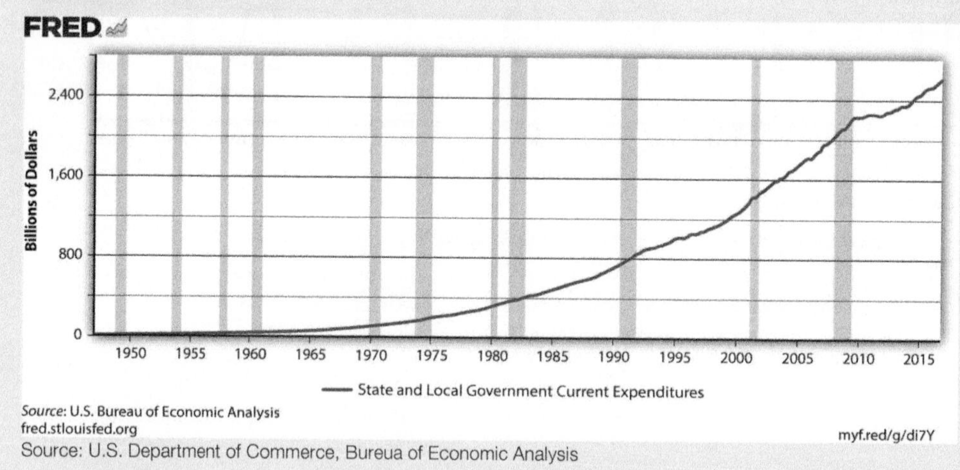

Source: U.S. Department of Commerce, Bureua of Economic Analysis

Key Takeaways

- The IS curve shows the points at which the quantity of goods supplied equals those demanded.
- On a graph with interest (i) on the vertical axis and aggregate output (Y) on the horizontal axis, the IS curve slopes downward because, as the interest rate increases, key components

of Y, I and NX, decrease. That is because as *i* increases, the opportunity cost of holding inventory increases, so inventory levels fall and +NPV projects involving a new physical plant become rarer, and I decreases.

- Also, high *i* means a strong domestic currency, all else constant, which is bad news for exports and good news for imports, which means NX also falls.
- The LM curve traces the equilibrium points for different interest rates where the quantity of money demanded equals the quantity of money supplied.
- It slopes upward because as Y increases, people want to hold more money, thus driving *i* up.
- The intersection of the IS and LM curves indicates the macroeconomy's equilibrium interest rate (i*) and output (Y*), the point where the market for goods and the market for money are both in equilibrium.
- At all points to the left of the LM curve, an excess supply of money exists, inducing people to give up money for bonds (to buy bonds), thus driving bond prices up and interest rates down toward equilibrium.
- At all points to the right of the LM curve, an excess demand for money exists, inducing people to give up bonds for money (to sell bonds), thus driving bond prices down and interest rates up toward equilibrium.
- At all points to the left of the IS curve, there is an excess demand for goods, causing inventory levels to fall and inducing companies to increase production, thus leading to an increase in output.
- At all points to the right of the IS curve, there is an excess supply of goods, creating an inventory glut that induces firms to cut back on production, thus decreasing Y toward the equilibrium.
- The IS-LM model's biggest drawback is that it doesn't consider changes in the price level, so in most modern situations, it's applicable in the short run only.

21.3 Suggested Reading

De Vroey, Michael and Kevin D. Hoover. *The IS-LM Model: Its Rise, Fall, and Strange Persistence.* Raleigh, NC: Duke University Press, 2005.

Young, Warren, and Ben-Zion Zilbefarb, eds. *IS-LM and Modern Macroeconomics.* New York: Springer, 2001.

Endnotes

1. en.wikipedia.org/wiki/John_Hicks

CHAPTER 22

IS-LM in Action

Chapter Objectives

By the end of this chapter, students should be able to:

1. Explain what causes the liquidity preference–money (LM) curve to shift and why.
2. Explain what causes the investment-savings (IS) curve to shift and why.
3. Explain the difference between monetary and fiscal stimulus in the short term and why the difference is important.
4. Explain what happens when the IS-LM model is used to tackle the long term by taking changes in the price level into account.
5. Describe the aggregate demand curve and explain what causes it to shift.

22.1 Shifting Curves: Causes and Effects

Learning Objective

1. What causes the LM and IS curves to shift and why?

*Policymakers can use the IS-LM model developed in*Chapter 21 *to help them decide between two major types of policy responses, fiscal (i.e., government expenditure and tax) or monetary (i.e., interest rates or money supply)*. As you probably noticed when playing around with the IS and LM curves at the end of the previous chapter, their relative positions matter quite a bit for interest rates and aggregate output. Time to investigate this matter further.

The LM curve, the equilibrium points in the market for money, shifts for two reasons: changes in money demand and changes in the money supply. *If the money supply increases (decreases), ceteris paribus, the interest rate is lower (higher) at each level of Y, or in other words, the LM curve shifts right (left)*. That is because at any given level of output Y, more money (less money) means a lower (higher) interest rate. (Remember, the price level doesn't change in this model.) To see this, look at Figure 22.1.

FIGURE 22.1 Effect of money on interest rates when output is constant

Mo' money means a lower interest rate, ceteris paribus.

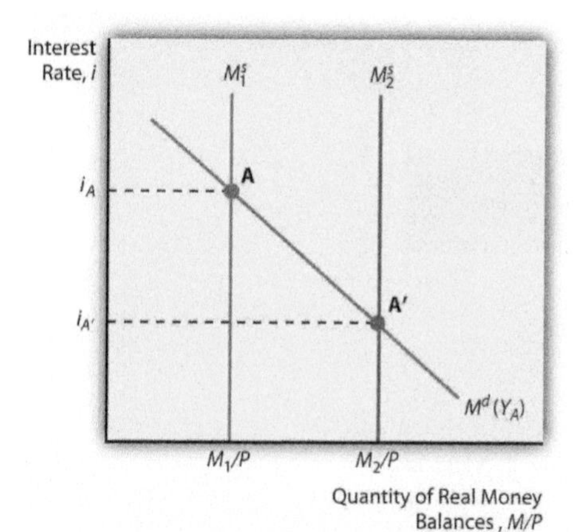

Effect on the market for money when aggregate output is constant at Y_A

FIGURE 22.2 Effect of an autonomous change in money demand when output is constant

More demand for money means a higher interest rate, ceteris paribus.

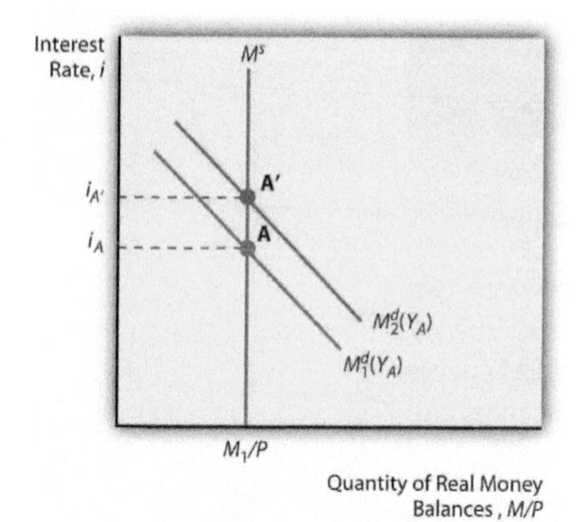

Effect on the market for money when aggregate output is constant at Y_A

An autonomous change in money demand (that is, a change not related to the price level, aggregate output, or i) will also affect the LM curve. Say that stocks get riskier or the transaction costs of trading bonds increases. The theory of asset demand tells us that the demand for money will increase (shift right), thus increasing *i*. Interest rates could also decrease if money demand shifted left because stock returns increased or bonds became less risky. To see this, examine Figure 22.2. An increase in autonomous money demand will shift the LM curve left, with higher interest rates at each Y; a decrease will shift it right, with lower interest rates at each Y.

The IS curve, by contrast, shifts whenever an autonomous (unrelated to Y or i) change occurs in C, I, G, T, or NX. *Following the discussion of Keynesian cross diagrams in* Chapter 21, *when C, I, G, or NX increases (decreases), the IS curve shifts right (left). When T increases (decreases), all else constant, the IS curve shifts left (right) because taxes effectively decrease consumption.* Again, these are changes that are not related to output or interest rates, which merely indicate movements *along* the IS curve. The discovery of new caches of natural resources (which will increase I), changes in consumer preferences (at home or abroad, which will affect NX), and numerous other "shocks," positive and negative, will change output at each interest rate, or in other words shift the entire IS curve.

We can now see how government policies can affect output. As noted above, in the short run, an increase in the money supply will shift the LM curve to the right, *thereby lowering interest rates and increasing output.* Decreasing the MS would have precisely the opposite effect. *Fiscal stimulus, that is, decreasing taxes (T) or increasing government expenditures (G), will also increase output but, unlike monetary stimulus (increasing MS), will increase the interest rate.* That is because it works by shifting the IS curve upward rather than shifting the LM curve. Of course, if T increases, the IS curve will shift left, decreasing interest rates but also aggregate output. This is part of the reason why people get hot under the collar about taxes.[1] (Of course, individual considerations are paramount!)[2]

Stop and Think Box

During financial panics, economic agents complain of high interest rates and declining economic output. Use the IS-LM model to describe why panics have those effects.

The LM curve will shift left during panics, raising interest rates and decreasing output, because demand for money increases as economic agents scramble to get liquid in the face of the declining and volatile prices of other assets, particularly financial securities with positive default risk.

Figure 22.3 *summarizes.*

FIGURE 22.3 Predicted effects of changes in major macroeconomic variables
I don't know about you, but I'd memorize this for the test!

Variable	Autonomous Change	Predicted Short-Term Response	Rationale
MS	Up	Y up, i down	i down LM shifts right
M_d	Up	Y up, i up	i up LM shifts left
C	Up	Y up, i up	C up Y_{ad} up IS shifts right
I	Up	Y up, i up	I up Y_{ad} up IS shifts right
NX	Up	Y up, i up	NX up Y_{ad} up IS shifts right
G	Up	Y up, i up	G up Y_{ad} up IS shifts right
T	Up	Y down, i down	T up C down Y_{ad} down IS shifts left

Stop and Think Box

Describe Hamilton's Law (née Bagehot's Law) in terms of the IS-LM model. *Hint*: Hamilton and Bagehot argued that, during a financial panic, the lender of last resort needs to increase the money supply by lending to all comers who present what would be considered adequate collateral in normal times.

During financial panics, the LM curve shifts left as people flee risky assets for money, thereby inducing the interest rate to climb and output to fall. Hamilton and Bagehot argued that monetary authorities should respond by nipping the problem in the bud, so to speak, by increasing MS directly, shifting the LM curve back to somewhere near its pre-panic position.

Key Takeaways

- The LM curve shifts right (left) when the money supply (real money balances) increases (decreases).
- It also shifts left (right) when money demand increases (decreases).
- The easiest way to see this is to first imagine a graph where money demand is fixed and the money supply increases (shifts right), leading to a lower interest rate, and vice versa.
- Then imagine a fixed MS and a shift upward in money demand, leading to a higher interest rate, and vice versa.
- The IS curve shifts right (left) when C, I, G, or NX increase (decrease) or T decreases (increases).
- This relates directly to the Keynesian cross diagrams and the equation Y = C + I + G + NX discussed in Chapter 21, and also to the analysis of taxes as a decrease in consumption expenditure C.

22.2 Implications for Monetary Policy

Learning Objectives

1. In the short term, what is the difference between monetary and fiscal stimulus and why is it important?
2. What happens when the IS-LM model is used to tackle the long term by taking changes in the price level into account?

The IS-LM model has a major implication for monetary policy: when the IS curve is unstable, a money supply target will lead to greater output stability, and when the LM curve is unstable, an interest rate target will produce greater macro stability. To see this, look at Figure 22.4 and Figure 22.5. Note that when LM is fixed and IS moves left and right, an interest rate target will cause Y to vary more than a money supply target will. Note too that when IS is stable and LM moves left and right, an interest rate target keeps Y stable but a money supply target (shifts in the LM curve) will cause Y to swing wildly. This helps to explain why many central banks abandoned money supply targeting in favor of interest rate targeting in the 1970s and 1980s, a period when autonomous shocks to LM were pervasive due to financial innovation, deregulation, and loophole mining. An important implication of this is that central banks might find it prudent to shift back to targeting monetary aggregates if the IS curve ever again becomes more unstable than the LM curve.

FIGURE 22.4 Effect of IS curve instability

If the IS curve is unstable, a money supply target will lead to less variation in output Y than interest rate target will.

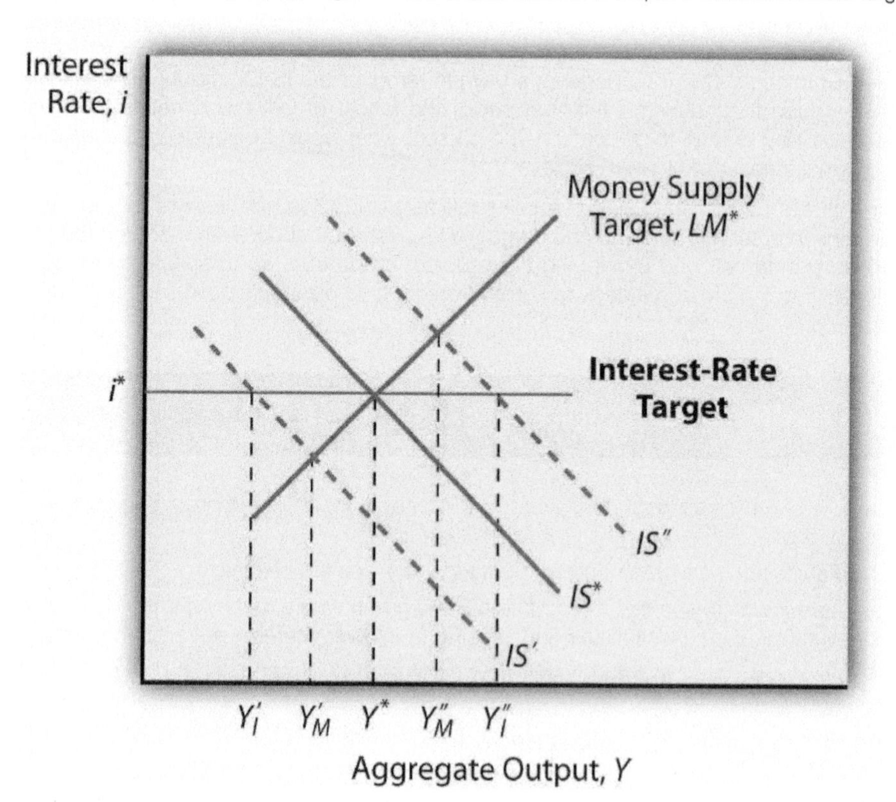

FIGURE 22.5 Effect of LM curve instability
If the IS curve is stable, an interest rate target will provide more stability in Y than a money supply target will.

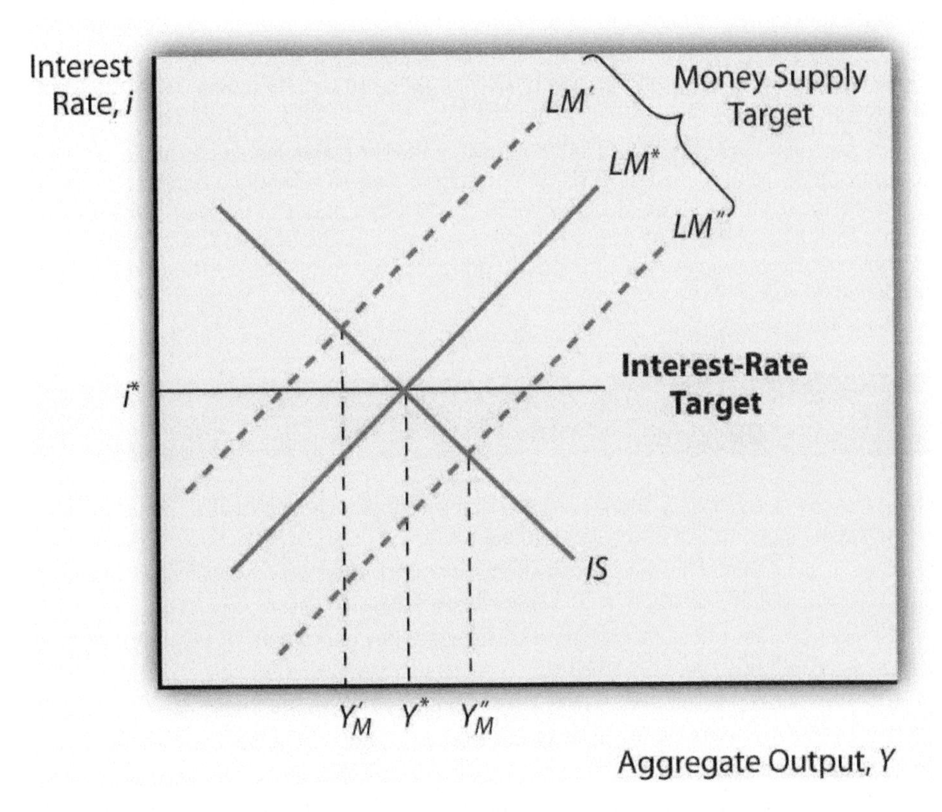

*As noted in*Chapter 21*, the policy power of the IS-LM is severely limited by its short-run assumption that the price level doesn't change. Attempts to tweak the IS-LM model to accommodate price level changes led to the creation of an entirely new model called Aggregate Demand and Supply.* The key is the addition of a new concept, called the **natural rate level of output**, Y_{nrl}, the rate of output at which the price level is stable in the long run. When actual output (Y*) is below the natural rate, prices will fall; when it is above the natural rate, prices will rise.

natural rate level of output
The rate of output at which the price level has no tendency to rise or fall.

The IS curve is stated in real terms because it represents equilibrium in the goods market, the real part of the economy. Changes in the price level therefore do not affect C, I, G, T, or NX or the IS curve. *The LM curve, however, is affected by changes in the price level, shifting to the left when prices rise and to the right when they fall.* This is because, holding the nominal MS constant, rising prices decrease real money balances, which we know shifts the LM curve to the left.

So suppose an economy is in equilibrium at Y_{nrl}, when some monetary stimulus in the form of an increased MS shifts the LM curve to the right. As noted above, in the short term, interest rates will come down and output will increase. But because Y* is greater than Y_{nrl}, prices will rise, shifting the LM curve back to where it started, give or take. *So output and the interest rate are the same but prices are higher. Economists call this long-run* ***monetary neutrality***.

monetary neutrality
The neutrality of money, or monetary neutrality, is the name given to the notion that changes in the money supply affect only nominal variables, like prices, interest rates, and exchange rates, and not real variables like real GDP.

Fiscal stimulus, as we saw above, shifts the IS curve to the right, increasing output but also the interest rate. Because Y* is greater than Y_{nrl}, prices will rise and the LM curve will shift left, reducing output, increasing the interest rate higher still, and raising the price level! *You just can't win in the long run, in the sense that policymakers cannot make Y* exceed* Y_{nrl}. Rendering policymakers impotent did not win the IS-LM model many friends, so researchers began to develop a new model that relates the price level to aggregate output.

Stop and Think Box

Under the gold standard (GS), money flows in and out of countries automatically, in response to changes in the price of international bills of exchange. From the standpoint of the IS-LM model, what is the problem with that aspect of the GS?

As noted, decreases in MS lead to a leftward shift of the LM curve, leading to higher interest rates and lower output. Higher interest rates, in turn, could lead to a financial panic or a decrease in C or I, causing a shift left in the IS curve, further reducing output but relieving some of the pressure on i. (Note that NX would not be affected under the GS because the exchange rate was fixed, moving only within very tight bands, so a higher *i* would not cause the domestic currency to strengthen.)

Key Takeaways

- Monetary stimulus, that is, increasing the money supply, causes the LM curve to shift right, resulting in higher output and lower interest rates.
- Fiscal stimulus, that is, increasing government spending and/or decreasing taxes, shifts the IS curve to the right, raising interest rates while increasing output.
- The higher interest rates are problematic because they can crowd out C, I, and NX, moving the IS curve left and reducing output.
- The IS-LM model predicts that, in the long run, policymakers are impotent.
- Policymakers can raise the price level but they can't get Y* permanently above Y_{nrl} or the natural rate level of output.
- That is because whenever Y* exceeds Y_{nrl}, prices rise, shifting the LM curve to the left by reducing real money balances (which happens when there is a higher price level coupled with an unchanged MS).
- That, in turn, eradicates any gains from monetary or fiscal stimulus.

22.3 Aggregate Demand Curve

Learning Objective

1. What is the aggregate demand (AD) curve and what causes it to shift?

Imagine a fixed IS curve and an LM curve shifting hard left due to increases in the price level, as in Figure 22.6. *As prices increase, Y falls and i rises.* Now plot that outcome on a new graph, where aggregate output Y remains on the horizontal axis but the vertical axis is replaced by the price level P. *The resulting curve, called the aggregate demand (AD) curve, will slope downward, as below. The AD curve is a very powerful tool because it indicates the points at which equilibrium is achieved in the markets for goods* and *money at a given price level.* It slopes downward because a high price level, ceteris paribus, means a small real money supply, high interest rates, and a low level of output, while a low price level, all else constant, is consistent with a larger real money supply, low interest rates, and kickin' output.

FIGURE 22.6 Deriving the aggregate demand curve
So IS + LM = AD.

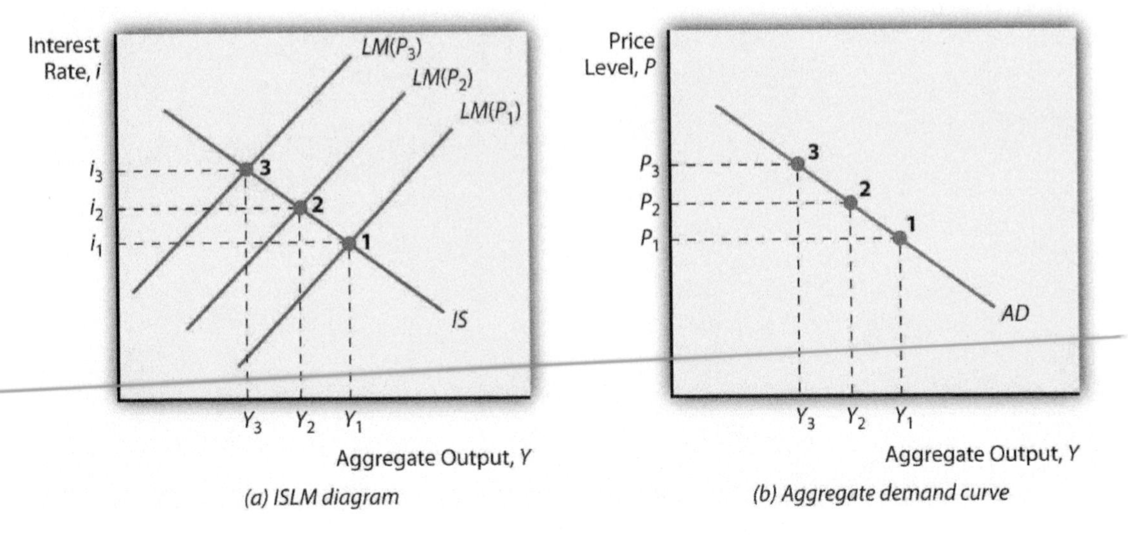

Because the AD curve is essentially just another way of stating the IS-LM model, anything that would change the IS or LM curves will also shift the AD curve. More specifically, *the AD curve shifts in the same direction as the IS curve*, so it shifts right (left) with autonomous increases (decreases) in C, I, G, and NX and decreases (increases) in T. *The AD curve also shifts in the same direction as the LM curve*. So if MS increases (decreases), it shifts right (left), and if M_d increases (decreases) it shifts left (right), as in Figure 22.3.

Key Takeaways

- The aggregate demand curve is a downward sloping curve plotted on a graph with Y on the horizontal axis and the price level on the vertical axis.
- The AD curve represents IS-LM equilibrium points, that is, equilibrium in the market for both goods and money.
- It slopes downward because, as the price level increases, the LM curve shifts left as real money balances fall.
- AD shifts in the same direction as the IS or LM curves, so anything that shifts those curves shifts AD in precisely the same direction and for the same reasons.

22.4 Suggested Reading

Mishkin, Frederic. *Macroeconomics: Policy and Practice* 2nd ed. New York: Palgrave Macmillan, 2014.

Rao, B. Bhaskara, ed. *Aggregate Demand and Supply: A Critique of Orthodox Macroeconomic Modelling*. New York: Palgrave Macmillan, 2014.

Endnotes

1. See, for example, www.nypost.com/p/news/opinion/opedcolumnists /soaking_the_rich_AW6hrJYHjtRd0Jgai5Fx1O
2. http://archives.politicususa.com/2011/07/01/polls-taxes-deficit.html. Note that the people supporting tax increases typically support raising other people's taxes: "The poll also found wide support for increasing taxes, as 67% said the more high earners income should be subject to being taxed for Social Security, and 66% support raising taxes on incomes over $250,000, and 62% support closing corporate tax loopholes."

CHAPTER 23

Aggregate Supply and Demand and the Growth Diamond

Chapter Objectives

By the end of this chapter, students should be able to:

1. Describe the aggregate demand (AD) curve and explain why it slopes downward.
2. Describe what shifts the AD curve and explain why.
3. Describe the short-run aggregate supply (AS) curve and explain why it slopes upward.
4. Describe what shifts the short-run AS curve and explain why.
5. Describe the long-run aggregate supply (ASL) curve, and explain why it is vertical and what shifts it.
6. Explain the term *long term* and its importance for policymakers.
7. Describe the growth diamond model of economic growth and its importance.

23.1 Aggregate Demand

Learning Objectives

1. What is the AD curve and why does it slope downward?
2. What shifts the AD curve and why?

The IS-LM model isn't entirely agreeable to policymakers because it examines only the short term, and when pressed into service for the long-term, or changes in the price level, it suggests that policy initiatives are more likely to mess matters up than to improve them. In response, economists developed a new theory, aggregate demand and supply, that relates the price level to the total final goods and services demanded (aggregate demand [AD]) and the total supplied (aggregate supply [AS]). *This new framework is attractive for several reasons: (1) it can be used to examine both the short and the long run; (2) it takes a form similar to the microeconomic price theory model of supply and demand, so it is familiar; and (3) it gives policymakers some grounds for implementing activist economic policies.* To understand aggregate demand and supply theory, we need to understand how each of the curves is derived.

The aggregate demand curve can be derived three ways, through the IS-LM model, with help from the quantity theory of money, or directly from its components. Remember that Y = C + I + G + NX. As the price level falls, ceteris paribus, real money balances are higher. That spells a lower interest rate. A lower interest rate, in turn, means an increase in I (and hence Y). A lower interest rate also means a lower exchange rate and hence more exports and fewer imports. So NX also increases. (C might be positively affected by lower *i* as well.) As the price level increases, the opposite occurs. So the AD curve slopes downward.

The quantity theory of money also shows that the AD curve should slope downward. Remember that the quantity theory ties money to prices and output via velocity, the average number of times annually a unit of currency is spent on final goods and services, in the so-called equation of exchange:

$$MV = PY$$

where

M = money supply

V = velocity of money

P = price level

Y = aggregate output

If M = $100 billion and V = 3, then PY must be $300 billion. If we set P, the price level, equal to 1, Y must equal $300 billion (300/1). If P is 2, then Y is $150 billion (300/2). If it is .5, then Y is $600 billion (300/.5). Plot those points and you get a downward sloping curve, as in Figure 23.1. The AD curve shifts right if the MS increases and left if it decreases. Continuing the example above, if we hold P constant at 1.0 but double M to $200 billion, then Y will double to $600 billion (200 × 3). (Recall that the theory suggests that V changes only slowly.) Cut M in half ($50 billion) and Y will fall by half, to $150 billion (50 × 3).

FIGURE 23.1 Aggregate demand curve
The whole AD curve shifts right.

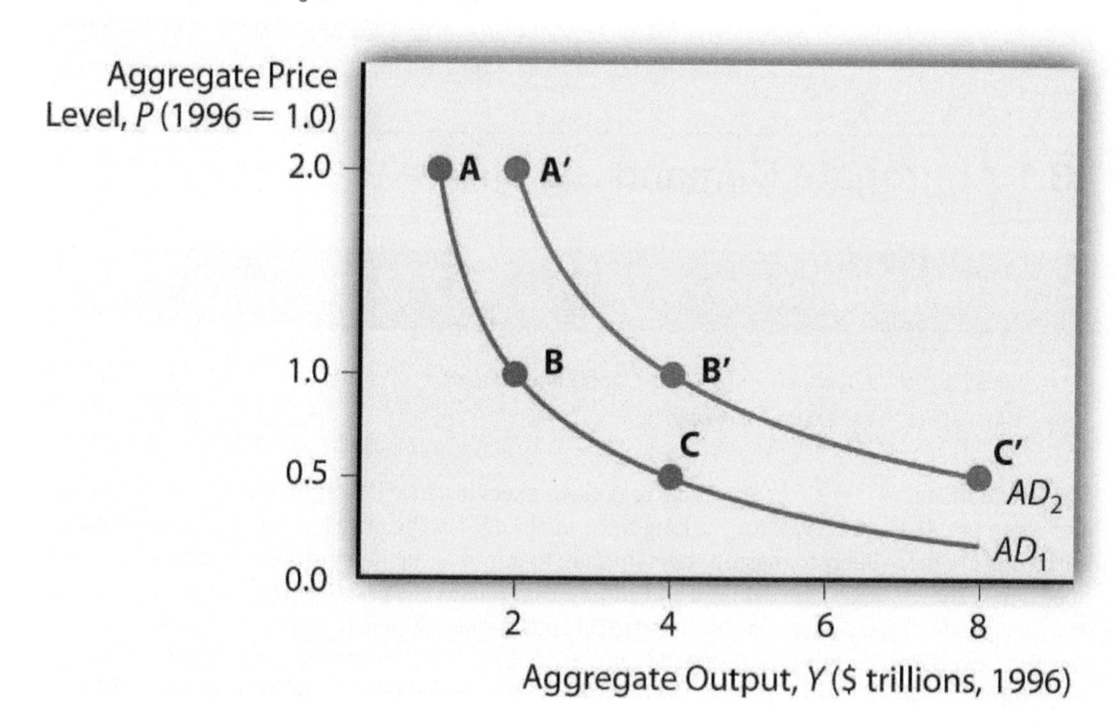

For a summary of the factors that shift the AD curve, review Figure 23.2.

FIGURE 23.2 Factors that shift the aggregate demand curve
Starting to see why T sucks?

Variable	Change in Variable	Change in AD
C	Up	Right
I	Up	Right
G	Up	Right
T	Up	Left
NX	Up	Right
MS	Up	Right

Key Takeaways

- The aggregate demand (AD) curve is the total quantity of final goods and services demanded at different price levels.
- It slopes downward because a lower price level, holding MS constant, means higher real money balances.
- Higher real money balances, in turn, mean lower interest rates, which means more investment (I) due to more +NPV projects and more net exports (NX) due to a weaker domestic currency (exports increase and imports decrease).
- The AD curve is positively related to changes in MS, C, I, G, and NX, and is negatively related to T.
- Those variables shift AD for the same reasons they shift Y_{ad} and the IS curve because all of them except taxes add to output.
- An increase in the MS increases AD (shifts the AD curve to the right) through the quantity theory of money and the equation of exchange MV = PY. Holding velocity and the price level constant, it is clear that increases in M must lead to increases in Y.

23.2 Aggregate Supply

Learning Objectives

1. What is the short-run AS curve and why does it slope upward?
2. What shifts the short-run AS curve and why?

The aggregate supply curve is a tad trickier because it is believed to change over time. In the long run, it is thought to be vertical at Y_{nrl}, the natural rate of output concept introduced earlier. In the long run, the economy can produce only so much given the state of technology, the natural rate of unemployment, and the amount of physical capital devoted to productive uses.

FIGURE 23.3 Short-run aggregate supply curve
And of course the short-run AS curve can shift left or right.

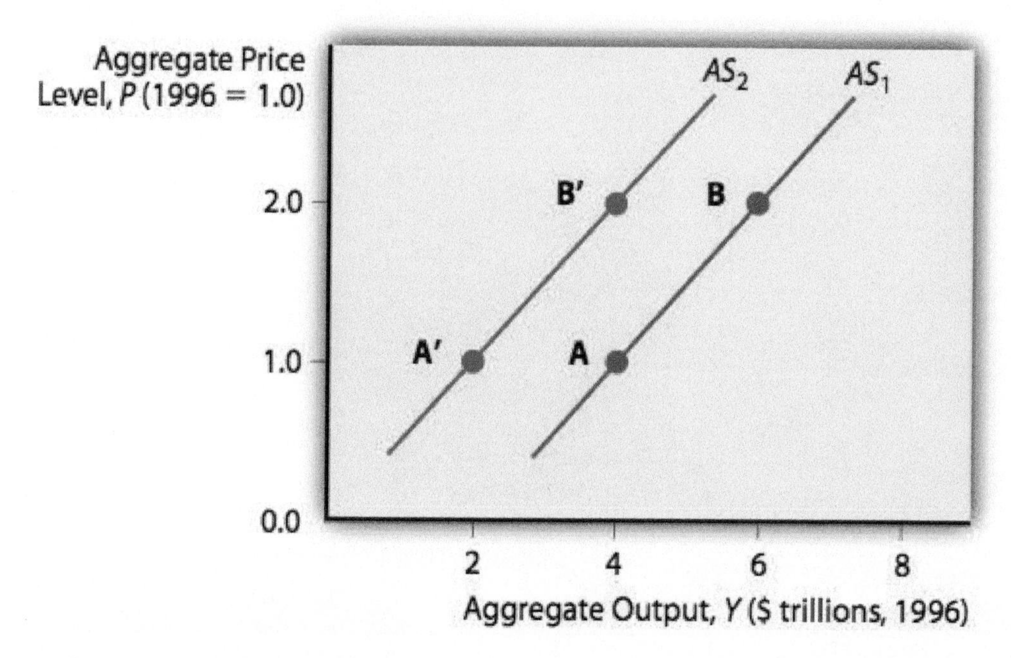

In the short run, by contrast, the total value of goods and services supplied to the economy is a function of business profits, meant here simply as the price goods bear in the market minus all the costs of their production, including wages and raw material costs. Prices of final goods and services generally adjust faster than the cost of inputs like labor and raw materials, which are often "sticky" due to long-term contracts fixing their price. *So as the price level rises, ceteris paribus, business profits are higher and hence businesses supply a higher quantity to the market. That is why the aggregate supply (AS) curve slopes upward in the short run, as in* Figure 23.3.

The short-run AS curve shifts due to changes in costs and hence profits. When the labor market is tight, the wage bill rises, cutting into profits and shifting the AS curve to the left. Any so-called wage push from any source, like unionization, will have the same effect. If economic agents expect the price level to rise, that will also shift the AS curve left because they are going to demand higher wages or higher prices for their wares. Finally, changes in technology and raw materials supplies will shift the AS curve to the right or left, depending on the nature of the shock. Improved productivity (more output from the same input) is a positive shock that moves the AS curve to the right. A shortage due to bad weather, creation of a successful producer monopoly or cartel, and the like, is a negative shock that shifts the AS curve to the left.

Also, whenever Y exceeds Y_{nrl}, the AS curve shifts left. That is because when Y exceeds Y_{nrl}, the labor market gets tighter and expectations of inflation grow. Reversing that reasoning, the AS curve shifts right whenever Y_{nrl} exceeds Y. Figure 23.4 summarizes the discussion of the short-run AS curve.

FIGURE 23.4 Factors that shift the short-run aggregate supply curve
This is a lot to chew on, but it all makes sense. Right?

Variable	Short-run AS Curve Reaction
Negative Supply Shock	Left
Positive Supply Shock	Right
Wage push	Left
Rise in expected inflation	Left
Decrease in expected inflation	Right
Tight labor market	Left
Loose labor market	Right
$Y > Y_{nrl}$	Left
$Y_{nrl} > Y$	Right

Key Takeaways

- The aggregate supply (AS) curve is the total quantity of final goods and services supplied at different price levels.
- It slopes upward because wages and other costs are sticky in the short run, so higher prices mean more profits (prices minus costs), which means a higher quantity supplied.
- The AS curve shifts left when Y* exceeds Y_{nrl}, and it shifts right when Y* is less than Y_{nrl}.
- In other words, Y_{nrl} is achieved via shifts in the AS curve, particularly through labor market "tightness" and inflation expectations.
- When Y* is > Y_{nrl}, the labor market is tight, pushing wages up and strengthening inflation expectations; when Y_{nrl} is > *Y, the labor market is loose, keeping wages low and inflation expectations weak.
- Supply shocks, both positive and negative, also shift the AS curve.
- Anything (like a so-called wage push or higher raw materials prices) that decreases business profits shifts AS to the left, while anything that increases business profits moves it to the right.

23.3 Equilibrium Analysis

Learning Objectives

1. What is the ASL curve?

2. Why is it vertical, and what shifts it?
3. How long is the long term and why is the answer important for policymakers?

Of course, this is all just a prelude to the main event: slapping these curves—AD, AS, and ASL (the long-run AS curve)—on the same graph at the same time. Let's start, as in Figure 23.5, with just the short-run AS and AD curves. Their intersection indicates both the price level P* (not to be confused with the microeconomic price theory model's p*) and Y* (again not to be confused with q*). Equilibrium is achieved because at any P > P*, there will be a glut (excess supply), so prices (of all goods and services) will fall toward P*. At any P < P*, there will be excess demand, many bidders for each automobile, sandwich, haircut, and what not, who will bid prices up to P*. We can also now examine what happens to P* and Y* in the short run by moving the curves to and fro.

FIGURE 23.5 Short-run equilibrium in the macroeconomy
Oh if only we could stop here!

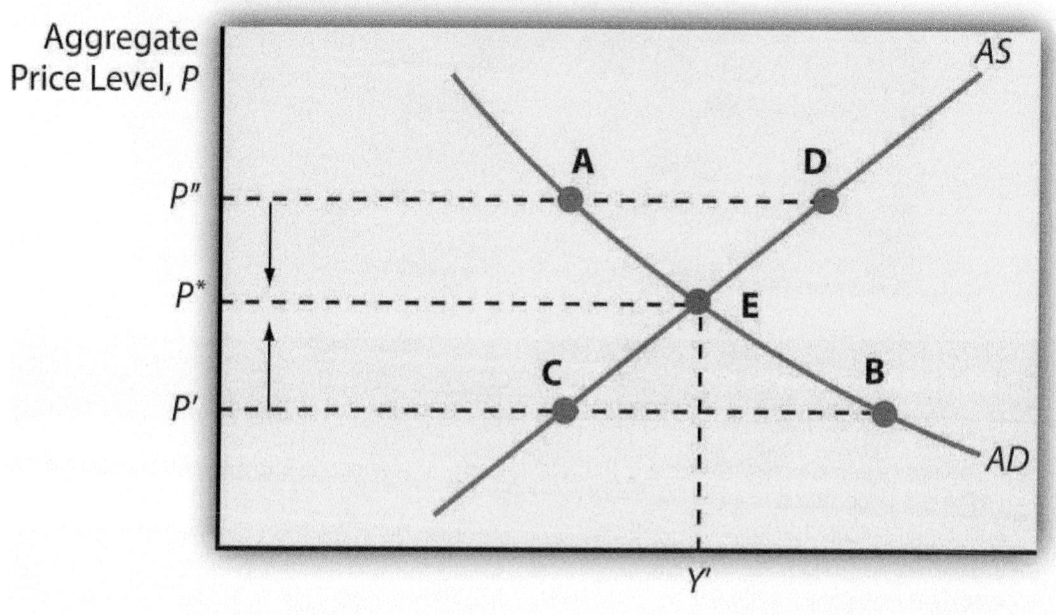

To study long-run changes in the economy, we need to add the vertical long-run aggregate supply curve (ASL) to the graph. As discussed, if Y* is > or < Y_{nrl}, the AS curve will shift (via the labor market and/or inflation expectations) until Y* = Y_{nrl}, as in Figure 23.6. So attempts to increase output above its natural rate will cause inflation and recession. Attempts to keep it below its natural rate will lead to deflation and expansion.

FIGURE 23.6 Long-run equilibrium in the macroeconomy

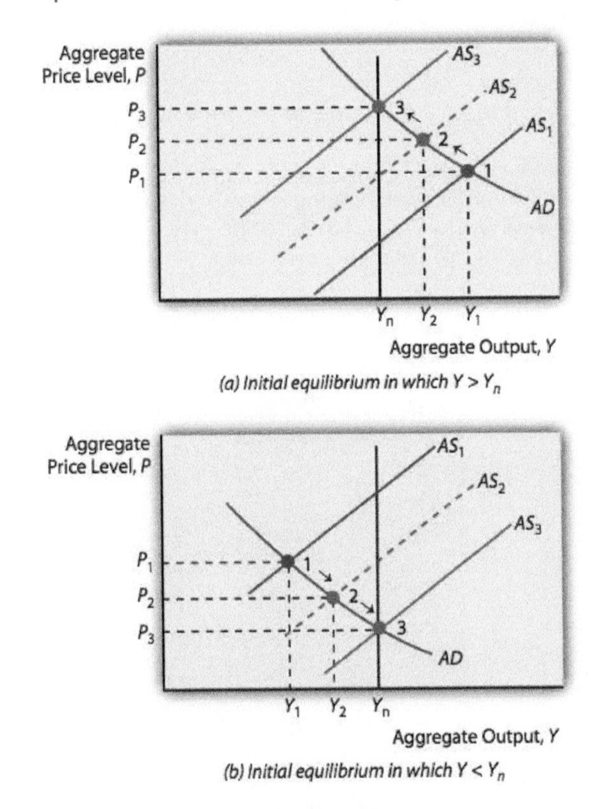

(a) Initial equilibrium in which $Y > Y_n$

(b) Initial equilibrium in which $Y < Y_n$

The so-called self-correcting mechanism described above makes many policymakers uneasy, so the most activist among them argue that the long-run analysis holds only over very long periods. In fact, the great granddaddy, intellectually speaking, of today's activist policymakers, John Maynard Keynes,[1] once remarked, "[The l]ong run is a misleading guide to current affairs. In the long run we are all dead. Economists set themselves too easy, too useless a task if in tempestuous seasons they can only tell us that when the storm is long past the ocean is flat again."[2] Other economists (non-activists, including monetarists like Milton Friedman) think that the short run is short indeed and the long run is right around the corner. Figuring out how short and long the short and long runs are is important because if the nonactivists are correct, policymakers are wasting their time trying to increase output by shifting AD to the right: the AS curve will soon shift left, leaving the economy with a higher price level but the same level of output. Similarly, policymakers need do nothing in response to a negative **supply shock** (which, as noted above, shifts AS to the left) because the AS curve will soon shift back to the right on its own, restoring both the price level and output. If the activists are right, on the other hand, policymakers can improve people's lives by shifting AD to the right to counter, say, the effects of negative supply shocks by helping the AS curve to return to its original position or beyond.

supply shock

A sudden change affecting production of goods, such as a change in technology or input (materials, labor) prices. A negative shock decreases production while a positive one increases it, ceteris paribus.

The holy grail of **economic growth** theory is to figure out how to shift Y_{nrl} to the right because, if policymakers can do that, it doesn't matter how short the long term is. Policymakers can make a difference—and for the better. The real business cycle theory of Edward Prescott suggests that real aggregate supply shocks can affect Y_{nrl}.[3] This is an active area of research, and not just because Prescott took home the Nobel Prize in 2004 for his contributions to "dynamic macroeconomics: the time consistency of economic policy and the driving forces behind business cycles."[4] Other economists believe that activist policies designed to shift AD to the right can influence Y_{nrl} through a process called hysteresis.[5] It's still all very confusing and complicated, so the author of this book and numerous others prefer bringing an institutional analysis to Y_{nrl}, one that concentrates on providing economic actors with incentives to labor, to develop and implement new technologies, and to build new plant and infrastructure.

economic growth

Real per capita GDP.

Stop and Think Box

People often believe that wars induce long-term economic growth; however, they are quite wrong. Use Figure 23.7 and the AS-AD model to explain why people think wars induce growth and why they are wrong.

FIGURE 23.7 **Inflation and output during and after two major U.S. wars, the Civil War (1861–1865) and World War I (1917–1918)**
Oh yeah, real output went up, but then it sank back.

Year	Inflation Rate	Real Per Capita GDP
1860	0	$2,296
1861	5.96	$2,277
1862	14.17	$2,497
1863	24.82	$2,624
1864	25.14	$2,592
1865	3.68	$2,606
1866	-2.53	$2,430
1867	-6.82	$2,418
1868	-3.91	$2,458
1869	-4.14	$2,473
1870	-4.24	$2,509
1914	0.94	$4,948
1915	0.52	$5,011
1916	9.24	$5,626
1917	20.49	$5,418
1918	17.47	$5,910
1919	14.87	$5,883
1920	15.84	$5,721
1921	-10.86	$5,483
1922	-6.31	$5,708

Y* often increases during wars because AD shifts right because of increases in G (tanks, guns, ships, etc.) and I (new or improved factories to produce tanks, guns, ships, etc.) that exceed decreases in C (wartime rationing) and possibly NX (trade level decreases and/or subsidies provided to or by allies). Due to the right shift in AD, P* also rises, perhaps giving the illusion of wealth. After the war, however, two things occur: AD shifts back left as war production ceases and, to the extent that the long run comes home to roost, AS shifts left. Both lower Y* and the AD leftward shift decreases the price level. Empirically, wars are indeed often followed by recessions and deflation. Figure 23.7 shows what happened to prices and output in the United States during and after the Civil War (1861–1865) and World War I (1914–1918; direct U.S. involvement, 1917–1918), respectively. The last bastion of the warmongers is the claim that, by inducing technological development, wars cause Y_{nrl} to shift right. Wars do indeed *speed* research and development, but getting a few new gizmos a few years sooner is not worth the wartime destruction of great masses of human and physical capital.

Key Takeaways

- The ASL is the amount of output that is obtainable in the long run given the available labor, technology, and physical capital set.
- It is vertical because it is insensitive to changes in the price level.

- Economists are not entirely certain why ASL shifts. Some point to hysteresis, others to real business cycles, still others to institutional improvements like the growth diamond.
- Nobody knows how long the long term is, but the answer is important for one's attitude toward economic policymaking.
- Those who favor activist policies think the long term is a long way off indeed, so policymakers can benefit the economy by shifting AD and AS to the right.
- Those who are suspicious of interventionist policies think that the long run will soon be upon us, so interventionist policies cannot help the economy for long because output must soon return to Y_{nrl}.

23.4 The Growth Diamond

Learning Objective

1. What is the growth diamond and why is it important?

Over the last two decades or so, many scholars, including the author of this textbook, have examined the link between financial development and economic growth. *They have found that financial repression, severe underdevelopment of financial intermediaries and markets, can stymie growth and that financial development paves the way for growth.* The reason is clear: by reducing asymmetric information and tapping economies of scale (and scope), the financial system efficiently links investors to entrepreneurs, ensuring that society's scarce resources are allocated to their highest valued uses and that innovative ideas get a fair trial.

The research agenda of some of those scholars, including the author of this textbook, has recently broadened to include more of the institutional factors that enhance or reduce economic growth, sustained rightward movements of Y_{nrl}. A leading model, set forth by two economic historians who taught economics at New York University's Stern School of Business,[6] is called the growth diamond or diamond of sustainable growth.[7] Imagine a baseball or softball diamond. At the bottom of the diamond is home plate, the most important base in the game, where the player both begins and, if successful, ends his or her journey. Looking out from home, first base is at the right corner; second base is at the top of the diamond, dead ahead; and third base is at the diamond's left corner. To score a run, a player must return to home plate after touching first, second, and third base, in that order. *Countries are no different than ballplayers in this regard. For a country to get rich, it needs to progress from base to base in the proper order.*

In the growth diamond, home plate is represented by government, first base by the financial system, second base by entrepreneurs, and third base by management. To succeed economically, as depicted in Figure 23.8, a country must first possess a solid home plate, a government that at a minimum protects the lives, liberty, and property of its citizens. Next, it must develop an efficient financial system capable of linking savers/investors to people with good business ideas, the entrepreneurs at second base. The managers at third take over after a product has emerged and matured.

FIGURE 23.8 The growth diamond

Play Ball! = Shifting the Long Run Aggregate Supply Curve to the right.

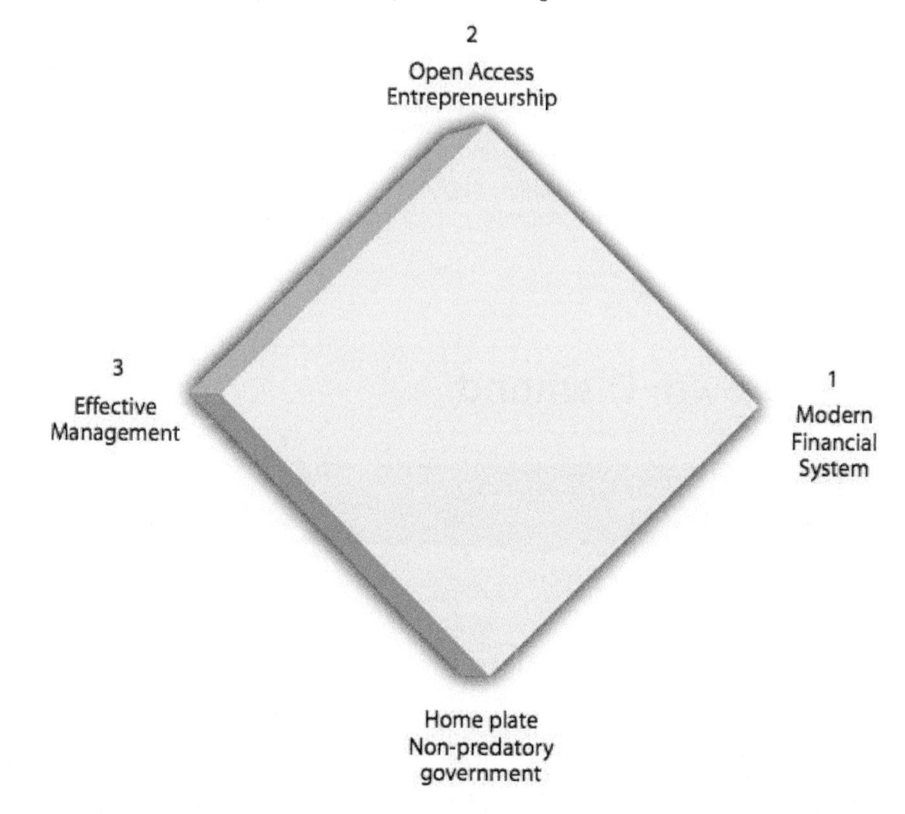

The growth diamond is a powerful model because it can be applied to almost every country on earth. The poorest countries never left home plate because their governments killed and robbed their citizens. Poor but not destitute countries never made it to first base, often because their governments, while not outright predatory, restricted economic liberty to the point that financiers and entrepreneurs could not thrive. In many such countries, the financial system is the tool of the government (indeed many banks in poor countries are owned by the state outright), so they allocate resources to political cronies rather than to the best entrepreneurs. Countries with middling income rounded the bases once or twice but found that managers, entrepreneurs, and financiers co-opted the government and implemented self-serving policies that rendered it difficult to score runs frequently. Meanwhile the rich countries continue to rack up the runs, growing stronger as players circle the bases in a virtuous or self-reinforcing cycle.

Stop and Think Box

In the early nineteenth century, Ontario, Canada (then a colony of Great Britain), and New York State (then part of a fledgling but independent United States) enjoyed (perhaps *hated* is a better word here!) a very similar climate, soil type, and flora and fauna (plants and animals). Yet the population density in New York was much higher, farms (ceteris paribus) were worth four times more there than on the north side of Lake Ontario, and per capita incomes in New York dwarfed those of Ontario. What explains those differences?

The growth diamond does. By the early 1800s, the United States, of which New York State was a part, had put in place a nonpredatory government and a financial system that, given the technology of the day, was quite efficient at linking investors to entrepreneurs, the activities of whom received governmental sanction and societal support. A nascent management class was even forming. Ontario, by contrast, was a colony ruled by a distant monarch. Canadians had little incentive to work hard or smart, so they didn't, and the economy languished, largely devoid of banks and other financial intermediaries and securities markets. As late as the 1830s, New York was sometimes "a better market for the sale of Canada exchange on London than Canada itself."[8] Only after they shed their imperial overlords and reformed their domestic governments did Canadians develop an effective financial system and rid themselves of anti-entrepreneurial laws and sentiments. The Canadian economy then grew with rapidity, making Canada one of the world's richest countries.

A narrower and more technical explanation of the higher value of New York farms comparable to Canadian farms in size, soil quality, rainfall, and so forth is that interest rates were much lower in New York. Valuing a farm is like valuing any income-producing asset. All it takes is to discount the farm's expected future income stream. Holding expected income constant, the key to the equation becomes the interest rate, which was about *four times* lower in New York (say, 6 percent per year versus 24 percent). Recall that $PV = FV/(1 + i)$. If FV (next year's income) in both instances is 100, but $i = .24$ in Canada and .06 in New York, an investor would be willing to lease the New York farm for a year for 100/1.06 = \$94.34, but the Canadian farm for only 100/1.24 = \$80.65. The longer the time frame, the more the higher Canadian interest rate will bite. In the limit, we could price the farms as perpetuities using the equation $PV = FV/i$. That means the New York farm would be worth PV = 100/.06 = \$1,666.67, while the Canadian farm would be worth a mere PV = 100/.24 = \$416.67 (which, of course, times 4 equals the New York farm price). Canadian land values increased when Canadian interest rates decreased after about 1850.

One important implication of the growth diamond is that emerging (from eons of poverty) or transitioning (from communism) economies that are currently hot, like those of China and India, may begin to falter if they do not strengthen their governance, financial, entrepreneurial, and management systems. Some of today's basket-case economies, including that of Argentina, were once high fliers that ran into an economic brick wall because they inadequately protected property rights, impeded financial development, and squelched entrepreneurship.

Although currently less analytically rigorous than the AS-AD model, the growth diamond is more historically grounded than the AS-AD model or any other macro model and that is important. As storied economist Will Baumol once put it,

> *We cannot understand current phenomena...without systematic examination of earlier events which affect the present and will continue to exercise profound effects tomorrow...[T]he long run is important because it is not sensible for economists and policymakers to attempt to discern long-run trends and their outcomes from the flow of short-run developments, which may be dominated by transient conditions.*[9]

Key Takeaways

- The growth diamond is a model of economic growth (increases in real per capita aggregate output) being developed by economic historians at the Stern School of Business.
- It posits that sustained, long-term economic growth is predicated on the existence of a non-predatory government (home plate), an efficient financial system (first base), entrepreneurs (second base), and modern management (third base).
- It is important because it explains why some countries are very rich and others are desperately poor.
- It also explains why some countries, like Argentina, grew rich, only to fall back into poverty.
- Finally, it warns investors that the growth trends of current high fliers like China could reverse if they do not continue to strengthen their governance, and financial, entrepreneurial, and management systems.

23.5 Suggested Reading

Acemoglu, Daron and James Robinson. *Why Nations Fail: The Origins of Power, Prosperity, and Poverty*. New York: Crown, 2013.

Baumol, William, Robert Litan, and Carl Schramm. *Good Capitalism, Bad Capitalism, and the Economics of Growth and Prosperity*. New Haven, CT: Yale University Press, 2007.

Easterly, Bill. *The White Man's Burden: Why the West's Efforts to Aid the Rest Have Done So Much Ill and So Little Good*. New York: Penguin, 2007.

Haber, Stephen, Douglass North, and Barry Weingast. *Political Institutions and Financial Development*. Stanford, CA: Stanford University Press, 2008.

Powell, Benjamin. *Making Poor Nations Rich: Entrepreneurship and the Process of Economic Development*. Stanford, CA: Stanford University Press, 2008.

Wright, Robert E. *One Nation Under Debt: Hamilton, Jefferson, and the History of What We Owe*. New York: McGraw-Hill, 2008.

Endnotes

1. http://en.wikipedia.org/wiki/John_Maynard_Keynes
2. https://en.wikiquote.org/wiki/John_Maynard_Keynes
3. www.minneapolisfed.org/research/prescott
4. nobelprize.org/nobel_prizes/economics/laureates/2004/prescott-autobio.html
5. http://www.economicshelp.org/blog/20144/concepts/hysteresis/
6. http://www.huffingtonpost.com/author/richard-sylla; http://winthropgroup.com/people/person/george-david-smith
7. w4.stern.nyu.edu/sternbusiness/spring_2007/sustainableGrowth.html
8. T. R. Preston, *Three Years' Residence in Canada, from 1837 to 1839*, 2 vols., (London: Richard Bentley 1840), 185.
9. Will Baumol, "Productivity Growth, Convergence, and Welfare: What the Long-Run Data Show," *American Economic Review* 76 (December 1986): 1072–1086.

CHAPTER 24

Monetary Policy Transmission Mechanisms

Chapter Objectives

By the end of this chapter, students should be able to:

1. Explain why structural models are generally superior to reduced-form models.
2. Describe the types of evidence that can strengthen researchers' conviction that a reduced-form model has the direction of causation right, say, from money (M) to output (Y).
3. Describe the evidence that money matters.
4. List and explain several important monetary policy transmission mechanisms.

24.1 Modeling Reality

Learning Objective

1. Why are structural models generally superior to reduced-form models?

We've learned in the last few chapters that monetary policy is not the end-all and be-all of the economy or even of policymakers' attempts to manipulate it. But we knew that before. The question before us is, *Given what we know of IS-LM and AS-AD, just how important is monetary policy? And how do we know? We've got theories galore—notions about how changes in sundry variables, like interest rates, create certain outcomes, like changes in prices and aggregate output. But how well do those theories describe reality?* To answer those questions, we need empirical evidence, good hard numbers. We also need to know how scientists and social scientists evaluate such evidence.

Structural models explicitly link variables from initial cause all the way to final effect via every intermediate step along the causal chain. Reduced-form evidence makes assertions only about initial causes and ultimate effects, treating the links in between as an impenetrable black box. The quantity theory makes just such a reduced-form claim when it asserts that, as the money supply increases, so too does output. In other words, the quantity theory is not explicit about the **transmission mechanisms** of monetary policy. On the other hand, the assertion that increasing the money supply decreases interest rates, which spurs investment, which leads to higher output, ceteris paribus, is a structural model. Such a model can be assessed at every link in the chain: MS up, *i* down, I up, Y up. If the relationship between MS and Y begins to break down, economists with a structural model can try to figure out specifically why. Those touting only a reduced-form model will be flummoxed. Structural models also strengthen our confidence that changes in MS *cause* changes in Y.

transmission mechanisms

How A leads to B in a causal chain; how A is transmitted, so to speak, to B.

Because they leave so much out, reduced-form models may point only to variables that are correlated, that rise and fall in tandem over time. *Correlation, alas, is not causation; the link between variables that are only correlated can be easily broken.* All sorts of superstitions are based on mere correlation, as their practitioners eventually discover to their chagrin and loss,[1] like those who wear goofy-looking rally caps to win baseball games.[2] Reverse causation is also rampant. People who see a high correlation between X and Y often think that X causes Y when in fact Y causes X. For example, there is a high correlation between fan attendance levels and home team victories. Some superfans[3] take this to "prove" that high attendance causes the home team to win by acting as a sixth, tenth, or twelfth player, depending on the sport. Fans have swayed the outcome of a few games, usually by touching baseballs still in play,[4] but the causation mostly runs in the other direction—teams that win many games tend to attract more fans.

Omitted variables can also cloud the connections made by reduced-form models. "Caffeine drinkers have higher rates of coronary heart disease (CHD) than people who don't consume caffeine" is a reduced-form model that probably suffers from omitted variables in the form of selection biases. In other words, caffeine drinkers drink caffeine because they don't get enough sleep; have hectic, stressful lives; and so forth. It may be that those other factors give them heart attacks, not the caffeine per se. Or the caffeine interacts with those other variables in complex ways that are difficult to unravel without growing human beings in test tubes (even more alarming!).

Stop and Think Box

A recent reduced-form study shows a high degree of correlation between smoking marijuana and bad life outcomes: long stints of unemployment, criminal arrests, higher chance of disability, lower lifetime income, and early death. Does that study effectively condemn pot smoking?

Not nearly as much as it would if it presented a structural model that carefully laid out and tested the precise chain by which marijuana smoking causes those bad outcomes. Omitted variables and even reverse causation can be at play in the reduced-form version. For example, some people smoke pot because they have cancer. Some cancer treatments require nasty doses of chemotherapy, the effect of which is to cause pain and reduce appetite. Taking a toke reduces the pain and restores appetite. Needless to say, such people have lower life expectancies than people without cancer. Therefore, they have lower lifetime income and a higher chance of disability and unemployment. Because not all states have medical marijuana exceptions, they are also more liable to criminal arrest. Similarly, unemployed people might be more likely to take a little Mary Jane after lunch or perhaps down a couple of cannabis brownies for dessert, again reversing the direction of causation. A possible omitted variable is selection bias: people who smoke pot might be less educated than those who abstain from the weed, and it is the dearth of education that leads to high unemployment, more arrests, and so forth. Unfortunately, bad science like this study pervades public discourse. Of course, this does not mean that you should go get yourself a blunt. Study instead. Correlation studies show that studying . . . .

Key Takeaways

- Structural models trace the entire causal chain, step by step, allowing researchers to be pretty confident about the direction of causation and to trace any breakdowns in the model to specific relationships.
- Reduced-form models link initial variables to supposed outcomes via an impenetrable black box.
- The problem is that correlation does not always indicate causation. X may increase and decrease with Y, although X does not cause Y because Y may cause X (reverse causation), or Z (an omitted variable) may cause X and Y.
- Reduced-form models can and have led to all sorts of goofy conclusions, like doctors kill people (they seem to be ubiquitous during plagues, accidents, and the like) and police officers cause crime (the number on the streets goes up during crime waves, and they are always at crime scenes—very suspicious). In case you can't tell, I'm being sarcastic.
- On the other hand, reduced-form models are inexpensive compared to structural ones.

24.2 How Important Is Monetary Policy?

Learning Objectives

1. What types of evidence can strengthen researchers' conviction that a reduced-form model has the direction of causation right, say, from M to Y? How?
2. What evidence is there that money matters?

Early Keynesians believed that monetary policy did not matter at all because they could not find any evidence that interest rates affected planned business investment. Milton Friedman and Anna Schwartz, another monetarist, countered with a huge tome called *A Monetary History of the United States, 1867–1960* which purported to show that the Keynesians had it all wrong, especially their kooky claim that monetary policy during the Great Depression had been easy (low real interest rates and MS growth). Nominal rates on risky securities had in fact soared in 1930–1933, the depths of the depression. Because the price level was falling, real interest rates, via the Fisher Equation, were much *higher* than nominal rates. If you borrowed $100, you'd have to repay only $102 in a year, but those 102 smackers could buy a heck of a lot more goods and services a year hence. So real rates were more on the order of 8 to 10 percent, which is pretty darn high. The link between interest rates and investment, the monetarists showed, was between investment and real interest rates, not nominal interest rates.

As noted above, the early monetarists relied on MV = PY, a reduced-form model. *To strengthen their conviction that causation indeed ran from M to Y instead of Y to M or some unknown variables A...Z to M and Y, the monetarists relied on three types of empirical evidence: timing, statistical, and historical.* Timing evidence tries to show that increases in M happen before increases in Y, and not vice versa, relying on the commonplace assumption that causes occur before their effects. Friedman and Schwartz showed that money growth slowed before recessions, but the timing was highly variable. Sometimes slowing money growth occurred sixteen months before output turned south; other times, only a few months passed. That is great stuff, but it is hardly foolproof because, as Steve Miller points out, time keeps on slipping, slipping, slipping, into the future.[5] Maybe a decline in output caused the decline in the money supply by slowing demand for loans (and hence deposits) or by inducing banks to decrease lending (and hence deposits). Changes in M and Y, in other words, could be causing each other in a sort of virtuous or pernicious cycle or chicken-egg problem. Or again maybe there *is* a mysterious variable Z running the whole show behind the scenes.

Statistical evidence is subject to the same criticisms plus the old adage that there are three types of untruths (besides Stephen Colbert's truthiness,[6] of course): lies, damn lies, and statistics. By changing starting and ending dates, conflating the difference between statistical significance and economic significance,[7] manipulating the dates of structural breaks, and introducing who knows how many other subtle little fibs, researchers can make mountains out of molehills, and vice versa. *It's kinda funny that when monetarists used statistical tests, the quantity theory won and money mattered, but when the early Keynesians conducted the tests, the quantity theory looked, if not insane, at least inane.*

But Friedman and Schwartz had an empirical ace up their sleeves: historical evidence from periods in which declines in the money supply appear to be exogenous, by which economists mean "caused by something outside the model," thus eliminating doubts about omitted variables and reverse causation. White-lab-coat scientists (you know, physicists, chemists, and so forth—"real" scientists) know that variables change exogenously because they are the ones making the changes. They can do this systematically in dozens, hundreds, even thousands of test tubes, Petri dishes, atomic acceleration experiments, and what not, carefully controlling for each variable (making sure that everything is ceteris paribus), then measuring and comparing the results. As social scientists, economists cannot run such experiments. *They can and do turn to history, however, for so-called natural experiments.* That's what the monetarists did, and what they found was that exogenous declines in MS led to recessions (lower Y*) every time. *Economic and financial history wins! (Disclaimer: The author of this textbook is a financial historian.)* While they did not abandon the view that C, G, I, NX, and T also affect output, Keynesians now accept money's role in helping to determine Y. (A new group, the real-business-cycle theorists associated with the Minneapolis Fed, has recently challenged the notion that money matters. In their view, the short-run is very short, so the SRAS curve is essentially irrelevant. Shifting the AD curve therefore leads only to changes in the price level, not output. All that changes output, they believe, are changes in productivity stemming from changes in the availability of raw materials, changes in government regulations, and inventions or new business processes, i.e., changes in the real economy.)

Key Takeaways

- Timing, statistical, and historical evidence strengthen researchers' belief in causation.
- Timing evidence attempts to show that changes in M occur before changes in Y.
- Statistical evidence attempts to show that one model's predictions are closer to reality than another's.
- The problem with stats, though, is that those running the tests appear to rig them (consciously or not), so the stats often tell us more about the researcher than they do about reality.
- Historical evidence, particularly so-called natural experiments in which variables change exogenously and hence are analogous to controlled scientific experiments, provide the best sort of evidence on the direction of causation.
- The monetarists showed that there is a strong correlation between changes in the MS and changes in Y and also proffered timing, statistical, and historical evidence of a causal link.
- Historical evidence is the most convincing because it shows that the MS sometimes changed exogenously, that is, for reasons clearly unrelated to Y or other plausible causal variables, and that when it did, Y changed with the expected sign (+ if MS increased, – if it decreased).

24.3 Transmission Mechanisms

Learning Objective

1. What are monetary policy transmission mechanisms and why are they important?

Most economists accept the proposition that money matters and have been searching for structural models that delineate the specific transmission mechanisms between MS and Y. The most basic model says the following:

Expansionary monetary policy (EMP), real interest rates (i_r) down, investment (I) up, aggregate output (Y) up.

The importance of interest rates for consumer expenditures (especially on durables like autos, refrigerators, and homes) and net exports (lower i_r spells depreciation of the local currency, which means fewer imports and more exports) has also been recognized, leading to the following:

$EMP, i_r \downarrow, I \uparrow, C \uparrow, NX \uparrow, Y \uparrow$

That might seem like enough, but many economists do not think those effects are strong enough to explain the effect of monetary policy on output, so they have developed other channels, causal chains, or **transmission mechanisms** to explain exactly how EMP works its way through the economy.

transmission mechanisms

The channels or causal chains by which monetary policy works its way through the economy, ultimately affecting output.

Tobin's q, the market value of companies divided by the replacement cost of physical capital, is clearly analogous to i and related to I. When q is high, firms sell their highly valued stock to raise cash and buy new physical plant and build inventories. When q is low, by contrast, firms don't get much for their stock compared to the cost of physical capital, so they don't sell stock to fund increases in I. By increasing stock prices, the MS may be positively related to q. Thus, another monetary policy transmission mechanism may be the following:

EMP, P_s ↑, q ↑, I ↑, Y↑

The wealth effect is a transmission mechanism whereby expansionary monetary policy leads to increases in the prices of stocks (P_s), homes, collectibles, and other assets (P_a), in other words, an increase in individual wealth. That increase, in turn, induces people to consume more:

EMP, P_s ↑, P_a ↑, wealth ↑, C ↑, Y↑

The credit view posits several straightforward transmission mechanisms, including bank loans, asymmetric information, and balance sheets:

EMP, bank deposits ↑, bank loans ↑, I ↑, Y↑

EMP, net worth ↑, asymmetric information ↓, lending ↑, I ↑, C ↑, Y↑

EMP, *i* ↓, cash flow ↑, asymmetric information ↓, lending ↑, I ↑, C ↑, Y↑

EMP, unanticipated P* ↑, real net worth ↑, asymmetric information ↓, lending ↑, I ↑, Y↑

Asymmetric information is a powerful and important theory, so scholars' confidence in these transmission mechanisms is high.

Stop and Think Box

The Fed thought that it would quickly squelch the recession that began in March 2001, yet the downturn lasted until November of that year. The terrorist attacks that September worsened matters, but the Fed had hoped to reverse the drop in Y* well before then. Why was the Fed's forecast overly optimistic? Where exactly did the structural models break down? (*Hint*: Corporate accounting scandals at Enron, Arthur Andersen, and other firms were part of the mix.)

The Fed might not have counted on some major monetary policy transmission mechanisms, including reductions in asymmetric information, being muted by the accounting scandals. In other words,

EMP, net worth ↑, asymmetric information ↓, lending ↑, I ↑, C ↑, Y↑

EMP, *i* ↓, cash flow ↑, asymmetric information ↓, lending ↑, I ↑, C ↑, Y↑

EMP, unanticipated P ↑, real net worth ↑, asymmetric information ↓, lending ↑, I ↑, Y↑

became something more akin to the following:

EMP, net worth ↑, asymmetric information — (flat or no change), lending —, I — , C —, Y —

EMP, *i* ↑, cash flow ↑, asymmetric information —, lending —, I ↑, C —, Y —

EMP, unanticipated P ↑, real net worth ↑, asymmetric information—, lending —, I —, Y — because asymmetric information remained high due to the fact that economic agents felt as though they could no longer count on the truthfulness of corporate financial statements.

The takeaway of all this for monetary policymakers, and those interested in their policies (including you), is that monetary policy needs to take more into account than just short-term interest rates. Policymakers need to worry about real interest rates, including long-term rates; unexpected changes in the price level; the interest rates on risky bonds; the prices of other assets, including corporate equities, homes, and the like; the quantity of bank loans; and the bite of adverse selection, moral hazard, and the principal-agent problem.

Stop and Think Box

Japan's economy was going gangbusters until about 1990 or so, when it entered a fifteen-year economic funk. To try to get the Japanese economy moving again, the Bank of Japan lowered short-term interest rates all the way to zero for many years on end, to no avail. Why didn't the Japanese economy revive due to the monetary stimulus? What should the Japanese have done instead?

As it turns out, i_r stayed quite high because the Japanese expected, and received, price deflation. Through the Fisher Equation, we know that $i_r = i - \pi^e$, or real interest rates equal nominal interest rates minus inflation expectations. If π^e is negative, which it is when prices are expected to fall, i_r will be > i. So i can be 0 but i_r can be 1, 2, 3...10 percent per year if prices are expected to decline by that much. So instead of EMP, i_r ↓, I ↓ C ↓ NX ↑, Y↑ the Japanese experienced i_r ↑, I ↓ C ↓ NX ↓, Y↓. Not good. They should have pumped up the MS much faster, driving π^e from negative whatever to zero or even positive, and thus making real interest rates low or negative, and hence a stimulant. The Japanese made other mistakes as well, allowing land and equities prices to plummet, thereby nixing the Tobin's q and wealth effect transmission mechanisms. They also kept some big shaky banks from failing, which kept levels of asymmetric information high and bank loan levels low, squelching the credit channels.

Key Takeaways

- Monetary policy transmission mechanisms are essentially structural models that predict the precise chains of causation between expansionary monetary policy (EMP) or tight monetary policy (TMP) and Y.
- They are important because they provide central bankers and other monetary policymakers with a detailed view of how changes in the MS affect Y, allowing them to see why some policies don't work as much or as quickly as anticipated.
- That, in turn, allows them to become better policymakers, to the extent that is possible in a world of rational expectations.
- Transmission mechanisms include:
- EMP, i_r↓, I ↑ C ↑, NX ↑, Y↑, EMP, q ↑, I ↑, Y↑
- EMP, P_a ↑, wealth ↑, C ↑, Y↑
- EMP, bank deposits ↑, bank loans ↑, I ↑, Y↑
- EMP, net worth ↑, asymmetric information ↓, lending ↑, I ↑, C ↑, Y↑
- EMP, i ↓, cash flow ↑, asymmetric information ↓, lending ↑, I ↑, C ↑, Y↑
- EMP, unanticipated P* ↑, real net worth ↑, asymmetric information ↓, lending ↑, I ↑, Y↑

24.4 Suggested Reading

Angeloni, Ignazio, Anil Kashyap, and Benoit Mojon. *Monetary Policy Transmission in the Euro Area: A Study of the Eurosystem Monetary Transmission Network*. New York: Cambridge University Press, 2012.

Friedman, Milton, and Anna Schwartz. *A Monetary History of the United States, 1867–1960*. Princeton, NJ: Princeton University Press, 1971.

Mahadeva, Lavan, and Peter Sinclair. *Monetary Transmission in Diverse Economies*. New York: Cambridge University Press, 2002.

Endnotes

1. www.dallasobserver.com/2005-09-08/dining/tryst-of-fate
2. en.wikipedia.org/wiki/Rally_cap
3. en.wikipedia.org/wiki/Bill_Swerski's_Superfans
4. www.usatoday.com/sports/columnist/lopresti/2003-10-15-lopresti_x.htm
5. www.lyricsfreak.com/s/steve+miller/fly+like+an+eagle_20130994.html
6. en.wikipedia.org/wiki/Truthiness
7. www.deirdremccloskey.com/articles/stats/preface_ziliak.php

CHAPTER 25

Inflation and Money

Chapter Objectives

By the end of this chapter, students should be able to:

1. Describe the strongest evidence for the reduced-form model that links money supply growth to inflation.
2. Explain what the aggregate supply-aggregate demand (AS-AD) model, a structural model, says about money supply growth and the price level.
3. Explain why central bankers allow inflation to occur year after year.
4. Define lags and explain their importance.

25.1 Empirical Evidence of a Money-Inflation Link

Learning Objectives

1. What is the strongest evidence for the reduced-form model that links money supply growth to inflation?
2. What does the AS-AD model, a structural model, say about money supply growth and the price level?

Milton Friedman claimed that "inflation is always and everywhere a monetary phenomenon."[1] We know this isn't true if one takes a loose view of inflation because negative aggregate supply shocks and increases in aggregate demand due to fiscal stimulus can also cause the price level to increase. Large, sustained increases in the price level, however, are indeed proximately caused by increases in the money supply and only by increases in the money supply. *The evidence for this is overwhelming: all periods of hyperinflation from the American and French Revolutions to the German hyperinflation following World War I, to more recent episodes in Latin America and Zimbabwe, have been accompanied by high rates of money supply (MS) growth.*[2] Moreover, the MS increases in some circumstances were exogenous, so those episodes were natural experiments that give us confidence that the reduced-form model correctly considers money supply as the causal agent and that reverse causation or omitted variables are unlikely.

Stop and Think Box

During the American Civil War, the Confederate States of America (CSA, or the South) issued more than $1 billion of fiat paper currency similar to today's Federal Reserve notes, far more than the economy could support at the prewar price level. Confederate dollars fell in value from 82.7 cents in specie in 1862 to 29.0 cents in 1863, to 1.7 cents in 1865, a level of currency depreciation (inflation) that some economists think was simply too high to be accounted for by Confederate money supply growth alone. What other factors may have been at play? (*Hint*: Over the course of the war, the Union [the North] imposed a blockade of southern trade that increased in efficiency during the course of the war, especially as major Confederate seaports like New Orleans and Norfolk fell under northern control.)

A negative supply shock, the almost complete cutoff of foreign trade, could well have hit poor Johnny Reb (the South) as well. That would have decreased output and driven prices higher, prices already raised to lofty heights by continual emissions of too much money.

Economists also have a structural model showing a causal link between money supply growth and inflation at their disposal, the AS-AD model. *Recall that an increase in MS causes the AD curve to shift right. That, in turn, causes the short-term AS curve to shift left, leading to a return to Y_{nrl} but higher prices.* If the MS grows and grows, prices will go up and up, as in Figure 25.1.

FIGURE 25.1 Inflation as a response to a continually increasing money supply
More money means more AD but that pesky SRAS curve keeps output muted and prices ever higher!

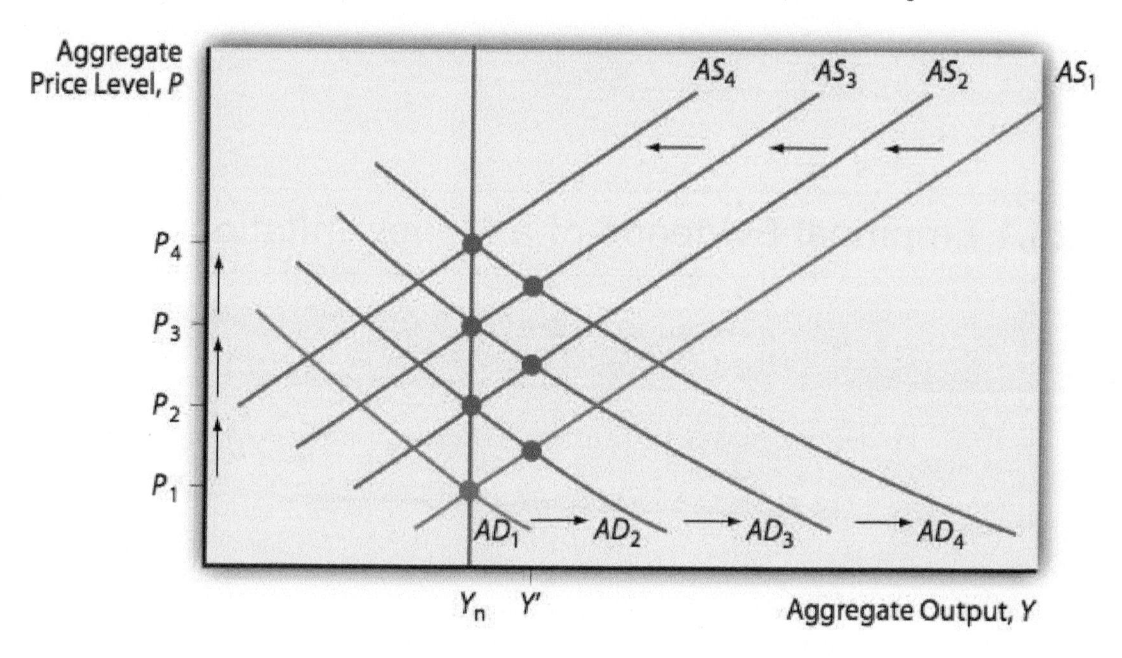

Nothing else, it turns out, can keep prices rising, rising, ever rising like that because other variables are bounded. An increase in government expenditure G will also cause AD to shift right and AS to shift left, leaving the economy with the same output but higher prices in the long run (whatever that is). But if G stops growing, as it must, then P* stops rising and inflation (the change in P*) goes to zero. Ditto with tax cuts, which can't fall below zero (or even get close to it). So fiscal policy alone can't create a sustained rise in prices. (Or a sustained decrease either.)

Negative supply shocks are also one-off events, not the stuff of sustained increases in prices. An oil embargo or a wage push will cause the price level to increase (and output to fall, ouch!) and negative shocks may even follow each other in rapid succession. But once the AS curve is done shifting, that's it—P* stays put. Moreover, if Y* falls below Y_{nrl}, in the long run (again, whatever that is), increased unemployment and other slack in the economy will cause AS to shift back to the right, restoring both output and the former price level!

So, again, Friedman was right: inflation, in the sense of continual increases in prices, is always a monetary phenomenon and only a monetary phenomenon.[3]

lagged

The time it takes for a policy to change on a variable, a cause to create an observable effect.

Stop and Think Box

Figure 25.2 compares inflation with M1 growth lagged two years. What does the data tell you? Now look at Figure 25.3 and Figure 25.4. What caused M1 to grow during the 1960s?

FIGURE 25.2 U.S. M1 and P growth, 1961–1972
Looks pretty highly correlated!

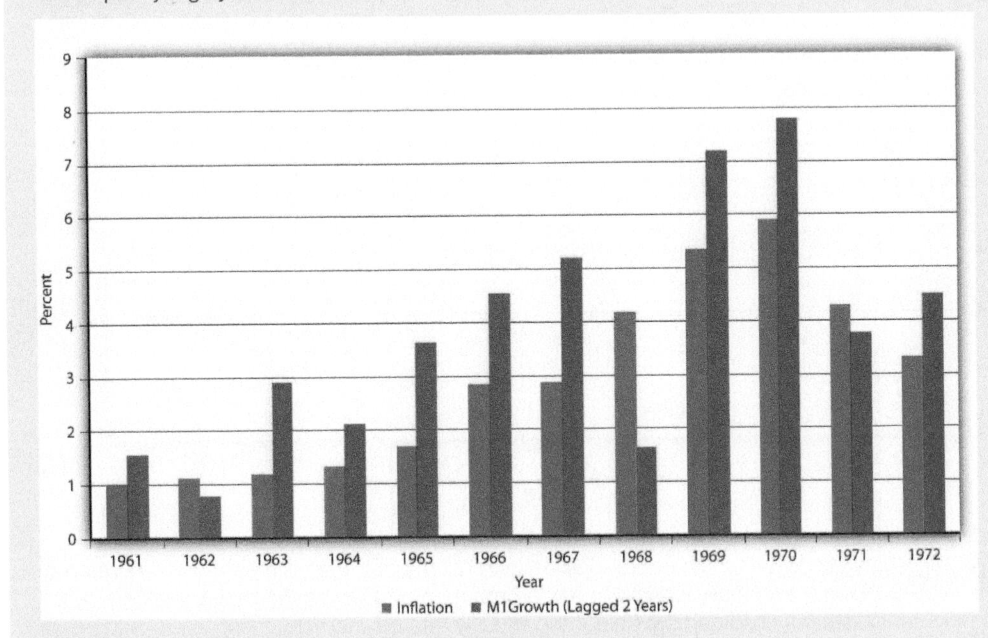

FIGURE 25.3 Government debt-to-GDP ratio, 1961–1972
Strong upward trend.

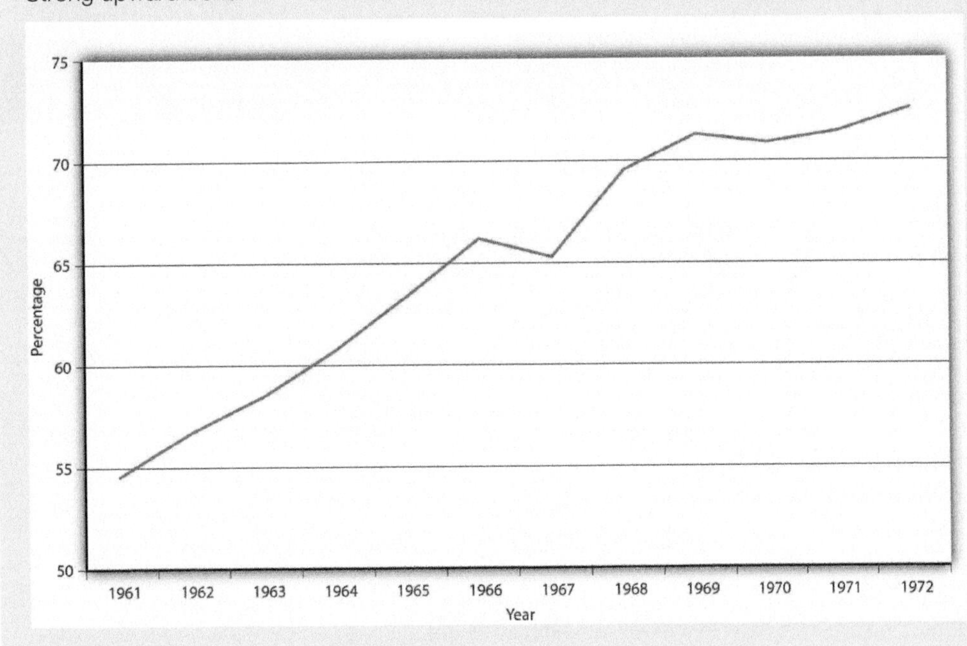

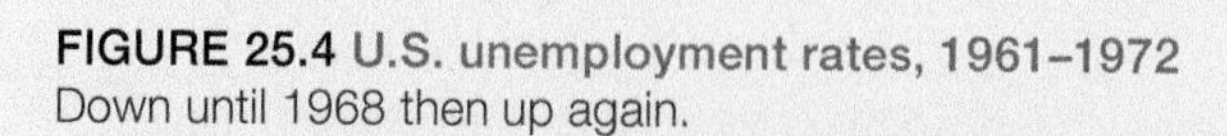

FIGURE 25.4 U.S. unemployment rates, 1961–1972
Down until 1968 then up again.

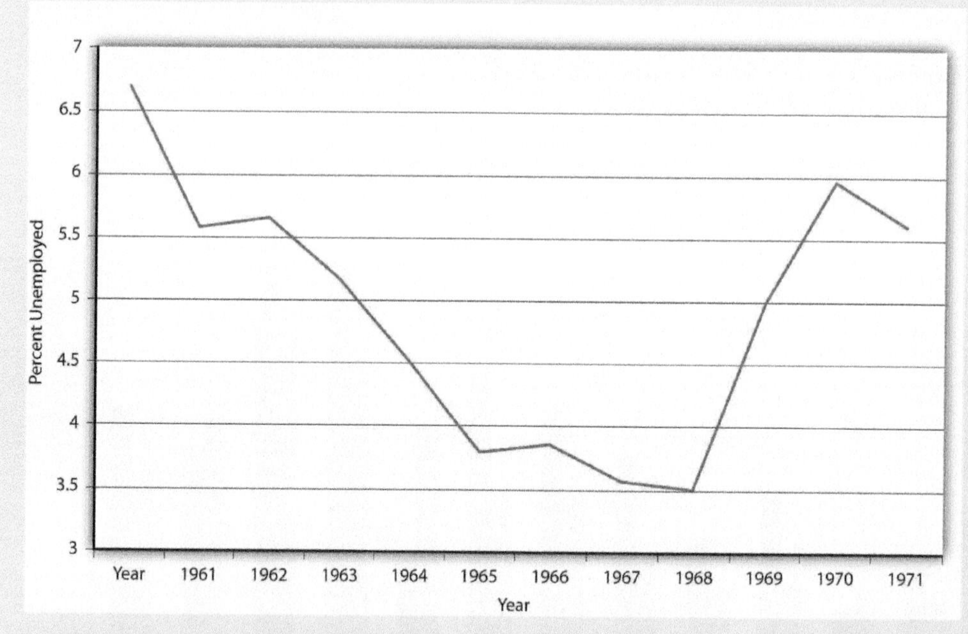

The data clearly show that M1 was growing over the period and likely causing inflation with a two-year lag. M1 grew partly because federal deficits increased faster than the economy, increasing the debt-to-GDP ratio, eventually leading to some debt monetization on the part of the Fed. Also, unemployment rates fell considerably below the natural rate of unemployment, suggesting that demand-pull inflation was taking place as well.

Key Takeaways

- Throughout history, exogenous increases in MS have led to increases in P^*. Every hyperinflation has been preceded by rapid increases in money supply growth.
- The AS-AD model shows that money supply growth is the only thing that can lead to inflation, that is, sustained increases in the price level.
- This happens because monetary stimulus in the short term shifts the AD curve to the right, increasing prices but also rendering $Y^* > Y_{nrl}$.
- Unemployment drops, driving up wages, which shifts the AS curve to the left, Y^* back to Y_{nrl}, and P^* yet higher.
- Unlike other variables, the MS can continue to grow, initiating round after round of this dynamic.
- Other variables are bounded and produce only one-off changes in P^*.
- A negative supply shock or wage push, for instance, increases the price level once, but then price increases stop.
- Similarly, increases in government expenditures can cause P^* to rise by shifting AD to the right, but unlike increases in the MS, government expenditures can increase only so far politically and practically (to 100 percent of GDP).

25.2 Why Have Central Bankers So Often Gotten It Wrong?

Learning Objectives

1. Given the analysis in this chapter, why do central bankers sometimes allow inflation to occur year after year?
2. What are lags and why are they important?

If the link between money supply growth and inflation is so clear, and if nobody (except perhaps inveterate debtors) has anything but contempt for inflation, why have central bankers allowed it to occur so frequently? Not all central banks are independent of the fiscal authority and may simply print money on its behalf to finance budget deficits, the stuff of hyperinflations. In addition, central bankers might be more privately interested than publicly interested and somehow benefit personally from inflation. (They might score points with politicians for stimulating the economy just before an election or they might take out big loans and repay them after the inflationary period in nearly worthless currency.) Assuming central bankers are publicly interested but far from prescient, what might cause them to err so often? In short, lags and high-employment policies.

A lag is an amount of time that passes between a cause and its eventual effect. Lags in monetary policy, Friedman showed, were "long and variable." Data lag is the time it takes for policymakers to get important information, like GDP (Y) and unemployment. Recognition lag is the time it takes them to become convinced that the data is accurate and indicative of a trend and not just a random perturbation. Legislative lag is the time it takes legislators to react to economic changes. (This is short for monetary policy, but it can be a year or more for fiscal policy.) Implementation lag refers to the time between policy decision and implementation. (Again, for modern central banks using open market purchases [OMPs], this lag is minimal, but for changes in taxes, it can take a long time indeed.) The most important lag of all is the so-called effectiveness lag, the period between policy implementation and real-world results. Business investments, after all, typically take months or even years to plan, approve, and implement.

All told, lags can add up to years and add considerable complexity to monetary policy analysis because they cloud cause-effect relationships. Lags also put policymakers perpetually behind the eight-ball, constantly playing catch-up. Lags force policymakers to forecast the future with accuracy, something (as we've seen) that is not easily done. As noted in earlier chapters, economists don't even know when the short run becomes the long run!

Consider a case of so-called cost-push inflation brought about by a negative supply shock or wage push. That moves the AS curve to the left, reducing output and raising prices and, in all likelihood, causing unemployment and political angst. Policymakers unable to await the long term (the rightward shift in AS because Y^* has fallen below Y_{nrl}, causing unemployment and wages to decline) may well respond with what's called accommodative monetary policy. In other words, they engage in expansionary monetary policies (EMPs), which shift the AD curve to the right, causing output to increase (with a lag) but prices to rise. *Because prices are higher and they've been recently rewarded for their wage push with accommodative monetary policy, workers may well initiate another wage push, starting a vicious cycle of wage pushes followed by increases in P^* and yet more wage pushes.* Monetarists and other nonactivists shake their heads at this dynamic, arguing that if workers' wage pushes were met by periods of higher unemployment, they would soon learn to stop. (After all, even 2-year-olds and rats eventually learn to stop pushing buttons if they are not rewarded for doing so. They learn even faster to stop pushing if they get a little shock.)

An episode of demand-pull inflation can also touch off accommodative monetary policy and a bout of inflation. If the government sets its full employment target too high, above the natural rate, it will always look like there is too much unemployment. That will eventually tempt policymakers into thinking that Y^* is < Y_{nrl}, inducing them to implement an EMP. Output will rise, temporarily, but so too will prices. Prices will go up again when the AS curve shifts left, back to Y_{nrl}, as it will do in a hurry given the low level of unemployment. The shift, however, will again increase unemployment over the government's unreasonably low target, inducing another round of EMP and price increases.

Another source of inflation is government budget deficits. To cover their expenditures, governments can tax, sell assets, borrow at interest, or borrow for free by issuing money. (Which would you choose?) Taxation is politically costly, as is selling assets. (Imagine the uproar over selling Mount Rushmore, or an aircraft carrier battle group!) Borrowing at interest can be costly too, especially if the government is a default risk. Therefore, many governments pay their bills by printing money or by issuing bonds, all of which their respective central banks then buy with money. Either way, the monetary base increases, leading to some multiple increase in the MS, which leads to inflation. Effectively a tax on money balances called a currency tax, inflation is easier to disguise and much easier to collect than other forms of taxes. Governments get as addicted to the currency tax as individuals get addicted to crack or meth. This is especially true in developing countries with weak (not independent) central banks.

Stop and Think Box

Why is central bank independence important in keeping inflation at bay?

Independent central banks are better able to withstand political pressures to monetize the debt, to follow accommodative policies, or to respond to (seemingly) "high" levels of unemployment with an EMP. They can also make a more believable or credible commitment to stop inflation, which is an important consideration as well.

Key Takeaways

- Private-interest scenarios aside, publicly interested central bankers might pursue high employment too vigorously, leading to inflation via cost-push and demand-pull mechanisms.
- If workers make a successful wage push, for example, the AS curve will shift left, increasing P^*, decreasing Y^*, and increasing unemployment.
- If policymakers are anxious to get out of recession, they might respond with an expansionary monetary policy (EMP).
- That will increase Y^* but also P^* yet again. Such an accommodative policy might induce workers to try another wage push. The price level is higher after all, and they were rewarded for their last wage push.
- The longer this dynamic occurs, the higher prices will go.
- Policymakers might fall into this trap themselves if they underestimate full employment at, say, 97 percent (3 percent unemployment) when in fact it is 95 percent (5 percent unemployment).
- Therefore, unemployment of 4 percent looks too high and output appears to be < Y_{nrl}, suggesting that an EMP is in order.
- The rightward shift of the AD curve causes prices and output to rise, but the latter rises only temporarily as the already tight labor market gets tighter, leading to higher wages and a leftward shift of the AS curve, with its concomitant increase in P^* and decrease in Y^*.
- If policymakers' original and flawed estimate of full employment is maintained, another round of AD is sure to come, as is higher prices.
- Budget deficits can also lead to sustained inflation if the government monetizes its debt directly by printing money (and deposits) or indirectly via central bank open market purchases (OMPs) of government bonds.

- Lags are the amount of time it takes between a change in the economy to take place and policymakers to effectively do something about it.
- That includes lags for gathering data, making sure the data show a trend and are not mere noise, making a legislative decision (if applicable), implementing policy (if applicable), and waiting for the policy to affect the economy.
- Lags are important because they are long and variable, thus complicating monetary policy by making central bankers play constant catch-up and also by clouding cause-effect relationships.

25.3 Suggested Reading

Ball, R. J. *Inflation and the Theory of Money*. Piscataway, NJ: Aldine Transaction, 2007.

Bernholz, Peter. *Monetary Regimes and Inflation: History, Economic and Political Relationships* 2nd ed. New York: Edward Elgar, 2016.

Bresciani-Turroni, Costantino. *Economics of Inflation*. Auburn, AL: Ludwig von Mises Institute, 2007.

Donovan, Paul. *The Truth About Inflation*. New York: Routledge, 2015.

Samuelson, Robert. *The Great Inflation and Its Aftermath: The Past and Future of American Affluence*. New York: Random House, 2010.

Endnotes

1. *A Monetary History of the United States, 1867–1960.*
2. In most of those instances, the government printed money in order to finance large budget deficits. The rebel American, French, and Confederate (Southern) governments could not raise enough in taxes or by borrowing to fund their wars, the Germans could not pay off the heavy reparations imposed on them after World War I, and so forth. We know that the deficits themselves did not cause inflation, however, because in some instances governments have dealt with their budget problems in other ways without sparking inflation, and in some instances rapid money creation was not due to seriously unbalanced budgets. So the proximate cause of inflation is rapid money growth, which often, but not always, is caused by budget deficits.
3. This is not to say, however, that negative demand shocks might not contribute to a general monetary inflation.

CHAPTER 26

Rational Expectations Redux: Monetary Policy Implications

Chapter Objectives

By the end of this chapter, students should be able to:

1. Describe how the new classical macroeconomic model differs from the standard, pre-Lucas AS-AD model.
2. Explain what the new classical macroeconomic model suggests regarding the efficacy of activist monetary policy.
3. Explain how the new Keynesian model differs from the new classical macroeconomic model.
4. Assess the extent to which policymakers can improve short-run macroeconomic performance.

26.1 Rational Expectations

Learning Objectives

1. How does the new classical macroeconomic model differ from the standard, pre-Lucas AS-AD model?
2. What does the new classical macroeconomic model suggest regarding the efficacy of activist monetary policy? Why?

Rational expectations is an economic theory that postulates that market participants input all available relevant information into the best forecasting model available to them. Although individual forecasts can be very wide of the mark, actual economic outcomes do not vary in a predictable way from participants' aggregate predictions or expectations. Perhaps Abraham Lincoln summed it up best when he asserted that "you can fool some of the people all of the time, and all of the people some of the time, but you cannot fool all of the people all of the time."[1]

That might sound like a trite insight, but the theory of rational expectations has important implications for monetary policy. In a quest to understand why policymakers had such a poor record, especially during the 1970s, Len Mirman (University of Virginia),[2] Robert Lucas (University of Chicago),[3] Thomas Sargent (New York University),[4] Bennett McCallum (Carnegie-Mellon),[5] Edward Prescott (Arizona State),[6] and other *economists of the so-called expectations revolution discovered that expansionary monetary policies cannot be effective if economic agents expect them to be implemented.* Conversely, to thwart inflation as quickly and painlessly as possible, the central bank must be able to make a credible commitment to stop it. In other words, it must convince people that it can and will stop prices from rising.

Stop and Think Box

During the American Revolution, the Continental Congress announced that it would stop printing bills of credit, the major form of money in the economy since 1775–1776, when rebel governments (the Continental Congress and state governments) began financing their little revolution by printing money. The Continental Congress implemented no other policy changes, so everyone knew that its large budget deficits would continue. Prices continued upward. Why?

The Continental Congress did not make a credible commitment to end inflation because its announcement did nothing to end its large and chronic budget deficit. It also did nothing to prevent the states from issuing more bills of credit.

Lucas was among the first to highlight the importance of public expectations in macroeconomic forecasting and policymaking. What matters, he argued, was not what policymakers' models said would happen but what economic agents (people, firms, governments) believed would occur. So in one instance, a rise in the fed funds rate might cause long-term interest rates to barely budge, but in another it might cause them to soar. In short, *policymakers can't be certain of the effects of their policies before implementing them.*

Because Keynesian cross diagrams and the IS-LM and AS-AD models did not explicitly take rational expectations into account, Lucas, Sargent, and others had to recast them in what is generally called the new classical macroeconomic model. *That new model uses the AS, ASL, and AD curves but reduces the short run of aggregate demand shocks to zero if the policy is expected.* So, for example, an anticipated EMP shifts AD right but immediately shifts AS left as workers spontaneously push for higher wages. The price level rises, but output doesn't budge. *An unanticipated EMP, by contrast, has the same effect as described in earlier chapters—a temporary (but who knows how long?) increase in output (and a rise in P followed by another when the AS curve eventually shifts left).*

Now get this: Y can actually decline if an EMP is not as expansionary as expected!* If economic actors expect a big shift in AD, the AS curve will shift hard left to keep Y* at Y_{nrl}, as in Figure 26.1. If the AD curve does not shift as far right as expected, or indeed if it stays put, prices will rise and output will fall, as in the following graph. *This helps to explain why financial markets sometimes react badly to small decreases in the Fed's fed funds target.* They expected more!

FIGURE 26.1 The effect of an unexpectedly weak EMP

If AD does not go all the way to AD2 as expected, output will fall and prices will rise (stagflation).

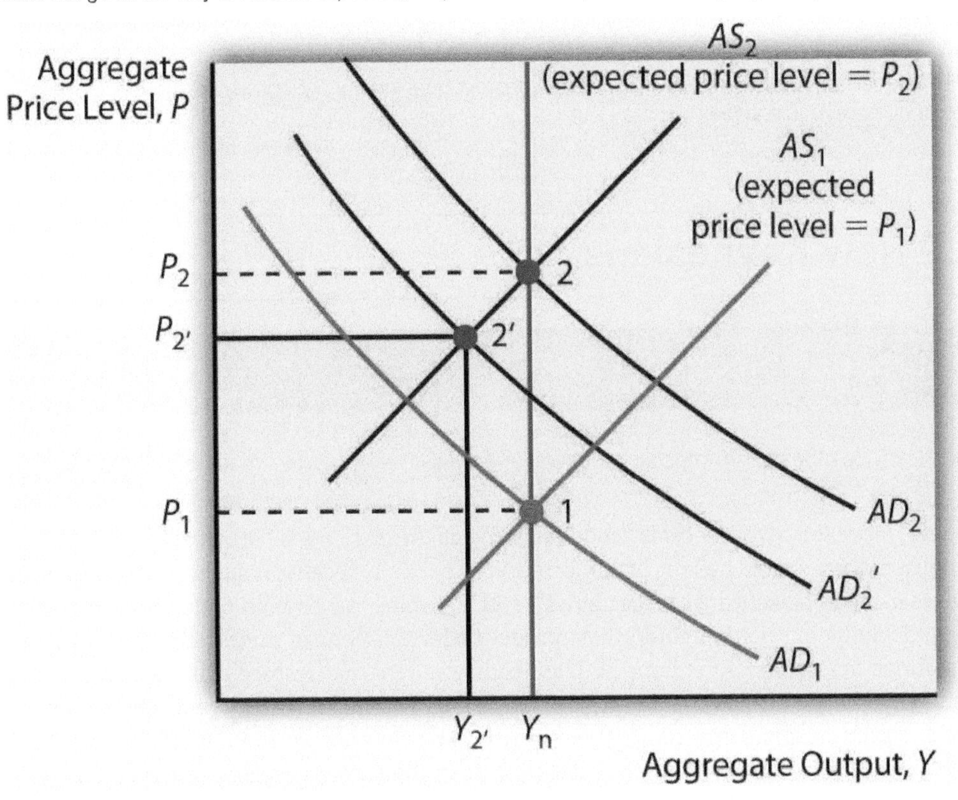

What this means for policymakers is that they have to know not only how the economy works, which is difficult enough, they also have to know the expectations of economic agents. *Figuring out what those expectations are is quite difficult because economic agents are numerous and often have conflicting expectations, and weighting them by their importance is super-duper-tough. And that is at T1.* At T_2, nanoseconds from now, expectations may be very different.

The "taper tantrum" of May 21, 2013 showed just how sensitive markets are to expectations. That day, the Fed merely *stated* that it would *gradually* wind-down an $85-billion-a-month bond-buying program (quantitative easing). Announcement of the unexpected policy caught market participants by surprise, which sent asset prices and currencies plunging around the world. Four years later, the ECB tried to avoid a repeat by leaking to the financial press that it was *contemplating* how to tell investors that it was *considering slowing* its own bond purchasing program, which was running about €60 billion per month, in an effort *to soften their expectations about how long the quantitative easing program would last.*

Key Takeaways

- The new classical macroeconomic model takes the theory of rational expectations into account, essentially driving the short run to zero when economic actors successfully predict policy implementation.
- The new classical macroeconomic model draws the efficacy of EMP or expansionary fiscal policy (EFP) into serious doubt because if market participants anticipate it, the AS curve will immediately shift left (workers will demand higher wages and suppliers will demand higher prices in anticipation of inflation), keeping output at Ynrl but moving prices significantly higher.
- Stabilization (limiting fluctuations in Y*) is also difficult because policymakers cannot know with certainty what the public's expectations are at every given moment.

- The good news is that the model suggests that inflation can be ended immediately without putting the economy into recession (decreasing Y*) if policymakers (central bankers and those in charge of the government's budget) can credibly commit to squelching it.
- That is because workers and others will stop pushing the AS curve to the left as soon as they believe that prices will stay put.

26.2 New Keynesians

Learning Objective

1. How does the new Keynesian model differ from the new classical macroeconomic model?

The new classical macroeconomic model aids the cause of nonactivists, economists who believe that policymakers should have as little discretion as possible, because it suggests that policymakers are more likely to make things (especially P* and Y*) worse rather than better. The activists could not stand idly by but neither could they ignore the implications of Lucas's critique of prerational expectations macroeconomic theories. The result was renewed research that led to the development of what is often called the new Keynesian model. That model directly refutes the notion that wages and prices respond immediately and fully to expected changes in P*. Workers in the first year of a three-year labor contract, for example, can't push their wages higher no matter their expectations. Firms are also reluctant to lower wages even when unemployment is high because doing so may exacerbate the principal-agent problem in the form of labor strife, everything from slacking to theft, to strikes. New hires might be brought in at lower wages, but if turnover is low, that process could take years to play out. Similarly, companies often sign multiyear fixed-price contracts with their suppliers and/or distributors, effectively preventing them from acting on new expectations of P*. *In short, wages and prices are "sticky" and hence adjustments are slow, not instantaneous as assumed by Lucas and company.*

*If that is the case, as*Figure 26.2 *shows, anticipated policy can and does affect Y*, although not as much as an unanticipated policy move of the same type, timing, and magnitude would.* The takeaway is that an EMP, even if it is anticipated, can have positive economic effects ($Y^* > Y_{nrl}$ for some period of time), but it is better if the central bank initiates unanticipated policies. And there is still a chance that policies will backfire if wages and prices are not as sticky as people believe, or if expectations and actual policy implementation differ greatly.

FIGURE 26.2 Effect of an EMP in the new Keynesian model

In the New Keynesian view unanticipated EMP > anticipated EMP > anticipated neo-classical EMP.

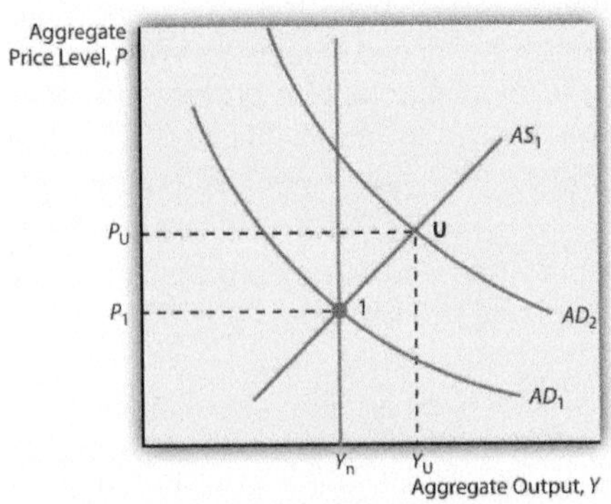

(a) Responses to an unanticipated expansionary policy

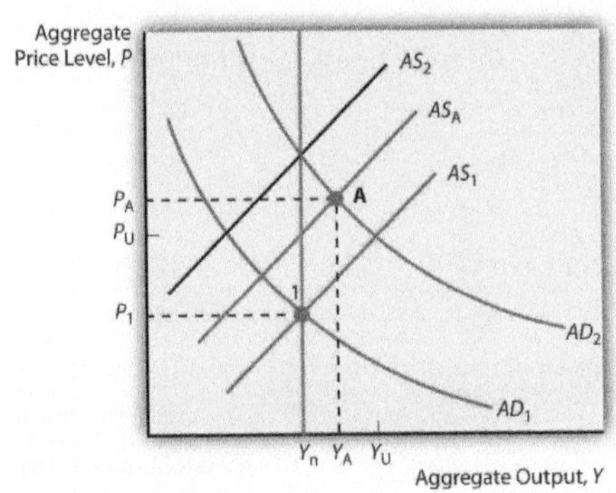

(b) Responses to an anticipated expansionary policy

Adherents of the new classical macroeconomic model believe that stabilization policy, the attempt to keep output fluctuations to a minimum, is likely to aggravate changes in Y* as policymakers and economic agents attempt to outguess each other—policymakers by initiating unanticipated policies and economic agents by anticipating them! New Keynesians, by contrast, believe that some stabilization is possible because even anticipated policies have some short-run effects due to wage and price stickiness.

Stop and Think Box

In the early 1980s, U.S. President Ronald Reagan and U.K. Prime Minister Margaret Thatcher announced the same set of policies: tax cuts, more defense spending, and anti-inflationary monetary policy. In both countries, sharp recessions with high unemployment occurred, but the inflation beast was eventually slain. Why did that particular outcome occur?

Tax cuts plus increased defense spending meant larger budget deficits, which spells EFP and a rightward shift in AD. That, of course, ran directly counter to claims about fighting inflation, which were not credible and hence not anticipated. But the Fed and the Bank of England did get tough by raising overnight interest rates to very high levels (about 20 percent!). As a result, the happy conclusions of the classical macroeconomic model did not hold. The AS curve shifted hard left, while the AD curve did not shift as far right as expected. The result was that prices went up somewhat while output fell. Eventually market participants figured out what was going on and adjusted their expectations, returning Y* to Y_{nrl} and stopping further big increases in P*.

Key Takeaways

- The new Keynesian model leaves more room for discretionary monetary policy.

- Like the new classical macroeconomic model, it is post-Lucas and hence realizes that expectations are important to policy outcomes.
- Unlike the new classical macroeconomic model, however, it posits significant wage and price stickiness (basically long-term contracts) that prevents the AS curve from shifting immediately and completely, regardless of the expectations of economic actors.
- EMP (and EFP) can therefore increase Y* over Y_{nrl}, although less than if the policy were unanticipated (although, of course, at the cost of higher P*; the long-term analysis of the AS-AD model still holds). Similarly, to the extent that wages and prices are sticky, some stabilization is possible because policymakers can count on some output response to their policies.
- The new Keynesian model is more pessimistic about curbing inflation, however, because the stickiness of the AS curve prevents prices and wages from completely and instantaneously adjusting to a credible commitment.
- Output losses, however, will be smaller than an unanticipated move to squelch inflation. Some economists think it is possible to minimize the output losses further by essentially reducing the stickiness of the AS by credibly committing to slowly reducing inflation.

26.3 Inflation Busting

Learning Objective

1. Can policymakers improve short-run macroeconomic performance? If so, how?

Fighting inflation requires the central bank to hold the line on AD, even in the face of a leftward shift in the AS curve that causes a recession ($Y^* < Y_{nrl}$). *The question is, How much will fighting inflation "cost" the economy in terms of lost output? According to the pre-Lucas AS-AD model, about 4 percent per year for each 1 percent shaved from inflation! The new classical macroeconomic model, by contrast, is much more optimistic.* If the public knows and believes that the central bank will fight inflation, output won't fall at all because both the AD and the AS curves will stay put. Workers won't fight for higher wages because they expect P* will stay the same. An unanticipated anti-inflation stance, by contrast, will cause a recession. *The moral of the story told by the new classical macroeconomic model appears to be that the central bank should be very transparent about fighting inflation but opaque about EMP!*

The new Keynesian model also concludes that an unanticipated anti-inflation policy is worse than an anticipated and credible one, though it suggests that some drop in Y* should be expected due to stickiness. A possible solution to that problem is to slowly decrease money supply growth rather than slamming the brakes on. If the slowing is expected and credible (in other words, if economic agents know the slowing is coming and fully expect it to continue until inflation is history), the AS curve can be "destickyfied" to some degree. Maybe contracts indexed to inflation will expire and not be renewed, new contracts will build in no or at least lower inflation expectations, or perhaps contracts (for materials or labor) will become shorter term. If that is the case, when money supply growth finally stops, something akin to the unsticky world of the new classical macroeconomic model will hold; the AS curve won't shift much, if at all; and inflation will cease without a major drop in output.

How can central bankers increase their credibility? One way is to make their central banks more independent. Another is not to repeatedly announce A but do B. A third is to induce the government to decrease or eliminate budget deficits.

Figure 26.3 summarizes the differences between the pre-Lucas AS-AD model, the new classical macroeconomic model, and the New Keynesian model.

FIGURE 26.3 The three major macro models compared

The neoclassical or New Classical and the New Keynesian are the major contenders today.

Model	Unanticipated EMP	Anticipated EMP	Activist Policy?	Unanticipated Anti-inflation	Anticipated Anti-inflation	Credibility of the Anti-inflation Policy
Traditional AS - AD	Y up, P up	No difference in sign or magnitude as unanticipated policy	Effective	Y down, π down	No difference in sign or magnitude as unanticipated policy	Not important
New Classical Macroeconomic	Y up, P up	Y same, P up	Ineffective or pernicious	Y down, π down	Y unchanged, π down more than when policy is unanticipated	Important
New Keynesian	Y up, P up	Y up less than when unanticipated, P up by more	Possibly effective	Y down, π down	Y down less, inflation down more than when policy is unanticipated	Important

Stop and Think Box

In Bolivia in the first half of 1985, prices rose by 20,000 percent. Within one month, inflation was almost eliminated at the loss of only 5 percent of gross domestic product (GDP). How did the Bolivians manage that? Which theory does the Bolivian case support?

A new Bolivian government came in and announced that it would end inflation. It made the announcement credible by reducing the government's deficit, the main driver of money expansion, in a very credible way, *by balancing its budget every single day*! This instance, which is not atypical of countries that end hyperinflation, supports the two rational expectation-based models over the pre-Lucas AS-AD model, which predicts 4 percent losses in GDP for every 1 percent decrease in the inflation rate. The fact that output did decline somewhat may mean that the policy was not credible at first or it may mean that the new Keynesian model has it right and the AS curve was a little bit sticky.

Key Takeaways

- Whether policymakers can improve short-term macroeconomic performance depends on the degree of wage and price stickiness, that is, how much more realistic the new Keynesian model is than the new classical macroeconomic model.
- If the latter is correct, any attempts at EMP and EFP that are anticipated by economic actors will fail to raise Y* and, in fact, can reduce Y* if the stimulus is less than the public expected. The only hope is to implement unanticipated policies, but that is difficult to do because central bankers can never be absolutely sure what expectations are at the time of policy implementation.
- On the other hand, inflation can be squelched relatively easily by simply announcing the policy and taking steps to ensure its credibility.

- If the new Keynesian model is correct, Y* can be increased over Y_{nrl} (in the short term only, of course) because, regardless of expectations, wages and prices cannot rise due to multi-year contractual commitments like labor union contracts and other sources of stickiness.
- Inflation can also be successfully fought by announcing a credible policy, but due to wage and price stickiness, it will take a little time to take hold and output will dip below Y_{nrl}, though by much less than the pre-Lucas AS-AD model predicts.

26.4 Suggested Reading

Gali, Jordi. *Monetary Policy, Inflation, and the Business Cycle: An Introduction to the New Keynesian Framework*. Princeton, NJ: Princeton University Press, 2008.

Lucas, Robert, and Thomas Sargent. *Rational Expectations and Econometric Practice*. Minneapolis: University of Minnesota Press, 1981.

Scheffrin, Steven. *Rational Expectations*. New York: Cambridge University Press, 1996.

Endnotes

1. www.econlib.org/library/Enc/RationalExpectations.html
2. https://www.econjobrumors.com/topic/why-didnt-brock-and-mirman-get-nobel-while-prescott-and-kydland-did
3. www.econlib.org/library/Enc/bios/Lucas.html
4. www.tomsargent.com
5. tepper.cmu.edu/our-faculty-and-research/about-our-faculty/faculty-profiles/bm05/mccallum-bennett
6. https://www.minneapolisfed.org/authors/edward-c-prescott

Index

Notes

Notes